The Seventeenth Century:

Europe in Ferment

THE
SEVENTEENTH
CENTURY
Europe in Ferment

A. LLOYD MOOTE

University of Southern California

D. C. HEATH AND COMPANY

A Division of Raytheon Education Company
Lexington, Massachusetts

cover design by Donya Melanson
maps by Richard Sanderson

Library of Congress Number: 76-92008

To My Mother and Father

Preface

Upper division and graduate courses on seventeenth-century Europe are very recent additions to the curriculum at most American and Canadian colleges. This book is designed, first of all, to meet the needs of such courses. To my knowledge, no American scholar has written a textbook limited specifically to the period from 1600 to 1715. Fortunately, we have been able to turn to surveys written by Englishmen, but British versions of seventeenth-century European history are not fully suited to the interests and background of American college students. They take for granted many basic facts about Europe which are not widely known on this side of the Atlantic. And, surprising as it may appear to those of us who consider England part of Europe, English academic circles treat the British Isles and continental Europe as separate subjects; hence they do not include their own country's past in European history courses and textbooks. In seeking to provide a broader picture of "Europe," I have brought England into the discussion and stressed central and eastern Europe more than has been the custom among western European scholars. And, while much of this book is devoted to the traditional subject of politics, my conviction that action cannot be divorced from thought has led me to place some emphasis on the science, religion, philosophy, political thought and culture of what is often called the "century of genius."

In addition to describing seventeenth-century Europe, I have sought to provide a synthesis and interpretation based on recent studies by scholars in continental Europe, England, Canada and the United States. The veritable flood of new books and articles during the past few decades has demolished many longstanding opinions about the political, social and intellectual life of seventeenth-century Europeans. Any advanced survey of the 1600's written today must depart sharply from the patterns laid down by historians who wrote in the nineteenth and early twentieth centuries, or even five or ten years ago. This book supports the current belief that we can no longer dismiss the so-called absolute monarchs as pure despots or their mercantilist regulation of economic affairs as wrongheaded. Nor can we condemn noble rebellions as acts of treason or the churches' misgivings concerning new science and philosophy as mere obscurantism. On the other hand, today's historians are equally reticent to treat every seventeenth-century scientist as a clear-sighted proponent of modern thought, every merchant as a progressive economist or every English parliamentarian as an exponent of liberty and popular government.

Unfortunately, it is easier to state what we can no longer say about the seventeenth century than to find alternatives to old interpretations. The present generation of historians holds to the traditional position that the seventeenth century was a major turning point in European history. But they are uncertain as to the nature of the turning point, the issues involved and the very attitudes held by seventeenth-century men as they grappled with the great problems of their day. Some historians have almost obliterated the distinctions which their forebears used to make between parliamentary England and the absolute monarchies of the continent. The once neat picture of seventeenth-century society as divided between a backward looking nobility and a forward looking bourgeoisie has become blurred by Marxists' emphasis on the role of the forgotten lower classes and by non-Marxists' stress on the bonds which cut across all class lines. What the nineteenth-century scholars saw as the "warfare between science and religion" now appears to have been a confused melée during which skepticism and Christianity were combined in a single person, and the scientist acted more like a "sleepwalker" groping in the dark than a conscious, rational searcher for the truth.

Within the last fifteen years it has become fashionable to make sense of this confusion by describing the 1600's as an age of crisis. I have been strongly influenced by the theme of crisis but have been wary of using a word which is more properly applied to very open breaks with the immediate past such as the Reformation and French Revolution. This book has been given the subtitle *Europe in Ferment* in the hope that it will more precisely describe the complexities of the seventeenth century

—an age which encompassed a wide range of events and movements in politics, economics, society, science, religion, philosophy and the arts, and which lacked the decisiveness and clear-cut alternatives that the Greek word *Krisis* (decision) implies. If we are to learn anything about an earlier period, we must surely see the age as its contemporaries saw it. There is rather strong evidence that seventeenth-century men sensed that their world was disintegrating but had no clear idea where they were heading nor where they could turn. It remains true that the word "crisis" is applicable to particular aspects of the seventeenth-century ferment, those in which the lines and issues between protagonists seemed to be clearly drawn. The most obvious of such "crises" were the cluster of political rebellions in the middle of the seventeenth century and the social and occasionally religious strife which accompanied them. Still, the reader should be alerted that even these were not followed by a sudden and fundamental break with the past but rather by a deepening of the century's ferment in somewhat altered form.

When I embarked on this project and divulged the title to an inquiring friend, she said, "But all ages are ages of ferment." I cannot recall my immediate response, but my answer now would be that although this may be true, some have greater ferment than others. It seems to me that when one sees the multi-faceted weakening of traditional bonds and beliefs and the profoundly unsettling effects it had on seventeenth-century men, one cannot help but to describe the politics and wars, social instability and economic difficulties, theological disputes and scientific "sleepwalking" as part of a general ferment of gigantic proportions. Not until many generations had come and gone would Europe gradually, painfully and with uncertainty and misgivings transform itself from a medieval to a modern civilization.

Specialists on seventeenth-century Europe will readily note how much the material included within the following pages owes to the work of many brilliant scholars. I have been particularly influenced by Paul Hazard, who first applied the word "crisis" to late seventeenth-century thought, as well as by men of such diverse interests as Roland Mousnier, Hugh Trevor-Roper, Eric Hobsbawm and John Wolf, all of whom have developed the crisis theme in other areas. Like other historians of the period, I discover something new in Sir George Clark's books every time I read them. Even when I have rejected the main thesis of a particular scholar or "school," I would be the first to admit that it has helped me to reexamine and alter my own views. This is true of the interpretation that makes Protestantism the key to change in science, economics and politics, a viewpoint which goes back to the work of the great sociologist Max Weber. It is also true of the exciting work by Marxist historians, who have reminded those of us who hold very different views of human destiny that we should not neglect socio-economic factors.

I cannot record all such personal debts, and am undoubtedly unconscious of many of them. In preparing a book of this scope, one assimilates so much from others that eventually an author tends to believe that more of his ideas are original than is actually the case. I do, however, wish to thank those who have read and criticized all or part of the typescript, saving me from a few of the errors which are bound to creep into any textbook, and compelling me to reexamine statements and views which were subject to debate or misinterpretation. Stephen Baxter has been particularly helpful, and present and former colleagues John Wills, Robert Anchor and Paul Christianson have taken time from their busy schedules to comment on chapters related to their fields. In addition, my graduate classes have listened to and raised important questions about several chapters; and it is a particular pleasure to thank those students of mine whose own research suggested ideas which altered some of my views: Erwin Sicher on Leopold I, Theodore Corbett on Spanish political thought, and William Roosen on French diplomatic organization and thought. I need hardly add that I am solely responsible for any factual errors and questionable interpretations which remain.

My family has also made a very important contribution to this book. The children followed its progress with great enthusiasm, if not infinite patience. My wife arranged her own, very full schedule so that she could type each chapter as soon as it was finished and helped me detect and eliminate many awkward phrases.

Los Angeles, November 17, 1968   A. LLOYD MOOTE

Table of Contents

Maps

✌ *Illustrations*

I.

The Weakening of Traditional Bonds and Beliefs

Like his medieval ancestors, seventeenth-century man envisaged the universe as a rigid, hierarchical order, a Great Chain of Being, in which every creature and thing had its divinely appointed place. This hierarchy stretched down from God and the angelic hosts of Heaven to God's special but sinful creature on earth (man), and then to the lower earthly orders of animals, vegetables and minerals. Human beings had their own hierarchies, both political and social. Above each ruler stood the idea that all nations were members of a family, the Christian Commonwealth of Europe, held together by religious bonds. Beneath each ruler were the social orders or estates of clergy, nobility and commoners, represented politically by parliaments or representative assemblies. Christian belief in an afterlife of heavenly bliss helped men accept these inequalities, living out their lives in an economic system of self-protecting corporations which were supposed to guarantee security if not prosperity.

This was the ideal world revealed in Shakespeare's *Troilus and Cressida*, where Ulysses proclaims:

> The heavens themselves, the planets and this center [earth],
> Observe degree, priority and place,
> Insisture, course, proportion, season, form,
> Office and custom in all line of order.

Unfortunately, reality was very different, since the bonds and beliefs which held together the parts of the Great Chain of Being were weakening. The fifteenth-century Renaissance and sixteenth-century Reformation had seriously undermined the intellectual and religious beliefs which made such a structured life intelligible. Politically, the authority of the seventeenth-century king within his state was weakened by religious disunity, while religious divisions throughout Europe destroyed the Christian Commonwealth. Society itself seemed in flux, as individuals rose and fell on the social scale at what seemed an unprecedented rate. The very hierarchy of the heavens was being questioned by scientists who saw imperfections on the surface of Sun and Moon, and who made the Earth part of the heavens rather than the center of the universe. Even the traditional economy turned against men, as sixteenth-century economic expansion was followed by uncertainty and depression. The disaster which Shakespeare's Ulysses saw as the inevitable result of a disintegrating hierarchy seemed all too real:

> O, When degree is shaked,
> Which is the ladder to all high designs,
> The enterprise is sick. How could communities,
> Degrees in schools, and brotherhoods in cities,
> Peaceful commerce from dividable shores,
> The primogeniture and due of birth,
> Prerogative of age, crowns, sceptre, laurels,
> But by degree, stand in authentic place?
> Take but degree away, untune that string,
> And hark what discord follows!

Few Europeans were directly or openly confronted with all these signs. Many a peasant, merchant, nobleman and priest lived out his days with no knowledge of the scientific revolution of his time, and the lower social orders were often untouched by theological disputes, civil disturbances and international wars. Even those who were thrust into the mainstream of the century's ferment rarely understood the full implications of the issues. Yet, every European was in some way affected by the weakening of traditional bonds and beliefs; and the statesmen, theologians and upper social orders shared the burden of putting Europe together again, socially, politically and intellectually. It was an awesome task.

I.

Economic and Social Conditions: Hard Times and Social Instability

If one wishes to understand the economic and social conditions that confronted seventeenth-century man, it is essential to stress the grim realities which stalked the European landscape and to pass lightly over the glimmerings of hope. The peasant, craftsman, merchant and nobleman who struggled with their "modern" times would have found little solace in the knowledge that their social patterns and economic enterprise occasionally anticipated the more affluent societies of later ages. One must also take all of Europe into account, rather than generalizing from examples drawn from the three most prosperous states—England, the Dutch Netherlands and France—as has been the habit of historians.

A generation ago, historians thought of the seventeenth century as a period of steady economic growth. Recently, this viewpoint has been severely modified by two less optimistic interpretations. The first holds that the century was one in which Peter was robbed to pay Paul; or, to put it in unemotional terms, there was a reorientation of industry, trade and commerce, with economic losses in some places balanced by economic gains in others. The second interpretation is still less sanguine, holding that the gains were outweighed by the losses, or at best came at the very end of the century after a prolonged period of economic contraction.

In discussing social conditions, the age can best be seen as a tug-of-war between a rigid social structure and the solvent of wealth. It should be kept in mind that social status determined attitudes toward wealth at least as much as wealth influenced the social structure. For those who think in terms of money breaking down the barriers to the "rise of the bourgeoisie," it is wise to remember the words of a distinguished social historian, Lawrence Stone. Writing on seventeenth-century society in the most "advanced" state, England, he warns, "Money was the means of acquiring and retaining status, but it was not the essence of it: the acid test was the mode of life, a concept which involved many factors."[1]

Ͼ The Faltering European Economy

The sixteenth century was a period of rising population and an almost unbelievable escalation of prices. The European population doubled between 1450 and 1650, and the prices of wheat and many other items rose between three- and six-fold. Both factors stimulated the economy, and help to account for the geographic expansion of Europe, including the more extensive cultivation of land in the east, the establishment of Europe as "overseer" of Asian maritime traffic, and her rapid thrust beyond the coastline of the New World. The volume of trade passing through the Baltic Sound between the agricultural east and the more industrialized west rose considerably, and there was a flourishing trade between Seville in Spain and the western hemisphere. There was also an increase in industrial production, accompanied by some technical improvements in mining, metallurgy and textiles. It was a period of fantastic profits for the great business families, the age of the mining, trading and banking Fuggers of Augsburg, the merchant-financier Simon Ruiz of Medina del Campo, and the peasant-turned-entrepreneur Stroganov family of Muscovy. It was a time that saw the beginnings of great urban guarantee banks around the year 1600 in Genoa, Venice, Amsterdam and Hamburg.

Sometime between the mid-sixteenth and the mid-seventeenth century, the European economy began to falter. In some areas the "boom" lasted from 1450 to 1650, allowing the great economic historian Fernand Braudel to coin the phrase "the long sixteenth century."[2] But here and there, trade, industry and agriculture were shaken by diminishing productivity, interrupted activity and recessions, starting with a temporary

1. L. Stone, *The Crisis of the Aristocracy, 1540–1640* (1964), 50.
2. See F. Braudel, "European Expansion and Capitalism: 1450–1650," in the Columbia University *Chapters in Western Civilization* (1961), vol. I, 245–287.

halt in Seville's Atlantic trade in 1551 and culminating in the pronounced dip in prices throughout most of Europe by 1640. The telltale signs of a severe and widespread slump by the 1650's and 1660's are to be found in the failure of large-scale trading companies, which were managed by the best businessmen of the most economically advanced countries.

In some instances, economic misfortunes were limited to one socio-economic group or to one geographic area; that was the price paid for the economic prosperity of other groups or areas. Thus Peter was robbed to pay Paul. In the east, noblemen met the western demand for grain by squeezing the peasants, tying them to the soil as serfs and forcing them to work more days per week on their huge estates. The once-flourishing Italian towns became economic backwaters in the wake of the emergence of northwestern Europe (England, the Dutch Netherlands and France) as the new center of world trade. Spain's apparent advantage in seizing the gold and silver mines of the western hemisphere helped other areas more than it did the Spanish monarchy. For Spain simply could not supply its colonies with the manufactures they needed, and the precious metals quickly passed into the hands of Genoese, Portuguese, and then Dutch, French and English merchant-financiers. The influx of bullion from Spanish America also ruined the prosperity of many south-central European mining areas, which had previously managed despite inefficient and costly methods of extracting silver.

If one takes a broader view of these particular situations, it becomes apparent that much more was at stake. If Peter was robbed, Paul was also placed in a precarious position despite his successful brigandage. Economic historians are still debating the nature and causes of the general depression that accompanied these shifts in economic fortune. Often more heat than light has resulted from the debate, and not a little of the Cold War has been injected into the controversy between Marxist and "capitalist" schools. Yet both sides have tended to agree that hard times descended on seventeenth-century Europe. And the ideological flags of the mid-twentieth century have at least spurred on Marxists and anti-Marxists to uncover far more facts than would have resulted from any dispassionate search for the truth.

We are reasonably sure of some facts about the depression that struck Europe. In general, hard times reached the Mediterranean shores, including Spain, Italy and southern France (but not Portugal) by the beginning of the seventeenth century, and then crept into northern Europe. Even the English and Dutch economies, which were the most prosperous ones of the early 1600's, showed signs of ill health. Charles Wilson states categorically that, in England, the period between 1603 and 1660 "was a time of painful readjustment in a darkening European context," not one of "conspicuous growth." [3] We know that the Dutch East India Company's dividends fell with every succeeding decade from the 1630's to the 1670's, although it is not yet clear whether this indicates a real decline in profits or merely the withholding of wealth from shareholders. In general, the low point was reached sometime between 1640 and 1680. Except in England there were few sure signs of major improvement until after 1715. The century's last decades were marked by especially gloomy economic forecasts in France, and it is possible that French conditions after 1680 were as bad as or worse than those of earlier years. We are less certain of the long-term pattern of prices, and it is safest to accept the suggestion that in many places the sixteenth-century price rise slowed down toward the end of that century, followed by an actual price fall in most areas by the 1650's. This trend was not to be reversed until the eighteenth century. Uncertain as are scholarly estimates of population figures, it is reasonable to assume that in most areas population declined or at least ceased to rise steadily during the course of the seventeenth century. The exceptions are a few administrative capitals and commercial centers like London and Amsterdam, and perhaps some countries like England, the Dutch Netherlands and Sweden. Frequently, these exceptions can be accounted for by population shifts, which depopulated surrounding areas. International trade also seems to have been the victim of serious recessions, not only in the Mediterranean backwater, but also in the Baltic and the Far East around the middle of the seventeenth century. The great bread basket of Europe, in the eastern Baltic and Slavic regions, continued to supply the west, but towards the end of the sixteenth century exploitation of the soil began to reach its natural limits. In Poland and East Prussia decreasing marginal yields are evident. The curves of industrial production are difficult to plot, but we do know that decline tends to set in at the slightest sign of faltering prices. Hence, the European decline in prices during the seventeenth century probably affected production adversely in many areas, despite the tenacity of industry, mining and metallurgy in Sweden, England, Switzerland and possibly the Spanish Netherlands. There are sure signs of disappearing industry in Italy, Spain's Castile, southern France and Germany, Bohemia and Poland, either in the late sixteenth or the early seventeenth century. There is no uncertainty about the slowing down of American silver imports from the avalanche of the late sixteenth century to the trickle of the mid-seventeenth. In early modern Europe, which was always hard

3. C. Wilson, *England's Apprenticeship, 1603–1763* (1965), xi.

pressed to secure an adequate supply of bullion, the drying up of that major source was an economic catastrophe.

Thus many of the elements of the sixteenth-century "boom" and some of its basic causes disappeared. Softer prices, population stagnation and dwindling supplies of new bullion meant less economic activity. Europe lacked the previous century's supply of men and metals, its expanding population's relentless demands for more goods, its incentives of high prices and sure profits. The seventeenth-century depression was all the more severe because the foundations on which the sixteenth-century "boom" had been built were shaky. The economic structure of Europe in early modern times was still basically the primitive one of the Middle Ages. The intense activity of the sixteenth century had obscured underlying weaknesses, not rectified them. It is possible that a collapse would have occurred earlier than it did had not governmental tampering with currency added a final artificial stimulation to the sixteenth-century "boom." The Thirty Years' War (1618–1648) in central Europe, and accompanying Franco-Spanish and Baltic conflicts may also have postponed the day of reckoning. Rising prices and war caught governments in a price-cost vise, forcing one after another to debase coinage in order to pay for ordinary and wartime goods and services. Debasement meant inflation, thus prolonging the momentum of the price rise at the very time when prices showed signs of slackening. Once the wars of the early seventeenth century ended and wartime economic activity halted, postwar readjustments aggravated the problems that set in.

ᐒ The Quasi-Medieval Economy of the Seventeenth Century

What were the underlying weaknesses in Europe's economic structure, which had been so long obscured and now came to plague the seventeenth century? Three factors can be stressed: the overwhelmingly agricultural nature of the economy, primitive methods of exploiting the soil and the elementary nature of industry. Together, these three conditions held down the supply of and demand for goods, and aggravated the misery of the depressed seventeenth century as they had prevented Europe from taking full advantage of the buoyant sixteenth.

The vast majority of Europeans gained their livelihood from agriculture. In England, the most industrialized country, 90 percent of the population was tied to agriculture in 1688. A few states had one city of between 100,000 and 500,00 inhabitants, but even in these the second largest city rarely had more than 25,000. Despite this overwhelming pre-ponderance of agriculture, the production of food was inadequate for Europe's subsistence. Those who lived on or from the soil had a hard time supplying themselves and the urban-commercial population with enough food even in years of favorable climates and bumper crops. In periods of crop failures, hunger, starvation and death hovered over the continent. It seemed unlikely that there could ever be a surplus of food-stuffs. Without such a surplus, it was impossible for the tiny urban population to turn its back on agriculture and concentrate on specialized, expanding industry and trade. Until Europe could solve its problem of food production, it would continue to be riveted to the land.

A variety of conditions explain this bleak picture. Ploughs were primitive, barely scratching the surface of the soil. The sowing of seed amounted to a race between germination and the birds, since grains were literally tossed on the surface of the ground. Crop yields were naturally very low when measured by modern standards. The lack of sophisticated methods of crop rotation compounded the problem, without suggesting a solution. Since yields were low, peasants had to concentrate on cereal grains, which gave the greatest yield; yet these were precisely the crops which depleted the soil most. Farmers preferred not to gamble with clover, turnips and other secondary crops which would have acted as natural fertilizers. The absence of such fodder crops also prevented Europe from producing the strong, healthy animals which would have allowed deeper ploughing and provided manure. Cows and oxen remained scrawny and weak, were killed in the fall because they could not survive rugged winters and were allowed to breed haphazardly.

The traditional methods of replenishing the soil seemed destined to remain the norm: the two-field system in the south, and the three-field system in the north, which left from one-third to one-half of the arable soil fallow each year. Forty percent of the land which was so desperately needed remained unused. Europeans knew as early as the sixteenth century the agricultural techniques used by antiquity, and "modern" books on farming were produced by Englishmen in the seventeenth century. But by and large, the persistently conservative and cautious peasant ignored their advice. The incentives provided by the high prices and demographic explosion of the sixteenth century had failed to shake Europeans out of their established patterns, and they had only extensive, not intensive, farming to show for the unprecedented opportunity.

Only the Dutch and Flemish peoples were famous in the seventeenth century for agricultural improvements, but their emphasis was not on greater production of staples for a mass market. The Lowlands concen-trated on market gardening (which utilizes technical advances most easily), and on crops for industrial products like beer, spirits and rope. By concentrating on these profitable items, the Dutch people became so successful that they actually had to import grain from the Baltic! It would have taken a much greater "agrarian revolution," complete with crop rotation, enclosure of common lands, improved breeding and concentration on staple crops for everyday consumption to free Europe from its subsistence living.

The backwardness of seventeenth-century industry posed a lesser threat to Europeans. They had enough to get by, even in hard times, although manufacturing methods and organization were too elementary to become the basis of an industrial society with its cheap, diversified, mass-produced goods. For most persons in the countryside and many in the towns, the basic necessities of shelter, clothing and household items were homemade, much in the fashion of the early American settlers. The paintings of seventeenth-century peasant and urban families which have survived to our day show the comfortable few as *they* lived, and one is struck with the limited number of household items and the crude workmanship which even they sometimes displayed.

Europe had previously had industries to supplement the work of a do-it-yourself society, and these continued into the seventeenth century. Yet manufacturing was carried on in very rudimentary fashion. Most manufactured goods were produced in small shops, by a master craftsman and a few journeymen and apprentices. The medieval organization of each craft into a guild continued, and the guild's emphasis on limited output by each member was still deeply imbedded in the mentality of seventeenth-century master craftsmen. These stifling restrictions on guild members had originally been based on medieval assumptions of equity and a stable, limited market. Like seventeenth-century attitudes toward agriculture, such assumptions seemed to fit well with a cautious urban mentality which feared that rugged competition might cause hardship rather than prosperity.

However, one should not disparage the attitudes of the guildsmen of the seventeenth century, who were faced with the real problem of a limited demand for their goods. The rural population which failed to ensure a regular supply of food for them was also a very poor market for their manufactures. The peasants were mostly poverty-stricken, lacking in money (often the only cash they possessed was handed over to the state tax collectors) and had sufficient resources themselves to do without manufactured items. Probably the poorest town dweller bought more from craftsmen than did the peasant, simply because he lacked self-sufficiency. However, the town market was too small to support the guildsmen, even if those scholars are correct who claim that the seventeenth-century price decline meant an increase in urban purchasing power. The limited market was all the more frustrating because the guild structure had a far greater capacity for production than was utilized, despite its small-scale units.

Production was limited not only because of the market, but by the limited number of potential workers. In eastern Europe, the situation was gravest, since the peasant population was becoming increasingly immobile as a result of serfdom. In the west, the peasantry had for centuries moved away from the serf status. Still, manufacturing had to compete with farming for the services of the technically free peasant. The repeated demand in seventeenth-century western Europe that "sturdy beggars" be put to work in industry is more a proof that peasants could not be lured from the countryside than a Calvinist doctrine of the virtue of labor and the sin of idleness.

Thus the industrial problem was tied to the agrarian one. Some way had to be found to increase food production for urban use, to free rural inhabitants for employment in the towns and to place in the hands of those who remained on the land the money to buy urban goods. A return of the price rise and the population explosion of the sixteenth century might have helped. Ultimately, however, such economic "windfalls" would not permanently strengthen European industry unless they resulted in an expanded industrial population, an adequate food supply and a mass market of human beings with a living standard at least of comfortable poverty.

On the surface, capitalism seemed tailored for reviving the economy. The capitalist was a person with relatively large financial resources, who placed profit-making over the security of limited production. His aim was to increase production, seek the best market, keep costs low and above all avoid guild restrictions. Since its beginnings in the late Middle Ages capitalism had played a far more important role than its small percentage of European economic activity would indicate. Yet it could not transform medieval Europe into modern capitalist, industrial Europe without coming to grips with the industrial and agrarian problems discussed. In the first place, capitalistic enterprise in the early seventeenth century was limited to enterprises in which the guild system could not operate, rather than elbowing local craftsmen out of its way. Brewing, book-making, mining and metallurgy were capitalistic enterprises because the guilds could not supply the enormous outlay of capital, buy and sell on an international scale or organize the several stages of manufacturing necessary for the finished product. With the major exception of textiles (where there was competition between capitalists and guilds), it would seem that the guilds cornered the market wherever it was humanly possible.

Then, too, early modern capitalism was largely commercial, not industrial. Historians have labeled it "commercial capitalism" with good reason, because its stress was on the trading of goods rather than on their production. It could organize, it could finance, but it had yet to prove that it could produce cheap goods in quantity. Perhaps its greatest advance over the guilds had been the late medieval "putting out" or domestic system. This system involved sending wool to cottagers in rural areas to be spun, transferring the wool to other cottagers for weaving, and so on down the line of finishing. This "putting out" relieved capitalists of the restrictions to which the guilds tenaciously clung inside the towns. More cloth could be manufactured, and rural wages were lower than those of urban workers. But this system was traditionally limited to the textile industry. It had just begun to play a major role in other industries during the late sixteenth century, and its future was uncertain. In any case, commercial capitalism, of whatever variety, had yet to invent the machines that would one day revolutionize output, and its means of harnessing energy were absurdly primitive—waterwheels (inoperable when the water froze in winter) and windmills (as unpredictable as the winds).

The great capitalistic trading companies which linked early modern Europe with the non-European world were in trouble in the mid-seventeenth century, and in any case their emphasis was on windfall profits from luxury items for the European elite. Until they shifted from imports of spices and silks to cotton and other everyday articles they could not revolutionize the European economy except at the very top of the social scale. There were non-European worlds to turn into markets for European goods, but in 1600 that development seemed far off, except in Africa. Europe had to balance its trade with Asia by exporting the one commodity that Asia really wanted—silver. And in the late seventeenth century trade with China was hampered by the Manchu seizure of power, and with Japan by the closing of its ports to all but a few Dutch traders. In the Americas, there was not even the necessary population to seduce into "buying European." The indigenous populations were declining; in Mexico there was an unbelievable demographic collapse from eleven to two million during the sixteenth century, and a further decline in the seventeenth century. In the words of one historian, America was in the throes of its own Middle Ages. There are, indeed, indications that the situation in Europe was but part of the first global depression. Undoubtedly, commercial capitalism could, given time and slow growth, change the European economy for the better by gradually forcing its goods and services on Europe, and making its own markets in spite of the poverty, conservatism and backwardness of the European peoples. In part, that is what occurred. But the process was too slow to affect Europe dramatically over the course of one short century.

❧ Short-Term Economic Cycles

The seventeenth century's economic problem was a prolonged recession which placed Europe at the mercy of a quasi-medieval economy, but it was also much more. The century was characterized, not by a simple levelling off or decline in economic activity, but by wild fluctuations within a broader pattern of decline—much like an obliquely descending spiral. These cycles were far more regional than the broader European recession, but they could take a decade or two to run their course. Historians have not yet sorted out the causes from the symptoms, but a glance at the characteristics of the cycles will show that they made a bad situation worse.

The first aspect worth noting is the demographic one. Seventeenth-century Europeans tended to have large families, averaging five children and ranging to as many as twenty. Europe had the potential to double its population in less than twenty-five years. Instead, the population oscillated between fixed limits. Poor diets, bad teeth and atrocious medical practices made for shockingly high mortality rates which placed absolute upper limits on population increases. Almost thirty percent of the population died in infancy, and about one-half before the age of ten. Despite these "normal" checks, the population would still have increased, but it was also cut back drastically by epidemics, crop failures or the simple fact that the food supply could not support more than a slight demographic rise. The seventeenth century was one of Europe's worst in terms of epidemics, and there is evidence that these were connected with famines which not only took lives but broke down resistance to disease. No area was free from the ravages of pestilence. Countries as distant as Russia and Spain were invaded by epidemics in the late sixteenth century. Englishmen still recall the Great Plague of 1665, which killed 100,000 in Greater London, at least twenty percent of its population. Few persons now remember that the same visitor struck Amsterdam and Frankfort around the same time. The Mediterranean was shaken by a series of plagues from 1646 to 1657, which killed off 130,000 persons in Naples alone. To this random list of epidemics can be added one of famines. The most severe and widespread occurred in the 1590's, between 1648–1652 and between 1693–1694; a series in 1709–1710 reached as far east as Russia and was accompanied by a severe winter.

Demographic instability and the vagaries of harvests were intimately connected with the short-run price cycles of the seventeenth century. Price cycles could take several forms. Normal increases in population induced by high birth rates would be followed by rising prices to offset the enlarged market. When the limited food supply caused starvation and death, prices would weaken in response to the shrinking market. There are sad examples of rural entrepreneurs trying to shift from one crop to another in a desperate attempt to follow prices, only to be struck down by low prices caused by a glut on the market. Or, crop failures would send the price of food items soaring, resulting in high mortality and a collapse of prices.

The effects of seventeenth-century wars on these price cycles are difficult to determine. War sometimes increased demands for war goods as well as for other commodities in towns where troops were stationed. But war also artificially inflated prices by destroying crops, and seems occasionally to have had little effect on the price of wartime goods (particularly during the wars in the west, late in the century). International trade between military foes often continued out of sheer necessity, with Dutch merchants being the least willing to forego profits. There were trade wars, but there was also war trade. On the whole, it seems that war was not a major factor in causing or altering price cycles.

Whatever the causes of the cycles, the results were disastrous for the economy. Rises in prices were too temporary to permit any advantage to agriculture or industry, and were too steep for the consumer to bear. The subsequent collapse of prices amounted to a minor recession within the long-term depression.

Capitalism and Economic Improvement

In describing the basic traits of the seventeenth-century economy, it has been necessary to paint a bleak picture. In concluding, it is only fair to touch on the improvements which took place during the century, in spite of hard times and in response to them. The real progress towards overcoming the depression and solving Europe's underlying problems was modest and uneven. But it would be as irresponsible to ignore the developments which eventually led to modern industrial society as to allow them to overshadow the essentially depressed conditions of the age.

The mercantilistic response of states to hard times can best be discussed in relation to politics.[4] Here, we can concentrate on the seventeenth century capitalists who engaged in agriculture, industry, commerce and finance. Conclusions are tentative, however, because of the lack of business records.

In agriculture, England made the surest gains, while the more spectacular Dutch improvements were receiving the bulk of attention. Enclosure of common lands was frequent in seventeenth-century England, and may well have been as common a practice among large landowners as the better known sixteenth and eighteenth century enclosure movements on the island. Enclosure often resulted in more intensive cultivation of crops for sale in London and other urban centers. The celebrated horse-breeding, root crops and clover of eighteenth-century England were well under way by the end of the seventeenth. At mid-century, the English were still looking to the Lowlands as the model for agricultural practices, as can be seen by Sir Richard Weston's *Discourse of Husbandry used in Brabant and Flanders* (1650). But by the end of the century, the country of the eighteenth-century "agrarian revolution" was beginning to feel more confident of its own accomplishments. John Woolridge's *Systema Agriculturae*, the first comprehensive treatise on husbandry in English, appeared in 1669 and went into its fifth edition during his lifetime.

There were also signs of change in scattered parts of the continent. Crop rotation became more sophisticated during the century in the Balkans, Bohemia and northern Italy (which had produced a handbook on the subject as early as the mid-sixteenth century). Traditional farming practices remained the norm elsewhere, including the rich soils of northeastern France. Yet, even where agriculture remained set in its ways, the gradual improvement in communication (especially by water) blunted the worst effects of inadequate crops. The disappearance of plagues in western Europe after 1721 is in part attributable to the west's ability to transfer surplus grain to areas of famine. A sound body and a full stomach made it easier for western Europeans to resist the plagues which had been the scourge of the seventeenth century. But most of the continent could not yet banish famine, as England did by 1700.

Industry also proved that it could survive, even in the agriculture-dominated east. In southeastern Europe, the emergence of great landed estates during the early modern period had strangled much of the remaining medieval industry. Fortunately enterprising western capitalists and opportunistic southeastern noblemen-landowners combined to find a

4. See Chapter 2, pp. 50–52, 62–64.

substitute. The landed serf remained the property of his lord, but in return for a fee he was permitted to contract out to foreign trading firms. In some cases, the putting out system was employed, but before the end of the century factories appeared here and there. As early as 1663 the Moravian mercantilist F. S. Malivsky established a woolen business which employed eighty workers and some foreign technicians. When the Bohemian textile firm of Horni Litvin was organized in 1715, it was able to employ eight hundred workers. Sweden, with a free peasantry, ambitious nobility and concerned monarchy had an easier time establishing large-scale mining and industry. And even Muscovy, the most backward state of Europe, with an outrageously oppressed peasantry, established factories by the sheer will power of Peter the Great, who forced drifters and serfs into state-controlled enterprises.

In the somewhat more urbanized west, Italy, England and the Spanish Netherlands exemplify the variety of responses to industrial problems. Because it clung to high quality cloths and the costly guild system which produced and controlled them, Italian industry never managed to offset the seventeenth-century depression. The contrast between the plight of the Italian towns and the English situation towards 1715 is startling. For the English broke down the control of guilds over industry, shifted from semi-finished woolens (the Old Draperies) to the lighter, brighter and cheaper New Draperies, and diversified their industry to include cottons, pottery and hardware. The putting out system was supplemented by far more factories than in southeastern Europe. English enterprise also began to add to the colonial luxury trade with finished products like refined sugar for a mass market. The introduction of new sources of power such as coal, and inventions like the Dutch loom for weaving several ribbons simultaneously also exemplify England's enterprise and imagination. Historians may be right in attributing the industrial growth of eighteenth-century Britain to the political revolutions which broke down governmental controls over English industry and trade during the late seventeenth century. Nevertheless, a comparison of the Italian and English experiences suggests that the latter's sharp break with the stifling guild system played an important and perhaps greater role in its rise as a great industrial state. It must also be remembered that the survival of English industry during the troubled early 1600's was partly due to the protection and monopolies created by the mercantilistic state. Midway between Italy's failure and England's success were the Spanish Netherlands. That area showed that industry could survive and even flourish under the aegis of the most paternalistic state in early modern Europe. Like the English, the Lowlanders made adjustments from depressed luxury articles to cheaper manufactures. But in addition to the mass market, they main-

Syndics of the Cloth Guild by Rembrandt (1662)

tained an elite market fed by high quality lace, tapestries, glass and printing.

While capitalism was making these scattered adjustments, it was undergoing changes in its organization and banking techniques. These changes did not ensure survival during the hard times, but they did provide some stability and financial security which improved the chances for continued existence and somewhat larger profits. And they provided the organizational foundations on which nineteenth-century industrial society was to be built.

The joint-stock company was one of the major achievements of seventeenth-century capitalism. The typical capitalistic organizations of previous centuries were the family business, small partnership and the regulated company. The regulated company was a collection of individuals who did most business separately but pooled their resources for essential, common needs such as warehouses, provisioning services, or legal counsel in foreign lands. The joint-stock company made an occasional appearance in the sixteenth century, but its continuous existence dates from 1600 when the English East India Company was formed, followed by its Dutch counterpart in 1602 and its French equivalent in

1604. It was a vast improvement over the regulated company, achieving greater unity and making better use of its members' wealth. Individuals bought shares in the company, drew their dividends and allowed the officers to run the firm as a unit. There were naturally variations from country to country, with the English coming closest to the model. The Dutch variety was really a cross between a regulated and a joint-stock enterprise, an amalgamation of several existing companies. The member companies continued to have their directors and operations, but all shareholders received the same dividend. The French companies were peculiar in that much of their capital came from the state. (Sir George Clark calls them "artificial creations of government.") [5] For a time joint-stock companies which were engaged in foreign trade raised capital for each voyage, and the English East India Company did not have a permanent, general capital fund until 1657. Nevertheless, this type of firm acquired a regular place in the western European economy by the end of the century.

Capitalism's achievements in banking and credit are less well known, but they actually affected a far greater area. Old family banking firms were joined by joint-stock, municipal and semi-state banks which could accumulate far larger amounts of money, guard more successfully against bankruptcy, and lower their interest rates gradually from above ten percent to below five percent. It is said that the Bank of Stockholm issued the first true bank notes, in 1661. Actually all the large new banks of the seventeenth century issued a kind of paper money in the form of bills of exchange or bank drafts which were endorsed by one person after another and hence substituted for coined money. The smaller financial enterprises of earlier centuries had done the same, but the larger banks could do it in larger quantities and with greater public confidence. The result was an increase in the stock of money during a period which was desperately short of coin. These great banks also helped to reduce the chaotic variety and fluctuations in Europe's coinage. After 1609, the Bank of Amsterdam used its bank florin as a standard for European monies. Coins from all over Europe poured in, to be converted into bank accounts or "bank money" listed in terms of the official florin. Near the end of the century, in 1696, the Bank of England provided a much more permanent service on a national level. With its assistance, the English government called in and recoined all existing coins to standardize the money of the country.

Although the improvements in capitalistic enterprise during the century were modest, it is tempting to speak of a "spirit of capitalism" which began to take hold over the businessmen of the age. This is the

5. G. N. Clark, *The Seventeenth Century* (Galaxy, 1961), 39.

most attractive feature of Max Weber's attempt to connect Protestantism with capitalism during the early modern period. For Weber admitted, as few scholars of his day did, that early modern capitalism was rare and relatively uninfluential. What he tried to prove was that a capitalistic "spirit" entered Europe at a time when capitalism itself was still unimportant, giving an enormous impetus to the growth of occidental capitalism in the long run.[6]

Weber contended that modern capitalism is an unnatural activity, and that what passes for capitalism during the late medieval and early modern periods was something quite different. Although this enterprise was dominated by the natural "impulse to acquisition" and "pursuit of gain," it was not capitalistic because it was too closely connected with a tendency to squander the acquired wealth. It could exist among waiters, physicians, coachmen, artists, prostitutes, dishonest officials, soldiers, nobles, crusaders, gamblers and beggars—an unlikely set of candidates for the label of capitalist. By contrast, modern capitalism was in Weber's words "identical with the pursuit of profit, and ever renewed profit, by means of continuous, rational, capitalistic enterprise."[7] This true capitalistic "spirit" was marked by the restraint, or at least the "rational tempering" of the natural impulse to spend. Its ethic was an ascetic, transcendental, irrational one, its duty that of making more and more money as an end in itself, the precise opposite of hedonism.

Having carefully prepared the groundwork, Weber went on to argue that this capitalistic spirit was the product of the "Protestant ethic," developed by the Calvinistic branches of early modern Christianity. For Weber, only the Calvinist belief in one's "calling" could explain the entry into Europe of the unnatural capitalistic spirit. The Calvinist believed that he should apply all his talents to the special work to which God had called him, offering his labor to the glory of God. It was this Protestant ethic which gave capitalism its *raison d'être* and its driving force.

Weber's thesis was so brilliantly argued and so carefully qualified that no one has been able to disprove his interpretation. In terms of the seventeenth century, it is a neat explanation of how and why Europe came out of its economic depression. A new spirit arose, stemming from Protestant ideas which were adapted and applied to capitalistic enterprise.

But although Weber cannot be disproved, one is certainly free to

6. See M. Weber, *The Protestant Ethic and the Spirit of Capitalism* (Scribner, 1958), especially 13–78.
    7. *Ibid.*, p. 17.

counter his hypothesis with another, providing it also fits the facts. While there was certainly a "Protestant Ethic" taking root in the capitalists of the seventeenth century, it is just as plausible that capitalists came first, and then the spirit of capitalism. As they became more and more involved in business, and for the sheer necessity of economic survival, capitalists gradually got into the habit of controlling their enterprises rationally, ploughing profits back into their businesses rather than squandering them. That they picked up some of the jargon of Protestantism may stem simply from the fact that it was "in the air," and that it fitted neatly what they were doing, as a sort of unconscious rationalization. There are too many intellectual gaps between the anticapitalist John Calvin of the sixteenth century and the (at best) nominally Calvinist Ben Franklin of the eighteenth, to suggest a linear descent from the one to the other.

Perhaps the greatest achievement of the seventeenth-century capitalists was in concentrating their resources in the face of depressed conditions. Capitalistic wealth, trade and industry were placed in the hands of a few people in a few prime areas of Europe. The banks of Amsterdam, Hamburg and England became giants, stock exchanges and bourses arose in the same cities, and industry located in areas close to ports, raw materials, capital and sources of power. It may well be that the hard times of the seventeenth century forced this realignment and in so doing helped to bring Europe out of its depressed condition. Thus Paul's robbing of Peter may have been in the long run to the advantage of the European economy. The agrarian and industrial revolutions were still several decades away in 1715, but capitalism was beginning to make the task of economic transformation look far less formidable than had been the case in 1600, or in 1650. As it began to break through the vicious agricultural, industrial and commercial cycles, it also weakened, ever so slightly, the habits and attitudes of individuals, groups and governments, which still placed the preservation of social order and economic security above economic innovations.

The Social Hierarchy

To seventeenth-century man, the arrangement of his society into a hierarchy of "estates" and ranks was perfectly natural; social "degree" was decreed by God and supported by human law. Protestants and Catholics alike thought that God placed human beings in one social station for life. Martin Luther's conception of the freedom of the Christian was rigidly limited to the "inner man" or Soul; the "outer man" was obliged to conform to the structure of society and his divinely ordained rung on the social ladder. John Calvin was almost as conservative socially. If some seventeenth-century capitalists tinged with Calvinism tended to break out of their allotted ranks through the power of their purses, it is doubtful that many of them questioned the idea of rank as such. Social legislation in all countries added to the forces of conservatism. Sumptuary laws, distinguishing social groups by their dress, were to be found in the Protestant city-state of Geneva and the Catholic nation-state of France. Frankfort-on-Main divided its townspeople into five groups, each with a distinctive dress. The town of Strassburg was even more meticulous. By a city ordinance of 1628, six broad classes were distinguished, and two of these broken down into further divisions. These divisions were accompanied by strict sumptuary rules.

This hierarchical arrangement was also deeply rooted in the concept of "estates." Medieval men had believed that their society was divided into those who prayed (the clergy), those who fought (the nobility) and those who worked (the commonality). It was assumed that the clergy, as guardians of men's souls, were the First Estate or Order, standing at the top of the social scale. The nobles, who were born to the second most important task of protecting society from its enemies, constituted the Second Estate. Beneath the nobility were the rest of the population, the Third Estate, who performed the ignoble task of looking after the material needs of society. The division into three estates was modified from time to time and from place to place. In England, the Lords Spiritual (bishops and abbots) and Temporal (noble peers) were united politically in the upper chamber of Parliament, the House of Lords. In parts of the Iberian Peninsula and in the Austrian Hapsburg domains the nobility was divided into two, or even three, groups for political purposes. In Sweden, the Third Estate was reserved to townspeople, and a Fourth Estate created for the peasantry.

Although the greatest social divisions were still among the estates, by the seventeenth century each estate had broken down into several ill-defined socio-economic-legal sub-groups as the simple medieval landed society evolved into the complex landed-urban society of early modern times. However imprecise the distinction between one sub-rank and another, and however secondary in importance they were, there was no doubt that seventeenth-century men were conscious of "degrees" and ranks within each estate. The English gentleman, Sir Roger Twysden, refused to take a place in public ceremonies ahead of his superiors, although he and they belonged to the broad English aristocracy. And the same Sir Roger apologized for copying a document in which the names of that aristocracy were listed out of their proper social ranking. The careful attention to the hierarchical arrangement of the French nobility at the court of Louis XIV was not the brainchild of that ruler, but rather the most elaborate example of a common trait.

We can pass lightly over the First Estate's place in the intricate seventeenth-century social hierarchy. Rather than maintaining itself as a distinct social class, the clergy mirrored the divisions of the outside world. The great church dignitaries tended to come from noble families, although in Spain, Sweden and Prussia it was not unusual for a commoner to attain high ecclesiastical office. At the other end of the ecclesiastical hierarchy, the parish priest or parson almost always came from humble stock. In between were the canons and other lesser dignitaries who were socially part of a broad urban middle class. The clergy was further weakened by the fact that the Reformation had broken down its religious unity. The lines between the confessions were often more important to seventeenth-century men than the obvious fact that all clergy, Protestant or Catholic, were Christians. Moreover, Protestantism had proclaimed the "priesthood of all believers," signifying that the layman was as important as the cleric in the eyes of God. Despite all their divisions and weaknesses, however, the seventeenth-century clergy retained some of the prestige and position which medieval society had recognized by calling them the First Estate.

In many ways, the seventeenth-century nobility were more respected as an order than the clergy. While the clergy's prestige depended in part on the performance of duties, the nobleman was nobleman by inheritance. His was still in theory the warrior class of European society, but in the seventeenth century he was not obligated to prove his status by fighting. And although titles were common, even these were not essential to noble status. The proud noblemen of Poland seldom had titles; it was enough that noble blood coursed through their veins. To be sure, the nobleman exhibited a certain "way of life," but that was his prerogative, not his duty. He had his special pew in the local church, and the right to defend himself against a fellow noble by a duel if his honor was slighted. While others were tortured by order of the law courts, the nobleman-criminal was spared. Even in death, he was set apart from the rest of society in many countries. The condemned nobleman was executed by decapitation, while the commoner ignominiously left this world swinging from the hangman's noose.

The ties of blood united diverse European nobility. Every country had its great nobles—the Spanish grandee, the English peer, the "great ones" in France. These great ones looked upon the impoverished country nobles as poor relations, yet accepted them as "their kind," whether they were the hobereaux of France, the hidalgos of Spain or the "seven-plum-tree" nobles of Hungary. Between the great nobles with their huge possessions and the petty nobility with their tiny plots of land were the middling nobility, or "gentry," to use the English term. In many countries, the entire nobility stemmed from a common conquering race which had become the ruling social class; in others there were subtle rankings according to race, with the descendants of "foreigners" ranked above "native" nobles. But racial differences, like financial ones, could not weaken the sense of a common identity which tended to unify all nobles politically, socially and linguistically. Even in England, where only the peers (and after their death, their eldest sons) were nobles in the strictest sense, one can include the gentry in the nobility.

The very fact that the nobility constituted a small percentage of the population also helped them to maintain an *esprit de corps*. Although in the remote northeast section of Spain the entire Basque population was reputedly noble, this was offset by parts of southern Spain where only 1 percent of the population was noble. On the national level, the Polish nobles (10 percent) and the Hungarian nobility (5 percent) were exceptions to the rule that only a tiny minority of a population was of noble stock.

Of the huge Third Estate, most were peasants of one sort or another. In western Europe, the gradual extinction of serfdom over the centuries gave rise to a variety of relationships with the noble landowners, and hence social ranking was a complex matter. Generally speaking, one can divide the western peasantry into the well-to-do, who paid nominal dues to their lord for the use of the land, sharecroppers who gave much of the produce of the land to its legal owner, common laborers who had at most a cottage and a garden patch, and the few remaining serfs who had no land and were virtually the slaves of their noble masters. From roughly the Elbe River eastward, the peasantry was being forced into a homogeneous serf-mold by the oppression of landlords and royal acquiescence. Yet, the change was so slow and the background of the peasantry so diverse, that there were still many gradations between free peasants and absolute serfs. In many eastern states, the monarchy had its own peasants, working on royal land. Generally, the "free" peasant was ranked highest, followed by the royal peasant and then the nobleman-owned serf. The chief distinction between east and west was that eastern peasants were obligated to work most of the week for their lords on their huge estates (*latifundia*). In the west, peasants were generally free to do what they wished with their time, provided they paid their dues.

Family of Peasants by Louis le Nain

Social gradations among urban commoners were so numerous and so divergent from place to place, especially in the more urbanized west, that it would take a volume to do justice to them. Wealth and occupation played important roles in determining urban status, but an ingrained European prejudice against money-making coupled with the centuries-old prestige of some professions pushed the money-lenders and many merchant-guild families several rungs below the lawyer-judges and the town hall oligarchs.

One of the best general guides to the hierarchical arrangement of seventeenth-century society was written in 1696 by the Englishman Gregory King. It should be noted that his *Natural and Political Observations and Conclusions upon the State and Condition of England* deals with the most complex and urbanized society of the period. However, with this qualification in mind, it is well worth noting how he ranked late seventeenth-century English society. His list reads as follows: temporal lords, spiritual lords, baronets, knights, esquires, gentlemen, persons in offices, merchants and traders by sea, merchants and traders by land, persons in the law, clergymen, freeholders, farmers, persons in sciences and liberal arts, shopkeepers and tradesmen, artisans and handicrafts, naval officers, military officers, common seamen, laboring people and out servants, cottagers and paupers, common soldiers, as well as a motley group of vagrants, gypsies, thieves and beggars.

☙ Social Mobility and Social Relationships

In any society, however hierarchical and rigid, there is always some social mobility. Social climbers move up the social ladder, other persons fall from the position held by their families. In the "class" society of the seventeenth century, the amount of mobility was probably somewhere between the minimum of a rigid caste system and the more common movement in modern western societies, where social distinctions run against the principle that all men are born and remain free and equal before the law.

Because of the combination of moderate social mobility and sharp disapproval of social climbing, Shakespeare and his contemporaries were particularly horrified by the internal displacements within their society. They exaggerated the amount of movement actually taking place, fretted about its effects on the rigid, hierarchical structure, and turned their ridicule on those who jumped several rungs on the ladder in a lifetime.

We can see several factors which led to the economic ruin and social fall of some individuals, and to the economic and social betterment of others. The price rise of the sixteenth century and the succeeding hard times were anything but stabilizing factors. War and monarchical policies were almost as unsettling. The Stuart monarchs in England early in the century awarded titles at an astonishing rate, and towards the century's end, the sons of Louis XIV's early ministers, who were tainted with middle-class background, were awarded noble status. The burgeoning of civil and military bureaucracies swelled the ranks of the nobility in virtually every state, as royal offices tended to provide personal nobility for the officeholder and hereditary nobility if the office was held for two or three generations in one family. The spoils of war frequently included lands, sometimes titles, and almost always a rise on the social ladder for successful captains of fortune. Frequently, but not always, one man's gain was another's loss. The settling of a new Swedish nobility in the conquered southeastern Baltic lands and the wholesale replacement of native Bohemians by a carpetbagger landed class after Bohemia's crushing defeat by the Austrians are but the most dramatic examples of the role of war as midwife to social mobility. There was also the pressure of a well-educated, university-trained middle class on a stagnating society which could not provide enough prestigious positions in church and state even with the flood of bureaucratic appointments. This last factor needs much further study, but it is clear that it heightened tensions between the "old guard" and the social climber in states as far separated as Spain and Sweden, and as socially different as England and France.

Just which specific social groups had a tendency to thrust their members upward, and what groups lost members to inferior ranks is a matter of fierce debate among today's scholars. The most satisfactory hypothesis is that some individuals in all groups rose and fell, but that economic fluctuations struck most savagely the poor at the bottom of the social scale and the marginally existing petty nobleman. The poor could of course descend very little socially, but the small landowner was in danger of losing what assets he had and ultimately his rank. By contrast, great noblemen with large estates to exploit or lease could usually survive, while the moderately wealthy and shrewd merchant-financier and the well-to-do peasant could often improve his social position by buying patents of nobility, acquiring an estate which carried a noble title, or moving into a less demeaning middle-class occupation. This picture is most accurate for the west, however. In eastern Europe, as a rule only the great nobles benefited in the long run. Not only were the rural poor depressed further (from free peasant to serf), but the tiny mercantile elements had a hard time holding their own economically and socially in the face of the nobility's efforts to put its landed interests ahead of urban and commercial enterprise. Around the year 1600, the once-thriving merchants of Poland were being run into the ground, while their brethren in Denmark, Sweden, Brandenburg and Muscovy were barely keeping their heads above water.

Relations among social groups are more difficult to determine than the movement of individuals from one group to another. The Marxist assumption that any society is composed of a few, simple "classes" who are naturally hostile to each other has provided an engaging social picture of three geographic areas during the seventeenth century: England, western continental Europe, and the east. In England, they interpret the scene as one of conflict between the bourgeoisie and feudal nobility, with the middle class remaking English society in its own image after its successful political revolutions of the 1640's and 1688. In the continental west, the bourgeoisie had yet to break with the lure of noble values. Hence the class conflict there was between the nobility plus the aristocratized or feudalized bourgeoisie on the one hand and the rural and urban poor (peasants and wage-earners) on the other. It is obvious that in such a struggle, the nobility was fated to retain its social ascendancy. In the east, there was a rather straightforward tyranny of the landed nobility over the depressed peasant-serfs, whose occasional insurrections were more pathetic than in the west.

The anti-Marxist view is not as clear, since many "western" historians disagree with the Marxists only in praising the "rising bourgeoisie," and many who have liberated themselves from a class interpretation have not substituted a new pattern of social relations. A few scholars, particularly in England, have emphasized the divisions within the "ruling class" of the seventeenth-century state. The family feuds, splits between the political "ins" of the royal court and political "outs" of the country, economic rivalries and the snobbery of the "haves" placed against the jealousy of the "have-nots" are all trotted out to give the lie to the Marxist hypothesis. Still, this argument does not refute any theory of class conflict, but merely contends that internal disputes within one class prevented the broader class struggle from taking its natural place in the forefront of social relations.

More persuasive is the positive argument of the few historians who question the existence of class conflict in seventeenth-century society. They agree that there were fairly distinct social classes, but they contend that social bonds lay not within a single class but between individuals in different classes. The slogan of the age was for them "patronage from above; clientage from below." For they see noblemen forging personal alliances with individuals in church, state and municipal office, securing a following among workers and the middle class in the towns, and continuing their hold over the peasants on their lands. They note that patronage was equally utilized by the upper clergy, high officials of states and members of urban patriciates to influence the lowest members of society. Their contention is that without taking into account the patron-client relationship which cut across class lines, the historian cannot explain the frequent coalitions of several classes against the monarchy during the seventeenth century. Both the class conflict thesis and its patron-client rival can be supported by factual evidence, but neither is acceptable as a generalization for any one seventeenth-century state, let alone for Europe as a whole. Each stresses one side of the coin, and hence distorts. For seventeenth-century society was dominated by the two forces of social rigidity and class antagonism, of a hierarchically conceived society in which every group accepted its place versus a social mobility which created tensions and violence. The class conflict theme ignores the deeply ingrained ideal of hierarchical harmony, while the patron-client interpretation fails to take into account the obvious and frequent breakdown of the hierarchy in practice.

If one dare generalize, it would be to say that the seventeenth century began with the generally accepted ideal of a harmonious hierarchy, followed by class conflict in the 1640's and 1650's, and ending with a conservative reaction in favor of an hierarchical arrangement. To this can be added the obvious point that the forces of class hostility, patron-client relationships and simple coexistence were all active in society at the same time, with circumstances determining which of the three factors dominated.

Placing seventeenth-century society in a broader historical setting, it is clear that the nobility of early modern Europe were trying to preserve their status, keep themselves financially solvent, and find the means to regain the political and social power which their medieval ancestors had held, but which seemed threatened by the authority of their rulers and the wealth of their social inferiors. In part, their response was one of "bastard feudalism," which entailed patron-client relationships with their social inferiors, and the acquisition of royal offices which were soon converted into family possessions. Often, they did not even think of their social inferiors except as chattels. There is a tragi-comic incident of a seventeenth-century English gentleman agreeing to let a neighboring landowner hang one of his "men" for petty theft—after the culprit finished harvesting the crops. Philanthropy was a common device to keep the rural poor quiet and working. If social inferiors attempted to move into their ranks or disputed their time-honored superiority, nobles combined savage repression, ridicule and sullen hostility to put them in their place.

Those lower on the social scale replied in kind, sometimes accepting patronage and charity, sometimes speaking of themselves as the nobles' equals, sometimes elbowing their way into the noble ranks. This was as true of Sweden as it was of France and Spain; and the most bourgeois of all countries, England, was far from immune to such varied relationships. One of the best contemporary accounts of social relationships shows how ambivalent commoners were toward their superiors. Grimmelshausen, in his novel on mid-century German society (*The Adventurous Simplicissimus*, 1669), described many examples of class hatred and patronage but noted that "there were peasants so Godless that if they were not thoroughly well and cruelly fleeced, they would sneer at other folks or even their lords themselves for simplicity."

Similar confusion dominated relations among non-noble groups. The haughty middle-class patriciate of the Dutch Netherlands and the city fathers of Paris sometimes looked after their inferiors, but usually were quick to use the urban militia to keep workers in their places. Poor laws were a convenient means to keep vagabonds in custody or put them to work in many countries. Conservative-minded philanthropy was widespread among wealthy English commoners, although it was sometimes so generous that one suspects that they had a more guilty conscience toward the poor than the rural aristocracy. Occasionally there are examples of tender Christian consciences who exhorted the wealthy to elevate their poorer brethren, even to the point of establishing job-training services. However, such hints of a seventeenth-century War on Poverty seldom meant that the middle-class townsman wanted his inferiors to improve themselves socially. The poorer townsfolk were evidently as confused as Grimmelshausen's peasant. They oscillated between the extremes of looting middle-class shops and cooperating with middle-class riots against royal tax collectors.

The most astonishing aspect of seventeenth-century society was the conservative result of social mobility. While noblemen had their eyes glued on the path of the *arriviste* who parlayed his wealth into the acquisition of noble estates and titles, they neglected to follow his family fortunes into the second and third generation. Had they extended their vision, they would have found that the former merchant's descendants washed their hands of the family's business associations and habits, and became indistinguishable from the "true" noblemen. It was unfortunate also that noblemen did not appreciate the fact that the "new nobles" brought fresh blood and wealth into the Second Estate. In effect, the nobility gained more than it lost through upward social mobility. Without the influx of new members, the nobility might well have been unable to survive as a class, since it was constantly losing wealth and members through the extinction of noble families or the squandering of family fortunes. Some nobles adapted themselves to shifting economic conditions, "manuring their gardens" by a convenient marriage with wealthy commoners, or leasing their peasants or mining rights to capitalists. Even in France, where nobles dared not openly participate in "business" for fear of social disgrace, they could secretly invest in commerce through middlemen. Still, the unsuccessful efforts of the French, Spanish and Papal states to overcome noble prejudices against engaging in business indicate that the nobility could not be trusted to save itself as a class.

Once social mobility had provided the needed transfusion, it brought in its train a marked social reaction. The *arriviste* who managed to achieve noble status then slammed the door on other would-be social climbers. By the middle of the seventeenth century, the flurry of land sales was over in England, and soon after on the continent. This reactionary trend is equally noticeable below the noble ranks. Early in the century there was a continuation of a sixteenth-century movement by commoners of low or middling rank to the upper bourgeoisie. The lawyer's son became a judge, the merchant slipped out of the degrading world of visible commerce by buying land, acquiring a municipal office, or investing in state bonds. By 1715, although these bourgeois families were still non-noble, their style of life set them off from their past. They were part of a political-social oligarchy in the local town, with a prestigious political position, a town house and country estate, and a safe and respectable income. And once they "arrived," they closed the door to advancement on their new social inferiors.

Thus in commercial states like the Dutch Netherlands and Geneva, one can see the same social reaction setting in among the upper bourgeoisie that one detects among the new nobles of the noble-dominated state of France. Perhaps the supreme example of the trend, if a bizarre one, is to be found in some Italian areas. The Italian nobles, whose ancestors had moved into the towns to mingle with commoners, now moved out into the countryside, adopting what Italians called *villeggiatura* or country living.

Economically, the seventeenth century witnessed a subtle shift towards capitalism, and by implication away from a predominantly rural and noble-dominated economy. Socially, there is a superficial resemblance to the economic trend. Social mobility pushed merchants, financiers, judges, lawyers, even peasants up the social ladder, usually one step per generation, but occasionally from lawyer or even peasant to nobleman within a single lifetime. Money, opportunism, education, war and the rulers' habit of ennobling commoners for money or service, all worked in this direction. But beneath the surface, the social trends are very different from economic ones. Contemporaries thought that their social hierarchy was falling apart. But the weakening of old bonds and loyalties, which had characterized the more primitive and less complex society of those who fought, prayed and worked, did not result in traditional society's collapse. Out of the confusion and seeming social chaos of the seventeenth century came a restored order, with the nobility and the non-noble urban and rural elite reasserting their authority and position with a combination of old and new weapons. It would take several generations, and the cataclysmic upheaval of the late eighteenth century revolutions before the hierarchical society of 1715 could be seriously challenged in the minds and actions of men.

2.

Politics and Inter-state Relations:
The Plight of Kings

As the seventeenth century opened, monarchy was as typical a form of government as it had been in the Middle Ages. The Dutch Netherlands had become a republic within the last half century, and the Swiss people were proud of their independence, but elsewhere kings ruled. Monarchical tradition stretched back into the distant past in the Iberian Peninsula, France, the British Isles, Scandinavia, Poland and the Balkans. On the eastern frontier of Europe, the grandiose title of Tsar (Caesar) had been held by the princes of Muscovy for half a century. In the Germanies, the titular head had an even more grandiose title, Holy Roman Emperor. Although his throne retained little of its authority, his office still radiated prestige, and he still hoped to restore its power. The princes of the states which made up his empire, however, held the authority and power which he lacked, and in many respects acted like kings. Even in the city states which dotted the Italian peninsula, the once common republican form of government had given way to rule by native despots or foreign monarchs. Republican Venice was an important exception, and yet it had a formal head in the Doge. The proud city of Florence, which had retained its republican facade under the early Medici leaders, was outwardly transformed into the Grand Duchy of Tuscany during the sixteenth century. Its ruling ducal family was connected by

30

marriage with the leading dynasties of Europe by the end of that century, and in 1600 it provided France with a second Medici queen in the person of Marie de Medici.

Yet this outward conformity to the monarchical principle could not hide the fact that early modern monarchies were undergoing a painful transition. New social tensions within the traditional estates made it difficult for rulers to know where to turn for domestic support. The Reformation and religious wars of the sixteenth and early seventeenth centuries weakened old bonds between king and subject. War and economic changes during the seventeenth century imposed greater demands on the craft of kingship and expanded the functions of the state at precisely the same time that rulers were finding it difficult to hold their own in the midst of social and religious ferment.

Estates and the State

To many seventeenth-century men, the problems facing monarchy centered on the relationship between the ruler and the estates or orders of his kingdom.[1] Twentieth-century man does not easily grasp the significance of that relationship. We think of the state as a political entity, in which the central government has sovereignty over the individuals and groups within its territorial confines. In 1600, this modern meaning of the term "state" was just beginning to enter the minds of Europeans. More frequently, they thought of the state in its medieval sense as a loose amalgam of king and estates (*Ständestaat*). The very word was often used to denote status or position, with the clergy, nobility and commoners as well as the king having their particular status to uphold and their peculiar role to play within the state in the broader, more political sense.

Since the fourteenth century, the social estates in most European countries had upheld their political position by means of representative assemblies. These national institutions formed by the combined estates differed in name from area to area, but their general role was similar. There was the Parliament in England, the Estates General in France, the *Cortes* in the Spanish principalities, the Diet in the Holy Roman Empire, *Landtag* in individual German states within that Empire. Everywhere, they influenced royal legislation, bargained with the ruler over the levying of taxes on the estates, and offered him some notion of the support which his subjects were willing to give him in his conflicts with

1. On the social aspects of estates, see Chapter 1.

the Pope and other foreign rulers. By the beginning of the sixteenth century, there were signs that these political arms of the estates were giving way to monarchical authority, and in danger of falling into disuse. Nevertheless, their tradition underlined the idea that the kingdom was not the king's domain, but a community of several interest groups, each of which had to be taken into account.

The social estates were also buttressed in most countries by regional parliaments. Sometimes these were more powerful than the national assemblies, since they were more closely associated with the local populace. Whether relatively strong or weak, their existence showed that the king could not dominate his estates even if he abolished or subdued national assemblies. Opposition would simply have shifted to the local political level. France's Estates General was rarely a major threat to the French monarchy, but the provincial estates in the outlying areas of the realm were virtual co-rulers with the crown in matters of taxation, bargaining with royal agents over taxes and administering them through their own machinery. England had regional parliaments in conquered Ireland and autonomous Scotland, which could prove as intractable as the Parliament in England proper. The German electoral prince of Brandenburg had no central parliament, but the *Landtag* in each of his territories was more powerful than the provincial estates in France. The same situation held for the family domains of the Holy Roman Emperor in Austria, Bohemia and Hungary. In 1609, the Bohemian parliament forced the Emperor into legally binding recognition of broad religious and fiscal autonomy for Bohemian subjects. The *reductio ad absurdum* of this situation was achieved in Brandenburg's Rhenish lands. In 1640 the elector had to agree that state officials in the Rhineland swear an oath to the local assembly rather than to the elector himself. The Spanish monarchy had little to fear from the *Cortes* in its largest and most important territory, Castile. Yet the *Cortes* in each of the remaining Spanish lands (Catalonia, Aragon, Valencia, Navarre) was so reluctant to concede any power to the monarch in the early seventeenth century that he hesitated to convoke an assembly.

Behind the collective assemblies of estates at the national or provincial level lay the individual social estates, with their own institutional arms. In Catholic France as in Protestant England, the clergy had their periodic assemblies. The French clergy had probably the most elaborate, efficient and powerful machinery of any social order in seventeenth-century Europe; its machinery for taxing the laity was superior to the financial administration of the French crown! In Muscovy, where the institutional bases of the individual estates were weaker than anywhere else in Europe, the Russian Orthodox church remained a major power within the state, thanks to the prestige and influence of its head, the Patriarch. In the early seventeenth century, this position was held by the Tsar's own father, who frequently dominated his son in public as well as private matters. A mid-century Patriarch, Nikon, proved so independent that the Tsar had to ask an assembly of the clergy to depose him. The Second Estate, the nobility, usually lacked the clergy's organization. Yet France's nobles were able to meet in national assemblies as late as 1651. In 1600, the Hungarian and Polish nobility were so autonomous that their right to self-protection by armed resistance was recognized by their rulers. The Third Estate was too diverse to create national institutions except as part of the national assembly. Nevertheless, towns and guilds in western and central Europe had their institutional defenses, including town councils, militias and regulatory powers in local matters of public order and economic welfare.

Throughout Europe, the political power of the individual estates was most easily seen in their stubborn resistance to royal taxation. In most countries, the clergy and nobility were exempt from direct taxation, the clergy contending that they paid by praying for the state's welfare, the nobility being excused on the assumption that it was the warrior class, paying with its blood. The brunt of taxation fell on commoners, but many a town managed to exempt itself from major taxes, and commoners in particularly autonomous provinces benefitted from the low rate of taxation wrested from the crown by the local assembly of estates.

The term used to describe the entrenched powers of seventeenth century subjects was "liberties." "Liberty" did not mean individual freedom in the modern sense, but the collective privileges of an area, an individual estate or the combined estates of the realm. The word was used in the plural, for "liberties" meant an exclusive right for all who lay within the group in question. Liberties constituted a preserve upon which neither an outside group nor the monarch should infringe.

The king swore to uphold these liberties at his coronation. In Denmark and Sweden, coronation oaths were used by the seventeenth-century nobility to protect their privileged position as well as to give them control of major offices of state. The Spanish king swore to uphold the privileges or *fueros* of his Aragonese subjects; the English monarch pledged himself to uphold the law of the land (i.e., of the higher social groups), and the French ruler agreed to protect the Catholic faith and clergy. In elective monarchies like Poland, Denmark, Bohemia and Hungary, it was easiest for subjects to wring new "liberties" in return for placing the new monarch on this throne. But even in hereditary monarchies like England, France and Spain, the coronation oath was a solemn pledge not to innovate in favor of royal authority at the sacrifice of subjects' liberties.

Even the most autocratic hereditary monarchy could be subjected to crippling limitations, if a dynasty became extinct. In Muscovy, the succession dispute known as the Time of Troubles (1605–1613) compelled one pretender for the throne to take two oaths: one to protect the nobility, and another to act only with the approval of a national assembly (*Zemski Sobor*).

The monarch's task of subduing the estates was complicated by the sixteenth-century Reformation. Whereas in 1500 it looked as if many European rulers were beginning to weaken the power of their national assemblies, the Reformation reversed that trend. The Tudor monarchy in England chose to effect its break with the Pope through parliamentary legislation in the 1530's. In France, the religious wars (1562–1598) rescued the Estates General from almost certain extinction. Militant Catholics and Huguenot Protestants as well as the vacillating king, Henry III, looked to that assembly as a potential supporter of their religious policies. The Estates General was so revived that it tried to codify French laws. Its attempt to block Henry IV's succession to the French throne in the 1590's was turned aside only because of astute manoeuvering by the new king and popular repudiation of its Spanish-backed candidate. The Holy Roman Emperor, Charles V (1519–1555), found that he could not settle the Catholic-Lutheran wars in the Germanies without recourse to the Imperial Diet. In desperation, he sought to convoke an international or national religious assembly to take up the issue. In the end, the Diet of Augsburg in 1555 dictated the terms which resolved the religious conflict.

In addition to the religious factor, the sixteenth-century price rise made it more difficult for monarchs to dispense with their assemblies. Joachim II of Brandenburg squandered his inheritance and threw himself on the mercy of his estates. The *Landtag* of Brandenburg responded by authorizing taxes, but it took their administration under its control, creating special parliamentary institutions to collect and disburse them. Perhaps the plight of Philip II of Spain (1556–1598) was even sadder. Although he had the Castilian *Cortes* under control, he could secure little financial relief from the several provincial *Cortes* of his Aragonese domains. He discovered that the costs of convoking those assemblies were greater than the taxes granted by his tight-fisted subjects.

As they attempted to maintain and enhance their royal authority, seventeenth-century monarchs ran headlong into the social confusion of their age. The apparent breakdown of traditional hierarchical society had its advantages for rulers, but it also had its perils. A wise or lucky king might be able to turn the antagonisms between the estates into a means to divide and rule. Parliaments were, after all, fragile alliances of separate estates. The Reformation had weakened the First Estate in countries which had shifted allegiance from Catholicism to Protestantism. Especially in northern Germany and Scandinavia, it had tended to turn clergy and nobles against each other, weakening their traditional political cooperation in national and regional assemblies. The nobles looked down on the Protestant clergy, recruited largely from non-noble ranks, while that clergy envied the social position of the nobles. The First Estate had also lost political power and a degree of independence to the crown because of the Reformation. Everywhere church lands had been confiscated by rulers who became Protestant. In Brandenburg proper, the First Estate disappeared entirely from the *Landtag*. In England, the lay lords dominated the upper chamber of Parliament, since the office of abbot had been abolished and only the bishops represented the Anglican church. Nevertheless, the clergy remained everywhere as a social order, and in the midst of such confusion, it was difficult for a ruler to determine whether an estate was friend or foe.

Social tensions and conflicts between crown and estates came to a head in the 1640's and 1650's. During those mid-century crises, rulers tried to undermine the parliaments and individual estates with varied results. The Scandinavian monarchs stood out as the most clever manipulators. In both Denmark and Sweden, they turned the non-noble orders against the nobility, and then imposed their will on both factions. In Brandenburg, Poland and Muscovy, the rulers tended to side with their nobility against the lower orders. However, they then found themselves faced with the most powerful nobility in Europe. Hence they had to divide their power, with the relative resources of the nobles, local circumstances and the relative ability of rulers determining who would gain most from the alliance. In western Europe, the situation was much more complex, reflecting the greater social complexities of that area. Royal policy in England, France and Spain seems to have been much less a matter of skillful manipulation than of drifting with events until social antagonisms became so clear that the monarchy could exploit them. Restoration of the English monarchy in 1660 after its temporary abolition, the survival of the Spanish crown and the enhancement of royal authority in France owed as much to the middle- and upper-class fear of social revolution from below as to royal manoeuvering.

Although monarchical fortunes during the mid-century crises varied from area to area, those crises did alter the general nature of the seventeenth-century state. Whether monarchy managed to subdue or abolish parliaments or had to cooperate more fully with them, the state as loose amalgam of ruler and estates had received a severe blow. For social tensions and political crises had divided the state only to unify it more completely than before 1640. The estate remained, but there was a noticeable tendency among the subjects to think of the state as sovereign in internal matters. Intrigue to influence state policies rather than rebellion against the head of state became common. The nature of this sovereign state might vary from country to country. In England, sovereignty consisted of cooperation between Parliament and crown; generally, it resided in the crown, tempered by lingering privileges of the most powerful estates and provinces. But in this so-called limited monarchy as much as in the so-called absolute monarchies of the continent, the state as such benefitted from the mid-century crises which had threatened rulers and subjects alike with disaster.

✺ The Vogue of Rebellion and the Cult of the King

In their conflicts with social estates, seventeenth-century rulers encountered opposition to their person as well as to the position of monarchy in the political hierarchy. It was not enough for them to divide and rule with political and social weapons. They had also to make subjects loyal to their person. This was an intellectual and emotional problem, a kind of ideological war. Seventeenth-century men had a profound respect for the institution of monarchy, a respect which was rooted in medieval political thought. Whatever the disagreement over the particular role of monarchy in relationship to the estates, subjects knew that monarchy was a fixed institution within the political hierarchy. But the Reformation had weakened the loyalty of individuals and groups within the state towards the ruler. The intensified religious zeal spawned by the Reformation forced Europeans to reinterpret respect for monarchy in the light of their greater loyalty to religious belief. Paradoxically, that reinterpretation consisted of accepting monarchy and urging violence against the person who sat on the throne.

To understand this paradox it is necessary to note first how medieval man viewed the monarchy. Traditionally, Europeans had believed in the divine right of kingship, taking their cue from Saint Paul's admonition that "the powers that be" were ordained by God, and hence should be obeyed (Romans, XIII, 1–7). This religious element in kingship was symbolized by the coronation ceremony or *sacre*, in which the king was anointed with holy oil by a leading churchman of his country. The effects of the mystique were to be seen in the healing powers or "king's touch" given by God to his secular representatives on earth. Both coronation and king's touch survived the Middle Ages, and became an integral element of early modern life. Louis XIV's *sacre* in 1654 was but the most spectacular of the seventeenth century's coronations. In the eighteenth, Queen Anne of England still plied the royal healing trade, and one gathers from the crowds she drew that many of her subjects believed in its efficacy. In the late Middle Ages, and especially during the Reformation, kings had strengthened the religious element of their office in order to combat papal authority. Popes claimed that their power came directly from God, implying that kings received their divine blessing indirectly, either through the Pope as God's vice-regent on earth or through divinely inspired election by their subjects. To counter this suggestion, rulers asserted that their office was directly sanctioned by God, independent of any earthly intermediary.

Unfortunately, the divinity which sheltered kings had one serious flaw. While his office was sacred, and monarchy was sanctioned by God, the ruler's person was not so sacrosanct. Presumably one could accept the institution of monarchy, while feeling free to attack the incumbent of the moment. Even before the seventeenth century, monarchs had tried to bridge the gap, but the danger was always there. The age-old cry, "The king is dead; long live the king," was an attempt to inculcate loyalty to a monarch from the moment he ascended the throne. In France, minor officials had to swear an oath to each new king as late as 1643. The royal funeral ceremony in the same kingdom shows even more dramatically how the rulers attempted to focus attention on the continuity of kingship from one royal person to the next. By the seventeenth century that ceremony had evolved to the point of cleverly obscuring the old king's passing. The continuation of the dynasty, not the royal death, was what counted.

The Reformation laid bare the Achilles' heel of monarchy. Kingship might be sanctioned by God, but He stood above each king, and the king was expected to support God's true religion. When the Reformation divided subjects of a state along religious lines, monarchs were compelled to take sides. No matter which confession they supported, they were criticized by followers of the remaining sects. If they persecuted the "right" religious cause, or were "soft" on the "wrong" ones, the hapless rulers were condemned as tyrants and ungodly creatures. It was but one logical step to the assassination of the offending ruler by an individual or a group of religious fanatics acting out God's will. Tracts on regicide poured from the European presses. Perhaps the most famous was the Huguenot-inspired *Defense Against Tyrants* (*Vindiciae contra tyrannos*, 1579). John Knox's *First Blast of the Trumpet against the monstrous regiment of women* was equally persuasive, and the Calvinist Knox felt strongly enough to write a *Second Blast*. Catholics were equally well represented. Indeed, the Jesuit order became anathema to European monarchs, because several of its members suggested assassination of Protestant rulers and Catholic monarchs who tolerated heresy.

Most partisan writers carefully qualified their attacks, often declaring that regicide was to be condoned only as a last resort, and that only state officials could take the initiative against crowned heads. Their reservations were ignored or overlooked by the masses. The vogue of regicide was in danger of jeopardizing monarchy itself. If one entrusted lesser officials with the task of opposing a king, it was a simple matter to say that those officials were equal to him in authority and could substitute for him. The staunchly conservative Martin Luther already pointed in this direction in the 1520's, by supporting the Lutheran German princes against the Holy Roman Emperor, a Catholic. The Dutch went further. As Calvinists, they viewed the Catholic Philip II as a tyrant, and through the officials of the States General drafted a document announcing his deposition. After searching in vain for a suitable (i.e., docile) successor, the Dutch created a republic.

The religious attack on kings was fortified by the secular argument of the social contract. This argument stressed the traditional "liberties" of subjects and contended that monarchy had originally been instituted to protect those rights. This distorted view of national history was held by Francis Hotman (*Franco-Gallia*, 1573) in France, George Buchanan (*The Rights of Royalty among the Scots*) in Scotland, and Juan de Mariana (*On the Authority of the King*, 1598) in Spain. As the seventeenth century progressed, this secular contract theory was divorced from the religious question and found new sources of strength.[2] The Spaniard Francisco Suarez (*On the Laws and God the Legislator*, 1612) was hinting at this division as the century opened. But the fusion of religious and political arguments against "tyrants" continued to frighten rulers far into the seventeenth century.

This religious-secular attack quickly found its way into the conflict between king and estates. Often depositions were carried out, or at least attempted, by noblemen who waved the flag of religion and pleaded their traditional "liberties" from the benches of a parliament. Duke Albert V of Bavaria (1550–1579) barely escaped this formidable combination after battling it for almost three decades. The Bohemian revolt of 1618–1619 against the Austrian Hapsburg line was almost identical; the only difference was that the rebels succeeded temporarily in deposing their ruler and electing a more congenial prince (Frederick, Elector Palatine). The Dutch revolt was an even more striking example. There nobles and

2. See Chapter 15.

commoners in the States General successfully opposed Philip II's religious persecutions and his disregard for traditional rights of the Lowlanders. But by far the most celebrated combination of these ideas was the one which led Puritan parliamentarians of England to overthrow the Stuarts in the 1640's. Where parliamentary institutions were weak, the estates had other means to make the combination of social and religious revolt effective. In the Scottish rebellion of 1567–1568 which unseated Mary, Queen of Scots, Presbyterian nobles and clergy acted partly through the Kirk, the institutional arm of the First Estate. It is significant that the staunch monarchist and propounder of the modern theory of sovereignty, Jean Bodin, could not escape this contemporary movement. The royal sovereignty expounded in his *Six Books on the Republic* (1576) was all but nullified by his emphasis on the traditional rights of the French people and the Estates General.

Thus rebellion, deposition and regicide came into vogue with the Reformation, reaching a peak in the last decades of the sixteenth century and the opening years of the seventeenth. Two kings of France met violent deaths, Henry III in 1589 and Henry IV in 1610. In England, Elizabeth faced plots on her life from aliens and Catholic natives from the 1580's on, and was formally (but ineffectively) deposed by the Pope in 1570. Mary Queen of Scots was deposed by her subjects, and her son James I ascended the throne of England only to escape narrowly the Gunpowder Plot of 1605, which sought to blow up the Parliament buildings and with them the king, his eldest son and the Royal Council. The deposition of Philip II by his Dutch subjects in 1581, and those by Rudolph II's Hungarian subjects in 1604 and Ferdinand II's Bohemian subjects in 1618–1619, showed how ubiquitous was the loosening of bonds between subject and ruler. The execution of Charles I of England in 1649, breaking dramatically with a strong monarchist tradition, made it obvious that no throne was safe. Medieval Englishmen had maintained the fiction that they did not kill kings, by first deposing and then murdering unpopular rulers. Charles I's opponents held to the fiction even more closely at first, contending that they were opposed not to the king but to his evil advisors. Finally, however, they had to recognize that their real enemy was Charles. When the Parliament turned against him, it executed him *as king,* not as a deposed monarch. It was a lesson that rulers in England and on the continent would not forget for a long time.

The ideological weapon that these rulers employed against the vogue of rebellion was the famous divine right of kings. It was a modernized version of the divine right of kingship, meant to plug the holes in that medieval principle. In essence, it was the belief that the king was somehow divine in his very nature as well as through his office. Saint

Paul had said that the "powers that be" were ordained by God. Seventeenth century divine rightists went further, declaring that kings were "God's lieutenants," who "partook in some way of divinity." French bishops, Anglican divines, Danish royal servants, university professors in the Germanies and legists trained in the French University of Toulouse all concurred in this principle.

The shift from the divinity of the office to the quasi-divinity of the person was in part achieved by sleight of hand, by obscuring the distinction between monarchy and monarch. Jacques-Bénigne Bossuet's *Politics Drawn From the Very Words of Holy Scripture* (published in final form in 1709) exemplifies this intellectual trick. The French bishop did not hesitate to overwhelm his reader with examples of the divine qualities of kings. Yet if one reads that work closely, it is immediately evident that Bossuet did not know precisely what monarchs received from God, or when they received it. Sometimes he thought that God gave kings special authority, while on other occasions he implied that special power was bestowed on them. Underlying the entire book is the still different assumption that superior wisdom was awarded them by God. Bossuet was equally evasive on the timing of God's gifts to kings. Did they become divinely blessed at birth, when their predecessors died, or when they were crowned and anointed with holy oil? Bossuet did not know, since God alone knew whether a royal baby would live long enough to ascend his father's throne. And what happened to God's blessing if subjects abolished monarchy and established a republic, or deposed a reigning king and placed someone else on his throne? It would have been logical to say that the republic or new king was divinely inspired. Indeed, many English theorists said precisely that when James II was overthrown and replaced by William III in 1688. It would seem that their God was a weathercock, shifting His blessing with the political wind.

To be sure, the supporters of the theory had other means to shore up belief in the divinity of kings. They drew heavily on contemporary belief in an orderly universe under God's direction, and by analogy showed that the king's person was just as important for the political realm as God was for the physical realm. As Bossuet noted:

> The power of God makes itself felt in an instant from one end of the world to the other: royal power acts similarly through all the realm. It keeps the whole realm in order, as God keeps the world. Let God withdraw His hand, and the world will fall into nothing; let authority cease in the realm, and all will be in confusion.

Using the complementary beliefs in a hierarchical universe and a hierarchical society, Bossuet attacked the idea that the estates could compete with their monarch. He declared that "Obedience is due to each according to his rank, and the governor must never be obeyed if his orders are detrimental to the prince's." To assure the continuation of the subjects' loyalty from one king to another without respect to personality, Bossuet drew on another argument. He noted that hereditary monarchy was in the image of God. Just as God had no beginning and no end, hereditary monarchy was "self-generating," continuing without a break from generation to generation.

If subjects still hesitated to respect the person of their king, the proponents of divine right could draw on history and mythology. Sir Robert Filmer's *Patriarcha* (1680) contended that the first man, Adam, was given political as well as personal dominion over man and the rest of creation. In this curious interpretation of Biblical history, Filmer assumed that God set up Adam in His own image, and leaped quickly to the conclusion that seventeenth-century monarchs were Adam's direct descendants, and hence inherited his patriarchal powers and divine sanction. It took little effort for Filmer's readers to infer also that monarchy was the only form of government sanctioned by God, since republics had never entered God's mind when He created the world and placed Adam in charge. In their eagerness to round out their arguments in favor of the divine spark in kings, some writers also linked them to the pagan gods. Bossuet, Christian that he was, did not hesitate to suggest that kings were "of the race of Gods." And at the court of Louis XIV, that most famous monarch of the age frequently masqueraded as Apollo or some other pagan deity. No one seemed to see the incongruity of a monarch who held the title of "Most Christian King" posing as a pagan god.

Although the proponents of divine right may have been shaky in their use of history and mythology, and their confusion of kings with kingship, they were anything but inept in driving home their conclusions, once subjects accepted their major premise. They put to good use the religious fervor which had been intensified by the Reformation, turning it against religiously inspired rebellion. If the king was quasi-divine, criticism of him was blasphemy, a sin which many Europeans hesitated to commit. Put indelicately, as it was by a French writer in the 1630's, this meant that "to curse the king is to spit on God." Writers were equally astute in playing on popular fears of social and political anarchy with their argument that kings were necessary to maintain an orderly, hierarchical system. And they could always pull out the plea that if a king was bad, that was God's punishment for men's sins.

As an intellectual weapon of self-defense, the divine right of kings proved an admirable supplement to the policy of dividing and ruling. It did not prevent all rebellion or stay the hand of every assassin. Yet it did gradually win back the loyalty of subjects to their rulers. Too often historians have looked on divine right as a mere apology for the growing absolutism of seventeenth-century monarchs, as if power and authority came first, and theory followed as a rationalization. If one wishes to understand the politics of the seventeenth century, it is essential that divine right be placed in proper context as a defensive weapon employed early in the century to shield monarchs against personal disaster. James VI of Scotland (James I in England) was certainly displaying his customary haughtiness in his divine-right tract, *True Laws of Free Monarchy* (1598). But he was also using that work to ward off the fate of his deposed mother, Mary Queen of Scots. And while Henry IV of France dismissed James' display of erudition, saying that he was too busy subduing his subjects to write about his divine right, theoreticians around the French monarch were scribbling their defenses of his divine qualities.

Once divine-right theory and the rulers' political-social manoeuvering began to pay dividends, the theory was put to another use. What had begun as a defensive weapon, came to justify the extension as well as the survival of royal authority. Built into the principle of the divine right of kings were ideas which could put monarchy on the offensive. For the theory declared that kings, coming from God, were accountable to God alone for their actions, and had full responsibility for directing the state. Subjects and estates had no rights, merely "privileges" which the monarch granted and could revoke. (It would seem that theoreticians forgot, at this point, that only God had "dominion," while kings like other mortals had mere "usufruct," or use on trust.) The medieval hierarchical system of law also lost much of its authority over monarchy. Saint Thomas Aquinas had divided law into four branches: eternal (God's plan for the universe); natural (principles appropriate for God's creatures, which humans could detect through God-given reason); divine (Biblical revelation, which supplemented but did not contradict reason) and customary (the application of natural law to specific instances). Since kings themselves were considered semi-divine, it was now possible for the School of Toulouse to contend that they could change customary law and interpret natural law through their superior wisdom. To be sure, kings were not God, and could not tamper with His plan for the universe or His holy word. But a breach had been made in the restrictions of natural and customary law.

It remains true that the divine-right theory which led to "absolute monarchy" did not and never was intended to justify arbitrary despotic government. Of this seventeenth-century rulers were well aware. To be sure, his subjects had no rights, and the law was not above him for he was responsible to no one but God for his actions; but his absolutism had theoretical restraints. Since he was accountable to God he knew that he would have to answer for his record in office. Louis XIV was to believe in his last years that God was already punishing him through military setbacks and economic disasters. Most absolutist supporters, including Bossuet, spelled out the do's and don'ts of kingship. The monarch might have the power, but never the right to take subjects' property or lives arbitrarily. Law, traditional practices and God's will were guidelines meant to restrain him. Machiavelli himself had admitted in the early sixteenth century that a prince was committing a moral wrong even when necessity required him to act arbitrarily. The divine rightists hesitated to go so far as the writer of *The Prince*. For them, morality, religion and politics were inseparable.

The distinction between absolutism and despotism was thus maintained, although tenuously, and proved to be a source of strength as well as weakness for seventeenth-century monarchs. Subjects, thrown into their outstretched arms by the anarchy and terror of the religious wars, were drawn toward absolutism by the feeling that the king knew his responsibilities towards them. Bossuet felt that self-interest alone would restrain the monarch from antagonizing his subjects. When, at the end of the seventeenth century, kings exploited absolutist thought so fully that they tended to go beyond its limitations, divine right began to lose its hold on European minds. In the meantime, it eased the transition from the religious strife of the sixteenth century and the old bonds and loyalties of a society of estates to the power and order of the late seventeenth-century state.

Growing Pains of Big Government

The governmental machinery of seventeenth-century states was not imposing by twentieth-century standards, but it was by comparison with the past. Without wishing to exaggerate the importance of the 1600's in the rise of modern bureaucratic government, it is plausible to think of that age as a major turning point in the evolution from the simple, personal government of medieval kings to the vast, impersonal machinery of present-day states. As authority which had been divided between king and estates became concentrated in the central institutions of the state, the functions, machinery and personnel of royal administration expanded at a rapid pace. The growing pains of big government were sharp and prolonged. Economic and military pressures urged the state to assume more and more functions and ever-increasing control over subjects' lives.

These pressures were in constant tension with the outmoded governmental ideals and institutions which the seventeenth century had inherited. Neither ruler nor subject, nor even the ministers and bureaucrats who were directly involved realized how much their government was changing. But in concentrating their attention on the tasks of the moment, kings and their officials made decisions which combined to produce the first big governments of modern times.

Medieval society had assumed that the king's role in internal affairs was limited to keeping peace and order. Since it was also believed that God had set down permanent guidelines for human laws (through revelation and man's God-given reason), this role was conceived very narrowly. Kings and their subjects simply adapted God's will to particular circumstances through customary law. There was scarcely a thought that the king could innovate or fundamentally alter a law. Nor was it thought necessary for a king to employ taxation to carry on his normal governmental tasks. He was supposed to "live of his own," that is, to rely on the products of his family lands except in emergencies. Military needs were similarly viewed. In a crisis, the king could call on his noble vassals to serve as his feudal host, but only for a very limited time. Thus legislation, taxation and the military, the main instruments of modern states, were barely part of the medieval vocabulary. Over the centuries, kings *had* begun to tax subjects, to legislate and to convert the short-term feudal host to a paid army of nobles and commoners which was maintained for several months or even several years. However, the underlying bias against those three branches of the government lingered on.

Medieval man had also assumed that royal government was a highly personal matter, with the king bearing the brunt of the work, assisted by a few ministers and lesser officials. In the course of time, the simple king's council or *curia regis* did split up into several more specialized organs of government: judicial courts, financial bureaus, and several councils to decide over-all policies. The number of ministers, who consulted with the king and his councils and supervised the various governmental branches, also increased, as did their staffs. Nevertheless, sixteenth-century government was still inadequately staffed. France, boasting the most numerous body of civil servants in Europe, had only one for every 1,250 subjects in 1505 (in 1934, it had a ratio of one to seventy), and only one official for every twenty-five square miles at a time when communications were greatly inferior to the present day.

Government was also poorly organized at the opening of the seventeenth century. In the course of time, one layer of officials had been superimposed on another, and at each level subdivisions had been created without any thought of clearly and rationally dividing topical and geographical responsibilities. Everything had been created to meet immediate needs, regardless of how the creation fitted into the over-all governmental structure.

Probably the greatest confusion existed in financial matters. Sources of revenue and bureaus to supervise them were overlapping and confused. There were royal domains, direct levies, sales taxes and tariffs, each divided into a bewildering variety of petty dues with their peculiar means of assessment and collection. Even the brilliant administrator of Louis XIV's finances, Colbert, felt that it was impossible to understand the French financial structure, and was happy just to make it work. Brandenburg, by no means a large state, had three treasuries—one for the prince's personal domains, another for war, and a third which defied categorization. James I sought without success in 1610 to simplify English taxation; it took an entire century and the revolution of the 1640's to sweep away even the most irrational aspects of the system.

The judiciaries of Europe closely rivalled the financial administrations in confusion. England alone had a common law for all its English territories, thanks to acts in the 1530's which had abolished independent jurisdictions and incorporated Wales into the English state. It was also unique in having supreme law courts for the entire English realm. But Ireland and Scotland had independent judicial systems still, although the Anglo-Scottish borderlands gradually came under the aegis of English law early in the seventeenth century. The continental states were composed of many areas, each with its peculiar laws, legal procedure and courts. Often, too, there was no clear geographical boundary between neighboring royal law courts, nor any clear division of functions between a lower court and a superior court in the same area. France had probably the most complex and confusing judicial system, with superior criminal-civil law courts (*Parlements*) vying with superior financial courts for control of litigation, and at the lower levels even greater confusion among the many highway, criminal-civil and fiscal courts. There was no supreme court for the entire realm, and a royal court for ecclesiastical affairs (the Great Council), which had pretensions to such a role, added to the chaos, since its authority was constantly challenged by the *Parlements*.

Even at the highest level of government, confusion existed. The concept of government by council vied with the rival idea of government by individual ministers, and it was often difficult to tell who made decisions. Over-all planning was made all the more difficult since responsibilities were divided territorially as well as topically. Spain's councils were mainly organized on geographic lines, with separate councils for each province or group of provinces. In France and generally in England, conciliar responsibilities were state-wide. Yet in both countries there existed secretaries of state, each of whom staked out a claim to supervise internal affairs in one geographic area of the realm. In Brandenburg, which fused Brandenburg proper, Prussia and Rhenish territories into the new state of Prussia during the course of the century, the obstacles to unity at the highest levels were almost insurmountable. The rulers could only hope that decisions made in the councils of the central Brandenburg territory would be accepted in the other areas, which were not legally bound by Brandenburg's policies. The Hapsburg rulers of the Holy Roman Empire had a somewhat different problem. During the seventeenth century, they saw the institutions of the Empire slip increasingly out of their hands into the control of its princes. Thrown back on the resources of their ancestral domains in Austria, Bohemia and Hungary, the Hapsburgs had to develop central institutions which would make a state out of them. Like the councils of Brandenburg, the Austrian councils made decisions, which they hoped would be accepted by the quasi-independent Bohemians and Hungarians.

The royal servants who tried to make these governmental institutions work presented another problem to their rulers. Theoretically, the king appointed, but in practice his choices were limited and his controls on the performance of duty restricted. Everywhere officials looked upon their positions as their personal, or even family, possession. The sale of offices, either by the king or by his favorites, ministers or lesser officials was practiced throughout most of Europe. It was most pronounced in France, where Henry IV extended the custom to its logical conclusion in 1604. By the privilege of the *Paulette*, for which an incumbent paid a small fee every year to the royal treasury, judges and tax officials were permitted to bequeath their offices at will. Although this system brought additional income to the French crown, it made it virtually impossible for the monarchy to dismiss its judicial and financial officials, since it never had the money to buy out the officeholder.

Whether venality existed or not, officeholders had an astonishing degree of independence, due to the very fact that monarchs normally made appointments from the upper and middle echelons of society. In England, local government was run by the gentry, chosen to serve as Justices of the Peace. Unpaid, solicitous of the interests of his social group and having immense influence on Parliament and the central government, the gentleman Justice of the Peace came close to ruling England in practice if not in theory. In the eastern part of the continent, the great nobles combined their economic and social control of an area and its people with the power of the highest offices of state. In Denmark and Sweden as well as in Poland, Muscovy, Brandenburg and the Austrian Hapsburg domains, the nobility had more power within the royal government than any other social group, and openly reflected their private interests in their performance of public duties. Where they did not actually serve in office, the chances were that those who did were in some way under their influence.

The demands of the seventeenth century placed a strenuous burden on these inadequate institutional resources. The steep price rise of the sixteenth century had made it more difficult for the king to "live of his own," since his own consisted largely of land rented out on semi-fixed leases. The unsettled conditions of the seventeenth century made his economic situation equally precarious. The obvious solution was to expand extraordinary, emergency taxation into normal, permanent and ever-increasing taxes, and to force privileged, tax-exempt groups to surrender part of their wealth to the king's coffers. The state had for centuries been replacing the guilds and towns in the regulation of economic matters. The seventeenth-century depression made state intervention all the more logical. But if the ruler wished to increase his revenues, he had first to provide economic security to his taxable subjects. Social tensions, religious disturbances and revolts against the king required more effective punishment through the law courts and surer maintenance of order through an expanded and more efficient army. A century of almost constant war also pressed hard on the financial resources of the state. All these activities necessitated an expansion of the royal personnel and a more thorough control of the various branches and echelons of government.

As monarchs attempted to expand government, they continually ran into opposition from social estates and representative assemblies, which balked at expanded or new taxes, and from the powerful groups which had infiltrated the government in order to keep themselves free from judicial, financial, legislative and military pressures from the crown. Thus the big government which was a response to the problems of the age increased the tensions which were rooted in those problems.

No state managed to streamline its government machinery entirely during the seventeenth century, but almost all managed to overcome the growing pains of big government and increase central power and governmental efficiency. The greatest progress was made in military and judicial matters, with somewhat less success being realized in financial and economic affairs.

During the early seventeenth-century wars, the army was a quasi-permanent force ultimately controlled and paid by the state, but much of the power over individual forces was held by the captains of fortune and rebellion-minded noblemen who led them. It was the local officer who recruited, provisioned and directly paid the soldiers, and who consequently could turn their allegiance to him rather than to the monarch. He was even given a special name, _condottiere,_ to signify his peculiar role of "conducting" (hiring and leading) troops. The spectacular careers of Wallenstein, who defied the orders of the Holy Roman Emperor, and of Condé, who turned French royal troops against the monarchy, can be found in miniature in the lives of less well-known _condottieri_. However, it should be added that Wallenstein was eventually assassinated for this disloyalty and Condé had to make his peace (although an honorable one). After mid-century, the day of the _condottieri_ was over. The state assumed much more direct control over its military arm, providing its own provisioning services and its own paymasters, and placing its royal ministers in charge of military policy. The nobleman might remain as captain or general, but he could no longer forge a personal link with his troops, and hence could no longer raise the standard of revolt. In internal affairs, the army settled down more and more to the minor task of crushing sporadic tax revolts.

The military could not restore order on its own, however, and hence monarchs had to work also through their judiciaries. Frequently, judges who balked at or delayed decisions against rebellious subjects or tax evaders were arbitrarily detained, exiled or even dismissed. These high-handed tactics assured control over the superior courts in England by 1637, and a measure of docility within the French judiciary during the same decade. However such policies provided at best only temporary assurance to the rulers. Hence, they relied heavily on special tribunals, which were packed with safe judges and worked rapidly without the delays and legal niceties of ordinary courts. The English monarchs before 1640 expanded the work of the Court of Star Chamber for criminal cases, and the Court of High Commission for religious disputes. France had its famous intendants, who tried criminal suits without recourse to the _Parlements,_ while Brandenburg and Austria used special, temporary commissions to try subjects who opposed taxation, religious persecution or loss of the right to armed resistance. Except in England, where revolutions swept away the special courts and made regular tribunals independent of the crown after 1688, monarchy was successful in imposing order through regular and special judicial channels. However, the regular courts continued to be staffed by the upper social classes, who persisted in bending the law subtly in their favor.

There was one striking by-product of the expansion of royal control of justice. The judiciary became more specialized, concentrating on its primary function of judging. Secondary duties which threatened to overburden judges were occasionally entrusted to the care of other institutions. For the first time in Europe's history, the idea arose of a regular police force, specialized and separate from the judiciary. The Paris police of La Reynie under Louis XIV became the wonder of the European world, and a model for other cities and countries. As the police and judiciary began to win the battle against crime and lawlessness, they also made it possible for rulers to establish new bureaus entrusted with re-habilitating the unfortunate, nameless people at the fringes of civilization. Unemployed males, wayward females, unhealthy living conditions and a host of other "items" were added to the list of governmental concerns. The states of the east were far behind the west in these matters, and even the west made only a halting beginning. Still, there was a sharp contrast to the conditions in the towns of late medieval Europe.

Seventeenth-century states won the battle to increase revenues, but without being able to overhaul tax structures. The power of the central government after mid-century is often linked by historians with the spec-tacular growth in the levying of indirect taxes, notably in England and Brandenburg. But while there is much truth in the saying that excise tax plus standing army equals the modern state, it should be kept in mind that the lower urban and rural groups bore the brunt of these and other expenses both in states with an important middle-class population (En-gland and the Dutch Netherlands) and in overwhelmingly agrarian countries like Muscovy. Denmark, England and parts of Brandenburg saw taxes laid on the nobility, but generally nobles, clergy and to a lesser degree the well-to-do bourgeoisie escaped. When Louis XIV, outwardly the most powerful ruler of the century, made a half-hearted attempt to impose income and poll taxes on the clergy and nobility at the end of his reign, he met his match and gracefully allowed them to buy back their exemptions with bribes.

Although the increased revenues allowed states to meet their grow-ing responsibilities, every state either experienced temporary bankruptcy (as did England, France and especially Spain) or barely managed to re-main solvent. The immediate solution lay not so much in streamlining fiscal administration or making taxation universal (although both would have proved major stabilizing factors) as in enabling states to borrow regularly at low interest rates. England and the Dutch Netherlands were probably almost as backward as their neighbors in fiscal administration, and England alone came close to taxing all subjects. Yet they had the soundest treasuries, the Dutch throughout most of the century, and the English by the century's end. In both countries this stability was due to the ability of the state to secure the confidence of the business com-munity. The Dutch regent class dominated both business and public life, and hence backed the semi-state Bank of Amsterdam, supplying provincial and national governments with money either directly or through the bank at an interest rate which steadily declined during the century until it reached 2.5 percent in Holland in 1729. England's revolution of 1688 brought about the cooperation of the crown, Parliament and business interests. That cooperation led to the creation of the semi-state Bank of England in 1694, and ultimately to an official interest rate of 5 percent in 1714. By contrast, the French monarchy, which had uncertain relations with the business community, struggled through the century without sound credit. It borrowed haphazardly from private bankers and its own tax collectors, and indirectly through the city government of Paris. It is ironic that the model absolutist state was financially far less absolute than the limited monarchy of post-1688 England or the republican Dutch state.

Everywhere, the state supplemented its financial activities with broader economic policies. For centuries, the state had been encroaching on the role of the town and guild as public regulators of economic activities. That process was greatly accelerated during the seventeenth century. What the local economic unit had done in regulating trade, manufacturing, prices and wages, the central government now did on a broader and more selfish scale. Like their medieval precursors, seventeenth-century officials assumed that the economy was static. But whereas the town or guild of the Middle Ages had tried to cut the local pie to suit the needs of producer, worker and consumer, monarchs now attempted to take a larger share of the international pie for their subjects, and use that share for state needs through taxes and goods requisitioned for the army. Little thought was given to the interests of the subject; what was important was that his industry and trade be protected and fostered so that the central government could meet its needs.

The realization that gold and silver were scarce, and the belief that the state with the greatest amount of bullion was the most powerful, were central to the formulation of seventeenth-century policy. This belief was based on the fortunes of the Spanish empire, which had flowed and ebbed as its supply of bullion from the American mines increased or dwindled. Not every state could secure a direct supply of bullion, but all adopted a modified form of bullionism, attempting to increase the amount of gold and silver inside the state. To prevent bullion leaving the state in return for foreign goods, to protect native industry so that subjects did not have to buy abroad, to regulate production so that the quality of goods was high and their sale abroad assured, to develop a native mer-chant fleet to carry world trade and bring in further treasure and to export more than was imported were among the various means to this end.

The name of these economic policies differed from state to state, according to which ones were emphasized, but the over-all policy was the same. Generally, historians have used the broad term *mercantilism* (or mercantile system). But Spanish bullionism, French Colbertism (after the minister in charge of economic matters, Colbert), and German cameralism (from the *kammer* or government chamber in charge of regulating economic matters) are terms that equally well describe the economic practices and policies of seventeenth-century states.

The most unique brand of economic policy was practiced by the Dutch. Lacking in raw materials and industry, the republic was shrewd enough to see that bullion could better be obtained through the exploitation of a free international market than through regulations. At mid-century, the Dutch were the carriers for the Europeanized world. They had taken over the Portuguese position as the trading nation *par excellence*, seizing most of the Far Eastern and Baltic trade, while cutting into the Spanish monopoly in the New World. Dutchmen were so bold that they landed on the shores of France's wine country and traded directly with local producers, much to the indignation of Colbert. Nor did the Dutch scruple to let money out of the state. By becoming a major exchange for European moneys and charging fees for their services, the Dutch were able to make the free movement of money pay a handsome profit.

France and England made attempts to cut into the Dutch trading monopoly by protectionist, regulatory policies. Legislation by Cromwell and Charles II in England and by Louis XIV and Colbert in France protected shipping, colonies and trading companies at the same time that it discouraged imports of goods and the exporting of money. In contrast to the Dutch, both governments supervised closely the manufacturing of native goods, although English controls of industry slackened towards the end of the century.

Towards the east, states were still more paternalistic and domineering than France and England, and their policies were in sharp contrast to the benevolent freedom allowed Dutch economic interest groups. Governmental regulation of native industry was mixed with the fostering of quasi-government enterprise. Brandenburg, Sweden and Muscovy all sponsored state-run mining, metallurgical and industrial plants. These three states also sought to make the best of their material resources by importing technicians. Austrian cameralism was equally paternalistic, but its stress was much more on austerity than on bolstering the economy. Farmers were urged to experiment with "every useful kind of plant under the sun," and told not to neglect "a single corner or clod of earth." Town-dwellers were lectured on the virtue of being "content for a while with their own manufacturers, however bad they be at first, and to refrain from foreign ones, keeping their good gold and silver in their

pockets." But even hoarding money was not enough, and Hapsburg subjects were admonished not to allow their money "to be buried in chests
and coffers," but to keep it in circulation.

Whatever the degree or variety of state control over economic enterprise, there was throughout Europe an enormous expansion of state
responsibility. Tariff boards, government inspectors of industry, government shipyards and state arsenals sprang up across the continent. States
as different in their economic policies as Muscovy, Sweden, France, Spain
and England developed councils, boards or bureaus to lay down guidelines
for everything from mining to industry and from commerce to colonies.

When all the changes within the machinery and functions of the
seventeenth-century state are put together, the full import of the emerging big government becomes clear. The most striking change resulted
from the merging of estates and monarch into the sovereign state, and
the growing respect for that state regardless of the succession from one
ruler to the next. As the king blunted the opposition of the estates and
gained loyalty to his person, he passed on his enhanced authority to the
ministers, bureaucrats and other organs of government. Medieval men had
been so wedded to the idea of personal rule by the king that they hesitated to obey orders from his agents. Seventeenth-century subjects still
retained much of that prejudice, but the tradition was dying. More and
more, Europeans came to recognize that the king could not personally
govern in every petty matter, and that his officials' actions and orders
should be respected, even if the king was not personally involved. Rulers
themselves came to realize that the impersonal state, run by bureaucrats,
was bigger than either subject or ruler. Louis XIV did not say, "I am
the state" (*L'Etat c'est moi*), a phrase often attributed to him. What he
said was that he would die, but the state would continue. In the most
backward state of the age, Muscovy, Peter the Great also saw the trend
of the century; he insisted that subjects swear an oath to the state as well
as to his person. Frederick William, the Great Elector of Brandenburg,
had a more limited vision, for he willed that the state which he had welded
together should be divided at his death among his children. However, his
heir, Frederick I, rectified that mistake by breaking the will and keeping
the north German state intact.

Christian Commonwealth, Sovereign Rulers and Inter-state Relations

It is ironic that the emerging sovereign state which made peace and
order possible within its boundaries undermined the forces contributing
to order and harmony among states. More than anything else, it was the

secular state which made a mockery of the medieval ideal of the Christian Commonwealth, which envisaged Europe as one political body composed of a family of nations held together by Christian bonds and devoted to international peace. For centuries, rulers had disputed the Pope's claim to the right to arbitrate disputes as the spiritual leader of Christian Europe, and had looked increasingly on their fellow monarchs as potential enemies rather than blood brothers. The Reformation shattered what was left of the bonds within the Christian Commonwealth. By 1600, neither Catholic nor Protestant kings accepted dictation from the Pope. The Reformation also made it impossible for states to agree on the medieval "law of nations" (customary law) which guided the conduct of states with respect to each other. Customary laws differed from country to country, but medieval man assumed that they could be reconciled, since custom was but the particular application of the divine law (Biblical revelation) and natural law (rational principles) which God had given to all nations. The Reformation left each state interpreting the Bible to suit its own needs, and by plundering the Old Testament it was an easy matter to find ample precedents for deceit, treachery and naked aggression. (Since the New Testament of the outcast early Christians had little application to the problems of interstate relations, the Sermon on the Mount could just as easily be ignored.) What the Reformation did not destroy of the law of nations, the Renaissance had already swept aside. For the fifteenth-century addiction to antiquity turned Europeans from the relevant customary laws of the immediate past to the virtually irrelevant statecraft of the Greeks and Romans. When the rulers of seventeenth-century states openly avowed their sovereign power over their subjects, there were no medieval restraints to stand between them and their neighboring rulers. Each ruler claimed that he had no superior but God, which meant in effect that the sovereign power he used to maintain internal order could freely be used to undermine the order within other sovereign states.

Faced with this lack of structure in interstate relations, seventeenth-century monarchs must have looked back with nostalgia to the Christian Commonwealth. Unfortunately the dead hand of the past blinded their vision of the present. During the Renaissance and the Reformation, rulers had been creating rudimentary instruments for handling relations with their neighbors, but all too frequently they had fitted them unconsciously into the outmoded concept of the Christian Commonwealth rather than applying them to current conditions. Rulers, diplomats and writers on international law acted as if the embryonic diplomatic arms of the sovereign states could somehow be used to revive the Christian Commonwealth which these states had destroyed.

By 1600 the leading states of Italy, the major northern states of Spain, France, England and the Holy Roman Empire all had ambassadors in residence at the leading courts of western and central Europe. Supervision of "foreign affairs" was assigned to one or more secretaries of state. There were even rudimentary collections of diplomatic correspondence, negotiations and treaties. Yet many ambassadors, rulers and writers clung to the fiction of the Christian Commonwealth. The flood of new books and reprints of old ones on the *Perfect Ambassador*, which deluged Europe around 1600, graphically illustrates the ambivalence of that age's statecraft. On the one hand, the large numbers of such books indicates a tacit recognition that interstate problems existed. On the other, their title clearly links them with the past; the "perfect" ambassador was one who represented not his ruler but the Christian Commonwealth, and who was supposed to uphold international peace even if this meant betraying his sovereign. The most famous of these writers on diplomacy, De Vera (*The Ambassador*, 1620), was aware that an ambassador had some allegiance to his king, but his slippery apologies for this reality suggest that he wrote with a guilty conscience. And he was quite clear that lying and spying on behalf of one's prince were beneath an ambassador's honor. At the end of the century, the same loyalty to the past can be found in a model treatise on diplomacy by Callières (*On the Manner of Negotiating with Sovereigns*, 1716), and in the secret correspondence of a leading practitioner of diplomacy, William III.

The great sixteenth-century Spanish writers on international law, from Vittoria to Suarez, and the more famous Hugo Grotius (*On the Law of War and Peace*, 1625), tried to grapple more forthrightly with the existence of sovereign princes. Grotius' work was novel in implying the equality of all sovereign states and in discarding theological arguments. Nevertheless, in seeking a new "law of nations," Grotius and his predecessors really fell back on the medieval belief in divine, natural and customary laws which had buttressed the idea of the Christian Commonwealth, and then, rather futilely, tried to adapt them to states whose relations could not be governed by those principles. Grotius even opened his book with the outmoded definition of the law of nations as being "concerned with the mutual relations among states or rulers of states, whether derived from nature, or established by divine ordinances, or having its origin in custom and tacit agreement."

The problem of regulating interstate relations in the seventeenth century was compounded by the vogue of rebellion and by the great religious issues which cut across political boundaries. Rebellions were an open invitation for foreign princes to intervene. The so-called Thirty Years' War in the Germanies (1618–1648) was a melee in which one prince after another, inside and outside the Holy Roman Empire, intervened in the civil war between Emperor Ferdinand II and his Bohemian subjects. So, to a lesser extent, were the French and Spanish civil wars of the 1640's, as French and Spanish monarchs gave assistance to rebels in each other's states. The nobleman who considered himself more than just the king's subject, the Calvinist, Lutheran or Catholic whose international religious ties transcended any loyalty to his prince and the foreign ruler who was torn between respect for divine right and his religious motivations, found it difficult to see interstate relations simply as a matter between two sovereign states. The twentieth-century observer may consider the great French nobleman-prince, Condé, a traitor for joining Spain's armies against France in the 1650's. But Condé, the French minister Mazarin and the Spanish minister de Haro, were all so convinced of the convention of a nobleman's independence that Condé's settlement with the French monarchy was made an integral part of the treaty of 1659 which ended that war. And while the twentieth century may see Emperor Ferdinand II as a hopeless and wrongheaded idealist for insisting on Catholicism in 1629 when it meant the destruction of his political dream of a powerful, united Holy Roman Empire, Ferdinand and his generation would have been baffled at such a separation of politics and religion.

How then could rulers find a solution to the problem of interstate relations, if traditional theory, contemporary principle and current social conditions provided no answers? Most historians have simply thrown up their hands, and declared that the vacuum caused by the disintegration of the Christian Commonwealth gave rise to "anarchy in international relations." There is some truth to this assertion. There was no authority superior to the sovereign ruler, no commonly accepted "law of nations." The very diplomatic institutions, such as the ambassadorship, which had painfully come into being in previous generations, threatened to disappear at the beginning of the seventeenth century. One state after another temporarily recalled its ambassadors because each seemed to be using its embassies to plot religious rebellion rather than to advance the cause of European concord. The projects for universal peace which were so important to men like Leibniz, Lisola and William Penn made little impression, whether the call was for a European confederation or a Christian alliance against the Moslem Ottoman Empire. And more than one historian has pointed out that the plea for a peace of mutual respect in the novel *Simplicissimus* [3] was put in the mouth of a demented god, Jupiter. (Actually Jupiter had another solution—deportation, liquidation and a peace of fear among those who escaped his sword!)

Yet, "anarchy" is a proper description for interstate relations in the

---

3. Written by Grimmelshausen about German society during the Thirty Years' War. Cf. p. 27.

seventeenth century only if we view Europe as a whole. If, instead, we look at the motives, policies and actions of individual European rulers, the statecraft of the seventeenth century takes on some meaning. It was not simply "irrational," standing in sharp contrast to "rational" domestic state-building, but rather an integral part of a king's political workings in an arena where he did not have the advantage of claiming the last word. If war is an extension of diplomacy, diplomacy and war are an extension of the task of ruling.

What, then, were the princely ambitions and interests which make sense of the international melee? In the early decades of the century, the most important driving forces were the religion of the ruler and his efforts to strengthen his position within his state. The religious factor needs little elaboration here. It dominated Emperor Ferdinand II's military and diplomatic policies during the first two decades of the Thirty Years' War, reaching its climax in 1629 when he tried to impose a Catholic territorial settlement on the Germanies. It influenced the decision of Sweden's Gustavus Adolphus to intervene in the same war on behalf of his fellow Protestants in northern Germany. It helped to end the tenuous peace between Catholic Spain and the Protestant Dutch Netherlands in 1621. And it goes far in explaining why Catholic France refused to join Protestant German states against the Catholic Emperor about the same time. The other major interest of rulers early in the century, to enhance their internal authority, can be seen from a few random illustrations. Spain's determination to cling to its far-flung and militarily vulnerable

A realistic view of war

The Hanging Tree by Jacques Callot

FROM JACQUES CALLOT, "MISÈRES DE LA GUERRE," 1633

An idealized version of war: Spaniards receiving the keys to the city from the Dutch in 1625

The Surrender of Breda by Velazquez (1635)

European possessions was anathema to France. It meant virtual encirclement of the French state, and seemed in the long run to threaten its very existence. Thus, to protect their territorial integrity, Spain and France ultimately went to war in the 1630's. To the northeast, Swedish intervention in the Thirty Years' War was founded, along with religious considerations, on the premise that the Baltic-based Swedish empire would collapse if the Emperor's advance into northern Germany were left unchecked.

The end of the Thirty Years' War in the Germanies in 1648, and the conclusion of the contemporaneous Franco-Spanish and Baltic conflicts a decade later constitute a watershed in the diplomatic and military history of the seventeenth century. That fact can be inferred from the usual text-book statement that the Thirty Years' War was the last of the religious wars and the first modern secular conflict. But one must examine more closely that generalization to see what it really means.

In the first place, it does not mean that war in 1618 was entirely religious, nor in 1648 entirely secular. It means rather that rulers early in the century, who waved the flag of religion, were compelled with increasing frequency to fight with very secular weapons. To gain their religious ends, they had to make alliances wherever they could, even if the ally was of a different faith. Religious motivations were still prominent in 1648, and one can see them in the resistance of Protestant states to the Catholic Louis XIV in the 1680's. However, religious interests increasingly had to take second place to secular-political strategy, until these secular means became an end in themselves by 1715.

The second meaning of the textbook generalization involves the emergence of the sovereign state. By surviving the civil and foreign wars of the early seventeenth century, rulers had already approached the sovereign status over their subjects which is clearly seen in 1715. As a result, European wars after 1660 were closer to simple conflicts between states than to the earlier melees of ruler, rebel subjects and foreign princes. Internal rebellions were rare late in the century, and rarer still was the intervention of foreign rulers on behalf of the rebels. When outside monarchs did intervene, they usually did so as claimants to the throne. The sovereignty of the state as such was respected; the only question was who had the right to be sovereign. Even the Glorious Revolution of 1688 in England, which superficially resembles a combined civil and foreign war, was really a War of English Succession which replaced James II with William III.

Thus far, we have arrived at the generalization that late seventeenth-century wars were secular conflicts between sovereign states. This generalization requires one major qualification, however. Although the days of supra-national interest based on religion were largely gone, the secular interests of the sovereign prince rather than those of the nation-state had taken their place. The ruler had not won the battle for sovereignty over his subjects in order to bend his policies to their desires and welfare. State interest was princely interest. And princely interest revolved around two prime considerations—dynasticism and *gloire*.

Dynastic concerns were based on the idea that the state's territory was the personal possession of the king. Because royal dynasties constantly intermarried, the concept of the state as a dynastic possession meant constant friction and frequent interstate wars. Rulers were not "Frenchmen," "Spaniards" or "Englishmen" by blood, but a mixture of many nationalities. It is almost as valid to call Louis XIV a Spaniard as a

Frenchman, or to declare William III an Englishman rather than a Dutch-man. A disputed succession to a royal throne, or the extinction of a ruling dynasty brought immediate claims from several "foreign" princes who had blood ties to the "native" line. While recognizing the sovereignty of the state in question, these foreign claimants legitimately looked upon them-selves as rightful sovereigns. The personal "union" of England and the Dutch Netherlands under William III looks unnatural only to a later age which thinks in terms of nation-states. To the Spaniards who were threatened with the partition of their empire on the death of Charles II without heirs in 1700, nothing could have been more logical than to save the state by giving it *in toto* to the grandson of the French monarch. The spirit of dynasticism was so strong that it even entered states with elected heads. Poland was the victim of intrigues by the French, Austrian, Swedish and Muscovite rulers to place on the throne a foreigner under their in-fluence. The Holy Roman Empire was on more than one occasion in danger of being headed by Louis XIV, who thought there was nothing wrong in attempting to buy the votes of the German electoral princes in charge of choosing each new Emperor.

The blurred lines of nationality in the ill-defined border lands betwen states also led to disputes. The Treaties of Westphalia in 1648 defined the rights of rival princes so vaguely that the inhabitants of Rhenish lands could claim allegiance to the French monarch, the Holy Roman Emperor and to petty German princes. This confusion was com-pounded by the fact that one of those German princes was none other than the king of Sweden, who was overlord of a Rhenish enclave! The boundaries between Muscovy and the Ottoman Empire on the one hand, and their westerly neighbors on the other, were equally confused. Tran-sylvania could be claimed by both Hapsburg Austria and the Ottoman Porte. The nomadic Cossack peoples were subjected to similar pressures by Muscovy, Poland and the Ottoman Empire.

The late seventeenth-century emphasis on *gloire* is far better known than that on dynasticism, but that term has been so distorted and mis-applied that twentieth-century men can scarcely grasp its real significance. *Gloire* (literally translated as "glory") has been equated with megalomania and its cultivation attributed solely to Louis XIV. In actuality, *gloire* in its seventeenth-century sense meant reputation, and it was accepted by Louis XIV's fellow monarchs as a fundamental aspect of statecraft. A ruler had to live up to the high station to which he had been born, or suffer loss of prestige and international influence. The difference between the "glory" of Louis XIV and that of his fellow monarchs lay in his ability to achieve that end, not in disagreement over its validity. Few historians can resist the urge to tell how the Spanish ambassador to France begged Louis' forgiveness for the loss of French reputation during a diplomatic proces-

sion in London.[4] Nor can a writer with an eye for the dramatic ignore
Louis' public humiliation of Pope Alexander VII, for a Roman mob scene
which almost proved fatal to the French ambassador's wife. (In an unprecedented act for the Papacy, Alexander sent a special Legate to make
an apology before Louis XIV, and agreed to commemorate the occasion
by erecting a pyramid in Rome.) What historians fail to say is that these
and other such international incidents would have been petty baroque
plays had it not been for the importance which Louis XIV's fellow princes
attached to *gloire*.

The search for and the attainment of *gloire* were both a substitute
for war and a major cause of the embittered international relations which
often led to war. Louis XIV shrewdly noted that "reputation alone often
achieves more than the most powerful armies." He might have added
that as one image-conscious ruler pressed further and further for *gloire*,
he tarnished the reputation of others to the point where they had to uphold their honor with armed retaliation.

The rulers who fought the Thirty Years' War for God and self-
defense, and their sons and grandsons who waged the wars of Spanish
and Swedish succession in the name of secular *gloire* and dynasticism,
never quite lost the medieval vision of a peaceful Christian Commonwealth. But to the historian looking back at the century of almost unbroken warfare, the records are a mockery of the hopes. Whether they
realized it or not, the overriding preoccupation of seventeenth-century
rulers was with their position as independent, sovereign princes. Although
princely interests shifted gradually from the religious to the secular realm,
and from a defensive posture to dynastic aggrandizement, the focus was
almost invariably a narrow one. The Christian Commonwealth had become a congeries of independent powers, each of which acted as if what
its leaders did was in the interests of all. From the vantage-point of each
throne, state-building appeared rational; from the European perspective
it looked at best absurd, and at worst a tragedy.

Towards Modern Diplomacy:
National Interests and the Balance of Power

While late seventeenth-century rulers looked on the game of diplomacy and war from a personal, selfish perspective, one can detect
subtle changes in the nature of interstate relations between 1661 and

4. The Spanish ambassador to England had made good his claim that he would
precede his French counterpart in the parade; a scuffle between the French entourage
and Englishmen in Spanish pay kept the French ambassador from joining the proces-
sion.

1715. Just as the quest for sovereignty in internal matters eventually placed the state above the ruler, so, too, dynasticism and *gloire* became merged with a more modern and impersonal approach to interstate relations. First, personal, princely interests gave way slightly to national interests. Secondly, Europe groped towards the concept of a "balance of power" among states, as a means of regulating relations between sovereign princes. In neither case did rulers intend to give up personal sovereignty for broader considerations, but military, economic and diplomatic pressures led them to take actions which made them the unconscious midwives of modern national interests and the modern balance of power.

As armies grew and became more dangerous, it became obvious that dynastic state-hopping could increase a state's military vulnerability. Rulers had to balance the legitimacy of taking territories far beyond the state's borders with the desirability of providing security for existing territories. Hence, there was a tendency to round out a ruler's domains along a defensible frontier rather than to pursue dynastic claims to distant areas. Louis XIV's famous siege expert, Vauban, was a leading figure in the movement to change borders from a hopping, zig-zagging line to a relatively straight one. Once such a line became established, and was fortified, the interior of France was far safer than it had been during the earlier Franco-Spanish conflict. The Austrian Hapsburgs did much the same thing, groping towards a defensible frontier after pushing the Turks out of the Hungarian basin in the 1680's. The most dramatic gesture in this direction was made by Muscovy's Peter the Great, who built his new capital of Saint Petersburg in the frontier area on the Baltic seized from Sweden.

Such developments in favor of the state as a solid block of land did not, of course, supersede dynastic concerns. The Austrian Hapsburgs not only rounded out their Danubian frontier in the 1680's, but made good their dynastic claim to the absurdly distant and non-Austrian territories of the Spanish Netherlands and Spanish Italy in 1714. No ruler thought of "natural frontiers" in the modern sense of a line which divided peoples according to race, language or culture. But it is interesting to note that Louis XIV had alternative schemes for dealing with the Spanish succession question. If he could not obtain the entire inheritance for his grandson, he was willing to make international agreements to round out his borders. Should the Spanish empire be partitioned, France would receive territories far removed from the French state; Louis intended to barter these lands in turn for territories contiguous with France.

When such bargaining took place, or areas near a state's borders were directly acquired, there remained the problem of assimilating the new subjects. Neither Louis XIV, nor Leopold I of Austria, nor Peter the

Great managed to truly nationalize these new nationals. Surprisingly enough in view of the French monarchy's power, Louis XIV was the least interested of the three in pressing for assimilation. Ex-Spanish Franche Comté retained its local customs, and ex-German Strassburgers were permitted to worship as Protestants at the very time when Protestantism was being stamped out elsewhere in France. Probably Sweden was the most advanced state in nationalizing new subjects. Yet it was successful only in the former Danish territories of southern Sweden; new subjects on the southeastern Baltic coast remained parochial and easily shifted allegiance to the Russian state when Peter the Great took over the area.

Undoubtedly the late seventeenth-century wars contributed to a sense of national identity. Spaniards fought for the integrity of the Spanish empire against the Austrian claimant, Charles, and Germans recoiled in horror at Louis XIV's brigandage of German territories. The Holy Roman Empire, supposedly a weak confederation of German states after 1648, actually declared war on the French monarch in the 1670's and 1680's. However, one should be extremely wary of confusing these occasional, poorly articulated, national feelings with modern nationalism, which became possible only when the late eighteenth-century revolutions enshrined the "sovereignty of the nation" and identified the state with its citizens rather than with its king.

Mercantilism was another factor which drew princely and national interests together. While few governmental economists were concerned about the economic well-being of subjects as such, they found that a sound national economy was a necessary means to the mercantilist end of a strong state. Neither Louis XIV nor Leopold I thought highly of businessmen, but their ministers, Colbert and Von Hörnigk, were highly conscious of the need to cultivate business interests as sources of taxes and military goods. At the end of the seventeenth century, mercantilism was still predominantly the pursuit of royal power through increased productivity, but the interests of the producers were beginning to color the decisions of the state.

There can be no doubt that princely-national mercantilism turned many of the late seventeenth century wars into economic conflict. Too often historians assume that mercantilists within a state wanted to sacrifice war to the peaceful pursuit of a state's economic well-being. It is commonly, and erroneously, asserted that Colbert was a man of peace, struggling to hold back the war-mongering of France's minister for war, Louvois. Such was not the case. Colbert was as addicted to war as a solution to internal economic problems as was Louvois to war as the extension of diplomacy. And Colbert was typical of late seventeenth century mercantilists.

Mercantilism was a form of warfare against outside states, and its logical extension was open military conflict. English attempts to cut into Dutch trade and shipping provoked a series of Anglo-Dutch wars which stretched from 1652 to 1674. Colbert's punitive tariff of 1667 against the Dutch was a major cause of the Franco-Dutch war of 1672–1678. Louis XIV's decision to fight in the Germanies rather than intervene in the English succession dispute of 1688 was also based partly on economic considerations. The French monarch assumed that the navy assembled by James II made the English a potential commercial foe of France, and that the succession dispute would involve James II and William III in a long war of attrition, during which Dutch and English commercial interests would suffer to the economic advancement of France. The War of Spanish Succession, which dominated the last decade and a half of the century, was a mixture of dynasticism and mercantilism. The French and Austrian rulers could see the economic windfalls to be picked up by seizure of Spanish territory. But neither the Dutch nor the English wanted a French monopoly of Mediterranean commerce, which would have been the price of letting France control Spain and Spanish Italy.

Perhaps the best way to demonstrate the mercantilist-war nexus is by describing the assumptions late seventeenth-century statemen made about money, trade and shipping. No one expressed those ideas more lucidly than Colbert. He assumed that there was "only a given quantity of money which circulates in Europe," and that "the trade of all Europe is carried on with about 20,000 ships of all sizes [whose] number cannot be increased, since the populations and the consumption of all the states remains the same." From this view of the static nature of European wealth and resources, Colbert went on to draw the conclusion that France must try to secure a larger slice of the economic pie. Colbert talked of a "war of money," and declared that "commerce causes a perpetual battle in peace and war between the nations of Europe, as to who will win the best part of it."

Colbert's position was in some respects the economic counterpart of the concepts of *gloire* and dynasticism. Trading companies were considered the king's armies, French industries and canals his "reserve corps," a favorable balance of trade with rival states constituted a "conquest," and results of the economic "wars" contributed to the "greatness and power of the state and the magnificence of the king." Like *gloire*, "this magnificence is so much greater in that it abases at the same time all the neighboring states." The economic sword-rattling of Colbert has its counterpart in Thomas Mun's *England's Treasure by Foreign Trade* (1669), and the pompous *Austria Over All If She Only Will* (1684) by von Hörnigk, which proclaimed that Austria could outstrip all her European rivals through cameralism and "in all probability win . . . a wealth and splendor such as she has never in her history had or even dared to hope for."

Not every subject could see that the economic *gloire* of the state provided material benefits for its inhabitants. Many Dutch merchants saw national interest in trade, not war, and insisted on trading with other states at the very moment that the Dutch Netherlands was locked in combat with them. Other commercial interest groups resigned themselves to wars, but grumbled at the loss of markets in hostile states. Still, many groups and individuals saw the fusion of economic and military conflicts as a national blessing. While merchants in the Dutch province of Holland complained of their wartime lot, those in the neighboring province of Zeeland thrived on war which legalized their piracy on the high seas and off the shores of the continent. Certainly French manufacturers of goods which competed with foreign imports had cause to rejoice when Colbert erected prohibitive tariffs against the Dutch and Louis XIV went to war to support those tariffs.

It is not as easy to determine the role of the other "modern" element in late seventeenth century wars, namely the concept of the "balance of power." Looking backwards from the nineteenth and twentieth centuries, historians have seen some signs of such a principle operating in the age of Louis XIV. Put simply, the idea is that whenever one state becomes so powerful that it threatens the power and existence of others, those states will combine to weaken the aggressor and restore a balance. Now there is no doubt that such a principle was at work during the late seventeenth century, but there are serious questions regarding some inferences that have been drawn from its existence. We need to examine, for example, whether rulers consciously thought of wars in terms of a balance of power. We should also ask ourselves whether the balance of power was really workable, whether European rulers succeeded in arranging the relative power of states so that they were in equilibrium.

In looking for the answers to these questions, one immediately runs into the stubborn fact that rulers were very slow to place the idea of a balance of power above their particular aggressive interests. Both wars and peace treaties show that each prince tried to seize as much as he could in the scramble, with little thought for a balancing of powers. Diplomacy looks very much like the "biggest dog getting the meatiest bone," and all others helping themselves in the order of size. As Sir George Clark has aptly commented, the balance of power principle which was defended as a means to preserve the *status quo* usually became "not a static principle, but a method of regulating and facilitating change." [5] For the "balance of power" was always restored not simply by taking away the gains of the aggressor, but by reassigning bits of territory in new ways, giving rise to new tensions and further wars.

One historian has countered this criticism by saying that at each stage of the continuing struggle for equilibrium, new states were added to the European states-system to prevent domination of the system by an aggressor. Thus England entered the European scene to tip the delicate balance against Louis XIV.[6] But this argument is also an admission that the area controlled by European statecraft became increasingly large, and hence more complex and difficult to regulate. In reality, the Europe of 1600 was three Europes (western, northern, southeastern), whose interconnected conflicts became fused by 1715 into one loosely connected states-system. The common use of a single modern diplomatic language (French), the perfection of the institution of the ambassador and the emergence of international peace congresses by the end of the seventeenth century do indicate that the instruments of diplomacy had improved considerably. However, they were instruments of an ever-enlarging number of predatory states, who made it more and more difficult to make sense on an international level of princely ambitions which were rational when viewed from the perspective of the individual ruler. If one wishes to eulogize the states-system of the seventeenth century as a creative force, one may do so by showing how wars compelled rulers to streamline their internal institutions, develop their internal economies and impose internal order on their estates, but surely not by implying a similar international product.

Finally, the "military revolution" which was a by-product of almost constant warfare made war a permanent European institution. During the religious-secular wars of the late sixteenth and early seventeenth centuries, rulers were in the process of turning their armies and navies into an effective and permanent branch of government. That process was accelerated between 1661 and 1715. There was a limit to the effectiveness of these later military machines, but it tended to prolong wars and make them indecisive, rather than discourage their outbreak. Armies were on the whole much larger than in the early seventeenth century, but rulers were wary of introducing universal military service for fear of placing too much power in the hands of their subjects. Voluntary enlistment, supplemented by some conscription and coercion (the famous press-gangs

5. G. N. Clark, *The Seventeenth Century* (Galaxy, 1961), 138.
6. L. Dehio, *The Precarious Balance* (Vintage, 1962).

of the English navy, for example) became the practice, soldiers coming from the bottom of society and almost as frequently from neighboring states. Discipline had to be fierce to make such an army effective; and if the army was risked in a major battle, and casualties high, it was difficult to secure replacements. With the improvement of firearms and their use by cavalry as well as infantry, statesmen became more conservative in their military objectives. Generals like England's Marlborough often wanted to risk all on a "sure" military victory, but politicians became addicted to sieges. It was easy to win battles and lose the war as a result. The brilliant victories of Marlborough at Blenheim and Ramillies were in fact followed by the bloody and senseless battles of Malplaquet and Audenarde which virtually destroyed both sides, and were not to be repeated before the battle of Borodino in 1812, and again in World War I.

Navies were even more difficult to maintain, and were subject to far more precipitous decline. It has been estimated that it cost twice as much to maintain one sailor as one soldier. Recruitment was necessarily far more limited, since sailors could be found only among the seafaring element of a state's population, a distinct minority. Many princes, including the ambitious but poor elector of Brandenburg, attempted to build navies, but only a few states managed to develop a respectable fleet— the English, French, Dutch, Swedes and, at the very end of the century, the Russians. Still, navies were an important weapon in the game of high politics. The navy which Cromwell and the restored Stuart dynasty developed played a major role in drawing England into continental wars; and the new Russian navy made Peter the Great feel confident in launching attacks on the Turks and Swedes. The French navy rose under Colbert in the 1660's and 1670's only to collapse before the imperious demands for the French army; nevertheless, it was a very significant factor in bringing about the Franco-Dutch war.

The combination of dynasticism, *gloire*, national interests and the balance of power made the wars of the late seventeenth century as complex as they were long. It has been suggested that in 1715 the first two motives were still more important than the others. But in making this generalization, one should not lose sight of the more important point that the old and the new were constantly vying with each other for the attention of statesmen. The confusion of princely interests and state interests, of dynastic aggressiveness and a search for the balancing of power in Europe, shows that the path from medieval ways to modernity was not a smooth one. The Thirty Years' War was in part a turning-point from religious to secular interests. But the complex of secular interests which unleashed the succeeding conflicts indicates all too clearly that Europe was still grappling with problems inherited from previous centuries. There were still no clear-cut, modern "solutions" to the difficulties caused by the weakening of traditional bonds. And the emergence of the sovereign prince made a difficult situation worse. The rulers of 1715 were strong enough to maintain some internal order, but too independent to permit a secularized version of the old Christian Commonwealth, and too powerful to give way before "national" interests.

3.

Post-reformation
Intellectual Currents

❧❧

B etween 1540 and 1640, Europe experienced the first phase of an
intellectual upheaval which ultimately revolutionized European
conceptions of God, man and the universe. That phase was largely a destructive one, which weakened the medieval Christian assumptions underlying the prevailing theocentric *weltanschauung* (world view). Within
a hundred years, Christian beliefs were subjected to bitter theological
disputes among the major confessions, challenged by religious "enthusiasm" and pagan free-thinking, and presented with an unexpected rival in
the form of modern science. The second, constructive phase of the
intellectual revolution saw the Age of Newton replace the shattered
theocentric world with a secular, centerless one which has been the
weltanschauung of the west ever since.

The shift from theological to secular concerns was both complex
and gradual. Because Christianity had assimilated much of ancient science
and continually allied itself with popular superstitious beliefs, the assault
on Christian doctrines was bound to involve far more than a few articles
of faith. At the same time, there was no outright "war" between Christians and anti-Christians. Even the most hostile critics of Christianity were
too steeped in Christian culture to make a clean break, as Carl Becker
noted in his witty *Heavenly City of the Eighteenth Century Philoso-*

phers. Many intellectual innovators consciously sought to reconcile their revolutionary ideas with traditional ones. Others unconsciously adopted the "double truth," accepting many traditional doctrines alongside new ideas without realizing that the old and new could not easily be reconciled. Even the greatest figure of seventeenth-century science, Newton, showed signs of the "split mind," discovering the immutable laws of physical science while writing a commentary on the apocalyptic Old Testament Book of Daniel. More astonishing is the tenacity of outright superstition and supernaturalism among the intellectual elite as well as the "common man." The astronomer Kepler scoffed at the way early seventeenth century astrologers plied their trade, but he was firmly convinced that astrology could yield secrets about the universe if rightly used. He could write to a friend that "nothing exists nor happens in the visible sky that is not sensed in some hidden manner by the faculties of Earth and Nature; these faculties of the spirit here on earth are as much affected as the sky itself." We can trace further that leading scientist's thoughts on astrology in another, revealing passage from his correspondence:

> In what manner does the countenance of the sky at the moment of man's birth determine his character? It acts on the person during his life in the manner of the loops which a peasant ties at random around the pumpkins in his field: they do not cause the pumpkin to grow, but they determine its shape. The same applies to the sky: it does not endow man with his habits, history, happiness, children, riches or a wife, but it moulds his condition.

Later in the century, we have the curious testimony of the novelist Grimmelshausen on witchcraft. He has his hero, Simplicissimus, say that "There be some, and indeed some learned folk among them, that believe not that there be witches and sorcerers, still less that they can fly from place to place in the air." What can one infer but that many intellectuals still persisted in the belief?

One must not suppose that the blurred lines between traditional belief and intellectual innovation made the seventeenth-century intellectual ferment a less severe problem than the contemporaneous socio-economic and political-international issues. Intellectual confusion reigned, as unsettling as any clear-cut conflict. It is no mere coincidence that the witch craze reached its zenith toward the middle of the seventeenth century, coinciding with the flourishing of new religious sects, the printing of many books on "atheism" and "libertinism" and the attempts of the giants of science to reduce the universe to fixed laws. For the mid-seventeenth century, which marked the close of the first, destructive phase of the intellectual revolution, saw Europeans grasping for any potential absolutes or at least for some compromise position which could make sense of the world of ideas and beliefs. Only in retrospect can we see that the mid-century confusion was to lead to the metamorphosis of European culture and the emergence of a new view of the world by the opening of the eighteenth century.[1]

❧ The Continuing Reformation and the Quest for Salvation

Because medieval European thought had centered on religion, the Reformation of the sixteenth century marked the first breach in the walls of the medieval *weltanschauung*. The medieval Catholic church had had its periodic intellectual crises and several major shocks to its institutional structure, its heresies from within and pagan challenges from without. It had survived them all, and continued to command the hearts and minds of virtually all Europeans. The Reformation shattered this institutional and intellectual unity. Instead of one catholic (universal) church, there were now four major confessions: the Roman Catholic (holding sway over Latin and southern Teutonic Europe as well as Ireland and the Spanish Netherlands), the Lutheran (predominant in northern Germany and Scandinavia), the Reformed or Calvinist (centered in Geneva, but with offshoots in the Dutch Netherlands, southwestern France, western Germany, England, Scotland, Hungary and Transylvania) and the Anglican (the official church of England). From the viewpoint of the twentieth century, the theological differences between post-Reformation churches may appear small. In his *Origins of Modern Science*, Herbert Butterfield goes so far as to dismiss the religious divisions of the Reformation as "mere episodes, mere internal displacements, within the system of medieval Christendom." [2] But to early modern Europeans, these internal displacements had a profoundly unsettling effect.

The most disturbing theological divisions of the Reformation concerned the question of man's salvation. On that issue medieval thinkers had suggested a variety of interpretations which could easily split Christianity if pressed to their logical extremes. One example can be found in the viewpoints of the fifth-century writer, Saint Augustine, and the giant of thirteenth-century thought, Saint Thomas Aquinas.

Aquinas and Augustine agreed on the basic Christian doctrines of Original Sin and divine grace. God had made man the special creature of his world, placing the first man, Adam, in the Garden of Eden, establishing the rest of creation for Adam's use, and allowing man an idyllic child-

---

1. The following sections of this chapter concentrate on the destructive phase of the intellectual revolution. On the constructive "Age of Newton," see Part IV.
2. H. Butterfield, *The Origins of Modern Science* (1950), viii.

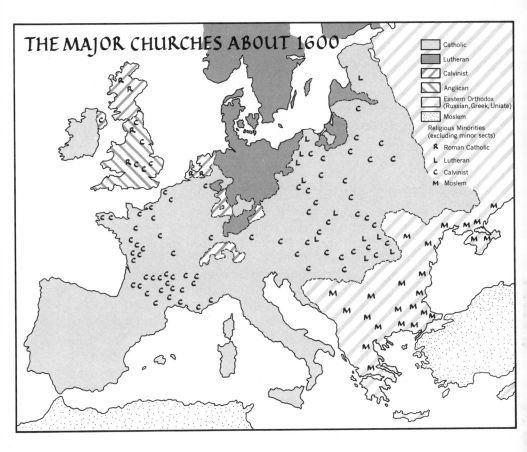

THE MAJOR CHURCHES ABOUT 1600

Catholic
Lutheran
Calvinist
Anglican
Eastern Orthodox
(Russian, Greek, Uniate)
Moslem

Religious Minorities
(excluding minor sects)
R Roman Catholic
L Lutheran
C Calvinist
M Moslem

like existence without the knowledge of good and evil. However, Adam
willfully sinned by eating the forbidden fruit of the tree of knowledge.
With that act, he asserted his desire to rival God. This Original Sin of
Adam became an innate trait of sinfulness in all human beings after him.
For this deed, Adam was banished from the Garden to a life of toil.
He and his descendants were condemned to know the difference between
good and evil without having the ability to eradicate evil. At best, they
could use their God-given reason to combat selfishness and strife through
human institutions like the state. Yet God did not leave man to struggle
through life on his own. He sent his Son, Jesus, to live on earth and to
show man how to love God and his fellow man. Central to Jesus' life
were his crucifixion and resurrection. The crucifixion revealed that God
loved his human creatures enough to sacrifice his own Son for them. At
the crucifixion, Jesus forgave man for the brutal act of killing him,
symbolically taking upon himself the sins of the world. Thus God revealed that He could be merciful as well as just. While punishing man
with original sin, He forgave men's sins. The resurrection of Jesus was
the climax of the crucifixion story. For Jesus proved that man could
conquer death, that death was not the sad end to a sad story, but pre-

liminary to an afterlife. God would decide whether to condemn an individual to an afterlife in Hell or to use His grace to award him salvation (the knowledge of and union with God) in Heaven. Meanwhile, when Jesus ascended to Heaven after his resurrection, he left behind his Church with the power to help Christians merit God's grace by leading an upright life on earth. The Church had its sacraments (outward signs of invisible grace) to serve this purpose. For example, the sacrament of baptism wiped away Original Sin from a baby, while the sacraments of penance (confessing one's sins to a priest and receiving absolution) and the Eucharist (reenacting the sacrifice of Jesus) helped to make men constantly aware of the effects of Original Sin which still remained and had to be combatted constantly.

Within this broad theological framework, Augustine and Aquinas differed somewhat on the effects of Original Sin, and the interplay of human will and divine grace. Augustine felt that Original Sin seriously impaired human reason, while Aquinas was much more optimistic about the rational faculty of post-Eden mankind. Augustine saw human institutions as exceedingly imperfect, while Aquinas was convinced that they were not just the result of Original Sin but also a means to improve the lot of the human race. When it came to salvation, Augustine so emphasized the role of divine grace that he came close to denying any role to man in the quest for a heavenly afterlife. It was possible to read into his writings the view that God predestined man to salvation or damnation, without regard to his merits. While Aquinas agreed that only God's grace could bring man salvation, he was much more willing than Augustine to admit that human reason and will employed in doing good works were noticed by God.

The Reformations of Luther, Calvin, England's Henry VIII and ultimately of the Roman confession unleased a torrent of disputation over the meaning of salvation. The division of Christianity into rival churches made it difficult to reconcile these theological differences as had been done in the unified medieval church. Luther and Calvin took their cue from Augustine, while the Catholic Council of Trent relied heavily on Aquinas. Calvin held an extreme interpretation of Augustine, stressing the will of God the Judge, who predestined a few humans for salvation and condemned the bulk of mankind to damnation in Hell. Luther's focus on the mercifulness of God kept him from such a harsh view, but his concept of "justification by faith" certainly implied that God's grace and not man's actions produced salvation.[3] The Catholic Tridentine position

---

3. Luther's discussions of "justification by faith" varied, but essentially he believed that the just man lived by the faith that God saved men in spite of their sinfulness.

was an avowed reaction to the Protestant emphasis on predestination. While not without its Augustinian elements, it declared that man had free will and a powerful rational faculty. Without God's prevenient grace, the Council affirmed, no man could hope for salvation. The individual did play a significant role, on the other hand, in accepting or rejecting that grace, as well as in meriting it by faith, hope and love (good works). Within the reformed Catholic church, these views were emphasized especially by the newly created religious order known as the Society of Jesus, whose members played a key role at Trent. But the older Dominican order, of which Aquinas had been a member, rivalled the Jesuits' zeal by propagating Catholic beliefs in the University of Alcala.

As the sixteenth century progressed, and the confessional divisions of Christianity hardened, the debate concerning salvation crept into each individual confession. At the beginning of the seventeenth century, free will remained the dominant view of Catholicism and predestination of Protestantism, but there were Catholic predestinarians and Protestants who believed strongly in free will. What probably happened was that as each confession tried to define an "orthodox" position for its members to counter rival churches, differences arose over what orthodoxy meant.

On the Catholic side, some Jesuits arrived at controversial conclusions in working out the details of free will. In order to present Catholicism in a more attractive light to a religiously confused Europe, they maintained that God's grace would make sweeping concessions to the frailty of human nature. Unfortunately, their advice that Catholics take communion frequently was misinterpreted; it was inferred by critics that the Jesuits were inviting individuals to sin, since they could light-heartedly go to Mass and feel that their sins were forgiven. The Iberian Jesuit Luis Molina's *Harmony of Free Will with Grace, Divine Fore-knowledge, Providence and Reprobation* (1588) shocked many fellow Catholics, since it seemed to exaggerate the free will of man and deal lightly with sinfulness. As Jesuits appeared to be opening wide the gates of heaven with arguments excusing many sins, they became the object of cruel jokes. Wags turned the liturgical phrase "Behold the Lamb of God that takest away the sins of the world" into "Behold the Fathers who have taken away the sins of the world." Acrimonious debate was added to ridicule. A Dominican-Jesuit controversy was glossed over by a papal decree of 1607 which imposed public silence on both parties. Silence could not be maintained, for the question of free will remained unresolved. Many seventeenth-century Catholics muttered that "the God of the Molinists is an Idiot," and the University of Louvain became a breeding place for a Catholic Augustinianism which took issue not only with Jesuit Molinism but with the Dominicans as well.

The Catholic Augustinian movement which started at Louvain became the famous Jansenism of mid-seventeenth century Europe, which took its name from Cornelius Jansen, Professor of the Bible at that university. Jansen was influenced by a late sixteenth-century critic of the Jesuits, Michael Bajus, and by his own reading of Augustine. Two years after his death, Europe was shaken by the appearance of his great work, *Augustinus* (1640). Jansenism spread quickly until it had followings in the Netherlands, Lorraine, Poland, Spain and Italy in addition to its most famous center at the convent of Port Royal outside Paris. Under the influence of the convent's advisor, Abbé de Saint-Cyran, and the Mother Superior's brother, Antoine Arnauld, the movement became fashionable among the political, social and intellectual elite of France.

In essence Jansen and Jansenism adopted a strict predestinarian position which was as controversial as the Jesuit stress on free will. Jansen declared that Jesus had not died for all men, and the emphasis his followers put on the awesomeness of the Deity came close to obliterating the roles of man and the church. The historian David Ogg could not resist the epigram that Saint-Cyran's philosophy was "one of perdition for the unfortunate many and ascetic gloom for the fortunate few," and added that the Abbé's theology "started with the Fall and ended with the Flood."[4] Saint-Cyran actually believed that the world had become so corrupted with sin that the true Christian should flee from it in order to avoid contamination. He was convinced that the true Church of Christ had also ceased to exist, through contamination. Arnauld's *On Frequent Communion* (1643) warned fun-loving noblewomen to abstain from communion until they were wallowing in despair for their salvation and ready to be truly penitent. The Jansenists were doubtful whether the door to heaven, which the Jesuits were leaving wide open, should be even left ajar. It is little wonder that one great Christian, Saint Vincent de Paul, asked how Arnauld could even think of celebrating Mass if Christians and their church were so debased and God so severe as he assumed.

In the heat of their controversies, Jansenists, Jesuits, Dominicans and successive Popes all missed the opportunity to stress the common beliefs which they all inherited from Catholicism's great traditions. The Papacy was particularly remiss, evading its responsibility for leadership in the Dominican-Jesuit debates and then taking a partisan position over the differences between Jesuits and Jansenists. The Papacy rejected Bajus' proto-Jansenism at the beginning of the century, and then condemned

4. D. Ogg, *Europe in the Seventeenth Century* (1959), 331–332.

Jansenist views in the papal bull *Cum Occasione* in 1653. Undoubtedly the Jansenists merited censure, and historians have found it difficult to forgive their argumentativeness and self-righteousness. But the fact remains that Popes were slow to criticize the ill effects of Jesuit casuistry, and the censure of 1679 was mild and limited. Nor was there a new Augustine or a new Aquinas to produce a theological synthesis which would take into account the variety of seventeenth-century Catholic thought.[5]

Seventeenth-century Protestantism was equally ineffective in dealing with the explosive issue of salvation. Neither the Lutherans' Formula of Concord (1580) nor the Calvinists' Heidelberg Catechism (1563) proved to be a synthesis satisfactory to all members of their respective confessions. Lutherans divided into at least three important factions over the question of salvation before the end of the sixteenth century. The Gneisolutherans of Magdeburg accused the Philippists of Wittenberg of saying that good works were necessary for salvation, while at Königsberg Andreas Osiander seemed too Catholic and anti-predestinarian for either contending party. Ironically, the Calvinist Heidelberg Confession was mild enough in its views of predestination to satisfy the Lutheran Philippists, but too mild to be accepted by those Calvinists who favored a rigid predestinarianism.

The greatest dispute among Calvinists took place in the Dutch Netherlands during the first two decades of the seventeenth century. The main contestants were a professor of theology at the University of Leyden, Jacob Arminius, and Francis Gomarus, his colleague. Gomarus held to the Dutch Reformed church's position that God not only predestined men to salvation or damnation, but had done so before the Fall of Adam (supralapsarianism). Arminius had originally examined Calvinist doctrines in an effort to learn how to combat free-thinking, anti-predestinarian Dutchmen. But as he delved into theology, he boggled at the idea that man's fallen state was part of God's original design; such a God had to be considered the author of human sin! Moreover, Arminius wished to work man's free will into the eternal quest for salvation. Before he was through his studies, the learned theologian opened the doors to heaven as wide as the Jesuits, hinting that Heaven could find room for those who combined works with faith, and even for virtuous non-Christians. The orthodox Gomarists won an official victory at the national Calvinist Synod of Dort (1618), but they could not silence the Arminians. The attendance at Dort of Calvinist observers from England, Scotland, Germany and

5. On Jansenist controversies in France, see also Chapter 10, pp. 267–268.

Switzerland made the breach between Gomarists and Arminians all the more serious. Catholics, too, watched the proceedings with intense interest, which prepared the ground for the Jesuit-Jansenist controversy over the same issue.

Some Calvinists ultimately found common ground in "covenant theology," which was set forth in John Cocceius' *Doctrine of the Covenant and Testaments of God* (1648). Covenant theology eschewed references to salvation, and by concentrating on the majesty of God emphasized that the Christian's chief aim was to glorify and worship Him. Still, this masterful resolution of the debate by shifting the focus of theological attention proved to be ephemeral. In 1686, the Dutch Calvinists returned to the controversy in a meeting at Dort. The bitterness of such divisions is evident in the fact that the French Huguenots, a Calvinist minority in a Catholic state, could not close their ranks even in the face of persecution. A Huguenot synod at Charenton in 1631 failed to define orthodoxy, and when the Huguenot Jurieu escaped Catholic persecution late in the century by going to the Dutch Netherlands, he promptly became a heresy hunter in the Huguenot colony of Rotterdam. The Huguenots who fled to England appalled the English with the fanaticism and internecine quarrels which they brought with them from France.

In England, the Thirty-Nine Articles of the Anglican church (1563) had a somewhat happier fate because they were vague and inconsistent, leaving the individual to interpret the matter of salvation as he wished. Still, Queen Elizabeth had her troubles. She suppressed Article XVII which dealt directly with salvation, because it seemed too Calvinistic and predestinarian. To her horror, she soon discovered that some Anglicans, including high church officials, wanted a more Calvinist article. Elizabeth rejected their proposed Lambeth Articles of 1595, and the subsequent Stuart monarchs avoided doctrinal controversy. But during the civil war of the 1640's the issue reemerged in the Westminster Assembly, packed with "learned, godly and judicious [i.e., Calvinist] divines." Its Confession of Faith and Shorter Catechism were a masterful summation of covenant theology, avoiding such emotionally charged words as "reprobation," and centering on the unifying theme that "Man's chief end is to glorify God and to enjoy him forever." This achievement of a decade of work and some eleven hundred sessions was for nought, nonetheless. Westminster was the work of a minority, and in any case its resolutions fell on barren ground when Cromwell's seizure of power placed England under a man who was hostile to creeds, particularly of the Westminster variety. Even John Milton, the Puritan poet of the Fall of Adam (*Paradise Lost*) scorned the work of Westminster, dismissing it as "plots and packing worse than those of Trent."

The storm over salvation was but one of many that disturbed the religious climate of seventeenth-century Europe. It has been stressed here because it was probably the most important "contribution" within Christianity to the breakdown of traditional thought. To most twentieth-century men, the debates on various types of grace, and the question of whether God predestined before or after Adam's Fall, are remote and almost incomprehensible. But to the seventeenth-century theologians in the universities, to the intellectual elite who read their huge rambling works in Latin and the vernacular and to the educated laymen who understood enough to follow the discussion, salvation was *the* intellectual issue. Granted, the question did not directly determine whether all things happen of necessity or are shaped in part by man. Indeed some predestinarians thought that in secular matters, man had free will. As Luther declared, any man can act as he pleases, milk the cow or not, as he chooses. Nevertheless, the debate over salvation indirectly affected European views of the secular as well as the religious life. By failing to come to an agreement, and by making so clear their differences, seventeenth-century Christians opened the way for the ultimate rejection of the idea that God intervened in the drama of human existence. The road leads to Voltaire in the eighteenth century, who wrote:

> I know to be sure that the Church is infallible; but is it the Greek Church or the Latin Church, or the Church of England, or that of Denmark and of Sweden? . . . In short, would it not be better not to lose ourselves in these labyrinths and simply preach virtue? When God judges us, I doubt very much if he will ask whether grace is versatile or concomitant. . . . Shall I not render a service to men in announcing to them nothing but morality? This morality is so pure, so holy, so universal, so clear, so ancient that it seems to come direct from God, like the light of day which we consider his first creation. Did he not give men self-love to insure their preservation; sympathy, beneficence and virtue to control self-love; mutual needs for the formation of society; pleasure in the satisfaction of them; pain which cautions us to enjoy with moderation; passions which lead us on to great things, and wisdom to curb passions?[6]

The variety of positions on salvation had another unexpected result. The Calvinist stress on the majesty of God led many to direct their entire life to His glory, but it also bore the possible inference that God was chained by His own will, a view which is easily accommodated to the seventeenth-century scientific conception of the universe as being governed by fixed laws which give no room for divine intervention. How

6. From *The Questions of Zapata*, a portion of Voltaire's *Miscellanies*.

close to the clock-like universe of eighteenth-century Deism are John Calvin's own words in *The Institutes of the Christian Religion*:

> We hold that God is the disposer and ruler of all things—that from the remotest eternity, according to His own wisdom, He decreed what He was to do, and now, by His power, executes what He has decreed. Hence we maintain that, by His providence, not heaven and earth and inanimate creatures only, but also the counsels and wills of men, are so governed as to move exactly in the course which He has destined.

The Jesuit accommodation to human frailty as well as the Arminian concessions to free will led equally logically towards the glorification of man without God. Arminius meant to attack the quasi-secular humanism of his fellow countryman Coonhert as well as the strict predestinarianism of the Dutch Reformed church. But it was easy to go from Arminius to Coonhert to pure Deism. Jesuit missionaries in China at the end of the seventeenth century were on sounder theological ground when they suggested that the Catholic church should tolerate secular Chinese customs. But the ensuing controversy over the "Chinese rites" led to confusion and even disbelief among European Catholics.[7]

One constructive by-product of the seventeenth-century interest in theology was a fresh awareness of what it meant to lead a Christian life. Europeans of the late sixteenth and early seventeenth century took their religion as well as their theology seriously. Many Catholics and Protestants became concerned with how to "know Christ," to lead a devout life, to love their fellow man. Commentaries on St. Matthew's Gospel, Chapter XXV, found their way into sermons and religious tracts. We can find that gospel message in St. Francis de Sales' *Introduction to the Devout Life*: "If you love the poor, mingle frequently with them, take pleasure in meeting them in your homes, in visiting them in theirs ... become their servant, go to the aid of the bedridden, I say with your own hands and at your own expense be their cook, their wardrobe keeper, their washerwoman." We can find that message acted out in French Catholic programs which combined material assistance, spiritual help and a willingness to become a part of the lives of the downtrodden. The same spirit is evident in the Lutheran break with the medieval view that the monk was necessarily more saintly than the average layman, and in the occasional philanthropy of English Puritanism. Modern research has also uncovered evidence of improved morality, more regular church attendance and a more frequent and serious participation in the sacraments during the period. Paradoxically, post-Reformation Europe was

---

7. On the "Chinese rites," see Chapter 16, pp. 422–423.

more Christian in its interests and conduct than it had been for centuries, at the same time that the quarrels among the major churches broke down the comprehensive Christian conception of human nature.

The Religious Frontier: Christian Enthusiasm and Pagan Free Thought

While the major confessions were undermining Christianity from within, two important intellectual currents were sapping its strength on the frontier. The religious "enthusiasm" of minor sects bred by the Reformation had very little in common with the unemotional pagan philosophies revived by the Renaissance. It is a far cry from the Quaker James Naylor's entry to Bristol in 1656 (in a manner disturbingly similar to Jesus' Palm Sunday triumph in Jerusalem) to Michel de Montaigne's skeptical motto "What do I know?". Naylor's frenzied companions who screamed "Holy! Holy! Holy! the Lord God of Israel! Hosanna in the highest!" *knew* that Naylor was Jesus himself. Montaigne was enough of a skeptic to be uncertain whether anything could be known in an absolute sense. Yet to Catholic, Lutheran, Calvinist and Anglican the religious fanatic and the free-thinker were twin monsters who subverted religion, society and state. It was, of course, easy for staunch churchmen to panic at the sight of individuals who wished to find their own road to truth at the very time when the controversy over salvation made the confessions internally insecure. Paranoic charges against "atheism" and "enthusiasm" were thrown out against almost anyone who placed conscience or reason above the collective wisdom of the church. In 1623 the *Illuminati* or *Alumbrados* of Spain were condemned on their own incoherent testimony for bypassing the Catholic church and the person of Jesus in attaining what they considered to be religious perfection. It is difficult to believe that the seven or eight thousand persons who reputedly "confessed" were all part of that heresy. But the fear of the illuminists survived into the next decade to frighten France's chief minister, Richelieu, when their number was estimated at 60,000. Late in the seventeenth century, the Anglican bishop George Hickes preached a long, shrill sermon against Fifth Monarchy Men, Muggletonians and Quakers, and published it as *The Spirit of Enthusiasm Exorcis'd* in 1709 against a fanatical group of French Calvinists who had been exiled to England. The word "atheist" was even more often on Christian lips during the century. The French cleric Marin Mersenne lumped together a wide variety of "free-thinkers" in his enormous tract, *The Impiety of Deists, Atheists and Libertines of this Time* (1624), in which he charged that Paris alone sheltered 50,000 atheists. Ironically, the Cambridge Platonist, Henry More, whose Christianity was somewhat suspect, was one of the century's writers against both enthusiasts and atheists (*Enthusiasm Vanquished*, 1659; *Antidote Against Atheism*, 1652).

While churchmen exaggerated the immediate influence of these "enemies" and defined their views imprecisely, there was good reason to be disturbed. Two problems were joined in the enthusiast-atheist "menace." One concerned the quest for certain knowledge, the other the search for moral standards.

The Reformation undermined religious certainty by denying the right of the Catholic church to determine religious truth. In the charges and countercharges which followed, it became clear that all churches were subject to the same skepticism. The Catholic church had reversed itself on many matters, and in any case who could tell whether the church was any more divinely inspired than the individual Christian? The Protestant might believe, with Luther, that religious truth was what the individual conscience felt compelled to believe from a sincere reading of the Bible. Yet who could tell whether one's reading of Scripture was truly divinely inspired?

The major Catholic and Protestant confessions soon fled from the specter of doubt and, as we have seen in the debate over salvation, buried themselves in the belief that true doctrine could be determined by the church. Luther and his fellow reformers came to the conservative position that the Bible had to be clarified by church authorities. Catholic Dominicans and Jesuits fell back on Aquinas' emphasis on reason and man's senses as vehicles for understanding and proving Biblical revelation, which of course came through the collective wisdom of the Catholic church. Luther's companion, Melanchthon, erected a systematic theology on Aquinas' methods in his *Main Concepts on Theological Matters* (1535 edition), and was followed by the great seventeenth-century scholastic theologian of Lutheranism, John Gerhard. Anglicanism was largely based on the similar rationalist work of Hooker, *The Laws of Ecclesiastical Polity* (1594–1597). Even the Jansenists had their authority in Augustine.

All these arguments were vain as far as the religious individualist was concerned. He knew that the churches disputed one another's religious truths. And he had Luther's own words to give him courage. In the excitement of the early Reformation Luther had himself declared, "No one can understand God or God's word unless he has it revealed immediately by the Holy Ghost; but nobody can receive anything from the Holy Ghost unless he experiences it." Who could say, then, that the religious enthusiast who found his own road to God was not filled with God's spirit?

The Renaissance interest in the skeptical writings of pagan antiquity added another dimension to the confessional churches' problems. Although lesser writers were known in the fifteenth century, it was not until the sixteenth that the giant of ancient skepticism was rediscovered. Sextus Empiricus' *Outlines of Pyrrhonism* appeared in a Latin edition in 1562, and was translated into English before 1600. Sextus Empiricus systematically showed that human reason and man's senses were deceptive; hence, there was no basis for believing that man could know the truth about anything. The revival of Pyrrhonism struck Europe like a bombshell, giving added force to Christians' doubts concerning religious truth. The churches, which were fleeing from the uncertainties of Biblical revelation to the seemingly surer ground of reason and the senses, were left with nothing but sheer institutional authority.

Among the followers of ancient Pyrrhonism, the major figure was Michel de Montaigne, whose *Essays* were published in final form in 1595, and who was widely read by Europeans of succeeding generations. In rambling fashion, Montaigne recited one skeptical argument after another. He concluded that since human senses and reason are uncertain, Christians should leave doctrinal disputes alone and let God's providence mold their lives according to His will. Montaigne was particularly disturbed by the religious fanaticism and intolerance which he saw turn late sixteenth-century France into a bloodbath of religious-civil war. "Reason has taught me," he wrote, "that to condemn anything so positively as false and impossible is to claim that our brains have the privilege of knowing the bounds and limits of God's will. . . . I have learnt too that there is no more patent folly in the world than to reduce these things to the measure of our own power and capacity."

Montaigne's view that one must suspend judgment, avoid theological debate, and trust in God has been labelled *fideism*. Outwardly, he was a Christian, and indeed he thought that the only solution to the religious ills of his day was to accept God's truths as interpreted by the Catholic church. Yet his skeptical means to this absolutist end bothered many fellow Catholics. Montaigne claimed that he meant to buttress his church by ending its internal disputes, thus strengthening its hand against the rival Protestant Huguenots. He was devoted to *fideism* as a means to end religious war and intellectual confusion. However, the doubting Thomases remained unconvinced of his sincerity. When he declared, "Either we must submit entirely to the authority of our ecclesiastical government, or we must dispense with it altogether," it was obvious to some that the latter was Montaigne's aim. Whatever his purpose, once Montaigne reduced religion to a leap of faith, he was encouraging men to balk at taking that leap.

Until Descartes came along in the 1640's with a radical reinterpretation of skepticism that changed the course of the great debate on religious truth,[8] many theologians directed their attention to Montaigne's *fideism*. The more they debated, the more ridiculous they looked. Among the most vicious and theologically inept rebuttals were those by Francis Garasse in the 1620's, which were so ignorant of theological niceties that they were declared heretical by the faculty of the University of Paris. Many persons who tried to bridge the gap between skepticism and dogmatism were branded by their contemporaries as either dogmatists who could not prove their case, or dangerous unbelievers. Lord Herbert of Cherbury (*On Truth*, 1624) became infamous because of the "common notions" which he presented as universally accepted religious ideas. When he declared that all men could accept belief in God, an immortality of happiness or suffering, and virtue, the critics pointed out that such opinions were not provable, and in any case were hardly the exclusive property of Christianity. The concepts he presented were actually much like those of the "natural religion" of eighteenth-century secular thought.[9]

The religious "enthusiasts"—Quakers, Molinosists, Quietists, Ranters, Labadists, some Baptists, and scores of other groups—were too nonintellectual to bother with revived pagan ideas. Yet there was an inner logic to their beliefs. The term "enthusiasm" means, literally, "full of God," and the enthusiast was convinced that God directly inspired his thoughts and actions. Those who believed James Naylor's body had been totally taken over by Jesus may have been eccentric, but their opinion stemmed logically from the concept of enthusiasm. So too did the late seventeenth-century Quietism of Madame Guyon, who claimed that God had so taken over her body that she was at complete rest. The trembling of the early Quakers when seized by the Holy Ghost, and some enthusiasts' habit of running naked in the streets of Europe and Salem, Massachusetts when "drunk with God," were equally logical.

We find these enthusiasts very peculiar people. It is certainly understandable why they were considered subversives by their contemporaries, particularly when their number grew rapidly around the middle of the seventeenth century. For despite the variety of outward customs and inner beliefs they were in agreement against the confessional churches on many issues. They usually had no use for any visible, institutional church (although some had a tendency to become institutionalized). They believed in individual religious experiences and direct inspiration. They stressed emotions as against rational thought. (The *Journal* of the Quaker leader, Fox, is humorously ungrammatical and at times incomprehensible.)

8. See Chapter 14, pp. 344–348.
9. On "natural religion" at the end of the seventeenth century, see Chapter 14.

They must have been amazed by the confessional squabbles over salvation, since that problem did not concern them at all. They *had* the inner light, they had experienced a "rebirth" and become "new men"; what need had they for theology? Some clung to the Bible as the source of their actions and attitudes, but most discarded even that authority as the dead Word of God in favor of the living presence of God in their souls. Fox argued against the Bible with the Calvinist leader, Richard Baxter, in the middle of the century, as the enthusiast Dutch Baptist Hans de Ries had with his more conventional coreligionary, Nittert Obbes, a quarter of a century earlier. Despite their very different roads to religious truth, the enthusiast and the skeptic also had some things in common. Both reacted to the dogmatic, intellectualized theology of their day, and both broke with the idea that society or a church had the right to compel religious conformity. Like the *fideism* of Montaigne or the "common concepts" of Lord Herbert, the Quaker way of reasoning anticipated the natural religion of the eighteenth century. Montaigne's belief in "universal reason, which is implanted in every man who is not corrupt by nature," has its echo in the writings of Fox's disciple Robert Barclay. In his *Apology for the True Christian Divinity* (1676) Barclay wrote:

> The divine revelation and inward illumination is that which is evident and clear of itself; forcing, by its own evidence and clearness, the well-disposed understanding to assent, irresistably moving the same thereunto, even as the common principles of natural truths do move and incline the mind to a natural assent.

The inner light of the religious enthusiast was still more disturbing to the major churches when it influenced his sense of moral values. Being filled with God, the enthusiast believed that He was guiding his actions as well as his thoughts. But the enthusiast's God could lead him to either an exaggerated moralism or an extreme permissiveness. No one could shake his finger at the Quakers' morality, however eccentric their customs. Shocked at the materialism of his age, Fox felt fortunate that God had made him morally perfect. He wrote in his *Journal*:

> Now was I come up in the spirit, through the flaming sword, into the paradise of God. All things were new, and all creation gave another smell unto me than before, beyond what words can utter. I knew nothing but pureness, innocency, and righteousness, being renewed up into the image of God by Christ Jesus, so that I was come up into the state of Adam, which he was in before he fell.

His moral rigorism was very different from the views expounded by the Quietists, Madame Guyon and Molinos, however. They preached that the person overcome by God was indifferent to life and his past sins. Indeed, sinning as a conscious act was impossible. If one sinned in a conventional sense, it was the work of God, not of His creature. Molinos and Madame Guyon may have led moral but strange lives; their followers sometimes acted in ways which were more than strange. Conventional society was shocked by the Quietists, uncomfortable with the Quakers, and uneasy that whatever the brand of enthusiasm, the enthusiast set his own moral standards without respect to the will of the churches or society.

The moral thought of skepticism and other post-Renaissance philosophies was more complex. Montaigne and other readers of antiquity had a habit of eclecticism, drawing at random from ancient moralists whatever they found suitable to their needs. Christian morality was placed alongside an increasing number of alternative views. Whereas Aquinas had contended with Aristotle, and the Renaissance with many more ancient authors, the seventeenth century was challenged by a veritable deluge of editions and commentaries on the ancients. Supposedly secular Italian Renaissance thinkers had tried manfully to reconcile the pagan past to the Christian present. But by 1600, it was becoming tempting for a few intellectuals to fit Christianity into a pagan mold. In the early sixteenth century the German Melanchthon and the Frenchman D'Etaples were still fitting pagan morality into Christianity through restatements of Aristotle's ethics. But late in that century, writings by the Dutch scholar Justus Lipsius and the Frenchman Guillaume du Vair treated revived Stoicism in a much more favorable light, as did the early seventeenth-century popularizer of ancient Epicureanism, Pierre Gassendi. Not satisfied with reading about the ancients through corrupted texts or hostile commentaries, they insisted on going back to the sources, which were naturally far more alluring and convincing. Lipsius' Stoicism, Gassendi's Epicureanism,[10] Cambridge Platonism[11] and Montaigne's hodge-podge of Pyrrhonism, Epicureanism and Stoicism were immensely popular reading in the seventeenth century.

All the pagan philosophies known to the seventeenth century gave incentives for morality, and frequently an apology for a contemplative as opposed to an active life. Nonetheless, the center stage of life was dominated by man, unaided by God. Opponents of post-Renaissance moralists indicted them for the greatest of Christian sins, human pride, and an intellectual libertinism which shaded into moral permissiveness. While Stoicism taught that the supreme good consisted in human virtue struggling against the passions, it threw man back on moral self-sufficiency. The stoical person seemed too aware of himself, and his virtue could be restricted to so few matters that expediency might become his

10. See Chapter 14, p. 354.
11. See Chapter 16, p. 412.

guide. Epicureanism was still less rigid. It posited a world of material atoms in which the passions of the body forced the movements of the soul. The Pyrrhonist knew that there was no way of arriving at absolute standards for morality; the best solution might be to ignore the question and follow local custom.

Montaigne flirted with several pagan views and settled provisionally for the position "I have not made any great efforts to curb the desires by which I have found myself assailed." He made it clear that he was not tempted by most vices, but his contemporaries wondered. Montaigne was in turn shocked by the impiety and vice which was discussed and advocated in scholarly circles at the University of Padua, and which spread to France and England early in the seventeenth century. The names of the Italians Caesarius Cremoni and Lucillo Vanini, who called Jesus and Moses imposters, still horrify some persons from the distance of the twentieth century.

The major confessions descended on the religious enthusiasts and pagan free-thinkers in full fury. Montaigne's works were placed on the Catholic Index of forbidden literature, while Vanini was burned at the stake after his tongue was removed for uttering blasphemies. The Quaker Naylor was flogged, pilloried and branded with a red-hot iron. Yet the churches could not halt the twin menaces. The more they reacted, the more hopeless they appeared. Indeed, the condemnation of the Quietists for their immoral views caused a ripple of laughter in French society, for the architect of their persecution was a leading ecclesiastical figure notorious for his transgressions of the Mosaic commandments. Had the churches concentrated on resolving their own differences, the course of European intellectual history might have been very different. The religious fanatic and the intellectual or moral libertine were a distinct minority, and might well have been assimilated ultimately into Christian culture or left innocuously on its fringes.

ℭ Medieval Cosmology and the New Science

While theologians, enthusiasts and free-thinkers grappled with medieval religious ideas, scientists were reexamining the medieval concept of the physical universe. From our perspective, that cosmology appears simplistic and wrongheaded, but it had lasted with minor variations for centuries and had the backing of both Christian theologians and the venerated ancient thinkers who had provided the foundation on which it was built. To see how it was finally destroyed, we must first examine its strengths and its weaknesses.

Like medieval politics and society, the medieval universe was an hierarchical, orderly one to both the common man and those who were trained to understand and popularize its workings. Every being had its allotted place in the system, depending on its degree of perfection. In metaphysical terms, this Great Chain of Being descended from perfect God and His angels through the physically perfect stars, planets, sun and moon to the four elements of this corrupt globe, starting with fire, followed by air, water and earth. In scientific terms, the universe was geocentric, with the central element, earth, surrounded by layers of water, air, and fire, followed by nine concentric spheres of the heavens which held in turn the Moon, Mercury, Venus, Sun, Mars, Jupiter, Saturn, the Fixed Stars, the "motor" of the system or Primum Mobile, and finally the Empyrean Heaven where God resided and from which he sustained the rest.

The hierarchical idea and the assumption that all parts of the universe had their particular "form" and "purpose" explained their movements. The spheres of the heavens moved in a circle, since that was the perfect form of motion. On this corrupt globe, the four elements were believed to have become mixed at creation. Each naturally sought to reach its natural place. Thus fire and air had the property of "levity" which made them attempt to soar upward, while the "gravity" of water and earth gave them a tendency to move downward. All non-circular movement in the heavens and non-rectilinear movement in the sublunary sphere was unnatural and required a special explanation.

Unless this scheme of the universe had approximately fitted the facts, it could never have been retained so long. The common man could tell that the sphere he inhabited was heavy and immobile, that gravity or levity applied roughly to its elements (water did "run" downhill to meet the ocean, and a ball thrown in the air fell downward), that the heavenly bodies were glittering jewels befitting their perfection, appeared light enough to whirl around the Earth, and did, indeed, pass across the skies. The greatest ancient scientists and their medieval successors were more aware that their picture was an hypothesis rather than a necessarily precise description of astronomy and physics, but they also knew that it was sufficient to plot the actual movements of the planets and to permit elementary calculations in physics. To accommodate the sometimes erratic movement of heavenly bodies, Ptolemy had added epicycles (little circles) to Aristotle's nine spheres. Aristotle thought the spheres carried the planets in piggy-back fashion. Ptolemy assumed that a planet moved uniformly on an epicycle, whose center moved around the circumference of the larger sphere. Ptolemy's device was a brilliant means for saving prevailing assumptions. The planet sometimes halted or retrogressed, but its path was still produced by a series of perfect, circular motions. The mind boggles at the forty-odd circles and epicycles which were employed by sixteenth-century scholars to explain the phenomena, but one cannot deny the ingenuity or relative accuracy of these cosmological architects.

The medieval cosmology was also very appealing to Christians. At once geocentric and theocentric, it dramatized the human story of Adam's Fall and man's salvation through divine grace. The hierarchical structure made all subordinate to the Creator and Preserver, who could intervene to save men as well as to keep His physical universe running. The position of the Earth and man at the physical center emphasized man as God's special creature, while the Earth's corrupt status was mirrored in Original Sin from which man could be rescued only after departing this imperfect globe for the perfect Heaven. Although medieval men had to play some tricks with the Bible, their cosmology was in agreement with certain Biblical stories and passages. Aquinas brushed aside the Old Testament description of the world as tent-shaped (like the Hebrew Tabernacle) as a myth which God had invented for the common man, who was unable to comprehend the concentric spheres of the scholarly world. But the Earth's position as the center of the universe and the Sun's motion around it were verified by Joshua's command that the sun stop (Joshua 10:12), by Ecclesiastes 1:4,6 and by several verses in the Psalms.

Historians have suggested several reasons for the early modern challenges to this medieval cosmology, but many of their interpretations are not entirely convincing when placed in historical context. It is doubtful that the main thrust of the scientific revolution was caused by more accurate observations, increased experimentation, revolutionary changes in mathematics which permitted rapid and precise calculations hitherto impossible or even the introduction of better scientific instruments. Certainly all these developments of the sixteenth and early seventeenth centuries played their part. However, much of the early spade work was done without their assistance. Copernicus relied heavily on Ptolemy's observations, while Galileo arrogantly declared that he needed experiments only to convince doubting Thomases and spoke favorably of reason's "rape of the senses" as the way to scientific knowledge. Kepler broke with the traditional belief in circular motion without the aid of a telescope, while Galileo, who used one, stubbornly held to that belief despite his knowledge of Kepler's views. Descartes, a brilliant mathematician, was a poor astronomer, while Kepler, ignorant of many mathematical advances, laboriously worked out his computations and even made schoolboy errors (which were happily canceled out by others).

The most plausible thesis is that the key to the new science lay in an unconscious intellectual revolution in which the great scientists of the late sixteenth and early seventeenth century blundered toward a view of the universe very different from that held by ancient and medieval scholars. It is not enough to say that that age simply produced an unusual number of brilliant men devoted to scientific truth. Intellectual brilliance in itself could not ensure that they would reject traditional assumptions. In large part it was a question of exceptional minds (and some plodding mediocrities) seizing on long-standing discrepancies between theory and fact, assisted by alternate hypotheses known to antiquity and revived by the Renaissance, and building as well on late medieval modifications of the prevailing cosmology. Aristarchus' belief that the universe was heliocentric and Archimedes' non-Aristotelian physics were well known by the late sixteenth century, and provided such alternatives. So, too, in a much more sweeping sense, did the revived Platonic-Pythagorean suggestions that the universe was a unit, to be understood in terms of numbers and mathematical relationships (not a hierarchy of "forms" and "purposes"). During the fourteenth and fifteenth centuries, scholars in the universities of Paris, Padua and Oxford had already come close to rejecting Aristotelian notions about "natural" rectilinear motion and approaching the modern theory of inertia which makes other types of motion equally natural. The Reformation added little to the intellectual aids at the disposal of early modern science. While many late seventeenth-century scientists were Protestants, notably with Calvinist leanings, Catholics were as prominent in scientific work up to roughly 1650. Moreover, the initial attacks on medieval cosmology had to take root before the Calvinist conception of God's inflexible laws could reinforce the new science's idea of nature's fixed, universal laws.

The initial phase of the scientific revolution, between 1540 and 1640, was a destructive one which broke down prevailing cosmological assumptions without providing a satisfactory, comprehensive substitute. Paradoxically, the great figures of sixteenth-century science either undermined prevailing views in their attempts to buttress them, or clung stubbornly to major parts of the traditional scientific picture while rejecting individual points. Stevin's work in physics and Vesalius' in anatomy were bizarre combinations of the old and the new. Nicolas Copernicus, whose name has been immortalized in the term "Copernican Revolution" was probably the most conservative of them all. He tried to conserve Ptolemaic astronomy by changing the place of the universe's center. The Ptolemaic geocentric system became the Copernican heliocentric scheme by juggling the positions assigned to the Earth and the Sun, and moving the Fixed Stars to a more remote part of the universe. Once Copernicus had made these important but isolated changes, he insisted on retaining the rest of the Ptolemaic system, which made little sense in a sun-centered universe. The perfect circular motion of the heavens, the nine main spheres of the finite universe, and the epicycles were retained by Ptolemy's disciple, despite the fact that no one could see in the Bible or through his senses what relation they had to the sun.

It was the sun-worshipping mystic, Johannes Kepler, who became the real revolutionary in astronomy by asking how the debris of Ptolemy's system could be squared with Copernicus' heliocentric hypothesis. Kepler's three famous laws concerning planetary motion appeared in his *New Astronomy* (1609) and his *Harmony of the World* (1619). The German scientist's first law, that the planet Mars described an ellipse with the Sun at one focus, broke with the idea of circular motion in the heavens. The second law, which demonstrated that the line joining Mars and the Sun sweeps out equal areas in equal times, applied the *coup de grâce* to the epicycles which had previously explained Mars' seemingly erratic behavior. That law also edged away from the hierarchical concept of the universe by describing how the parts of the universe worked in mathematical, quantitative terms rather than asking what quality or "form" of an object "caused" it to act out its assigned role. Kepler's Italian contemporary, Galileo Galilei is more famous, but his contributions to astronomy were a complement to rather than an advance on the work of the German scholar. With his self-made telescope, Galileo provided sensory support for the heliocentric system. His discovery of the moons of Jupiter and his finding that the Moon "is not robed in a smooth and polished surface but is in fact rough and uneven . . . like the earth's surface" are presented in his immensely readable *Messenger from the Stars* (1610). Jupiter's satellites showed that the Earth was not the sole center of heavenly activity, and the Moon's corruption removed with a stroke of the pen the distinction between the "perfect" heavens and the imperfect Earth. Copernicus had made the Earth part of the heavens, Kepler had described the heavens in quantitative terms, and Galileo made them appear like the Earth.

For all their daring, neither Kepler nor Galileo broke cleanly with medieval cosmology. Both hesitated to move all the way from a hierarchical, limited universe to an infinite, centerless one. Galileo refused to budge from his belief in perfect, circular motion in the heavens. Kepler was not entirely free from the ingrained habit of looking for qualities and forms in physical nature. At least he could write, "The Sun alone appears, by virtue of its dignity and power, suited for this motive duty [of propelling the planets] and worthy to become the home of God himself."

Terrestrial physics offered one means of destroying utterly the

Galileo being visited by Milton in Florence

hierarchical universe, but the physicists of the early seventeenth century were unable to link their findings in dynamics with the new hypotheses in astronomy. Galileo went far beyond Stevin's work in breaking with Aristotelian ideas of terrestrial motion. His examination of the flight of projectiles showed that non-rectilinear motion was "natural." He even arrived at the theory that a body in motion on earth continued in a straight line until some force acted on it, an enunciation of the law of inertia. Galileo's work in hydrostatics banished the Aristotelian idea of "levity," showing that weight is a relative thing. In the broader sense, Galileo had discovered that the Earth was subject to an invariable order, written in the language of mathematics, just like Kepler's heavens. What he was unable to do was link his laws of terrestrial physics to the celestial physics of astronomy, and show that the same laws applied to both realms.

Galileo's contemporaries had no greater success in applying their discoveries in physics to astronomy. In 1600, the Englishman William Gilbert proposed the theory that the Earth was a magnet, but no one at the time could carry that hint of universal gravitation to its logical conclusion. René Descartes' flights of fancy destroyed the usefulness of his discoveries on terrestrial motion, when he applied them to astronomy. He assumed wrongly with Aristotle that "nature abhors a vacuum." Thus to explain the movements of the heavenly bodies, he had to assume the interaction of material particles. The result of their interaction was a series of whirlpools, each of which trapped a planet and carried it around in a circular motion. Many contemporaries believed Descartes, and he had his followers as late as the eighteenth century. But it was immediately pointed out that his vortex theory could not fit with Kepler's law of elliptical motion, and that it was at odds with some of his own laws of terrestrial physics.

Little change was made in the traditional assumptions of other sciences, with the exception of physiology, during the age of Copernicus, Kepler and Galileo. The reason was in part the absence of previous comprehensive systems as a starting point, in part the fact that the mathematical approach so successful in astronomy and physics could not be readily applied to chemistry, geology and biology. Even in physiology, William Harvey's findings on the circulation of the blood (1626) were of limited importance in the general breakdown of the medieval cosmology. To be sure, Harvey and his immediate successors tended to fit man into a new universe of mechanical motion, but he made little use of the contemporary advances in physics and his writing was most certainly not that of a mathematician. Although he dismissed the ancient Galenic belief in the "natural," "vital" and "animal" spirits of the blood, he could write in semi-Aristotelian terms of the heart as an animate object. Harvey's heart, "like the prince in a kingdom, in whose hands lie the chief and highest authority, rules over all; it is the original and foundation from which all power is derived, on which all power depends in the animal body."

The early, destructive phase of the scientific revolution had a mixed and confused reception among the intellectual and social elite of Europe. The English poet John Donne summed up the one common element in this varied response, when he wrote:

> And new philosophy calls all in doubt;
> The element of fire is quite put out;
> The sun is lost, and th' earth, and no man's wit
> Can well direct him where to look for it.
> And freely men confess, that this world's spent

When in the planets and the firmament
They seek so many new; then see that this
Is crumbled out again to his atomies.
'Tis all in pieces, all coherence gone;
All just supply and all relation.[12]

The new questioning of ancient authorities in science added to the uncertainties which the free-thinkers had raised about absolute truth. From
Montaigne to the mid-seventeenth century, the skeptics who were interested in science almost unanimously invoked the names of Copernicus
and Galileo to show, not that they were right, but that no scientific
authority could now be believed. Many of the most prominent scientists,
theologians and other thinkers either remained neutral in the dispute on
the various "systems of the world," or tentatively accepted the compromise between the Copernican and Ptolemaic systems propounded by
Kepler's teacher, Tycho de Brahe.[13]

Far better known, but only superficially, is the furor which the
scientists' attack on the medieval cosmology aroused within the Christian
churches. Much research needs to be done on this emotionally charged
and complex subject, but recent reappraisals suggest that it was not a
simple, black-and-white contest between "religion" and "science." Again,
Donne's phrase that all was in doubt sets the tone. For it was fear and
uncertainty, more than implacable hostility, which were the moving
forces behind the religious reaction.

The early scientific revolution was only belatedly and slowly seen
as another challenge to orthodox belief. While Luther, Melanchthon and
Calvin had some caustic words for Copernicus' heliocentric views, this
did not stop Lutherans from being sympathetic to and utilizing the data
advanced by Copernicus and Kepler. The trouble arose indirectly from
the fear that Copernicus' theory unconsciously undermined cosmological
views which buttressed Christian belief. By the opening of the seventeenth
century, several objections had been raised. Often they combined sensa-
tionalism and literal-mindedness. If the heavenly bodies were not different
from the earth, did human beings inhabit them? If so, did God visit
them all in an endless series of incarnations like that of Jesus? Where
could Heaven and Hell now be placed, if the Earth and man were not
at the center of the universe?

Still, there was no real hostility between science and religion as long
as the new astronomy was viewed as an hypothesis (as the Ptolemaic
structure had consistently been viewed). Nor need there have been. The

12. J. Donne, *An Anatomy of the World* (1611).
13. Brahe proposed that the planets revolved around the Sun, and the Sun with
the planets revolved in turn around the Earth!

medieval church had coped with as difficult problems, chiefly the Biblical conception of the universe as a giant tabernacle. Nor was it necessarily wedded to ancient scientists, for in the thirteenth century French and English ecclesiastical circles had condemned Aristotelian theses which the scientific revolution was now questioning in turn (for example, Aristotle's belief that God could not create an infinite universe or a plurality of worlds). If medieval cosmology fitted in with Christian concepts, it was possible that other cosmologies could do so, too. However, it would be *difficult* to contend with a science which undermined that cosmology, especially if men took their Bible and the implications of science as literally as they did. Hence, the insistence by Galileo that his science was the truth, and not just another hypothesis as Copernicus' work had suggested, brought the latent issue to a head. And Galileo's cleverness and arrogance antagonized even many churchmen who welcomed and supported his and his contemporaries' scientific findings. Galileo insisted in his famous letter to the Grand Duchess of Tuscany (1615) that the Bible need not be taken literally when it proclaimed the geocentric view, but that his science *was* literally true. He tried to put the burden of proof on the Catholic church at a time when he could not prove his own system, when all the alternatives to Aristotle and Ptolemy were in doubt.

For their part, the highest Catholic authorities in Europe fell into his trap. One of their reasons is understandable, the other deplorable. Cardinal Bellarmine summed up the first point when he said that to proclaim the heliocentric theory "is a very dangerous attitude and one calculated not only to arouse all scholastic philosophers and theologians [i.e., those who clung to the ancient authorities like Aristotle and Ptolemy] but also to injure our holy faith by contradicting the Scriptures." Essentially, Bellarmine feared that the society of his day could not make such an intellectual leap suddenly, and that if it were forced to do so in the wrong way, its faith, which could be gradually accommodated to the heliocentric theory, would be destroyed. He felt it was not worth the price of pushing the issue. Bellarmine even suggested a way to cushion the intellectual revolution, if at a future date, Galileo was proved right. "If there were a real proof [of the heliocentric system], . . . then we should have to proceed with great circumspection in explaining passages of Scripture which appear to teach the contrary, and we should rather have to say that we did not understand them than to declare an opinion to be false which is proven to be true." The second reason for the clash with Galileo was far less intellectual. The church authorities, including Jesuits who had supported and even improved on Galileo's work, were stampeded into a witch hunt against him by the clever manipulations of a few clerics who personally hated the upstart scientist-theologian.

The actual pronouncements which the Catholic authorities made on the heliocentric theory and their treatment of Galileo were surprisingly mild in view of the deepseated issues. The initial action taken in 1616 did not officially involve Galileo, but Copernicus and the heliocentric view itself. One bright bishop wanted Copernicus jailed, not realizing that he had been dead for some seventy years. Calmer heads prevailed, and Copernicus' works were placed on the Index of forbidden books for four years until trifling "corrections" were inserted. It was also clearly stated that the heliocentric view could be used as a working hypothesis, although it was equally clear that no one should describe it as scientific fact and Galileo received a personal warning to that effect. There the matter rested until Galileo wrote a clever polemic which led the reader to discount Ptolemy for Copernicus (*Dialogue on the Two Principal Systems of the Universe, the Ptolemaic and Copernican*, 1632). The Catholic university of Salamanca had recommended Copernicus' works for its students since 1594, and Galileo had been invited to the staunchly Catholic Spain of Philip III. After 1632, the Catholic church felt compelled to take a new look at its decision of 1616, and the pro-Galilean Pope Urban VIII was urged in this direction by malicious gossip that the ridiculed Ptolemaic figure of the *Dialogue*, Simplicio, was none other than himself. Galileo did not receive a fair trial, although the rectitude of the proceedings is clouded by contradictory evidence about his earlier warning. Galileo was publicly humiliated through a forced recantation of his heliocentric views and the prohibition of his *Dialogue*. Mild house arrest and a punishment of reciting the penitential Psalms periodically were added barbs to an old man who had only a decade to live.

Compared with the churches' treatment of religious heresy and intellectual free thought, the attack on Galileo was hardly an all-out assault on the new science. The immobility of the Earth did not become an article of faith, nor the immobility of the Sun a heresy. What the church accomplished, as Arthur Koestler astutely remarks, was a tragic divorce of science and religion in the popular imagination, where none was necessary or inevitable. The church's condemnation of Galileo "conveyed to simple sons of the Church . . . that to talk of the Earth's motion was a Bad thing and contrary to faith; and . . . to the skeptic . . . that the Church had declared war on Science." [14] Once again, as in dealing with religious enthusiasts and intellectual free-thinkers, confessional Christianity appeared foolish. It also appeared inept, since scientists continued their work, even in Italy. Galileo himself turned his attention exclusively to physics after his trial and produced his greatest work, *Dialogues*

14. A. Koestler, *The Sleepwalkers* (Universal Library, 1963), 458.

Concerning Two New Sciences. The work was smuggled to a printing house in the Dutch Netherlands, but it had the blessings of a Jesuit in Catholic Vienna, and could have been published in that most Catholic city of mid-seventeenth century Europe. Divided and confused over the "crime of Galileo," the Catholic church and Christianity in general had lost the opportunity to take the new science into its fold when that science was still in its early, destructive phase. It would be much more difficult to handle when the pieces of the scientific picture were put together by Newton and his fellow scientists late in the seventeenth century.[15]

༅ *Intensified Supernaturalism and the Witch Craze*

As the new science struck at the roots of medieval cosmology, a wave of supernaturalism which was an exaggerated form of that cosmology swept Europe. The assumptions of medieval science left ample room for superstitions. A world in which even inanimate objects seemed alive with "purposes" and souls, which so reduced natural motion that supernatural forces were needed to explain most activity, and which blurred the distinction between the natural and supernatural by placing both in the hierarchy of the physical universe, quite logically crammed the heavens and the Earth with spirits. The attempt to understand the workings of nature was inextricably connected with efforts to determine where and how supernatural forces of good and evil interfered with nature. Astrology and astronomy were closely connected, as were mathematics and divination, chemistry and alchemy. By the seventeenth century, alchemy was going out of fashion, but other pseudo-sciences of the supernatural were even more common than had been the case in the heyday of medieval cosmology. Astrology thrived, and with it the belief in palmistry and oracles. Medieval man gave his nodding assent to belief in witches, but early modern Europe brought into being a veritable witch craze.

We know much about these superstitions, but little of the causes of their increased popularity during the sixteenth and early seventeenth centuries. The revival of Platonic-Pythagorean ideas during the Renaissance may have made men more aware of spiritual forces in the material world, but basically those ideas fitted into the efforts to reduce the universe to quantitative, mathematical order. The Reformation is a more likely culprit. The Protestant stress on providence made post-Reforma-

15. See Chapter 13.

tion Europe see every event in life as a "sign" of God's pleasure or anger. God was always warning, rewarding or punishing men; men had only to read into the workings of nature the proper supernatural message. The heightened interest of both Catholic and Protestant in salvation made human existence a perpetual fight between God and the Devil over man's immortal soul. No doubt, religious strife and the existence of religious minorities within a hostile community fanned the flames of superstition. Religious foes were often looked upon as being in the clutches of the Devil, for otherwise there could be no explanation for their refusal to accept the faith set down by God's "true" church. Thus while seventeenth-century Spanish inquisitors continued to persecute Jews and Moslems, the rest of Christian Europe frequently identified religious heretics and social misfits as witches in league with the Devil. The economic and political instability of the times may also have made men grasp at supernatural explanations of events otherwise inexplicable.

Leading theologians and parish priests, kings and their ministers, secular scholars and men, women and children of humbler circumstances were swept along by the intensified supernaturalism. Frequently, precisely those learned souls who pretended to universal knowledge were unquestioning believers in the popular superstitions of the day. The pedant-scholar, King James VI of Scotland, and the Rector of the University of Utrecht, Gisbert Voet, believed in the malevolent power of witches. As the novel *Simplicissimus* [16] shows so forcefully, those who played on the credulity of others by peddling patent medicines, casting horoscopes and impersonating the Devil could be duped in turn when confronted by events in their lives which appeared unnatural. While confessions of supernatural activities were often forced by torture, many were so imbued with popular demonology that they were convinced that their visions of visits to the Devil were concrete events. It has been amusedly pointed out that witches exist where people believe in their existence. It is no wonder that more witches existed in the period between 1550 and 1650 than at any other time in European history.

The most fascinating and blood-curdling manifestation of this intensified superstition was the witch craze. It took on the appearance of a Great Fear in area after area, often coinciding with the conquest or reconquest of territories by one major confession or another. In the sixteenth century, former Catholic areas turned up batches of witches for Protestant fires and torture chambers. By the turn of the century, the revival of Catholic fortunes brought to light further witch cells in lands returned to the Catholic fold. At mid-century, the witch craze struck

16. See reference on p. 27.

England like a pestilence during the unsettling time of the civil wars, and in the 1660's it reached hitherto immune Sweden just as the Swedish authorities were trying to define and defend Lutheran orthodoxy against the dangers of the new science and new philosophy. The witch craze roamed Europe from Scotland to the Balkans, and penetrated Spanish Mexico and the English colonies to the north.

Witchcraft was tied to belief in the Kingdom of the Devil, who had his special hierarchy of demons and their human assistants who had become witches. At the Witches' Sabbath, inverted Christian rites took place, with witches renouncing baptism, parodying the Eucharist, and having sexual relations with the Devil. The witches then returned to human society to disturb the course of nature at the bidding of the Devil. They caused epidemics and death, spread crop failures and famine, and even deprived would-be parents of the ability to produce children.

It was an easy matter for good Christians to reconcile witch-hunting with Biblical truth. The New Testament writers had been fascinated with evil spirits, and the stories of Jesus banishing them from human bodies were well known. The Old Testament revealed that Saul had called on the Witch of Endor for help in his wars (I Samuel, 28) but it also had the stern message, "Thou shalt not suffer a witch to live" (Exodus 22:18). The theology of witch-hunting bordered on heresy, but early modern Christianity managed to hold the line to orthodoxy and retain its holy war against witches. The Devil was as much on the lips of the faithful as God himself. But it was argued that the Devil was not God's equal (as had been maintained by the heresy of Manichaeism); provided an individual remained steadfast in his Christian faith, the Devil could not lure him from God's church to the Evil Kingdom.

Demonology and other superstitions were so rooted in medieval cosmology and so responsive to the needs of early modern man that they died a slow death. Piecemeal attacks on particular superstitions were ineffectual because they left intact the medieval assumptions on which they were based. Historians speak highly of Balthasar Bekkar's *The Enchanted World* (1690), but Bekkar stopped short of denying the existence of evil spirits. His criticism of the witch craze followed closely in the footsteps of John Weyer (*The Tricks of the Devils*, 1563) and Friedrich Spee (*Caution in Criminal Procedure against Witches*, 1631). At best, the craze's critics denied the ability of the Devil to influence events outside his kingdom, and their most frequent approach was to recognize witches but deny their "crimes" or their torture-induced confessions. The attacks by state and church authorities were still less effective. The Roman Inquisition curbed the worst excesses of witch trials in 1657, and France's Colbert forbade magistrates to receive confessions concerning Witches'

Sabbaths in 1672. Both actions were attempts to contain the prejudices of society by sheer weight of authority rather than by undermining their intellectual foundation. The papal bull of 1631 which condemned astrologers who had predicted the Pope's death was obviously little more than an attempt to protect one individual.

Hugh Trevor-Roper is convincing when he contends that the demise of witch-hunting in the late seventeenth century was the result of the scientific revolution which banished supernatural forces from the natural world of quantity and mathematics.[17] Once again, Christian society was caught napping. Many Christians saw any attack on spiritual forces as an attack on religion. Sir Thomas Browne cried out that to disbelieve in witches or the Devil was tantamount to being an atheist: "They that doubt [the existence of witches] do not only deny them, but spirits; and are obliquely and upon consequence a sort not of infidels but atheists." [18] Thus when Newton and the second generation of seventeenth-century scientists added the new scientific synthesis to their predecessors' attacks on medieval cosmology, Christianity was so tied to non-Christian superstition that it was in danger of being discarded along with witches, horoscopes and oracles.

17. H. Trevor-Roper, "Witches and Witchcraft," *Encounter*, vol. xxviii, no. 6 (1967), 29, 34.
18. T. Browne, *Religio Medici*. Browne's attitude was expressed in almost identical language by many contemporaries. See S. I. Mintz, *The Hunting of Leviathan* (1962), 107, 153.

II.

Secular States in Tension:

1600–1660

We have already seen that seventeenth-century states were plagued with internal and external problems which made their future uncertain. The tensions were most pronounced during the first half of the century, when the authority of rulers and the very existence of the "state" were subjected to dissent from below and attacks from outside. It is convenient to divide that half-century into two periods, 1600–1625 and 1625–1660. During the first, new rulers on old thrones tried their best to overcome the tensions resulting from the weakening of traditional bonds. In general, tensions remained constant or increased, but few major rebellions or large-scale wars erupted. The exceptions were the Time of Troubles in Muscovy, the civil-foreign wars of Poland and Sweden, the Bohemian revolt against Austria and a religious-civil crisis in the Dutch Netherlands. The second period was far more turbulent, as tensions mounted and resulted in mid-century crises in almost every state of Europe. Minor conflicts between states escalated into major conflicts (notably the Thirty Years' War) which strained the internal structures of the warring principalities. These wars were accompanied by widespread rebellions or crises which verged on revolution. It was the time of the Great Rebellion or Puritan Revolution in England, the Fronde in France, the Catalan and Portuguese revolts in Spain. It was also a period of political upheaval in Denmark, Sweden,

Poland and some German states. In Muscovy, it was a time of political and religious disturbances, and in the Dutch Netherlands, a period of political unrest. The mid-century crises profoundly altered the relationships among the states of Europe. In the west, France emerged as the greatest power, while to the east the three states of Austria, Brandenburg and Muscovy began the transformation which would make them the great powers of the Danubian monarchy, Prussia and Russia by the end of the century. These crises also brought order out of domestic chaos. Problems remained for the rulers late in the century to resolve, but there was no doubt that the secular state had survived the earlier challenge. The secular state in tension gave way to the triumph of the secular state.

4.

Western Europe
at the Crossroads

In 1600, the major states of western Europe were at the crossroads of political fortune. Spain, France, England and the Dutch Netherlands all were variously affected by the tensions which had swept across Europe in preceding decades. In each of these states, a fundamental change in national destiny loomed as a distinct possibility, but its direction was not at all clear. The Golden Age of Philip II's Spanish Hapsburg empire and of Elizabeth I's England had left major problems unresolved, obscured by the greatness of Spanish gold and arms and by the daring exploits of Elizabethan merchant-pirates. Now the day of the Spanish galleons brimming with bullion and of the English buccaneers who preyed on them was coming to a close, revealing the underlying tensions which had been half-forgotten. Such superficial greatness could turn quickly into military, naval and economic decline, and the sense of national purpose and pride could fade before internal divisions and external dangers. In France and the Dutch Republic, the end of long and costly wars brought Dutchmen and Frenchmen face to face with the agonizing uncertainties of post-war reconstruction. Who could say how well the once-mighty French monarchy would bind up the wounds of religious-civil war, or how the young Dutch state which had united to overthrow its Spanish masters would adapt that artificial unity to the task of forging a new governmental structure?

EUROPE IN 1600

ATLANTIC
OCEAN

MUSCOVY

●Moscow

SCOTLAND

NORTH

DENMARK

SEA

SWEDEN

BALTIC SEA

Copenhagen

IRELAND

ENGLAND

London ●

BRANDENBURG

●Warsaw

POLAND - LITHUANIA

Boundary of the
Holy Roman Empire

Danish lands

Swedish lands

Venetian lands

Spanish Hapsburg lands

Austrian Hapsburg lands

SAXONY

PALAT-
INATE

AUSTRIA

●Paris

BAVARIA

Vienna

FRANCE

SWITZ.

TYROL

STYRIA

SAVOY

PAPAL

STATES

OTTOMAN

Constantinople ●

BLACK SEA

PORTUGAL

●Madrid

SPAIN

Rome ●

EMPIRE

MEDITERRANEAN

SEA

In all four states, the task of charting a new course was thrust on leaders who were either new to the task of ruling or unaccustomed to the problems of peacetime politics. Henry IV of France (1589–1610) and Maurice of Nassau of the Dutch Netherlands (1586–1625) discarded their military dress for the uncomfortable clothing of civilian leaders. In Spain and England, death carried away able rulers and brought to their thrones the untried Philip III (1598–1621) and the Scottish king who became James I (1603–1625), unfamiliar though he was with English politics. In France and England, the rulers were further hampered by the fact that they were the founders of new dynasties, the Bourbon Henry succeeding the old Valois kings, the Stuart James following the Tudor line.

Spain: The Legacy of Philip II

From the economic theorists (*arbitristas*) of the 1600's to today's historians it has been fashionable to speak of the "decline of Spain" after Philip II. But while the decline was certainly real, it was neither so sudden, so complete nor so inevitable as was once believed. It is more accurate to say that the Golden Age of Philip II bequeathed an ambiguous legacy which his frail successor did little to resolve.

Philip II wielded enormous personal power within Spain, added Portugal and its colonies to his empire in 1580, and won a great naval victory over the Turks at Lepanto in 1571. In Italy, he held Milan, Naples, Sicily, Sardinia and the coastal towns or *presidios* of Tuscany; in the Lowlands, the southern provinces were firmly under Spanish control, and the rebellious northern provinces were still battling for their freedom in the face of the greatest existing army of Europe. However, Philip never managed to harness the potential power within his huge empire. He bequeathed to his son, Phillip III, a loosely knit group of territories which had been held together by the precious metals of Spanish America and the resources of Spain's major area, Castile. Philip II's Castile could hardly bear the strain, even with the windfall of American treasure; Philip III's Castile could not. In the last years of Philip II's reign bullion imports decreased and the Castilian economy was depressed by a declining population, faltering commerce and industry, and neglected agriculture. By 1610 the financial situation in the empire was critical. Of the 15,500,000 ducats of state revenue, the non-Castilian parts of Spain contributed a mere 700,000, Naples and Milan only 1,600,000. The Spanish Netherlands and Sicily paid only for local defense. Castile could not continue to shoulder such a heavy burden.

The inordinate reliance on Castile was symptomatic of the governmental weaknesses which Philip II passed on to his son. Castilian by upbringing and persuasion, Philip II had naturally been pro-Castilian in his political views. However, he had arrived at an illogical half-Castilianization of Spanish government which infuriated non-Castilians without bending them to the will of the crown. Officials of the central government were Castilians, as were the viceroys. Catalan, Valencian, and Aragonese Spaniards envied their favored position at Madrid, and all non-Castilians hated their viceregal overlords. In their anger, these provincials conveniently forgot that Castilianization had progressed no further than excluding them from central power. The Castilians had to pay for their privileged position with taxation and military service. The non-Castilians kept their local "liberties," including immunity from heavy fiscal and military burdens and the right to be judged under local law.

Philip II even carried his policies into the conciliar structure of central government. He inherited an empire with separate councils for Castile, Aragon and the Indies. Instead of combining them or placing the council of Castile over the others, he added still more territorially organized councils: for his Italian possessions, the Spanish Netherlands,

Portugal and the Philippines. To be sure, this was one solution to the problem of running a multi-territorial state. But as Vicens Vives once noted, the solution provided autonomy at the expense of efficiency.[1] Philip II made the system work by taking over-all charge of imperial affairs, and by relying heavily on his personal secretaries. It was a rather indirect way of centralizing imperial government, and even placing all the councils in the capital city of Madrid did not alleviate the difficulties of coordinating their work. Meanwhile, the viceroys proved to be untrustworthy conciliar agents, fleecing the local populace and proving far from amenable to the royal will. Obviously the organization of the empire needed overhauling.

Unfortunately, Philip III had neither the ability to make his father's system work, nor the imagination or will to change it. He had only the name and good looks of his predecessor. His minister-favorite, the Duke of Lerma, was not without talent, but he, too, tended to let the empire run its own course. Perhaps the economy of Castile was beyond recall and the slowdown of bullion imports from the Americas impossible to reverse. Yet some things could have been done, even by men of modest talents. If the Castilians could not run the empire on their own, the rest of the empire might have been brought into the mainstream of Spanish politics, sharing decisions in return for shouldering burdens. And if Castile could not pay for imperial commitments, those commitments should have been curtailed.

The beginning of the new reign provided some faint signs that Philip III and Lerma were prepared to sacrifice imperial grandeur to internal strength. In 1604, Spain ended Philip II's lingering war with England, and in 1609 a Twelve Years' Truce was arranged with the Dutch Republic of the northern Netherlands. Already, in 1598, Spain had withdrawn from the civil wars in France. France was permitted to work out its own destiny under Henry IV, the English were allowed free trade in most of the Spanish empire, and the Dutch Netherlands was given de facto recognition as an independent state. These concessions were a heavy blow to Spanish pride as well as a loss in potential wealth and security. But they were a mere beginning of the continuous pacific policy which alone could relieve Spain of its financial ills.

In the end Philip III's foreign policy proved to be too hesitant, and his pacific intentions foundered on the shoal of decentralized government. Spain was saved from the lure of a new war with France in 1610 by the

1. J. Vicens Vives, "Estructura administrativa estatal en los siglos XVI y XVII" *XIe Congrès International des Sciences Historiques* (Stockholm, 1960), *Rapports*, IV, 10–15.

assassination of Henry IV.[2] But while fate kept Lerma and Philip from reversing their peaceful posture, opportunistic agents of the crown made independent decisions elsewhere which dragged the monarchy into new imperialistic ventures. In northern Italy, French and Spanish troops jockeyed for position in the strategic Alpine passes. The Spanish involvement seems to have been due to the whims of the Castilian viceroy in Milan, Fuentes. From his perspective, it made sense to control the Alps, for they linked Spanish Italy with the other branch of the Hapsburg family in Austria, and ultimately with the Spanish Netherlands. Fuentes ignored the fact that his actions also antagonized the French and Dutch states. The Spanish envoy to Austria, Count Oñate, committed the crown to still more grandiose designs in the Germanies. In 1616–1617, Oñate secured Austria's promise to turn over to Spain the key territories of Alsace, Tyrol, Finale and Piombino. The promises were never kept, but they committed Oñate to a triple policy of linking Spanish Italy territorially with the Spanish Netherlands, hemming in the French and Dutch states, and involving Spain in Austria's religious troubles with the rest of the Holy Roman Empire. By 1621, Oñate had gone on to oust from the Austrian government those who were conciliatory towards Protestant Germans, thus paving the way for the outbreak of religious war in the Germanies.[3] As the Austrian forces began to triumph over rival states in the Holy Roman Empire, Oñate persuaded the Austrians to allow Spanish troops entry into the strategic Rhineland territory of the Calvinist Palatinate. This series of bellicose actions by Spanish agents was rounded out by war with the Dutch. The Twelve Years' Truce, about to expire when Philip III died, was not renewed. The military leader of the Spanish Netherlands, Spínola, had so prepared for the resumption of war with the Dutch that war was inevitable. Castilian pride and the independence of local administrators and diplomats were too much for Philip III's initial policy of military detachment.

Meanwhile, the central administration proved impossible to regenerate. Lerma did attempt to cut through conciliar divisions by relying on royal secretaries who were his creatures. He also placed capable persons in the councils. But that was the limit of his governmental reform. He quickly fell into the pattern of royal favoritism, staging costly extravaganzas which pleased the king, ate into the royal treasury and created the illusion that all was well in the Empire.

Lerma's solution to the deep-seated problem of religious minorities in Spain was still less helpful. The immediate fear was that the Moriscos,

2. See Chapter 5, p. 153.
3. For the central European developments, see also Chapter 5, pp. 150–157.

who were officially Christian but actually Moslem, might join forces with Spain's Mediterranean enemies: France, the Ottoman Empire, the North African Moors and roving pirates. The landowners of Valencia tried to protect their hard-working Morisco tenants, but the clergy and other Christian Spaniards envied and feared the industriousness of urban and rural Moriscos alike. Lerma could have stood firmly against public opinion or weakened Morisco treachery and undermined Christian opposition by punishing a few Morisco leaders. Instead, between 1609 and 1614, he attempted to expel all Moriscos from Spain. The loss of population has sometimes been exaggerated (probably 275,000 Moriscos actually left Spain), and in some cases job-hungry Christians probably assumed vacant positions. But it was difficult for Castile to absorb the loss of 45,000 urban menials or for Valencia to recover from a 25 percent drop in its population. Whatever the specific consequences, Lerma did not improve the economic conditions of Spain.

Lerma was equally incapable of resisting the temptation to meet imperial financial needs by tampering with the currency. Philip II had occasionally defaulted on state debts, but he had managed to retain some stability in monetary values. Under Philip III, the crown began the disastrous policy of constantly debasing the content and increasing the nominal value and quantity of coins. The copper *vellón* currency of the early seventeenth century helped the crown in the short run, but ultimately it was so cheapened that it hurt the Spanish economy and the royal treasury. Inflationary Spain was an excellent place for foreigners to send their goods and secure temporary employment, but Spanish products were priced too high for European markets. Taxes paid in *vellón* could buy abroad only half the goods and services which they were nominally supposed to provide for the monarchy.

Lerma was disgraced in 1618, and Philip III died in 1621. Under them, Spain lost a great opportunity to retrench and reorganize after the peace treaties of 1598, 1604 and 1609. Her armies were still considered invincible, her generals—like the Lowlanders, Tilly and Buquoy, and the Italian, Spínola—had won respect. The English crown was so impressed that James I's heir, Charles, tried to woo a Spanish princess. Favorable marriage alliances were made with France and the Austrian Hapsburgs. Outwardly, one cannot therefore speak of the "decline" of Spain in the early seventeenth century. But increasing foreign commitments and decreasing resources would soon create more than institutional and economic weaknesses. The 1640's were to bring a crisis which would shake the foundations of the Spanish empire.[4]

4. See Chapter 7.

France: Reconstruction Under
Henry IV and Marie de Medici

The Edict of Nantes which ended France's religious-civil wars in 1598 revealed a country whose religious divisions offset underlying strengths far greater than Spain's. Post-war France was more compact territorially, more unified institutionally, and more fortunate in its economic resources and royal leadership than its western neighbor. But Spain had no problem to compare with the hatred between France's Catholic majority and Protestant Huguenot minority, nor anything approaching the disrespect which Protestant and Catholic Frenchmen alike had come to show for a monarchy which had constantly vacillated on religious issues for several decades. Although French centralization compared favorably with Spain's divisions, the civil wars had weakened France's territorial unity. While royal leadership faltered, the great French nobles who served as royal military governors in the provinces had gone their own way. In the midst of anarchy, they had turned their military authority into political power, and made their provinces into quasi-independent principalities. When the Valois dynasty became extinct with the assassination of Henry III in 1589, the French kingdom appeared headed for disintegration.

Between 1589 and 1598, the new king and founder of the Bourbon dynasty, Henry IV, had saved France from that fate, but without destroying the forces which made it an ever-present danger. It was miracle enough that he could rise from leader of a small band of Protestant soldiers to be the respected ruler of all Frenchmen. That political miracle was fashioned by military victories over the army of the French Catholic League, and a shrewd mixture of threats and bribes to the Catholic majority of France. Astutely aware that he alone could save France from perpetual civil war and foreign intervention, Henry made himself palatable to French Catholics by becoming a Catholic, while proving that he was his own man by exiling the Jesuit order for alleged subversive activities against the crown.

The Edict of Nantes of 1598 was the new king's masterpiece. The royal decree forced an unwilling Catholic majority to allow limited privileges to the Huguenots, and reconciled the Huguenots to a permanent position as second-class subjects. It recognized Catholicism as the state confession, and preserved for Catholics the lion's share of public offices. Huguenots were legally entitled to worship in several specific places, and to be eligible for state offices. By a separate, less binding agreement, Henry allowed Huguenots to keep their political organizations, to maintain armed forces and to retain one hundred fortified places within the realm. Thus Protestantism became a state within a state, complete with the guarantee of financial support from the crown; but Protestants were no longer a separate power, divorced from the rest of France. To complement the royally imposed settlement within France, Henry IV negotiated peace treaties with Spain (1598) and Savoy (1601).

The Edict of Nantes marked the real accession of Henry IV to the French throne which he had claimed and clung to for ten years. He quickly showed that he was as great a politician-ruler as he had been a warrior-politician. Yet he could not fashion miracles. Protestants and Catholics were to remain bitter foes for decades to come, except at the highest levels of royal government where Henry's engaging personality helped to heal old wounds.

Henry's former Huguenot co-religionaries were not pleased with his abjuration, and remained uneasy with their second-class status. The king never fully trusted them. Even the Edict of Nantes which he had forced down Catholic throats was more than he thought Protestantism deserved, although far less than the Huguenots had envisaged. They had blackmailed the king into last-minute additions to the settlement by withdrawing their troops from the French armies fighting the Spaniards in 1598. To make up for that concession, Henry edged towards the re-catholicization of France in his last years. The Jesuits were recalled, and one, Father Coton, was appointed confessor to the monarch. Although the Huguenots did not rebel during the second decade of the reign, they grumbled that Henry had "cotton in his ears," and many of them were ready to take up arms against their monarch if he went much further in betraying them.

The position of the Catholics was more complex. The French clergy faced in two directions: towards their spiritual leader, the Pope, at Rome; and towards their political master, the king, in Paris. Quite understandably, there were several brands of French Catholicism which ranged from pro-papal ultramontanism through clerical Gallicanism to pro-royal Gallicanism. The ultramontanists (taking their lead from the Pope, "beyond the Alpine mountains") placed religious devotion above state interest. They implicitly questioned the principle of royal divine right by declaring the king to be subject to papal directives on religious issues. They made a flexible foreign policy difficult by demanding a consistently pro-Catholic stance. Henry IV was expected to side with Catholic states like Spain and Austria against Protestant ones, whether they were a potential menace or not. Royal Gallicanism went to the other extreme, placing divine right and royal authority over the obvious necessity of making some accommodation to the powerful ultramontanist wing of French Catholicism. To side with one group or the other, to adhere rigidly to divine right or to weaken that instrument of royal authority, was to court new religious and political trouble in the realm. Clerical Gallicanism was, unfortunately, no happy compromise between these extremes. For the clerical Gallicans wished to play Pope against king, making the French or Gallican "church" quasi-independent of papal directives and royal demands alike. The universal trimmer, as Henry in essence was, barely managed to hold to a fuzzy line which placated all three Catholic positions. His widow and son would be forced by continuing religious passions and external problems to face more forthrightly the issues which he had managed to evade.

As an administrator, Henry IV proved also to be a consummate politician. Rather than destroying institutional, provincial and social opposition, he undermined his enemies by making compromises which often amounted to open bribery. He dared not remove any but the most rebellious noble governors, choosing to blunt their powers by appointing safe lieutenant-governors to share their authority. Towns were allowed to continue the tradition of electing their officials, but royal pressure often ensured that loyal subjects were elected. Similar interference with the electors of provincial estates weakened regional opposition to royal fiscal demands.

The most obstinate institutional opposition came from the law courts and taxing bureaus which administered justice and taxation in the king's name. By extending the sale of offices to include the right to bequeath them (the *Paulette* of 1604)[5] Henry in effect tried to bribe these officials into loyalty. The king did benefit from the transaction, for judges and tax collectors knew that he might revoke the privilege if they proved too independent. The king also used the *Paulette* to keep the ever-dangerous nobility from packing the law courts and taxing bureaus with their members; many nobles could not afford the price. Yet the *Paulette* did not ensure total obedience. The tax collectors still had ample opportunity to assess and collect royal taxes inequitably to favor their relatives and friends, and even to divert taxes to their own pockets. The law courts had no trouble bending the multiform and confusing laws of the realm to suit their own interests. The high courts, especially the *Parlement* of Paris, also turned their privilege of registering new laws into a judicial review of tax legislation. In examining legislation prior to registering it, the high courts often added crippling amendments or declared an outright veto which made a mockery of royal authority. Henry IV was

5. See Chapter 2, p. 46.

too much of a realist to make an issue of every act of embezzlement, or every tampering with the laws. He let his officials have their way in most instances, while bringing all the pressures at the crown's command to bear on key issues. Sometimes he pleaded, sometimes he threatened, occasionally he imprisoned or exiled. It took all his forebearance, tact and persuasiveness to compromise in this way with his own officials. The luxury of his relatively quiet last years, devoid of civil and foreign war, helped to make such limitations on his legislative, judicial and administrative powers tolerable.

Henry was more fortunate than Philip III in the executive organs and personnel with which he worked. France's councils were divided topically, and it was relatively easy to form an inner working council of devoted servants within the leading council of state. Without a mother or brother or strong-willed wife in his last years, Henry had only to contend with career ministers in making key decisions. His policy of persuading his servants while insisting on the last word allowed him to work them hard and to utilize the services of Sully, who was addicted to agrarian reforms, as well as Laffemas, who stressed industrial output. One should not exaggerate the effectiveness of Henry's political machine, however. The restoration of peace to a country well endowed with natural resources did far more than executive fiat. But the encouragement and protection of luxury industries (especially silk), the draining of marshes, improvement of land and water routes, even the planting of trees to protect roads from greedy farmers, were without their equal in early seventeenth-century Europe. Ironically Henry was cut down by the assassin's knife in 1610, just as he was about to embark on a major war with the Hapsburgs. Had war come, it would have hampered the economic recovery of France and drained the treasury of the surplus which Sully had managed to wring from the dishonest and self-seeking tax collectors. As it was, Henry is remembered as one of the greatest of France's rulers, the architect of peaceful reconstruction.

The interlude between Henry IV and Richelieu (1610-1624) is not a pleasant memory for Frenchmen. While Henry IV's successor, Louis XIII, passed unnoticed through his childhood and youth, much of the first Bourbon's work seemed to be undone by those who ruled in Louis' name.

Under the regency of the queen-mother, Marie de Medici (1610-1617), the monarchy looked almost as weak and indecisive as the regime of Philip III and Lerma in Spain. Marie hastened to keep peace with the Spanish Hapsburgs by a marriage which tied France to Spain's coattails. Henry IV had been on the point of going to war with Spain at his death; his widow allowed Spain to continue its encirclement of France in return for a Spanish bride (Anne of Austria) for Louis XIII. The meeting of the Estates General in 1614–1615 was the culmination of a dreary series of humiliations at home. The great nobles alternated between accepting huge pensions and rebelliously wringing more money from the hapless regent. Marie bribed the Huguenots by confirming the Edict of Nantes, and then had to allow them more elaborate self-government on the model of the Protestant Dutch state. Some Huguenots were still not satisfied, and joined the nobles in revolt. The convocation of the Estates General which followed these cycles of bribery and rebellion was forced on a reluctant regent by the great nobility of France. Its sessions opened up old wounds. Pro-Gallican representatives argued with ultramontanists over divine right, and noble delegates attacked the judicial officials' privilege of the *Paulette*. Even the Franco-Spanish marriage pact was bitterly criticized.

Marie managed to dismiss the Estates General before these debates split France into armed camps once more, but she could not resolve the problems which had been raised. Just when a group of able ministers (including the later First Minister, Richelieu) began to take firm military action against a new round of revolts, political disaster struck the regent from an unexpected quarter. The neglected young king and his companion, Luynes, asserted their authority. The upshot was the assassination in 1617 of Marie's minister-favorite, Concini, by a royal agent. Marie and Richelieu fell from power. But Louis XIII only succeeded in destroying those around his mother who wanted to strengthen royal authority. The Duke of Luynes proved a weak successor to Concini and Richelieu as minister-favorite (1617–1621), and Louis XIII, lacking the common sense of his father, immediately pardoned the noble rebels who were on the verge of suffering total military defeat. Under Luynes, the monarchy vacillated between coexistence and petty civil wars with nobles and Huguenots, while allowing the Spanish and Austrian Hapsburgs to further their encirclement of France.

This summary does not do full justice, however, to the interlude of Marie and Luynes. Marie's policies were negative, and Luynes vacillating. Yet they brought France through a very difficult period after the sudden death of Henry IV and before the young Louis XIII had reached maturity. At worst, France's interlude was less dismal than the Spanish counterpart under Philip III. Marie's foreign policy was actually an intelligible one. She bought continuing peace with Spain at a time when France was too weak internally to risk foreign war. Her ministers played a dangerous game of dividing and ruling during the Estates General of 1614–1615, but the policy paid political dividends. They allowed the divine-right and *Paulette* issues to divide the assembly, and then hurriedly swept them under the rug before they could destroy France. The famous divine-right "Gallican article" of the Estates General was tabled by royal orders, pending royal action which never came. The *Paulette* was temporarily abolished to frighten the judicial and financial officials and placate the nobility; then it was restored, to the relief of the officials, with the promise that it would be permanently abolished at a later date. Marie's mass bribery of the nobility with pensions frittered away the surplus which Henry IV and Sully had amassed in the treasury, but it also bought time. During Luynes' last months in power, and increasingly between 1621 and 1624, the French monarchy stumbled towards a religiously inconsistent but pragmatic policy in foreign and internal affairs. For all his Catholic conscience, Louis XIII began to align France with Protestant Europe against Catholic Spain and Austria, while pressing military action more continuously against noble and Huguenot rebels at home. When Richelieu became Louis XIII's chief minister in 1624, there were at his disposal the ingredients of the policies which would make him one of the great figures in the history of the French monarchy.[6] The same could not be said for the policies which Philip IV inherited from Philip III and Lerma in 1621.

England: The New Stuart Dynasty

Legal, territorial and religious unity made England unique among the western states of the early seventeenth century. Had these factors alone counted, the Stuart dynasty which replaced the Tudors in 1603 might well have attained the political stability which it was denied. English common law contrasted with the legal diversity which divided continental states. England had neither the autonomous provinces of Philip III's multiterritorial state, nor the quasi-independent provincial governors who weakened the territorial unity of Henry IV's France. England did have her religious minorities, the Catholics on the right and the Calvinistic Puritans on the left; however, she had shifted with relative ease from Roman Catholicism to national Catholicism, and thence to a half-Catholic, half-Protestant Anglicanism which was acceptable to the vast majority of English subjects. The inevitable religious tensions and fiscal ills of the late sixteenth century had been unable as yet to undermine England's unity, thanks to the ability of Elizabeth I to rally Englishmen to her person.

The representative institutions which were the bane of early seventeenth century monarchies had been kept in check by the Tudor Elizabeth. Her last parliaments were by no means docile, but she had contained

6. On Richelieu's administration, see Chapter 7.

their restiveness by several devices. The Speaker of the House of Commons was a royal agent with enormous power to direct and halt debates.
Members of Elizabeth's executive Privy Council sat regularly in the Commons and frequently introduced legislation which the crown wanted.
Elections were influenced by royal backing of safe candidates, and disputed election returns were subject to royal review. Thus Parliament
was still largely a royal institution. Indeed, one continental historian,
Roland Mousnier, has contended that the Tudor monarch as "king in
Parliament" was far less limited than his continental counterparts.[7] While
he swore at his coronation to uphold the laws of the land, the "king
in Parliament" could alter any law. There was no English distinction between changeable statutory law and unalterable "fundamental law"; on
the continent it was commonly believed that certain fundamental principles (such as hereditary male succession to the throne, or the inalien-
ability of royal lands) could not be overriden by any power on earth.
Provided the English crown controlled Parliament, its legislative acts were
subject only to interpretation by the common law courts. Although those
courts were as independent-minded as Parliament, their members, holding
office at the king's pleasure, were also subject to royal pressures.

The naval and military exploits of Elizabeth's England also placed
her in an enviable position. The victory over the Spanish Armada in
1588 not only made Englishmen feel that they were God's chosen people,
but secured England's shores against the only naval power which then
posed a threat. Closer to home, the troublesome Irish were being crushed
by 1603, and with the accession of the Scottish king James to the English
throne in that year, Anglo-Scottish relations were improved. While imperial commitments weakened Spain's fiscal and institutional structure, and
France faced encirclement from Spain, little England seemed secure.

Nevertheless, internal unity and external security did not tell the
whole story. While England was unified by continental standards, its
governmental machinery was grossly inadequate to turn that unity to the
advantage of the crown. After 1603 the ruling dynasty was less endowed
with political ability than either the Bourbons or the Hapsburgs. And,
ironically, the very unity which had helped the monarchy could also
place power in the hands of an opposition. On the continent, disunity
made rebellions likely, but a united revolution difficult. In England, an
opposition might be kept together by the territorial and legal unity of
the realm. The Stuarts would have to make serious mistakes before such
an opposition could emerge, but if they stumbled, they courted disaster.

7. F. Hartung and R. Mousnier, "Quelques problèmes concernant la monarchie
absolue," X Congresso Internazionale di Scienze Storiche (Florence, 1955), Relazioni,
IV, 4–15, 21–29.

The Stuarts did stumble. One need look no further than the personality of the first Stuart, James I. When he succeeded Elizabeth, James was not yet the buffoon that the portraits of his later years show. But his somewhat crude and cruel wit, and his scholarly pursuits were but a shadow of Henry IV's earthy humor and practical wisdom. James was also mistrusted because of his Scottish background. Whenever he favored those Scots who came to the English court, Englishmen were confirmed in their prejudices against Scots in general and James in particular. The king had other traits which weakened his cause. He was lazy and pleasure-loving. While the king was chasing game, the government was left in the hands of others. This problem was not disastrous at first, since an Elizabethan bureaucrat, the Earl of Salisbury, filled the breach until his death in 1612. But James could neither rule nor let others rule for him. He demanded daily written reports from Principal Secretary Salisbury, and whenever there was a crisis, James stepped in personally to make it worse. His sharp rebuke to moderate Puritan reformers at the Hampton Court Conference in 1604 ("no bishop, no king") was indicative of his ability to envenom his relations with his subjects.

Such a "system" of governing was ill-suited to the machinery of English administration and to the problems that were crying for attention in 1603. Elizabeth's Privy Council, state secretaries and Exchequer had served her well. Yet they constituted a bureaucracy which was too small to bear the burden of seventeenth-century government, unless given energetic and imaginative leadership. Although G. R. Elton speaks of a modern, national, bureaucratic government in the 1530's,[8] the English bureaucracy of the 1600's still appears rudimentary, badly overworked and grossly underpaid by continental standards. And if the bureaucracy was light at the top, it was even lighter at the bottom. The Justices of the Peace tended to represent the interests of the "establishment" of their localities. Well they might, since they were not paid by the crown, and although chosen by the ruler, were picked from the landed families. The absence of the large armies of the continent (since insular England had only the Scottish threat) made it all the more difficult for James to enforce his will.

Historians usually stress two other limitations on the English crown of the period—the common law courts and Parliament. Both have already been described as agents of royal power in the preceding pages. The truth is that although the judiciary and legislature did serve the crown, they might also be used in opposition to it. Before the civil wars of the 1640's, no one came out into the open to declare that the king was beneath the

---

8. G. R. Elton, *The Tudor Revolution in Government* (1953).

law in all circumstances, or that Parliament was in itself, without the king, "sovereign." In fact, one leader of parliamentary opposition, Coryton, admitted in 1628 that the king had power from God, was the supreme feudal seigneur and absolute in his own sphere of government (foreign affairs, war and peace, money, convoking and dismissing parliament) and also had discretionary power when the safety of the state was in jeopardy. Sir Edward Coke, the great defender of the common law and common law courts, liked to think that lawyers passed on constitutional issues; nevertheless, there could be no real sovereignty of common law. Even Sir John Eliot, in prison after 1629 for aiding parliamentary opposition, declared that a king could tax arbitrarily if necessary and that a bad king must be obeyed to avoid greater evils. Yet the common law courts and Parliament had to be watched very closely lest they grope towards a policy of parliamentary or common law sovereignty without realizing it. The common law courts could well provide a ground for opposition rather than royal initiative. A single Parliament in which there were no sharp divisions between town and country, noble and non-noble, could equally serve as a focal point of opposition.

Common law and Parliament were thus the Achilles' heel of the Stuarts. The crown lacked an elaborate executive machinery and the subjects had a ready-made institutional base from which an opposition could challenge its power. Under James I festering religious issues and critical financial problems made the common-law courts and Parliament the centers of political disputes. The question was, who would control those agencies, the crown or a national opposition?

The effects of the late sixteenth-century price rise placed the Stuarts in direr straits than either the Bourbons or Spanish Hapsburgs. In France and Spain the non-noble urban and rural well-to-do paid taxes at least in the central, populous areas. In England the wealthy were grossly under-taxed, and the machinery for putting the subjects' money in the king's pocket appears shockingly primitive compared with that of contemporary continental monarchies. In the 1620's Normandy paid as much to Louis XIII's treasury as the ordinary income Charles I of England received from his entire kingdom. French taxation *per capita* was four times that in England. Elizabeth had already begun to live on capital by selling crown lands. James continued her short-sighted policy only to find that in 1621 the remaining crown lands brought in rent only 50 percent of what Elizabeth had originally harvested. James ended Elizabeth's Irish war, and generally stayed out of continental conflicts, thereby reducing extraordinary costs. But his court was lavish where Elizabeth's was frugal, and he had inherited a public debt from his predecessor.

James' efforts to increase royal revenues were both clever and impolitic. They succeeded temporarily, but at the cost of alienating the political and social elite of the realm. Unfortunately for the new king, the one fiscal reform which would have helped the treasury without antagonizing subjects fell through. Salisbury's Great Contract proposal of 1610 was a sound one. The crown was to relinquish antiquated fees such as wardship (income from lands while the holder was a minor) and purveyance (royal purchase of supplies for the king's household at below-the-market prices) in return for an annual income of £200,000 guaranteed by Parliament. But crown and Commons were suspicious of each other's motives. After preliminary negotiations each side decided it would lose more than it gained by the transaction, and the reform died. As a result James I had to use his prerogative to bolster his treasury, shunning parliamentary tax legislation and acting by executive decree backed by rulings of the common law courts in favor of his right to bend existing laws. The custom duties were turned into a gold mine by an upward revision in rates. The royal prerogative of awarding aristocratic titles was also exploited, since the new aristocrats paid for their honors. Between 1616 and 1628, the number of noble peers rose from 81 to 126, and the number of earls from 21 to 65. Grants of monopolies, at a price, to certain merchant and industrial interests also paid handsome dividends. Meanwhile, parliamentarians complained that the king was twisting the law and making a mockery of parliamentary rights. The well-to-do commoners were irritated at their increased tax burden. The established nobility were horrified at the "inflation of honors" which cheapened their ranks, and the new nobles found themselves with empty titles lacking corresponding public functions. Bitterness was mixed with humor. Rumors circulated that James I was trying to rival King Arthur's creation of the thousand knights of the Round Table. One local genealogical "expert" actually tricked an official into granting a coat of arms to a common hangman.

Tragically for the early Stuart monarchy, these expedients did not benefit the royal treasury as much as they should have. Royal favorites and courtiers often gained control of the patronage involved in the sale of titles, awarding of monopolies and other windfalls. At best, the system was a means whereby the impoverished crown kept a key segment of the population loyal. But too few individuals benefitted from this legal embezzlement. Under Charles I's early favorite, Buckingham, corruption became the virtual monopoly of one family. The crown lost desperately needed revenue, and a large element of the political-social establishment was alienated from the king.

The same amateurish approach to finances was evident in the system of paying royal officials. To supplement meager salaries, the crown permitted its servants to extract exorbitant fees from its subjects in the course of performing their duties. Perhaps the system had its advantages, for the crown was relieved of the task of wringing still more money from reluctant subjects to provide decent salaries. However, it did not endear the government to them. It may also have deprived the crown of a source of income which the French monarchy was to exploit throughout the seventeenth century. Even with their fees, English offices were not as desirable as French ones, which combined adequate salaries with ample opportunity for illicit profiteering. Under the French system, the very wealthy were attracted to royal offices and then forced to pay huge fees to the crown in return for their share of corruption. The Stuart monarchy had no such well-to-do bureaucratic class to exploit.

James' religious predilections also alienated part of the English establishment. The Anglican king had sound political reasons for favoring the Catholic right-wing element and fearing the Puritan Calvinist left. He was anxious to live at peace with continental Catholic states in order to avoid the extraordinary financial burdens of war. He had seen the Presbyterian brand of Calvinism go hand in hand with opposition to royal authority in Scotland. However, he let his emotions override political reality. As a result, he lost opportunities to keep the Puritan left within the broad Anglican church.

Too much has been made of Puritanism as a cause of the English civil wars of the 1640's. But it is true that James pushed the religious left into a more militant, self-righteous and popular mold by his inflexible posture. Radical Puritanism in turn became one cause of civil disobedience, parliamentary intransigence and outright rebellion. At the beginning of his reign, some Puritans presented James with the mild Millenary Petition which advocated a less ritualistic Anglicanism and restrictions on the power of the Anglican church's bishops. The subsequent Hampton Court conference between the king and the Puritans broke up when James misinterpreted mild Puritan reformism within the Anglican church as a radical attack on the church's government. He wrongly felt that English Puritans wanted to replace the Anglican system of bishops with the Scottish church's looser system of presbyters. Consequently, he ignored virtually all of their suggestions, and although many Puritans stayed within the Anglican church, many others began to turn against Anglicanism and the crown.

James I was equally unable to balance the requirements of peaceful foreign policy with the necessity of placating anti-Catholic sentiment in England. One can sympathize with his desire to avoid turning the anti-papal hysteria aroused by the Gunpowder [9] and other Catholic "plots" into a witch hunt against all English Catholics. But if he did not act against

9. See Chapter 2, p. 39.

Catholics, he should also have been accommodating to the Puritans. Being "soft on Catholicism" and touchy on every Puritan issue did not help the causes of religious harmony or monarchical authority. James' religious partiality also made his seemingly pro-Catholic foreign policy raise eyebrows. When his son and heir, Charles, returned to England after an unsuccessful pursuit of a Spanish Hapsburg bride, London went wild with joy. James ignored the warning and found a Catholic wife for Charles in the person of Henrietta Maria, a French princess. While Philip III and Lerma gave in to the religious prejudices of their day, and Henry IV reconciled and trimmed, James I divided and antagonized.

In the course of his tortuous political career, the first Stuart king managed to maintain control of the common law courts, although at the expense of respect for the crown. We have already seen that he cloaked his financial expedients with their legal sanction. In 1605, the Exchequer court ruled that the king could increase custom charges without parliamentary sanction. In 1615, the King's Bench, including Coke, agreed to a preliminary polling of their opinions by the crown, although the case in question went eventually against the crown. The following year, the king insisted on having a case delayed until the judges could hear the royal side. Coke refused, and was dismissed. But as surely as royal control of justice increased, parliamentarians instinctively increased their veneration for common law as a necessary bulwark for individual liberty and property.

Parliament proved more obstinate. James found himself compelled to dissolve it to cut off opposition to executive taxation and seemingly pro-Catholic royalism. A real break in royal-parliamentary relations came in 1614; the session concluded on an angry note, something that Elizabeth had avoided. In 1621, James tore from the Commons Journal a petition outlining parliamentary rights. As he lost his temper, he also lost his "initiative" in the House of Commons. In 1621, Parliament impeached (i.e., tried in the upper house) Lord Chancellor Bacon for bribery, and Mompesson as a monopolist. In 1624, Lord Treasurer Cranfield was impeached, and the Commons took the radical step of earmarking taxes for war, thereby asserting parliamentary right to control foreign policy. The House of Commons also managed to streamline its machinery in ways which placed it beyond the clutches of Privy Councilors and the Speaker, and at the same time groomed its members to take over state affairs. In committees and subcommittees, members of the House familiarized themselves with legislative issues, prepared legislation and came close to forming a parliamentary cabinet. By forming the Committee of the Whole House, the Commons found a way to escape the tyranny of the royalist Speaker, who was replaced by a chairman of their own choice when they sat as the Committee. And as early as 1604, the Commons wrested from Chancery the right to decide disputed elections. Ominously, too, an element in the House of Lords began to shift in the same direction as the lower house. At the end of James' reign, the Earl of Southampton, a member of the Lords, led the opposition of the Commons.

When Charles I succeeded his father in 1625, a crisis was in the offing, just as there was in France in 1624, and in Spain in 1621. Tensions were increasing, the battle lines beginning to be drawn. James had managed to keep revenue rising to match increases in prices, and to rule without parliamentary "supply" between 1610 and 1621. But it remained to be seen whether his even less competent son could continue the game of hide and seek with Parliament.[10]

❧ The Dutch Netherlands After Independence

The Dutch Netherlands is often denied the prominent place in seventeenth-century histories that it deserves. The uniqueness of its political experience should merit close study; unfortunately, many historians have neglected that story because it fitted neither the pattern of monarchical absolutism prevalent on the continent, nor that of violent and decisive constitutional conflict which was England's fate. The ephemeral but spectacular rise of the Dutch state to the status of a great power after gaining independence is a fascinating subject, but the greatness of the early seventeenth century Dutch Republic has all too often been obscured by its commercial and military decline at the century's end. Anyone who wishes to know seventeenth-century Europe must take into account the unusual Dutch people, who baffled outsiders with their strange institutions which somehow worked.

The birth of the independent Dutch state was in itself a political miracle. Of the original twenty-one provinces in the Lowlands, only seven managed to make good their revolt against Philip II's great Spanish empire. Their success was as much due to their flooding of the dykes on the seacoast and the unchivalrous piratical activity of the so-called Sea Beggars, as to military exploits. The leading noble House of Orange contributed great leaders to the Dutch revolt. But the first great Orangist, William the Silent, did more for the Dutch cause by dying a martyr's death by assassination, than he ever had as a rebel chieftain. His successor, Maurice of Nassau, achieved a great military reputation in Europe for carrying the Dutch on to *de facto* independence in 1609; in reality, how-

10. On England under Charles I, see Chapter 8.

THE DUTCH AND SPANISH
NETHERLANDS, 1609-1648

1 Holland   5 Overyssel
2 Zealand   6 Groningen
3 Utrecht   7 Friesland
4 Gelderland   8 Drenthe

Dutch Netherlands
Dutch acquisitions in 1648
Spanish Netherlands
Bishopric of Liège

ever, he was overly cautious, and his love of siege warfare prevented him from annihilating his Spanish foes. The stirring saga of the Dutch revolt presented in John Motley's partisan history [11] is closer to a Hollywood movie plot than to the confusion, internal division and sheer tenacity which actually characterized the drive for independence.

The new republic's institutional framework was as puzzling as its achievement of independence. On paper, the Dutch state was a model of decentralization and particularism. The retention of Spanish centralizing institutions (notably military governorship or Statholderates in each province) seemed to be pointless in a federal state where every province and town had its separate history and age-old "liberties." At least one distinguished historian, David Ogg, has wondered how the new republic escaped disintegration.[12]

Power lay at the base of the governmental pyramid rather than at the top. In theory, the power lay in the States General, but that body was actually little more than a gathering of representatives who followed the orders of their provinces instead of dictating to them. Each provincial

11. J. L. Motley, *The Rise of the Dutch Republic.*
12. D. Ogg, *Europe in the Seventeenth Century* (1959), 408–411.

assembly was as important as the States General, and those assemblies were accountable in turn to a small "regent" class of oligarchs and aristocrats who controlled the towns and countryside of the Republic. Thus power resided in the hands of a small and scattered portion of the population, perhaps 1,000 out of 2,000,000. The regent class was as corrupt as any bureaucracy of that time.

Nor was there military centralization to offset political decentralization. The Dutch army was a coalition of provincial armies, each of which was subject to local control by regents who appointed its commanders and set aside funds for its upkeep. The navy was similarly organized.

Despite the victory of Dutch Calvinism over Spanish Catholicism, the new state was as divided as any neighboring country on religious matters. Other states had religious minorities, but the Catholic "minority" of the Dutch Netherlands constituted almost half the population! In the leading province of Holland, where the state church (the Reformed church) was most deeply entrenched, 25 percent of the population was Catholic. Moreover, the Reformed church was threatening to break into the rival Arminian and orthodox (Gomarist) factions [13] at the same time that the Truce of 1609 with Spain assured its survival.

Despite the particularism, corruption and divisiveness of the new state, the Dutch political system had its advantages. While the regent groups which controlled the system were narrow, they were not isolated from the life of the Republic. Indeed, the same men who gave directives to provincial and national assemblies, dominated the political life of the towns and controlled the commercial and financial companies of the nation. Commerce, local politics and national concerns were thus closely coordinated. Furthermore, decentralization and parochialism could be offset by shrewd manipulation. Two methods were devised to bend the seemingly inflexible constitution. One was employed by the House of Orange, the other by the regent class in the province of Holland.

Because of its great banking and commercial interests, the province of Holland was assured of far greater influence in Dutch politics than the institutional structure of the Republic intended. Hollanders paid 58 percent of the state's taxes. By insisting that their province determine how that percentage was spent, they could, in effect, dictate national policies. Holland also had a unique official, the Advocate or Grand Pensionary. He was legal advisor to the province, president of the provincial assembly and head of its delegation to the States General. When a man of purpose and decision assumed the position of Advocate in Holland, he became a sort of national Prime Minister. The great Advocates of

13. See Chapter 3, pp. 75–76.

the seventeenth century (Oldenbarnevelt in the early years, John de Witt at mid-century), were so powerful that they took over the Republic's correspondence with its ambassadors and thus controlled both foreign and internal policies of the state.

The methods of the Orangists were very different. While the Hollanders' power was largely based in one province, the Orangist party drew its strength from the national prestige of the House of Orange. By leading the Dutch to independence, William the Silent and Maurice of Nassau made theirs the leading family of the Dutch state. During the seventeenth century, the family name was more than upheld by one distinguished Orangist after another: Maurice (1586–1625), Frederick Henry (1625–1647), William II (1647–1650) and William III (1672–1702). With the backing of the family name, the Orangists were able to control major offices, and, through them, influence all levels of Dutch politics.

The key to their power lay in the tradition of bestowing provincial Statholderates on members of the Orange family. Normally, the leading member of the house was made *Statholder* by five of the provinces, and a relative was given the office for the remaining two. These Statholderates gave the Orangists enormous influence over provincial life, since they carried the obligation to maintain law and order. It was easy for the House of Orange to manufacture or exploit political turmoil, and use their authority as *Statholder* to purge town councils of hostile or independent regents. Having seized control at the bottom of the institutional pyramid where political power lay, the Orangists could influence elections to provincial and national assemblies. This chain of indirect power made the States General the agent of the Orangists. It became traditional for national assemblies to appoint the leading Orangist Captain General of the armies and Admiral General of the navies, although these offices were more difficult to exploit because of the decentralized military establishment.

But the greatness of the Dutch political system of the seventeenth century was neither in the enlightened particularism of Holland and its Advocate, nor in the absolutist potential of the Orangist camp, but the ability of the Dutch to shift from one power base to the other in accordance with internal and external needs. In 1609, Advocate Oldenbarnevelt and Holland's commercial interests seized power, and forced a badly needed truce with Spain on the Orangists. In 1618–1619, the Orangists managed a purge of the regent class, just before the truce expired, thereby strengthening the unity and military direction of the Dutch Republic. The pattern continued throughout the rest of the century. As Ernst Kossman has pointed out, the Dutch underwent several political upheavals

.during the century, but without civil war or violent revolution.[14] Perhaps the absence of kingship served the Dutch well, for they could adapt their republican institutions without the violence and confusion which the English experienced in shifting from monarchy to republic and back to monarchy.

After 1609, the Dutch needed all the flexibility their system could provide. By 1610, the divisions within the Reformed church hardened and the Republic was split into religious-political factions. That year the Holland assembly, with Advocate Oldenbarnevelt's backing, sided with the Arminians. The Orangists, led by Maurice of Nassau, quickly backed the opposing orthodox religious faction. Religious divisions, the fortunes of the two great political "parties," and the destiny of the Republic converged in a major crisis two decades before the Spanish, French and English states experienced the same fate.

Both political arms of the religious factions were treading on dangerous ground. The Arminian Hollanders realized the need for religious tolerance and compromise in a multi-sectarian state whose lifeblood was international commerce. They also saw behind the orthodox position the clergy's challenge to secular authorities for control of Dutch life. In the parable of the Arminian playwright Samuel Coster the world was a headstrong horse, ridden by the state with the aid of a whip (law) and a bridle (religion). If the bridle were seized by a second rider (the church), the horse would bolt. The Arminians felt the country would be torn asunder if narrow orthodoxy asserted itself. To the orthodox Orangists, on the other hand, Arminianism threatened the very existence of the Republic, which had been founded on Calvinism and was constantly threatened with the Catholic Spanish desire for reconquest. The Arminian belief that salvation was not the monopoly of a few made them appear no different from the Catholic Jesuits.[15] Indeed, their religious tolerance seemed suspiciously like the first move towards restoring Catholicism. Had not Oldenbarnevelt made peace with the hated Catholics of Spain in 1609? Where would he turn next? At stake also in the debate was the relationship of the free Dutch Netherlanders with the southern Netherlanders who remained under Spanish control. There was some hope that common history and culture might encourage them to break with Spain and join the Dutch Republic. However, religious considerations were crucial. Since the southern Netherlanders were overwhelmingly Catholic, only an Arminian victory in the north and the religious tolerance which would accompany it could reconcile them to joining a

14. E. H. Kossman, "The Dutch Republic," *New Cambridge Modern History,* V (1961), 275–300.
15. See Chapter 3, p. 78.

Protestant state. A triumphant orthodox party would end all prospects of reunion between the Dutch and Spanish Netherlands.

The religious crisis threatened not only to divide the Dutch into two implacable national groups, but to turn province against province, and town against town. In The Hague, the orthodox were called "Mud Beggars" because they could not worship inside the town gates. In Amsterdam, it was the orthodox who did the persecuting. In debating the issue of predestination, the two sides seemed between them to be denying every Christian the prospect of Heaven.

The crisis reached its climax when the estates of Holland authorized Arminian towns to raise troops for the cause of Arminian "tolerance." The Orangists took advantage of this threat to "law and order." In a veritable *coup d'état* the Arminian regents were purged in the provinces of Guelderland and Overyssel, and then in Utrecht. The States General had Oldenbarnevelt arrested, and he was condemned to death by an orthodox-packed national tribunal which looked suspiciously like an extra-legal court of the English Tudor-Stuart type. Meanwhile Maurice marched around Holland with troops, purging local magistracies.

The *coup* of 1618–1619 was capped by the national religious synod of Dort, monopolized by orthodox clergy, and Orangist by persuasion. Not only was strict predestination proclaimed to be doctrinal truth, but Arminians, Catholics and other "sectarians" were subsequently denied the right to worship or hold political office. But the orthodox victory was not fated to be complete. It was not the religious fanatics, but their Orangist political allies who really won. Many Netherlanders had supported orthodoxy to rid themselves of political opponents, and were now willing to wink at evasions of religious and civil restrictions. Maurice was quite conscious of the danger that the orthodox clergy posed to his own power. That clergy continued to stir up trouble, especially in Holland, but the secular power of the Orangists overrode them through the town councils. Ironically, too, Maurice found himself faced with the dilemma of heading the orthodox and anti-Catholic party at home at the very moment when the Twelve Years' Truce came to an end in 1621. To combat Spain, Maurice solicited the aid of Catholic France. By his death in 1625, Maurice was subordinating religious belief to secular considerations far more completely than had the tragic Oldenbarnevelt.

The crisis of 1618–1619 was thus resolved with a minimum of bloodshed, and with national unity preserved. In fact, the victory of the Orangists over the Arminians, the orthodox clergy and the province of Holland gave the Dutch state of 1625 greater internal strength and stability than the larger, monarchical states of Spain, England and France. The young republic had proved that it could overcome the tensions which were yet to test its more illustrious neighbors. With both civil and military institutions directed by a military leader, the Dutch were well prepared to preserve their independence against the Spanish attempt at reconquest.[16]

The Forgotten Italian Peninsula

The greatness of the Italian peoples in the seventeenth century lay in their ability to combine cultural and intellectual vitality with political stability in the midst of an economic depression which was as severe as anywhere during the period. Historians have universally overlooked or discounted the achievements of seventeenth-century Italy, seeing only cultural decadence, economic decline, social eccentricity and political stagnation. But this peninsula produced Galileo,[17] Campanella[18] and Sarpi,[19] and survived the tensions of the age without the violence and confusion which were so common in the rest of Europe. No one would deny that the great commercial empires of Venice and Genoa were now but a memory, or that the brilliance of Renaissance Tuscany and Rome could not be restored. But it is surely a distortion to dismiss seventeenth-century Italy as merely a tourist attraction and a "backwater."

One of the reasons for seventeenth-century Italy's political stability was the Spanish rule which historians condemn as a malevolent influence. Between 1559 and 1713, Spain directly governed three-fourths of the Italian peninsula. While Spanish viceroys and governors diverted some wealth from Milan, Naples and Sicily to their own pockets, they did develop an imperial policy of divide and rule which kept political instability and social discontent to a minimum. Institutions of government were left virtually as they had been when Spain assumed control, and offices were awarded to the native elite in town and countryside. If taxes appeared high, that was because the Spanish regime courted the favor of nobles and clergy by allowing them tax-exempt status. The hard lot of the peasant was largely due to oppression by noble landlords, winked at by Spanish overlords. The poor complained, but normally they could do nothing against the coalition of the viceroy and the native establishment. If the countryside suffered from low profits, the causes were the low food prices maintained by the Spaniards to keep the townspeople docile. Even the military service which Spain demanded from its Italian

16. On the Dutch Republic during its war with Spain, see Chapter 8.
17. See Chapter 3, pp. 89–95.
18. See Chapter 15, p. 393.
19. See Chapter 16, p. 417.

subjects was a stabilizing factor. For the inclusion of the Italian subjects
in the far-flung Spanish empire greatly increased their chances for employment as soldiers and diplomats.

Troubles arose only when the Spanish overlords made temporary
tactical errors in their policy of divide and rule. Emergency levies of
exorbitant taxes on the urban and rural poor, combined with Spanish-
backed oppression of the poor by the local elite, could spark rioting
against nobles, tax collectors and viceroys. The Neapolitan disturbance
of 1621 was little more than a bread riot, during which the viceroy's
carriage was mobbed and pelted with bad bread. The larger and longer
rebellions of 1647–1648 in Naples were triggered by a tax on fruit. The
rioters at first proclaimed their loyalty to their Spanish monarch. Ultimately the rebellions got out of hand, and a short-lived republic was set
up in response to Spanish treachery after a negotiated settlement. Still,
the main attention of the urban and surrounding rural rebels seems to
have been directed against the local nobility. The revolt collapsed due
to the support which the well-to-do townsmen and nobles gave to the
Spanish regime, and a confirmation of local "liberties" by a new viceroy.
A Sicilian uprising in Messina in 1674–1675 was caused when Spain permitted merchants to raise the price of bread. This was the one major
revolt to turn into a conflict by all classes against Spanish rule, a unity
which may have resulted in part from Spanish preference for the rival
city of Palermo. The revolt was put down, and the "liberties" of the city
were withdrawn. However, this list of revolts does little to support the
almost universal opinion of historians that the Spanish Hapsburgs were
oppressive rulers. The early modern epigram that the Spaniards "nibbled
in Sicily, ate in Naples and devoured in Milan" is too quaint to ignore
but too exaggerated to believe. The Spaniards were oppressive only in
the sense that all seventeenth-century regimes victimized the downtrodden.

The stability of the independent states of Venice, Genoa and
Tuscany is attributable to time-honored constitutions which could muffle
or divert discontent. The tranquility of these commercially minded
states is remarkable, nonetheless. The Dutch and English peoples, with
equally complex institutions and comparable commercial interests, could
not avoid some political instability. Venice was the most stable state in
Europe, thanks to the institutional structure which it had perfected during
the course of several centuries. A tiny oligarchy controlled Venice's
executive institutions. The bulk of the commercial nobility, socially equal
to the oligarchs, vented their frustrations in the perfunctory debates of
the Grand Council. Any sign of disaffection among disgruntled nobles
or outcast commoners resulted in swift "justice" by a three-man In-

quisition. The subject peoples of the Venetian countryside were excluded
from decision-making, but were left with autonomy in local affairs and
used as a buffer against rival states rather than as a source of revenue.
James Davis is undoubtedly correct in censuring the early modern Venetian nobility for becoming increasingly exclusive and politically
apathetic;[20] however, they managed to ease Venice into a period of
economic and military decline without political upheaval. It is also
doubtful that the group of reformist nobles called the *giovane* would
have improved matters if their cries for an aggressive foreign policy and
greater power to the Grand Council had been heeded. The oligarchy
that ran Genoa had greater difficulty in preventing feuds between old
and new nobles. However, after a particularly ugly feud in 1628, the
oligarchs eased the state's tensions by appointing Inquisitors of the State
on the Venetian model. Tuscany, under the Medici Grand Dukes, was
a model of tranquility, thanks to the gradual fusion of republican and
ducal institutions that had occurred in the previous century. Only a few
bread riots and the squabbles within the ducal house, marred its peace.

The Pope, who was religious head of Catholic Europe, also ruled as
secular prince over the most peculiar Italian principality, the Papal States.
In the seventeenth century, Popes tried to use their remaining religious
prestige and their territorial base to play a political role in Europe and
Italy. But their importance in European affairs, already a pale imitation
of Pope Innocent III's position in the thirteenth century, continued to
decline. Urban VIII (1623–1644) tried to contain Spanish and Austrian
Hapsburg power by supporting Catholic France and Lutheran Sweden
during the Thirty Years' War. However, his successors were not a party
to the treaties which ended that war nor to the negotiations which concluded its Franco-Spanish sequel. Urban also sought to make the Papal
States a strong military power on the Italian peninsula. He succeeded in
raising a formidable army and in annexing Urbino. But the costly military
machine plunged his state deep into debt, and the neighboring states of
Tuscany and Venice fought successfully to halt his territorial expansion.
Thereafter the Papacy became a second-rate Italian power.

Within the Papal States, a degree of stability was achieved. This
accomplishment was significant, in view of the fact that the papal office
was elective, and the electoral College of Cardinals tended to choose old
and weak men. It has been said that the Papal States were run in the
seventeenth century by dependent nephews and independent women.
There is much truth in that witticism, for virtually every Pope of the
century bestowed offices and wealth on his nephews, and one Pope's

20. J. C. Davis, *The Decline of the Venetian Nobility as a Ruling Class.*

sister-in-law shamelessly dispensed patronage at the papal court. Yet rule by Cardinal-nephews provided the Popes with agents whose loyalty was assured, and gradually they were replaced by still abler Cardinal-Secretaries. Popes also strengthened their government by the use of annuities called *Monti*. *Monti* were really offices, purchased by well-to-do Romans, Tuscans and Genoese. The officeholders, or *Montisti*, received interest on their investment as well as a prestigious social position. The Popes, on the other hand, helped the treasury and created a new social elite which was loyal to the state. The Roman palaces and country villas of seventeenth century papal relatives and *Montisti* still remind today's tourist of the glories of that aristocracy. To the support which they secured from the elite, the Popes added the loyalty of plebian Romans, bought by preferential economic and fiscal treatment. The rural areas retained the tradition of misgovernment, fiscal oppression and brigandage, but they still remained firmly under papal control. A Venetian observer suggested that "it must be God's will that the Papacy should keep its States; no other power that governed it so badly could do it."

Under Innocent XI (1676–1689) the Papacy showed outward signs of revival, but that great Pope could not significantly alter its fate. Elected by a reformist group of Cardinals called the Flying Squadron, Innocent exploited to the fullest the remaining power and prestige of his office. Thanks to his perseverance and the still substantial income the Papacy derived from Catholic Europe, interest rates on state debts were lowered to 3 percent. Innocent also resisted with courage and dignity the attempts by Louis XIV to dominate him on the Gallican issue of 1682.[21] Innocent's dynamic direction of the coalition of Catholic states in the war of the Holy League against the Moslem Ottoman Empire gave the Papacy a brief moment of glory which it was not to recapture until the late nineteenth century.

Of all the seventeenth-century Italian states, Savoy had the brightest future. Half French and half Italian, it resembled the transalpine monarchies far more than it did the commercially oriented republics and dukedoms of northern Italy. Its potential greatness was due largely to Duke Emanuel Philbert I (1553–1580), who freed it from French occupation and fused ducal authority with French institutions to produce a cohesive military state. Through his encouragement of agriculture, industry and mining, Emanuel Philbert turned the inhospitable highlands of Savoy and Piedmont into a land which could support a high rate of taxation and a professional army manned largely by native commoners. The nobility remained a danger, but they were encouraged to commute

21. See Chapter 10, pp. 266–267.

military service into a war tax, and their fortification of castles was discouraged. Although the Estates General was not destroyed, the Duke ceased to call it into session.

Emanuel Philbert's successors had to contend with family feuds at home and play off the French and Spaniards against each other to escape foreign domination. Despite many temporary setbacks, they managed to overcome both problems. During the 1620's and 1630's, French arms and diplomacy almost succeeded in making the Savoyard state a military outpost of France. From 1637 to 1663 the state was subjected to princely intrigues, civil war and an extravagant court life under the dowager duchess, Christine of Bourbon. But it reemerged stronger than ever under Charles Emanuel II (1637-1675) and Victor Amadeus II (1675-1730). Charles Emanuel's finance minister, Trucchi, played an important role in the political, financial and economic improvement of the state. Nobles and clergy were subjected to taxation, and corruption by state officials was checked. State regulation of the economy combatted the economic problems of the age. After a troublesome minority and near-catastrophe from a French invasion, Victor Amadeus turned the War of the Spanish Succession into the most brilliant coup of his family's history. At the Treaty of Utrecht in 1713,[22] Savoy became more Italian by the annexation of territories to the east. The gift of Sicily by the same treaty (later exchanged for Sardinia) brought with it a royal title. The new royal state of Savoy was still far from being the Italian power which would lead the peninsula to unification in the nineteenth century, but it had become a great Italian principality and a respectable, second-ranked European power.

As a group, the Italian states experienced problems similar to those which beset the major western states during the first quarter of the seventeenth century. Noble factionalism, popular unrest, economic uncertainty, fiscal difficulties and foreign threats troubled western principalities to the south as well as to the north of the Alps. Italian reactions varied, just as did the responses of Spain, France, England and the Dutch Republic. But as this survey of Italy from 1600 to 1715 indicates, peninsular solutions came earlier and more peacefully than elsewhere. The mid-century crises which are the subject of later chapters scarcely troubled the Italian scene. In 1625, England and the Dutch Netherlands were relatively stable, but during the succeeding decades they experienced dramatic internal changes. By contrast, the Venetian Republic, which had a constitution of equal complexity, quietly absorbed the shocks of political discontent and economic malaise. Savoy's troubles mirrored those

22. See Chapter 9, pp. 257-258.

of France. However, her involvement in the very wars which intensified the Bourbon kingdom's problems during the 1630's and 1640's failed to halt the Savoyard dukes' state-building. The experience of the Papal States is even more revealing. Like the Spanish monarchy, the Papacy had to adjust to the chilling reality of reduced power and prestige. Philip III and Lerma were unable to make that adjustment, and in 1621 Spain was only two decades away from a major upheaval. While Urban VIII brought the Papal States dangerously close to an internal crisis by aggressive policies during the 1630's, his successors concentrated on fiscal responsibility. As a result, Innocent XI brought to the Papal lands the efficiency which Spain acquired only under the new Bourbon dynasty after 1700.

5.

Central and Eastern Europe: Civil Strife and International Instability

Central and eastern Europe occupy far less space than western Europe in traditional texts on the seventeenth century. Yet in the first quarter of the century, the states to the east of the Elbe were the storm centers of the continent. Western states had their share of internal problems, but in the east, internal difficulties were compounded by the accidents of geography and the primitive way of life, which made the day to day existence of the monarchs precarious. Eastern states frequently lacked even a bare subsistence in revenue. It was not uncommon for a state to receive taxes in agricultural products, or to pay its civil and military servants in land or produce. Moreover, the landed aristocracies were far stronger than in the west, often deliberately keeping the monarchy elective; thus each new ruler had to barter away what little power he had in return for election by the nobility. And finally, the immense, flat plains which gave Poland its name (from *Polska*) stretched forth in all directions. Natural, defensible frontiers were rare. No western state found its capital besieged or captured as were Copenhagen, Stockholm, Warsaw and Moscow in the seventeenth century. Occasional mountain ranges like the Carpathians slowed down the advance of hostile powers, but did not prevent invasion. The sea was a barrier, but in the northeast it froze over in winter to become a natural military route, as the Danes

discovered to their regret. Given primitive internal structures and virtually no natural external protection, it was little wonder that civil turmoil
was common, and civil strife intimately connected with international
instability. Civil-foreign wars became bewilderingly complex, as armies
marched back and forth at will, and states entered or left the conflict
or changed sides, with a casualness incomprehensible to western statesmen
used to some pattern of alliances and enmities.

To make eastern European politics intelligible, one can only fall
back on the fact that certain arenas of conflict existed. The major storm
centers of the century's first decades were the Baltic Sea and the collection of German principalities known as the Holy Roman Empire. In
addition, there were constant, underlying tensions in the northern Slavic
world of Poland and Muscovy, as well as in the borderlands between
the Moslem Ottoman Empire and its neighboring Christian states.

Denmark, Sweden and the Baltic

The Baltic Sea was intensely alive in the early seventeenth century.
Eastern products of forest, plain and stream were shipped through the
Baltic, into the narrow straits (the Sound) at the western end, and
thence out into the North Sea. There, these primary goods were exchanged for the manufactures and colonial luxuries of the west. It was
obvious that the state which controlled the Sound would perforce be a
great power. The countries which managed to cling to part of the Baltic
coastline could always hope for a bright future.

The petty medieval powers which had once dominated the Baltic
disintegrated or faded from the scene in the course of the sixteenth
century. In the place of the old military crusading orders (Teutonic
Knights, Knights of the Sword) and the coalition of port towns (Hansa),
more viable powers contended for control of the Baltic. Muscovy, Poland
and the north German principality of Brandenburg (which claimed East
Prussia as its own, under the overlordship of Poland) entertained hopes of
being great Baltic powers. However, the Scandinavian states of Denmark
and Sweden were the main actors in the Baltic drama of the early seventeenth century. The fifteenth-century state of Denmark-Norway-Sweden
had divided into the Danish-Norwegian and Swedish-Finnish states during
the sixteenth century, and no love was lost between these former partners.
In 1600 Denmark's territories made it the dominant power in the Baltic,
but Sweden was envious of its position.

Tiny Denmark was a most unlikely candidate for great power
status. The mainland of Jutland was sparsely populated and economically

unpromising. The islands by the Sound were only slightly more inviting. Their soil was fertile, but the nobility dominated the peasantry and over-shadowed the middle-class population. The greatest asset of the islands was the capital city of Copenhagen, on the main island of Zealand. The position of the monarchy was far from enviable. Although the crown was held by the Oldenburg dynasty, it was an elective one, and the powerful nobility sought at each election to wring concessions for them-selves in return for continuing the line. The ruler could not expect the slender resources of the country to yield much revenue to the treasury, unless the nobility relinquished the "liberty" of tax exemptions. When the Danish Reformation of the sixteenth century turned Denmark from Catholicism to the new Lutheran confession, the treasury had been bolstered by the seizure of church lands. But that was a windfall which could not be repeated.

The Danish monarchy and state were saved from oblivion by the country's strategic location on the Baltic and the leadership of the Olden-burg dynasty. The political division of Scandinavia into two states left the Danes with control of both shores of the Sound and other key pos-sessions in the Baltic. Dominating the Sound from the island of Zealand and the southern Swedish province of Scania, the Danish monarchy had been able to collect tolls from all ships passing through it after 1544. The tolls were a precarious but lucrative substitute for natural resources and national taxation. They made it possible for the Oldenburgs to maintain a sizable fleet and a respectable army of German mercenaries. Denmark hemmed in Sweden from Danish Norway, the Danish provinces of Hal-land, Scania and Bleking on the southern tip of the Swedish peninsula, and the Danish-held islands in the Baltic. With the assistance of anti-Swedish Poland and Muscovy, it was conceivable that Denmark might try to force Sweden back into the late medieval Scandinavian union. And the Oldenburgs even had ambitions on the European mainland, where they were overlords of Germanic Holstein. The great Oldenburg king, Christian IV (1588–1648), also managed to keep the powerful Dan-ish nobility loyal by a marriage of convenience with them. His coronation oath (*Handfaestning*) legalized the aristocratic nature of the government, but left the crown free to pursue an ambitious foreign policy. And while the nobility enlarged their domains, tightened their grip on the peasantry and monopolized royal offices, Christian balanced their power somewhat by his strong support of Denmark's middle-class interests. Overseas trading companies were chartered, harbor facilities improved, and the teaching of physics, mathematics and natural science fostered by the monarchy. It was questionable whether even a great monarch like Christian could continue to satisfy his nobles, maintain Denmark's Baltic

position and at the same time pursue an ambitious policy in northern
Germany. However, Denmark held the sources of power; any rival would
have to dislodge it to become a great northern state.

Between 1598 and 1629, Sweden prepared the ground for such a
challenge, but it was not until the middle of the seventeenth century that
the Swedish royal house of Vasa could overcome internal and external
weaknesses. The prospects looked none too bright for the Vasa dynasty
or the Swedish people in 1598. Hemmed in on the south, west and north
by Denmark, with hostile Muscovy and Poland holding most of the
remaining southern Baltic shores, Sweden was not a great trading or
naval power. Her economy was backward. Her peasants paid taxes in
kind because of lack of currency, her internal commerce was conducted
frequently by barter and her immense mineral resources in iron, copper
and silver were exploited in a primitive manner. The government in the
sixteenth century was haphazard and elementary in organization, and
the crown hard pressed to contend with a four-estate assembly (*Riksdag*)
of nobles, clergy, townsmen and peasants. In 1568 a family feud between
king Erick IV and his brothers John and Charles, had emasculated royal
power. John replaced the deposed Erick, and his accession was ratified
by the *Riksdag*. Thus that national assembly, more truly representative
than most contemporaneous parliaments, now emerged as one of the
important elements in Sweden's political life. However, it was the Swedish
nobles who were the chief beneficiaries of the palace revolt. The crown
exempted them from indirect taxes, and they began to monopolize the
chief posts in the central government. On the local level they were even
more triumphant. The nobles' peasants (as distinct from free peasants and
peasants on royal estates) were freed from taxation, and the nobles were
placed in charge of the local law courts. In effect the nobles became
virtually a state within the state.

The fortunes of the Vasas began to improve as a result of a weird
succession dispute in the 1590's. When King John died in 1592, his son
and successor, Sigismund, unwittingly destroyed his own political career
and at the same time enhanced the position of the royal family. Sigismund
was already king of Poland, by election in the Polish Diet. He thought
that he could easily use his combined power as ruler of Poland and
Sweden to become a strongman in his Swedish kingdom. However, he
made two tactical errors. In the first place, he tried to restore the Lutheran
Swedish state to the Catholic fold, thereby antagonizing many Swedes
who saw the move as a scheme to subordinate Sweden to Poland. In
addition, he relied too heavily on support from a few friendly Swedish
and Finnish noblemen, which he thought was sufficient to give him a
stranglehold over the Swedish people.

To the consternation of Sigismund and his noble allies, many Swedes refused to accept domination by a Polish Catholic king, even a Vasa. When in 1598 Sigismund imported Polish troops to Sweden and leading Swedish and Finnish noblemen sided with him, a national resistance movement resulted. The Swedish people rallied behind Sigismund's uncle, "Charles Crooknose," who swiftly turned the rebellion into a *coup d'état* which made him king and master. The nobles who had supported Sigismund were now cast in the role of traitors. The *Riksdag*, with Charles as prosecutor, purged local government and even the royal council of these enemies of the state by condemning them to death (the so-called Linkoping massacre). The many nobles who had stood by Charles remained in power, of course, but the new king was at least rid of the most independent noblemen. Instead of being torn apart in a religious war, Sweden was united more firmly than ever behind the Lutheran church. State and church systematically did away with the pockets of Catholicism remaining from Sweden's pre-Reformation days.

As Charles IX (1598–1611), the victor over Sigismund now cast his eyes towards the Baltic. Sweden was still too weak to dislodge Denmark from its stranglehold on the Sound, but Charles was able to circumvent the Danish tolls by building the port of Goteburg just outside the strait. Charles decided to test his army against the weaker powers of the eastern Baltic. He fared poorly against the Polish cavalry, and was forced to abandon his campaign to conquer Polish Livonia. However, a civil war in Muscovy made a successful campaign against the Muscovite state possible. In 1610, Swedish troops marched into Moscow and plans were made to place Charles' heir, Gustav Adolph, on the throne of the Tsars. Charles died with success in the east within sight, but with the nagging problem of Denmark still unresolved. Quick to take advantage of the Swedish involvement with Muscovy, the Danes had launched an attack which began a new Danish-Swedish war.

The new Vasa monarch, Gustav Adolph (1611–1632), continued the work of his father with far greater success. Gustav Adolph was one of the great statesmen of the seventeenth century, bringing monarchy and nobility together in a remarkable alliance which was far more effective than Christian IV's capitulation to the Danish nobility. Like Henry IV of France, he was a gifted leader of men, and turned his father's bitter relations with the Swedish nobles into an agreement based on trust. His accession oath placed great power in the hands of the royal council, which was headed by an aristocratic chancellor, Axel Oxenstierna. The following year, the nobles' powers over their tax-free peasants were extended, and in 1617 the formal coronation oath (on the king's assumption of his majority) further ensured the virtual monopoly of the nobility over high state offices. But Gustav Adolph turned these apparent liabilities into strengths. While the nobles held high offices and dominated the council, they knew that their king had ultimate direction of affairs. They became a service nobility, kept in power because they were willing to follow the lead of their monarch. Even Oxenstierna was not in on the secrets of the king's foreign policies. The *Riksdag* was used as a platform from which the king could appeal to his great and humble subjects alike, and Gustav Adolph had the gift of rallying the country to his side. Before the assembled estates at his coronation, the monarch declared that he relied only on "trust in God, and the power which derives from the loyalty of Swedish men," a marvelous blending of divine right and popular monarchy.

As years passed, the central and local governments were gradually reorganized, adding efficiency to popularity. The great offices of state were transformed into government boards (colleges), after the Dutch model. Permanent governorships were established for local affairs. The judiciary was systematized, with a hierarchical organization complete with courts of appeal. The governmental organization outlived the great king, and helped Sweden survive the difficult regency period which followed his death in 1632.

Gustav Adolph's greatness was partly due to fortunate circumstances, but it was to his credit that he took advantage of every favorable turn of events. At a time when Swedish and foreign demands for metals were quickly outrunning the supply, Gustav Adolph had the vision to exploit his country's untapped mineral resources. Under royal direction, Dutch and other foreign entrepreneurs used their wealth and technical skills to organize Swedish mining and metallurgical enterprise. The economic domination of Lowlanders like Louis de Geer was so great that Sweden became in some respects a "colony" of the Dutch. However, the Swedish king and people also benefitted. The treasury was bolstered by the export of copper to western European countries which were converting from silver to copper currency. Iron exports for European armaments provided further income. In 1613, copper and iron accounted for 80 percent of all Swedish exports. Needless to say, the shrewd Swedish monarch was careful to see that some mineral resources were diverted to the needs of his own military machine.

It has been argued that Gustav Adolph squandered his country's new wealth by embarking on an overly ambitious and reckless foreign policy. The truth of the matter is that Sweden had to expand territorially if the country were to survive and the monarchy remain strong. The king also set priorities in laying down the lines of his imperialism. At war with Denmark on his accession, Gustav Adolph wisely negotiated a set-

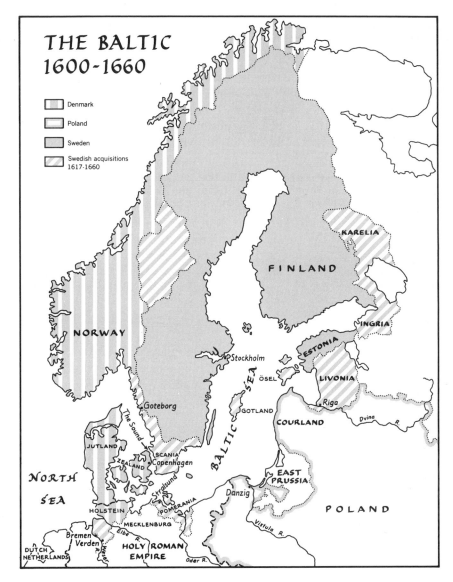

THE BALTIC
1600-1660

Denmark

Poland

Sweden

Swedish acquisitions
1617-1660

KARELIA

FINLAND

INGRIA

NORWAY

ESTONIA

Stockholm

ÖSEL

LIVONIA

Riga

Goteborg

GOTLAND

COURLAND

Dvina R.

The Sound

BALTIC SEA

JUTLAND

SCANIA

ZEALAND

Copenhagen

EAST
PRUSSIA

NORTH
SEA

Stralsund

Danzig

POMERANIA

HOLSTEIN

MECKLENBURG

Vistula R.

POLAND

Bremen

Verden

Elbe R.

HOLY ROMAN
EMPIRE

Oder R.

DUTCH
NETHERLANDS

tlement within two years. The Danish-Swedish treaty of 1613 deprived
Sweden of its Arctic trade via Goteburg, but it also exempted Swedish
goods from the Danish Sound dues. More significantly, the peace removed
the danger of Danish attack from the rear, and freed Sweden for new
wars against the weaker powers of the eastern Baltic. War with Muscovy
brought rich rewards at the Treaty of Stolbova (1617). The Swedish
coastline was extended from Finland to Narva, and Muscovy agreed to
divert all trade with the west (except exports from the Arctic port of
Archangel) through Swedish territory. Next, Gustav Adolph turned his
attention to the port of Riga, eastern Poland's window on the Baltic, at

the mouth of the Dvina River. In 1621 the Swedish army stunned the vaunted Polish cavalry with a crushing defeat, and Riga was added to Sweden's chain of Baltic ports. By the time Poland was ready to negotiate the Treaty of Altmark (1629), Sweden was firmly in control of all the major ports and river mouths of Poland, with the exception of the free port of Danzig on the Vistula.

In the campaigns against Poland, the Swedish army became the best military machine in Europe, "fed" by a conscription policy far more advanced than that of other states. By combining the best features of the Polish cavalry with the Dutch system of small, mobile units, and employing the new Swedish cannon to protect the army's flanks, Sweden revolutionized military tactics. The conquered peoples of the Baltic contributed additional troops and supplies to the Swedish state. Moreover, the tolls which Sweden charged at its newly acquired Baltic ports greatly increased the resources of the royal treasury. It has been estimated that the tolls from Polish Prussia provided 30 percent of the total Swedish royal income.

By 1629, Gustav Adolph was in the peculiar position of having to wage new aggressive wars to preserve the empire which he had created while defending Sweden's integrity. The Swedish monarch once muttered that he was "suspected of wanting to drink up the entire Baltic, just because he had been constrained to take one pail of water from it." In reality, whether he had foreseen the result of his defensive expansion or not, his critics had accurately predicted the result. There was no possibility of turning back. Sweden's empire had made it a great power; to defend that empire, Gustav Adolph would have to expand his state indefinitely.[1]

໑ Poland and Muscovy: Giants of the East

Outwardly, the two giant states of Poland and Muscovy seemed in 1600 equally destined for greatness, and far more likely to achieve it than tiny Denmark or Sweden. The size of the united state of Poland-Lithuania was immense, and the already large principality of Moscow was constantly expanding its borders in all directions. Each of these giants had perhaps ten times the population of Denmark or Sweden proper. Each was blessed with fertile lands which yielded an immense harvest in grain, and Muscovy also had rich mineral resources in the interior which

---

1. On Sweden and Denmark during the Thirty Years' War, see Chapter 6.

had scarcely been touched. Although the commercial-industrial classes in each state were weak, so were their counterparts in Scandinavia.

The seventeenth century was to see Muscovy capitalize on its opportunities and Poland fail to realize its potential. Polish historians generally argue that wars with predatory neighbors turned Poland's promise into ultimate disaster. There is some truth in this interpretation, but Russian scholars have been quick to point out that their state, too, was faced with dangerous enemies. The best explanation for the diverging fortunes of Poland and Muscovy in the seventeenth century seems to be the particular tradition which each state had been developing in the preceding decades. By 1600, there were already signs that their political and cultural differences were molding their future. By 1715 the ultimate destiny of Poland and Muscovy was much clearer. In the intervening decades, Poland's monarchs had proved incapable of altering tradition, while Muscovy's Tsars were able to exploit and alter it sufficiently to meet the pressing problems of the century.

Historians wonder whether the Muscovy of the early seventeenth century was a European state. Contemporaries knew that it was not. To them, Poland was the last outpost of European civilization, while Russia was outside the pale. Muscovy had diplomatic relations with states to the west, and was on the trade routes between Persia and Europe. Observant westerners knew a lot about the Muscovite state, even if cartographers used the terms "Scythia" and "Tartary" to identify it. There was still closer contact through the so-called German quarter of Moscow, where Europeans had settled and Muscovites could come to pick their brains. Still, Muscovy was essentially an isolated principality which had developed its own traditions as an expanded fortress-town.

The Dukes of Moscow had gradually risen from the status of petty, tax-collecting agents of the Asian Tartars to independent Grand Dukes of the surrounding countryside. During the fifteenth and sixteenth centuries, the Muscovite state had thrown off the Tartar yoke, followed the rivers which ran to the northwest and southeast and gradually swept into its protective net the nearby towns and primitive tribal communities. Under Ivan IV, called "the Dread" or "the Terrible" (1533–1584), Muscovite expansion had temporarily reached the Baltic, and that audacious ruler had hopes of marrying Elizabeth I of England. However, the most significant thrust of his conquests was towards the southeast, along the Volga river to Kazan, Astrakhan and eventually to the landlocked Caspian Sea.

Moscow seemed incapable of freeing itself from its heritage as a fortress-state under the Tartars. The military and Tartar traditions

MUSCOVY OR RUSSIA IN 1682

blended together to stamp Muscovy in a non-European autocratic mold. The Dukes of Moscow looked on their subjects' lands as a ducal patrimony owned by right of conquest. Their haughty titles and pompous language may have seemed laughable to westerners, but they had real meaning in Muscovy. The state was the prince's. That tradition was strengthened by the influence of Byzantium, the eastern remnant of the ancient Roman Empire. Moscow acquired close personal, religious and cultural ties with that eastern empire in the late Middle Ages. When the capital and last possession of Byzantium, Constantinople, fell to the Ottoman Turks in 1453, Moscow saw itself as the heir of the Byzantine tradition. A national myth arose: two Romes (Rome and Constantinople) had fallen, and Moscow was the third Rome, inheriting the greatness of the ancient Empire. The Dukes of Moscow drew upon the Byzantine tradition of state domination of religious affairs, thereby avoiding the painful struggles between church and state which plagued European monarchs. The Muscovite dukes came to consider themselves God's agents on earth far more firmly than any divine-rightist ruler in the west. And eventually, in 1547, Ivan the Dread exchanged the ducal title for the imperial and imperious name of Tsar (Caesar).

The state church of Muscovy, known as the Russian Orthodox church, also helped to further the isolation of Muscovite traditions from European culture. Muscovites were proud of the fact that their church was an offshoot of the Greek Orthodox church, the state church of Byzantium. They looked to the Greek church for inspiration when the latter continued its existence under Turkish rule; and they sealed themselves off from the religious and cultural ferment of the west, looking on Catholic and Protestant Europe with contempt.

The autocratic tradition of Muscovy was enhanced by the absence of strong institutional opposition within Muscovite society. Muscovy had a very powerful aristocracy, composed of great nobles (*boyars*) with freehold estates and service nobles (*opritchniki*) who were paid in land by the Tsars. The Patriarch of the Russian Orthodox church could also wield great influence in political affairs if he had a strong will. But Muscovite society lacked the provincial liberties and assemblies so common in European states. (Indeed, it would be an error even to say that "provinces" existed in Muscovy.) Nor were there strong institutional offshoots of society at the central level. The assembly of the *boyars* (*Boyarskaia Duma*) claimed the right to participate in the Tsar's decisions, but its influence had been circumvented by Ivan the Dread's reliance on the service nobility. The assembly supposedly representative of all society (*Zemski Sobor*) was still weaker. In times of grave national emergency, it played a major political role, but it never was able to overcome the powers of autocratic tradition and provincial impotence.

Only in the southern borderlands of Muscovy did the Tsars face a constant threat to their political power. That threat came from the semi-nomadic Cossack bands of the Dnieper, Don and Volga rivers, which had carved out quasi-political states. In 1600, the Dnieper Cossacks were loosely associated with the Polish-Lithuanian state, while the other bands showed some slight deference to Moscow. Nevertheless, the Cossacks could not achieve more than primitive political organization and loose control over the local peasantry. The Cossacks could turn their military power against Moscow or Poland, or fight on behalf of those states against the Ottoman Empire and its tributary Khanates of the Black Sea. But while they could threaten or ally with Moscow, they had no hope of replacing the Tsarist regime within Muscovy as a whole.

The Tsars had to temper their autocratic political tradition to accommodate the socio-economic power of their mightiest noble subjects. In so doing, they managed to keep political power in their hands. *Boyars* and *opritchniki* were left tax exempt, but the Tsars were able to turn the lucrative external trade in grain into a state monopoly. In addition, revenue could be drawn from the Tsars' personal estates. A haphazard and inefficient, but nonetheless profitable, system for taxing peasants and townspeople also existed. The royal bodyguard of musketeers (*Streltsi*) was somewhat unreliable but it *could* be contained by Tsarist bribes. Boris Godunov showed how easily an opportunistic politician could put the national assembly to work for the Tsarist regime. When the ruling dynasty became extinct in 1598, he summoned a *Zemski Sobor* which was little more than a gathering of state officials embellished with the common folk who happened to be in Moscow at the time. Although he was only the brother-in-law of the deceased Tsar, Boris was "elected" by the will of the people as shown in this assembly. Political power, financial windfalls and compromises with the social elite thus placed the Tsars in an enviable position. One could argue that the Muscovite rulers had all the advantages of Sweden's kings, without the Vasas' limitations. Muscovy had the same resources as Sweden in far greater abundance, and boasted a unique autocratic tradition unencumbered by a *Riksdag* or a noble-dominated royal council.

In contrast, Poland's tradition combined the disadvantages of Muscovite society with the tensions of European political-cultural life. The fifteenth and sixteenth centuries had been a great period in Polish history, but they gradually gave way to discord and decentralization. The union of Lithuania with Poland gave the state a single head (ruling as king in Poland, and grand duke in Lithuania) and started the process of Polonization to accustom the Lithuanian nobility to Polish habits. Unfortunately, the nobilities of the two peoples combined their economic and social power, which was as great as that in Muscovy, with institutional arms as strong as anywhere in Europe. The Polish-Lithuanian Diet (*Sejm*) became the tool of the nobility, and checked every move made by the monarchy to enhance royal power. Church and state dignitaries of noble lineage dominated the Diet's upper house, while the lower house was packed with the petty nobility or *szlachta*. There were also numerous regional assemblies (*Sejniki*) which elected delegates to the Diet's lower house, thereby ensuring that the Diet would protect the interests of local nobles.

While the extinction of the ruling family in Muscovy in 1598 did not destroy the principle of hereditary monarchy, the disappearance of the Jagellon dynasty in Poland (1572) did. The Polish-Lithuanian nobility seized the opportunity to strengthen their institutional base by making the monarchy elective. Many of the Polish rulers of the seventeenth century were able men, but the elective principle coupled with the nobles' institutional power gave them little margin for human error. The fact that the nobles called in one foreigner after another to wear the Polish crown did nothing to help Poland's kings build up a national royalist party.

By the early seventeenth century, the monarchy had only a shadow of the power exercised by kings elsewhere. Instead of permanent tax revenue, there were temporary taxes, so narrowly allocated by the Diet that it was impossible for the crown to maintain a large, standing army. The military consisted of a small royal guard and a large but unwieldy volunteer army of noble cavalrymen which could not easily be turned into a disciplined arm of the monarchy. Meanwhile, the nobility were permitted to place the peasantry firmly under their control, and to ruin the commercial populace by placing landed interests above middle-class commerce and industry. Without independent military and fiscal resources, it was difficult for the monarchy to resist this extension of the nobles' socio-economic power; and without the means to build up non-noble classes as a counter to the nobility it was still more difficult to divide and rule. The Lithuanian nobles found themselves in a particularly advantageous position. As a reward for accepting Polonization, they acquired a virtual blank check to control their peasants.

Cultural ties with the west gave Poland advantages which isolated Muscovy lacked, but they also created diversity which caused tensions among its peoples. The intellectual and cultural ferment in early modern Poland may have been as intense as its western versions. The Reformation had taken Poland by storm. Lutherans, Calvinists and unitarian Socinians vied with Catholics. There was also the Greek Orthodox faith to contend with, deeply imbedded in the life of the Polish-Muscovite borderlands. The University of Cracow was a great center of learning, and Polish nobles frequently studied abroad, adding to the diversity of ideas. Lithuanian nobles were assimilated, but the Cossack bands and peasants of the east were not, while people of German and Jewish ancestry mingled without merging with the Poles. Such diversity can be far healthier for a state than bland homogeneity, but the combination of a multicultural and particularist, decentralized state is fraught with grave problems. It is tempting to speculate on the fate of the culturally diverse Dutch people, had they found no way of circumventing a decentralized political structure very similar to that of Poland.

In the early seventeenth century, both Poland and Muscovy underwent internal crises which tested the strengths and weaknesses of royal authority. Before long, these internal troubles became merged in conflicts between the two states. In Poland, the occasion of the trouble was the accession of a militant Catholic as ruler in 1587. In Muscovy, the death of Boris Godunov in 1605 led to succession disputes which became known as the Turbulence or Time of Troubles.

When Sigismund III (1587–1631) was elected to the Polish throne, he resolved to reimpose Catholicism and royal authority on his subjects. It was a valiant attempt to exploit what remained of waning royal authority and prestige, but it fell short of its ultimate objective. Sigismund

was far more successful in recatholicizing Poland than he was as king
of Sweden (1592–1598).[2] He packed the upper house of the Polish Diet
with bishops who were both Catholic and royalist, and appointed Catholics as local governors. In 1607–1608 he put down a rebellion by
Protestant nobles which had some support in the Diet's lower chamber.
Poland became a predominantly Catholic state as a result. Unfortunately,
Sigismund was unable to exploit his religious and military victories to
the permanent advantage of the monarchy as Charles IX did in Sweden.
His Catholic appointees were given lifetime positions, and in time became as independent of the Polish crown as the rest of the clergy and
nobility. The nobles who volunteered to put down the Protestant uprising refused to relinquish their control of military affairs to the king.
The power of the purse and over the provinces remained outside royal
control. Sigismund became known as the "Philip of the North," fighting
for Catholicism like Philip II of Spain. The title is not entirely appropriate, because the Spanish monarch's greatness rested on his control
over his subjects as well as his devotion to the Catholic faith.

Sigismund's pro-Catholic internal policy also dragged the Polish
state into new troubles on its borders. He was fortunate that the hatred
which oppressive landlords and Catholic crusaders aroused among his
Orthodox subjects in eastern Poland did not lead to outright rebellion
until after his death. His crusading ventures in Muscovy had more immediate repercussions. Tempted by the succession disputes in Moscow,
Sigismund decided to place a Catholic Polish puppet on the throne of the
Tsars with the aid of Poland's noble army. The Poles were temporarily
successful, but in the long run their venture helped to unite Muscovites
behind a new native dynasty, thereby strengthening the autocracy of the
rival Muscovite state. If Sigismund was really aiming at protection of his
valuable Baltic coastline, it would have been wiser to concentrate Poland's
military forces on the Baltic, than to employ the rather indirect and
impolitic strategy of striking at the heart of Muscovy. By chasing a
will-o'-the-wisp in the Muscovite interior, the Polish monarchy missed
a great opportunity to unite crown and nobility in a successful venture.
At stake also were the trade and natural resources of the Baltic, which
might have been placed under royal control. Poland might not have
been able to become a great power on the autocratic Muscovite model,
but it was conceivable that the Polish crown could have utilized the
Baltic resources which became such an important instrument of Swedish
imperialism under Gustavus Adolphus.

2. See pp. 134–135.

Meanwhile, the Time of Troubles (1605-1613) brought to the surface all the tensions within Muscovite society, which had been held in check by autocracy. Tsar Boris Godunov (1598-1605) discovered that his election could not obliterate his non-regal *boyar* background. The *boyars* would not respect his authority, and he embittered relations by having his enemies executed or exiled. Without a "legitimate" autocrat, autocracy failed. Boris died with the country in turmoil, while many persons rallied behind a pretender to the throne who claimed he was Dmitri, the previous Tsar's half-brother (murdered in 1591 in a cloak-and-dagger scene which encouraged rumors of his "escape"). After Boris' death, the turmoil enlarged into the Time of Troubles. A rash of pretenders vied for the succession, but none could prove his regal pedigree and the country divided into a number of warring factions. Various elements of Muscovite society tried to seize power and subject other groups to their tyranny. The *boyars* were split into rival parties, peasants rose up against their noble masters, and Cossacks tried their hand at fighting and pillaging. The *reductio ad absurdum* of the "Turbulence" was reached when Polish forces seized Moscow and a native *boyar* leader, Basil Shuisky, called in the Swedes for help.

For all its engendering of social divisions and political chaos, the Turbulence emphasized the tenacity of Muscovite autocracy. No politico-social party had a strong enough institutional base to control its candidate or impose him on the country. When Moscow and other areas turned against the foreign powers, a grass-roots movement led to an extremely representative *Zemski Sobor* in 1613. The national assembly after much wrangling found a candidate who had kinship with the old Tsarist line. Michael, first of the Romanov dynasty (1613-1645), was not a great man, but Vasili Klyuchevsky is probably right in stressing his legitimacy as the solution to the Turbulence.[3] Once they had discovered their "legitimate" ruler, Muscovites fell in line under continued autocracy.

On the surface, Michael's reign appears pitifully ineffectual, as Sweden wrested away Muscovy's Baltic coastline and Poland held its own on the Dnieper. Institutionally, the splintering of state departments or *prikazi* into bewilderingly overlapping administrations makes one wonder whether there was any unity to internal policy. The return of Michael's father from captivity in Poland in 1619 provided Moscow with further problems. As Patriarch and Co-Tsar, Philaret virtually dictated Muscovy's foreign policy. His relentless hatred of the Poles dragged Moscow repeatedly into futile conflict with Poland. In turn, this policy

3. V. O. Kluchevsky (or Klyuchevsky), *History of Russia*, III (1960), 63.

necessitated a rapprochement with the two more dangerous foes on the flanks: Sweden and the Ottoman Empire. It was Muscovite subsidization of Gustavus Adolphus [4] as much as French assistance which was to free the Lion of the North from his concerns with Poland, and make Sweden a great European power in the Thirty Years' War. Sweden would long be the main external obstacle to the modernization and Europeanization of Muscovy.

Nevertheless, under Michael Romanov, Muscovy recovered from internal chaos and Muscovite autocracy began to bridge the chasm opened between crown and nobility. Desperate to find men and money to fill the vacuum left by the flight of peasants during the Time of Troubles, Michael moved towards a marriage of convenience with the nobles. The tendency of the nobility to tie the peasantry to the soil became more pronounced, and received the sanction of the Tsar. The Tsarist regime realized that if peasants and other commoners were rendered immobile, they could not escape their obligations to the state. The statist end seemed to justify placing the lower orders of society under the tyranny of rapacious landlords. It was a policy which would become a permanent trait of Muscovite society under Michael's successors.[5]

✎ The Ottoman Empire: Sleeping Giant

To the south of Poland and Muscovy lay the formidable Ottoman Empire. Since the fourteenth century, that Moslem state had been expanding from its center in Turkey. In 1600, it had control over the Christian peoples of the Balkans, overlordship of Tartar Khanates on the Black Sea and nominal suzerainty on the southern shores of the Mediterranean. In 1529 it had startled western and central Europe by laying siege to the city of Vienna. Virtually no seventeenth-century European state could ignore the Sultan who ruled this vast empire from its capital in Constantinople.

Europeans frequently talked of new Christian crusades against the infidel Turks, but normally they alternated between uneasy peaceful coexistence and secular territorial wars. The Austrian Hapsburgs clung to a narrow strip of Hungarian soil on the condition that they pay annual tribute to the Sultan. Despite this agreement, Ottoman rule in neighboring Turkish Hungary and Transylvania resulted in intermittent warfare with the Porte. As the seventeenth century opened, one of these Hapsburg-Ottoman wars was dragging to a close. Poland's flank was equally threat-

4. See Chapter 6, p. 164.
5. On Poland and Muscovy at mid-century, see Chapter 6.

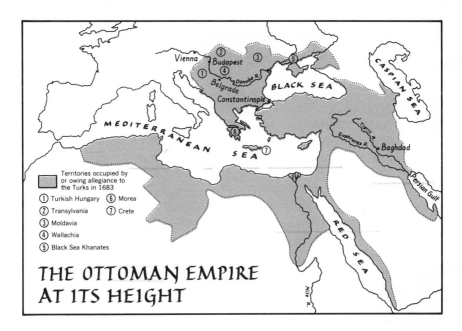

Territories occupied by
or owing allegiance to
the Turks in 1683

① Turkish Hungary ⑥ Morea
② Transylvania   ⑦ Crete
③ Moldavia
④ Wallachia
⑤ Black Sea Khanates

THE OTTOMAN EMPIRE AT ITS HEIGHT

ened by the Turkish protectorates of Moldavia and Wallachia. Muscovy was blocked from access to a warm-water port by the Turkish Khanates of the Black Sea. Venice's once-great empire had receded before Turkish military and naval power, but the Venetian republic held on grimly to its Mediterranean outpost of Crete while trying to trade with the Porte. England, France and Sweden all tried to reach agreements with the Ottoman Empire. In the early sixteenth century, France had begun an uncertain tradition of commercial and diplomatic relations with Constantinople. The Turks were a dangerous foe, but the French also realized the advantages of a commercial link with them and the possibility of turning them against France's Hapsburg enemies. Elizabeth I was equally unscrupulous in her relations with the Porte. She tried to secure trade concessions, and had the nerve to suggest an Anglo-Turkish alliance against their common foe, Hapsburg "idolatry" (i.e., Catholicism!). Faraway Sweden flirted with the Ottoman tributaries to the south of Poland, hoping to weaken its Polish rival from the rear.

One of the great strengths of the Ottoman Empire was its unique military system. An elite corps of 8,000 called the Janissaries (literally the New Troops) was the backbone of the army. It was composed of sons of Christian subjects, who were converted to the Moslem faith, put in uniforms, placed in barracks and subjected to rigid discipline. To supplement the Janissaries, the Sultan granted land to Moslems on the condition that they supply a quota of soldiers when called upon by the state. In a sense, the Empire was an army on the move. As long as it seized new territories and acquired new Christian subjects, its security seemed assured. When the army ceased to extend its territorial and human base at the end of the sixteenth century, the Ottoman Empire was weakened. However, it was not until the 1680's that this weakness, combined with the degeneration of the Janissaries into a corrupt collection of place seekers, spelled disaster for the state. The navy was inferior to the army, and at the battle of Lepanto in 1571 had suffered a crushing defeat at the hands of the Spaniards and Venetians. Nevertheless, the Ottoman Empire had the will and the resources to replace its lost fleet almost overnight and regain hegemony over the eastern Mediterranean.

The commercial and agrarian life of the Empire was dominated by non-Osmanli, yet the Sultan took his share of their profits. Moslem peasants paid taxes and met other obligations. Christians paid a poll tax and dues on virtually every product of their labor. Egypt supplied grain. The Sultan was able to maintain a court ceremonial which was colorful and impressive, and boast of a capital city of dazzling splendor with a population exceeding that of the largest European cities. The early modern palaces and mosques of the capital impressed any European who did not regret the lack of crosses. Constantinople was also the hub of a flourishing trade between Asia and Africa on the one hand and Europe on the other.

The vagaries of Ottoman government made the political life of the Porte seem barbaric, bloody and anarchic, yet behind all the tumult was a highly effective governmental system. When there was no strong Sultan or prime minister (Grand Vizier), imperial politics degenerated into an almost endless round of intrigues; spiritual officials, court favorites, the princess-mother (Valide Sultan), the Janissaries and the harem jostled each other for influence, and in the process one Sultan and Vizier after another were chosen, deposed and assassinated. Powerful Sultans and Viziers tended to rule by mass terrorism and political murder. Particularly gruesome was the "law of fratricide," whereby suspicious Sultans had their brothers murdered to ensure palace stability. In 1595, the reigning Sultan had nine brothers dispatched to "save the state." The efficient bureaucracy of well-trained civil servants (often non-Osmanli) managed to carry on the state's affairs in the midst of outward anarchy, or until a tyrant passed from his inaugural bloodbaths to political sanity.

The sheer inability of the Osmanli to assimilate subject peoples also contributed to the strength and greatness of the Empire, by keeping subjects loyal or at least docile. There is some evidence that the Christian subjects, especially on the periphery of the Empire, were treated more gently than the lower orders in neighboring Christian states. Taxes on Christians were heavy, but probably less onerous than the obligations of Austrian Hungary's peasants to their political and social superiors. Occasionally a Sultan would take his faith too seriously and give orders for the extermination of all Christian subjects, but they were not carried out. In general, the large numbers of Protestants in the Empire enjoyed greater toleration than their co-religionaries in nearby Catholic states. The distance of the Christian Balkan peoples from Constantinople and the barrier of mountains normally allowed these subjects to maintain their native customs. In the borderlands between the Ottoman Empire and Europe, the Porte also ruled through native governors; these often proved to be irritatingly independent.

During the early seventeenth century, the Turkish state became a sleeping giant, giving Europe time to resolve its own problems. The Ottoman Empire dozed through Muscovy's Time of Troubles, and did little to interfere with Austria's internal turmoil and her involvement in the Thirty Years' War. Had the Porte been aggressive at this time, the course of European history might have been very different. Instead, internal instability and external dangers turned the Turks away from Europe. A prolonged period of internal blood-letting and weak Sultans made new wars difficult. More important was the challenge from the state of Persia. Under Shah Abbas the Great, that state began a relentless war against the Turks after 1602. By 1623, the Persians had swept through to Baghdad and posed a threat to the Ottoman Empire's existence.

To meet the Persian challenge, the Ottoman Empire reduced its pressures against Europe. The lingering war with the Austrian Hapsburgs was concluded with the Treaty of Sitva-Torok in 1606. The Hapsburgs were freed from paying tribute, and Transylvania was given the ambiguous rule of a Turkish protégé under Hapsburg overlordship. Under a self-made prince, Bethlen Gabor (1613–1629), Transylvania stirred up troubles in Austria and Poland, but the Turks could neither subdue Bethlen nor capitalize on his intrigues against those Christian states. Rebelliousness by the puppet state of Moldavia caused further troubles, which the Turks were not free to quell. A border war between Poland and the Ottoman Empire over Moldavia resulted, during which the insufficient Turkish forces were defeated by Sigismund's Polish cavalry. By the Treaty of Chotin in 1621, Moldavia was converted into a buffer state, a clear loss for the Turks.

Only when Sultan Murad IV (1623–1640) attained his majority in 1632 did the Ottoman Empire's fortunes take a turn for the better. True to the law of fratricide, Murad unleashed a reign of terror which claimed the lives of two brothers, the Patriarch of the Greek Orthodox church and many foreigners at court. The terror gave way gradually to order. The army was overawed, the laws codified, and finances reformed. By 1639 the Persians were put on the defensive. Baghdad fell to the Turks, and the estimates of the deaths inflicted on the garrison range as high as 30,000. Persia was forced to sue for peace. The sleeping giant was once again free to harass and terrify Christian Europe.[6]

༒ The Austrian Hapsburgs and the Holy Roman Empire

Two outstanding problems faced the Austrian Hapsburg family during the first quarter of the seventeenth century. As territorial princes in Austria, Bohemia and Hungary, they were confronted by entrenched religious, social and institutional opposition within each of their lands. As the dynasty that continually provided the nominal rulers of the Germanic Holy Roman Empire, they were responsible for seeing that constitutional weaknesses and religious tensions did not destroy it. In the process of seeking solutions to both problems, the Hapsburgs brought on the so-called Thirty Years' War of 1618–1648, and made the German lands the focal point of the major issues in the neighboring Baltic, Rhenish and Balkan regions. This shift of the Holy Roman Empire from a regional storm center to the European cockpit began in 1596, when Ferdinand von Hapsburg assumed control of the Styrian third of the Austrian Hapsburg domains. By 1625, Ferdinand had solved the Hapsburgs' problems within his own lands, but as Holy Roman Emperor he had turned his backyard squabbles into a Germanic-European holocaust.

The underlying problem of the Austrian Hapsburgs was the imperial one. In 1555–1556 Emperor Charles V had divided his Hapsburg domains, titles and prerogatives between his "Spanish" son, Philip II, and his "Austrian" brother, Ferdinand I. Since that time, the Austrian branch of the Hapsburg dynasty had been plagued with its dual role as elected Emperors of the Holy Roman Empire and direct rulers of Austria-Bohemia-Hungary. Undoubtedly, they would have had an easier time had they relinquished the imperial mantle and concentrated on turning their family possessions into a powerful state. The neighboring Wittelsbachs of Bavaria were able to achieve a degree of ducal authority in the late sixteenth century without the imperial crown. The princes of Brandenburg were to acquire still greater authority within their north German state in the late seventeenth century, also without the imperial title. However, a Hapsburg had sat on the imperial throne without interruption for centuries. The Austrian Hapsburgs simply could not shake tradition and family pride. At the death of each Hapsburg Emperor, the family persuaded the seven electoral princes of the Empire to elect a Hapsburg as successor, even when there was no direct heir in

---

6. See Chapter 6, pp. 166–167, 170–171 for Turkish affairs at mid-century.

the family. Thus, after Ferdinand I, the imperial title passed to his son
and grandson, then to his grandson's brother, and finally in 1619 to his
grandson's nephew in the person of Ferdinand of Styria.

Having kept the imperial title in their grasp, the Austrian Hapsburgs
were faced with difficulties which would have baffled the kings of Poland.
The Holy Roman Empire was essentially a loose confederation of petty
and large principalities, far less united than Poland-Lithuania. Its Emperor
had roughly the same degree of institutional, fiscal and military authority
as the Polish monarch. The Imperial Diet was, if anything, less of a
centralizing force than the Polish one. It was composed of three chambers, whose interests often clashed: the Electoral College, composed of
the great princes, who elected the Emperor and convoked the Diet; the
remaining princes, who were jealous of the electoral princes; and the
imperial free towns, which were under the shadow of both these groups.
Moreover, many princes refused to be bound by any decisions even when
the Diet managed to reach accord, unless they had individually given
their consent. Militarily and administratively, the Empire was divided into
ten regional "circles." Since the president of each circle tended to be the
dominant prince of the area, it was he, rather than the Emperor, who
held the power. For justice, each principality had its own courts. Normally, appeals went to the Imperial High Court (*Reichskammergericht*),
in which the Emperor nominated six of the twenty-four members. However, the great princes were strong enough to ignore it in many instances.
It was impossible to disguise the fact that the Empire gave unity only
to its hundreds of petty principalities (towns, free imperial knights,
small ecclesiastical and secular territories). The great princes tended to
go their own ways. Thus, the Empire was really a confederation of the
great princes: the secular Electors of Saxony, Brandenburg and the
Palatinate; the ecclesiastical Electors of Mainz, Trier and Cologne; the
Duke of Bavaria; the King of Denmark in his capacity as Duke of Holstein and the Austrian Hapsburg Emperor in his family capacity as
Elector-King of Bohemia, Archduke of Austria and King of Hungary.

Bedevilled by political near-impotence, the Emperor was nonetheless drawn into the religious troubles which the Empire had inherited
from the sixteenth-century Reformation. The Peace of Augsburg (1555)
had ended a series of religious wars between Catholic and Lutheran
German princes, but the settlement itself created new problems. Consistent with the federal nature of the Empire, the peace had allowed each
prince to impose his brand of Christianity on his principality. The first
problem arose because, while there could be Catholic or Lutheran princes,
Calvinism was outlawed in the Empire. When Calvinism moved into the
Empire after the peace, some princes adopted it. By the early seventeenth

century, one of these, Frederick of the Palatinate, was actually compelling all subjects to conform to the illegal Calvinist faith. Quite naturally, Frederick and other Calvinist princes wanted to legalize their position by tearing up the Augsburg settlement; Catholic and Lutheran princes in turn stood for the legal *status quo* against the Calvinists. Moreover, Lutheran princes also had ignored the spirit and letter of the settlement. The Peace of Augsburg had stipulated that a Catholic ecclesiastical principality could not become Lutheranized. The ecclesiastical head, be he archbishop, bishop or abbot, might renounce the Catholic faith, but his church lands must then be bestowed on a new head who was Catholic. Ignoring this provision, Catholics had embraced Lutheranism, secularized their states, and forced Lutheran worship on their subjects. Secular Lutheran princes had simply taken over Catholic church lands and enforced Lutheranism within them. Much of the power of the great Protestant principalities (especially Brandenburg and Saxony) was based on these thefts from the Catholic church. Protestant princes naturally wanted to keep their gains; Catholic princes and Catholic Emperors who wished to support their church and at the same time weaken rival principalities in the Empire, tried to return Germany to the legal situation of 1555. If Lutheran and Catholic opposition to Calvinist princes threatened the existence of the Palatinate, Catholic hostility to secularization of Catholic lands could destroy the power of a Brandenburg or a Saxony.

These tensions made the Empire a powder keg, ready to explode at any moment. If war came it would really be two, interrelated conflicts: a religious contest between Protestantism and Catholicism, and a secular conflict between princely autonomy and imperial absolutism. Catholic Emperor would be pitted against Protestant princes, with Catholic princes vacillating between support of the Emperor on religious grounds, and sympathy for their Protestant counterparts on the secular, constitutional issue. The result of such a confused, religious-constitutional war might be revived imperialism, princely independence or sheer anarchy.

During the first two decades of the seventeenth century, these religious tensions broke down what remained of the central imperial institutions. A Protestant and a rival Catholic military party emerged outside the constitution, each headed by a militant prince. To meet his own needs, the Emperor so bent the imperial institutions that in effect he also built up an unconstitutional base of power.

By 1608, the constitution of the Empire was rendered totally unworkable. Catholics boycotted the Imperial High Court because a Protestant had become its president. The Calvinists walked out of the Imperial Diet, fearing that Catholic and Lutheran members would enforce the Augsburg prohibition of Calvinism. About the same time, the Emperor began to bypass the High Court, which he could not control, and issue judicial decrees on religious matters through an agency amenable to his will (the Aulic Council or *Reichshofrat*).

The emergence of rival Protestant and Catholic parties among the princes resulted from one such decision by the Emperor. In 1606, the Aulic Council, packed with Catholic imperialists, asked the Catholic Duke of Bavaria to "investigate" a Lutheran-Catholic altercation in the city of Donauwörth. Duke Maximilian brushed aside the wishes of the Lutheran majority in Donauwörth and annexed the city. Unable to secure redress within the Empire's institutional framework, Protestant leaders formed the defensive military group known as the Protestant Union (1608). Its leading figure was none other than the powerful Calvinist, Elector Frederick of the Palatinate. Duke Maximilian of Bavaria formed the military Catholic League (1609) to meet the challenge. Other European states gave their moral support to one military party or the other, threatening the Holy Roman Empire with foreign war as well as civil strife. In 1610, a succession dispute over the Germanic principality of Julich-Cleves almost pitted the Protestant Union, France, the Dutch Netherlands and England against the Catholic League, Holy Roman Emperor, and Spain. The death of Henry IV and a tentative division of the inheritance between a Catholic and a Calvinist prince (Treaty of Xanten, 1614) postponed the Thirty Years' War.

As is so often the case, it was not the great issues which started the war. The German powder keg existed, but the spark which ignited it came from within the family domains of the Austrian Hapsburgs. In 1564, those domains had been divided into three blocks, each under a separate member of the Hapsburg family. Jealousy within the dynasty and raids by the Ottoman Turks combined to weaken the patrimony. The local nobility, provincial diets and Protestants combined to force the Hapsburg princes into major concessions. The absolutist, Catholic ambitions of the House of Hapsburg gave way before the religious-fiscal-military "liberties" of the people. Emperor Rudolph (1576–1612) tried feebly to enforce Catholicism in his third of the patrimony, but his Austrian, Bohemian and Hungarian subjects resisted. In 1608, the Protestants in Hungary and Austria revolted against Rudolph, supported by the Emperor's own brother, Matthias. Upper and Lower Austria, Hungary and Bohemian Moravia all renounced their allegiance to Rudolph, and accepted Matthias as their ruler in return for sweeping concessions to their "liberties." The hapless Rudolph was left with only the imperial title and a truncated Bohemia. In order to keep his Bohemians from breaking away also, he conceded to them the Letter of Majesty in 1609, which confirmed their "liberties." The Hapsburg cause improved slightly on Rudolph's death in 1612. Matthias became Holy Roman Emperor

(1612–1619), and reunited the Austrian-Bohemian-Hungarian complex. However, he respected the concessions previously granted to his subjects, and the Tyrolese and Styrian lines of the Hapsburg dynasty remained separate.

The family fortunes were rescued by Ferdinand of Styria. At the turn of the century, this remarkable prince had already shown his true colors. Educated by the Jesuits at the University of Ingolstadt, he learned quickly that the Catholic cause must be foremost in his thoughts. As ruler of Styria after 1596, he was determined to combat the Moslem Turks and convert his Protestant subjects to Catholicism. It made no difference that he had to deal with both enemies simultaneously. His advisors wondered how he could secure financial help from his Protestant-dominated estates against the invading Turks, if he persisted in persecuting them. To their astonishment, Ferdinand did secure his money, drove the Turks from the heart of his domains and forced Catholicism on most of his people. His success was a striking illustration of the role personality can play in history. Ferdinand's interpretation of the events was slightly different. Convinced that he was God's agent on earth, he had believed that divine help against the Turks would come only after he returned his subjects to God's Catholic church. His victory over the Turks was obviously God's doing.

Ferdinand of Styria quickly emerged as the strongman of the Austrian Hapsburg family. His strong will and religious fervor stood in sharp contrast to the compromising tactics of his uncles, Rudolph and Matthias. It was Ferdinand who represented Rudolph at the Imperial Diet of 1608, at which the assembly tried to force Calvinism out of the Empire. And it was he who was chosen by the Hapsburgs to inherit the scattered and divided possessions of the family. Upon the death of Matthias in 1619, Ferdinand claimed the vacant throne of the Holy Roman Empire. When Protestant princes who feared his religious intolerance and Catholic princes who disliked having a strong imperial opponent of their authority, failed to agree on a non-Hapsburg candidate, Ferdinand of Styria became Emperor Ferdinand II (1619–1637). In the meantime, he began to gather in the family patrimony. In 1617, the estates of Bohemia were persuaded to make him heir-apparent to the Bohemian throne. In 1618, he was elected king of Austrian Hungary by the Hungarian estates. By 1621, he could claim lordship of all the Austrian Hapsburg domains which had been divided in 1568, and lay down a will which prohibited their dismemberment.[7] Thus Ferdinand II, Holy Roman Emperor, became also a powerful prince in his own right, as ruler of Bohemia (including

---

7. Ferdinand disregarded his own will and ceded Tyrol to his brother in 1621. However, it reverted to the main Austrian Hapsburg line in 1665.

Lusatia, Moravia and Silesia), Upper and Lower Austria, Styria (including Carinthia and Carniola) and Hapsburg Hungary (with a claim to Turkish Hungary).

It was not to be expected that Ferdinand II would countenance the existence of religious liberties and powerful provincial Diets within his vast personal domains. It was equally certain that his spectacular successes in Styria could not be repeated with as little opposition in Austria, Bohemia and Hungary. A violent clash of ruler and territories was inevitable. It came even before Matthias' death and Ferdinand's formal succession to all of his lands. The weak link in his chain of possessions was Bohemia, where he was only heir-designate. When Ferdinand began to restrict Protestant liberties, an insurrection took place. This famous Defenestration of Prague (1618) began as a badly acted comedy. Local nobles led by Count Thurn thrust two Hapsburg agents from a window of the local palace. Thanks to their cries for help to "Holy Mary" and a cushion of refuse into which they fell, the agents escaped with their dignity hurt but their lives spared. One even boasted of the number of times he had bounced in landing! But the comedy became a tragedy and the miracle a hoax. By 1619, the Defenestration had led to a civil war between Bohemian Protestant subjects and their Catholic ruler which attracted European attention and support for both sides.

The Bohemians deposed Ferdinand and elected the Calvinist Frederick of the Palatinate as their king. Recognition of the rebel regime came from Sweden, Denmark, Venice and the Dutch Netherlands. Frederick sent troops to aid the rebels, and the unpredictable Transylvanian prince, Bethlen Gabor, brought his own Protestant forces to the very gates of Vienna. Lower and Upper Austria as well as Hungary erupted in revolt, and the provinces associated with Bohemia either rebelled or tottered on the edge of insurrection. On the other side, Ferdinand created a powerful coalition which included the Spanish branch of the Hapsburg dynasty, Poland and several Lutheran and Catholic princes of the Holy Roman Empire. The Emperor's cause appeared just and his actions constitutional to many German princes. After all, the issue was an "internal" one within his personal domains. It was Elector Frederick of the Palatinate who appeared the villain, for he had broken the peace of the Empire and illegally seized Ferdinand's Bohemia. Duke Maximilian of Bavaria was also influenced by the prospect of seizing part of the Palatinate, and the Emperor had even illegally promised the transfer of the electoral vote from the Palatinate to Bavaria. The Lutheran Elector of Saxony was enticed into the Imperialist camp by the promise of Bohemian Lusatia and Ferdinand's agreement to respect the rebel Bohemians' Protestant faith. The Spanish monarchy wavered, but its representatives in central-western Europe joined the Emperor in return for the Rhenish portion of the Palatinate.

Emperor Ferdinand's greatest advantage was occasioned by French diplomatic blundering in the midst of the Bohemian crisis. Louis XIII's advisors tried to restrict the fighting as much as possible to keep Haps-burg Spain and Austria from becoming too great a threat to France. By the Treaty of Ulm (1620), French negotiators persuaded the Catholic League and Protestant Union to neutralize the western part of the Holy Roman Empire. Unfortunately for the French, neutralization in western Germany merely freed the Catholic Duke of Bavaria to move his troops into Bohemia. Victory was assured for Ferdinand. At the Battle of White Mountain in 1620, the armies of Bethlen, Frederick and the Bohemian rebels under Count Thurn were annihilated. Bohemia stood helpless be-fore Emperor Ferdinand, and the hapless Frederick lost his new Bohe-mian crown.

The road was clear for Hapsburg-Catholic absolutism within Ferdinand's patrimony. Ferdinand did not destroy local institutions, but placed them in the hands of loyal Catholics. In the Austrias and Bohemia the local Estates remained, but Catholic conversion was forced on many subjects, the universities were packed with Jesuit teachers, and obstinate Protestant noblemen lost their lands to Catholic carpetbaggers from out-side and turncoat Protestants from within. In 1627, the formally elective crown of Bohemia was made hereditary in the male Hapsburg line of Ferdinand. Hungary was too close to the Turks for Ferdinand to risk comparable measures against the Magyar nobility, who might resist with a Turkish-Hungarian alliance. Moreover, some of the Hungarian nobles eased the path to a compromise peace by voluntarily becoming Catholic. As a result, other nobles were allowed to remain Protestant, and the Magyar nobility as a whole continued to control the Hungarian Diet and their own peasants. Ferdinand had to be satisfied with the nucleus of a Hapsburg Catholic party in Hungary. Through Archbishop Pazmany and Governor Esterhazy (the latter a Hungarian Protestant, turned Catholic), the Emperor hoped to work against Hungarian "liberties" within the institutional structure of the country.

White Mountain and its aftermath should have ended the fighting in central Europe. But it was only the beginning. The Bohemian revolt of 1618–1627 became the first phase of the Thirty Years' War. The ill-fated French settlement at Ulm made a Germanic peace impossible, while it ensured Ferdinand's victory in Bohemia. Frederick, Elector Palatine, found that he had not only lost his new Bohemian crown, but left his ancestral lands defenseless as well. The treaty kept the Protestant Union neutral in western Germany, while Catholic Bavaria seized the Upper

Palatinate and Catholic Spain the lower, Rhenish Palatinate. Even the electoral title was wrested from the hapless Calvinist prince, Ferdinand illegally bestowing it on Duke Maximilian of Bavaria. The fate of the Palatinate forced several Protestant states in the Empire to continue fighting with the Catholic brigands, and others to join the Protestant cause. Moreover, in pursuing Frederick, the Catholics moved into northern Germany and threatened Denmark and Sweden. By 1625, the Bohemian civil war, now a German war, was merging with the Baltic Scandinavian problem as well. The second phase of the Thirty Years' War, known as the Danish phase, was about to begin.[8] Finally, Spain's seizure of the Rhenish Palatinate next to France threatened to merge the Baltic and Bohemian-German issues with the Franco-Spanish one in the west.[9] Already at war with the Dutch Netherlands after 1621, Spain was simultaneously threatening France with encirclement. In 1625, the fate of Europe depended on the way in which the Holy Roman Empire and its Emperor adjusted to Germany's central position in European affairs.

8. See Chapter 6.
9. See Chapter 4, pp. 104–105.

6.

The Thirty Years' War:
Central and Eastern Europe

W e have seen how the Bohemian crisis of 1618 escalated into the
Thirty Years' War which concerned all Europe by 1625.[1] It remains to be shown how that continuing conflict and its sequels affected
the two halves of the continent between 1625 and 1660. Traditionally,
historical accounts have pulled together east and west in a single discussion
of the Thirty Years' War. While there is some justification for such an
approach, it has the weakness of subordinating central and eastern European politics to those of the west. To be sure, no historian can write
about the war without saying something about the fate of the German
peoples. Nevertheless, by implying that the war was a conflict between
Hapsburg Spain and Austria on the one hand and Bourbon France on
the other, historians tend to subordinate everything else to the emergence
of France as *the* great power of mid-century Europe. And if Germany
and Hapsburg Austria are made secondary characters in this drama, the
Baltic, Slavic and Balkan areas are treated still more peremptorily. A
better balance can be achieved by treating the continuing war on the
two halves of the continent separately. In the following pages, there is

1. See Chapter 5, pp. 150–157 for the German background and the Bohemian
phase of the war, 1618–1625.

no attempt to divorce events in the west from those in the east, but there is a conscious effort to show that the western and eastern theaters of war had fairly distinct problems. Indeed, while the Thirty Years' War and its sequels continued to be a European problem, they never fully merged into one European war.

One of the strangest paradoxes of the Thirty Years' War was the fact that diplomatic and military intervention by the two halves of the continent in each other's theater of war actually prevented the merging of those arenas. France was able to concentrate on the Spanish Hapsburg threat, because it kept the Austrian Hapsburgs occupied east of the Rhine River with French diversionary forces and French-subsidized Swedish troops. The Austrian branch of the Hapsburg dynasty continually made decisions which prevented Austria from coming to the aid of the Spanish branch of the family. Spain's plan to make the Baltic into a Hapsburg lake in the late 1620's was taken over by Austria. As a result, Austria turned increasingly towards the Baltic and away from the Franco-Spanish theater. Spain's military assistance to Austria at the battle of Nördlingen in 1634 had the effect of prolonging the Austrian-Swedish conflict in the east, thereby continuing the essential separation of eastern and western problems. During the sequels to the Thirty Years' War (the Franco-Spanish conflict of 1648–1659 and the Little Northern War of 1655–1660), the western maritime states did intervene directly in the Baltic war, but only to settle it before it could expand into an all-European war.

War in central and eastern Europe between 1618 and 1660 affected both the international situation and the internal affairs of individual states. When the smoke cleared from the battlefields, the Holy Roman Empire was clearly under the shadow of emerging France. Equally significant were the birth pains of three new states east of the Rhine River. The Emperor's failure to revive his power within the Holy Roman Empire was more than balanced by his conversion of the Austrian Hapsburg patrimony into an embryonic Danubian monarchy. Swedish imperialism on the Baltic was at last contained, but at the same time Brandenburg started on its way to becoming the new state of Prussia, and Muscovy underwent external and internal shifts which began its conversion into the new state of Russia. Internally, the states of central and eastern Europe were shaken by social and political crises which, although they lacked the violence of the civil war crises of the mid-century western states, were equally important. The tensions which had threatened to tear apart German, Scandinavian and Slavic states gave way before the ascendancy of the secular state at mid-century. The ravages of war certainly had some adverse effects on the central and eastern European peoples. But the historical cliché that Germany was set back politically, economically and socially for decades or even centuries must be modified to show that war, economic dislocation and social instability also were midwives to a new political order in Germany, Scandinavia and the Slavic east. This positive result of four decades of war is, in the last analysis, far more significant than the ascendancy of the west after the Thirty Years' War.

Hapsburg Austria and Denmark at War

Denmark entered the Thirty Years' War in 1625 with high hopes. The Danish Lutherans were determined to help German Protestants turn back the advance of Emperor Ferdinand II and the Catholic League. Their king was eager to expand his toehold on northern Germany to make his Danish Baltic state a great power within the Holy Roman Empire.[2] Specifically, Christian IV laid claim to the Catholic church-states of Bremen and Osnabrück, since they would round out his over-lordship of German Holstein and his son's administrative control over the Catholic church-states of Verden and Halberstadt. In 1625, all this seemed within Christian's grasp. England, France and the Dutch Netherlands assured him of financial backing. The Protestant north German princes made the Danish king (as duke of Holstein) the president of their Lower Saxon circle; he thereby became the administrative and military leader of north German Protestantism. To attack the rampaging Catholic armies was a gamble, but Christian was an ambitious and confident man.

But the gamble was greater than he had imagined. He had to face not only the old Catholic League controlled by Maximilian of Bavaria and led by General Tilly, but also a newly constituted army pledged to Emperor Ferdinand II. Ferdinand had previously relied on Maximilian's Catholic League. However, he began to fear that Bavaria might become a threat to his own imperial authority. Hence, he allowed a soldier of fortune to recruit a mercenary army in the name of the Emperor. The soldier of fortune was the brilliant organizer of men and resources Albrecht von Wallenstein. A Bohemian Protestant who had gone over to Ferdinand before the Bohemian crisis, Wallenstein had acquired vast possessions during the massive land transfers after the Bohemians' defeat. Now he used his wealth and brains to create a huge army, which grew with its military successes. Wallenstein could not be fully trusted by the Emperor, since the imperial army was really the general's creation and creature. Time alone would tell whether Wallenstein would serve as loyal subject of the Emperor or as a quasi-feudal war lord. In the meantime,

2. For background on Denmark, see Chapter 5, pp. 132–134.

Wallenstein and Tilly combined to give Catholic Germans military strength which was greater than Christian of Denmark and the Lower Saxon circle could muster. Only if Christian's western supporters kept their financial promises could the Protestants hope to dominate the battle-field. But the French, Dutch and English, having incited Christian to wage war in the Germanies, turned their backs on him and kept their money and troops as insurance against the Spanish menace.

Thus Danish hopes gave way to disaster. In 1626, the Protestant troops were humiliated in two battles. By 1628, Wallenstein was master of northeastern Germany. His troops occupied Danish Holstein, and lived off the lands of the hapless Protestant principalities of Brandenburg and Saxony. Wallenstein was made duke of the German Baltic state of Mecklenburg by imperial decree, and laid siege to the great Baltic port of Stralsund in neighboring Pomerania. The Emperor and his general were also making use of Spain's plan to wrest the Baltic from the Scandinavian powers. An imperial fleet and a trading company for the Baltic were projected. Denmark was in danger of losing not only its German possessions but also its position in the western Baltic. And Sweden's recent gains in the eastern Baltic[3] were equally menaced. Germany's problem was now a Baltic crisis. Gustav Adolph relieved the tensions somewhat by sending Swedish forces to break the siege of Stralsund. The king of Denmark was not so fortunate. He was lucky to negotiate the Treaty of Lübeck (1629) with the Emperor. His German lands and ambitions disappeared, but he was left with his Danish possessions and somewhat reduced Baltic aspirations. As Christian crept into his Danish shell, Sweden's Gustav Adolph prepared to challenge the Hapsburg position on the German Baltic coast.

The Emperor did not know it, but 1629 was to be the high-water mark of imperial Catholic fortunes. In order to meet the attack from Sweden that Wallenstein's Baltic victories had invited, Ferdinand needed to secure peace within the Holy Roman Empire as well as with Denmark. The situation was complicated, and no easy solution to the German problem was apparent. Yet twice before, Ferdinand had acted forcefully in similar circumstances, and prevailed. Unfortunately, the German problem was not the Bohemian one, or the Styrian one.[4] This time, sheer determination and trust in God were not enough. In fact, they were the instruments of Ferdinand's failure in 1629. His insistence on a Catholic imperial solution to the Holy Roman Empire's problems robbed him of what political wisdom he possessed. He terrified Protestant princes in the Empire by issuing the Edict of Restitution (1629). That decree

3. See Chapter 5, pp. 136–138.
4. See Chapter 5, pp. 154–156.

stated that all Catholic ecclesiastical states seized by Protestants since 1555 were to be relinquished, and outlawed Calvinism within the Empire. Protestant princes were thereby threatened with substantial losses in territory, and Calvinist principalities with the extinction of their church. Moreover, the Edict of Restitution was an act of the Emperor alone. Neither the great German princes nor the Imperial Diet were a party to the decision, and enforcement was in the hands of an imperial commission, under the Emperor's command. By acting against the Protestants, Ferdinand drove Protestant German princes away from a peace settlement. By acting on imperial authority, he alienated Catholic German princes, who liked his religion but were adamant against any peace settlement which would leave the Emperor with the greatest territorial and legal power in the realm. Ferdinand was taken aback by the almost universal hostility to his action. To add to his problems, the Pope questioned his plan to administer the land transfer. Ferdinand wanted the lands for his family and friends; the Pope wanted to turn them over to pro-papal bishops and religious orders.

Ferdinand discovered that he could not carry out his Edict of Restitution. The Catholic League's army, under Tilly, refused to permit recatholicization of the lands in question, obviously on orders from the Catholic Duke of Bavaria. Even Wallenstein, who had made the Edict of Restitution thinkable by his military victories, made its execution impossible by dragging his feet when the Emperor asked him to take charge. The general had his own vision of imperialist power. Wallenstein hoped to secure peace within the Empire by forcing Protestants and Catholics to tolerate each other. Once religious peace was achieved, the Empire could become a great, united state under a powerful Emperor (and his equally powerful general!). Thus, when Wallenstein took over former church lands in Ferdinand's name, he refused to let in Catholic missionaries who would only increase religious tensions and make peace impossible.

The storm over the Edict of Restitution reached its peak in 1630 at the belatedly convoked Imperial Diet. Ferdinand still had a chance, but he threw it away. Although the leading Protestant states of Brandenburg and Saxony refused to send representatives to the Diet, a compromise could have been struck which would have left Ferdinand's power greater than it had been in 1618. Veronica Wedgwood quite rightly points out that Ferdinand could have bargained by revoking the hated Edict of Restitution and dismissing the almost as universally hated Wallenstein.[5] Ferdinand did agree to his general's ouster (although more out of fear

5. C. V. Wedgwood, *The Thirty Years War* (1957), 233–235.

of Wallenstein's growing power than in the interest of a German peace). But he refused to rescind the Edict of Restitution. To the end, his religious convictions remained paramount, and they were his political undoing. The Catholic Duke of Bavaria led the opposition at the Diet of 1630 to veto the election of Ferdinand's son as heir-designate, and left the princes suspicious of or hostile towards the Emperor. Fatefully, too, the Diet refused to give military aid to Spain, which was fighting the French in northern Italy and the Dutch in the Netherlands. Eastern and western conflicts remained separate. Spain had to battle alone against the French and Dutch. Hapsburg Austria continued to grapple with the thoroughly confused German problem, which was at this moment drawing the attention and the invading troops of Lutheran Sweden. Ferdinand II still had the title of Emperor, and an army, but he had to face the Swedes without the support of most of the German princes.

᪣ Hapsburg Austria Versus Sweden and France

When Gustav Adolph swooped down on the German Baltic shores in 1630, he began the so-called Swedish phase of the Thirty Years' War (1630–1635). Sweden's entry marked far more than the mere replacement of one Scandinavian state on German soil by another. Sweden's king had stronger religious and territorial interests than his Danish counterpart. While his troops sang Lutheran hymns, Gustav Adolph sought to overturn the religious balance in Germany by imposing Protestantism on Catholics wherever his army was victorious. Christian IV had been determined to create a north German-Danish state; Gustav Adolph eyed the same territories, and the entire Baltic Sea. In dragging the eastern Baltic into the German question, the Lion of the North indirectly tied Muscovy and Poland to his fortunes.

Gustav Adolph's imperialistic mission can best be described by his own words: "Pomerania and the Baltic coast are the outworks of Sweden —they are our guarantee against the Emperor." Wallenstein's threat to Pomeranian Stralsund had been ended temporarily by a Swedish expeditionary force in 1628. The imperialist threat to the Baltic as a whole remained. But how could Sweden engage in a land war in Germany, while its long war with Poland continued? Moreover, the Hapsburg Emperor was involved in that war, constantly encouraging the Poles. The simplest solution was to make peace with Poland. In negotiating the settlement, Gustav Adolph drew into his orbit Muscovy on the east, and the maritime states of England, France and the Dutch Netherlands to the west.

As in the past, Gustav Adolph's policies were aided by favorable circumstances. The interests of the western maritime states in the Baltic coincided with Sweden's. They wanted to restore normal commercial activity in the Baltic. They also wanted to free Swedish troops to fight against the Austrian Hapsburgs, and thus keep Austria from joining the Spanish side of the western European conflict. Through the good offices of the anti-Spanish western states, Sweden was able to secure a truce with Poland in 1629.[6] Because Gustav Adolph was still fearful that Poland would break the truce, he turned to Muscovy. Sweden provided the Tsar with military aides and the secret of the Swedish cannon, in the hope that Muscovy would fight a diversionary war against Poland. However, the Muscovite campaign against Poland (the Smolensk War of 1632–1634) came too late and ended too abruptly to provide the kind of guarantee that the Swedish king wanted. Gustav Adolph decided to risk his army in the German-Baltic war in any case, but he always had half his thoughts on the Swedish-Polish border.

Sweden was more fortunate in securing financial assistance for its German campaigns. The great army which Gustav Adolph led on the German battlefields was subsidized, first by Muscovy and then by France and the Dutch Netherlands. Tsar Michael was more than willing to oppose the Polish state if someone else did the fighting. By subsidizing the Swedish campaigns against Poland's ally, Austria, Muscovy struck indirectly at its enemy. Between 1628 and 1633, Muscovy exported grain in great quantity, and without the normal crown tariff, to Sweden. Sweden reexported this grain to the west at a handsome profit. The total sudsidy was equal to one-fourth of the total Muscovite budget, and one-half of the subsidy came in the crucial year of 1630, when the Austro-Swedish fighting began. Beginning in 1631, the French and Dutch states added their own monetary subsidies. Thus Gustav Adolph's Sweden had the financial support which had been withheld from Christian IV's Denmark. This difference, combined with the ouster of Wallenstein after the Danish phase of the Thirty Years' War, helps to explain why Sweden succeeded where Denmark had failed.

By 1632, Sweden was the dominant power in the Holy Roman Empire. The would-be neutralist princes of Brandenburg and Saxony joined the Swedish side to avoid another imperialist Catholic tidal wave. Gustav Adolph proved a brilliant general, defeating the imperialists under Tilly at Breitenfeld in 1631. Although vulnerable to a possible Polish attack, the Swedes managed to terrify Catholic Germany in the following year. The German allies of Gustav Adolph stormed into the heart of

6. See also Chapter 5, p. 138.

the Austrian Hapsburg lands, while the Swedish king-general marched into the rich ecclesiastical states of the Rhineland known as the Priests' Alley. Even France's chief minister, Richelieu, began to regret French subsidization of the Lion of the North. The Swedish monarch had promised to avoid the Rhineland and to respect Catholic worship in return for the subsidy. Now he seemed bent on carving out a Protestant Swedish protectorate in western Germany. It was embarrassing for Catholic France to have an ally who persecuted German Catholics at the same time that the French were quarrelling with the Catholic Spaniards. It was positively dangerous for this ally to control the Rhineland, which connected Spanish Italy with the Spanish Netherlands. France wanted the Rhenish area for itself, to break Spain's chain of possessions. But Richelieu could only wait to see where Gustav Adolph's secular ambitions and religious principles would lead him.

The unexpected happened, but it did not fit into Richelieu's plans. Gustav Adolph did not live to make the next move. At the battle of Lützen in 1632, the Swedes forced the Catholic imperialists to withdraw, but the Swedish king was killed during the fighting. There was relief in some quarters at the news of his death. Swedish imperialism had become such a threat to Gustav Adolph's unwilling German partners and his French ally, that some persons wondered whether the bullet came from the front or the rear! After Lützen, the Swedes fought on without their great leader, under the direction of Chancellor Oxenstierna. But the imperialists held the upper hand, militarily, even surviving a bizarre series of changes in the leadership of their forces. Their general, Tilly, had died of wounds before Lützen, but Wallenstein had been recalled in time to fight the battle and withdraw without a rout. When Wallenstein became too independent after the battle, and sent peace feelers to his Swedish-German opponents, fortune again smiled on the Emperor. Wallenstein was stripped of his command by Ferdinand, and murdered by his own subordinates. He was replaced by more trustworthy and, luckily, relatively competent generals. To add to Ferdinand's blessings, the imperialist forces fought the key battle of Nördlingen in 1634 against a temporarily weakened Swedish army with the aid of Spanish forces. Nördlingen was near the Rhine, and Spanish troops that were moving down the river to the Dutch theater of war took time out to augment the Catholic German forces. By a coincidence, the War of Smolensk between Poland and Muscovy had just ended, and some Swedish troops had been removed from the Rhenish area to safeguard Sweden's Polish borders. It was not surprising that Nördlingen was one of the greatest military victories of the war for Hapsburg Austria. After the battle, the German princes allied with Sweden came to terms with the Emperor, one by one. Ferdinand was willing to compromise in 1635, where he had been intransigent in 1630. The Peace of Prague (1635) between the Emperor and his princely German foes was a settlement which all could live with. It modified the Edict of Restitution, so that some of the secularized church lands remained with Protestant princes, while other church-states were reserved for the Catholics.

The Peace of Prague was to be the model for the later Peace of Westphalia which ended the German-Baltic conflict in 1648. Tragically, what the Germans had settled for themselves, could not be so easily ended. The war in Germany was too intimately connected with the Rhineland and Baltic issues. France and Sweden would not leave the Holy Roman Empire alone. After Lützen, Richelieu had seen the Rhenish Priests' Alley slip out of Swedish control only to fall into Spanish and Austrian hands. The battle of Nördlingen was fought too close to the Rhine for comfort, and the fact that Spanish troops had played a major role in the Hapsburg victory underlined the Spanish threat to France. A much bolder French foreign policy was required in 1635, if France were to keep Spanish and Austrian Hapsburgs from joining forces. Richelieu negotiated a new settlement between Sweden and Poland, which extended the precarious truce of 1629 into a twenty-five-year nonaggression pact. While Sweden gave up its lucrative tolls on the Polish Baltic, it was able to forget Poland and throw its full military might into the German campaigns. In addition, France officially declared war on the king of Spain and the Holy Roman Emperor (although not against the Holy Roman Empire). On the surface, France and Sweden were equal partners against the Hapsburgs. In actuality, Sweden played the greater role against the Austrian Hapsburgs, while France took the former Swedish Rhineland under its "protection" and fought to break Spain's chain of possessions between northern Italy and the Spanish Netherlands.

The last phase of the Thirty Years' War is called the Franco-Swedish phase (1635–1648). Although Poland and Muscovy did not intervene, the official declaration of France more than compensated for their neutralism. Moreover, two other problems complicated the last years of the war. The first concerned the Balkans. France and Sweden befriended the new prince of Transylvania, George I Rakockzy, and tried to involve both that underling of the Ottoman Empire and the Turkish state itself in a diversionary campaign against Hapsburg Austria. Fortunately for Austria, the Turks were not interested. Fresh from their victorious war against Persia,[7] they began a long war against Venice

7. See Chapter 5, pp. 149–150.

(1645–1669) and turned their backs on the Austrian lands. But the Hapsburgs had still to deal with the pesky Transylvanian prince, who helped the Swedes and French by invading Hungary in 1644. The second problem was a renewal of the old Swedish-Danish rivalry in the Baltic. In 1643, Denmark allied with its former Austrian foe against Sweden. The Danish intervention proved to be another mistake. Sweden won the short war, and by the Treaty of Brömsebro (1645) strengthened its position in the Baltic as well as in northern Germany. The Danish Baltic islands of Gotland and Ösel became Swedish possessions, and Sweden staked out its claim on the northern German church-states which Denmark had formerly aspired to control. Thanks to the Transylvanian diversion and the Swedish-Danish war, Sweden was in an excellent position to bargain at the German peace conferences which now began.

Swedish and French military campaigns in the Holy Roman Empire, plus unexpected developments in the western theater of war, brought those negotiations to a head. Sweden made raids deep inside the Empire, and in 1645 even reached the gates of Vienna. A combined Franco-Swedish thrust in 1648 forced Catholic Bavaria to desert the Emperor. That same year, the Dutch Netherlands and Spain negotiated a settlement of their long war of 1621–1648. Deprived of its major ally against Spain, and determined to continue the war against the Spanish Hapsburgs, France was compelled to withdraw from the German conflict. Franco-Swedish marches against Austrian Vienna and Prague forced Ferdinand II's son (Emperor Ferdinand III, 1637–1657) to settle his disputes with France, Sweden and the German princes. The result was the Peace of Westphalia which ended the Thirty Years' War in the German-Baltic arena.

The Central-Eastern European Settlements: Westphalia, Vasvar and Oliva

The Peace of Westphalia in 1648 was the most important of three settlements which brought peace to central and eastern Europe between 1648 and 1664.[8] Westphalia stamped Germany in a decentralized mold which was to remain formally until the dissolution of the Holy Roman Empire in 1806, and actually until the division of Germany into a German Empire and an Austro-Hungarian Empire in 1867–1871. The hope of a united German empire under Austrian Hapsburg control, which had been a distinct possibility in 1629, vanished in 1648. Within the Holy Roman Empire, power remained in the hands of the great princes, and

8. See Chapter 7, p. 195 for the Westphalian articles affecting Western Europe.

the Emperor had to concentrate on his position as prince of the Austrian-Bohemian-Hungarian complex on the Danube River rather than as imperial ruler. The shift in Austrian interests became more apparent when the Emperor went to war with the Turks in the 1660's, and then concluded the Austro-Turkish Truce of Vasvar (1664). Meanwhile, the Westphalian settlement of the Baltic problem was tested by the Little Northern War of 1655–1660, and modified by the subsequent Peace of Oliva (1660–1661).

The religious and territorial clauses of Westphalia recognized the fact that the Holy Roman Empire of the German Nation was really a confederation of German princes. The principle of 1555 that the individual prince could enforce conformity to his faith was recapitulated and expanded. Calvinist rulers could exist legally alongside Catholic and Lutheran ones. Hence, Calvinist Brandenburg was added formally to Catholic Bavaria, Catholic Austria and Lutheran Saxony, as a great princely state within the Empire. The son of the ill-fated Elector Frederick was given back a truncated Palatinate (the Lower or Rhenish portion of the Calvinist state of 1618). Saxony kept Hapsburg Lusatia, which had been its reward for joining the Emperor against the Bohemians in 1620. Bavaria gave back to the Emperor his Lower Austrian land, which had been under Bavarian occupation since the Bohemian crisis, but retained the Upper Palatinate. In addition, a compromise over the Edict of Restitution strengthened the territorial position of both Brandenburg and Saxony. The former Catholic church-states of the Empire were distributed as they had been held in 1624. The date was crucial, since Catholic reconquests of those disputed territories had taken place mainly after that time. Saxony retained sizeable holdings. Brandenburg held on to its pre-1624 church lands, and also won the succession to scattered northern German bishoprics (Minden, Kammin, Halberstadt and Magdeburg).

Of the non-Austrian principalities within the Empire, Brandenburg emerged in the best position. The Palatinate was too small and too shaken by military defeats to pose again as the leader of German Protestantism. Saxony was the leading Lutheran principality, but war had made the Estates so strong that the prince was forced to share power with them. Moreover, the attempt late in the century to forge a dynastic union of Saxony and Poland undermined the German position of the Saxon principality. Under Duke Maximilian, Bavaria had made its move to rival Austria as the leading Catholic state of the Empire, but in 1648 Bavaria was under the influence of France and the shadow of the Hapsburg Emperor-prince. By contrast with these states, Brandenburg looked strong. The Great Elector (Frederick William, 1640–1688) had transformed Brandenburg from a helpless victim of surrounding states to a respected German power through deft diplomatic manoeuvering in the last years of the Thirty Years' War. The Great Elector did not receive all that he wanted in 1648, for Sweden acquired many of the north German lands which he coveted. Still, Brandenburg's possessions stretched across northern Germany from the Rhine River in the west to the Niemen River in the east. In addition to the nucleus of the state in Brandenburg proper, there were the Rhenish acquisitions of 1614 (Cleves, Mark and Ravensberg), East Prussia (under the nominal overlordship of Poland), Eastern Pomerania, and the scattered secularized lands. Brandenburg's territories did not ensure future greatness, but they were the foundation on which the Prussian state of the eighteenth century was to be built.

The battered and abused central institutions of the Holy Roman Empire all survived the settlement at Westphalia, but they could no longer be forged into weapons of Austrian Hapsburg imperialism. Legally, the Emperor still retained some authority through the constitutional structure of the Empire. Actually, he could enforce his will only on the many petty German principalities. While the great princes were not supposed to make foreign alliances or enforce state laws outside of the constitutional framework, they had little difficulty bypassing the constitution and acting on their own. The Emperor was compelled to recognize the *de facto* atomization of his power. In so doing, he admitted to himself and to the Holy Roman Empire that his family's destiny lay with the Hapsburg patrimony in Austria, Bohemia and Hungary. Ferdinand III and his successors would still make attempts to revive their power as Emperors, but after 1648 there was an unmistakable shift in interest from imperial to patrimonial concerns. In the future, the Emperors found themselves engrossed in three problems: to disentangle the institutions of their family lands from those of the Empire; to weld the multinational patrimony into a Danubian state with the aid of those patrimonial institutions; and to protect that state against the Ottoman Empire and France.

Ferdinand II and III had already worked towards these ends before Westphalia. In 1620, the Austrian chancellery was separated from its imperial counterpart. Originally an institution in charge of Austrian records and correspondence, it began to frame policy for the entire Hapsburg complex from its seat in Vienna. When the Bohemians were defeated in the 1620's, their chancellery was moved from Prague to Vienna as a second branch of the Austrian office. Under Ferdinand III, the Imperial Privy Council also became insignificant. The main advisory board for the Hapsburg domains became first the Emperor's personal Privy Council, and then the smaller Privy Conference. Both were staffed by men from various parts of the Hapsburg patrimony. The division between Empire and patrimony became all the more marked when the Ferdinands increased the number of electors in the Holy Roman Empire from seven to eight (the Bavarian duke becoming the seventh elector, and the restored Palatinate prince the eighth). Less clear were the implications of the territorial settlement with France. At Westphalia, France received complicated rights to some Hapsburg and imperial lands to the west of the Rhine River. Although these rights might reduce Hapsburg involvement in the contentious Rhenish problems of the Holy Roman Empire, they could also involve Austria in new disputes between the Empire and France over their interpretations.

Within the Austrian-Bohemian-Hungarian complex, the Hapsburgs began to establish the base of power which they had been unable to achieve as Emperors. To be sure, the Ferdinands bartered away Bohemian Lusatia to Saxony and guaranteed religious toleration in Bohemian Silesia. But these concessions were more than balanced by the war settlements in Bohemia and Austria. The rebellions of the 1620's had forged Bohemia-Austria into a relatively cohesive core for the future Danubian monarchy. Local diets remained in most Austrian and Bohemian lands, and some noblemen clung to the Protestant faith of their fathers. But, essentially, Catholic religious unity was achieved, and the initiative in military and fiscal matters came from the Hapsburg institutions in Vienna. Hungary, however, remained virtually separate.

After Westphalia, the Austrian Hapsburgs turned their attention to the Hungarian peoples and the Ottoman Empire. A new Transylvanian prince, George II Rakockzy (1648-1658) followed the imperialistic pattern set by Bethlen Gabor and George I Rakockzy. Austrian Bohemia and Hungary, and the Turko-Polish borderlands of Moldavia and Wallachia were threatened by Transylvanian imperialism. The Ottoman Empire was also beginning to meddle in Balkan affairs. A palace revolt placed a new dynasty of able Grand Viziers in charge of the Sultan's state. The first was Mohammed Kiuprili, a vigorous septuagenarian who had spent most of his life as provincial governor, administrator of the palace and the treasury and then assistant to the Vizier. In 1656 he became Grand Vizier on his own terms, and placed the Ottoman Empire under tight personal control. It has been estimated that as many as 60,000 were purged from court and government by death or dismissal. The head of the Janissary troops and the Greek Orthodox Patriarch were killed, the Moslems' religious leader and the head of the Sultan's harem deposed. Provincial uprisings in Asia Minor were ruthlessly suppressed, and thirty-one heads were put on public display in Constantinople as a grisly warning to future malcontents. After this initial reign of terror, Mohammed turned to foreign affairs. The prolonged war against Venice (1645-1669) was pursued with new vigor, and the Dardanelles fortified to stop Venetian attacks on the capital. Mohammed's son, Grand Vizier Ahmed Kiuprili (1661–1676) was able to turn his attention to the troublesome Transylvanian prince who was as much of a threat to the Turks as to the Austrian Hapsburgs. By 1663, Ottoman soldiers had him at their mercy. Transylvania, which had been nominally under Austrian Hapsburgs since 1606, reverted to its sixteenth-century status as a vassal state of the Porte. Immediately, the Turkish forces invaded the Hungarian and Bohemian possessions of the Hapsburgs, and threatened Vienna.

A new Emperor, Leopold I (1658–1705), had to face this Turkish challenge. Fortunately, the poorly trained and inexperienced Hapsburg ruler had a brilliant general, Montecuccoli. He held the Turks at Saint Gotthard in 1664, with the assistance of troops from France and other Christian states. Leopold wisely decided to use this military victory to force a truce on the Turks, rather than to risk his emerging Danubian state's future in a premature all-out war. The Truce of Vasvar (1664) guaranteed peace between the Austrians and Turks for twenty years. Leopold had to recognize Ottoman overlordship in Transylvania, but he could now concentrate on his Danubian subjects without fear of Turkish intervention.[9]

Westphalia brought only an uneasy peace to the Baltic. Sweden emerged after 1648 as the dominant power in the north, but its gains antagonized neighboring states. By obtaining the German lands of Bremen, Verden and Western Pomerania on the Baltic and North Seas, Sweden achieved a virtual stranglehold over trade on the Weser, Elbe and Oder rivers. The rulers of Brandenburg, Poland and Muscovy were understandably eager to challenge Swedish hegemony. Brandenburg's Great Elector felt that he should have received all of Pomerania, rather than just its impoverished eastern section. Frederick William particularly eyed the Swedish Pomeranian port of Stettin, which would give him a window on the Baltic. The new king of Poland, John Casimir (1648–1668), had old scores to settle with Sweden which went back to Gustav Adolph's conquest of the Polish Baltic coastline. In 1635, Poland had freed its ports in Courland from Swedish tolls, but Sweden still occupied Livonia. Moreover, the Polish king resumed an old claim to the Swedish throne. Under Tsar Alexis (1645–1676), Muscovy also renewed its interest in the Baltic, willing to fight either Poland or Sweden. Even Denmark, smarting from the humiliating treaty of 1645 with Sweden, sought revenge under a new king, Frederick III (1648–1670). Since Frederick William, John Casimir, Alexis and Frederick had all ascended their thrones in the

9. On developments within the Austrian state after Vasvar, see Chapter 11.

1640's, they were all eager to test their new authority at the expense of Sweden.

Their eagerness was scarcely greater than that of their Swedish opponent, Charles X (1654–1660). Charles was king of a land seething with discontent stemming from the Thirty Years' War. The nobility who had been so loyal to Gustav Adolph had virtually dominated the Swedish government under Queen Christina (1632–1654). Charles ran into stiff opposition when he tried to curb their power, and turned to foreign adventure as a means to keep them occupied and docile. In addition, he was interested in continuing Gustav Adolph's imperialism in the eastern Baltic. Above all, he came to the conclusion that the old Danish-Swedish rivalry should be ended once for all; his "solution" was an attempt to incorporate Denmark in the Swedish state!

The Little Northern War of 1655–1660 was precipitated by a renewal of old Polish-Muscovite feuds. Muscovy took advantage of a Polish Cossack uprising in 1654, and soon its troops swept into the heart of Polish Lithuania. Charles X of Sweden had to act quickly, or lose the Polish-Lithuanian Baltic coast to the Tsar. In 1655 he occupied northern Poland. The Great Elector of Brandenburg was forced into a military alliance with Sweden, and compelled to recognize the Swedish king as overlord of East Prussia. In 1656, the armies of Sweden and Brandenburg crushed the Polish forces at the battle of Warsaw. These events changed the complexion of the Baltic problem. Charles X looked like another Gustav Adolph. Sweden's neighbors forgot their own rivalries and united against the threat. Denmark quickly entered the war against Sweden, eager to share in the expected plunder. Muscovy and Brandenburg changed sides and allied with Poland against Sweden. Even Hapsburg Austria, fearful that Sweden was on the point of becoming its neighbor, worked behind the scenes to strengthen the anti-Swedish coalition. The war also attracted the attention of the western maritime states. The Dutch sent a fleet to protect Denmark and the Baltic from Swedish imperialism. England prepared to side with Sweden. France wanted a balance of power in the Baltic, and was fearful that a sudden Swedish collapse would result in Hapsburg domination of northern Germany as had been threatened in the days of Wallenstein. The Little Northern War was in danger of becoming more widespread than the Thirty Years' War itself, and the Westphalian settlement was clearly in jeopardy.

Quick action by Sweden and diplomatic intervention by the western states prevented major conquests and a new European holocaust. While Charles X's one sure ally, Transylvania, harassed the Poles and Austrians from the rear, the Swedish monarch struck against Denmark. A Swedish engineer discovered that the ice between Denmark's mainland and its islands could hold soldiers and cannon. Charles exclaimed melodramatically, "Now brother Frederick, we will speak in plain Swedish!" Swedish troops on the continent crossed the ice and approached the defenseless Danish capital of Copenhagen. Frederick III sued for peace, but the truce was short lived. New Swedish campaigns were launched against Denmark and Brandenburg. At this moment, France, England and the Dutch Netherlands forced a compromise peace on the Baltic states while the question was still negotiable.

The peace treaties of Oliva (Copenhagen, Oliva and Kardis, 1660–1661) constituted an important alteration of the Westphalian settlement. Sweden gained territory, but she was denied her ultimate goal—possession of the entire Baltic coastline. Sweden's neighbors at last set limits to Swedish imperialism. Denmark ceded its south Swedish provinces, but escaped incorporation in the Swedish state. Henceforth, Sweden and Denmark would face each other across the Baltic Sound. Finland and Livonia were retained as part of the Swedish empire, but Polish Prussia and Courland escaped the clutches of Charles X. Above all, East Prussia became an integral possession of Brandenburg. Formerly held by the Great Elector as a fief under Polish overlordship, temporarily placed under Swedish overlordship during the Little Northern War, it now returned to Brandenburg free of all ties to either Poland or Sweden. Having seen the Polish Baltic tolls slip from its grasp in 1635, and East Prussia escape its overlordship, Sweden was forced to realize that the Baltic was not a Swedish lake. All it could do in future was cling to its existing possessions on the Baltic and North seas, and hope that its neighbors would not try to roll back these frontiers.

Oliva not only set limits to Swedish expansion, but marked the beginning of the Polish state's decline as a great power. In 1660, Poland still appeared to be the most dangerous foe of Sweden. In reality, Brandenburg and Muscovy were the powers which were to challenge Sweden in the future. Poland had led the coalition against Sweden during the Little Northern War, had borne the brunt of the Swedish attacks, and had emerged with its lands intact. That it did so was as much due to shifts in the foreign policies of Tsar Alexis and Great Elector Frederick William as to Polish heroism. Muscovy had at last begun to see Sweden, not Poland, as its greatest northern enemy. In the future, Muscovy would be the surest guarantee of the continuing existence of Poland through its hostility to Sweden. To be sure, Muscovy embarked on a new war against Poland after Oliva, and at the Treaty of Andrussova (1667) acquired huge territories on the Dnieper River, including Kiev. But thereafter Muscovy protected Poland and set its sights on Sweden's Baltic possessions and the Black Sea outposts of the Ottoman Empire. During

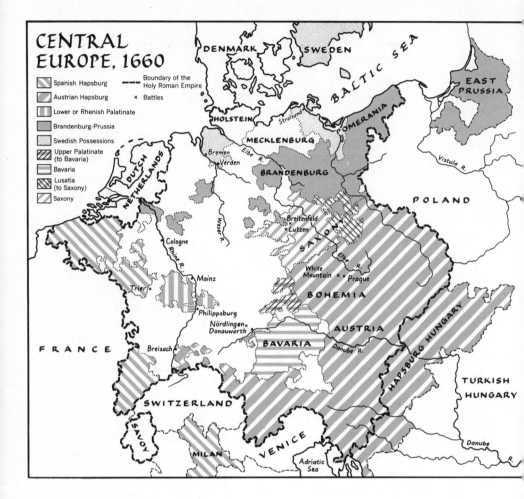

CENTRAL
EUROPE, 1660

Spanish Hapsburg
Austrian Hapsburg
Lower or Rhenish Palatinate
Brandenburg-Prussia
Swedish Possessions
Upper Palatinate (to Bavaria)
Bavaria
Lusatia (to Saxony)
Saxony

Boundary of the Holy Roman Empire
× Battles

DENMARK SWEDEN BALTIC SEA EAST PRUSSIA

HOLSTEIN Stralsund POMERANIA

MECKLENBURG

Bremen Elbe R. Vistula R.
Verden BRANDENBURG

POLAND

DUTCH NETHERLANDS

Weser R. Breitenfeld × × Lutzen SAXONY

Cologne Elbe R.

Rhine R. White × Prague
Mainz Mountain BOHEMIA

Trier

Philippsburg HAPSBURG HUNGARY
Nördlingen × AUSTRIA
Donauworth ×

FRANCE Breisach BAVARIA Danube R.

TURKISH HUNGARY

SWITZERLAND

SAVOY Danube R.

MILAN VENICE

Adriatic Sea

the Little Northern War, also, <u>Brandenburg</u> showed that it had the <u>military capacity</u> to keep Sweden in check, and the wisdom to keep <u>Poland intact as a buffer against Swedish</u> imperialism. After Oliva, the emerging states of Brandenburg-Prussia and Muscovy-Russia were all that kept Poland in being. When they turned against Poland in the late eighteenth century, the state was doomed to dismemberment and extinction.

Central and Eastern European States at Mid-Century

The peace treaties which settled scores among the states of central and eastern Europe were complemented by settlements within each state. The internal tensions in the first quarter of the seventeenth century had frequently centered on religion. During the course of civil and foreign wars, the <u>religious issues</u> had been somewhat <u>resolved</u>—in the Holy Roman Empire by an extension of the right of the prince to determine the religion of his subjects; in Sweden by the victory of the Lutheran Charles IX and his estates against the Catholic Sigismund of Poland; in Austria and Bohemia by the military victory of the Catholic League and Emperor; in Poland by the agreement by Polish-Lithuanian nobles to accept the king's Catholic religion and by the king to accept the nobles' "liberties"; in some German states, by the *de facto* recognition of religious minorities. During the course of the Thirty Years' War, as religious interests became overshadowed by secular concerns, princes and subjects inevitably found themselves fighting religious battles with secular weapons.[10] Tensions remained within individual states, and rulers still vied with their estates for control, but the tensions increasingly took on a social-political rather than a religious-political form. The mid-century crises in the German, Scandinavian and Slavic states were in part a continuation of the earlier tensions, but their main ingredients were the economic and social repercussions of international and civil war.

Historians still argue over the economic effects of the Thirty Years' War, but there can be no doubt that war intensified the underlying social tensions of early modern central Europe. War temporarily reduced the peasant population, and gave hard-pressed landlords all the more reason to exploit their remaining workers to combat economic depression. War helped some urban centers by providing war industries and war refugees eager to work; but it also dislocated the urban economy elsewhere, and made townsmen envious of the noblemen who survived as captains of fortune, and who fostered competing rural industries. One can sympathize with the plight of these commoners, without condemning the nobility out of hand. Noblemen were fortunate in escaping most of the state taxes which fell on commoners, but they were hard pressed to live in the fashion to which they had been accustomed, unless they exploited their social inferiors.

Where could nobleman or commoner turn when faced by "popular" insurrection or landlord oppression? The state was the obvious vehicle for resolving economic ills and social tensions. The precise nature of political alignments was not so obvious. Peasants, townsmen and (in some cases) the clergy were almost as hostile to the war policies of their princes as they were towards the nobility. After all, the state's armies not only killed and looted, but also demanded supplies (a disguised form of taxation). While the fiscal demands of the "warfare state" were often less of a grievance than those of the nobles, they were equally often the proverbial straw that broke the camel's back. Moreover, the warfare state frequently sided with the nobility in return for their military services, legalizing

10. See Chapter 2, pp. 57–58.

landlord oppression and awarding them crown lands and high civil offices. Wherever possible, notably in Sweden and Denmark, commoners tended to side with royalty as the lesser of two evils, hoping to turn crown against nobles in return for their support of the state. However, there were instances where peasants, faced by the fusion of political and social authorities, rebelled against both state and nobility. This occurred in the Swiss cantons, in Muscovy and occasionally in Austria and Bohemia. There were also times when peasants combined with nobles against the prince's taxing of peasants and requisitioning of men, supplies and money from nobles. While townsmen rarely allied directly with country nobility against the crown, both groups were known to rebel simultaneously (in East Prussia, for example).

The political attitudes of nobles were also ambivalent. For the most part they hoped that they could continue their privileged existence under princely protection. However, they could never be sure. In addition to war requisitions, they were sometimes threatened with loss of tax exemptions and former crown lands, as the desperate state sought to meet its war needs. During the Little Northern War, the prince of Brandenburg tried to tax his nobles, and Charles X of Sweden sought to restore crown lands. Even when the prince honored the fiscal privileges of his nobles, his troops had no qualms about imposing taxes on them as they marched through the countryside. Furthermore, there was always the danger that crown and commoners would combine against the nobility, forcing them to protect their "liberties" with their swords.

Denmark presents the best example of a popular-royal alliance which played into the hands of the monarchy. The disastrous Little Northern War which followed the ill-fated Danish phase of the Thirty Years' War turned the lower Danish estates against the nobility. Christian IV and Frederick III had not been blameless in the defeats. But it was sensed that the nobility were the real power in the state, and that they, not the ruler, should be chastised. The fact that Frederick III had been forced into confirming the nobles' political and economic powers in order to win election in 1648 reinforced popular royalism by 1660.

At the end of the Little Northern War, Denmark had to solve the dual problem of war debts and the loss of the Sound dues.[11] It was no longer a great power, and drastic measures were mandatory. When the estates met in 1660, the urban and clerical representatives demanded that the tax system be overhauled and the nobles forced to share financial burdens. The nobles were outmanoeuvered, and Grand Treasurer Sehested

11. On Denmark's internal conditions before the war, see Chapter 5, pp. 132–134.

instituted sweeping changes. In the 1660's a land census was undertaken, and a general land tax imposed on town and countryside, including the noble holdings. Tax reform was accompanied by administrative changes. The creation of several ministries (colleges) within the central government reduced the power of the noble-dominated royal council. The semi-feudal *len* was superseded by the administrative *amt* as the local political unit, and the local officials or *amtsmenn* were restricted to civil functions. Military duties escaped their control, and tax collection was entrusted to separate *amt*-secretaries. This popular-royal revolution did not entirely destroy the nobles' power, and certainly did not benefit the Danish peasantry in economic matters. Economically and socially, the nobility still dominated the countryside, and politically, they were simply transformed from a ruling elite to a service nobility under the control of the crown. However, the monarch held the greatest political power in the state, exploiting the "popular" anti-noble feeeling and dividing the spoils more favorably between king and nobles. The capstone of the new monarchical edifice was the transformation of the elective monarchy into an hereditary one in 1660. Freed from bargaining on the death of every king, the crown could now take advantage of the improved administration and its hold on the service nobility. However, Denmark also had to tailor its ambitions to fit its reduction to a second-rate power. A smaller army, modest economic improvements and heavy reliance on subsidies from the western maritime powers (especially England and the Dutch Netherlands) were to be the keys to the next half-century.[12]

The fusion of popular frustrations and royal opportunism in Sweden produced more modest dividends for the Vasas. The three restive estates of clergy, burghers and free peasants were as angry at the Swedish nobility as were their Danish counterparts. Gustav Adolph's personal authority over the Swedish nobles[13] had given way to a thoroughly noble-dominated regency and reign by his successor, Christina. The Oxenstierna family alone held three of the five major ministries, and the rank and file of nobles had eagerly taken over crown lands and royal taxes in return for providing ready cash and soldiers for the state's wars during the 1630's and 1640's. Nevertheless, certain factors militated against a thorough popular-royal backlash. Unlike Denmark, Sweden had achieved military victories and territorial gains during the Thirty Years' War. While commoners resented the war profiteering of the nobility, they could not accuse the nobles of plundering the state to the detriment of the wars. Nor was the Swedish crown as financially desperate as the Danish monarchy. It

12. See Chapter 11.
13. See Chapter 5, pp. 135–136 for Swedish internal affairs under Gustav Adolph.

could hope to exploit its newly acquired lands. And, unlike Denmark, it had been fortunate enough to receive outside financing for its wars, through western and Muscovite subsidization as well as the temporary tolls at the Polish ports. What the Swedish crown wanted was some modest increase in revenues to offset the loss of the tolls and foreign subsidies (revenues having dropped from 6.36 million silver dollars in 1644 to 3.79 million in 1653). Finally, Queen Christina was not a royal revolutionary by temperament or design. She was not interested in increasing her power, but merely wished to abdicate and transfer the crown to her cousin Charles without damaging royal authority. As a result, Christina's exploitation of popular unrest in Sweden was more cavalier and less thorough than the actions of Frederick III in Denmark.

Christina's political manoeuvering in 1650 was nonetheless a remarkable feat. On the one hand, the great nobles were a power in the state not to be easily outwitted. On the other, popular discontent seems to have been far more volatile and unpredictable than in Denmark. Peasants complained of being degraded to "a Livonian slavery," and even the Oxenstiernas were afraid of an uprising. Preachers denounced the nobles for taking over church lands, and for allowing their horses to eat the very grain that kept the peasantry from starvation. The leading burghers, who were rising from merchant status to positions in civic government, begrudged the nobles' hold on high state offices. Royal and noble circles were fearful that such discontent might even trigger a political upheaval which would drag down the crown. Christina was well aware of the contemporary revolts in western Europe, where, she declared "neither king nor *parlement* have their proper power, but the common man, the *canaille*, rules according to his fancy." A leading nobleman-statesman put it more colorfully, saying that the restive Swedes "want to do as they have done in England, and make us all as like as pigs' trotters."

The crown's salvation was the decision by the three estates of clergy, burghers and free peasants to seek royal support against the nobility. The heart of the opposition's grievances lay in the nobility's domination of political and economic power to the detriment of the crown and the other estates. When the dissatisfied estates called for a royal policy of "reduction" (resumption of alienated lands and taxes), Christina brilliantly seized the opportunity. First she supported vigorously this attack on the nobles, placing them at her mercy. Then she shifted abruptly, dropping the matter of reduction in return for the nobles' political support. Somehow, the nobles kept their social and political power, while all four estates accepted Charles as hereditary prince and heir. Charles succeeded Christina in 1654, and the following year forced a very modest reduction on the nobles. Perhaps he might have gone further, as did

Frederick III of Denmark. But his death in 1660 ushered in a long regency period under his widow and the nobleman-chancellor, de la Gardie. Further extension of royal authority had to await the personal rule of Charles XI after 1672.[14]

No generalization can describe all the principalities which made up the Holy Roman Empire at mid-century. In Bavaria and Austria-Bohemia the crisis stopped short of reaching a political phase. The military triumphs of the Emperor in the 1620's and the successful struggle of the Bavarian prince with his estates at the beginning of the century probably account for this unique situation. The Elector of Bavaria had to compromise somewhat with his nobles after 1648, but there was no doubt that he was the chief power within the state. In Bohemia-Austria, the military defeat of the estates and the sharing of power by Emperor and carpetbagging noble landlords placed princely authority in a strong position. Against this coalition, the peasantry could do little. During the 1640's and 1650's, peasants rebelled occasionally against marauding armies, noble landlords and the prince, but their uprisings were doomed.[15]

In the leading Protestant states of the Empire, princes were forced to make new concessions to their estates. The Great Elector of Brandenburg was most adept at making gains in return, but he had to wait until the 1660's to turn the tide against his subjects in the Rhineland, Brandenburg and East Prussia. What he gained on the eve of the Little Northern War was the authority to levy temporary taxes and recruit a small army which fought well against the Poles and then the Swedes.[16] In many respects, the princes of Saxony and Württemberg were in a better position than the Great Elector to deal with social tensions and political opposition. In both states there was a balance of social and economic power among towns, peasants and nobles which Brandenburg lacked, and which was comparable to the situation in both Bavaria and Sweden. But instead of dividing and ruling, the Saxon and Württemberg princes saw much of the power which their dynasties had achieved at the beginning of the century turned over to their Estates during the Thirty Years' War. After 1648, the Saxon nobles wrested from their prince the legal right to forbid peasants to leave their villages or engage in household industry. In 1661, the estates of Saxony were allowed to meet without princely summons. Historians may well be correct in their contention that the difference between Brandenburg and the other Protestant states was due to the personality of the Great Elector, a man who was determined to have mili-

14. See Chapter 11.
15. On Austria at mid-century, see also pp. 169–170. Austrian developments after 1664 are discussed in Chapter 11.
16. See also Chapter 11.

tary power and who knew how to bargain with his subjects to achieve that end.

In Poland, the fate of the crown was sealed during the middle decades of the seventeenth century.[17] John Casimir was able to survive the Little Northern War, but he had neither the institutional power nor the social allies to keep his nobility in check at home. Between 1648 and 1651, the country was wracked by peasant unrest, but the peasants were too weak to offer a serious challenge to their social betters and too disorganized to protest to the monarchy against increases in their obligations to the nobility. When the war with Sweden came, the Polish nobles proved to be frighteningly resourceful in finding ways to destroy the slight authority left in the king's hands. Leading Polish nobles went over to the Swedish side, and a group of Lithuanian nobles offered to place their part of the state under Swedish suzerainty. Within the Polish Diet, decentralization at last reached the absurd point whereby programs were vetoed by the vote of a single deputy (the *liberum veto*). As a contemporary said in disgust, "With a single word, God created the world; with a single word, veto, we destroy Poland." John Casimir tried to outmanoeuver the nobles over the royal succession issue, but that, too, failed. Had he been able to secure the election of a successor while he was still on the throne, a degree of stability might have been achieved. However, the king's plan was ruined by a noble revolt led by the Grand Marshal of the army, George Lubomirski. The civil war of 1662–1663 ended when the soldiers were rewarded by church and state "gifts." But France and Austria added their intrigues to the continuing succession dispute.

Victimized by noble self-centeredness from the inside, and intrigues by the great European states from the outside, the Polish state was in no position to handle the Cossack rebellion which erupted on its eastern borders. Long-standing grievances of these nomadic peoples against Catholic persecutors and Polish-Lithuanian landlords came to a head in 1654. The Dnieper River Cossacks and their peasant followers secured military support from their co-religionaries in Muscovy. The Little Northern War of 1655–1660 temporarily overshadowed this confused civil-foreign war, but in the 1660's the Tsar's troops reentered and occupied much of eastern Poland. The Treaty of Andrussova (1667) dismembered the once mighty semi-state of the Dnieper Cossacks, placing most of the Cossack peoples under the authority of the Tsar.[18] Those who remained under Polish rule were too unruly and bitter to make them worthwhile subjects. The only

17. On background, see Chapter 5.
18. On the connection between the Russo-Cossack-Polish wars and the Little Northern War, see also pp. 172–173.

consolation for Poland was that the Tsar now also had his share of Cossack problems.[19]

The mid-century crisis in Muscovy was the most unexpected and unique of all the troubles which visited the central and eastern European states. When Alexis succeeded Michael Romanov in 1645, he found a Muscovy which had healed many of the political wounds and resolved some of the economic and social problems inherited from the Time of Troubles.[20] No election charter was imposed on the new Tsar. The *Zemski Sobor*, after a brief flurry of legislative activity under Michael, declined in importance. It approved a new law code in 1649, but after 1653 the Tsarist government worked through committees of experts who were advisory and not representative. The old *boyar* class was steadily diluted by the elevation of new men to aristocratic and political position. Its political instrument, the Boyar Duma, also continued its demise. In 1668, the Duma was composed of persons who were chosen by the Tsar for life, and only twenty-six of the sixty-eight were of the old, important *boyar* families. The haphazard central government of Michael was reduced to some order by a reorganization of the *prikazi*. Thanks to Swedish technical assistance in the 1630's and an influx of foreign military aides from other states, the army began to approach the size and effectiveness of Peter the Great's later military force. In the 1630's and 1640's, German, Dutch and English adventurers assisted in the exploitation of copper and iron resources; the importation of foreign arms was supplemented by native-manufactured weapons.

Alexis' immediate problems were fiscal and social. He needed revenue to maintain his court and army, and he had to ensure that the structure of Muscovite society would serve the state as well as the nobility. The two problems were interrelated. The Tsarist regime was capable enough of inventing schemes to wring money from its subjects—debased copper coins flooded the country and an oppressive salt tax was added to the already oppressive taxes on the lower social orders. What remained to be discovered was the means to impose these fiscal expedients on society. The "solution" was a comprehensive Law Code in 1649. It was the culmination of Michael's efforts to reconstruct society in the wake of the Time of Troubles. The Code forced individuals into fixed classes according to their current occupation or the needs of the state. Muscovite society became frozen occupationally and geographically. The Tsar could determine easily where he might dip into his subjects' pockets for money, and be equally sure that his victims would be in their assigned locality when he did. He was also assured that he could find men for his army

19. On Poland after 1667, see Chapter 9 especially pp. 252, 255.
20. See Chapter 5.

when he needed them. In Muscovite towns, there was now less likelihood that temporary residents could exist, free of taxes. In the countryside, slaves and free peasants were merged in a serf class, members of which were tied to the soil and to noble masters; it was obvious that they could not escape the call of the army or the treasury. The Law Code of 1649 was pressed to completion in the astonishingly short time of six months, but was to become the foundation of the Tsarist regime until the late nineteenth century. Not even Peter the Great would alter it in any major way.

Fiscal expedients and the Law Code stood the test of time, but in the short run they unexpectedly triggered uprisings by townsmen and peasants. In 1648, Moscow and other cities were scenes of massive demonstrations. Two years later, revolts erupted in Pskov, Novgorod and nearby peasant communities. As late as 1662, the Tsarist regime had to face disturbances in the capital. These rebellions coincided with revolts by the new Cossack subjects on the Dnieper in the 1650's and a more widespread insurrection by the old Cossack subjects of the Don River during the 1660's. The Don Cossack revolt, under Stenka Razin, drew to its banners all the discontented elements of Muscovy. Fugitive peasants, impoverished nobles, village priests, unpaid mercenary soldiers and non-Russian nomads joined the Cossack bands. All these rebellions were aimed at corrupt Muscovite courtiers, local Tsarist governors and great landlords. At times, rebellion became tinged with xenophobia. Foreign residents were accused of undermining the Orthodox religion and profiteering from the grain trade; their very lives were endangered.

The sheer severity and crudity of the Tsarist reaction had no parallels in other states east of the Rhine River. At first, the Tsar responded to the rebellions with clemency. But as the crisis mounted, the rebels were hunted down and uprisings crushed with brutal force. Alexis' political power remained intact, and the defeat of the rebels placed Tsarist autocracy in an impregnable position. Undoubtedly, the division and confusion among the dissident elements of society and the firm support by the nobility of the Tsarist regime helped to save the state from dismemberment. On the other hand, the mid-century crisis in Muscovy revealed some basic weaknesses in Tsarist autocracy. The personal authority of the Tsar and the deeply entrenched autocratic tradition of his country were a poor substitute for the more organized, bureaucratic governments which were helping the states of central and western Europe carry on in the midst of their upheavals. The Muscovite crisis also showed that the Tsar was crude and backward in his handling of political problems, by comparison with the sophisticated manoeuvers of a Christina, a Frederick William or a Frederick III.

In another, still more important, respect, the Muscovite crisis was unique. The rebellions coincided with a religious controversy which struck at the very roots of the Muscovite way of life. While the western and central European states were finding political solutions to religious tensions, Muscovy was just beginning to encounter them. Muscovy had not only escaped the sixteenth-century Reformation, but had been untroubled by either the Renaissance or the scientific revolution. It was a complacent Muscovite society, cut off from and contemptuous of European ways, which suddenly found itself in the midst of cultural-religious turmoil in the 1650's. The so-called "German quarter," the foreign suburb of Moscow, affected few Muscovites. The trickle of foreign technicians and military aides in the 1630's and 1650's served to show a few Tsarist administrators the need for at least partial adaption of European ways, but few men understood the necessity of broad but discriminate westernization as Alexis' foreign minister, Ordin-Nashchokin, did. Tsar Michael's habit of cramming his chambers with clocks, and Tsar Alexis' fancy for "German" music and ribald western comedy show little more than a superficial delight in the externals of western culture. The Muscovite court was simply dazzled by noise and color, as evidenced by the curious description of Alexis' dinner hour, when "Germans did play upon horns, and blow upon trumpets, and beat upon drums." How naive was Tsar Michael's unsuccessful attempt to lure a Leipzig professor into permanent residence with the invitation: "Unto Us, the Great Tsar, is it known that thou art exceeding learned and skilled in astrology and in geography, and in the heavenly courses, and in the measuring of the earth, and in many other like masteries and subtleties. Of a wise man of this sort have we need."

This limited contact with and interest in things western undoubtedly helped develop a pro-western climate of opinion at the Tsar's court. However, it was the sudden upheaval in the Orthodox church in the 1650's which shocked Muscovite society out of its complacency, isolation and sense of superiority. The conflict between Orthodoxy and Catholicism in the Polish-Muscovite borderlands was directly responsible for the reform movement of Patriarch Nikon (1652–1658). To combat Catholic rivals, Kievan Orthodox scholars had studied their Latin works. Under Patriarch Joseph, Nikon's predecessor, the Kievan scholars came to Moscow and began to criticize Muscovite deviations from Greek Orthodox practices. A controversy soon raged over whether it was right to practice polyphonic recitation of services (i.e., to have several persons recite different portions simultaneously, to save time), as was done in Muscovy. Under Nikon, the controversy spread, and by 1654 the Boyar Duma together with a church council adopted a new service book. The reforms

of Nikon, such as giving the sign of the cross with three fingers instead
of two, and altering the number of Hallelujahs and genuflections, do not
appear fundamental. But the Muscovite Orthodox Church placed great
emphasis on ritual, and little on theology or social issues. To criticize
accepted church custom as a deviation from the Greek Orthodox services
was to question the essence of Muscovite religion. Moreover, it was to
challenge the deep inertia and complacency of Muscovite society which
took its lead from the church. The resulting schism (*Raskol*) between
the Old Believers and the Greek reformers stiffened the opposition of
many Muscovites to any change, religious, intellectual or political. But
that schism also made it possible for Peter the Great to administer a second
shock to Muscovite institutions and society at the end of the century,
and may have determined his own hostility to tradition which now was
equated with schism and thereby with revolt against the authority of
church and state. One is tempted to say that the Petrine revolution would
have been impossible without the mid-century schism.

The schism also undermined the authority of the one Muscovite
institution still capable of challenging the Tsar's authority, the Orthodox
church. Nikon had no intention of limiting the reform movement to
purely religious matters. Even as head of the church, he was probably
more concerned with upholding his authority than with steering the
church onto the path of revitalization and genuine religious life. His bitter
vendettas against religious leaders who dared to challenge his will soon
broadened into a personal quarrel with the Tsar. Michael's father, the
Patriarch Philaret, had been co-Tsar and virtual director of foreign
policy. Nikon tried to attain a similar position with Alexis and to harden
it into a dogma. At first he succeeded. When Alexis was with his soldiers
fighting the Poles in 1654, the Patriarch acted in his stead. Alexis also
supported Nikon's reforms, probably from far more genuine religious
feeling than was manifested by the Patriarch. The line was drawn by
1656, when the Tsar saw where Nikon's ambitions were taking him. It
was made clear to the Patriarch that his role was within the church, and
that the state stood over the church in secular matters. Nikon resigned
his post in 1658, and in voluntary exile tried to carry on the battle. But
the state stood firmly against his political position at the same time that
it supported the church reforms. At an ecumenical council of Muscovite
and Greek Orthodoxy in 1666–1667, the Old Believers were excommuni-
cated and Nikon formally deposed. With the fall of Nikon, a great barrier
to Tsarist autocracy and further political-intellectual reform was shattered.

The mid-century crisis in Muscovy was both unique and typical. It
involved social revolt and political upheaval, as was the case in Denmark,

Sweden and the Germanies. It led to the strengthening of the state, as occurred to the north and west. It formed the lines for future relationships between social classes. But it also began a transformation of Muscovy which had no parallel elsewhere. It would not be an exaggeration to say that the Muscovite crisis constituted a turning point of a magnitude unequalled even in western European states like England and France. In the crisis, the non-European Muscovite state began to change into the semi-European state known as Russia.[21]

21. On the emergence of the new Russia under Peter the Great, see Chapter 11.

7.

The Thirty Years' War:
Spain and France

Between 1624 and 1659, France and Spain fought their own version of the Thirty Years' War.[1] It was a conflict which neither state wanted, and which neither had the capacity to wage. Spain saw as its enemy the Dutch Republic, and was bent on victory in the Spanish-Dutch war of 1621–1648. France would have liked to avoid involvement in that war, but it was not to be. When the Count-Duke of Olivares became the chief minister in Spain in 1622, Spain's ambassadors and generals were already provoking France by setting up a chain of possessions from northern Italy to the Spanish Netherlands. Ostensibly these claims were to channel Spanish troops and supplies to the Dutch war, but in the process they threatened France with encirclement. When Olivares' counterpart, Cardinal Richelieu, took over French affairs in 1624, the French monarchy was wavering between neutrality and cold war with Spain. A series of localized conflicts between France and Spain after 1624 escalated into an open war by 1635. The war continued under their successors, Luis de Haro in Spain and Jules Mazarin in France, outlasting the central European version of the Thirty Years' War by eleven years.

---

1. On the Thirty Years' War in central and eastern Europe, and its connections with the Franco-Spanish conflict, see Chapter 6.

The war altered the destiny of western Europe in a way which neither Olivares nor Richelieu could have foreseen in the mid-1620's. The preponderance of Spain in western European affairs was swept away, and France took its place. The war also shook the foundations of both states. Once they were drawn into a bitter and protracted war, the two ministers strained the internal structures of their states so badly that they created in each a violent mid-century crisis. In 1640 Olivares was faced with provincial rebellions and a palace intrigue which toppled him. Richelieu was able to keep minor rebellions from merging into a general revolt while he lived, but he also set the stage for the major rebellion of the Fronde (1648–1652) which his successor, Mazarin, had to face. Mazarin and de Haro managed to put down the revolts in their states, but the rebellions left scars and an uncertain legacy for Louis XIV of France and Charles II of Spain.

ᴄᴓ Spain and France at War

In the mid-1620's, Spain was internally weak but outwardly in a much better position than France to wage war in the west. Under Philip III, Spain had failed to solve its economic ills or the problem of governing a far-flung empire. It had, however, jockeyed itself into an excellent geographic position to wage war on the Dutch Republic when the Spanish-Dutch truce of 1609–1621 expired.[2] It was too much to expect that the Spain of Philip IV (1621–1665) would give up that position, and with it the chance to reverse the outcome of the sixteenth-century war of Dutch independence against Spain. It was equally tempting for Spaniards to forget their internal problems by concentrating on a foreign war. And in the royal favorite and first minister, the Count-Duke of Olivares (1622–1643), Spain had a leader who thought that it was possible to attempt domestic reform and external conflict at the same time.

Olivares was a bold and brilliant administrator, whose upbringing gave him an unusual understanding of Spain's traditions and the inspiration to recapture the grandeur of Philip II's reign. His family had a tradition of service to state and church. He was originally groomed for a career in the church, and educated at the University of Salamanca. The death of an older brother changed his family's plans, for since Olivares became heir to the family estates, he was compelled to pursue a secular career. During Philip III's reign, Olivares was placed in the household of the future Philip IV. When Philip IV became king in 1621, Olivares was

2. See Chapter 4, pp. 104–105.

THE SPANISH
ROUTE FROM MILAN
TO THE NETHERLANDS
1619-1648

NORTH
SEA

DUTCH NETHERLANDS

SPANISH
NETHERLANDS

HOLY ROMAN EMPIRE

LUXEM-
BOURG

Rhine R.

① Philippsburg

②

BAVARIA

Spanish Hapsburg

Austrian Hapsburg

Catholic church lands

Bavaria (pro-Hapsburg)

① Lower or Rhenish Palatinate

② Upper Palatinate

③ The Grissons

④ Valtelline

⑤ Montferrat

⑥ Mantua

— — Boundary of the
Holy Roman Empire

FRANCHE
COMTÉ

Brisach

Rhine

SWITZERLAND

TYROL

③

④

FRANCE

SAVOY

MILAN

Casale

⑤

VENETIAN REPUBLIC

Pinerolo

⑤

GENOA

⑥

ADRIATIC SEA

PIEDMONT

PAPAL
STATES

already in his favor. Within a year, the pleasure-loving mediocrity who
sat on the throne had made Olivares his chief minister and the real ruler
of Spain.

The Count-Duke was probably aware of the gamble that he took
in pursuing the new war against the Dutch, but he was not one to retreat.
He was a man of immense self-confidence and an autocrat by nature. It
seemed only logical for him to use Spanish bases in northern Italy, the
Rhenish Palatinate and the Spanish Netherlands against the Dutch Netherlands. By controlling Alpine passes, especially in the Valtelline, he could
send troops and supplies by land down the Rhine River to the Dutch

theater. Those same passes also gave the Spanish Hapsburgs a link with their Austrian Hapsburg relations in Germany, and the hope that Austria's Thirty Years' War in the German theater could be coordinated with the Spanish effort against the Dutch. In addition, Olivares began to revive the Spanish navy, which had gone into decline under Philip III. Spanish ships could put into neutral English ports, and, when the Dutch fleet let down its guard, slip across the English channel to the Spanish Netherlands. With land and water supply routes to the Dutch theater, who could stop Spain from crushing the upstart Dutch republicans? France was a potential enemy, but it was virtually surrounded by Spanish possessions. And Olivares counted on the French to see that their best course of action was to remain surrounded—and neutral. In 1620, France had taken that course. The Treaty of Ulm of that year, fashioned by French diplomats, had neutralized the anti-Hapsburg principalities of the Rhineland in order to keep the German war from spreading to the French borders. Why should France not continue its neutrality? The prospects for Spain were very bright around 1624.

The French situation was obviously very different from that of Spain. Spain not only held the key territories, but seemed certain to prove a still greater threat to France if it reconquered the Dutch state and combined its power with an already victorious Austria in the German lands to the east of France. If France remained neutral, its territories and its very existence as a state might eventually be placed in jeopardy. However, if France decided to enter the Dutch war against Spain, there were still greater problems. The greatest was the religious one. Catholic Spain was fighting the Protestant Dutch. By seventeenth-century standards, it would be wrong for Catholic France to take the Protestant side against a Catholic state. The dilemma was increased by France's internal problems. The French monarchy was continually faced with rebellions by Protestant Huguenot subjects. How could it fight Catholics abroad while trying to subdue Protestants and strengthen Catholicism at home? In the early 1620's, the king of France, Louis XIII, had begun to resolve the problem without regard to religious logic; repression of Protestant rebellions was combined with occasional military manoeuvers in northern Italy against Spain. The foreign ventures were nonetheless fitful and hesitant. France tried to avoid direct contact with Spain on the battlefield. While Spain supported the Catholic inhabitants of the Valtelline, France tried to dislodge Spanish forces from the area by backing the military action of the valley's Alpine enemy, the Protestant Grisons.[3] This indirect warfare was made difficult in 1623, when Spain placed the Valtelline under the pro-

3. The name applied to several communities loosely associated with the Swiss Confederation.

tection of the head of the Catholic church. If France wished to continue action in the valley, it would henceforth have to deal with the troops of the Pope which occupied it. Even if France defied religious principles, there was the nagging question of whether the French army was strong enough to deal with Hapsburg and Huguenot foes simultaneously.

At the head of the French government was a man who was Olivares' equal in self-confidence and vision, Cardinal Richelieu (1624–1642). In 1624, Richelieu lacked one qualification of his Spanish counterpart. He was not free to pursue his own policies. Richelieu had risen and fallen and risen again with the fortunes of Louis XIII's mother, Marie de Medici. A member of her government while the king was too young to rule in his own name, Richelieu had fallen into disgrace and exile when Marie was ousted from power by Louis XIII in 1617.[4] He had helped to reconcile mother and son during the following years, receiving a cardinal's hat in 1622 and entering the royal council in 1624. By the end of 1624, Richelieu had undermined and succeeded the chief minister. But he was distrusted by Louis XIII, and beholden to Marie de Medici. What particularly limited him in foreign affairs was the religious position of Marie and her "party," the Devout Ones. The Devout Ones were determined to exterminate Protestantism in France and to support the advancement of the Catholic cause in Europe under the leadership of the Spanish and Austrian Hapsburgs. Having clawed his way to the top of France's government, Richelieu had to swear that he would remain Marie's "creature," and would cooperate with other members of her party, who controlled the ministries of justice and finance, and even wielded a marshal's baton. Richelieu could work only gradually to free himself from this entrenched ultra-Catholic, pro-Spanish group. Between 1624 and 1630, he quietly and slowly won the confidence of Louis XIII, built a base of power independent of Marie and shifted subtly from the inflexible Devout foreign policy.

With French foreign policy entangled in domestic intrigue, it is not surprising that Spain continued its ascendancy in western Europe immediately after 1624. While Spanish forces made headway against the Dutch, France could accomplish only limited intervention in northern Italy. The first of these limited wars took place in the Valtelline in 1624–1625. The outbreak of a Huguenot revolt, secretly encouraged by Spain, and Richelieu's hesitation to escalate the Italian campaign to the point of a major war with Spain, made a fiasco of the enterprise. In 1626, Spain and France signed the Treaty of Monçon, which theoretically placed the pro-French Grisons in control of the Valtelline, but in actuality permitted

4. See Chapter 4, pp. 111.

Spanish troops to remain in control of the valley and its Alpine passes. The treaty had immediate repercussions in Italy. France's Italian allies, Venice and Savoy, felt betrayed. The ambitious Duke Charles Emanuel I of Savoy (1580–1630) henceforth determined to expand his state through friendship with Spain. The Venetian ambassador summed up his state's position in bitter words:

> Broken faith, false promises, secret intrigues, plain trickeries, "Yea" in the mouth, and "Nay" in the heart, have between them ended in a treaty . . . full of prejudice and injury to Venice, Savoy and the Grisons, with the sole end of satisfying Spain, since all the advantages are on her side.

The death of the Duke of Mantua-Montferrat was followed by a second small war, the Mantuan succession conflict of 1627–1631. Spain and Savoy agreed to divide the inheritance between the Savoyard Duke and a pro-Spanish candidate. The Austrian Hapsburgs backed their stand with troops from the Holy Roman Empire's Catholic army, the Emperor arguing that as overlord of the Mantuan duchy he had every right to take part. France supported the candidacy of the pro-French Duke of Nevers, but it was not easy for Richelieu to impose Nevers on the Savoyard-Spanish-imperialist coalition. The support of the pro-French Pope, Urban VIII, in Italy was offset by a Huguenot uprising in France. Even when Richelieu ended that rebellion by the compromise Peace of Alais in 1629,[5] the French troops released from civil combat could make little headway against their Italian enemies. Moreover, Richelieu did not want a direct, military confrontation with Spain or the Empire. France and Spain avoided direct combat, attacking instead the lands of each other's Italian allies. Ultimately, France had to respect the Emperor's authority to decide the Mantuan succession.

France was fortunate to emerge from the Mantuan war with a slight improvement in its position. French victories over Savoy and the Imperial Diet's decision to withdraw its troops from Italy resulted in a draft treaty negotiated at the Diet, modified by the secret Treaty of Cherasco (1631) between France and Savoy. The pro-French candidate received the Mantuan and Montferrat lands, and France occupied the fortresses of Casale in Montferrat and Pinerolo in Savoy. Pinerolo gave France an entry to Italy, and the combination of French-occupied Casale and pro-French Mantua allowed France to hem in Spanish Milan on both sides.

Nevertheless, Spain was the real victor of the war. It continued to hold the all-important Valtelline, despite the peace settlement which called for Spanish withdrawal. France could harass Spain's Italian possessions

5. See pp. 205–206.

after 1631, but Spain was able to keep sending troops and supplies across the Alps to the Rhineland and the Netherlands. It was from Milan and the Valtelline that Spain sent the army which won the battle of Nörd-lingen for Austria in 1634 and which strengthened Spain's position in the Rhenish Lowlands area.[6] To add insult to injury, the Protestant Grisons renounced its alliance with France in 1637, and went over to the Spanish side.

In one important sense, the Italian wars marked a change in French policy and fortune. By combining a lenient peace with French Huguenots with the Italian campaigns against Spanish interests, Richelieu forced a showdown at home with the Catholic Devout party. The Devout Ones were furious with him for allowing the Huguenots to continue prac-ticing their faith, equally angry with his support of the Protestant Grisons and opposition to Spain, and above all jealous of his ability to secure Louis XIII's support for such anti-Catholic actions. While engaged in the Man-tuan war, Louis XIII became seriously ill. Marie de Medici tried to coerce her sick son into dismissing the cardinal-minister, but Louis re-served judgment until after he recovered and returned to Paris. On the famous Day of Dupes in 1630, a final confrontation between Marie and Louis took place at the Luxembourg palace in Paris. When Richelieu in-terrupted the queen-mother's emotional outburst against him, the king dismissed both him and Marie from his presence and then requested the cardinal to meet him at his hunting lodge at Versailles. Richelieu almost decided to flee, convinced, as were the Devout Ones, that his political career had come to an end. But a close friend persuaded him to visit the king, and at Versailles Louis XIII informed the cardinal that he would support him against all his enemies. The Devout party was duped. Marie soon went into exile in the Spanish Netherlands, and the Devout elements in the royal government were purged by execution, exile and imprison-ment. Richelieu was to face further governmental crises, and he was never completely sure that Louis XIII's support would continue. But after the Day of Dupes the cardinal-minister dominated the French government and guided its foreign policy free of the Devout party.

While Richelieu was freeing himself from the ultra-Catholic party in France and achieving limited success in northern Italy, he was also busy trying to keep Spain occupied with the Dutch. In 1624, he initiated a policy on the Spanish-Dutch war which continued until 1635. France subsidized the Dutch fighting forces, but stayed out of the war. After 1631, the use of money as a substitute for war was expanded. French grants to Sweden enabled that state to fight Hapsburg Austria in Ger-

6. See Chapter 6, pp. 165-166.

many, thereby preventing the Emperor from joining the Spanish Hapsburg war against the Dutch. These subsidies probably saved the Dutch
Netherlands from disaster, although they did not stop the Spanish offensive. It is also noteworthy that alliances with Protestant states did not
stray far from the Devout policy of supporting Catholicism. The French
alliance of 1624 with the Protestant Dutch gave France the use of Dutch
ships, which were employed against the Protestant French rebels. And the
alliance with Protestant Sweden stipulated that Catholic worship was not
to be disturbed by the Swedes (although the clause was disregarded).
An alliance between the French and English monarchies in 1624 also
brought private Catholic worship to the English court, when the Catholic
princess Henrietta Maria married the future Charles I. France failed,
however, to secure English naval assistance against the French Huguenots,
and in 1627–1628, an English fleet actually fought with the Protestants
against the French monarchy.

By 1635, Richelieu had to modify drastically his quasi-Devout position on foreign affairs. The Dutch Netherlands seemed on the point of
negotiating an end to its war with Spain, and the Hapsburg fortunes had
been greatly improved by the Spanish-Austrian victory at Nördlingen.
Consequently, France openly entered the war, through military alliances
with the Dutch (against Spain) and with Sweden (against Austria). The
French still relied heavily on the armies of its allies, subsidized more than
ever by the French treasury. However, there was no way to disguise the
fact that France was openly and directly at war with Spain and Austria.
French troops, bolstered by German mercenaries, fought in the Lowlands,
the Rhineland and even in Bavaria and the Austrian domains. As might
be expected, Richelieu tried to ensure toleration of Catholicism in lands
occupied by the Dutch and Swedes. However, it was difficult to square
this position with the policy of waging open war on Catholic states. Pope
Urban saw the war against Spain and Austria as a purely secular conflict;
many Catholics must surely have seen it as the last stage in Richelieu's
retreat from ultra-Catholic Devout policies.

The cautiously escalated and secularized war policy of Richelieu
brought extreme hardship and popular and noble revolts to France, but
it succeeded in containing the Hapsburgs. The French army became first
the equal and then the superior of the Hapsburg forces. The inefficient
tax system managed to yield enough money to keep the army in being,
thanks to ruthless collection of taxes by royal intendants supported by
troops, and royal loans bearing high interest. Richelieu's naval reforms
made the French navy a rival of the Dutch and English fleets, and an
able fighting arm against Spain. While the French monarchy reformed its
military and managed to keep isolated revolts from merging into a major

rebellion, Spain buckled under the strain of war. Dutch ships cornered a
Spanish fleet off the English coast in 1639, and virtually destroyed it.
Olivares had breathed new life into Spain's navy just as Richelieu had
done, but Admiral Tromp's victory undid his work. Spain could no longer
hope to roam the northern waters and supply the Spanish Netherlands
by sea. In the Rhineland, France's troops and her German mercenaries
took Breisach in 1638. It was a greater victory than the annexation of
Pinerolo in 1631. In 1639, the sudden death of the German mercenary
leader who had claimed Breisach as his own, gave the area to France.
Breisach was on the east bank of the Rhine River. From that strategic
position, France could easily occupy the rest of the west bank, cut off
Spanish supplies from Milan to the Lowlands, and advance into Germany
against the Austrian Hapsburg forces. Still worse fortune was in store
for Olivares. His attempt to make the non-Castilian provinces of the
Spanish empire contribute to the war led to Catalan and Portuguese
uprisings in 1640. Portugal, supported by France, declared its independence. The Catalans swore allegiance to Louis XIII and French forces
joined the rebels. Olivares wrote in a memorandum that "this year can
undoubtedly be considered the most unfortunate that this Monarchy has
ever experienced." A scapegoat had to be found. In 1643, Philip IV banished Olivares to his estates; two years later, reduced to insanity, the
would-be restorer of Spain's greatness died. With the death of Richelieu
shortly before, in 1642, and Louis XIII, shortly after, in 1643, the Franco-
Spanish war entered a new phase, under new leaders.

Between 1643 and 1659, the Franco-Spanish conflict became an
almost completely secular one. The new chief ministers of Spain and
France were skillful, secular diplomats, and the course of the war reinforced their proclivities. Spain's de Haro (1643–1660) was determined
to pull the tottering Spanish empire together and prevent the emerging
power of France from destroying it. Cardinal Mazarin (1643–1661) was
bent on capitalizing on French military might and subordinated everything to the defeat of Spain. Neither had the vision nor the domineering
quality of his predecessor, but both were adept at playing the game of
secular statecraft.

Luis de Haro was overshadowed by Mazarin, but he managed to
make the best of a bad situation and prevent Spain from collapsing completely. While he patched up the Spanish monarchy's differences with its
internal foes, he took every advantage of the new problems which confronted France after the death of Richelieu and Louis XIII. The first
break for Spain came early in 1648. The Dutch were willing to negotiate
a settlement of their long war. De Haro had to make major concessions,
including the recognition of Dutch independence and the transfer of

additional land from the Spanish Netherlands to the Dutch Republic. But peace was worth the price, because the Dutch deserted France and left Mazarin to fight Spain alone. Late in 1648, Mazarin countered with the Peace of Westphalia, which freed French troops in Germany for the war against Spain. Westphalia brought peace between France and Austria and at the same time kept Austria from joining the Spanish side of the Franco-Spanish conflict. That German settlement also strengthened France's position in the Rhineland. Acquisition of rights in Alsace (to the west of the Rhine River) and the fortress-towns of Breisach and Philippsburg (on the east bank) broke Spain's encirclement of France, and made a future French advance into western Germany possible.[7]

The second opportunity for Spain came later in 1648 when a major rebellion—the Fronde—erupted in France. Before the Fronde collapsed in 1652, the French war effort was seriously weakened by the virtual collapse of the monarchy's local administrative machinery which resulted in a sharp fall in tax revenue. De Haro was able to invade France on several occasions, and at times to coordinate his troops' movements with the manoeuvers of French rebel armies. When the Fronde was put down, the rebel chieftain, Condé, slipped across the border to Spanish territory and became commander of Spanish forces. However, Mazarin was able to revive French fortunes somewhat after the Fronde, by bringing England into the war against Spain. Spain was placed once more on the defensive, but de Haro held on until France agreed to negotiate a peace treaty.

The Peace of the Pyrenees (1659) marked the end of Spain as a great power in western Europe, but saved it from the disintegration which had seemed likely in the last years of Olivares. France strengthened its borders, supplementing the Westphalian gains with lands in the Spanish Netherlands and on the Franco-Spanish border. The danger of Hapsburg aggression through encirclement was thus virtually ended. Spain had to realize that it could not achieve Olivares' dream of grandeur, and reconcile itself to the somber task of holding on to what remained of Philip II's great empire. The Dutch Netherlands was lost forever, and in 1668 Spain finally recognized the independence of Portugal. There remained the Castilian core of the empire, the Catalonian, Valencian and Aragonese provinces of Spain proper, the Italian territories, the Spanish Netherlands and Franche Comté as well as the Spanish territories overseas (minus the Portuguese lands). Spain's hope was that it could solve its internal problems without further interference from France.

The most celebrated part of the treaty was a marriage alliance be-

7. On Westphalia, see also Chapter 6, pp. 167–171.

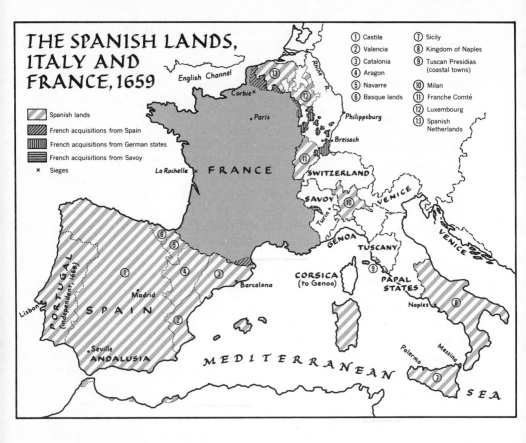

① Castile ⑦ Sicily
② Valencia ⑧ Kingdom of Naples
③ Catalonia ⑨ Tuscan Presidias
④ Aragon   (coastal towns)
⑤ Navarre ⑩ Milan
⑥ Basque lands ⑪ Franche Comté
⑫ Luxembourg
⑬ Spanish
   Netherlands

Spanish lands

French acquisitions from Spain

French acquisitions from German states

French acquisitions from Savoy

× Sieges

English Channel

Corbie ×

Paris

Philippsburg

Breisach

La Rochelle × FRANCE

SWITZERLAND

SAVOY

VENICE

Turin

GENOA

TUSCANY

VENICE

CORSICA
(to Genoa)

PAPAL
STATES

Naples

PORTUGAL
(Independent, 1668)

Madrid

SPAIN

Barcelona

Lisbon

Seville
ANDALUSIA

MEDITERRANEAN

Palermo

Messina

SEA

tween Spain and France. More than any territorial concessions, it symbolized the shift in the relative positions of the two states. Fifty years
before, France had humbled itself by marrying Louis XIII with the
Spanish princess, Anne of Austria. In the Peace of the Pyrenees, Spain
was the humble party. Philip IV gave his daughter, Maria Theresa, in
marriage to Louis XIV, and with her went a future Bourbon claim to
the Spanish succession. The new queen of France officially renounced
her position in the Spanish Hapsburg line, but no treaty could change
her blood relationship to the king of Spain. De Haro was so anxious to
make the match that Mazarin was able to make Maria Theresa's renun-
ciation conditional on Spanish payment of a large dowry. Since impoverished Spain soon defaulted on its payments, Maria Theresa's re-
nunciation was voided. In 1665, Philip IV was succeeded by a sickly son,
Charles II. Although Charles confounded Europe by living until 1700,
while he lived, the shadow of France hung over the Spanish empire. Louis
XIV used Maria Theresa's position as half-sister of Charles to advance
French claims to portions of that empire. And he, along with other
rulers, struggled with the awesome question of who should succeed the

childless king of Spain when he finally gave in to death. The full details of the Spanish succession problem were not known when Mazarin and de Haro concluded the marriage alliance of 1659, but even at that early date it was evident that Spain was a second-rate power and the potential victim of France and Europe rather than the great state which Philip II had ruled and which Olivares had sought to revitalize.

Spain Under Olivares and De Haro

Although Olivares' great ambition was to revive Spain's external greatness, he never lost sight of the internal means to that end. He knew that in order to wage war against the Dutch and the French he would have to overcome the Spanish empire's economic and administrative weaknesses. He was not concerned that those problems had baffled Lerma and Philip III.[8] His natural instinct for reform, his boundless optimism and his dream of grandeur combined to make him one of the most ambitious administrators in Spanish history. Many historians have even concluded that his internal goals could have been realized had he resisted the lure of revived imperialism. We cannot pass such judgment on him, however, for sweeping reforms and aggressive foreign policy were inseparable for the Spanish minister. It is true that the strain of war led eventually to an upheaval in Spain. But without the initial demands of diplomacy and war, the inspiration, nature and direction of reform would have been much weaker.

Like Richelieu, Olivares knew how to combine self-advancement with statesmanship. The first years of his ministry brought forth a veritable flood of reform projects designed to cut back unnecessary state expenses, stimulate the economy and ruin his rivals. Philip III's courtiers and ministers were hounded until they disgorged the wealth they had acquired in office, expenses in the royal household were halved and an attempt was made to reduce municipal offices by two-thirds. Married men were relieved of tax burdens and bachelors over twenty-five were penalized, in order to encourage population growth. Restrictions on the teaching of Latin were aimed at diverting young men from careers in government, law, medicine and the church to more "productive" employment. Emigration without royal approval was forbidden, nobles were asked to live on their estates rather than off the court and industries were protected from foreign competition.

All these measures were worthwhile. But even an Olivares could

8. See Chapter 4.

not revive the Spanish economy or reduce expenditures to match income overnight. Some historians have accused him of sabotaging the reform program by allowing Philip IV and the Castilian court to spend freely on entertainment. It is more likely that population stagnation, rural impoverishment and the understandable rush of desperate fortune-seekers into court, bureaucracy and church were virtually impossible to halt, than that Philip IV's court costs were the cause of Olivares' failure.

Undaunted, Olivares sought to unite the Spanish empire by means of his famous "Union of Arms." A common reserve of 140,000 soldiers was to be supplied and maintained by the Iberian, Italian and Lowlands territories of the empire. Each area would contribute according to its wealth, thereby breaking down the privileges of tax-exempt areas like Portugal and Catalonia. Soldiers from the different provinces would fight together, thereby eroding the separatism and provincialism which had survived Philip II and Philip III.

The Union of Arms was merely the first part of Olivares' grand scheme to unify the Spanish empire. He also aimed at bringing more non-Castilians into the central government, shifting administrators and clergy from province to province, exposing the king more frequently beyond the confines of Castile by state visits, and modifying local laws to eliminate provincial differences. The Count-Duke hoped to reduce provincial opposition to his ambitious program by gradual reform, and by holding out the prize of local participation in state concerns in return for the loss of autonomy. Nor could it be said that he favored Castile, since tax burdens in that province actually increased during the era of reform.

The grand scheme proved too grand to be accepted by the non-Castilians, and royal visits to Aragon, Valencia and Catalonia in 1626 were far from joyous occasions. The Aragonese and Valencian Cortes grudgingly voted token subsidies for the Union of Arms, but refused to allow troops recruited in their provinces to fight elsewhere. The Catalonian Cortes was so opposed to any concession that Philip IV left the assembly and returned to Castile while the delegates were still in session.

After this first setback in 1626 until the revolts of Portugal and Catalonia in 1640, Olivares tried one scheme after another to achieve unity and a full treasury. The loose conciliar system of government was coordinated by the appointment of able men, amenable to Olivares' will. The cumbersome councils were also bypassed by the creation of a series of special Juntas. In 1634 an executive Junta was formed, which virtually replaced the Council of State as the chief policy-making body for the empire. This reordering of the central government was in itself a significant achievement, but without fundamental fiscal reform and control over the provinces, its effectiveness was blunted. Olivares tried to win over the local elite in Catalonia and Portugal, but to no avail. Princess Margaret was made governor of Portugal to counter Portuguese complaints that they were neglected by the crown. A Catalan was installed as viceroy of Catalonia, to avoid the charge of Castilianization. But the Portuguese soon discovered that the arrival of the princess was an excuse for infiltrating the Portuguese administration with Castilian "advisors," and excluding the native elite. And well-to-do Catalans suspected their viceroy of being a weak-willed tool of Castile. Resistance to Olivares among the alienated aristocratic and merchant families of Portugal and Catalonia naturally increased. In those provinces and elsewhere on the Iberian peninsula, the urban and rural poor were driven to despair by Olivares' monetary policies. Prices fluctuated wildly as the crown constantly changed the quantity and value of its coins. A sudden 50 percent deflation in 1628 was caused by an official reduction of the value of vellon currency. In 1636, vellon coins were stamped at three times their previous value. Such measures relieved the royal treasury, but at the price of ruining the already weak economy, and inciting the poor to revolt.

The earliest insurrections against Olivares' regime proved abortive, since they were limited to the lower orders of Spanish society. But the revolts of 1640 were regional uprisings of both rich and poor. Olivares could not cope with the Portuguese revolt, which rallied around the legitimate heir to the old Portuguese throne, John of Braganza. In 1668, Spain finally recognized the independence of Portugal. Luckily for Spain, the Catalan revolt degenerated into a war within a war, as peasants and poorer townsmen turned their wrath on all persons in authority, including rich Catalans. However, Olivares fell before the monarchy could take advantage of the divisions within the Catalan revolt. With Andalusians plotting their independence from Castile, French troops, Catalan rebels and Castilian forces bringing anarchy to Catalonia, and Portugal severed from the empire, Olivares' enemies at court seized the opportunity to strike. The queen played a leading role in the intrigue, which included relatives of Olivares. The *coup d'état* had all the ingredients of France's Day of Dupes, except for the outcome.[9] Had Olivares been able to win military victories abroad as Richelieu had during the Mantuan war, he might have survived the provincial revolts and court intrigues. But the Spanish military campaign of 1636 had reached Corbie, and endangered Paris, only to end in retreat and humiliation. Later campaigns against the French

9. See p. 192.

also failed. Philip IV was not Louis XIII. In 1643 he gave into the wishes of his wife and dismissed the man who had the vision of Richelieu and perhaps a more original mind, but who lacked the Frenchman's luck and ability to concentrate on what was possible.

Ironically the fall of Olivares probably helped to save what was left of the Spanish empire. The new favorite, Luis de Haro, Olivares' nephew, lacked the grand design of his uncle, and his apparent mediocrity as an administrator served to calm the courtiers and provincials who had disliked Olivares' arrogance. Fiscal policies did not improve. Bankruptcy was declared in 1647 and again in 1653, tampering with the coinage continued and the supply of silver from the Indies was cut off by the English in 1657. De Haro had to face new revolts in Naples and Sicily (1647) and new plots in Aragon (1648). But with the help of local viceroys, he was able to combine successfully military repression with royal clemency. In 1652, Barcelona fell to Spanish forces, and Catalonia was granted a renewal of its old privileges. The Neapolitan and Sicilian revolts were little more than desperate outbursts by the poor against new taxes and famines. The nobilities remained aloof from these Italian uprisings, terrified by mob scenes and realizing that they had been very favorably treated by the Spanish regime. By rescinding the new taxes and confirming the privileged position of the nobility, the local Spanish officials soon restored order.[10] Spain was also saved by the high-handed tactics of the French invaders in Catalonia, who made many Catalans prefer Spanish rule to that of France. Above all, as John Elliott has noted, Spain and de Haro survived the revolts because of the stability of Castile and the weaknesses of its control over the empire. Castile did not revolt; hence the heart of the empire remained immune to internal problems. But neither could it tyrannize the outlying provinces, and once they returned to the fold, they could enjoy a degree of autonomy which reconciled them to their secondary position.[11]

The so-called decline of Spain was therefore an accommodation to the fact that the crown could not weld the loosely organized and controlled empire into a united and powerful state. While elsewhere in mid-century Europe rulers played on social divisions, the pressures of war and economic troubles and emerged more powerful than before, the Spanish monarchy at least survived the mid-century crisis, although with no increase in its power or authority. In view of the political and economic weaknesses of Spain, that achievement may have been as great as the more spectacular and surer gains of its neighbors.[12]

10. See also Chapter 4, p. 126.
11. J. H. Elliott, *Imperial Spain: 1496–1716* (Mentor, 1966), 346–350.
12. On Spain's internal affairs after 1665, see Chapter 10.

France Under Richelieu

Few public figures in Europe's past have been as fortunate with historians as Cardinal Richelieu. Many have disliked the man, but rarely have they questioned his accomplishments. His iron self-discipline, his ability to summarize lucidly in writing the problems before him and his solutions and his victories against foreign and internal foes have made a legend of his name. Yet that legend has badly distorted the real Richelieu, turning a gifted human into an implausible superman.[13]

If we are to understand the cardinal-minister who dominated France between 1624 and 1642, we must first of all realize that he was a practical politician. Richelieu's reform proposals came while he was still opposed to Louis XIII's government between 1618 and 1623, and during his first years in power while he was as yet inexperienced with the hard world of practical politics. As he gained increasing control over Louis XIII, Richelieu the reformer gave way to Richelieu the administrator. Power and responsibility sobered the early visionary. So, too, did his fear of Hapsburg Spain. In 1629, he wrote to Louis XIII that France should cling to its Italian conquests, but that in following such a policy, "one must leave behind all thought of peace, economy and order within the realm." Richelieu realized, as generations of historians have not, that he was sacrificing all possibility of basic internal reorganization on the assumption that the Hapsburg menace transcended internal problems.

While Olivares was arrogant and offensive to those around him, and became bolder and more sweeping in his reform projects as time went on, Richelieu kept the French government and state together by his remarkable handling of persons and his sense of political expediency. Both traits are nowhere more evident than in his treatment of internal administration. After the Day of Dupes in 1630,[14] Richelieu had an opportunity to overhaul the central government. Instead he simply placed reliable and able "creatures" in the most important positions—Sublet des Noyers as secretary of state for war, Bullion and Bouthillier as superintendents of finances, Chavigny as secretary of state for foreign affairs, Séguier as chancellor (minister of justice). These men, whom he trusted, were given tasks which went far beyond the formal functions of their offices. Those whom he distrusted were either removed from office or given only perfunctory tasks. This highly personal "system" did little to eliminate the divisions of governmental authority which had plagued

13. See Chapter 4 for the problems which Richelieu inherited.
14. See p. 192.

France in the past. What it achieved, as Orest Ranum has pointed out, was a remarkable unity and flexibility at the highest level of decision-making.[15] Richelieu's men not only worked hard to give him responsible advice and to execute the decisions made by the cardinal and his "team"; they also smoothed the relationship between the principal minister and the king. Unlike Philip IV, Louis XIII was no cipher. He wanted to rule, and his ever-changing temperament made it essential for Richelieu's creatures to protect the minister against the king's moods. They submitted Richelieu's proposals to the monarch when he was receptive, placated him when he was angry, warned Richelieu of his illnesses and moods when these turned him against the minister.

Relations between the central, ministerial government and the myriad of institutions beneath were subject to the same pragmatic approach. Richelieu's great rival within the government between 1624 and 1630, Michel de Marillac (of the Devout party), tried his best to change the institutional framework which had troubled Henry IV and Marie de Medici, but Richelieu did not support his reforms. As minister of justice, Marillac drafted a series of reform regulations culminating in the ill-fated law code known as the Code Michau. Marillac wanted to place the royal councils firmly over the *Parlements* (high courts), introduce royal tax officials (*élus*) from the central provinces (*pays d'élections*) into the more independent outlying provinces (*pays d'états*), crush the estates or parliaments of the latter provinces, and in general stamp out local rebellions and weaken the institutions which made them possible. Richelieu's refusal either to support his colleague, or to make the reforms his own after the Day of Dupes had resulted in Marillac's fall, are typical of the cardinal's actions. He was not above petty politics, foresaking Marillac's projects because he was a rival. But he also refused to adopt them because he knew they would increase tensions within the state by alienating the *Parlements*, provincial estates and other elite groups of French society.

While Olivares attempted his Union of Arms,[16] Richelieu bargained and compromised with *Parlements* and provinces. The hated *élus* were withdrawn, and the provinces which had rebelled against Marillac were granted the confirmation of most of their privileges, including that of negotiating subsidies through provincial estates. Provincial governors were replaced by more loyal men if they rebelled, but the important and quasi-independent office of governor was retained. The *Parlements* proved less amenable to such tactics. The French monarchy came to realize that the law courts would not condemn treason by the great nobles and princes

15. O. A. Ranum, *Richelieu and the Councillors of Louis XIII.*
16. See p. 198.

of France, and that the judges were determined to refuse registration of
fiscal legislation. Richelieu did not hesitate to try crimes of lese-majesty
by special, hand-picked commissions, nor to hold royal parlementary
sessions (*lits de justice*) to override judicial review, nor even to imprison
and exile the most hostile judges. But he never allowed such contests of
strength to get out of hand. Often he kept the king from giving vent
to his anger at the *Parlements*, while quietly negotiating a settlement with
the judges. He was willing to withdraw particularly objectionable taxes,
and to accept compromises over other financial expedients. Louis XIII
thundered at the judges in the *Parlement* of Paris that they were not to
interfere in the affairs of *his* state. Richelieu felt that the state was doing
well when it kept such interference to a minimum. A royal regulation
in 1641 institutionalized this modification of old royal-parlementary
relations by placing limits on judicial review. But this reform came only
at the end of the reign, and did not eliminate the right of review. The
Parlements were by no means rendered impotent; after 1643, under a less
skillful manipulator of men and institutions, they would prove just how
ephemeral had been the achievements of Richelieu.

The emergence of intendants was the one major institutional development under Richelieu. Intendancies had their origin in the traditional
royal practice of commissioning officials and private persons to take
charge of special problems on a temporary basis. Masters of Requests,
for example, were frequently detached from their positions in the royal
councils and sent to the provinces to report on corruption and disobedience by tax officials and petty law courts. The commissions entrusted
with treason trials under Richelieu were also an outgrowth of this practice. Before Richelieu's time there had been a few instances of commissioners staying on in a locality after their commissioned work was
accomplished, becoming the local officials' permanent rivals and threatening to supersede them. It is doubtful that Richelieu desired to turn a
useful, but temporary, check on officials into another echelon of the
already complex and confused government. Permanent intendancy was
not in keeping with his approach to administrative problems, nor his
relations with the *Parlements*. What probably happened during his ministry was that the incessant financial demands of war and the interminable
revolts and plots which the law courts proved unable and unwilling to
curb, led naturally to the creation of quasi-permanent commissions in
virtually every province of the realm. Whatever the causes, the period
between 1630 and 1635 was crucial in the transformation of commissioners into intendants. By Richelieu's death, intendants existed everywhere, and were entrusted with very wide discretionary powers which
virtually permitted them to tax and judge with the assistance of local

judges and tax bureaus. In several instances, the intendants went beyond their commissions and tried rebels, collected taxes and in general upheld royal authority without regard to local authorities. The lesser law courts and taxing bureaus were virtually deprived of their major functions, and the *Parlements* lost control of appellate jurisdiction. There were cries of anguish by the judicial and financial officials, who had bought their positions and now saw their prestige, power and opportunities for corruption eroding. Although they were too divided and too demoralized to counterattack under Richelieu, they were rapidly reaching a point of desperation which would lead to rebellions after the cardinal-minister and his king died.

Just as Richelieu avoided reforming political institutions, he had no intention of disturbing the hierarchical structure of society. Being of petty noble stock, he yearned to enhance the position of the nobility. He was a member of the clerical estate, as bishop of Luçon and then cardinal, and at the Estates General of 1614–1615 had been the clergy's orator and an impassioned apologist for the participation of clerics in politics. His exemplary handling of diocesan affairs in impoverished Luçon, and his orthodox writings on theological issues gave no hint that a secular politician hid behind the priest's dress. Richelieu was certainly more knowledgeable in economic matters than appears at first glance, but he had no intention of elevating the merchant and financier above the traditional pillars of society—the nobility and clergy. His many economic projects of the 1620's compare favorably with Olivares' schemes for revitalizing the Spanish economy; but they were meant to strengthen France's commerce, industry and agriculture, not to elevate the Third Estate. The tariff protection of native industries; creation of trading companies for the Atlantic, Mediterranean and Pacific waters; permission for nobles to engage in maritime commerce without loss of noble status; elevation of ship owners and wholesale merchants to the nobility and the consolidation of naval and commercial affairs under Richelieu's personal direction were all conceived as means to break the commercial might of England and the Dutch, and to provide more wealth for France's military needs. As for the poor in the towns and countryside, the cardinal viewed them in very traditional terms, when he thought of them at all. They were meant to work, and to be kept poor. Richelieu believed that luxury and leisure made the lower classes restless, arrogant and a threat to social stability. Like his counterparts elsewhere in Europe, he was fearful that social inferiors might escape their destined lot through education. "The great number of colleges which exist in our realm permits the poorest [parents] to have their children educated," he wrote with sadness. The undesirable consequence was that "Few can be found who will engage in trade or war."

In fact, Richelieu's highest hopes were dashed and his deepest fears realized. The cardinal discovered that although the nobility, particularly the great nobles and princes, wanted a return to grandeur, they were unwilling to pay the price of serving under the state. Before he died, many of their castles were torn down, their symbol of independence—the duel—was punished by execution of the worst offenders, arch rebels were executed, the princes excluded from the inner circle of royal advisors and nobleman-generals subordinated to non-noble civilian administrators like Sublet des Noyers. The greatest offender, Gaston d'Orléans, could not be touched, since he was brother of the king and until 1638 heir presumptive to the throne. But Gaston's noble followers, who used him as the figurehead for plots and rebellions against Louis XIII and Richelieu, were mercilessly dispatched from this world by order of special commissions. When the king shrank from giving "justice" to the great nobles, whom he viewed as part of his family, Richelieu persuaded him that mercy had to be tempered by punishment when crimes against the state were involved. While central and eastern European monarchs were playing on social divisions and forcing the "great ones" into the mold of a service nobility, the French nobles were cut adrift from the body politic. It was little consolation to them that they retained their social position and exemption from most taxes. They had been humbled, humiliated and weakened; the only way they knew to fight back was with their swords. During Richelieu's last years, noble revolts were fewer and, with the exception of Cinq Mars' conspiracy in 1642, less dangerous. The nobility were biding their time, until their friend-turned-tormenter passed from the scene.

Richelieu was more successful in his manipulation of religious issues. While the Devout party was virtually destroyed, the Catholic church in France retained its strong position within the framework of the secular state. The crown saw that religious men who were also loyal to the state were placed in charge of bishoprics and abbacies. These men did much to elevate the religious and moral life of their charges. Moreover, in the periodic assemblies of the clergy they could be counted on to increase the so-called "free gift" that the church paid to the state in lieu of regular taxation. The Gallican-ultramontanist question [17] was not resolved, but was kept quiet by Richelieu's practice of curbing pro-papal, anti-divine-right literature and dissuading the anti-papal *Parlements* from launching their own investigations of such tracts.

The royal seizure of Protestant La Rochelle and the subsequent Peace of Alais in 1629 did not "solve" the Catholic-Protestant conflict in France, but it went far towards restoring religious-civil peace in the

17. See Chapter 4, pp. 108–109.

kingdom. At Alais, the Edict of Nantes [18] was confirmed, and Huguenots were left with most of their churches and the right to worship. The military privileges which Henry IV had bestowed in addition to the Edict, and the political assemblies which had developed under Marie de Medici, disappeared. Ultra-Catholics were angry at Richelieu for this compromise, but the Day of Dupes left them without power in the royal government. Transformed from a state within the state to mere subjects, the Huguenots began to lose their separateness, and were singularly unmoved by the revolts of Richelieu's last years and the rebellions against Mazarin.

Far less fortunate was the cardinal's experience with the lower echelons of society. His grand schemes for encouraging commerce, industry and agriculture, his hopes of keeping the base of society submissive and respectful of political and social superiors, all foundered. Once he persuaded Louis XIII to place war with Spain before internal reform, there was no hope for economic prosperity or social harmony. War merely added to the underlying economic and social problems of the time. To finance the campaigns, the crown resorted to measures which were economically disastrous, fiscally unsound and morally questionable. Indirect taxes on beverages and meats raised the cost of living for poor townsmen to dangerous heights. Peasants not only were hounded by intendants bent on wringing land taxes from them, but also had to house and supply troops who were frequently quartered on French soil between campaigns. Blocks of new offices in law courts, taxing bureaus, town governments and guilds were put up for sale; the purchasers quickly tried to secure a return on their investment by charging the public for their services. Not even the well-to-do members of the *Parlements* and taxing bureaus were immune to financial pressures. Salaries were withheld, and fees had to be shared with new colleagues. Despite these desperate measures, the treasury was still short of cash. The crown had to float loans bearing exorbitant interest rates (and often including the right of the lender to collect taxes) in order to balance the budget. Richelieu resignedly admitted that tax farmers and state creditors were virtually left "to treat the king's subjects according to their boundless appetites," and he predicted disorders comparable to those which Olivares faced in Spain.

Disorders did occur in province after province during the 1630's, usually taking the form of peasant uprisings against tax agents, but occasionally gaining the support of the urban poor and even the tacit approval of the *Parlements*, which failed to take strong repressive measures. Luckily

18. See Chapter 4, pp. 107–108.

for Richelieu, these provincial rebellions did not all occur at the same time, and he was careful to avoid antagonizing the populace of Paris and to compromise with the chief *Parlement* which met in that city. When revolts occurred, he was quick to call the rebels "wicked men," who set a "bad example." Military repression and summary trials without the slightest legal formalities discouraged others from such wickedness. If Richelieu's is the most fascinating of public careers in the seventeenth century, it is difficult to ignore the fact that his foreign and domestic policies were executed at the sacrifice of innocent men, and that they led to a mid-century crisis in France which came closer to sheer anarchy than did those in any other European state, including England and Muscovy.

❧ *Mazarin and the Fronde*

When Louis XIII followed his minister to the grave in 1643, he was succeeded by a king five years of age, who ruled through a regency government headed by the queen-mother, Anne of Austria, and her advisor, Cardinal Mazarin, a protégé of Richelieu. It was an unfortunate time for a change in government personnel. Anne and Mazarin had little opportunity to learn how to deal with the crisis which faced them. Anne was determined to maintain royal authority for the young Louis XIV, but her fits of temper served to intensify the antagonisms inside the realm. Mazarin was very different from Richelieu. His policy of dividing and ruling, of buying off the opposition, of exiling and imprisoning rather than using the executioner's axe, ultimately undermined the rebel forces which he faced. Initially, however, it made a bad situation worse. The great nobles and parlementary judges who had feared and respected Richelieu, had nothing but contempt and hatred for his successor. Mazarin's Italian birth was a fact which he could not live down, even though he had become a naturalized Frenchman. Nor was he able to mold his own creatures into a harmonious team, as Richelieu had done.

The result was the series of reform movements and rebellions known collectively as the Fronde, and more precisely as the First or Parlementary Fronde (1648–1649) and the Second or Noble Fronde (1650–1653). While provincial rebellions continued to erupt as they had under Richelieu, the contagion now spread to Paris, capital city and seat of the most prestigious *Parlement* as well as three other high courts. Attempts to force new fiscal measures through the *Parlement* of Paris, and to impose new taxes on Parisians through special commissions, were resisted by parlementary veto and street demonstrations led by poor and wealthy alike. In the summer of 1648 an assembly of representatives from the four law courts in Paris drafted a series of reform proposals for Anne's approval. She could not recall troops from the Franco-Spanish conflict, and her attempt to arrest leading judges was thwarted by a massive riot in the heart of the capital. In October, 1648, the *Parlement* of Paris secured her approval of most of the reforms. A belated effort to recall troops during the following winter when seasonal conditions halted the fighting with Spain was fruitless. Paris and the *Parlement* were beseiged by royal forces, but the city held out, and in the spring of 1649, Anne had to reconfirm the reforms. Mazarin thought that the "best part of the monarchy" had been abolished; certainly the reforms wiped out the gains which Richelieu had so cautiously and painfully made. Taxes in town and countryside were slashed, and in many parts of the realm it became impossible to collect any taxes. The intendants, except in six border provinces, were removed. Guarantees against arbitrary detention of judges and ordinary subjects were made. It was stated that in future tax legislation must be subjected to judicial review in the appropriate law courts. Royal authority virtually collapsed, and the crown's financial position had already forced a declaration of bankruptcy in mid-1648.

Anne and Mazarin had no time to regroup their forces against the reforms of 1648. The princes and great nobles began making their own demands, first as the generals of the rebel parlementary army which defended Paris in 1649, and then in 1650 on their own. Two noble factions emerged. One, headed by the king's cousin, Condé, was most interested in raising revolts in the provinces; its leading members seemed bent on strengthening the power of their provincial governorships. The other, grouped around the Cardinal de Retz, was more concerned with ousting Mazarin, making Retz the chief minister, and securing other ministerial positions for his followers. It is impossible to follow the chaotic course of this second, noble Fronde. In 1651, the two factions and the *Parlement* of Paris combined against the crown, forcing Mazarin's exile from France. On other occasions Retz joined the queen-mother in a civil war with Condé's party. The rest of the population was equally confused and divided. Unlike mid-century crises in east-central Europe, and to a greater extent than in England's revolution;[19] the Fronde degenerated into near anarchy. Divisions between social groups hardened, and within each group there were royalists, rebels and would-be neutralists. The havoc created by royal and rebel troops, the subjection of districts to forced taxation by both sides, the dislocation of merchants' business, the

19. For a fuller comparison with England's revolution, see Chapter 8, pp. 215–216, 218.

demoralization of the urban poor—who hated Mazarin more than did any other group, but who wanted most of all to escape starvation—made an indelible impression on an entire generation of Frenchmen.

In the midst of this terrifying experience, surrounded by enemies, Mazarin used his talents with consummate skill. He turned the noble factions against each other, and managed an extensive network of spies and secret agents which bribed key individuals in the *Parlement* of Paris and other law courts, municipal governments and merchant groups. What bribery could not accomplish, was achieved by the gradual build-up of royal armies against the noble rebels, the war weariness of the population, and the growing hostility of parlementary judges to the lawlessness and haughty attitudes of the noble rebels. In 1652, Condé's army was virtually wiped out before the gates of Paris, and the temporary reign of terror which he and the survivors unleashed in the capital turned Paris against him. When Mazarin agreed to return to exile, few could see any reason for holding out against the crown. In October of 1652, Louis XIV and Anne made a triumphal entry to the capital. Condé held out in southern France for a few months, but in 1653 the last provincial rebellion was put down and Condé was forced to carry on his personal fight as a commander in the Spanish armies. That same year, Mazarin felt safe enough to return to Paris, and the man whom most Frenchmen had come to detest was given a tumultuous welcome.

The Fronde was over, but the crown still was hampered by the reforms of 1648, most of which remained in force. During Mazarin's last decade in power, he did little to undo the work of the *Parlement* of Paris and the other courts. Eradicating the reforms was not as simple as it might seem. No one wanted another civil war, and it was inconceivable that the French nobility could undertake one. But the *Parlements* at Paris and in the provinces, protected by the offices which their members had bought and by the refusal of many subjects to endure new taxes, new intendants and new judicial commissions, were prepared to resist encroachments on the reforms of the Fronde. Mazarin's brilliant, energetic personal secretary, Jean-Baptiste Colbert, urged the chief minister to take the initiative against the law courts, but Mazarin's cautious personality and his more optimistic interpretation of conditions would not permit him to yield to the pleas of the future minister of Louis XIV. Here and there intendants did creep back into the provinces, sometimes to stay, sometimes to be chased away by the populace, the local estates or the law courts. Some taxes were approved by the *Parlements,* but others were successfully resisted by judges and ordinary subjects. It was left for Louis XIV and Colbert to take advantage of the demoralization of French society and the divisions among and within social groups which lingered on long after the Fronde. Perhaps Mazarin himself realized that the future Grand Monarch, untainted by the rebellions, might accomplish what he—a foreigner and one too closely identified with the horrors of the Fronde—could not do.[20]

20. On France under Louis XIV, see Chapter 10.

8.

Republicanism in England and the Dutch Netherlands

The temporary abolition of monarchy by the English in 1649 and the reassertion of republicanism by the Dutch in 1650 remind us that the mid-century crises were not universally favorable to the monarchical cause. Why was it that the Stuart and Orange dynasties suffered such serious setbacks, while the French Bourbons and Spanish Hapsburgs survived comparable tensions and perhaps bloodier civil wars? In answering that question, it is not enough to say that Dutch republican institutions made Orangist authoritarianism impossible, or that England was so different from continental monarchies that Stuart "despotism" was bound to fail. To do so would be to ignore the power of the Stuarts and Orangists in the first quarter of the seventeenth century. If James I could rule England virtually without Parliament from 1610 to 1621, and Maurice could use the Arminian-orthodox religious quarrel of 1618–1619 to enhance his position in the Dutch Republic, there was obviously some hope for their successors during the second quarter of the century. Much depended on how they responded to the tensions which continued to plague their states after 1625. We must also look to the broader results of the English and Dutch crises to see how much they damaged the Stuart and Orange lines. Finally, it is important to see how the misfortunes of the princely families affected the state. A close look at these questions will reveal that neither the Stuarts nor the Orangists were irreparably weakened, and that the state itself was actually strengthened by the mid-century crises.

England Under Charles I

In 1625, Charles I became king of England amid hopes that his reign would be happier than that of his father.[1] Apart from his tendency to drift with events, there was little indication of the flaws in his character which would bring him to the scaffold in 1649. In fact, the young Charles was a pleasant contrast to James I. Charles' unhappy childhood, an unfortunate speech impediment and a certain slowness of mind made him more reserved, less self-assured and generally less obnoxious than his garrulous, pompous and pedantic father. Time would harden and distort those traits, and turn the reluctant king into a suspicious, uncompromising and deceitful ruler. But Charles' first years were marked by the continuation of James I's problems, without his irritating personality.

Although Charles did little to influence the course of public events between 1625 and 1629, circumstances played into his hands. At first, his favorite, the Duke of Buckingham, almost destroyed the good will of the political and social elite. The patronage-conscious Buckingham continued James' mismanagement of finances, to the sole benefit of his family circle. As Lord Admiral, he also involved England in futile, petty wars with Spain and France. England suffered little more than a loss of prestige; but at a time when the Thirty Years' War was advancing the cause of the Spanish and Austrian Catholic states, it was damaging to the English monarchy that it could do nothing on behalf of Protestantism. Parliament, which had been revived during James' last years, continued to obstruct and criticize the foreign and domestic policies supported by Charles and Buckingham. Fortunately, the assassination of Buckingham in 1628 removed the man who had swayed the king and had done so much to weaken royal finances and popularity. The seasoned leaders of parliamentary opposition also disappeared from the scene: Eliot died in jail, and Coke of old age, while Wentworth defected to the side of the crown.

Parliament overplayed its hand by its obstructionism. The plight of the leaders in the House of Commons is evident. They thought in terms of conserving what they considered to be traditional checks on the crown, not of making a conscious bid for parliamentary sovereignty. Their hesitant tactics had the effect of starving the monarchy of the money neces-

---

1. See Chapter 4 for James I's reign.

sary for running the state while falling short of giving Parliament the power to carry out its own policies. Thus Parliament in the name of tradition and responsibility seemed to be violating traditional royal rights and making all government impossible.

Parliament began Charles' reign by refusing to grant the revenues (especially customs duties) which were traditionally renewed at the outset of each reign. Having impoverished the treasury, the parliamentarians then demanded a vigorous war effort against Catholic Spain. This was followed by the Petition of Right in 1628, which condemned the crown for financing ordinary and wartime needs by "illegal" (i.e., executive) means. That famous petition attacked forced loans, the arbitrary imprisonment of those who resisted them, the compulsory billeting of troops in private houses while they waited to embark for the continent and the use of martial law in settling disputes between soldiers and civilians. Charles tried to halt parliamentary criticism by a grudging assent to the petition and the prorogation of Parliament. But when it was reconvened in 1629, the House of Commons became more daring. The royalist Speaker of the House was held in his chair while three inflammatory resolutions were passed. Payment of custom duties was equated with treason. Royal advisors responsible for their collection were branded as public enemies. The quasi-Catholic tendencies of the Anglican church (High Church policies) were condemned in harsh language. While the Commons' leaders thought that these three resolutions were implementations of the Petition of Right, they were in fact far more radical than the spirit of the petition. When Charles dissolved Parliament in protest, he undoubtedly had widespread sympathy in the realm. This sympathy, coupled with the conclusion of the ill-fated and costly continental wars, placed the king in an excellent position to rule. In 1630, Charles was probably in a better position than either Olivares in Spain or Richelieu in France.

The period from the dismissal of the Parliament of 1628–1629 to its next convocation in 1640 is variously known as the "eleven years' tyranny" and the "personal rule" of Charles I. Neither description is fair or accurate. Charles was no tyrant, nor was he his own first minister. Factionalism emerged within his government, and Charles' personal feelings were obscured by his habit of vacillating between the thoroughness expounded and practiced by Wentworth and Laud, and the desire of his French wife, Henrietta Maria, and her coterie to get rich and absolute quickly. Towards the middle of the 1630's, Laud came close to being the dominant figure in the administration, but by the end of the decade the king was supporting his wife's desire to run roughshod over all opposition. Consequently, his government combined irresponsible despotism and benevolent paternalism to fall short of effective tyranny. G. E. Aylmer has summarized the situation cleverly: "Charles' trouble was that he willed the end without always willing the means to achieve it; he wanted to be an absolute monarch without all the bother and unpleasantness involved." [2]

Despite the limitations inherent in Charles' vacillation and the rivalries within his administration, the 1630's were a remarkable period of royal resurgence. The brains and determination of William Laud and Thomas Wentworth made their "thorough" policy highly effective. Although it was often brutal and reprehensible, their attitude can be termed responsible authoritarianism. The historian finds himself torn between sympathy for the goal of effective, efficient government and revulsion at the means which were deemed necessary to the end. Neither Laud nor Wentworth hesitated to override common law principles and human considerations. As Wentworth wrote to Laud, "a little violence and extraordinary means" were justifiable. In the more antiseptic language of modern historians removed from the moral issues, "thorough" stood for vigorous, economical and disinterested government, based on the legal and financial resources which the constitution provided.

As head of the Irish government after 1632, Wentworth cleverly stepped outside the common law which protected the English settlers' defrauding of church and state. He achieved the rare feat of making the Irish government self-sufficient, while restoring church lands and incidentally increasing his personal fortune. As Bishop of London and then Archbishop of Canterbury, Laud strengthened the Anglican church's financial position and made it a bulwark of religious orthodoxy and royal authority. For example, Laud sought to make nominal tithe-giving an actual 10 percent tax on the Anglican laity. He also tried to elevate the church in dignity and authority—to make it a High Church. The importance of the sacraments and clergy was stressed by railing off the communion table from the congregation. Well-educated, orthodox priests were appointed to bishoprics. Meanwhile, Laud persecuted Puritans within the church, who equated his High Church tendencies with Roman Catholicism, and countered with their own emphasis on preaching, upright living and service to the community. The church's special Court of High Commission was effectively used to hound those who opposed Laudian High Church principles. Puritan holders of church "lectureships" were harassed, and Puritan pamphleteers were whipped, pilloried, branded and even mutilated by loss of their ears.

No less spectacular were the efforts of Charles' servants to improve

---

2. G. E. Aylmer, *A Short History of 17th Century England: 1603–1689* (Mentor, 1963), 87.

the position of the treasury. Buckingham's misuse of royal patronage gradually gave way to a reduction in government spending and an increase in revenues. The customs duties were increased above the level achieved under James I, and the farmers of some customs were forced to increase the amount they paid to the crown for the privilege of administering the system. Half-forgotten laws and royal rights were revived as fiscal expedients. Fines were imposed on those whose ancestors had encroached on royal forests. Persons whose annual income exceeded forty pounds were liable to the "privilege" of being knighted (for a fee, of course). The most controversial of the old laws which were adapted to current fiscal needs was "ship money." The crown had the right to demand ships or money from coastal areas for commercial and national defense. In 1636, ship money payments were requested not only from ports, but from inland areas as well, on the argument that the navy protected all Englishmen. Since the levy was made on clergy as well as laity, and was administered in a relatively efficient manner by sheriffs rather than by less amenable authorities, it proved very lucrative. All told, royal revenues rose some 40 percent during the 1630's, although it proved impossible to forego borrowing to balance the budget. Neither Richelieu nor Olivares came close to achieving the reduction in costs and the increase in revenue which were realized in England during that decade.

❧ The Collapse of Royal Authority

To discover why Stuart authority collapsed so quickly after the 1630's, we must look first of all at the opposition to Charles which grew in the late 1630's and came into the open in 1640–1641. The core of that opposition came from the political and social elite of England, and to a degree from conquered Ireland and the Scottish kingdom which was under Charles I's nominal rule. The political-social establishment had been uneasy about James I's tendency to run roughshod over them. During the 1630's, English merchants and landowners, Scottish lairds and English settlers in Ireland were further alienated by the "thorough" policy which threatened their freedom, wealth and influence. There was little likelihood that all the social groups who considered themselves the natural leaders of the realm would break completely with Charles. There was, however, a general disenchantment with him which gradually turned a sizeable percentage of the political-social elite against him. Such a split in the governing classes was more serious in the British Isles than in any continental monarchy, because of the institutional, legal unity of England proper and the relatively mild social divisions within the English elite.

When civil war came to England in 1642, the division between royalists and rebels was not primarily one of class, and hence Charles had a harder time dividing and ruling than did the Spanish monarchy. Moreover, social cohesion among the rebels kept them from splitting until after they had Charles at their mercy. This situation was in contrast to that in France, where the Fronde was really two revolts led by the rival groups of old nobles and newly ennobled judges, a situation which allowed the French monarchy to win the civil war. Moreover, when revolution came to England, the legal, institutional unity of the government gave the rebels a much better chance of seizing power than was the case in the more loosely organized French and Spanish states.

If more were known about the role of the lower social orders in the 1630's and 1640's we would be in an even better position to analyze Charles' collapse. It seems that the poor in town and countryside played a relatively small role, compared with the elite in and out of Parliament, and with the lower classes of continental western Europe. But it also appears that this minimal role was important, both in a positive and a negative sense. In the positive sense, lower-class demonstrations against royal conscription and agitations by the London "mob" against Charles' ministers, goaded (and perhaps frightened) the rebellious elite into a more radical attack on monarchy than they would have undertaken on their own. It is true that those lower-class movements and the rioting against the wealthy landowners' enclosure of common lands also probably turned many of Charles' would-be opponents into reluctant royalists; nevertheless, they did not save the monarchy. In negative terms, the limited involvement of the lower orders in the struggle between Charles and the elite saved England from the anarchy of the continental civil wars, anarchy which could have swung opinion towards the monarchy and helped the ruler to win the civil wars, as it did in France and Spain. (The shift of sentiment back to monarchy did come, but largely after the monarchy had been abolished.)

The role of Puritanism in uniting the lower and upper social orders of England is still more debatable. It is probable that Puritanism (in the broadest sense) did play a role in rallying many people against the High Church intransigence of Laud, and against the king who supported him. We can also speculate that Puritanism may have given its supporters an élan which was lacking in the continental rebellions. For the Puritans were tinged with the Calvinist belief that they were on God's side, predestined to Heaven after death, and His divinely blessed agents while on earth. This belief in the rightness of their cause, this optimistic fatalism, was held by only a minority of the opposition to Charles, but a minority with a mission can often dominate.

For the opposition to realize its potential, a crisis was needed which would undermine royal authority and at the same time solidify objections to Charles. That crisis came in the form of a revolt in Scotland. Instead of sputtering out like the revolt of Catalonia against Spain, the Scottish uprising became a struggle for power in England itself. Charles precipitated the crisis by ruling through a dangerously small native elite of courtiers and bishops. This antagonized the majority of Scotsmen, who were left out of political power. When Charles tried to alter the church service in Scotland in 1637, a national resistance movement sprang up overnight. Acting forcefully for once, the king made the ill-fated decision to raise an English army against the rebellion. There were immediate repercussions in England. War upset the delicately balanced budget of the 1630's, drastically increasing the treasury's needs and at the same time encouraging English opposition to existing taxes. Despite a decision by the Court of Exchequer that ship money could be collected without parliamentary approval (the Hampden Case of 1637), English taxpayers balked at paying their assessments. Before the Hampden Case, all but 3.5 percent of ship money assessments were paid; in 1638, the level of payments dropped to 39 percent; by 1640, the tax revolt reduced income from the levy to a trickle. Nor did Charles have an easy time conscripting Englishmen into his army. Rioting took place in several areas. What had started as a crisis comparable to that of Spain was fast becoming a national uprising similar to the Fronde.

At this critical moment in 1640, Charles' true character began to emerge. He mixed vacillation, duplicity and stubbornness to ruin what chances he had of extricating himself from the mess he had created. Charles had two alternatives—to make a firm peace with the Scots, or to convoke the first English Parliament in a decade and request financial support to put down the Scottish revolt. The policy which was developed by Charles and his advisors was neither one nor the other, but a bungling combination of both. With the Scots Charles tried duplicity, securing a truce by promising concessions which he had no intention of making. With Parliament, he used a mixture of vacillation and obstinacy. He had excellent advice from Wentworth, who was recalled from Ireland to handle the Scottish-English troubles. Wentworth knew Parliament from his days as a parliamentary opponent of Charles; he advised keeping it in session until it gave way to the king's financial demands. But at the first sign of opposition, Charles discarded Wentworth's plan and abruptly dissolved Parliament. A potentially conciliatory assembly became the Short Parliament.

After the Short Parliament, Charles and Wentworth agreed that the truce with the Scots should be broken and the war resumed. The Scots were too strong for Charles' underpaid and mutinous army, and carried the war into northern England. Charles was not only compelled to end hostilities and disband his army, but forced by the Scots, leading English peers and some of his own councilors to call another English Parliament to meet the indemnity the Scots demanded. The new assembly was the famous Long Parliament, which destroyed royal authority and by its intransigence proved that it had been a tragic mistake for Charles to dissolve the Short Parliament.

The initial reform measures of the Long Parliament, during 1640 and 1641, closely resemble the parlementary or reform period of the Fronde in France (1648–1649).[3] In England as in France, the collapse of royal finances and widespread dislike of the crown's policies allowed a major institution, controlled by the opposition, to force sweeping reforms on the monarchy. The fact that the institution was an assembly of estates in England and a high court of law in France does not detract from the similarity. The attack by the *Parlement* of Paris on royal councils, intendants, arbitrary justice and taxation differed little from the parliamentary measures. The Long Parliament abolished special royal tribunals, ended arbitrary imprisonment and made taxation subject to parliamentary approval. And while the Parlement of Paris outlawed the chief minister and forced the dismissal of the finance minister, the English Parliament put Laud in prison and Wentworth to death. In both countries, the initial reform period of the revolution destroyed the most objectionable instruments of arbitrary rule and struck at those who were most likely to use the remaining royal powers in an authoritarian way.

After the initial reform period, however, the path pursued by the English revolution was very different from the course of the Fronde in France. In both cases, divisions within the realm led to civil war between crown and opposition. However, the English rebels managed to put together a coalition which overwhelmed the monarchy, while the Frondeurs divided and quarrelled among themselves and permitted the crown to win the war.

The hardening of the lines in England began during the reform period. Religious and political issues pushed some parliamentarians into a more radical opposition to the untrustworthy Charles, while they made reluctant royalists out of others. A radical Puritan "Root and Branch" petition, which aimed at destroying the power of the Anglican bishops, drew the ire of Anglicans and moderate Puritans in both houses of Parliament. Many moderate foes of Charles became royalists when radical parliamentarians put a new royal army, raised to fight an Irish rebellion,

---

3. See Chapter 7, pp. 207–208.

under parliamentary control. When the radical parliamentarians went on to demand legislative control of the remaining prerogatives of the crown, civil war was almost inevitable. Charles failed in a last attempt to regain control over Parliament. He tried to arrest the ringleaders of the opposition, only to discover that they had escaped to safety in London. Having made himself look like the fool playing tyrant, he decided to withdraw from the capital, rally the parliamentary moderates and other royalists to his side, and decide the contest by civil war.

Charles proceeded to lose the civil war (1642–1646) as well as the battle for control of Parliament. He failed to take advantage of his military strength while it lasted. His army was far superior to the hastily assembled forces of the parliamentary radicals and might have struck decisively at London, or advanced steadily from the royalist-controlled areas of the north and west. Instead of concentrating on one of these objectives, the royalists tried both strategies and failed to realize either. The war became one of mild attrition, during which the rebels drew on their superior resources. They fully exploited their control over the wealthier, southeastern area of England, and organized a New Model Army of "Roundheads" which was well paid, well disciplined and recruited on the basis of ability to fight. By contrast, Charles' "Cavalier" army suffered increasingly from the weak economic base of the area under his control. The rebels also kept religious disputes and rivalries between parliamentarians and generals from coming into the open. The Presbyterian majority in Parliament (desiring a loose organization of individual congregations) got along with the army's Independents (who wanted each congregation to have full autonomy). Both agreed to make an alliance with the Presbyterian Scots. This Solemn League and Covenant placed the Scottish army on the side of the English rebels, on the understanding that the Anglican church would be given a Presbyterian organization. The Scottish-Roundhead armies were simply too much for the weakened Cavaliers. After losing the initial battles due to incompetent leadership, the rebels found a military genius in Oliver Cromwell. In 1646, Charles turned himself over to the mercy of the Scots.

The Republican Experiment and Royal Restoration

In 1646, Charles I still had a chance to save his throne and his life, since virtually all his opponents were willing to bargain over a peace settlement and few dreamed of suggesting a republican solution. The king's most hostile enemies, the Roundhead Independents, wanted strong guarantees of religious toleration, and firm checks on what remained of royal authority after the reform period of 1640–1641. The Presbyterian majority in Parliament were willing to trust Charles far more, provided he convert the Church of England into a Presbyterian church. The Scottish forces wanted to be paid for their part in the civil war; they were willing to settle for money and a Presbyterian state church in England.

It is difficult to look back on the events of 1646–1648 and determine what Charles should have done in bargaining with the victors in the civil war. All we know is that the monarch did the logical thing and that it proved to be the last and most fatal mistake of his tragic life. Charles took advantage of the divisions within the opposition, and made a deal with its moderate elements, the Parliamentary Presbyterians and the Scottish army. Unfortunately this pitted Charles against the Roundhead Independents, who were not only his most radical foes but also the most powerful militarily. A brief war in 1648 between Charles' new coalition and the Independents under Cromwell resulted in victory for the latter. Thus Charles unwittingly resolved all the issue of the English mid-century crisis to the advantage of those most hostile to his cause. Moreover, his willingness to side with Presbyterianism and limited monarchy after opposing both in 1642 made him seem unprincipled. The Independents had particular reason for distrusting him. They began to believe that no agreement with Charles would last, and that he had to be killed to save the revolution's gains. Thus Charles not only threw power into the hands of his most extreme enemies, but made them far more radical than they had been two years earlier.

The repercussions of the debacle of 1648 were immediate. In 1648–1649, the House of Lords was abolished, the House of Commons reduced to a Rump of Independent members by the expulsion of its Presbyterian majority (Pride's Purge) and Charles executed as a "tyrant, traitor, murderer and public enemy of the good people of this nation." His death was followed by the proclamation of a republic. While Cromwell and his Roundheads struck at royalty and moderate revolutionaries, they also lashed out at the left wing of their own group, the "Levellers." This movement had gained strong support among the common soldiers of the Roundhead army as well as within the lower social orders in London. Cromwell and the commanders were but the victorious element of the political-social establishment, which had split in 1640–1642. The Levellers wanted to bend that establishment so that parliamentary elections would be based on a broader suffrage. They also wanted to protect the interests of the poor against the rich; they requested toleration for minor Protestant sects which even the tolerant Independents opposed; and they desired an end to the most glaring abuses of economic power wielded by the wealthy against the poor. The Levellers stopped short of full political democracy and far short of economic equality, but their demands frightened the Cromwellians. Cromwell's fellow generals confused the political Levellers with a much smaller and rather harmless group of social Levellers (Diggers) and feared an attack on the principle of private property. Cromwell himself feared political and social anarchy, although he was tolerant of radical Protestant sects. He put the situation strongly to his peers, "You have no other way to deal with these men but to break them in pieces. . . . If you do not break them they will break you." In 1649, the generals put down mutinies within the army and purged the military of its Leveller elements.

Victories against the right and left in 1648–1649 ensured that the Roundhead Independents would control England in the next few years. And since Cromwell was the leader of the Roundhead army, he became the real ruler of the state. The republic was in reality a military dictatorship, disguised by a facade of Parliaments and constitutions. It achieved order, and it attempted to rule on behalf of the principles of the revolution, but it never acquired legitimacy or popularity. Without these qualities, the regime could never be assured that it would survive after the death of its great leader.

Cromwell was a convinced parliamentarian, but he failed in his efforts to transform military rule into a legitimate parliamentary system. In his new capacity as head of the state, Cromwell experienced Charles I's problem of obstructionist Parliaments. Added to his difficulties was the fact that the republican Parliaments expected a much larger role in politics than they had under Charles and were hopelessly divided over the means to achieve true republicanism. Until 1653, Cromwell tried to rule with a makeshift republican structure consisting of the Rump Parliament and a Council of State composed of army officers, parliamentarians and himself. Cromwell overthrew that system when the Rump failed to work out a constitutional, legal and religious settlement, which was an unfinished legacy of the Long Parliament. For a few months in 1653, Cromwell ruled with the advice of a Nominated Parliament, chosen by Independent congregations and the military. Cromwell hoped that its godly members would succeed where the Rump had failed. The Nominated Parliament had many ideas, but was badly divided; Cromwell reluctantly abolished it before the year closed. From 1654 until his death in 1658, Cromwell ruled England as Lord Protector, within the framework of a written constitution, the Instrument of Government, drawn up by the army. The constitution was unworkable. It provided for a Parliament elected by pro-Cromwellian property owners, but both Parliaments convoked by Cromwell under the new constitution quarrelled with the Lord

Protector and opposed the Instrument itself. Not even a modification of the document healed the breach between executive and legislature. As a result, Cromwell continued to rely heavily on the army throughout his "civilian" career, at times openly governing and taxing England by means of regional military governors.

Cromwell also failed to reconcile the country to his regime. He could not broaden the base of support which had been narrowed so dangerously by his victories over the Cavaliers and his purging of the Presbyterians. As time went on, Cromwell made those groups still more hostile to his government, while alienating many of his Independent supporters. All three were unhappy with Cromwell's necessary but arbitrary taxes. Merchants discovered that custom duties were no less burdensome than they had been under Charles I. Landowners found to their sorrow that a Cromwellian property tax exceeded the hated ship money levies which it replaced. All three were equally disturbed by Cromwell's religious policies, which ultimately reduced the state church to a mixture of Presbyterianism and Independent Congregationalism, and envisaged toleration of minor Protestant sects as well. The old governing classes either refused to serve as Justices of the Peace, or used their local offices to obstruct the republican tax machinery and to persecute those sects which Cromwell tolerated.

Cromwell was not unsympathetic with the plight of the poor, but his suppression of the Levellers in 1649 and his continued reliance on his fellow generals thereafter made an accommodation with the old left of the revolution impossible. Cromwell's Independent supporters sabotaged his support of lower-class religious sects and failed to reform the unfair, costly and slow legal system despite his urgings. Excise taxes, which had been created by the Long Parliament, pressed heavily on the poor during the republican years. The small master craftsman and the common worker discovered that the Long Parliament had dismantled industrial monopolies, only to leave a mass of privileged guilds run by tight oligarchies. Despite agitations for a more open economic system, the Cromwellian regime actually began to strengthen the forces of privilege in its last years. State machinery for relief of the poor and private philanthropy continued, but society's belief that the poor should be kept alive, docile and at work was if anything strengthened by the Puritan tone of the revolutionary decades.

The greatest Cromwellian successes came in external affairs. The Irish rebellion was crushed in 1649, the Scots subdued by 1652. Ireland came under the grip of an oppressive regime, with Irish Catholics subjected to a harsh penal system and Anglo-Irish settlers losing lands to Cromwellian carpetbaggers. The Highlands of Scotland were also treated as a conquered land. The Scottish Lowlands were more fortunate; the Presbyterian church was recognized and free trade with England sanctioned. However, the Lowlands were subjected to control by English officials and the Presbyterian establishment was weakened by English toleration of other Scottish sects. Cromwell's regime also raised the prestige of England on the continent by a vigorous foreign policy which contrasted with the timid, ineffectual forays of James I and Charles I. A commercial and naval war against the Dutch (1652–1654) weakened England's greatest commercial rival.[4] The alliance with France in the last stages of the Franco-Spanish war started England on its way to being an important European power which would rival France itself by the end of the century. Under Cromwell, England began to acquire the security and sense of purpose which were to make it the envy of the continent in the eighteenth century.

When Cromwell died in 1658, the order which he had established gave way to the divisions in the realm which he had merely kept in check. In a sense, the Cromwellian regime fell by default, since Cromwell's son and successor, Richard, proved incapable of controlling either Parliament or the army. In 1659, the army toppled Richard and restored the old Rump Parliament. However, that *coup d'état* did not resolve the problem of finding a workable replacement for the Cromwellian experiment. The army quarreled with the Rump and split into factions, driving the country into near-anarchy. The restoration of the monarchy was one obvious solution to the country's troubles, but it took an intelligent and personally unambitious Cromwellian general to steer England back from the republican experiment. General Monck brought his troops down from Scotland to London and secured the election of a new Parliament, based on the pre-civil war suffrage. This propertied electorate showed its distaste for military rule and its hope for a repentant Stuart dynasty by choosing a moderately royalist Parliament. The Parliament in turn was heartened by the Declaration of Breda, a very conciliatory political manifesto issued by Charles I's exiled son. Parliament called him back to rule as Charles II.

The Restoration of 1660 gave the impression that the revolution had been in vain. Charles II was given a tumultuous welcome on his entry to London, and is said to have exclaimed, "I never knew that I was so popular in England." Appearances were deceiving, and most Englishmen (including Charles) knew it. For the political-social establishment which had turned against Charles I and hampered Cromwell's efforts was obviously not prepared to allow Charles II to rule on his own. It was,

4. See pp. 229–230.

indeed, likely that the new monarch, lacking the personal magnetism and military power of Cromwell, would have to be far more accommodating to the establishment than the upstart Lord Protector had been. Moreover, the power of that establishment was enhanced by the Long Parliament's abolition of the special royal courts. Since those courts were not restored in 1660, law enforcement became more than ever the domain of local officials who came from the social elite of England. If Charles needed any reminder that he was not a free agent, he had only to recall the fact that his father had been executed for his sins of commission and omission. The tragic end of the father was a lesson which the son never forgot.

Changes in the religious life of England during the 1640's and 1650's also made a return to royal authoritarianism difficult. The old Church of England, which had been a prop of Charles I's throne, lost its overwhelming ascendancy in religious affairs after 1640. Its Presbyterian and Independent elements were removed at the Restoration, and its Anglican structure was restored. However, no one could make the Anglican church the religious monolith which Laud had sought to realize. Protestant sects had survived persecution, and the spirit of dissent could not be willed away. After 1660, the so-called Dissenters were an important counter to the Anglican state church. The position of the Church of England in the political structure of the realm had also been altered by the revolution and the republican experiment. Whereas the church had held the privilege of voting its own taxes for the state, the revolution had taken away that power. And whereas Laud and Charles I had dictated the form of church service and determined orthodoxy, Parliaments dabbled in those matters after 1640. At the Restoration, ultimate control of taxes on the clergy and of religious matters was given to the Restoration Parliament, not to the restored monarchy and the restored church.

The revolutionary and republican decades left an uncertain fiscal legacy for the restored monarchy. Cromwell had been far more successful than Charles I in securing income, but the revolution had strengthened (or if one wishes, given birth to) the tradition of parliamentary control over taxation. Cromwell realized a moderate streamlining of the tax structure, including more rational assessments; Charles inherited this improved machinery, but his Parliaments were to determine how it would be used. Cromwell also had utilized expedients such as the confiscation of royalists' lands and income to swell his treasury; obviously no king could continue such practices. With all the power that Cromwell had wielded, the republican regime had left an enormous deficit. Charles II was promised a fixed annual income which fell short of the Lord Protector's revenue from ordinary sources. It was impossible for the new monarch to run his government without turning to Parliament for additional money.

Thus Charles II, though he dated his reign from the moment of his father's martyrdom, could not turn back the clock to that moment in 1649, much less to 1639. The state had been strengthened between 1640 and 1660 by greater external security and greater financial resources. There was also the prospect of greater harmony internally, since Englishmen wished to avoid a recurrence of the horrors of division and bloodshed. But the monarchy was not the major beneficiary of these developments.

The social and political establishment benefitted most. Although that establishment had split after 1640, the victorious element had not destroyed the defeated ones. Nor did the royalists within the establishment treat the revolutionaries harshly at the Restoration. The two decades of turmoil probably resulted in a shift, but only a moderate one, of opportunity and power from the upper to the middling ranks of England's elite. Many Stuart controls of commerce and industry had been removed, and commercial interests were to have more influence in politics. Royalist landowners could not recover lands which they had "voluntarily" relinquished during the two decades of strife, and they were even harder hit ultimately by indebtedness, which forced many of them into disaster in succeeding decades. But many were able to struggle through and even regain some lands, including those which had been confiscated by the revolution.

The revolution and the Restoration left the urban and rural poor where they had been. In this respect, England's path during the mid-century crisis was the path of the continent. The social Levellers who preached egalitarianism during the revolution were bypassed, then forgotten. The political Levellers, who in any case would have confined the franchise to far less than universal male suffrage, were destroyed. The England of 1660 was still the England of the political, economic and social elite.[5]

The Dutch Netherlands: Orangist Ascendancy and Republican Revival

England's war with Scotland divided the English people and undermined Stuart rule. The long Spanish-Dutch war of 1621–1648 had a very different effect on Dutch politics.[6] War did not end internal tensions,

5. On post-Restoration England, see Chapter 12.
6. See Chapter 4 for the background of the war and Dutch politics before 1621.

but it subordinated them to the popular conflict against the Republic's traditional enemy, and enhanced the position of the House of Orange. The landward provinces and the seafaring population of Zeeland combined patriotism with profiteering. The small native nobility were employed as officers in the state's armies, and the Zeelanders plundered Spanish shipping. Merchants in the anti-Orangist province of Holland were less enthusiastic. They complained that the war harmed their commercial activities, and that they bore the brunt of war taxes while the landward provinces failed to meet their modest quotas. Nevertheless, the Hollanders continued to finance the war. They also watched anxiously as war played into the hands of the Orangists. Frederick Henry (1625–1647) built on the foundations of princely authority laid by his predecessors. The Dutch navy was too decentralized to become the tool of the prince, but he commanded the armies and packed them with Orangist officers. Control of foreign policy, which had once been in the hands of the anti-Orangist Advocate of Holland, was bestowed on Frederick Henry. That prince was too cautious to destroy the civil institutions of the Republic, but he worked patiently and unobtrusively to bend them to his will. As *Statholder* of five of the seven provinces (six after 1640), he influenced the choice of local officials and provincial delegates to the States General. The national assembly consequently became an Orangist institution. The delegation from Holland and the Hollanders' States Provincial alone retained a degree of independence. The Hollanders also suffered the humiliation of losing control over their most important office. The office of Advocate became an Orangist possession in 1636, when the brother-in-law of a leading Orangist assumed the function. Meanwhile, the other provinces were constantly under the shadow of Orangist authority; whenever they fell too far behind in their contribution to the war, their magistracies were purged by Orangist agents, backed by the Orangist armies.

At The Hague, Frederick Henry surrounded himself with the pomp and ceremony befitting a head of state. The Republic had all the trappings of a monarchy, short of a royal crown. The title "Your Excellency" was replaced by the more grandiose "Your Highness," thanks to French influence at the capital. Dutch nobles were joined at the court by English, French and German noblemen who became mercenary officers in the Dutch armies. Exiled royalty also arrived, the Stuarts from England and the ex-king of Bohemia from the Palatinate. Frederick Henry brought royalty into his own family; his son, William, married the daughter of England's Charles I. And the more prestigious French language replaced Dutch at The Hague. Less calculated to give the outward appearance of royalty, but more important in terms of power, was an Orangist succession settlement. Frederick Henry persuaded province after province to promise that his son would inherit his Statholderates. The Republic now had the makings not only of a monarchy, but of an hereditary regime.

The prince of Orange met frustration only when he attempted to turn the Spanish-Dutch war into a vehicle of Orangist imperialism. Frederick Henry hoped to join France in partitioning the Spanish Netherlands, to support his Stuart relations in the English civil war and to join Denmark in its short war of 1643–1645 against Sweden. He succeeded only in negotiating a military-political alliance with France against Spain in 1635. To his sorrow, he discovered that Dutch naval and land victories over Spain did not break the Spanish will to fight, and that French assistance in the war was a mixed blessing. Dutchmen began to look with suspicion on the Franco-Dutch plan to partition the Spanish Netherlands, which would substitute a strong French neighbor for the weaker Spaniards. Dutch merchants refused to consider the acquisition of towns like Antwerp, which would bring their economic rivals under the protection of the Dutch state. For a while there was some hope that a native uprising in the Spanish Netherlands might automatically hand over that area to the Dutch in spite of their objections. However, no uprising took place. Spain retained the loyalty of the Spanish Netherlands by respecting local privileges, including what amounted to a virtual tax exemption. And while Frederick Henry tempted the Catholic southern Lowlanders with hopes of religious toleration, the Dutch people frightened them away by their determination to persecute Catholics. Despite an agreement with the French that conquered Catholic territory would be spared religious persecution, Frederick Henry's forces proved intolerant when they seized Maastricht and Hertogenbosch.

By 1648, Frederick Henry's grand design was a lost cause. The usually compliant States General blocked Dutch support of Stuarts and Danes, and compelled the Orangist leader to begin peace negotiations with Spain. Frederick Henry died before peace was concluded, but his son and successor, William II, had to sign a treaty. The war which had done so much to raise the fortunes of the House of Orange was at an end. The Dutch people could congratulate themselves on ending once for all the Spanish threat to their independence, and on a modest acquisition of land in the Spanish Netherlands. The Orangists had less cause to rejoice.

The new prince of Orange was not prepared to let his dynasty's position in the Republic be weakened simply because he had lost the battle to continue the war. The young William II (1647–1650) was, if anything, more determined than his father to carry on the family tradition. Had he escaped the attack of smallpox which cut short his life, he might well have destroyed the republican institutions which Frederick Henry had bent to his will. William II closely resembles his near-contemporary, Charles X of Sweden, who died suddenly after a short but vigorous reign. In both countries, the enhancement of princely authority had to wait another two decades.

In his three years as Dutch leader, William II made the best of his circumstances. He could not expect the wartime unity to continue automatically, and he knew that the anti-Orangist province of Holland would try to use the peace as an argument for dismantling his military machine. On the other hand, William had possession of the native armies, and the support of the French regiments which remained on Dutch soil after 1648. He could also count on strong Dutch support after the execution of Charles I in 1649 turned many Dutchmen against republicanism. William's grand design was far more grandiose than his father's. He planned to help Charles II fight his way to the English throne, use French subsidies to crush internal resistance from Holland, join France in its continuing war with Spain and partition the Spanish Netherlands in accordance with the old Franco-Orangist plan of 1635.

Success for William hinged on his handling of Holland. The internal crisis came to a head in 1650, when the States Provincial of Holland ordered the disbanding of some of the many troops in its pay. If carried out, the order would have greatly reduced the Dutch armies, and encouraged the national assembly to slash the Republic's general military budget. William had to act quickly before the military base of his power disappeared. He was able to secure the States General's vague authorization to act against Holland. The prince failed in his efforts to frighten the town governments of Holland into dismissing anti-Orangist members. However, he managed to seize six leading opponents in the States Provincial of Holland, and laid siege to the city of Amsterdam. To avert a civil war, the opposition in Amsterdam made what amounted to a capitulation. Military reductions were renounced, the mayor of Amsterdam agreed to resign and the imprisoned deputies were freed only on condition that they withdraw from political life. The crisis was not entirely resolved, however. Holland's assembly continued to oppose William's foreign policy and actually thwarted his plan to drag the Republic into the Franco-Spanish war.

With the issue still in doubt, William was struck down by smallpox, before he reached his twenty-fifth birthday and before he could produce an heir. In contrast to the situation under William's father, there was no provision for a succession. William's wife was pregnant at the time of his death, but when the baby was born a week later, he had to face a hostile republican world which had no place for him. The tiny prince had no rights, and quarrels within his family prevented his uncle (the *Statholder* of Friesland) from taking his place. The baby would one day restore the Orangist fortunes as the great William III. But in 1650 the Orangists were in eclipse.

The jubilant anti-Orangists in Holland and elsewhere took full advantage of the sudden turn of events. During the 1650's, the sources of Orangist power were removed. In 1651, the republicans in Holland took charge by convoking a special assembly of delegates from the seven provinces, thereby bypassing the still Orangist States General. The assembly abolished the offices of Captain General of the army and Admiral General of the navy, and left the provincial Statholderates vacant. Holland emerged as the leader of the Republic once more under a forceful, anti-Orangist Advocate, John de Witt (1653–1672).

De Witt proved to be a capable "successor" to William II, steering the Republic through a difficult period. He had to face internal hostility to the continuation of the military machine inherited from the Orangists, and an external threat from the aggressive Cromwellian state. Due to his perseverance, the military and naval budgets suffered only minor reductions. He was helped by the lowering of interest rates on state debts, made possible by the close connection of business and government. The province of Holland, for example, was able to reduce the interest rate on its debt to the astonishingly low level of 4 percent, thanks to the business community's confidence in the government. De Witt was less fortunate in dealing with the English. He was forced into the Anglo-Dutch war of 1652–1654, which ended in the humiliating Treaty of Westminster. The settlement upheld the English Navigation Act of 1651, which discriminated against Dutch shipping, and Dutch ships also recognized the precedence of the English flag on the seas.

The war with England placed a severe strain on the constitutional settlement of 1650–1651. Cromwell tried to use victory on the seas as an excuse for interfering with the Dutch Republic's internal affairs. De Witt rejected the Englishman's demands for a united Anglo-Dutch state (under English domination), but the province of Holland secretly agreed to another Cromwellian proposal. By their Act of Seclusion, the Hollanders agreed never to appoint a member of the House of Orange as Captain General of the Republic. On the surface, the Act of Seclusion strengthened the republican cause. It is possible also that it was a price the Dutch had to pay to end a war which was threatening to revive Orangist sentiment. During the war, feelings against republican handling of the conflict grew so strong that recruiters were harassed and one town flew the Orange flag from its towers. Nevertheless, the exclusion of the Orangists by foreign dictate was a bitter price for even the most anti-

Orangist republican. The fact that Holland acted on its own in the matter was resented by the other provinces, further straining the unity of the republic.

The Treaty of Westminster marks also the beginning of the decline of Dutch commercial power in the European world. The greatness of the Dutch depended largely on their position as the middleman of international commerce. They exchanged the moneys of other European states for a modest but sure profit; they carried in their ships the goods of one state to another; they commanded one-half of the Baltic trade; they had challenged the Portuguese in Latin America, and taken from Portugal her East Indies empire; they entered the lucrative Mediterranean center of commerce. Against Spain (and Portugal until it broke from Spanish control in 1640), the Dutch were able to compete on favorable terms. But new English shipping was beginning to make inroads on the Dutch position, and during the Anglo-Dutch War the Portuguese took back the Brazilian conquests which the Dutch had made earlier in the century. It is one of the supreme ironies of history that the republican regents, so closely identified with the Dutch mercantile community, reasserted their political power at home only to find that their international, commercial position was disintegrating before their eyes. The Dutch regent class would continue to play a role in the commerce of Europe and the wider world, for the decline was a gradual one, and there remained the Dutch power in international monetary and banking circles. But the days of real greatness were gone.

In the future lurked the shadow of the Orangists. In 1660 William III was but a decade away from adulthood and a potential reversal of the settlement of 1650. In 1660 also, Charles II was restored as king in England; with the return to power of the Stuarts in the person of the young Dutch prince's uncle, pressures for an Orange "restoration" began to rise across the sea as well as within the Dutch Republic. No Act of Seclusion, no vacant Statholderates could ensure the indefinite ascendancy of republicanism in a republic which had already found a way to accommodate its decentralized institutional framework to Orangist centralism under a Maurice of Nassau, a Frederick Henry and a William II.[7]

7. See Chapter 12 for Dutch affairs after 1660.

III.

The Age of Louis XIV:
1661–1715

The political climate in Europe between 1661 and 1715 was very different from that of the preceding half-century. The confusion and violence of an age suffering from the weakening of traditional bonds gave way to new order imposed by the secular state. The age of the Three Musketeers was followed by the Age of Louis XIV. The function of the prince was no longer just to survive, but to build on the foundations of royal authority which had emerged from the mid-century crises. Few rebellions occurred between 1660 and 1715, and most of these had no chance of success. Huguenots, Hungarians, Catalans and the Cossacks all demonstrated the futility of trying to oppose with arms the growing power of their sovereigns. The two major internal upheavals of the half-century, in England in 1688 and in the Dutch Netherlands in 1672, were not so much revolutions as palace coups which actually strengthened the central government. Foreign wars were different also. The generation which had lived through the Thirty Years' War had seen foreign wars combine with internal rebellion in a frightening assault on the individual state's existence. Early seventeenth-century warfare was really a glorified melée of jostling internal and external authorities, made possible by the breakdown of traditional bonds and loyalties. But in the mid-century crises the state had brought internal order out of confused loyalties. The wars of Louis XIV tended to be simple conflicts between sovereign states, with rulers rarely allying with their opponents' rebellious subjects. This type of war, which was the result of the triumph of central authority, became in turn an agent of the further enhancement of the state. War accelerated the transformation of Austria into the powerful Danubian monarchy, of Brandenburg into the Kingdom of Prussia, of Muscovy into the quasi-Europeanized state of Russia, and of England into the strong royal-parliamentary state known as the United Kingdom of Great Britain. War also tended to merge the regional storm centers of the century's early decades into one European system of states.

We often refer to this period as the Age of Louis XIV. For it was the Sun King of France who was at once its symbol and its dominant figure. His government is considered the "model" absolute monarchy, symbolizing the ascendancy of the secular state over its subjects. And it was he who was most responsible for the series of great interstate wars which also symbolized the ascendancy of the secular state. At the same time we should not give the Grand Monarch all the credit for the historical processes at work during his lifetime. In the externals of courtly splendor, Louis XIV's fellow monarchs did imitate him. Frederick I of Prussia even had an official mistress in open imitation of the Grand Monarch, and many a petty German prince fashioned his palace and gardens in the image of Versailles. But when we probe beneath the veneer of courtly life and culture, we see very little which would justify the commonly held belief that Louis XIV's state was the "model" for other states. Leopold I of the Danubian monarchy and Charles II of England greatly admired Louis' power, but they built their states in accordance with English and Austrian needs and conditions. In distant Sweden a priest referred to Swedish absolutism as "a damned French system." Yet Sweden was actually the institutional model for many of its neighbors. The country which was most transformed during this period was Muscovy-Russia; but its political-institutional models were not France but the Swedish, Dutch and German states. The one country that consciously copied French absolutism was Spain, where the importing was done by Philip V on the orders of his grandfather, Louis XIV! Nor did Louis XIV hesitate to learn from other states in areas which were most crucial to royal power. At the end of his reign, he introduced to France an income tax similar to levies which had proved successful in England, the Dutch Republic and the Spanish Netherlands. This is not to say that we should not designate this as the Age of Louis XIV. But it should be remembered that the age was one in which general European conditions were conducive to state-building, and that all rulers, including Louis XIV, acted in response to these conditions and to the particular needs of their countries. Louis and his state remain the symbols of the age, the most spectacular and celebrated example of absolutist state-building. But we should be aware that if his fellow monarchs were fortunate to have reigned in the Age of Louis XIV, Louis XIV was equally fortunate to have lived in his "age." In foreign affairs, this period may more meaningfully be called the Age of Louis XIV. Yet again we must be wary of overstating the case. The motivations which drove Louis to war so often in western Europe were felt equally by his neighbors. Moreover, what historians call "his" wars were merely part of much broader conflicts which involved many areas of Europe. Ironically, too, the "Wars of Louis XIV" ushered in a European balance of power, rather than leading to French hegemony. Although we should not discard the term, Age of Louis XIV, we should realize that his was also the age of other rulers, of their absolutism and their wars.

9.

The Emergence of a
European States-System

The late seventeenth century was a period of almost continuous war between rival secular states. With the power of central administrations enhanced by 1661, and with new impulses to aggression to replace the ones of the previous half-century, interstate war became a regular institution in European affairs. Dynasticism, *gloire*, mercantilism and a vague interest in achieving a "balance of power" [1] all conspired to upset the settlements of 1648–1664 which had brought an uneasy peace to the regional storm centers of Europe.[2] In the 1660's, the west, the Baltic and the Balkans all threatened to erupt in new violence. In the west, victorious Bourbon France faced erstwhile allies (England and the Dutch Netherlands) and continuing rivals (Hapsburg Spain and Hapsburg Austria). In the northeast, Sweden had been contained, but was viewed with envy and distrust by its neighbors, Muscovy, Poland, Brandenburg and Denmark. To the southeast, the still powerful Ottoman Empire was feared by its Christian neighbors, Austria, Venice, Poland and Muscovy. To make sense out of the confusion of wars which plagued Europe in the succeeding decades, it is convenient to divide them into four sub-periods.

1. On these underlying causes of war, see Chapter 2, pp. 58–67.
2. See Chapter 6, pp. 167–174, and Chapter 7, pp. 195–197, for the treaties of Westphalia, Vasvar, Oliva and the Pyrenees.

1661-1679
WAR OF DEVOLUTION
DUTCH & SCANIAN WARS

1680-1688.
SEIGE OF VIENNA
GLORIOUS REVOLUTION
ENCROACHMENT BY FRANCE

1688-1699
WARS IN WEST
& BALKANS

1700-1721
WARS OF
SPANISH &
SWEDISH
SUCCESSION

From 1661 to 1679, minor wars erupted in each of the three regions (notably the War of Devolution and the Dutch and Scanian wars). Accompanying them was a realignment of the warring parties in each area. Then, between 1680 and 1688 Europe experienced three diplomatic crises: the Turkish siege of Vienna in 1683, the English succession issue of 1688 and persistent juridical-military encroachment by France on the lands situated on its eastern borders. The result was a decade of major wars in the west and the Balkans (1688–1699). This was followed closely by still greater conflicts between 1700 and 1721, the wars of Spanish and Swedish succession.

Out of the half-century of secular wars came a reordering of the relations of European states. The three regions became so entangled in each other's affairs, that by 1715 they had virtually merged in what is commonly called the European states-system. Within that system, some states had enhanced their power, others had declined and a few held their ground. Austria, transformed into the powerful Danubian monarchy, replaced the Ottoman Empire as the greatest power in the southeast. Muscovy, now the quasi-westernized state of Russia, took Sweden's place in the north. In the west, France held its own, but was kept in check by the rising English state, known since 1707 as the United Kingdom of Great Britain, as well as by the Danubian monarchy. Although Poland, Spain and the Dutch Netherlands played important roles in the wars, they were unable to maintain or increase their power within the European states-system. Poland contributed to the wars against both the Ottoman Empire and Sweden, but its leader, John Sobieski, was unable to resurrect the Polish state in the process. The Dutch were in some respects the western counterpart of the Poles. William III was the head of the coalition which checked the power of Louis XIV's France, but the Dutch state itself continued the military and economic decline which had already become evident by 1661. Spain was the great victim of the wars. Its Italian and Lowlands possessions were bestowed on the French and Danubian monarchies, its Iberian lands devastated and its throne awarded to a Bourbon, Louis XIV's grandson. Its internal revival under Bourbon rule was not matched by external power, and it remained an important, but second-rate, European state. Thus, in 1715, the European states-system was dominated by four states: England, France, the Danubian monarchy and Russia. A fifth great power, Prussia, was to join the list a half-century later. During the wars of the late seventeenth century an internal transformation of the old Brandenburg electorate into the new Prussian kingdom foreshadowed the military victories of the 1740's. This states-system, born of the wars of 1661–1715, was to last until the First World War of 1914–1918.

EUROPE IN 1721

Great Britain
France
Danubian monarchy
Savoy
Russia
Brandenburg-Prussia
Boundary of the
Holy Roman Empire
× Battles

SCOTLAND
IRELAND
ENGLAND
NORTH SEA
DENMARK-NORWAY
SWEDEN-FINLAND
RUSSIA
HANOVER
Bremen
POLAND
SAXONY
Cologne
Ramillies
Malplaquet
Blenheim × BAVARIA
AUSTRIA
VENICE
OTTOMAN EMPIRE
BLACK SEA
FRANCE
PORTUGAL
SPAIN
Minorca (Br.)
PAPAL STATES
Cadiz
Gibraltar
MEDITERRANEAN SEA

⚓ *The Realignment of States, 1661–1679*

The changes in the world of high politics during the 1660's and 1670's were produced by many causes. The most important factor was the personality of the young Bourbon king of France, Louis XIV. Hence it is important to analyze his aims from the time when he took personal charge of his state in 1661 until his death in 1715.

Some historians assert that the Grand Monarch had one constant aim, namely to turn the troublesome Spanish succession question to his Bourbon dynasty's advantage. There is no doubt that this issue was important for him. When the sickly Hapsburg, Charles II, became king of Spain in 1665, it was almost certain that he would die soon without direct heirs. Many European dynasties had Spanish Hapsburg blood, but the closest blood relationship lay in the French Bourbon line. Louis XIV's wife, Maria Theresa, was half-sister to Charles, and the oldest child of their father, Philip IV of Spain. Louis XIV entertained three prospects.

Seventeenth-century view of Versailles by P. Menant

First, the entire Spanish inheritance might be willed to a descendant of Louis and Maria Theresa, when Charles II died. Secondly, Louis could use the principle of "devolution" to claim a portion of the Spanish empire for his wife while Charles was still on the Spanish throne. A private law of inheritance in parts of the Spanish Netherlands stipulated that the female offspring of a first marriage took precedence over the male children from a second marriage. Thus Louis could claim that although Charles should inherit elsewhere, Maria Theresa had legal title in those parts of the Spanish Netherlands where the private law was recognized. Thirdly, Louis realized that other claimants to the Spanish succession (notably the Austrian Hapsburg Emperor, Leopold I, in the 1660's) would dispute the Bourbon claim to the entire empire. Hence, he could seek to reach an international understanding which would divide the entire inheritance between his family and rival dynasties.

We should be wary of fixing Louis XIV's foreign policy so rigidly, however. While keeping his eye on the Spanish succession issue, Louis XIV had other objectives in sight. He always was concerned about the defensibility of France's frontiers, and whether he looked to the Spanish Netherlands or Spain itself, to the Rhineland or northern Italy, he saw the possibility of expanding the frontier to make his realm safer. He might also place himself on the throne of the Holy Roman Empire. Since that was an elective position, there was a chance that, on Leopold's death, the

EXPANSION OF FRANCE
1661 - 1713

ENGLAND

ENGLISH CHANNEL

SPANISH
NETHERLANDS

Rhine R.

Cologne

Mainz

Trier

Strassburg

Paris

F R A N C E

SWITZERLAND

SAVOY

GENOA

MEDITERRANEAN
SEA

S P A I N

France in 1661
Acquired in 1668
Acquired in 1678
Acquired during 1680's
Acquired in 1713
Ceded to Savoy in 1696

① Saarland
② Alsace
③ Franche Comté
④ Papal territory

electoral princes in the Germanies might choose Louis XIV as their new Emperor. There are some who go so far as to say that the Sun King's ultimate goal was "universal empire"; others reduce his foreign policy to his desire for *gloire*.

One can generalize by saying that the Sun King tried to achieve limited objectives most of the time, while keeping more grandiose possibilities in mind. In a sense he tried to do too little and too much simultaneously. On the one hand he was pragmatic, adapting his immediate interests to changing circumstances, in order to take advantage of every opportunity which came his way. Thus in the 1660's and 1670's he nibbled at the Spanish Netherlands soon after the accession of Charles II, then made an agreement with Emperor Leopold to partition the entire Spanish empire, went to war with the troublesome Dutch, and finally attacked both the Spanish and German territories on his eastern borders. However, as he leaped from one immediate objective to another, he failed to keep all the interrelated problems in perspective and allowed the over-all situation to slip out of his control. Despite this shortsightedness, he was forever attempting to place all the important states in Europe within his sphere of influence by a combination of bribes, threats, informal understandings and formal alliances. The result all too often was that potential friends became suspicious of this double-game, and turned into bitter foes. In the 1660's and 1670's, for example, Louis tried to play England, Spain and the Dutch Netherlands against each other and to link each state to France, with rather unfortunate repercussions. He used the same ill-fated approach to Baltic and Balkan affairs, although he had only a superficial understanding of the rivalries there. In all three areas he played a major role in the realignment which took place during the first years of his personal rule.

In mid-century western Europe, there were family ties between Hapsburg Spain and Austria, and diplomatic connections between France and the English and Dutch states. The wars of previous decades had frequently pitted the two groups against each other. Louis XIV sought to keep all these states occupied with each other's troubles, to make himself the arbiter of western European affairs, and at the same time to achieve limited territorial gains amid the confusion. The long Portuguese war for independence against Spain continued into the 1660's. Louis professed benevolent neutrality in order to keep Spain friendly. Secretly, he encouraged England to send troops to aid the Portuguese cause, and provided those soldiers with French subsidies and a French commander. He was equally slippery in dealing with an Anglo-Dutch war which began in 1665, managing to remain friendly with both combatants. French troops fought on the continent against England's petty German allies, thereby endearing Louis to the Dutch. Meanwhile, he carefully avoided provoking the English. Louis had to declare war on England, but he did not engage in major battles with his formal enemy. With England, Spain and the Dutch Netherlands tied down, Louis unleashed the War of Devolution (1667–1668) against Spain to make good his wife's claim to parts of Spain's Netherlandish territory.

The War of Devolution turned out to be a disagreeable surprise for Louis. The English and Dutch hastily concluded their war, and Spain recognized Portuguese independence. Spain could not hold back the invading French armies in the Spanish Netherlands, but it was saved by the diplomatic intervention of a Triple Alliance. The English, Dutch and Swedish states put pressure on France to negotiate a settlement. By the Treaty of Aix-la-Chapelle (1668), France limited its acquisitions to several towns in the Spanish Netherlands on or near the French border. The new, zig-zagging border was not rational, and it was certainly not considered definitive. It did, however, reduce the danger of invasion for France. Unfortunately for the French monarch, the forced settlement indicated a potential shift in alignments within western Europe which threatened to offset his limited gains.

Louis' obvious step was to break up the Triple Alliance, patch up his differences with as many states as possible, and expand his network of friendly states. His objective was to isolate and crush the Dutch state, which had inspired the Triple Alliance and was a serious commercial rival of France. For a time, everything proceeded smoothly. Impecunious Sweden was brought into line with a bribe. Charles II of England agreed to join France in war against the Dutch in return for a handsome subsidy. Agreements were reached with several German princes. Emperor Leopold I agreed to a Spanish partition treaty and then pledged his neutrality in the Franco-Dutch dispute.

The Dutch War of 1672–1678 was an even more disagreeable surprise for Louis XIV than the Devolution excursion. France quickly invaded the Dutch Netherlands, only to be thwarted by the courageous Dutch who flooded the potential battlefields by opening the dykes on the seacoast. Still more trouble was in store for Louis. An internal upheaval within the Dutch Republic placed the state in the hands of the young William III, who rallied his people against the French invaders. In England, Charles II deserted his French ally and became neutral, under pressure from Parliament, which feared commercial reprisals by France's enemies. Alarmed German princes turned against France, the Diet of the Holy Roman Empire declared war, and Leopold himself made an alliance with Spain against the French. Louis and his generals were thus confronted by a loose coalition of states. They could count only on Sweden and, as we shall see, the Swedes had too many troubles of their own to be of any help.[3]

By 1674, the Dutch war was in reality two wars, both of which had little direct connection with the disputed Dutch territories. France withdrew from Dutch soil and fought two western campaigns: one against the Dutch and Spaniards for control of the Spanish Netherlands, another against Austria and the Holy Roman Empire in the Rhineland. The French managed to slip into Spanish Franche Comté (below the Rhenish theater) in the confusion which followed, but met stiff resistance elsewhere. When it became clear that England would join the coalition against France unless Louis moderated his ambitions, the French monarch agreed to the Peace of Nijmwegen (1678–1679).

France achieved something by the peace. Its eastern borders were strengthened by the acquisition of Franche Comté, and made more rational by the swapping of lands in the Lowlands to straighten the bound-

3. See pp. 242–243.

ary with the Spanish Netherlands. But France also sustained serious losses. Louis XIV had to grant the Dutch a commercial treaty which included the reduction of a high French tariff against Dutch goods. The Rhenish border problem remained unresolved. France held on to some conquests, but gave up one of the bridgeheads across the Rhine which it had seized during the Thirty Years' War.

The most important result of the war was not written into the peace settlement. This was the stubborn fact that the alignment of 1661 was in disarray. Louis XIV was able to negotiate the peace separately with each of his enemies, and still had hopes of tying all western European states to his coattails. Yet a precedent had been set for future coalitions against him. In effect, the War of Devolution and the Dutch War undermined the old Anglo-French-Dutch alignment against the Spanish and Austrian Hapsburgs. The Dutch had become hostile and the English unreliable, while Spain was more wary than ever and Austria's Leopold I bitter and angry.

The shift in alignments was not as complete in the Baltic, but there, too, France lost ground between 1660 and 1679. Since the 1630's France and Sweden had frequently been in diplomatic and military alliance against the Austrian Hapsburgs. Louis XIV counted on a strong and friendly Swedish state. His wars in the west, and his mishandling of Franco-Swedish relations worked against his assumptions.

During the War of Devolution, Sweden joined the Triple Alliance against France. Although French money brought Sweden to its "senses" at the conclusion of that war, the Dutch War again altered Franco-Swedish relations. When Brandenburg entered that war against France in 1674, Louis XIV called on the Swedes to attack the German state from the rear. The Swedes were more than willing to attack Brandenburg, and thereby strengthen their territorial position on the north German coast. But to their displeasure, this northern phase of the Dutch War became the near-disastrous Scanian War of 1674–1679. Sweden was driven from the continent by German enemies headed by Brandenburg. Brandenburg's spectacular victory at the battle of Fehrbellin gave notice that Brandenburg was the military equal of Sweden. Denmark was not the great power which it had been in 1600, but with Dutch naval assistance the Danes drove the Swedes from the Baltic Sea and barely missed reconquering Scania in southern Sweden. Sweden was saved from immense territorial losses only by luck and the French alliance. Fortunately, Poland and Muscovy were too occupied with wars against the Ottoman Empire to join the coalition against Sweden. And Louis XIV used the threat of force to make Denmark and Brandenburg return their conquests. The Treaty of Saint-Germain (1679) obscured the real changes brought about by the war. While Sweden recovered all its territory, it was now obviously a great power only because of Franco-Swedish friendship. And that friendship was shattered by Louis XIV's settling of the terms of peace without even consulting his ally. Within a few years a realignment of states took place which benefitted neither Sweden nor France. Sweden turned to the English and Dutch states for support, and France made an alliance with Brandenburg and Denmark. This alignment left Sweden virtually defenseless against its many Baltic enemies, because the English and Dutch states were too involved in western affairs to protect Swedish interests. Moreover, France could not count on its new allies. Frederick William of Brandenburg declared in 1679: "In the present state of affairs, so far as human prudence can judge, it seems that no prince will henceforth find security and advantage except in the friendship and alliance of the King of France." Like the Danes and many petty German princes, Frederick William rushed into Louis' arms after the Dutch and Scanian wars, but with the intention of gaining what he could until "human prudence" induced him to turn against French aggression once again.

Southeastern Europe was less troubled than the north and west during the 1660's and 1670's. Yet there, too, the stage was set for the startling changes of later decades. The Ottoman Empire remained the great power of the Balkans, but its neighboring Christian states edged towards cooperation against the infidel Turks. Leopold I's Austria concluded its mid-century war with the Turks through the twenty-year truce of Vasvar (1664), but prepared for the inevitable renewal of hostilities. Meanwhile, Poland and Muscovy ended their long-standing rivalry with the Treaty of Andrussova (1667),[4] and turned their attention to the Turkish menace. A series of petty wars with the Ottoman Empire failed to push back the Turkish frontier, but strengthened the resolve of Muscovy and Poland to crush the Turks. During the wars, internal Polish weaknesses were obscured by the emergence of a great national figure, the soldier-king John Sobieski (John III, 1674–1696). Poland added to its strength by resisting the temptation to be drawn into the Scanian War to the north. Moreover, the Poles improved their relations with Austria by withholding support of Austria's rebellious subjects in Hungary. Thus by 1680, southeastern Europe had the makings of a triple alliance of Austria, Poland and Muscovy against the Ottoman state. The Osmanli had little to show for the past two decades. Their major achievements had been the seizure of Crete from Venice and the conclusion of a long war with that Italian republic.

One outside power could have slowed down or taken advantage

4. See Chapter 6, p. 173.

of the shift in Balkan affairs. This was Louis XIV's France. Unfortunately the Grand Monarch had little understanding of southeast European politics. He tried everything and accomplished nothing. His very aims were contradictory. Louis tried to keep Austria isolated and weak so that it could not rival France; yet he also wanted Austria's friendship to keep it from interfering with France's Spanish policies. He wanted to maintain diplomatic and commercial links with the Ottoman Empire, but he was unwilling to give up the pretense of supporting Christian crusades against the Moslem state. To attain all these objectives, the French ruler intrigued with the Poles, Turks and Hungarians to stir up troubles against Leopold I, and also gave military assistance to Austro-Venetian campaigns against the Turks. Such vacillating, deceitful half-measures prevented Louis from forming a strong, pro-French party in southeastern Europe. He might have established a Franco-Austrian-Polish alignment, which would have kept the Turks in check while opening the way for a firm settlement of the Spanish succession issue. Or he could have thrown his full support behind the Turks as a counter to Austria. Instead he alienated Austria, while failing to give adequate security to the Turks. The Franco-Austrian agreement of 1668 over the Spanish succession was virtually repudiated by Leopold I and Austria, Poland and Muscovy drifted toward an alliance against the isolated Ottoman Empire.

Three European Crises, 1680–1688

Three European crises in the 1680's brought the realignments of the previous decades into the open, and precipitated major wars. The first to come to a head was the Austro-Turkish problem. As the Truce of Vasvar was expiring, the Ottoman Empire came under the control of Grand Vizier Kara Mustafa, third of the great line of Kiuprili ministers. Kara Mustafa decided to end the truce with an assault on the Austrian state of Leopold I. By mid-1683, the Turks had stormed through the Hungarian plain and were at the gates of Vienna. All Europe was surprised at the rapid thrust of the Turks, and most Christian states feared that the Moslems would make Europe a Moslem dependency. Contemporary reports exaggerated the size of the invading Turkish forces, but the some 250,000 persons (including the civilian attendants of the soldiers), and the many mules, camels, tents and cannon, gave Christian Europe a scare that would not be equalled until Napoleon's Grand Army swept through it over a century later. Leopold I fled from Vienna, leaving its defense to bolder souls.

To the astonishment of Turks and Christians alike, the siege of Vienna turned into a nightmare for the Turks. John Sobieski brought

Polish forces to the relief of the city, and with the assistance of Bavarian and Saxon troops routed Kara Mustafa's great army. Once the Turks turned their backs on Vienna, their only course of action was to keep retreating over the indefensible plains. A coalition of Christian states, the Holy League, was organized by Pope Innocent XI. It included the Austrians, Poles, Venetians and Muscovites, as well as petty German states and volunteers from every corner of the continent. This last Christian crusade was climaxed by the fall of Buda, Belgrade and Athens before the end of 1688. The Turks retained control of the core of their empire, but no one could fail to realize that they were no longer the greatest power of southeastern Europe. A series of court purges, beginning with the strangling of Kara Mustafa and culminating in the deposition and imprisonment of the Sultan, left new men to save what they could from the disaster.

While the Turks were being routed, a second crisis developed, this time in England. The Restoration settlement of 1660 had placed Charles II of England on a shaky throne. His successor, James II, alienated large numbers of Englishmen by his pro-Catholic policies. When the birth of a royal son ensured a Catholic succession in England, the opposition to James requested the intervention of William III, who was the son-in-law of the English king as well as leader of the Dutch Republic.[5] These events of 1688 brought England directly into the delicate western European diplomatic picture. If William III and James II fought a long civil-foreign war, the two great maritime states of England and the Dutch Netherlands would be removed from continental affairs, leaving Louis XIV virtually free rein in the west. If James' position should collapse completely and William III become ruler of England, a very different situation would face France. For the Dutch and English governments would be controlled by one man. Since that man was an implacable foe of Louis XIV, the Grand Monarch would be faced with a more formidable situation than he had seen during the War of Devolution or the Dutch War.

The king of France was very concerned about the Turkish and English crises, since each threatened his position in a vital part of Europe. However, he was most concerned about his self-made crisis in the Rhineland. After the Dutch War, Louis XIV pursued a half-legal, half-military policy of pushing back the eastern frontiers of France. Overlapping rights in the Rhineland made the French borders vague. Louis claimed sovereign control of any areas which had a legal-historical connection with France. French Courts of Reunion determined what areas should be "reunited" to France; French troops occupied them. Place after place in the Spanish Netherlands, Germanic Alsace and the German Saarland fell to the French.

5. For greater detail, see Chapter 12, pp. 311-312.

The most spectacular acquisitions took place in 1681, when French forces marched into Strassburg on the Rhine River and Casale in northern Italy.

It is difficult to determine the ultimate aims of Louis XIV's aggression. Quite probably he was interested mainly in the immediate objective of strengthening the eastern frontier against future invasion. However, France's expansionist activities made German princes fear the worst. Quite naturally they saw Louis' nibbling at borderlands as the prelude to universal empire, since there was no logical limit to the policy of "reunion." If he seized a "dependency" as French territory, could he not claim that the dependency of that dependency was also French soil?

The Rhenish crisis quickly became linked with the Turkish one, as Louis sought to exploit the Turkish question to his advantage in the Rhineland. Even before the siege of Vienna, he had encouraged the Turks to attack Austria, to prevent Leopold I from intervening against the policy of reunion. When the siege became a reality, Louis used the situation to secure international authorization of his Rhenish conquests. In return for German and Spanish recognition of his seizures, Louis would promise to stop sending troops into neighboring countries. To the French monarch, this offer seemed reasonable. All his opponents had to do was give up the territory he already possessed, and he would not harass them from the rear as they concentrated on the Turkish war. France's opponents had little choice. The Truce of Regensburg (1684) guaranteed the French conquests for twenty years.

The irony of Louis' negotiations over the reunions was that they succeeded in their immediate objective while harming France's broader prospects. For Louis had exploited the Turkish crisis without solving it. When the Truce of Regensburg freed Leopold I to concentrate on the Turkish war (now the War of the Holy League), the crisis became a Turkish—and French—nightmare. Had Louis joined the Ottoman Empire in a war against their common enemies, the Turkish collapse might well have been averted. Instead Leopold I drove back the Turks, greatly expanded his state, and by 1688 was ready to turn his attention to France. Contemporaries saw Louis XIV as a monster, and denounced the Most Christian King as the Most Christian Turk. What they did not see was that he had been hesitant rather than bold, and had missed his chance to contain Austria in the southeast and the west.

After 1684, Louis saw that the Balkan situation was deteriorating, but his interest in the Rhineland distorted his vision. He wanted to make the Truce of Regensburg into a definitive peace before the anti-Turkish forces could turn against him. This time he tried to blackmail his opponents by intervening in a succession dispute concerning the Rhenish Palatinate and a disputed election in the Rhenish Archbishopric of Cologne. Resistance to him stiffened. A Germanic League of Augsburg was formed against him, and a still more important defensive alliance between Brandenburg and Austria was formed.

The climax came in 1688, when the English succession issue came to a head and became entangled in the Rhenish and Turkish crises. Louis had to make a choice. Should he intervene in England to save James II's throne? Or should he escalate his aggression in the Rhineland to force concessions there before the Ottoman Empire was swept entirely out of European affairs? The Grand Monarch did not trust James II. Despite James' Catholicism, he was not a reliable ally, and his interest in rejuvenating the English navy seemed as much a threat to France as to its enemies. Louis decided to let James fight his own battles, assuming that a long Anglo-Dutch war would keep the Dutch and English states from becoming involved in France's Rhenish problems. In 1688, the French king stepped up his campaign in the Rhineland. His brutal war minister, Louvois, sent French troops across the Rhine, systematically burning, pillaging and extorting contributions within the Palatinate in an effort to terrify the Germans into making peace.

Neither the English nor the Rhenish gamble worked. As soon as French forces moved against the Germans, William III knew that he could leave his Dutch state without fear of French attack. He slipped across the English channel, James II fled to the continent, and the bloodless Revolution of 1688 made William and his wife, Mary, joint rulers of England. When James II persuaded Louis XIV to help him regain his throne, William III was able to rally England for a war against France. Meanwhile, French war atrocities in the Rhineland angered all Europe. Even the cautious Leopold I decided that he could fight Louis XIV and the Turks simultaneously. The Rhenish war became the War of the League of Augsburg, which merged with the War of English Succession and became closely connected with the War of the Holy League against the Turks. And Louis XIV's France was confronted by a grand coalition which included England, the Dutch Netherlands, Spain, Savoy, Austria and Brandenburg. Even the Holy Roman Empire made a formal declaration of war, as other German princes joined Austria and Brandenburg in a display of unity rarely achieved by that weak, confederate state.

War in the West and Southeast, 1688–1699

Historians have not discovered a suitable title for the western-southeastern wars of 1688–1699. Western historians have simplified matters somewhat by neglecting the post-1688 phase of the War of the Holy League (1683–1699). The western conflict, which lasted from 1688 to 1697, has been variously described as the War of the League of Augsburg

(referring to the Franco-Germanic theater of war), the War of English
Succession (involving Louis XIV's attempt to reverse the Revolution of
1688), King William's War (the North American phase of the Franco-
English struggle), and (probably in desperation) simply the Nine Years'
War. Fortunately, the Baltic did not have its own theater of war to add
to the confusion, although some northern states were involved formally
in the western contest. The term "First World War" has recently been
employed to show the global nature of the fighting. This title is useful,
if one remembers that it was the European powers that were fighting in
the western hemisphere, Africa and India (in contrast to what is commonly called the First World War of 1914–1918, when non-European
states were first involved in a global conflict on their own initiative).

Whatever the terminology employed, these were conflicts for high
stakes. Louis XIV's enemies claimed to be fighting to restore the settlements of Westphalia, the Pyrenees and Nijmwegen. In a sense they were
groping towards a western European balance of power. They were also
attempting something more grandiose as a group, and something more
limited as individual states. Collectively, the anti-French and anti-Turkish
states were using war as a crude instrument to regulate the affairs of
Europe as a whole, although they had difficulty agreeing on how the
western and southeastern pieces of the puzzle should be put together. As
individuals, these powers had overlapping and sometimes conflicting aims.
Protestant countries liked to think of the war against Louis XIV as a
Protestant crusade, especially after his persecution of Huguenot subjects
flooded Protestant principalities with French religious refugees. Yet the
same Protestant states did not hesitate to ally with Catholic Austria, which
had recently attempted savage measures against its own Calvinist subjects. The English and Dutch were very interested in undermining the
French commercial challenge, but they disagreed on the degree of punishment to be administered. The English wanted to destroy French commerce. The Dutch wanted a balanced commercial world, in which they
could enjoy favorable trade relations with France. Leopold of Austria had
ambitions which were as contrary to a balance of power as Louis XIV's.
The Emperor desired three things: to ensure his gains from the Turks by
driving them still farther from the Hungarian basin, to restore French
conquests to the proper members of the Holy Roman Empire and to
gain support from his Anglo-Dutch allies for his family's own claim to the
Spanish succession. Brandenburg fought against France for a reason which
belied its interest in a "balance of power." The Brandenburgers' main
ambition still was to crush Sweden; since that goal had been denied them
by Louis XIV, they acted partly out of revenge. Denmark and Sweden
played a more cautious game. Both had gone over to France's enemies,

but they placed commercial interests above their new alliances. While technically members of the anti-French coalition, the Scandinavian states acted like neutrals, and Sweden tried to negotiate a western settlement. Little Savoy unashamedly shifted from one side to the other, with the object of soliciting European support for Savoyard expansion. Poland and Muscovy saw the War of the Holy League as an opportunity to share the spoils to be had from the tottering Ottoman Empire.

Appetites were huge, but the expansion of the Turkish war into a broader conflict was a sobering experience. The French army was a superb machine which was able to tie down the coalition's armies in the west and divert the Holy League's troops from the southeastern theater as well. Moreover, France had possession of the territories in dispute. The French were driven from the high seas, but land battles and sieges seemed endless and inconclusive. All that was proved was that limits could be placed on French expansion, and that the anti-French states could match the power of the absolutist model.

The most spectacular development during the war in the west was the internal transformation of England. William III achieved outward harmony between crown and Parliament. Through the cooperation of king, Parliament and commercial interests, and with the added incentive of financing the expensive war, England became the great financial power of Europe. With some assistance from the Dutch, the English played the role of the "coalition's banker"; English money kept the Germans and the Spaniards fighting against France. While Dutch resources were badly strained by the war effort, the English survived a threat of bankruptcy and established the Bank of England in 1694. The semi-state bank enormously strengthened the state's credit. England also enhanced its commercial position as the Dutch continued to decline. Colonial conflicts with France were inconclusive in North America, the Caribbean and India; but England's navy destroyed Colbert's dream of a Europe dominated by French sea power. In the Mediterranean English shipping cut into French commerce, and the use of Spain's Cadiz as a naval base anticipated the later development of Gibraltar as the English key to that sea. Closer to home, the English closed their grip on Ireland by defeating Irish rebels and the expeditionary forces of James II at the battle of the Boyne (1690).

The war also affected the fortunes of Leopold I's Austria. The decision to fight a two-front war in 1688 was a courageous one, and Austria had a hard time against the Turks and French at first. The French held their ground in the Rhineland, and a Turkish counteroffensive pushed the Austrians out of Belgrade. Eventually the war in the west helped Austria's Turkish campaign. Louis XIV had to neutralize northern Italy in order to free his forces for the Rhenish theater. In 1696, France and Savoy signed the Treaty of Turin. This was a stroke of luck for Leopold, who was able to withdraw troops from Italy and send them to the Turkish front. The bolstered forces of the Holy League won a striking victory against the Ottoman Empire the following year (the battle of Zenta). After this battle, the Turks were willing to accept the loss of Balkan territory to Austria. Leopold wanted to turn his attention to the west where peace was being restored and the Spanish succession issue was becoming the overriding concern. With diplomatic help from England and the Dutch Netherlands, Leopold ended the Turkish conflict. He had reason to be satisfied. An Austrian-dominated Holy Roman Empire, which had been denied on the battlefields of the Thirty Years' War, found its substitute in the great Danubian monarchy of Leopold's reign. To Austria, Bohemia and Hapsburg Hungary were added the Turkish territories of Hungary and Transylvania. This multinational state was to last until the First World War of 1914–1918 conspired to break it up into the states of Austria, Czechoslovakia, Hungary, Yugoslavia and Rumania. Although Leopold could not foresee the future greatness of his new Danubian monarchy, he was confident of its ability to challenge France over the Spanish succession.

The Treaty of Carlowitz in the southeast (1699), and the Treaties of Turin and Ryswick in the west (1696, 1697) underlined the emergence of England and the Danubian monarchy as great European powers, while setting limits to French expansion. In the west, France recognized William III as king of England and scaled down French mercantilist curbs on English commerce. The Spanish Netherlands was protected against French aggression by a barrier of Dutch-held fortresses facing France inside Spanish territory. Further south, France retained Strassburg, but restored some of its recent acquisitions in the Rhineland and another Rhenish possession dating from the Thirty Years' War. In northern Italy, it relinquished its hold on Casale, and awarded to Savoy the key Alpine fortress of Pinerolo, which had also been held since the Thirty Years' War. A humbled and much smaller Ottoman Empire faced a powerful Danubian monarchy in southeastern Europe. The other enemies of the Turks received scraps from the Sultan's table. Poland gained Podolia, Venice the Morea and Muscovy Azov. Of these exchanges of territory, only Azov symbolized an important change. Venice's greatness was past, and it was soon to lose what it had gained. A new succession dispute in Poland in 1696 did not augur well for the weak Polish state. The Poles fended off a determined French bid to place a French prince on their throne, only to accept the candidate advanced by Austria, Brandenburg and especially Muscovy. The new king, Augustus the Strong, was already elector of Saxony, but he was little more than a pawn in the hands of the ambitious new ruler of Muscovy, Peter the Great.

The arrival on the European scene of Peter the Great pointed to the future. Legally co-Tsar with a weakling half-brother since 1682, and under the domination of a half-sister, Sophia, until 1689, Peter made the closing stages of the War of the Holy League the first important concern of his great reign. Sophia and her minister Golytsin had been unable to realize their ambition of combining westernization of their backward state with military triumphs over the Turks. Peter was equally determined, and more successful. After failing to take Azov from the Turks in 1695, he drew on western European technical assistance to reorganize his army and to build a fleet on the Don River. The following spring, the Muscovite ships, soldiers and batteries overwhelmed the Turkish outpost. Peter wanted much more than Azov; indeed, he tried to secure diplomatic support for a major offensive against the Turks which would give his country access to the Black Sea. But Europe was too interested in the Spanish succession issue, and too contemptuous of Muscovy to lend a receptive ear. Peter had to settle for Azov and a thirty-year truce with the Ottoman Empire. Nevertheless, it was a beginning which gave Peter the encouragement and inspiration to transform the old Muscovy into the new Russia that was to emerge in the last wars of the century.

ꝃ Wars of Swedish and Spanish Succession, 1700–1721

Europe did not remain long at peace. The long-expected death of Charles II of Spain in 1700, and the accession to the Swedish throne of fifteen-year-old Charles XII in 1697, precipitated another round of armed conflict. The succession issues in Spain and Sweden were European diplomatic problems of the greatest magnitude. The end of the Spanish Hapsburg line threatened Europe with either a] return to the Austro-Spanish hegemony of the early sixteenth century, or the union of France and Spain under the French Bourbons. For the two claimants with the best chances of success were the grandson of Louis XIV, Philip, and the second son of Leopold I, Charles. The Baltic powers could not dispute Charles XII's right to succeed his father in Sweden, but they could take advantage of the new king's youth and inexperience to dismember his empire. Sweden was no longer protected by the Turkish threat to its neighbors. The Treaty of Carlowitz freed Poland and Muscovy from their southeastern entanglements and permitted them to join Sweden's other enemies, Denmark and Brandenburg-Prussia. Moreover Sweden had broken her ties with the one state which had saved her from dismember-

ment during the War of Scania, France. Finally, the few allies which
Sweden had in the west (the Dutch and the English) were soon to be so
involved in the Spanish succession question that they, too, could give
Charles XII little assistance. It seemed that northern Europe was on the
threshold of a fundamental shift in power.

Most historians have focused their attention on the succeeding War
of Spanish Succession (1701–1714), while neglecting the War of the
North (1700–1721). If one looks at the results of the wars, however, it
is evident that the northern conflict changed Europe far more than did
the western one. Hence it is appropriate to begin with the War of the
North.

The war was launched almost simultaneously by Denmark, Poland
and Muscovy. Charles XII turned out to be a most unwilling victim.
Brave, insensitive to pain, the very embodiment of a soldier-king, he provided the aggressors with a disagreeable surprise. Taking advantage of
momentary assistance from the English and Dutch fleets, he besieged
Copenhagen and forced Denmark out of the coalition. Later in 1700,
he turned his tiny army of 8,000 against a Muscovite force of 40,000 in
the midst of a blinding snowstorm (the battle of Narva). Peter the Great
was so taken aback that he left the battle in the hands of a foreign officer,
and the Muscovite troops were defeated. But Charles XII decided to strike
out against the Poles rather than follow up his rout of the Petrine army.
By 1707, the Swedes had invaded Saxony, forced the king of Poland-
Saxony to abdicate, and placed a puppet, Stanislas Leszczinski, on the
Polish throne. Charles XII was now a potential Gustav Adolph and had
all the appearances of being the arbiter of the continent. Indeed, both
sides in the Spanish succession dispute tried, although without success,
to bring this new Lion of the North into the western conflict.

Meanwhile, western statesmen had found it impossible to settle the
succession to the Spanish throne. Louis XIV was most to blame, although
the complicated nature of the problem and the actions of other rulers
played their parts as well. The Franco-Austrian partition agreement of
1668 was no longer relevant in the late 1690's. Leopold of Austria insisted
that the entire inheritance belonged to his son Charles; the aging Charles
II of Spain had just enough will power to oppose any partition of his
lands; and across Europe, three decades of princely procreation had
added many new candidates to the field. The English, French and Dutch
governments decided to draw up a new international settlement and hope
that it would be accepted by their neighbors. The first partition treaty
of 1698 met immediate failure. The Bavarian prince chosen to inherit
most of the Spanish empire died unexpectedly, frustrating the plan to
bypass the major claimants. In 1700, the English, French and Dutch

attempted a second partition treaty. Prince Charles of Austria was to become Charles III of Spain, while France was to annex Spanish territories in Italy. The treaty was a reasonable one, but the Austrians and Spaniards rejected it. Leopold demanded that Charles be awarded the entire Spanish empire. And Charles II of Spain died, leaving a will which gave all his possessions to Louis XIV's grandson Philip. Louis XIV and his council wavered between accepting the will and honoring the second partition treaty. In the end, the Sun King decided to accept the will, and proclaimed his grandson Philip V of Spain. It was a perfectly logical decision. The will stipulated that if the French waived Philip's claim, the inheritance would be given to Charles of Austria in spite of the partition treaty. It seemed folly for Louis to hold out for a partition which was opposed by both the Spaniards and the Austrians.

The accession of the Bourbon Philip in 1700 did not make a major war inevitable, but it did mean that Louis XIV needed extreme caution and tact to avoid such a conflict. It is here that the Sun King erred, committing a blunder equal to the Palatinate atrocities of 1688. When Philip V took over the Spanish inheritance, Louis XIV could count on Leopold I and the Austrians to be against him. But he could also depend on the support not only of the new Spanish king, but of the Spanish populace as well. Moreover, the English and Dutch soon decided to recognize Philip V. Hence, Louis XIV counted on the neutrality of the two maritime powers. However, those powers made an important stipulation: Spain and France were to remain separate, legally and in fact. Under no circumstances were French civil and military officials to take over the reins of Spanish power, especially in the Spanish Netherlands. It was also understood that the Bourbon king of Spain should not grant special privileges to French commercial interests. Louis XIV ignored those provisos. His troops took over the Dutch "barrier" inside the Spanish Netherlands, his merchants were given a virtual *carte blanche* to trade with the Spanish empire and the Sun King told his grandson how to run the Spanish government. Louis' recognition of James II's son as king of England when the ex-Stuart monarch died in 1701 added insult to injury, but the damage was already done. A grand coalition was formed against France, almost as formidable as the coalition of 1688. England, the Dutch Netherlands, the Danubian monarchy, Brandenburg-Prussia and the Holy Roman Empire joined to prevent the union of France and Spain under Bourbon control. Each foe of France had its particular interests, which added up to a balance of power. Paradoxically, at least two of those foes were interested in achieving their own preponderance of power (England in commerce, the Danubian monarchy in territory) in the name of preserving that balance!

As in 1688, France held the disputed territory. But unlike 1688, France had outside support for its claims from Bavaria, Cologne, Portugal and Savoy. However, Louis found it impossible to retain possession of the disputed lands, or to keep his allies from drifting to the other side. When William III died in 1702, the Duke of Marlborough took over as commander-in-chief of the English and Dutch armies, and head of Queen Anne's English government. Marlborough was a great general, and at Blenheim (1704), and Ramillies (1706) decisively defeated the French in the German and Lowland theaters of war. Leopold I's equally great general, Eugene of Savoy, crushed the French at Turin (1706) and dislodged them from northern Italy. Savoy and Portugal went over to the coalition, and France's German allies found their territories occupied. In Spain, Philip V was faced with invasion from Portugal and revolt in Catalonia. The western Mediterranean became almost an English lake, as the English seized the Rock of Gibraltar and the island of Minorca. By 1707, war had resulted in as startling a turn of events in the west as in the north.

After 1707, the fortunes of war dramatically shifted in the north. Many historians have criticized Charles XII's ill-fated decision to risk another showdown with Peter the Great in 1708–1709, by invading Muscovy from the south. Actually, Charles XII had already made a serious blunder, and was trying to extricate himself. In retrospect, it was obvious that the Swedish king should have followed up his victory of 1700 against the Muscovites, rather than plunging into Polish politics. His decision had proved to be an error in judgment rivalling that of Louis XIV in 1688. No matter how much Polish territory the Swedes occupied, they were faced with hostile confederacies of Polish noblemen. While Charles pursued a will-o'-the-wisp in Poland, Peter the Great began to transform backward and militarily weak Muscovy into the powerful state of Russia. Slowly but surely, Russian forces swept the occupying Swedes from the southeastern shores of the Baltic.

Charles XII's strategy in 1708–1709 was to drive Russia from the Dnieper River. He counted on linking his own forces with the rebellious Russian Cossacks and another Swedish army which had been fighting in the Baltic. It was a daring plan, which looked foolhardy only when circumstances turned against the Swedish monarch. The failure of the Cossacks to give Charles as much support as promised, a Russian thrust at the relieving Baltic army before it could join the Swedish king, the unusually harsh winter and the refusal of the Russians to fight until the Swedes had been drawn far into Russia explain the disastrous battle of Poltava in 1709. Before the encounter, Peter the Great had tried to negotiate a peace on degrading terms. After Poltava, it was Sweden which faced humiliation. Charles managed to put off the day of reckoning by bringing the Ottoman Empire into Sweden's war with Russia in 1711. The Turkish forces surrounded Peter's army, and had him at their mercy. Fortunately for Peter, the Turks agreed to spare the Russian army from certain slaughter and to sign a peace treaty. This settlement of 1711 restored Azov to the Turks, leaving Peter free to continue his pursuit of the Swedes.

The last decade of the northern war brought one state after another into the conflict against the hapless Swedes. Poland (under the restored Augustus the Strong) reentered the war, as did Denmark. Brandenburg and Hanover joined the coalition. Charles XII refused to admit defeat and fought on courageously and stubbornly. Only his death in 1718 and English pressure on Peter the Great brought Sweden and its enemies to the conference table. The result was a series of treaties known collectively as the Peace of Nystad (1719–1721).

The Peace of Nystad reduced Sweden to the status of a minor power. Its German territories, which had been won during the Thirty Years' War, were awarded to German princes. Its lands on the eastern shores of the Baltic, which dated from a still earlier period, went to Russia. The hope of making the Baltic a Swedish lake had vanished. Russia benefitted most from the settlement. Peter the Great lost Azov to the Turks, but he gained an outlet on the Baltic, a new capital of Saint Petersburg (built during the war on former Swedish soil in Ingria) and control of Baltic lands stretching from the border of Swedish Finland in the north to the Dvina River in the south. Western statesmen were puzzled by Peter the Great's outlandish behavior during his diplomatic missions to Amsterdam and Paris late in the war, but they also respected Russia's new power. Brandenburg was the other important state to improve its Baltic position by the peace settlement, realizing its long-held ambition to acquire part of Western Pomerania from Sweden, and with it the excellent Baltic port of Stettin. By contrast, Denmark remained the weak power that it had been in 1700, and Poland suffered from both internal weaknesses and reliance on Russia. Augustus the Strong's restoration to the Polish throne after Poltava caused new troubles. The Poles treated their king's Saxon troops as invaders, and a civil war ensued between king and nobles, which was ended only by Peter the Great's intervention. As the price of peace, Poland accepted Augustus as a Russian puppet as well as a weak constitution "guaranteed" by the Russian ruler.

France was much more fortunate than Sweden after 1707. The resources of the French state combined with circumstances to save it from Sweden's fate. The French survived the heavy financial cost of the war, a series of crop failures and the bloody battles of Oudenarde and Malplaquet, which killed thousands of soldiers on both sides. Like Peter

POLAND-LITHUANIA
AND MUSCOVY (RUSSIA)

▨ Poland-Lithuania

▢ Muscovy (Russia)

▥ Polish lands acquired by Sweden
in 1629, and by Muscovy in 1720

▨ Polish lands acquired by Muscovy in
1667

▨ Sweden

▨ Swedish in 1617, to Muscovy in 1621

▥ Ottoman lands and dependencies

① Karelia   ⑥ East Prussia
② Ingria   (Polish overlordship
③ Estonia   relinquished to
④ Livonia   Brandenburg
⑤ Courland   in 1660)
             × Battles

the Great, Louis XIV was on the point of offering generous terms to save his state from further punishment. However, his Anglo-Dutch enemies toughened their conditions to the point of asking the French king to drive his grandson from the Spanish throne. This Louis refused to do, and the war continued. The coalition against him began to fall apart. Philip V and his Castilian subjects showed that it would be difficult to change the succession by withstanding the forces of the Austrian prince Charles and the Catalan rebels. The English and Dutch also lost their interest in Charles' Spanish pretensions when he inherited the Austrian lands as Emperor Charles VI in 1711.[6] To fight for Charles in Spain would only result in the union of the Austrian and Spanish empires under the new Emperor. That prospect pleased the Anglo-Dutch coalition no more than did a united France and Spain. The English also underwent a palace upheaval which thrust Marlborough from power and replaced the war ministry with a peace party. The English and French worked out a

6. His father, Leopold, had died in 1705, and his older brother Joseph in 1711.

settlement of the Spanish succession issue. The Dutch Netherlands accepted the agreement in 1713, and in 1714 Austria gave up its attempt to continue the war against France singlehandedly.

The Peace of Utrecht (1713–1714) strengthened the settlement of 1697–1699 which had made England and the Danubian monarchy great powers and contained Louis XIV's France. France lost little in territory, but was hemmed in by buffer states and separated from Spain. The peace recognized Philip V as king of Spain on the condition that the Spanish Bourbon line and the French Bourbon line would remain distinct. Spain's possessions in the Netherlands and Italy were ceded to Austria as compensation to Charles and also as a check against French aggression on France's eastern borders. The Dutch retained a reduced "barrier" in the new Austrian Netherlands. Savoy's duke was awarded new lands to check France in the south, and a royal crown. Brandenburg expanded its territory near France by acquiring Spanish Guelderland, and its elector acquired the title of "King in Prussia."

The English made the greatest gains, taking over France's privileged commercial position in the Spanish empire through the Asiento agreement. This treaty gave England control of the African slave trade with Spanish America, and an opening in other Spanish trade. England had already obtained a favorable trade treaty with Portugal during the war (the Methuen Treaty of 1703). The Peace of Utrecht also gave England the Rock of Gibraltar and Minorca, thereby opening Mediterranean commerce to English merchants. England's North American possessions were expanded to include French Acadia. England's position was all the more impressive because the war had ruined its Dutch rival financially and commercially. The Dutch turned away from their role as Europe's middlemen and invested their money in English enterprises. In a sense, the Dutch were as tied to the coattails of England after 1714 as the Poles were to the Russian state after 1721. Two additional effects of the war on England should be mentioned. During the conflict, England and Scotland were merged in the United Kingdom of Britain. This ended the precarious century-old arrangement under which the two independent kingdoms were held together only by the fact that the same monarch wore both crowns. And at the conclusion of the war, Louis XIV recognized the Hanoverian succession of 1714, which placed George of Hanover on the English throne as George I. The Hanoverian succession had advantages and drawbacks for England. It avoided a return to the direct male line of James II by settling on the German relations of the Stuarts after the death of William III in 1702 and Anne (James II's second daughter) in 1714. However, it tied England more closely to continental problems than the English wished. In theory, Hanover and England remained separate. But since George I of England was also Elector George of Hanover, the British government was occupied with the German state's affairs in practice. The fact that Hanover had emerged from the wars of 1688–1714 with an electoral title in the Holy Roman Empire and possession of Swedish Bremen and Verden in northern Germany, did not compensate the English for their added responsibilities.

The legacy of the war for the Danubian monarchy was more ambiguous than that of England. Austria had been unable to achieve Leopold I's wish to restore most of Louis XIV's Rhenish conquests to their rightful German princes. The addition of Spanish lands in the Netherlands and Italy to the huge Danubian monarchy weakened rather than strengthened the state. Charles VI could not tap the wealth of the Austrian Netherlands because the English and Dutch placed restrictions on its international commerce. And the Italian provinces brought still another language and many additional provincial "liberties" to the already multi-provincial and multi-linguistic Danubian state. Perhaps it was fortunate for Charles VI that he was unable to become Charles III of Spain as well! On the other hand, there could be no doubt that the great-power status achieved by the Danubian monarchy between 1683 and 1699 was retained during the war of 1701–1714. The Austrian Hapsburgs fought well during the war, put down a Hungarian revolt in the process and went on to crush a Turkish attempt to reverse the settlement of 1699 during a short Austro-Turkish war concluded by the Treaty of Passarowitz (1718). Thus at the end of the seventeenth century the Danubian monarchy held its place with England, France, Russia and the emerging kingdom of Brandenburg-Prussia as one of the major powers which would regulate the European states-system of the eighteenth and nineteenth centuries.

10.

Louis XIV's France and
Hapsburg-Bourbon Spain

Historians continue to argue over Louis XIV's personal reign in France (1661–1715).[1] The most persistent and popular interpretation depicts the Sun King as the "perfector and destroyer" of the French monarchical state, a great king who secured political obedience and grandeur, but a mediocrity as a man, who "refused to prepare for the future," who left "a sort of anarchy under the beautiful appearance of monarchical order," who exhausted the French monarchy by his wars, his egotism, his fairy-tale flight from reality.[2] This interpretation, rendered most eloquently and persuasively by Ernest Lavisse at the beginning of the twentieth century, has its roots in the French Revolution of 1789 and the liberal-democratic legacy. It assumes that because the Revolution occurred seventy-four years after Louis XIV's death (scarcely more than the length of his reign), Louis was to blame for that unheaval. Of course, one cannot ignore the fact that revolution did overthrow the monarchy at the end of the next century. However, if it is unhistorical to ignore 1789, it is bad history to condemn a regime for not anticipating problems

1. See Chapter 7, pp. 207–210 for Louis XIV's minority, 1643–1661.
2. E. Lavisse *et al.*, *Histoire de France depuis les Origines jusqu'à la Révolution*, vol. VII, part 1 (1905), pp. 119–138. For this and other interpretations of Louis XIV, see W. F. Church, ed., *The Greatness of Louis XIV: Myth or Reality?* (Heath, 1959).

seventy-four years in advance. It is equally dubious history to write off absolute monarchy as "bad" simply because it did not conform to the liberal-democratic ideals of a much later age.

Many scholars have preferred to see Louis XIV as the epitome of his times, a ruler who answered the almost universal desire of Frenchmen for order under a king who ruled personally, a reaction to the turbulence of the Fronde. Such an interpretation does not close the debate on Louis XIV, however, for it begs the question of whether he was too dull witted to do more than dutifully play his assigned role, or whether he capitalized on popular feelings to give Frenchmen the order and security which no mere following of opinion could have achieved. In short, this second interpretation leads straight to a third: that Louis XIV was a highly successful and innovative politician-statesman. In the words of the most distinguished contemporary historian of seventeenth-century France, Roland Mousnier, Louis XIV was "both autocratic and revolutionary." [3] In the less bold, but equally cogent phraseology of an earlier historian, Louis XIV's greatest achievement was in being an "administrator." [4] Both views agree that Louis XIV's greatness lay in his ability to bring order out of chaos, to achieve stability as well as grandeur. This interpretation recognizes the weaknesses of Louis XIV's state, in addition to its strengths. But it is true both to Louis' times and to the revolutionary future in emphasizing the bureaucratic-police state as a lasting achievement, which survived the monarchy's fall and provided the framework for the modern state which we know. It is this interpretation which provides the soundest framework for discussing the accomplishments of Louis XIV between 1661 and 1715.

♫ The Sun King's Experiment: Personal Rule

The most revolutionary act of Louis XIV's life was his decision to be his own First Minister after Cardinal Mazarin died in 1661. That decision can almost be compared with the Revolution of 1688 in England, for both events placed the authority of the state on a new and more powerful basis. In England, royal-parliamentary cooperation enhanced the authority of William III's state. In France, personal rule by Louis XIV performed a similar function. Under Richelieu and Mazarin, government had been "a matter of family, birth, titles and office." Public

---

3. R. Mousnier, *Les XVIᵉ et XVIIᵉ Siècles* (1965), 252.
4. P.-E. Lemontey, *Essai sur l'établissement monarchique de Louis XIV* (1818), 333.

positions from First Minister down to the pettiest tax collector were regarded as the private possession of the incumbent. By assuming direct control of his government, Louis XIV made it known that all governmental positions were subject to his wishes and commands, and paved the way for the subordination of functionaries and subjects to the state which his person symbolized. Louis XIV, who did not and could not have said "I am the State," recognized at least dimly the emergence of a new loyalty to the impersonal state on his death bed, declaring, "I die, but the state goes on." [5] There is much irony in the fact that this king, whose name is almost a synonym for personal autocracy, cleared the way for an impersonal, bureaucratic state which survived even after the fall of monarchy in the 1790's. Nevertheless, the irony does not detract from the importance of Louis' personal rule.

Louis XIV was well qualified to rule as well as reign. His intelligence was far from superior, but he had an inquisitive and retentive mind and much "good sense." Even the hostile courtier, the Duke of Saint-Simon, wrote enthusiastically of the qualities of leadership which Louis possessed: "his courage, his grace, his beauty, his grand mien, even the tone of his voice and the majestic and natural charm of all his person." He was by nature and upbringing made for his role. He had been brought up by his mother and Mazarin to enjoy as well as endure the hard labor which a king's *métier* (craft) entailed, and which he felt God had assigned to him as a sacred trust. As Louis wrote to his own son, "the *métier* of a king is great, noble and enjoyable, when one feels worthy of doing well everything which it involves. But it is not free of burdens, weariness and anxieties." Above all, he knew that God had placed a heavy responsibility on his shoulders, and that, if subjects had no right to tell him how to perform his tasks, he had to devote all his energies and talents to his work.

Fortunately, Louis XIV had an uncanny knack for securing the loyalty, devotion and cooperation of functionaries and subjects. Mazarin had done little to eradicate the tensions which lived on after the revolts of the Fronde had been put down. French society and government bristled with hostilities and uncertainties in the 1650's. It took a singular personality to change the atmosphere of the country. How else can one explain the relative ease with which Louis XIV transformed the central government from a series of overlapping councils and rival ministries into a relatively orderly and efficient administrative machine commanded by an inner group of ministers who worked harmoniously with each other, with the king, and with the councils themselves? In changing his

5. See also Chapter 2, p. 52.

Portrait of Louis XIV by N. Pitau

government, the king had his problems. His finance minister, Nicolas Fouquet, was so powerful and corrupt that it seemed he was destined to succeed Mazarin as chief minister. The Brienne family were firmly entrenched in one of the four secretaryships of state, yet Louis considered the father stubborn and the son incapable of keeping government secrets. The king acted slowly, quietly and deliberately to seize, try and condemn to permanent imprisonment the would-be master, Fouquet. The proceedings took three years, but there was no new civil war or attempted palace revolt by Fouquet's followers. Louis was still more cautious in dealing with the Briennes. He deliberately left them in office, but gave the real power of secretary to the trusted Hugues de Lionne. Shortly after, the Brienne dynasty quietly sold their office to Lionne. Thus, Louis avoided forcibly dispossessing the family, an act which would have engendered distrust and insecurity within his civil service. By the late 1660's, he had a working personal government of himself and three intelligent, loyal ministers: Michel Le Tellier for war, Lionne for diplomacy, and Jean-Baptiste Colbert for finances and internal affairs. From this inner council and the formal, administrative councils, Louis excluded also those whose birth and high station gave them some claim to partake in government: his mother and brother, the great princes of the blood and the leading French clergy. Thus no rebellions could arise in the name of the royal family, as they had under Richelieu and Mazarin.

Throughout his reign, Louis XIV clung to this personal rule. Within his central government, new family dynasties did emerge, family rivalries fester and the balance of royal favor shift from one family to another. Nevertheless, the king remained in charge, and everyone knew it. He may have encouraged rivalries between the Le Tellier and Colbert dynasties, but he insisted that they and others work as a team under his guidance. In the first years, Colbert was the dominant servant of the king, as secretary of state over Catholic affairs and the royal household, and director of finances, the navy and royal buildings. Colbert was a clever, unassuming "clerk" who could persuade the king to follow his views while convincing him that he was making the real decisions. Yet Louis kept him in check, and on occasion scolded him for being too independent. During the 1670's and even more after Colbert's death in 1683, the Le Tellier family predominated. Le Tellier was "retired" to the chancellor's office, but his son, the Marquis of Louvois, amassed even greater power and influence than Colbert had attained; he was secretary of state for war, superintendent of postal services and royal buildings, and royal minister, while one of his supporters took charge of finances. Louvois came closer to being "first minister" than any one else under Louis XIV, but fell short of achieving that distinction. After his death in 1691, no one royal servant came close to emulating him and Colbert, although the high functionaries of Louis' last years were more competent than historians have suspected, and although the two great families retained the important offices of war, finances and foreign affairs. The grandsons of courtiers who were amazed to see Colbert, Lionne and Le Tellier leave council meetings in one carriage at the beginning of Louis' reign were astounded by the old king's maintenance of harmony and obedience within his councils.

Nor can there be any doubt that Louis XIV stamped French society as well as his ministers in his own mold. Colbert and Louvois were ruthless, imaginative men who wished to ride herd on vested interests, whether they were clergy, judges, Huguenots, military commanders, master craftsmen or city bosses. The king was more interested in acting by persuasion, and even by compromise, provided his authority was upheld and public order and unity maintained. His revocation of the Edict of Nantes in 1685, which abolished Protestant worship, is the major exception. But it should be remembered that Louis tried to moderate Louvois' brutal methods of harassing the Huguenots before that time and that he decided on formal revocation only when he thought most Huguenots had been converted by persuasion to Catholicism. He also overruled Colbert's decision to codify French legal procedure without the assistance of the parlementary judges. Nor can it be claimed that the king deliberately ruined his nobility by encouraging them to gamble away their fortunes at Versailles and Paris. On the contrary, he was careful to deny compulsive noblemen-gamblers access to gambling dens. His famous *lettres de cachet* were most often used politically to strengthen family bonds by allowing wayward children, wives and husbands to mend their ways in jail. As father of his people, Louis XIV was far from the despot he is often painted. His rather quiet methods and the tone of his administration created a climate of order which was as remarkable an achievement as the more spectacular revolution from above which his Russian contemporary, Peter the Great, unleashed, or the transformation of England under William III and his Parliaments. Scarcely a year passed during Louis XIV's long reign without a few tax revolts and uprisings by the lower social orders against France's political-social elite. However, the almost complete absence of such disturbances during the early and middle decades of the eighteenth century shows how well Louis had done his work of taming and civilizing France.

The Unification of France: Economic, Legal and Religious

While Louis disagreed with his servants' method of unifying France, he fully supported their aim. The monarchical motto of the late seventeenth century—"one king, one faith, one law"—was particularly dear to the French ruler and his functionaries. Colbert was the driving force behind the efforts to bring some order and unity to economic and legal matters, while he, Louvois and Louis were all concerned with one or more of the religious issues which divided France.

In economic matters, Colbert was not a sweeping reformer, but an indefatigable and persistently optimistic administrator who wished to make some sense of the chaotic conditions which he inherited from Fouquet, Mazarin and Richelieu. Colbert failed to abolish all internal tariffs and create a free trading area inside France's boundaries. Instead France emerged as three tariff areas: the newly conquered Rhenish lands with free trade in the Germanies but separated from the old France by a tariff barrier; a second area of privileged provinces on the periphery of old France which had tariff walls with both the new France and central France; and central France itself, within which most tolls were eliminated but which retained tariffs with the rest of France. Colbert also tried to impose regulations on French industries. Here he was pragmatic, sometimes establishing state industries, sometimes subsidizing existing private enterprises and on other occasions making them part of the old local guild structure, which could be more easily watched than the independent entrepreneurs. Behind this diversity could be seen Colbert's mercantilistic aim of increasing production and trade to bring greater wealth and power to the state. Colbert's self-righteousness and his penchant for order blinded him to the interests of businessmen (except where their interests happened to coincide with his). Still less did he have sympathy for the plight of workers, whose attempts to organize and to strike he thwarted. He had little but contempt for agriculture, which explains why he left it to the vagaries of laissez faire. Nineteenth-century free traders have assailed his brand of mercantilism, as did some business interests and ministers after his death. However, it is likely that Colbert's directives and leadership benefitted the French economy as a whole. His passion for laying down standards for production in textiles, for example, resulted in a high quality of workmanship which encouraged foreign states to buy French products. It was after Colbert's death that regulations became hopelessly complex and an end in themselves, leading to the gradual easing of state interference during Louis XIV's last years.

Colbert wanted the codification of French laws to be Louis XIV's supreme achievement. The Sun King was to be a new Justinian, doing for France what the Justinian Code had accomplished for the Roman Empire. The task was staggering, and it is doubtful that any twentieth-century state could have accomplished as much as the seventeenth century minister, given the same multiplicity and diversity of local laws and procedures. Only the genius of a Napoleon, backed by the French Revolution's cataclysmic break with the past, brought Colbert's work to completion. Working with a hand-picked commission of legal experts including his uncle, Colbert brought forth a code for civil procedure (1667) and a code for criminal procedure (1669). The laws themselves, both civil and criminal, were left uncodified. Unfortunately, the *Parlements* were hostile to both codes, and frequently paid little more than lip service to the regularized procedures. But beyond a doubt, the codes at least provided a greater impulse for political unity in France. There followed other codes: forest (1669), commerce (1673), marine (1680), colonies and slaves (1685). While the civil and criminal codes strengthened the grip of the state over its subjects by reinforcing brutal punishments and limiting defendants' rights, the later codes had a broader and more humanitarian vision. Slaves were still considered to be chattels, but the rights of their owners were circumscribed. The commercial code hedged on the legality of loaning money at interest in deference to traditional Catholic opposition, but by this fence-sitting permitted the practice of usury to continue unpunished. The forest code's attempts to protect national woodlands against predatory local interests often broke down in practice during the next century, but it helped to preserve a national resource for the state. As a whole, the codes did bring some order and a little light into the legal world, as much as the society of the day would permit. It was to be a century before major states in central Europe embarked on codification comparable to that achieved by Louis XIV and Colbert.

No problem of Louis XIV's reign was as complex as that of religious affairs. Under Louis the Huguenot minority was proportionately as large as the Negro American population in the present-day United States, and the Catholic laity and clergy were deeply prejudiced against what was officially termed the "So-Called Reformed Religion." Within the Catholic church, there were tensions between Jesuits and Jansenists, and between Gallicans and ultramontanists. It would have taken the wisdom of a Solomon to find solutions to these religious controversies, and the wisdom of Louis XIV was deeply rooted in the prejudices of his own age. Louis XIV's religion may well have been limited to "superstitions and petty, superficial practices," and a fear of Hell rather than of God, as one fervent Catholic critic complained, but he was certainly no neutral in religious issues. He wished to make France entirely Catholic, in deference to his coronation oath, his religion, and his title as "the Most Christian King." In disputes within the Catholic church, his religion gave him no guidelines, and personal prejudices, pride and obstinacy as well as purely pragmatic considerations influenced his decisions by turns. He was fortunate that the politician in him frequently tempered other less desirable traits.

The most serious religious disputes were those within the Catholic

church. Louis inherited the French monarchy's control of most high
clerical appointments, and relatives of his leading ministers were archbishops, bishops, abbots, and priors. Many were mere placemen, secular
men in ecclesiastical dress. When an observer of the clergy's national
assembly declared that it resembled Heaven, a wag replied, "Ah, no,
madame, there are not so many bishops up there." Still, there were
some fervent religious souls among the high clergy who proved to be
obnoxiously independent of Louis on religious matters. When the king
tried to expand his control of vacant bishoprics' incomes to include all
bishoprics in the realm, two clerics protested to Rome. Louis had merely
wanted to supplement his revenues, but now he had to face the Pope
as well as some of his clergy over the broader issue of Gallicanism (national control of the church) versus ultramontanism (papal control). In
1682 he assembled the French clergy in special session, and had them
draw up four Gallican articles. The language was deliberately vague to
avoid a complete break with the international Catholic church, but the
articles substantially asserted the French clergy's independence of the
Pope on religious matters, and the French king's independence in secular
ones. The Gallican articles even touched on the question of papal infallibility with the ominous statement: "The Pope has the principal part
in deciding questions of faith, and his decrees extend to all the churches
and to each particular church; yet his judgment is not irreversible unless
confirmed by consent of the church [i.e., the French clergy]." Louis was
practising brinksmanship, but he eventually had to compromise with the
Papacy, which refused to ratify his appointments of bishops after 1682.
The compromise was effected quietly a decade later, and it was a model of
complexity. In essence, Louis withdrew support of the Gallican articles
and the clergy of France made an apology to the Pope. The king retained
his control over vacant bishoprics (régale), in reality a minor matter.
The ultimate line between loyalty to state and to church, to king and
Pope, remained unclear.

One of the reasons for the compromise over the régale was Louis
XIV's need for papal support on another religious issue. Louis disliked
ultramontanism, but he disliked Jansenism even more.[6] Ever since the
Jansenist movement had entered French Catholic circles in the 1640's, it
had contributed to religious and political divisions within France. Jansenists opposed the pro-papal Jesuit order, questioned the authority of
the Pope and became involved in the revolt of the Fronde against Mazarin.
That minister had been unable to subdue them, and in the 1660's they still
plagued Louis XIV. In 1669 the Pope and the French minister Lionne

6. On Jansenism, see Chapter 3, pp. 74–75.

worked out a settlement which satisfied no one. The center of the controversy was the convent of Port Royal, whose nuns embraced Jansenist views of doubtful orthodoxy. The settlement asked them to repudiate "sincerely" five heretical ideas to be found in a certain Jansenist work. The nuns agreed that the ideas were heretical, but maintained a "mental reservation," arguing that the condemned points were *not* in the controversial tract. Neither Pope nor king was satisfied with this evasion, and Jansenists disliked having to resort to a subterfuge to escape persecution. This issue simmered for two decades and came into the open again in the 1690's. To put pressure on the anti-Jansenist Papacy and gain support from the French crown, Jansenism joined forces with Gallicanism. In attempting to crush the Jansenists, Louis had to renounce his former Gallican stand as well. Indeed the old foe of ultramontanism had no choice but to adopt an ultramontanist position and appeal to the Pope for support. In 1713 the Papacy obliged by issuing the bull Unigenitus, which condemned Jansenist ideas. Outwardly, Louis had restored order and orthodoxy to the Catholic church in France, but the bull did not destroy Jansenism. The pro-Gallican *Parlement* of Paris did not register the bull until after Louis XIV's death, and during the eighteenth century, Jansenism was embraced by many French clerics and laymen. The Jansenist controversy is a case study of Louis XIV's difficulties with religious division and of the supposedly absolute monarch's willingness to play politics in an effort to gain outward conformity.

Louis XIV's fight with the Protestant Huguenot minority in France is a favorite topic of historians, but it was not as explosive an issue as those which tore apart the Catholic majority in the realm. When he began his personal rule the Grand Monarch satisfied his Catholic conscience by permitting only the narrowest legal interpretation of Huguenot privileges. This had the effect of persecuting the Huguenots, who had managed to live with the religious settlements of Henry IV and Louis XIII (the Edict of Nantes and Peace of Alais[7]). Soon the king and his advisors stepped up their campaign to convert all Huguenots to the Catholic faith. A special "conversion fund" was established to bribe wavering souls, and Huguenot children were permitted to join the Catholic church without parental consent at the age of "reason" (i.e., seven)! Persecution, harassment and exclusion from public life and important professions followed. Louis' minister Louvois and a local intendant were so zealous in their efforts to please the king that they went beyond the limits he deemed prudent. Troops were quartered in Huguenot households. After experiencing the company of the soldiers for a few days,

7. See Chapter 4, pp. 107–108, and Chapter 7, pp. 205–206.

many Huguenot families were more than willing to embrace the Catholic faith. By 1685, Louis was convinced that there were few Huguenots left and that he need only formalize the change by revoking the Edict of Nantes. His general Edict of Fontainebleau in that year stopped just short of forcing all Huguenots to join the Catholic church. Huguenot worship was prohibited and Huguenot pastors were expelled from France, but Huguenot laymen were allowed freedom of conscience (i.e., they could keep their beliefs, as long as they did not reveal them in word, worship or deed). Louis clearly believed that his "generosity" would result in the conversion of all remaining Huguenots. His edict stipulated that they were not to be "subjected to molestation or hindrance . . . pending the time when it shall please God to enlighten them." At the same time he was less than sincere in leaving conversion to God and the Huguenots. The restrictions on them remained and the Huguenot laity were forbidden to leave the kingdom.

Neither Louis' "generosity" nor his deity nor Huguenot "enlightenment" worked in the manner that he predicted. Many Huguenots became Catholics to survive, but many more escaped beyond the borders or took up guerrilla warfare against the Catholic state. We should be wary of making sweeping generalizations about Louis' "settlement" of the Catholic-Huguenot problem. Louis remained convinced to his dying day that he had earned God's thanks for his act of revocation. Many of his Catholic subjects hailed the act as the greatest achievement of his reign, and most Catholics thought it was the right decision. The economic effects of the revocation have also been exaggerated by historians until recently when Warren Scoville made an exhaustive study of the subject.[8] It is now clear that the harm done to France by the mass exodus of skilled Huguenot tradesmen was indirect. Huguenot refugees bolstered the economy of rival states such as Brandenburg, England and the Dutch Netherlands. But within France, Catholics were able to fill the void and keep the French economy running. The guerrilla activity within France also had a limited impact on the state. It tied down royal troops which were badly needed in Louis' foreign wars, but it had no chance of endangering the state and had little bearing on the life of most Catholic communities. In retrospect, Louis' persecution of the Huguenots seems typical of the treatment religious minorities received wherever the state felt powerful enough and righteous enough to persecute. France's Huguenots were treated as England's Irish Catholics and Austria's Hungarian Protestants were. In the last analysis, the decision to persecute unpopular minorities was a matter of power and ingrained

8. W. C. Scoville, *The Persecution of the Huguenots and French Economic Development, 1680–1720.*

prejudice against a higher conscience which said that there was a better way.

The Bureaucratic and Privilege Groups

Louis XIV and his chief ministers of the 1660's and 1670's assumed that France could be run by a few persons. The king thought that he could rule personally, with advice from a select few. Colbert looked suspiciously on the multiplication of offices in the law courts and taxing bureaus, and even opposed the emergence of the intendants as a new echelon of royal servants above the judges and tax collectors. Colbert's plan was to reduce drastically the number of judicial and financial officials (redeeming their purchased offices), and to place those who remained under strict royal control. As for the intendants, who had emerged in the 1630's only to be swept aside by the Fronde's reforms in the 1640's, Colbert wished to restore them with a much reduced role. The new intendants were to be merely census-takers in the provinces and observers of maladministration in the courts and bureaus.

The expansion of state functions and power made purely personal monarchy difficult to maintain. Louis had to rely increasingly on his secretaries and ministers to wade through the mass of paper and problems which came to their desks. Thus situations frequently came to his attention predigested, with solutions already formulated. Louis kept over-all control, but personal monarchy gradually became royal-ministerial monarchy. Moreover, the volume of business was too much for Louis' advisors to handle. The ministers and secretaries of state leaned heavily on ever-expanding bureaus of civil servants. When Louis XIV assumed personal charge of the state in 1661, his secretaries had only a few scribes and clerks to assist them. When the government personnel moved with the royal court from Paris to Versailles in the 1680's, two separate buildings were erected in front of the palace's wings to accommodate them. To-day's tourist at Versailles will probably miss those buildings, which are closed because they are considered unimportant by comparison with the palace and gardens. The curious visitor who manages to peek inside them unnoticed will probably also miss their importance, for their offices are small, dingy and uninspiring. Yet, in Louis XIV's day, the two government buildings symbolized a revolution of formidable proportions. For even as the state increased its control over subjects' lives, the bureaucracy acted as a brake on royal-ministerial initiative. Louis XIV ruled his state with a surer hand than had Henry IV and Louis XIII; but his bureaucrats set up their own routine which checked the will of the master and his advisors.

What was true at the center of government was also true in areas where the central government reached into the affairs of the provinces. Colbert's monotonously repeated admonitions that intendants should co-operate with law courts and tax officials show how frequently his words must have been disregarded. Instead of cooperating, intendants competed with the local venal officials. As the personal reign of Louis continued, the intendants expanded their functions and powers so much that they, like the central ministers, had to increase their staffs. They also tended to remain in the chief town of the locality, delegating many of their important duties to *subdélégués* or sub-intendants in surrounding towns. At first, the intendant had only one or two of these lieutenants. By the 1690's the number of *subdélégués* had risen to twenty in Dauphiné, and before the end of the reign there were no less than eighty-six in Brittany. The *subdélégués* developed their own staffs and routine, corresponding with the local intendant and with the finance minister at Versailles. Alongside this local bureaucracy emerged a special office of lieutenant general of police to assist the intendants and *subdélégués*. The experiment began in Paris under La Reynie, in 1667. In 1699, it was extended to other cities and towns. This local bureaucracy, like that at Versailles, tended to limit the initiative of the king and his ministers. Intendants who lived for years, even decades, in a locality, came to see France from a regional perspective. During the wartime distress and economic troubles of 1688–1714, the intendants did not hesitate to argue, sometimes successfully, for exemptions from taxes for their areas.

But the emergence of the state as a bureaucracy meant more than controls on royal and ministerial initiative. The other side of the coin shows the bureaucracy controlling the king's subjects as they had never been controlled before. Louis' personality and leadership set the tone for a society which was becoming less brutal and more orderly. His bureaucracy reinforced that tendency. The intendants, *subdélégués*, police chiefs and their staffs maintained order with a minimum of military force. They controlled town governments by influencing elections and taking over municipal finances. They brushed aside the old confusion of municipal, judicial and clerical authorities in matters of censorship. They helped royal inspectors of industry enforce mercantilistic regulations. They bribed members of local parliamentary estates and influenced those assemblies to vote supplies. Sometimes they acted in concert with the old judicial and financial officials, but increasingly they bypassed them and even incorporated the most docile of them in their own bureaucracies. When one looks at France at the end of Louis XIV's reign, one cannot help being struck by the contrast with the local governments of England and the Dutch Netherlands, which were still small-scale, and still controlled by the economically and socially predominant classes.

This does not mean that the rise of the French bureaucracy made the monarchy totalitarian in its powers and influence over subjects. Indeed, as we shall see, the combination of monarchy and Parliament in England gave that state far greater resources and power in fiscal matters. The French monarchy, even when bureaucratized, could neither gain the confidence of its powerful middle-class subjects, which was essential for a strong treasury, nor sweep away the inherited "liberties" of aristocratic groups and privileged provinces. Instead, Louis XIV's state increased its control over privileged and unprivileged subjects to achieve a negative kind of absolutism. The king, personally and through his bureaucracy, was powerful enough to prevent any massive rebellion. Yet adjustments were made to balance royal demands with local interests. The underlying strength of privilege which made such compromises necessary can be illustrated by examining some of the more important seats of privilege—the nobility and clergy, the *Parlements* and the provincial estates.

The greatest independence of the nobility and Catholic clergy lay in their exemption from most taxes. Not even Colbert seriously considered a direct assault on this bulwark of privilege. What he wished to do was to reduce the number of clergy, perhaps nationalize some of the church's lands, and place on the tax rolls commoners who falsely claimed noble status and hence exemption from taxes. Only that last aim was realized. Colbert's nephew, Desmaretz, attempted a far more direct attack on tax exemptions after 1695, when he found that Louis XIV's wars could not be financed by taxes on commoners alone. First came the graduated head tax (*capitation*), which fell on all subjects except the hopelessly indigent and the clergy. It had two flaws. Rates were based only on guesses as to the wealth of individuals, and many well-to-do social groups and even entire provinces purchased exemption through moderate bribes. Hence Desmaretz turned in 1710 to a 10 percent income tax which was based on the actual resources of subjects and which fell on both the nobility and the clergy. Although this levy was superior to the head tax, and continued in modified form throughout the eighteenth century, it still failed to tap the wealth of the rich. Fully 25 percent of the population managed to secure exemptions by one ruse or another. Like the *capitation*, the income tax in effect became a surcharge on the taxes already paid by the poor.

For all their weaknesses, Desmaretz's tax schemes at least undermined the idea that the nobles and clergy were by nature free of obligations to the state. His work went hand in hand with the monarchy's insistence that both groups accept an inferior political status in return for the continuation of privileges. The nobles' practice of holding national assemblies ended with Louis XIV's assumption of power; the lawlessness of petty noblemen-bandits was challenged by special courts (*Grands Jours*) which seized, tried and punished lawbreakers in remote districts of the realm; and the great nobles were virtually excluded from the central and local bureaucracies of the state. The clergy continued to hold their periodic assemblies every five years, but in the areas of public order and taxes they had less power than they did in religious matters. Louis XIV gradually increased the so-called free gift or subsidy paid by the clergy to the state, even while he failed to impose the income tax on the church. Assembly sessions, which had lasted for a year and a half in 1650, were reduced to four months by 1665, elections to the assemblies were influenced by royal pressure on archbishops, and docile delegates were paid for voting in the king's interests.

Versailles symbolized the aristocracy's strange combination of docility and privileged status. By creating that imposing palace, attracting the great ones to it, and developing an elaborate court ceremonial centering on himself, Louis XIV educated the aristocracy to accept the monarch and the state as above themselves. Yet, Versailles also placed the aristocrats at the top of society. In a sense, the court ceremonial which permitted them to participate in Louis' personal-formal activities (such as rising from bed in the morning and retiring at night) was a conscious attempt by the monarchy to show that the aristocrats were above other subjects. The same technique was applied to the high officials of the church (archbishops, bishops, abbots, priors, canons, archdeacons). Most of these men came from aristocratic or well-to-do bourgeois families. Louis XIV pandered to their vanity and divided the spoils of the church with them. The parish priests, who came from humble backgrounds, were excluded from the assemblies of the clergy, and denied a role in diocesan affairs. The king also gave his bishops the authority to keep the lesser clergy in their place. Bishops could revoke the right of priests to preach or hear confessions. If necessary, they could punish priests with temporary exile or indefinite imprisonment for criticizing royal actions or espousing the cause of democracy in church affairs.

The Fronde had demonstrated the dangerous political power of the *Parlements*, lesser law courts and taxing bureaus. Colbert's dream of reducing the number of judicial and tax officials, and even of ending the sale of offices and the *Paulette* [9] remained a dream. The treasury could not afford to redeem offices, and in fact the number and variety of petty saleable offices were sharply increased to finance Louis' later wars. The political power of the *Parlements* was sharply reduced without being

9. See Chapter 2, p. 46.

abolished. Vetoing or amending legislation was forbidden. Remonstrances were curbed by insisting that the *Parlements* register royal laws before remonstrating against them. Under a king who insisted on obedience, there was little chance for the *Parlements* to use their remaining powers to block major royal programs. Nevertheless, the *Parlements* knew how to use the law, legal procedure and remonstrances to slow down the implementation of many royal programs. The parlementarians were also a far greater force than the church or monarchy in molding public opinion on social and moral matters. They were the ones who by their judicial decisions did most to strengthen the family unit and paternal authority in paranoic fear of the disintegration of that basic social institution. The monarchy had greater success in controlling the corruption of tax officials. Nevertheless, royal intendants were continually frustrated by powerful local personages and petty tax assessors who persisted in shifting the burden of taxes from their relatives, friends and peasants to the shoulders of their enemies and neighbors. More than one intendant wrote to Versailles about the "cocks of the parish" who eluded all their plans for equitable taxation.

In the outlying provinces of France which retained provincial estates the central bureaucracy and the intendants struggled with similar problems. The provincial estates blocked attempts to raise taxes to the level of the central provinces which lacked representative assemblies. The monarchy succeeded in increasing taxes far above previous levels, but it did so by working within the framework of the local assemblies— influencing elections, bribing delegates, and curtailing the length of sessions. Astonishing as it seems, Louis XIV was very accommodating to local traditions and institutions in his newly acquired provinces. His officials entered Alsace and Franche Comté, but acted more as supervisors than administrators. In Franche Comté only natives could become judges. In Alsace, Louis XIV personally forbade his functionaries to disturb Protestant worship or oust Protestants from their offices at the very time he was abolishing the Edict of Nantes in the rest of France. This policy was in sharp contrast to the English parliamentarians' persecution of Catholics in Ireland after the revolution of 1688.

Despite their continuing privileges, many noblemen of Louis XIV's last years dwelled morbidly on the erosion of their political power during the reign. Like the Duke of Saint-Simon, they believed that the long personal reign had been one dominated by the "vile bourgeoisie." Historians have echoed their sentiments, although with greater sophistication. It is popular to say that Louis XIV "balanced" classes, elevating the bourgeoisie to important positions in government as a counter to the nobles' continuing place at court. It would be more accurate to say that individual commoners rose within Louis XIV's system of government, but that their rise had the effect of strengthening the nobility's privileges. For the commoner-turned-bureaucrat became a nobleman and left his middle-class origins far behind. The first generation of middle-class officials attained personal nobility; by the time their offices had been handed down through three generations, their family had attained hereditary nobility. This was true of the families that staffed the *Parlements*, and equally true of the ministerial families—the Colberts and the Le Telliers—that formed an administrative nobility. Louis XIV's massive creation of new venal offices to finance his wars brought still more middle-class persons into the governmental nobility. Unconsciously, the Grand Monarch consummated Mazarin's defeat of the noble Fronde only to infuse his government with an aristocratic, privilege-mongering atmosphere. To be sure the old "nobles of the sword" no longer raised the standard of revolt. When Henry IV's nobles left the court, it had been a sure sign of imminent rebellion; when Louis XIV's nobles left Versailles, it was a sign of disgrace. But tamed as they were, the nobles retained their influence. During the eighteenth century, they were to retain their privileges by intrigue and legalistic resistance. Hostile ministers fell before court intrigues, and anti-aristocratic legislation was blocked by the new noble judges in the *Parlements*. These were far more effective weapons than the open rebellions of the age of Richelieu and Mazarin.

Although commoners slipped into the government, Louis XIV's regime remained cold towards the world of commerce, finance and industry. Colbert exploited the bourgeoisie, and even his Council of Commerce did little to build a bridge of communication between the governmental and business worlds. In 1700, the Council of Commerce was revived as a vehicle for drawing commerce and government together. Unfortunately, it was used more as a safety valve for the pent-up feelings of the bourgeoisie than as a means to bring them into government. Commoners remained suspicious of the monarchy, since they had no control over taxes and little influence over economic policies. While England's commercial interests established the Bank of England to help finance the wars against Louis XIV, the Sun King had to rely on private loans, frequent tampering with currency, creation of new offices, and taxes which burdened the poor and discouraged commerce and industry. Even private bankers could not continue to meet the demands of the state. Their terms were extortionate (35 percent, 40 percent, 50 percent), but interest payments were badly in arrears, and the great banker, Samuel Bernard, suspended his advances in 1709. The Monarchy turned to paper money in 1701, establishing a loan bank (*caisse des emprunts*) to issue notes in place of coin. But there was no cash to back the notes. Businessmen refused to handle them, and they depreciated to less than half their nominal value. In 1710, Desmaretz tried to create a semi-state bank run by a syndicate of bankers. Unfortunately, he could not find men who were willing to subscribe the necessary 200,000,000 *livres* to fund the experiment. Taxes could not be used as backing, for the monarchy had already pledged future revenues to meet an alarming state deficit (45,000,000 *livres* on a budget of 119,000,000 in 1715). Only a true income tax comparable to England's post-1688 land tax, and control of taxes by the merchant-banking interests as in England, could have induced French bankers to make the bank of 1710 a success. When the War of Spanish Succession came to a close, the French monarchy was bankrupt, its deficit an astronomical 2,328,000,000 *livres*, while England managed a national debt of only £34,400,000. Only a prolonged period of peace after 1715 and the resiliency of a basically sound economy saved the state which was outwardly the strongest in Europe.

Spain Under Charles II and Philip V

The Spanish monarchy, which had survived the shock of external defeat and internal rebellion in the 1640's and 1650's,[10] could not rival the achievements of Louis XIV's personal rule. Spain lacked France's economic resources, its institutional base, and above all a ruler with the capacity for work and a flair for leadership. During the long reign of Charles II (1665–1700), Spain slumbered through a period when virtually every other state in Europe was recovering from a mid-century crisis and undertaking major internal reforms. Charles II was a pathetic figure, physically misshapen, subject to serious physical and psychological disturbances, incapable of running the state which desperately needed direction and purpose. He came to be known as Charles the Bewitched. Government fell into the hands of his self-seeking mother, Mariana, assisted first by her Austrian confessor, Father Nithard, and then by a page-turned-paramour, Fernando de Valenzuela. When the queen-mother's influence waned, the government became burdened by the Spanish succession question, and the intrigues of the Austrian and French factions surrounding the monarch. Spanish historians turn in dismay from the reign. Altamira y Crevea declared that "under the rule of favorites, the internal political life of Spain was utterly reduced to internecine intrigues." [11]

10. See Chapter 7, pp. 193–200.
11. R. Altamira y Crevea, *Historia de España y de la civilización española*, vol. III (1913), 249.

Although recovery did not take place until after 1700, when the Bourbon Philip V ascended the throne, there were already some hopeful signs during Charles' reign. After 1686 the currency was stabilized following a long period of wild fluctuations. Little could be done to halt the economic decline of Castile, but other provinces began to recover. Barcelona's trade increased 50 percent between 1680 and 1700. Between prolonged periods of rule by worthless favorites, an occasional minister or prince with ability and vision emerged to show what could still be done to save Spain. Charles II's half-brother, Don Juan José, proved to be a capable governor of Aragon, and also succeeded in ousting both of the queen-mother's favorites from central positions of power. He became virtual head of state between 1677 and 1679. However, his earlier enthusiasm for fiscal and economic reform gave way to a life of intrigue. Much more was accomplished by the Count of Oropesa, who as principal minister from 1685 to 1691 made a strenuous effort to reduce taxes and government expenses. During the course of Charles' reign, repeated efforts were also undertaken to make the state an agent of national economic recovery. Immigration was encouraged by waiving religious restrictions on foreign artisans, nobles were permitted to take charge of industrial enterprises without losing status, workers and employers were given tax relief and freed from some mercantilistic regulations, bishops were discouraged from ordaining an excessive number of priests, and a Council of Trade and Currency was established and placed over the guild structure.

Under Philip V, major administrative changes took place. The Bourbon king had his weaknesses. He had to be dissuaded by Louis XIV from harsh treatment of his rebellious subjects in Barcelona, and he had a tendency to yield to the influences of courtiers. But he brought Spain back to a sense of national purpose during the War of Spanish Succession by leading its armies against the Austrian claimant. The war also gave the Bourbon king an opportunity to deal more effectively than any Spanish Hapsburg monarch with provincial privileges. The Catalans and Aragonese sided with the Austrian pretender in hopes of strengthening their provincial liberties. Their miscalculation proved to be disastrous. When Philip V won the war, he could impose a new order on the privileged provinces. In the words of the leading historian of seventeenth-century Spain, his victory "marks the transformation of Spain from a collection of semi-autonomous provinces into a centralized state." [12] The Council of Aragon was abolished, and the Council of Castile became the chief administrative organ for unified Spain. Fusing Spanish and French administrative traditions, Philip V reformed the new Bourbon state

12. J. H. Elliott, *Imperial Spain: 1469–1716* (Mentor, 1966), 371.

from top to bottom. Viceroys ruled the provinces, aided by intendants as well as Spanish *corregidores*. With the disappearance or growing impotence of the various *Cortes*, which had in most instances ceased to meet under Charles II, came the opportunity for the Spanish monarchy to insist that all parts of the state pay their share of taxes. The Frenchman Jean Orry took charge of finances. Under his guidance, a central treasury (*caisse*) was established and tax farming was consolidated. The old, inefficient councils began to take on the shape of ministries, in conscious imitation of the French system.

These remarkable reforms did not take full effect until after 1715, but they were well under way by the end of the War of Spanish Succession. They did not obliterate provincial attachments, nor rid the non-Castilian provinces of their hatred for Castilianization; but they did give Spain a degree of unity comparable to that of other continental states. They did not enable Spain to become a great power again, but did make her a formidable second-rate power, with an army of 58,000 and a respectable fleet. Even the territorial losses at Utrecht[13] were a gain in terms of internal strength. The Spanish Netherlands and Spanish Italy had been costly to defend, and the attempt at defense had enticed Spain into a century of wars which its resources could not support.

The Spanish Bourbons' attempt to recapture their Italian lands during the two decades which followed Utrecht is an interesting footnote to Philip V's reign. Once again, as in the days of Lerma and Olivares, Spain appeared to throw away an opportunity to concentrate on internal state-building. Yet, absurd as was this new flight from reality, it underlines the success of the Bourbon reforms. The fact that the other European powers awarded Naples and Sicily to one of Philip's sons in 1735 is not as significant as the Spaniards' capacity to wage new wars after the exhausting War of Spanish Succession. That a second-rate power could undertake such a struggle without causing internal chaos is dramatic proof of the rise of the modern, secular state. While the emergence of strong central government in Spain was overshadowed by the far greater achievements of Louis XIV's bureaucratic-police state, the Spanish example of state-building in the late seventeenth century should not be overlooked.

13. See Chapter 9, p. 257.

II.

Central and Eastern Europe:
New States in the Making

State-building in Brandenburg, Austria and Muscovy after 1660 [1] differed in one important respect from the process in France and Spain. In the western lands, rulers, ministers and bureaucrats were able to build on the foundation of existing states. In the east, there was the nucleus of power, but as rulers built from that center they changed their countries so much that we can describe the process as the creation of "new" states. When we refer to Austria and Brandenburg in the first half of the seventeenth century, we think of Austria proper and Brandenburg proper rather than the complex of territories held together by the Austrian Hapsburg and Brandenburg Hohenzollern dynasties. The state-building of 1661–1715 in these areas was largely a matter of pulling together the nucleus and other family domains to constitute a more cohesive and more powerful state. Austria became transformed into the Danubian monarchy, united geographically around the Danube River basin. Brandenburg united Rhenish, Brandenburgian and Prussian lands into the new kingdom of Brandenburg-Prussia (more commonly known as the kingdom of Prussia). The Austrian Hapsburgs also looked less and less to their position as Emperors of the Holy Roman Empire of the German

1. See Chapter 6, pp. 167–185, for the situation within central and eastern European states at mid-century.

Nation, as they welded together their Danubian holdings on the southern fringes of the Empire. The Hohenzollerns thought less and less of their position as electoral princes of the Holy Roman Empire as they acquired a royal crown to symbolize the distinctness of their north-central European state. While France and Spain had problems with outlying provinces, the French and Spanish states were already historic entities with strong nuclei which could carry the state through any period of difficult provincial relations. By contrast, Austria and Brandenburg would never have survived as important, viable states without some control over their provinces. The case of Muscovy is slightly different. The task of the Tsar in the late seventeenth century was not so much to change the relationship between the parts of his empire as to alter the nature of his autocracy over the entire state. The transformation of Muscovy into Russia was a cultural-intellectual one. The term "Muscovy" conjures up the image of the original, non-western and backward frontier-fortress of Moscow (if one wishes to avoid the still more contemptuous names of Scythia and Tartary used by western cartographers). The term "Russia" implies a more modern and powerful state which was adapting western techniques and institutions to the conditions of the Slavic world. The transfer of the capital from the "backward-looking" interior town of Moscow to the brand new metropolis of Saint Petersburg facing the Baltic and Europe was symbolic of the transformation of the Muscovite state, just as the acquisition of a Prussian crown was for Brandenburg and the drive down the Danube River was for Austria.

Brandenburg: From German Electorate to Prussian Kingdom

The late seventeenth-century state of Prussia was an unexpected and most unlikely creation. The main territory of Brandenburg with its electoral vote in the Holy Roman Empire had been held by the Hohenzollern family since the fifteenth century. But the other major parts of the Prussian states came to the Hohenzollerns only in the early seventeenth century, and under freakish circumstances. The daughter of a petty Rhenish prince persisted in marrying the Duke of East Prussia, even after she learned that he was mentally unbalanced. The daughter of that strange couple married in turn the Elector of Brandenburg. Two generations later, the real founder of the Prussian state succeeded to this crazy-quilt congeries of territories, which hopped across north-central Europe from Cleves, Mark and Ravensberg [2] in the Rhineland to electoral Brandenburg

2. The rest of the original principality of Jülich-Cleves was awarded to another prince by the Treaty of Xanten (1614). See Chapter 5, p. 153.

straddling the Elbe and Oder rivers and thence to East Prussia lying between the Vistula and Niemen rivers. The Hohenzollern lands were geographically separated, economically uninviting and virtually landlocked
because of the absence of good ports on East Prussia's Baltic shoreline.
The young man who inherited this pathetic consolation prize of the
central-eastern European world was Frederick William, known to history as the Great Elector (1640–1688).

Between 1640 and 1660, the Great Elector clung to his inheritance,
and added to it Eastern Pomerania, Kammin, Minden, Halberstadt and
Magdeburg. In so doing he survived the last years of the Thirty Years'
War and the Little Northern War. He also took advantage of a mid-
century crisis, playing off nobles against peasants, and town against
countryside. In the process, he raised a small army, collected taxes and
maintained internal order. But he had yet to deal conclusively with the
entrenched localism and privileges of his scattered possessions, which
blocked his path to united and absolute rule. All of his territories had
their local assemblies, or *Landtage*, which held the power of the purse
(and in some cases had their own machinery to assess, collect and disburse
the money they voted as well as independent foreign policies). In East
Prussia the landed nobility or Junkers and the guildsmen of Königsberg
could also reject the elector's demands by securing the veto of their overlord in Prussia, the king of Poland. The elector's status as vassal to the
Polish ruler was abolished formally by the Treaty of Oliva, and after
1660 Frederick William was the sovereign authority in East Prussia. However, the Prussians still tried to protect their privileges by requests for
judicial or military intervention from Warsaw. In Cleves-Mark, Frederick
William was faced by equally intransigent townsmen and nobles in the
assembly. In 1653, he had made a humiliating agreement with the Rhenish
estates. When he disregarded the compact and collected taxes illegally,
leading natives took their case to the Holy Roman Emperor. Frederick
William arrested one such offender and confiscated the lands of another,
but finally compromised by removing the penalties in return for a ransom.
In Brandenburg proper, such appeals concerning the hereditary elector's
demands were made illegal in 1648. Nevertheless, the nobles who dominated the *Landtag* drove a hard bargain with Frederick William in 1653.
A subsidy was finally voted, but it was to end in 1659, and in return the
elector legalized the growing control of the nobility over their peasants.

During the 1660's, the Great Elector dealt more effectively with
such local privileges. In East Prussia, the "Great Landtag" of 1661–1663
was forced to back down after the elector placed a merchant leader
under house arrest. Frederick William recognized Prussian liberties
only insofar as they did not infringe on his sovereignty. What this sovereignty implied became clear in the next ten years. A young nobleman

who incited the *Landtag* of 1669 to refuse a subsidy, was made an object lesson. He was kidnapped in Warsaw, to which he had fled. Despite cries for mercy from Prussians and the elector's advisors, Frederick William had him tortured and executed in defiance of Prussian law. During the next reign, the city of Königsberg settled down to paying a permanent excise tax, and Prussian nobles, peasants and small towns agreed to a permanent land tax. The *Landtag* disappeared except for formal occasions. In Brandenburg, the single *Landtag* was replaced by regional *Kreistage* in the 1660's, and the elector gradually wore down their resistance to taxation. A compromise with the nobility helped to divide the opposition in Brandenburg. The nobles escaped taxation while agreeing to a land tax on their peasants, administered by themselves in the *Kreistage*. The townspeople in Brandenburg also agreed to a permanent excise tax. The conflict was more dignified in Cleves-Mark. There the local assembly survived by agreeing in 1661 that it would vote supplies regularly and waive all appeals to the Emperor. The estates' granting of such a major concession was due largely to the elector's "invasion" of the area with troops to emphasize his power.

The taxes which Frederick William wrung from his possessions after 1660 allowed him to maintain a standing army. Only persistence, occasional acts of brutality and a willingness to compromise with the local nobilities over their right to rule the peasant population made such an achievement possible. Even so, the Great Elector's army was always close to disbandment for lack of funds. It dipped as low as 12,000 after the Scanian War and levelled off at the end of the reign to 30,000. This still amounted to 3 percent of the population, an enormous burden on a small and economically backward state, and the percentage is even more striking by comparison with Louis XIV's army, which amounted to 1.5 percent of the much larger French population.

The army, war taxes and wars of the Great Elector were the real driving force behind the unity which he was able to impose on his state. Without the constant presence of the army and the ever-present danger of invasion, provincial "liberties" would have remained even stronger than they did. Frederick William did not dare to interfere with the exclusive right of "natives" to hold office in each separate territory. Nor could he superimpose on his outlying possessions all of the organs which he and his predecessors had created for Brandenburg proper. Instead he quietly expanded the roles of a few key institutions at the center and drew provincials from all areas of the state into the central government.

This unifying trend was most notable in fiscal and military matters. Nothing could be done to unify the bewildering variety of treasuries dealing with ordinary income from both royal domains and miscellaneous sources. Brandenburg proper kept two separate treasuries, while similar treasuries sprang up in the other lands. However, a General War Chest for military expenditures was established for the entire state, and a Court State Chest had some authority over local treasuries in making allocations for the prince's personal needs. More important was the General War Commissariat. It emerged as an administrative clearing house for the war taxes imposed on the various provinces during the 1660's. Ultimately, the Commissariat became a rather complex structure, combining the functions of France's finance ministry and intendancies. The Commissariat imposed economic regulations on each area of the state, looked after the recruiting, provisioning and quartering of the army, handled disputes between soldiers and civilians, and acted as a general police force. The Commissariat also employed special officials in the towns and countryside. Its land councilors administered the rural land tax. Its town commissioners looked after the urban excise and eased town councils out of the administration of urban affairs. The army was "nationalized" to a greater extent than any other arm of the state. The General Staff ran the army of the entire state as a unified operation. In sharp contrast was the operation of the Privy Council for Brandenburg proper. Although it attempted haltingly to formulate policies for all provinces, it had neither the authority nor the power to enforce them.

Developing centralized princely institutions was one thing; luring individuals from the various provinces into them was quite a different matter. Since the Great Elector respected the right of "natives" to monopolize offices in their own areas, he could not develop a general Prussian bureaucracy in the strictest sense of the term. Only in the army did he insist that regional differences be obliterated. Soldiers from every part of the state marched shoulder to shoulder and took orders from common commanders. In the civil service, Frederick William's approach was more subtle and patient. He drew local burghers and nobles into the intendant-like offices of land councilor and town commissioner in their regions. Often, he chose precisely the local political-social elite which had traditionally served in the local *Landtag*. These men could not bear the strain of serving two masters simultaneously. In time, their loyalty to their province waned and their attachment to the state filled the vacuum. By the eighteenth century, Frederick William's grandson and namesake was at last free to place state servants indiscriminately in any area of the realm, regardless of the province from which they had come. It is easy to overlook one other long-range result of the Great Elector's bureaucratic work. In contrast to Louis XIV, Frederick William insisted that nobles as well as commoners share the burdens of government. Perhaps he was fortunate in having a nobility which was too impoverished to resist the lure of paid state offices. In any case, they did not look suspiciously on the Prussian state as a rival or potential enemy, as Saint-Simon's generation did at the end of Louis XIV's reign in France. While Richelieu had French bluebloods decapitated and Louis XIV made them ornaments of his Versailles showcase, Frederick William made Prussia's nobles full partners of his state. And while the French nobility intrigued and filibustered against their kings in the eighteenth century and ultimately revolted against them in 1788, the Prussian nobles remained loyal to their rulers even in the dark days of the military collapse before Napoleon's triumphant army.

A distinguished scholar, Frederick Nussbaum, has said that "the Great Elector succeeded in creating the state as machine, but not the state as organism." Perhaps it is true that "the state remained external," and that there was no complete fusion of subjects' and ruler's interests.[3] But as a machine, the Prussian state was as effective as any in the seventeenth century. It was the ruler with his officials who forced the Lutheran majority to tolerate Calvinist and Catholic minorities, a notable achievement in the religiously divided Germanies. It was the central government which provided the impetus for economic development by a conscious policy of attracting religious refugees from neighboring Catholic and Protestant states (an immigrant population which composed one-sixth of the scant 1,000,000 souls in the Prussia of 1688). The Prussian brand of mercantilism was sometimes visionary (Frederick William was naive in thinking that he could make his state a world commercial-naval power), sometimes debilitating in its controls over industry (far greater than in Colbert's France). Nevertheless, it is inconceivable that Prussia could have rebounded so quickly from the Thirty Years' War or become as united as it did by the end of the Great Elector's reign, had it not been for state-imposed mercantilism. And the vision of commercial greatness at least drove Frederick William to realize two major achievements. A canal linking the Oder and Elbe river systems avoided the tolls charged by Swedes and Danes in the Baltic. Use of the East Frisian port of Emden gave Prussia a major outlet to the North Sea. Except for inferior ports in East Prussia and Eastern Pomerania, Prussia was a landlocked state; it desperately needed the means to utilize the major German waterways which passed through its territories but which were blocked at their mouths by the Swedes and petty north German states. Thanks to Frederick William's initiative, Prussia gained control of major trading routes from Poland and the Danubian monarchy to the west. Its capital, Berlin, changed from a sleepy, provincial town to a thriving city.

3. F. L. Nussbaum, *The Triumph of Science and Reason, 1660–1685* (1953), 121.

Frederick I (1688–1713) lacked the vigor and vision of the Great Elector, but in his own peculiar way added to his father's achievements. The new prince is remembered for the cruel witticism tossed his way by his famous grandson, Frederick the Great, who declared that his grandfather was great in little things, but little in great ones. The remark is accurate, but it misses the important results of Frederick I's pettiness. His obsession with the trappings of monarchy greatly enhanced the prestige of Prussia. On the eve of the War of Spanish Succession, the Prussian ruler wrung from the Holy Roman Emperor a very important concession. Leopold I was given the use of Prussian troops in the war against France, but in return authorized Elector Frederick to become King Frederick. It was the supreme moment of Frederick I's life when he transported an enormous retinue from Berlin to Königsberg in 1701 and crowned himself "King in Prussia." Not even that awkward royal title tarnished the crown which he now wore. To accommodate the Emperor, who refused to create a monarchy within the Holy Roman Empire, Frederick avoided the title King of Brandenburg. Hence he turned to East Prussia, which was outside the Empire. But he still had to mollify the Polish ruler, who held West Prussia and did not want anyone else being called King of Prussia. Thus Frederick diplomatically called himself "King *in* Prussia!" The title was bizarre, but late seventeenth-century Europeans were impressed by any royal crown, and Prussian subjects undoubtedly felt a new sense of unity and collective pride. Gradually, the preposition "in" was conveniently dropped, and the Prussian Hohenzollerns became commonly known as kings *of* Prussia.

Frederick I had a flair for the pomp, ceremony and culture of royal life, whether it was in preparing for his coronation of 1701 or in working out the details of courtly etiquette. His coronation was meticulously copied from Scottish, Danish and Polish ceremonies. His royal court was fashioned in the image of Louis XIV's Versailles, just then taking its place as the new wonder of the European world. Frederick had to have his own official mistress (like Louis XIV), his wigs (in Louis XIV's personal style), an enlarged palace and an embellished capital city, Berlin (renovated in Baroque style by French, Dutch and Prussian architects, painters, sculptors and musicians). To his superficial cultural interest was added the intellectual curiosity of his wife, Sophie Charlotte. It was she who attracted the intellectual giant Leibniz to Prussia as founder of the Berlin Academies of Sciences and Arts. She also made possible the development of the new University of Halle, with its refreshingly unpedantic approach to jurisprudence and theology, and its interest in modern scientific and historical subjects. It was to suit her tastes also that Charlottenburg was made a pleasant suburb of Berlin, complete with its own palace, park and opera house.

BRANDENBURG-
PRUSSIA

Possessions in 1618

① Cleves (1614)
② Mark (1614)
③ Ravensburg (1614)
④ Minden (1648)
⑤ Halberstadt (1648)

⑥ East Pomerania (1648)
⑦ Kammin (1648)
⑧ Magdeburg (conceded 1648, occupied 1680)
⑨ Spanish Gelderland (1715)
⑩ West Pomerania (1720)

Frederick I lived beyond his income and chose to let other states use his armies in return for subsidies. In these respects his reign marked a sharp departure from that of his predecessor; for the Great Elector had lived frugally and insisted on controlling his armies, whether subsidized by other states or not. The next ruler, Frederick William I, was to give Frederick I a magnificent funeral and then fire two-thirds of the state's court officials to bring Prussia closer to financial reality. Even so, Frederick I had built on the foundations laid by his own father, making the state look like a kingdom, continuing its mercantilism and religious toleration and creating a supreme law court for his miscellaneous provinces (although not for the major ones). An indication of the unity attained under Frederick I can be found in the share of taxes allotted to the various parts of his state. Brandenburg paid one-third, a major burden but not an inordinate one in view of the area's importance. East Prussia contributed 16 percent, Cleves-Mark 10 percent, and the rich territory of Magdeburg 15 percent. Whatever his faults, Frederick I came closer to seeing the Prussian state as an abstraction, rather than as a family possession, than had the Great Elector. Frederick William had divided his lands among the offspring of his two marriages. Frederick I annulled the will, ensuring that all of the family lands would remain part of the Prussian state.

Austria: From Weak Imperialism to Danubian Monarchy

The Great Elector's Austrian counterpart was the Holy Roman Emperor Leopold I (1658–1705). Leopold was a strange figure as a statebuilder. He has been compared unfavorably with his great antagonist, Louis XIV, and his personal traits mark him as the inferior of the other great rulers of the day, William III, Frederick William and Peter the Great. One could well argue that the creation of Leopold I's Danubian monarchy was due to external events which thrust greatness on the Hapsburg monarch in spite of himself. Certainly it was the unexpected collapse of Turkish power after 1683 and the military victories of the coalition of Christian states which made a new monarchy on the Danube possible. Historians have wondered how the self-conscious, indecisive and morbidly fatalistic Leopold could be so lucky. For he was forever putting off decisions, and always quick to say that it was God's will whether catastrophe or good fortune came his way. If we look more closely at Leopold's character, however, it is possible to see traits which had something to do with his good fortune. Leopold's devotion to the Austrian Hapsburg cause and his deep religious convictions carried him through the Turkish siege of Vienna in 1683 and the interminable conflicts with Hungarian heretics and Ottoman infidels. Other personal traits helped Leopold to take advantage of the Turkish collapse. To be sure, the ruler was frequently saved by the decisions of able ministers. Yet we should not forget that he chose those servants and that he was able at crucial moments to take their advice over that of corrupt ministers who looked only to their self-advancement. For example, Leopold relied heavily on spiritual advisors who warned him against self-seeking courtier-ministers.[4] It was Leopold himself who made the decision to give up the bankrupt ministerial policy of savage repression against the Hungarian rebels. And when external events gave Leopold his opportunity to create the Danubian monarchy in the 1680's, he did not try to escape his destiny.

When Leopold was crowned Holy Roman Emperor and succeeded to his family's lands in Austria, Bohemia and Hapsburg Hungary in 1658, the creation of the Danubian monarchy was just beginning. It was clear that the base of power in the state could no longer be the imperial title and the nominal leadership of the Germanic empire. But little had been done since the Thirty Years' War to shift the center of power to the Danubian complex of Hapsburg territories.[5] Leopold could draw little satisfaction from the fact that the Austrian Hapsburg lands had been united under his family for many generations (in contrast to the recent gathering-in of the Hohenzollern lands of the Rhineland, Brandenburg and East Prussia). The process of dividing the Austrian chancellery into chambers for each of the major territories had just begun. Austria's war council and treasury had to contend with rival authorities in the other provinces. In all parts of the realm there were privileged assemblies that

4. Historians have believed the vitriolic comments of the priest-haters in Leopold's entourage, failing to notice that the confessors, priests and monks around the ruler were often his best advisors.
5. See Chapter 6, pp. 169–171.

retained the right to bargain over taxation with the Hapsburgs, and in some cases actually controlled the administration of direct taxes through their own officials. The Hungarian estates were the most independent, but the Bohemian Diet retained some privileges despite the defeat of a Bohemian revolt in the 1620's. Everywhere, the landed nobility used the provincial estates to legalize their control over the hapless peasantry. Religious and linguistic divisions within the state were far more serious than in the Hohenzollern state to the north, for they coincided with (and hence reinforced) provincial borders. The one main advantage of the Austrians over the Hohenzollern rulers of Brandenburg-Prussia was geographic. While the northern state was composed of separated areas, the Hapsburg domains were a bloc of contiguous territories.

The immediate concern of Leopold was to keep Hapsburg Hungary from breaking away from his rule. The Truce of Vasvar with the Turks in 1664 gave him his opportunity to act without fear of arousing a Hungarian-Turkish alliance. A conspiracy by leading Hungarian noblemen was answered by swift reprisals. In 1671 the rebel leaders were executed with all the fury the English exercised in Ireland, and a military regime was imposed on Hapsburg Hungary. The architect of this "pacification" was Wenzel Lobkowitz, who had masterminded the attack on Bohemian independence in the 1620's. Now, as an old man, Lobkowitz meant to "put the Hungarians in Czech trousers." A Hapsburg governor took the place of the native Palatine, and ruled with a mailed fist from Pressburg. The Hapsburg Archbishop of Gran presided over a special tribunal which disregarded local law and meted out penalties for Hungarian "treason." An army of Jesuits spread through the towns and countryside, forcing Catholicism on Protestant Hungarians.

These methods proved to be too sweeping and premature. Hungarian rebels continued to hold out with the assistance of Polish mercenaries and French "advisors." Leopold became more conciliatory and tried to patch up his differences with the Hungarians through a compromise settlement in 1681. However, reconciliation could not take place overnight. Lobkowitz's methods had made Hungarians bitter, suspicious and hostile. When Kara Mustafa's Turkish army invaded the Hapsburg lands in 1683, Hungarian malcontents stirred up new troubles. It was not until 1687 that a lasting settlement of the Hapsburg-Hungarian problem was possible. By then, the Turks had been thrown back, the Hapsburg Hungarians defeated and the Turkish territories in Transylvania and Hungary conquered. Vienna was now the center of a huge Danubian state, Leopold was master of the situation and, fortunately, he was willing to compromise once more with Hungarian "liberties."

The Hapsburg-Hungarian settlement of 1687 was largely a modification of the abortive compromise of 1681. The brutal Lobkowitz had been removed from power, the hated Hapsburg governorship abolished and open religious persecution tempered. Leopold's new advisors were the more realistic chancellors of Austria and Bohemia. They thought in terms of political centralization, but under the ruler's tempering influence settled for something far short of sweeping religious and social changes. The medieval charter of Hungarian liberties (the Golden Bull of 1222), which stood in the way of political control from Vienna, was modified. Instead of a formally elective crown, the Hungarian throne now became hereditary in the male Hapsburg line. Instead of the traditional right of Hungarian nobles to resist Hapsburg "tyranny" with armed rebellion, the nobility were to confine their opposition to the chambers of the Hungarian Diet. This settlement was almost a carbon copy of the political peace imposed on Bohemia in the 1620's. In social and religious matters, the Hungarian nobles were spared the rude treatment given the Bohemians. There was no wholesale confiscation of lands. Religious changes were moderate. Catholics continued to undertake missionary work, but systematic destruction of Protestant churches was forbidden. Although Protestant nobles might have felt that the treason- and heresy-hunting of the 1660's and mid-1680's could be resumed at any moment, they were in the meantime relatively safe from the priest and the executioner. The Hapsburgs had gained what they wanted most of all, political power. The Hungarian Diet began to increase its share of taxes to the Danubian state under the influence of Hapsburg officials who interfered with elections in the manner of contemporary rulers in England, France and the Dutch Netherlands. To contain the power of the Hungarians, ex-Turkish Transylvania was placed under separate jurisdiction, with its own assembly and even its own native prince. Since the Transylvanian Diet was closely watched by the Hapsburgs and the prince was raised and educated under Hapsburg influence at Vienna, it was clear that the Transylvanians were part of the Danubian monarchy just as the Hungarians were.

The new Danubian monarchy of Austria-Bohemia-Hungary-Transylvania fell short of the unity achieved by the Brandenburg-Prussian state. Nevertheless, its accomplishments were impressive. At Vienna, the Austrian and Bohemian chancelleries were joined by new chancelleries for Hungary and Transylvania. The important fact was not that these organs remained separate from each other but that the internal and external policies of every region were set in the capital and not in the provinces. The Austrian treasury and war council did not go as far as their counterparts in Brandenburg in centralizing taxation and the army, but they did initiate fiscal and military policies for the provinces to consider. The development of a central Danubian bureaucracy was still more suc-

THE DANUBIAN MONARCHY

× Battles
1 Upper Austria
2 Lower Austria
3 Styria
4 Tyrol
5 Carinthia
6 Carniola
7 Croatia
8 Temesvar (1718)
9 Wallachia
10 Austrian Netherlands (1714)

cessful. To Vienna were drawn nobles and commoners from throughout the state as well as many foreigners. They were an impressive group, bringing their various talents and backgrounds to bear on Danubian problems, while leaving their parochialism behind them. No other late seventeenth-century state, with the possible exception of Russia, could rival the fusion of political interest and cosmopolitanism which was displayed in Vienna.

The situation at the local levels of government was less pleasing to the Hapsburgs. Since the estates did not fade away as they did in the Prussian state, it was difficult to turn country nobles into a local service nobility. A governor, whose title varied from area to area, acted as a poor imitation of the French intendant and the Prussian land councilor. He took orders from Vienna, but he was also responsible to the local assembly of estates. And the estates, not the central government, chose the working officials who assisted him. At the county level also, the same type of government by assembly persisted. The native nobles, clinging to their privileges, dominated the county and provincial estates and offices. On their own property these nobles still ruled as little kings. Leopold tried to curb their controls over the peasantry, but he had to concede defeat. Even in Bohemia, he agreed in 1680 that the noble-dominated estates should control noble-peasant relations and that no appeals against landlord oppression could be made to him.

The compromise solution of Leopold I in the 1680's was just as effective as it had to be. That is, it was effective enough to keep the Danubian monarchy running for over two centuries. It was strong enough to weather a new Hungarian uprising between 1703 and 1711. It was flexible enough to tolerate virtual autonomy in the Italian and Netherlandish territories obtained from Spain in 1713–1714. And it was able to withstand the tensions inherent in a state which retained three separate crowns, the imperial, the Bohemian and the Hungarian. Joseph I (1705–1711) had to travel to Pressburg and Prague for his Hungarian and Bohemian coronation ceremonies, but this inconvenience could be tolerated, since it gave those areas a direct attachment to the Hapsburg dynasty. Charles VI (1711–1740) went a step further. In 1713 he repeated the Hapsburg formula that all parts of the state were inseparable and went on to emphasize the hereditary succession of his family to all kingdoms, provinces and counties of the Danubian monarchy. There was one flaw in this Pragmatic Sanction of 1713, but it was rectified by the War of Austrian Succession a generation later. The flaw was that succession was guaranteed only in the male line. If Charles had no sons, it was questionable whether a daughter could succeed him. When the hypothetical situation became a reality in 1740, Charles' daughter (Maria Theresa) had to fight against neighboring states and plead with Hungarian subjects to maintain the integrity of her state. She succeeded in retaining everything but Silesia. Her success is proof enough of the lasting achievement of Leopold I.

ꙮ Russia: The Westernization of Muscovy

One cannot tell the story of Muscovy's transformation into the Russian state without concentrating on the ruler who effected that change. More than Frederick William and far more than Leopold, Peter the Great (1682–1725) was the creator of his state. Historians will probably always disagree over the originality of Peter, and certainly will argue over the wisdom of his methods. But of the importance of the Romanov ruler there can be little doubt. He stands out not only as the greatest Tsar of the seventeenth century, but as one of the great rulers in Russian history, taking his place with Ivan IV, Catherine the Great, Alexander II, Lenin and Stalin. Indeed, there has been a tendency in Russian historiography to divide Russian history into two periods, the pre-Petrine and the post-Petrine. For many scholars believe that the basic change in Russian history occurred during Peter's reign, and that this change was his personal work. Although Marxist historians have tried to rewrite the Petrine era with the aim of sweeping aside the Great Man theory of history, they cannot blot out Peter's achievements by attributing them to economic, social and national "forces."

Among the prominent rulers of the late seventeenth century, Peter the Great was unique in his way of ruling. In contrast to Leopold's manner of putting off decisions, Peter made decisions constantly and quickly. William III compromised with the representative institutions of England and the Dutch Netherlands, which at times hampered the effectiveness of his military and diplomatic plans; one cannot conceive of Peter the Great doing so, even had he been in William's place. Louis XIV had a sense of decorum and a mildness in his actions; Peter was forever restless and nonconformist. The Great Elector was closest to the Tsar in methods, but even his brutal attack on privileges appears mild by comparison with Peter's habit of overwhelming the forces and individuals lying in his path.

There is singular agreement over Peter's personality. He was a human dynamo, with unbelievable energy, an immense appetite, and a rugged constitution which allowed him to tackle a day's task after an evening of carousing which felled his fellow merry-makers. His habit of gesticulating wildly with his hands when talking and a nervous disorder which frequently gave his face and eyes a savage appearance could intimidate and terrorize those around him. Ceremony and etiquette were completely foreign to his nature. In an age when rulers were becoming sedentary administrators who carefully thought out their statecraft, the Tsar seemed an anomaly with his constant wanderings, his calloused carpenter's hands and his pragmatic response to fundamental problems which begged for broader, comprehensive solutions. Probably the best description is Vasili Klyuchevsky's brilliant portrait, which paints Peter as an "artisan-Tsar." [6]

Peter's personality was a rude shock to the Muscovites. The out-

6. V. O. Klyuchevsky, *Peter the Great* (Vintage, 1961), 33–56.

moded, semi-feudal army, the confused and overlapping central institutions and the poorly developed human and economic resources which he inherited were to be subjected to rough treatment from the impetuous, naive, boorish ruler. As a youth he had escaped the dull and proper courtly life at the Kremlin. His contact with the merchants, artisans and military men in the foreign suburb of the capital reinforced his natural antipathy towards the backwardness and sluggishness of Muscovite society. His experience with court intrigue as a ten-year-old made an equally lasting impression. After the mildly reformist regime of Tsar Alexis, Moscow was subjected to a succession dispute between the offspring of Alexis' two marriages. The eldest son of the first marriage, Fedor, succeeded peacefully in 1676, but his death in 1682 triggered a palace struggle between the supporters of Fedor's brother and sister (Ivan and Sophia) on the one hand, and his half-brother (Peter) on the other. The Petrine faction lost, and Sophia became the regent and acting ruler, with Ivan and Peter as figurehead co-Tsars. The coup was engineered by the corrupt, backward-looking musketeers (Streltsi), and involved disorderly demonstrations by the Old Believers, passive acceptance by the Orthodox clergy, and the massacre of Peter's relatives and the ineffectual old nobility (boyars). Peter never flinched at the bloodbath, which he saw with his own eyes, but the events of 1682 made him hostile to Old Believers, Orthodox clergy, boyars and Streltsi—in short, to all the forces that stood in the way of political and cultural change. Ironically, Sophia turned out to be a reformer. She increased Muscovite contacts with European culture, maintained the army of 100,000 which had gradually been formed under foreign influences and attempted without success to defeat the Turks who blocked her state's path to the Black and Mediterranean seas. Ironically, too, a second coup which ousted Sophia in favor of Peter in 1689 was supported by reactionary noblemen who wished to put a stop to the regent's westernizing and modernizing schemes. Little did they know that Peter would be far more sweeping in his assault on the Muscovite past. While the corrupt and self-seeking followers of Peter's mother proceeded to undo Sophia's work, the young Tsar continued his unorthodox education. He picked the brains of the Swiss, Scottish and Dutch soldiers of fortune and savants in Moscow's foreign suburb, organized his Muscovite playmates into two western-style regiments and became fascinated with boats and sea power.

Peter's personal reign did not really begin until 1695 when he broke out of the foreign ghetto and unleashed a military-naval attack on the Turks at Azov. The action was typical of the artisan-Tsar. All Peter had was a vague plan to secure a commercial outlet to Asia and Europe. Azov was a most unlikely "window to Europe," but Peter attacked it because it was the weakest Turkish outpost. The capture of Azov in 1696 did not accomplish much, since Peter had to cut short his drive to the Black Sea for lack of allies. He quickly adjusted to the changed international situation. When neighboring states decided to attack Sweden, Peter dropped his interest in the Black Sea and made the Swedish-dominated Baltic his goal. The Baltic Sea would be his window to the west. This was an astonishing change in direction, even if it seemed to be the only course of action open to the Tsar. To concentrate on the War of the North against Sweden (1700–1721), Peter abruptly halted several programs oriented towards the southern border of his state. His new dockyards on the Don River, his dream of uniting the Don and Volga rivers by canal and his plans for a Black Sea fleet were all sacrificed for a war of uncertain outcome. The Russian army was ill-prepared for the difficult land campaigns against the seasoned Swedish forces, and incapable of sustaning the long twenty-one-year war ahead without drastic military changes. Without knowing it, Peter had naively thrown his subjects into a conflict which would turn his state upside down before it ended.

The War of the North unleashed on Russia a torrent of internal reforms sometimes described as the Petrine Revolution. Klyuchevsky has given us a vivid picture of what this period of reform was like for Peter: "He lived from day-to-day, trying to cope with fast-moving events and trying to deal with the most urgent requirements of state without having time to think things out or make a plan."[7] Is it any wonder that one historian has compared the Petrine Revolution to Roosevelt's New Deal in its confusion and sense of urgency? The peripatetic warrior-Tsar remained constantly with his army, while expecting his civilian government several hundred miles away to decipher his barrage of cryptic, sometimes incomprehensible, orders. At first, Peter thought exclusively in terms of military and naval needs, then grasped at any idea which would bring more men, money and resources to bear on the war effort, and eventually turned to administrative reshuffling in a desperate effort to make the backward autocratic state an effective weapon. Peter's victory over Sweden at Poltava in 1709 relieved some of the urgency and gave the Tsar time to devote more attention to the institutional framework of his state. However, it was only in the last year or two of his reign that the confusion began to take on some semblance of order.

The Petrine Revolution was not, strictly speaking, a sharp break with the past. Rather it was an acceleration of tendencies already visible in the reigns of Michael, Alexis and Sophia. What distinguished Peter

7. *Ibid.*, 31.

from his predecessors was his insistence on carrying through his reforms, and the brutal methods and shock to Russian society which accompanied them. His headlong assault on tradition was made possible only because a mid-century religious schism had broken down traditional habits. Yet his assault reverberated throughout the state far more than had the mid-century Nikonian crisis.[8]

The most celebrated aspect of the Petrine Revolution was its so-called Europeanizing or westernizing of Muscovite culture. Actually, Peter had no intention of making his society a European one in thought or word. He was interested in making use of European technical advances, not in transplanting western ideas. If he tried to make Russian courtiers and officials look and act like Europeans, this was to shake them out of their lethargy and parochialism so that they would be receptive to western techniques. Thus the Tsar made the cream of his society dress like Europeans, smoke pipes and shave their beards, but when it came time to send them to school they entered technical institutes. Under Peter there arose an academy of "mathematical science and navigation," an academy for engineering and an academy for artillery. As Paul Miliukov notes, elementary and general education were sacrificed to professional training.[9] Only the diocesan schools, teaching grammar, rhetoric, philosophy and theology to future Orthodox priests, kept Russia from becoming an intellectual wasteland. Peter was also interested in discovering at first hand how Europeans plied their trades. He made two extensive trips to the west (1697–1699 and 1716–1717) and sent scores of young noblemen tramping across the continent to pick the brains of Europeans. It is an amusing commentary on Peter's travels that he knew more about how ordinary Europeans lived than their own rulers did. When he returned to his native land, he brought back technical skills as well as foreign technicians and teachers to train his people.

Politically, Peter wanted to combine the old Tsarist autocratic tradition with centralized power and decentralized action. As he ran roughshod over existing institutions, however, only the autocratic element remained discernible. In 1711, he replaced the old Boyar Duma with an executive senate. Somehow, the senators were meant to translate the Tsar's suggestions for reform and his imperious orders into action. The poor senators had neither the intelligence to make sense of Petrine commands nor the initiative and honesty to carry them out efficiently. Hence Peter had to subordinate the senate to a special official, known as the

8. See Chapter 6, pp. 183–185.
9. See the translated excerpt from Miliukov's *Essays in the History of Russian Culture*, in M. Raeff, ed., *Peter the Great: Reformer or Revolutionary?* (Heath, 1963), 61–67.

Procurator General. Peter also knew that something was wrong with the Muscovite system of overlapping, chaotic ministries (*prikazi*), and replaced them by a series of colleges on the Swedish and German models. These colleges had some advantages. All members of a college shared responsibility for its decisions, whereas the head of each *prikaz* had tended to act arbitrarily. And the colleges tended to be more specialized than the old *prikazi*. But since Peter kept abolishing old colleges, adding new ones, combining some and dividing others, there was an element of confusion which looked disturbingly similar to the old pattern. At the local level, disorder and order went hand in hand. Eight (eventually twelve) huge provinces were created and run by governors. These governors had a staggering responsibility, for they were to see that taxes were collected, soldiers recruited and order maintained. The efficient Prussian bureaucrats would have been dumbfounded by such a confusion of powers. It is impossible to describe the constant changes and the variety of forms these governors created at the county level. But somehow they managed to work.

Peter tried to establish a chain of command from Tsar to Procurator General, through the senate and the colleges and on down to the governor and his underlings. So frustrating was the attempt that the Tsar had to rely heavily on personal agents: the Procurator General, to watch the senate; foreign vice presidents in the colleges, to watch the native presidents and the other councilors; and above all the glorified spies known as fiscals who infiltrated every level of government, to watch everybody. There is a very famous example of how the system of fiscals "worked." The chief fiscal of the realm had the governor of Siberia sent to his death for stealing from the state and its subjects, only to be broken on the wheel for his own corruption.

Peter insisted that all subjects serve the state in some capacity, and hence his social "reforms" have to be discussed in a political context. Actually, the most striking political-social achievement was also the most ephemeral. Peter broke down the rigid hierarchy of noble ranks based on birth and status, and created a service nobility which drew both hereditary nobles and ex-commoners into military and civil service. Promotions were based largely on merit, and social ranking was based rigidly on the specific function of the individual state servant. This emphasis on service to the state as the basis of social status was not new, but Peter made it work far more effectively than his predecessors. The difficulty was in securing enough loyal and efficient state servants. During his lifetime, Peter constantly had to supplement native servants with foreigners, especially Germans, Silesians and Bohemians. We have already noted his reliance on foreigners as vice presidents in his colleges. The military had more than its share of foreign commanders. A Holsteiner and a Silesian were instrumental in organizing and staffing the administrative colleges. During his reign, Peter relied increasingly on natives, and he even came to see the day when his Russian officers fought rather than fled at the sound of the first shot. Unfortunately, the will of one man could not be transferred easily to the entire state and society. During the course of the eighteenth century, the Russian nobility retained their noble status while evading the very state service on which that status was based.

One of Peter's greatest tasks was to make the untapped resources of his Russia serve the insatiable appetite of the army and navy. The commercial population was small and the great mass of his subjects were serfs riveted to the soil. Thus it was difficult for him to find persons with the ability to run his mines, foundries, arsenals and cloth factories, and even more difficult to find a ready supply of workmen. At first, the Tsar concentrated on state-owned enterprises, run by foreigners and native nobles and commoners. Eventually he began to rely on private entrepreneurs, although their enterprises were limited by tight state regulations. He had to scour Russia in search of potential laborers. Fugitives, retired soldiers, soldiers' children, the poor and "vagabonds" were all pressed into service. Peter also resorted to the expedient of attaching entire villages of serfs permanently to state and private businesses.

Marxist scholars like Peter Lyashchenko are correct in noting that Peter built his state on the foundations of serfdom.[10] Instead of altering the base of the social structure, he actually strengthened the institution of serfdom. Serfs were kept under the control of their lord in order to be of service to the government as well. Tied to the soil, they could easily be found by the tax collector and the army recruiter. The worker in the mines and in industry was really only a different type of serf, since he too was frozen to his job in the service of the state. The Tsar was disturbed by the debasement of his subjects, but was trapped by the needs of his "warfare state." His only attempt to improve the lot of the masses was to declare that serf families should be sold as a unit, not as individuals. His basic fiscal "reform" was to shift the burden of taxation from households to individual males (including infants!). The effect was to make taxation all the more inequitable for large families with low incomes.

Peter's attitude to the state Orthodox church is a study in contrasts. He hated the backwardness, obscurantism and hypocrisy of the clergy, and he was suspicious of the lingering political power in the hands of the Patriarchal head of the church. It is not surprising that the Tsar and his boon companions established what was called the Most Drunken Synod

10. P. I. Lyashchenko, *History of the National Economy of Russia to the 1917 Revolution* (1949), 267.

of Fools and Jesters, to parody ecclesiastical ceremonies. Nor is it surprising that he left the office of Patriarch vacant in 1700. He went so far
as to divert some of the clergy's wealth to the poor (and also to the state
treasury). In 1721, Peter agreed to restore the control of church revenues
to the clergy, only to place the Orthodox church itself under a state-
controlled Holy Synod. On the other hand, Peter was apparently a
devout man who spoke of God with more sincerity and less superstition
than did Louis XIV. Peter was determined that the church should be
reformed, not destroyed. He laid down regulations which struck at
superstitious practices and unseemly conduct in church services. He also
established elementary parochial schools rivalling his secular "cipher"
schools.

Peter the Great made his state a great military-political power, and
transformed non-European Muscovy into semi-European Russia, adapting
western techniques and culture to Russian needs. It is obvious that he did
so at a great sacrifice of his subjects. His new capital at Saint Petersburg
was the symbol of the new state, but what he called his "paradise" was
also a mass grave for thousands of workmen who died building the "window to Europe" on a marsh. Every year his army absorbed a fresh batch
of recruits, sometimes numbering as many as 30,000. Many of these unwilling soldiers did not survive the wars, epidemics, cold and other hazards
of military life. He tripled state revenues between 1710 and 1724, and
balanced his budgets without a state bank or deficit financing. But so
great was the hardship on his subjects that many fled to areas where they
could not be traced by the tax collector. He made courtiers and bureaucrats look like Europeans, but widened the gulf between them and
most Russians, who kept their beards, wore their traditional dress and
sullenly resisted westernization. Outwardly, Peter was obeyed, and on
his death he was proclaimed as a new Samson, Japhet, Moses, Solomon
and David, who had "given birth to Russia and nursed her." Yet to
many Christians he was Anti-Christ. His innovations drove the *Streltsi*
into rebellions which were not finally suppressed until 1700. His taxes
and military conscription were so disliked by the Cossacks that their
revolts had to be put down savagely.

One cannot condone such by-products of the new Russia. Fortunately, we are far enough removed from the misery to be able to see
the positive side of Peter's state-building. Peter treated his subjects as
inanimate objects, bullied his closest friends and played cruel practical
jokes, but he also loved his country. One may disagree with Mikhail
Bogoslovskii's emphasis on Petrine "benevolence," but there is an element of truth in that historian's picture of Peter "leading the people

and reconstructing its life in accordance with the dictates of reason."[11] If the Tsar drove his people, he led them as well. If his decrees are filled with threats they are equally crammed with explanations of why things should be changed. While provincials went their own way, those at the center of Russian life could not shake off their western habits and dress; and in the next few generations, western techniques were reinforced by western ideas and literature. For all that the post-Petrine nobility shirked state service in practice, they could not destroy the idea that they owed service to the state. For good or for ill, society was now bound to the state as the sovereign authority. Even the Tsar began to perceive that the Russian state was above everyone, including himself. Peter wrote into his decrees the notion that the interests of the state were supreme, and insisted on an oath to the state separate from that sworn to his person. Out of the turmoil, misery and ferment of Peter the Great's reign came a more modern concept of the state to replace the traditional idea of the state as the Tsar's personal possession.

ᴄᴀ Sweden, Denmark and the Lesser German Principalities

Political changes in the Scandinavian and lesser German countries after 1660 are almost crowded out of the central-eastern European picture by the more spectacular emergence of the Prussian, Danubian and Russian states. We should not ignore these secondary powers, however, for their experience sheds light on the historical processes at work within their greater neighbors. Their story also exemplifies the late seventeenth century trend towards monarchical absolutism and the development of the impersonal bureaucratic state. Certainly, it is more instructive to study Sweden and Denmark than to dwell on the sad plight of Poland and the Ottoman Empire. While the Scandinavian principalities adapted their institutions to contemporary conditions, the Polish and Turkish states failed to do so and became European problems rather than viable powers.[12]

The most interesting developments took place in Sweden. After a twelve-year regency dominated by the great nobles, Sweden was transformed during Charles XI's personal reign (1672–1697). Historians now believe that Caroline reforms were unpremeditated, but their opinion does not detract from Charles' achievements. He built on the foundations of

11. Quoted in M. Raeff, ed., Peter the Great, 29.
12. See Chapter 9, pp. 244–245, 250–251, 255, 258.

Swedish absolutism laid by Gustavus Adolph and completed the work cut short by Charles X's untimely death in 1660. The Caroline absolutism achieved after 1680 was so effective that its institutions were copied by both Russia and Prussia. Its reforms were accomplished without the terror and hardship which were the lot of the Prussian and Russian people. So effective was Charles XI's state-building that it carried Sweden through the catastrophe of Charles XII's War of the North and was accommodated to the noble-dominated Age of Freedom which followed.

The great nobles who ran Sweden between 1660 and 1680 committed serious errors which played into the hands of Caroline absolutism. They continued past practices of taking over crown lands and diverting state revenues from the hard-working petty bureaucrats who came from the lesser nobility and professional families. They also involved Sweden in the near-disastrous Scanian War of 1674–1679. Meanwhile, young Charles XI performed well on the battlefield and became something of a national hero. In 1680 the king called a national assembly to solve post-war problems. He vaguely compared the country to a ship which had escaped stormy seas, but had returned to harbor in need of repairs. Probably Charles was as astonished as the great nobles by the response of the *Riksdag*. The traditionally anti-noble estates of clergy, townsmen and free peasants demanded an absolute monarchy to check the nobles. When the bureaucrats, who had remained neutral in a similar crisis in 1650, threw their support to the disaffected estates, the coalition became invincible.

With the support of the majority in the *Riksdag*, Charles XI achieved a political and social revolution between 1680 and 1693. A "reduction" (restoration of crown lands) left the holdings of the great nobles reduced to their ancestral estates. Instead of owning two-thirds of the state, they now owned only one-third. A Great Commission of the *Riksdag* investigated the record of the toppled noble regime, and mercilessly fined the regents on the assumption that their personal wealth had been illegally acquired while in office. With the income from fines and restored lands, Charles XI was able to rebuild the Swedish army and navy, streamline treasury procedures, reduce the national debt by 75 percent and avoid new loans or reliance on subsidies from Sweden's allies. It was an astonishing achievement, which might well have left the loan-mongering west European statesmen incredulous and Frederick William or Peter the Great wondering how it could be done without force. Charles' reorganization of military recruitment and support was an equally masterful stroke. The army became "territorial, self-recruiting and self-supporting" by a few primitive but effective devices. Soldiers and officers stayed in the area from which they were recruited, supported directly by the income from that area's land. There was no need for a costly centralized administrative system like the French intendancies or the Prussian Commissariat. Between reviews, soldiers could be spared for productive work on the land. Thus the state, the economy and all classes except the great nobility benefitted from Charles' revolution. Even the great ones managed to survive, round out their remaining domains, and take their place in the ranks of the military and civil service.

Officially, Charles XI became an absolute monarch, equal in rights to the most absolute monarchs of late seventeenth-century Europe, including Peter the Great and Louis XIV. In 1693, the *Riksdag* declared that Charles was "by God, Nature, and the crown's high hereditary right . . . an absolute sovereign king, whose commands are binding on all, and who is responsible to no one on earth for his actions, but has power and might at his pleasure, as a Christian king, to rule and govern his kingdom."

In practice, absolute monarchy by divine right was based on substantial cooperation between king and subjects. Charles XI probably did not know it, but he was really combining the best of the post-1688 English system and its continental absolutist antithesis. His major reforms were accomplished through the *Riksdag*, not by executive fiat. Occasionally he placed pressure on his judiciary, but normally common law prevailed and even royal civil servants were placed beneath the laws. At the center of government, the famous Swedish colleges worked effectively under the principle of collective responsibility within each college. The fact that Prussia and Russia imitated the collegial organization with a degree of success, indicates its greatness among the many administrative experiments of the century. At the local level of government, the royal governor cooperated with popular representatives and allowed the locality to take the initiative in assigning tax liabilities for its inhabitants. Peter the Great's confused and inefficient adaptation of Sweden's local government [13] underlines the point that it takes more than naked autocracy to make institutions work well.

Not the least of Charles XI's achievements was his Swedification of Sweden's outlying areas. The accumulation of former Danish, German and Russian provinces around the Baltic Sea had turned the Sweden of 1600 into a great power at mid-century. With those territories, Stockholm was the center of a thriving state; without them, it would be reduced to a border town. Since the south Baltic provinces provided as much as one-third of the state's revenue, they had to be kept loyal. The former Danish area of Scania at the southern tip of the Swedish peninsula

13. See p. 296.

was equally important. Pro-Danish feeling remained, and during the Scanian War, guerrilla tactics were employed by anti-Swedish "free shooters." Charles XI attempted some harsh measures against provincial attachments, including confiscation of noble lands and the use of intendant-like officials. On the whole, however, his Swedification was mild in its methods and thorough in its results. The state Lutheran Church and new Swedish universities were used to preach and teach Swedish customs. Wherever possible, Swedish law and the Swedish language took the place of the native idiom. Swedish institutions were introduced, but native assemblies were still allowed to play an important role in local affairs. Swedification was most successful in Scania, which was integrated with the rest of Sweden and remained loyal during the War of the North. The process of assimilation was successful enough in other areas to prevent an uprising by the Livonian patriot Patkul. If Livonia and the rest of Sweden's south Baltic shoreline were lost during the war, it was because of faulty strategy, not disloyalty from within. Swedification as such was an eminently sound policy. It was milder than the English, Prussian and Russian attempts to assimilate restive areas, and more successful than either the Austrian or French experiences with new provinces.

The most remarkable aspect of Charles XI's state-building was its adaptability to the changed political circumstances of the eighteenth century. Charles XII (1697–1718) almost destroyed his father's system by the ruinous fiscal policies and political experimentation brought on by the War of the North. Yet the system survived. Outwardly, the death of Charles XII without heirs brought about the overthrow of absolute monarchy and the beginning of the Age of Freedom. Formally, Sweden was ruled after 1718 by the *Riksdag*, with Charles' sister as a do-nothing queen. But change was more apparent than real, and reminds one of the results of England's Glorious Revolution in 1688. While the *Riksdag* controlled appointments to high civil office, in practice it shared power with the bureaucracy. During Charles XI's reign, the bureaucrats had become less and less servants of the king and more and more servants of the state. They were in many respects the underlying power in the post-Caroline state, and many even secured seats in the *Riksdag*. Thus in Sweden as elsewhere, the end of the seventeenth century saw the emergence of the impersonal, bureaucratic state, standing above ruler, ruling classes and ordinary subjects. As Michael Roberts so aptly said: "King and Riksdag have changed places: the game goes on as before. And behind and around their authority, as around his, lay the massive, immortal *pondus* of the civil service." [14] Since the Swedish civil service and the

14. M. Roberts, "Charles XII," *History*, vol. L (1965), 185.

Riksdag represented a broader segment of the population than did the post-revolutionary governing class in England, it is tempting to suggest that the Swedish government bequeathed by Charles XI was in some respects the best which the seventeenth century produced.

In Denmark, absolute monarchy had come into being two decades earlier than its Swedish version, and it was outwardly strengthened under Christian V (1670–1699). The principles of absolutism were worked out and justified in the *Kongelov* (king's law), written by Peter Schumacher in 1665, and published after Christian became king and Schumacher his chief minister. The *Kongelov* openly declared that "the more power and authority a lord and king possesses, the safer are he and his subjects from external foes."

For all its outward authority, the Danish brand of absolutism appears to have lacked the effectiveness of the Swedish variety. It is difficult to reconcile the facts with Frederick Nussbaum's assertion that "in principle and in reality Denmark had become the most finished example in Europe of the absolute state." [15] To be sure, the national assembly ceased to meet, a common law was established for Denmark (1683) and another for Norway (1687), mercantilist regulations were elaborated, and a degree of toleration for Catholics, Calvinists and Jews was forced on the Lutheran majority. But against these real accomplishments, one has to set the shaky financial position of the royal treasury. The Danish monarchy was saved from bankruptcy by self-defeating measures which included sizable alienations of crown lands. Huge foreign subsidies were also necessary to keep the state solvent. Even so, Christian could not afford to pay for a large army; he resourcefully let the English employ and maintain some of his troops. The underlying financial weakness which these policies reveal was partly due to the modest resources of Danish society. It would seem, however, that the real weakness lay in the Danish monarchy's concessions to the nobility. The economic and social power which the nobles were allowed to retain in return for permitting absolutism in the 1660's came to haunt the monarchy in the 1680's and 1690's. While Charles XI of Sweden forced reduction on his nobles, Christian V permitted his to exploit the labor of the Danish peasantry to their benefit. It was a terrible price to pay for the outward signs of absolutism.

No survey of seventeenth-century Europe can do justice to the lesser German states of the Holy Roman Empire. The Empire was composed of some 360 principalities, plus 1,500 free imperial knights. The Empire had lost its last chance to work as a unit when the Austrians turned from Catholic-German imperialism to work on the creation of the

---

15. F. L. Nussbaum, *The Triumph of Science and Reason*, 135.

Danubian monarchy after the Thirty Years' War. Most of the petty rulers within the Empire eked out an existence, while the larger states tended towards a modest form of absolutism. The power which the Great Elector forged in Prussia can be seen in miniature in the other electoral principalities. In Bavaria, for example, Ferdinand Maria (1651–1679) ruled through a privy council and an intendant-like *rentmeister*. A modest standing army waś maintained by taxes which were authorized and administered by twenty "deputies," a permanent rump of the electoral assembly which had ceased to meet. The Saxon princes had to wait until the eighteenth century to achieve that degree of control over their parliaments, but in the meantime they established a respectable court at Dresden and a standing army which fluctuated between 10,000 and 20,000. Hanover was a pale reflection of those great eastern European states which combined a degree of princely power with social and economic privileges for the nobility. It managed to round out its domains by seizing Bremen and Verden from Sweden during the War of the North. The real plight of these third- and fourth-rate powers is shown by their vacillation between two practices: dividing the principality among the sons of the prince, and becoming tied to the coattails of outside states. The *reductio ad absurdum* of the latter policy was Augustus the Strong's conversion from Lutheranism to Catholicism in order to add the Polish crown to his Saxon electoral title. The Hanoverians were more fortunate in ascending the English throne with George I, but it is debatable whether Hanover gained by its association with a maritime power which considered its German territories a nuisance and a liability. Whichever of the two principles a lesser German state tended to pursue, it remained a pale reflection of the absolutism achieved by Prussia, the Danubian monarchy and Russia. The petty German state became an anomaly in a Europe where great powers had to be territorially large and rulers astute to achieve and retain an important place. One cannot help calling the Hanovers, Bavarias, Palatinates and Saxonies of 1715 political freaks. In John B. Wolf's words, they were "political units that had no geographic or cultural basis, that were mere segments carved from the mass of central Europe by the accidents of heritage." [16]

16. J. B. Wolf, *The Emergence of the Great Powers, 1685–1715* (1951), 127.

12.

The British Isles and the Dutch Netherlands: Change and Continuity

꧁ ꧂

During the first half of the seventeenth century, England and the Dutch Netherlands experienced the same tensions as other states without producing absolute monarchies. After 1660 the English and Dutch states continued to escape the outward pattern of monarchical authority which prevailed throughout most of Europe. The Restoration of monarchy in England in 1660 was followed not by monarchical absolutism but by the Revolution of 1688, which placed serious legal restrictions on royal authority. In the Dutch state, princely authority was revived under William III (1672–1702), but the prince of Orange had to work with republican institutions and to cooperate with a republican regent class. His power was personal rather than institutional. With his death, when no strong family figure took his place, the republic reverted to direct rule by republican regents.

To state the above is merely to relate the obvious facts about English and Dutch politics after 1660. If we are to understand the full import of the Revolution of 1688 and the Orangist Dutch regime after 1672 we cannot be satisfied with the simple truth that monarchical absolutism "failed" in both instances. We have to look beneath the surface of events to see how that supposed failure affected the state and its relations with its subjects. This is not an easy assignment. We must get beyond the

305

nonsense which generations of Whig historians have written in praise of 1688 as a revolution on behalf of the "people" and individual liberty. And we must get beyond no less than two narrow interpretations of the Orangist regime: the pro-Orangist one which praises William beyond all reason, and the republican one which ignores his achievements. Fortunately, historians in the twentieth century are sufficiently detached to begin to raise the writing of history above the level of partisanship. In the late seventeenth century, monarchical "failure" did not necessarily mean popular rule. Government under William III in England and the Dutch Netherlands was government by oligarchies. In this respect, the English and Dutch states had social bases somewhat comparable to the formally absolute monarchies. The English and Dutch socio-economic elite tended to govern directly; the French, Prussian, Danubian and Russian nobility were ruled by monarchs who acted largely in the nobles' interests. There is another comparison with so-called absolute monarchy. We need to discard the old-fashioned contrast between "weak" limited monarchy and "strong" absolute monarchy as pure myth. The England of William III and Anne was actually a more effective warfare state than was Louis XIV's France or Peter the Great's Russia. For cooperation between the socio-economic elite and the crown gave post-1688 England a far sounder fiscal structure than the irrationally constructed tax system of France or Russia. The Dutch state was not so fortunate, but the fault did not lie with republican institutions. The Dutch Republic simply could not compete indefinitely with the European giants, which had far greater human and natural resources at their command. Even so, the Dutch state contributed far more to the wars against Louis XIV than its size and resources seemed capable of bearing.

❧ The Uneasy Reign of Charles II

The reign of Charles II (1660–1685) in England strongly resembles the in-fighting characteristic of seventeenth-century Dutch politics. English institutions had been so modified during the revolutionary period of 1640–1660 [1] that monarchical absolutism was virtually impossible. At the same time, the unsettling experience of revolution made subjects wary of further violence. The new Stuart king knew his place and the political-social elite which had overthrown his father knew theirs. King and Parliament might jockey for position, bending the constitution in favor of the monarchy or the elite-controlled legislature. But both sides were un-

---

1. See Chapter 8, pp. 223–225.

likely to break the Restoration settlement of 1660 with the sword of absolute monarchy or parliamentary sovereignty. For his part, Charles II was a witty, intelligent, self-indulgent and lazy man. He had no desire to be dictated to by Parliament, but as he flippantly remarked, he had no intention of resuming his travels. His long exile on the continent following Charles I's execution in 1649 had sobered him to the realities of English politics rather than making him bitter and eager for revenge when he ascended his father's restored throne in 1660. Nor did the dominant social groups in England desire to press their power against the king to the point of unleashing another round of civil war. The noble peers, landed gentry and commercial interests knew all too well that conflict between crown and Parliament might bring to power another Cromwell who would threaten their liberty and property. Still more did they dread civil unrest which might unleash a new lower class movement against them like the Leveller movement of the 1640's. Consequently, Restoration England experienced an uneasy peace and a degree of stability for negative reasons. During the first half of Charles II's reign, the political pendulum swung slightly towards parliamentary authority; then it swung back somewhat towards royal preponderance.

The parliamentarians who dominated the first part of the reign were a small segment of the political-social elite of the realm, which in turn was a minority of the English population. Perhaps 3 percent, or at most 6 percent of the families in England constituted the governing class in Parliament and local government. Parliament itself was a particularly exclusive group, controlled by "less than 2,000 active men" according to one contemporary observer. And within Parliament, it was the still more restricted "Cavalier" element which controlled the legislative process. The Cavaliers were royalists, but they were above all devoted to the Anglican church, landed wealth and social stability. The so-called Cavalier Parliament of 1661–1678 kept close watch on the king as well as on the lower social orders.

The Cavaliers mixed social conservatism and staunch Anglicanism to keep religious and social dissent in check. The parliamentary acts known as the Clarendon Code were much harsher for non-Anglican Protestants than either Charles or his minister Clarendon desired. The Anglican church became the narrow, exclusive club that Laud had tried to make it in the 1630's. Protestant Dissenters who refused to conform to its narrow orthodoxy were subjected to persecution and repression. They could not worship on their own or hold public office. Moreover, the press was subjected to censorship by Parliament. Dissent was stifled by the local elite as well as by Parliament. The militia, controlled by local Anglican authorities, harassed Dissenters' meetings. Charles could point out to the Quakers, for example, that the troops which broke up their meetings were under the orders of the Lord Mayor of London. An act against "tumultuous petitioning" to king or Parliament placed mass petitions at the mercy of the local rural and urban establishment. Taxation also reflected the sympathies of the Cavaliers. The heaviest tax burden fell on the shoulders of the poor and some commercial interests, through the excise and hearth taxes, while the landed interests protected themselves by drastically reducing the Cromwellian taxes on income from land.

Charles' treatment at the hands of the Cavaliers was milder than that experienced by religious Dissenters and the lower orders of society. Still, there was no doubt that the Cavalier Parliament and not he held the upper hand. Parliament controlled the state's purse strings, could impeach royal ministers and could even override the king's will by legislation. All three weapons were used against Charles' attempts to pursue an independent course. The crown's financial position was particularly precarious during his first years. Since the sum allotted to him for life was inadequate, the king had to beg Parliament for special grants and supplement these with gifts from Louis XIV and loans at rates which went as high as 10 percent. Moreover, the House of Commons began after 1665 to specify how its grants could be spent and to set up its own accounting procedures for public funds. On religious and diplomatic matters, clashes also occurred. Charles was sympathetic to Catholicism, although he did not become a Catholic until just before his death. He also hoped to gain support from Dissenters by supporting their cause. Hence he tried on occasion to suspend the legal restrictions on both Catholics and Dissenters, to the point of appointing men of both backgrounds to high executive office. The Caroline policy of religious toleration at home was combined with a foreign policy which made Protestant England the ally of Catholic France. The sale of Dunkirk to France and England's involvement in the Dutch War on the side of France between 1672 and 1674 did not sit well with many Parliamentarians. Parliament countered with measures which frustrated one Caroline plan after another. The Test Act of 1673 restricted civil and military offices to Anglicans and forced Charles to abandon his toleration of non-Anglicans. Opposition to the military alliance with France forced Charles to withdraw from the Dutch War the following year. Moreover, on three occasions parliamentary manoeuvering broke up Caroline ministries. Chief minister Clarendon went into exile in 1667. The ministry of Dissenters and Catholics known as the Cabal was broken up by the Test Act in 1673. At the same time the king's own brother, an avowed Catholic, was compelled to resign his post as Lord High Admiral of the Navy. Finally, in 1679, the financial wizard and strong man of the executive after the

Cabal, Danby, was so viciously attacked in Parliament that he was put in the Tower of London to save his skin.

Charles II managed to cling to power and to persist in a mildly pro-French foreign policy. Gradually he began to discover means to manipulate Parliament and public opinion in favor of the crown. The beginning of the royalist revival took place under the unfortunate Earl of Danby. During his administration (1674–1679), king and minister took advantage of an improvement in royal finances. The treasury had already weathered a financial crisis by suspending payments of interest on state debts (Stop of the Exchequer, 1672). A remarkable recovery of English industry and commerce, including an increase in foreign trade of 50 percent between 1662 and 1688, greatly increased the yields from custom duties and excise taxes. The gradual conversion of tax administration from private contractors to government officials after 1671 also helped the crown. With such financial strength, Charles II was able to maintain a small standing army, while Danby used a secret service fund to buy the votes of parliamentarians. The king also altered the charters and administrative personnel of several towns, including London. The result was an expanded base of royal power, including influence over elections to the House of Commons. Charles had stormy scenes with the three Parliaments that succeeded the Cavalier Parliament, but by the time of his death he had established the machinery which would make his successor's Parliament very favorable to royal authority. The Caroline political strategy strongly resembles the Orangist manipulation of Dutch institutions. By 1685 the English crown was in a position quite comparable to that which was being achieved across the channel by the Dutch prince William III.

The royalist revival was also due to a fortuitous alliance of the crown with some of the old Cavaliers against more hostile elements in and out of Parliament. The allies of Charles became known as Tories, the opposition as Whigs. Both parties came from the same broad establishment, but they had different leanings religiously, politically and socially. The name "Tory" was inappropriately borrowed from the term used to describe Irish Catholic insurgents against English rule. The English Tories were staunch Anglicans and royalists, who tended to put royalism above Anglicanism. They did not oppose Charles' proto-Catholicism to the point of rebellion against him. Consequently they developed the political theory of non-resistance. Aylmer has quite properly described this theory as a negative version of the divine right of kings, for it declared that rebellion against a divinely ordained king was never justified.[2] The Whigs also received their name from a foreign source.

2. G. E. Aylmer, *A Short History of 17th Century England* (Mentor, 1963), 203.

The original Whiggamores were Presbyterian Scots who attempted a futile revolt against Charles II. The English Whigs were as aristocratic as the Tories and some were Anglicans, but the party also contained strong mercantile and Dissenter elements. They were militantly anti-Catholic and willing to press resistance against the crown to the point of demanding new limitations on royal authority.

The clash between the Caroline-Tory alliance and the Whigs focused on the Exclusion Controversy of 1678–1682, and the so-called Popish Plot. These two emotional issues were almost Charles' undoing, but in the end the Whigs became the victims of their own plotting. A pathological liar named Titus Oates convinced many Englishmen that a Popish Plot was afoot. Sinister Catholic forces were supposedly planning to murder Charles, place his avowedly Catholic brother James on the throne of England and launch a reign of terror against Protestantism and English liberties. In Parliament the Whigs, led by the Earl of Shaftesbury, took advantage of the national hysteria which followed. A bill to exclude James from the succession was placed before Parliament. Charles II proved that he could be shrewd as well as lazy. He deftly outmanoeuvered the Whigs by offering to limit in advance the future James II's authority in religious matters, while dismissing one Parliament after another before legislative action could be taken on the bill. The republication in 1679 of civil war tracts by the royalist Robert Filmer [3] added ideological support to Charles II's cause.

The opposition disintegrated before Shaftesbury's eyes. Rather than a monolithic party, the potential opposition to the king and the Tories included Trimmers who fluctuated between Whig and Tory principles, as well as moderate Whigs, militant Whigs and outright republicans. Most of the Whigs were afraid to press the Exclusion issue too far. They were reminded during the crisis that in the 1640's radicalism had eventually turned against the very members of the socio-political establishment who had begun the attack on royal authority. They were bluntly told that "the gentlemen, the knights of the shires, may be kicked out by mechanics, by citizens and burgesses, for he who practiseth disobedience to his superiors teacheth it to his inferiors." Shaftesbury's apparent involvement in further conspiracy, and a plot against Charles by republican extremists completed the debacle. Shaftesbury had to flee to the continent, two supposed plotters were executed, and Charles emerged more powerful and popular than ever. Even the Whig writer and critic of Filmer, John Locke, had to retire to the Dutch Republic for safety. When James II became king in 1685 the English political scene was still tense. The con-

---

3. Most famous for his *Patriarcha* (1680). See Chapter 2, p. 41.

fusion of parties—Tory, Trimmer, Whig and republican—made the future uncertain. But James had an excellent base of power, a deep reservoir of good will in the country, the negative support engendered by dread of civil war and a crown on his head. It was up to him to prove that he could wear that crown as graciously as his brother had.

The Glorious Revolution in England, Ireland and Scotland

If any ruler lost a throne by his own actions, that ruler was James II (1685–1688). Charles II once predicted that his brother would not last four years; it was an uncanny prognosis. More stubborn and stodgy than Charles II and more principled than Charles I, James II worked hard at alienating the entire English population. He destroyed the bonds between divine-right monarchy and Tory non-resistance while failing to secure support from Whigs or middle-of-the-road Trimmers. The key to this disaster was the new king's uncompromising Catholicism. Charles had never pressed his proto-Catholicism to the point of alienating the staunch Anglican Tories. And only on his deathbed did he acknowledge that he was actually a Catholic. By contrast, James II openly avowed his Catholicism before his accession, and when placed on the throne tried to go far beyond Charles II's early moves in favor of toleration. Charles had not gone beyond openly supporting private worship and limited office-holding for Catholics. For James, nothing short of total Catholicization of church and state would suffice. When his Tory-royalist Parliament refused to give way, the king acted on his own. He suspended religious laws, including the Test Act, by executive decree. He purged the common law courts of "snivelling Trimmers." And he proceeded to pack the army, local urban and rural governments and even the universities with Catholics.

James discovered that his policies were resented by persons of every conceivable background. Even Catholics in England and on foreign thrones thought he was acting unwisely. The Tory-royal alliance was shattered. Most Anglican Tories felt they had gone far enough in their non-resistance by accepting a Catholic king and giving him an initial income twice the amount allowed Charles in 1660. Seven Anglican bishops headed by the Archbishop of Canterbury rejected royal orders to read an executive decree of toleration at Anglican church services. The fact that they were thrown into the Tower of London, tried for seditious libel and acquitted by the jury, made James II look like a foolish anti-Anglican tyrant. James' overly clever attempt to woo Protestant Dissenters by tolerating them along with Catholics also backfired. Few

Dissenters, Whig or republican, were duped into favoring Catholic authoritarianism under the guise of religious toleration. More than religion was at stake. Catholicization of the army dramatized too openly James' reliance on a standing military force; memories of Charles I's misuse of standing armies were quickly revived. The social establishment, both Whig and Tory, saw Jacobean toleration as the beginning of social subversion. After all, the dismissal of college heads and other officials was, to the seventeenth-century mind, an invasion of property rights. Moreover, the non-Anglicans who were appointed in their stead turned out to be well down the social scale; the establishment was naturally uneasy about this form of social mobility.

Although James II forfeited his crown by alienating the establishment, William III of the Dutch Netherlands was the one who seized it. The Whig and Tory lords could not and dared not use the weapon of revolution against James. They lacked the military means. That fact had been proved on James' accession, when the army stood with the king against a rebellion by Charles' illegitimate son, the Duke of Monmouth. They dared not call on other Englishmen to rebel for fear that their "private" quarrel with James might turn into a social upheaval. Fortunately for James' gentlemanly opponents, they were relieved of the agony of civil war by William III. When the birth of a male Catholic heir in 1688 deprived James' Protestant daughter Mary of her right to succeed, the opposition turned to Mary's husband, William. It is difficult to tell precisely what the opposition had in mind other than a military demonstration by William to bring James to his senses. For his part, William was a staunch monarchist, less interested in chastising James than in bringing England into a continental coalition against Louis XIV's France. But once leading Whigs and Tories invited the Dutch prince to come to England and he accepted, events rushed ahead of plans. William landed on English soil with 15,000 seasoned troops, and James fled for his life. The unlikely alliance of Tories, Whigs and the king's son-in-law was now confronted with an unoccupied throne.[4]

The virtually bloodless triumph of William's army and the ensuing settlement of the problem of the vacated throne has been called the Glorious Revolution of 1688. Actually the way that the entire affair was handled bears little resemblance to any political revolution, and none whatsoever to the revolution of the 1640's in England. It was really a palace coup, started by a handful of the political-social elite of the realm, accomplished by an army recruited from the continental Protestant states and directed by a Dutch prince more interested in European diplomacy

4. See also Chapter 9, pp. 245, 247.

than in the crown of his father-in-law. The "revolution" has often been considered a popular one, but the role of the civilian masses and the rank and file of James' army was to stand by and let William take over. It has been described as a movement for English liberties, but those who were in on the coup clearly were thinking of liberties in the seventeenth-century sense of the privileges of the political-social elite. Moreover, that establishment was so divided and confused about the unexpected issue of the vacated throne that we can scarcely call the events of 1688 *their* revolution. Tories, Trimmers, Whigs, and republicans all puzzled over the dilemma of a monarchy whose incumbent was on the run. Some thought of making William and Mary regents for James' infant son; some considered offering the crown to Mary alone, since she was James' eldest daughter; some perhaps speculated on establishing a republic. In the confusion, it was William who decided the issue. His overriding interest had been to bring England into the great European alliance then being formed against Louis XIV. But if the English throne were to be auctioned off, he was now determined to have it. William would not hide behind a regency or his wife's skirt. He had the military power and he also had English royal blood in his veins. A new Parliament proclaimed William and Mary as joint rulers in 1689.

Although the implications of the accession of William and Mary were more "revolutionary" than the original *coup d'état*, one must qualify the oft-repeated generalization that 1688 marked the collapse of divine-right monarchy. Only a few die-hard Anglican Tories refused to accommodate themselves to the coup, and contended that James was still king. While they did not attempt a counter-coup, they refused to take the oath of allegiance to the new monarchs and became Jacobite Non-Jurors. By contrast, many moderate Tories used a modified version of divine right to justify the accession of William and Mary. Hereditary divine right was obviously upset in 1688, since James was the rightful king and his infant son the rightful heir. Mary was second in line, and William was far down the list as the grandson of Charles I. Yet resourceful Tories discarded hereditary divine right only to substitute "divine right of providence." They contended that divine providence, and not human—especially parliamentary—will, had determined the succession. Parliament declared in deference to these Tories that God had made William "the glorious instrument of delivering this kingdom from popery and arbitrary power." One post-revolutionary Anglican tract was actually entitled *God's Ways of Disposing of Kingdoms!* Obviously God had not accompanied James when he fled from England. Tory belief in non-resistance was also conveniently assuaged by James' flight. Tories could write into the parliamentary election of William and Mary the interpretation that the late king had "abdicated," obscuring the fact that he had really been forced off his throne.

If divine right were not destroyed, what remains of the traditional Whig interpretation that the revolution of 1688 was a victory for parliamentary-popular sovereignty? The fact is that the Whigs also wrote their interpretation into the election of William and Mary. Parliament declared that James had "abdicated" and God had chosen William as his instrument, but the parliamentarians also stated bluntly that James had "endeavored to subvert the Constitution of the Kingdom" and that he had thereby broken an "original contract between King and people." Assuming that there was such a contract and James had broken it, Parliament had obviously deposed James and chosen William, whatever God's desires might have been. As one Whig indelicately informed William, he was king by the grace of Parliament, not by the grace of God.

This Whig interpretation of 1688 was popularized in John Locke's *Second Treatise of Civil Government* (1690).[5] Locke stripped government of its divine sanction and saw it as a human creation meant to protect individual "natural rights" of life, liberty and property. He felt that curtailment of those rights by any branch of government, but particularly by the crown, justified resistance by the people. Ironically, as Peter Laslett has shown, Locke's treatise was originally composed during the Exclusion Controversy of Charles II's reign to justify a Whig uprising which failed to materialize.[6] When the revolution of 1688 succeeded, Locke dusted off his unpublished manuscript, made a few changes to make it fit the events of that year, and published it to justify them. Locke became known as *the* Whig philosopher and the Lockean interpretation of 1688 gradually became the accepted version, while the Tory view was forgotten.

The attempt to rationalize the accession of William and Mary in 1688 was followed by a series of parliamentary laws which we can call the "revolutionary settlement." They include the famous Bill of Rights in 1689 and many other laws which were passed during the reign of William and Mary (1689–1702) and the succeeding reign of Mary's younger sister, Anne (1702–1714). This settlement has not escaped the ravages of partisan history. Many historians still cling to the Whig view that it gave Parliament sovereignty over the crown. But such a view is too one-sided. It would be fairer to say that the settlement greatly enhanced the power and authority of Parliament, but left the monarchy the option of either succumbing to parliamentary will or using it to royal

5. For a detailed discussion, see Chapter 15.
6. P. Laslett, "The English Revolution and John Locke's 'Two Treatises of Government,'" *Cambridge Historical Journal*, vol. XII (1956).

advantage. The settlement left the ruler in control of the executive branch of government, although that control had to be exercised cautiously. Provided the ruler cooperated with Parliament and the political-social elite, his actual power could be quite extensive. To be sure, the settlement made it impossible for the monarch to suspend laws or levy taxes without parliamentary consent. He could not successfully maintain a standing army without the military discipline authorized annually by Parliament. He could not keep a pliable Parliament in session indefinitely by putting off new elections. Nor could he interfere with the judicial branch of government, its judges and its juries. Yet monarchs could—and William and Anne did—maintain a full treasury, a strong military-naval force and even a foreign policy along the lines they desired, by cooperating with the people who controlled Parliament and local government. The rules of the game of English politics had been changed, but the game went on. A James II, who disregarded the legislative and judicial branches of government, could not have operated under the new rules. But a powerful William III, who was willing to attain power by bargaining with the political-social establishment, could exist.

William III saw that he had to work within the framework of the revolutionary settlement just as he worked within the republican system in the Dutch Netherlands. Parliamentary sessions were short, but they became the center of English political activity. The king placated Parliament by honoring its control of the state's purse strings. In fact, he went so far as to open state budgets to the scrutiny of parliamentary committees. But there was another side to the coin. William continued Charles II's habit of building royalist parties within Parliament. After 1689, Charles' men, Danby and Sunderland, managed the post-revolutionary Parliaments, awarding government contracts and favors. Corruption became a mainstay of executive influence in the legislature. There was always a bloc of King's Men, legislators who could be counted on to vote the right way. William supplemented these sure votes with temporary support from one or another of the many independent factions that developed in his Parliaments. He tended to look to the Whigs, who were more firmly committed to his person than were the divine-right Tories. The Whig party continued to be an amalgam of petty, rival factions vying for power and influence with the crown. Anne leaned more towards the Tories because of their mutual belief in divine right. However, her death resulted in the collapse of that party as a viable alternative to the Whigs. Many Tories refused to recognize the Protestant Hanoverian George as the childless Anne's successor. By sympathizing with the candidacy of James II's son, the Tories in effect turned against the revolution of 1688. Under George I and George II in the eighteenth century, the Tories sat in Parliament as proud but outcast gentlemen, while the King's Men and Whig factions held the favor of the Hanoverian dynasty.

William learned to live with the revolutionary settlement, although he begrudged parliamentary interference with finances and foreign policy. In the end, he was too long absent from England during the wars with Louis XIV and too narrowly interested in European diplomacy to attempt any fundamental change in the system. Although reluctant to follow parliamentary dictates in the choice of his ministers, he tended to choose those whom parliamentarians either liked or could be bribed to support. Anne was still more aloof from English politics. She played the same game with Parliament over her ministers, but she relied heavily on those ministers to rule in her name and to manage Parliament. The way was prepared for the Hanoverian period, during which George I and George II let the governing class of patronage-dispensing Whig ministers and patronage-receiving parliamentarians dominate the internal political life of England.

William III received full value for his transactions with Parliament. Parliaments continued to pass the necessary authorizations of military discipline to maintain a strong army. They gave him financial support for his wars, sometimes grudgingly but often willingly. Taxes on rents from land reached the satisfactory level of 20 percent after 1688, whereas the Cromwellian experiment with land taxes had been almost forgotten during the Restoration. Parliament also provided more efficient machinery for levying indirect taxes. Continental states, including the Dutch Republic, relied heavily on indirect taxes; but the English land tax was unique, as Wolf has shown: "It was levied upon the very people who could best afford to pay: the country squires and the landed nobility."[7] Expanded parliamentary taxation also provided the security for wartime loans which could never have been floated on the king's credit alone. In 1694, the practice of raising loans backed by the security of excise taxes was institutionalized through the creation of the Bank of England. The Whig businessmen who held the state's purse strings in Parliament were quite willing to put up the initial capital of £1,500,000 for the bank. Thus the commercial interests added their financial contribution to those of the landed gentlemen, and the poor, who suffered heavily from excise taxes. Of course, the businessmen received interest on their investment, unlike the taxpaying gentlemen and lower classes. The Bank of England became "the most important single economic institution in the kingdom."[8] It loaned money to the state and became the paymaster of English and

7. J. B. Wolf, *The Emergence of the Great Powers*, 189.
8. *Ibid.*, 191.

continental allied armies. It helped the English state achieve monetary stability. It undoubtedly gave an added thrust to the late seventeenth-century expansion of the English economy. One can safely say that through the cooperation of the business community, the legislators and the crown, the English monarchical state became the most awesome financial power in Europe at the end of the seventeenth century. Who could have predicted in 1688 that the flight of an unpopular ruler could have so enhanced the position of the royal-parliamentary state?

The revolutionary settlement left the political-social elite to rule in their own interest in areas where they were most affected. Tory and Whig were in lasting agreement on one thing, that they alone should continue to control the offices which enforced law and order and kept their social inferiors in their place. Positions in the militia, the judiciary, the town governments and other judicial-administrative agencies were their reward for 1688. The Whigs tended after 1688 to stem from the great noble landowning families and to dominate high positions in the Anglican church, while the Tories were slightly down the social scale as country squires and Anglican parsons. The Whigs and moderate Tories gravitated towards the royal court, while the intransigent Tories became rooted to the soil. But they all felt a common bond in being part of the establishment. The revolution of 1688 was anything but the first step toward democracy, politically or socially. Indeed, the century following 1688 saw the liberty, property and security of the establishment strengthened. One can even argue that the "revolution" forestalled radical changes in politics and society. Had James stayed on his throne, a much sharper clash between crown and subjects might well have taken place as the establishment feared. It is unlikely that the 250,000 persons who voted in parliamentary elections could have denied some share of power to the rest of a nation of 6,000,000, had a real civil war occurred. The English establishment was also fortunate that it was not divorced from the commercial interests as were its counterparts on the continent. Of course, commercial interests had to buy land and live as country gentlemen before they were fully accepted as part of the establishment. But they could make such a move, and even if they did not, the establishment in Parliament was much more favorably inclined to the needs of the businessman than was true in most continental countries. An alliance between middle-class interests and the poor in town and countryside, such as the one which overthrew the political and social structure of France in 1789, was possible in eighteenth-century England, but it was unlikely.

Safeguards against any political or social upheaval were to be found everywhere in the political-social structure of post-revolutionary England. "In matters of public order," as Aylmer admits, "there was not much of a victory for the populace." [9] Decisions as to when law and order were flouted were placed in the hands of local officials to an even greater extent than had been true in 1660. Licensing of publications ceased, and political debate was thereby enlivened. Yet literature was still closely scrutinized by the common-law courts, which were staffed by very uncommon persons. The judges were particularly hostile to any works which smacked of blasphemy or sedition. To borrow the words of Christopher Hill, "There was a tendency in William's reign for the law to be made more savage in protection of private property." [10] Shoplifting and theft of furniture by tenants were crimes punishable by death. The already harsh debtors' law was made still harsher.

In the early eighteenth century, the witty author of the *Fable of the Bees* [11] which eulogized laissez faire could write of the poor in England:

> Yet, it was thought, the sword she bore
> Checked but the desperate and the poor,
> That, urged by mere necessity,
> Were tied up to the wretched tree
> For crimes which not deserved that fate
> But to secure the rich and great.

One should not end a discussion of the revolutionary settlement in England on such a negative note. The cynic can remark that late twentieth-century American society has advanced little beyond the maintenance of law and order as a means to "life, liberty and the pursuit of happiness." But the lot of the English masses three centuries ago was probably better than that of their continental counterparts; and where property was not concerned, the barbarities of English law were fading more surely and quickly than those across the channel. One may smile on learning that no Englishwoman was burned alive for political offenses after 1688, but the fact is that such inhuman punishments had taken place in preceding decades. The same is true of flogging to death, which had occurred as late as 1685, but ended after the Bill of Rights ruled out "cruel and inhuman punishments." In religious matters, 1688 marked a sharper break with the past than it did in the political and social sphere. Non-Anglicans, with the exception of Catholics and Unitarians, were now allowed to worship. Toleration did not mean full civil status, to be sure. Only Anglicans could hold local offices, attend the universities or enter the Royal College of Physicians. However, Dissenters could evade such discrimination by occasionally attending Anglican services. When a Lord Mayor of London

9. G. E. Aylmer, *A Short History of 17th Century England*, 228.
10. C. Hill, *The Century of Revolution, 1603–1714* (1961), 289.
11. See also Chapter 15, p. 395.

went to a Presbyterian chapel in his mayor's robes during William's reign, many objected to this act of an "uppity Dissenter"; the fact that he could do it at all revealed the difference which the revolution of 1688 had made in English life.

The lot of the English masses appears much happier by contrast with that assigned to the Irish by the revolutionary settlement. The brutal Cromwellian treatment of Ireland as an inferior, conquered land had not been significantly modified between 1660 and 1688. The English revolution of 1688 raised the hopes of impoverished Irish Catholics and well-to-do Anglo-Irish Protestants, only to bring further troubles to both restive groups. A rebellion by both groups against colonial status was ruthlessly ended by William III's military forces. The post-revolutionary English Parliament followed with harsher laws than those of Cromwell's time. One can understand why there was such hostility towards the Irish Catholics. William and the Protestant English feared a coalition of Irish rebels, the exiled James II and France. Engaged in the long European war of 1688–1697 against Louis XIV, the English could ill afford a second front so close to home. Nevertheless, the severity of the English treatment of the Irish is astonishing; it ranks with that meted out to the Rhinelanders by Louis XIV's minister, Louvois, about the same time. Irish Catholics were barely able to worship under the English revolutionary regime. They were forbidden to send their children abroad for an education. Family estates were to be broken up on the death of the head of the family, and divided equally among the children. There was a slight exception to this last rule: if one of the sons became a Protestant, he could inherit the entire family property! Treatment of the Anglo-Irish Protestants was mild only by comparison with that received by their Irish Catholic neighbors. Only English settlers who belonged to the Anglican church had any reason to be moderately satisfied with their lot. They were left in control of public and private life, including the Irish Parliament. But they paid a heavy price for this privileged position in an unprivileged colony. They, like all other inhabitants of Ireland, were constantly subjected to interference in their affairs by the English Parliament. Just how meddlesome the English could be was shown by the Draconian economic restrictions imposed on the Emerald Isle. At the end of William III's reign, the English Parliament forbade the export of Irish woolen goods except to England, and then promptly placed a prohibitive tariff on woolen goods destined for English use. Thus all inhabitants of Ireland—Irish and Anglo-Irish, Catholic, Anglican and Dissenting Protestant—were equally oppressed by a conscious colonial policy aimed at destroying the core of the Irish economy. The people of Ireland were left with only their sense of humor. Since Ireland was still permitted to trade with the south European wine-producing countries, Jonathan Swift could remark wryly: "Though England has constrained us to be poor, they have given us leave to be merry."

The fate of the Scots after 1688 was better. The majority, who lived in the Scottish Lowlands, had seen their state Presbyterian church modified along Anglican lines under Charles II and threatened by James II's Catholic beliefs. Hence the Lowlanders offered the Scottish throne to the Calvinist Protestant, William. In return, the Scots were left with their own law, their church and their native Parliament. The weak point of the settlement was that the Scottish and English states were united only by the fact that William wore both the Scottish and English crowns. When Anne succeeded William, the English began to worry lest the two thrones be mounted by different rulers on her death. The Scottish Parliament, in fact, passed an act in 1703 which differed from the English provision in 1701 for a German Hanoverian successor to Anne in England. The Act of Union (1707) was the result. It brought the two successions together and created a United Kingdom of England and Scotland. The Scots were assimilated into English life by the election of Scottish members to the English Parliament and the creation of a "common market" within the Anglo-Scottish state. The Scots had to give up their own Parliament, and some Scottish merchants had a difficult time competing with their English counterparts. Still, the Scots could be relatively happy with the settlement. They retained their local political, legal and religious institutions, and they obtained one-eleventh of the seats in Parliament while assuming only one-fortieth of the United Kingdom's financial burdens. It should be noted that the Lowlanders were the Scottish beneficiaries. The minority of Scotsmen, living in the Highlands to the north, were treated differently. These proud and primitive clansmen clung desperately to James II after 1688. Only the coldblooded massacre of the clan MacDonald after it had entertained English troops brought order to the wilds of the north. The Highlanders remained sullen, but subdued. A few revolted on behalf of James II's family in 1715 and 1745, but their quick defeat demonstrated the strength of the new Anglo-Scottish state.

✄ The Dutch Republic Under William III and After

The republican institutions of the Dutch Netherlands were better adapted to republican rule than was the makeshift institutional framework of Cromwellian England. While the royal restoration took place in England by 1660, it was another twelve years before the House of Orange was able to regain its place in Dutch politics. The Regime of True Liberty, a government by anti-Orangist regents, managed to surmount one obstacle after another from 1650 to 1672.[12] The republican regents were able to keep religious issues among Calvinist, Dissenting Protestant and Catholic groups from tearing the republic apart. They stayed in power despite the two Anglo-Dutch wars of the 1650's and 1660's, which weakened the Republic's commercial position in the world. Only a major external crisis in 1672 brought about the collapse of the republican regime. That year, the Dutch War against France and England began. The republican leader, John de Witt, found his state isolated diplomatically in Europe and his armed forces too weak to hold back the French. Louis XIV's army occupied three of the state's provinces, and seemed on the point of pushing the Dutch into the sea.

It was the young prince of Orange, William III, who took advantage of the republican regents' plight in 1672. Although the offices which his family had traditionally held had been denied him on the death of his father in 1650, memories of the Orangists as national saviors lingered. The English and French tried to tempt William with a plan whereby their states would take over most of the Dutch Netherlands and he would be placed at the head of the remainder. William turned his back on the foreign "devils," only to succumb to the temptation to play politics at home. It is not clear whether he personally took part in the sordid events which followed, but he did nothing to halt them and his followers certainly played an active role. As national hysteria swept across the Dutch polders, Orangist elements gained control of the States General and the provincial assemblies in the key provinces of Holland and Zeeland. William was given the all-important positions which his ancestors had held. He became *Statholder* in Holland and Zeeland, Captain General of the armies of the Republic and Admiral General of its navy. Just as the Dutch frenzy elevated a would-be hero, it had to have its scapegoat. An ugly mob at the capital city of The Hague took out its wrath on John de Witt. He resigned his office, but could not save his life. The mob murdered the ex-Advocate and his brother, took their fingers as "souvenirs," and left their bodies to hang in the public square.

William took full advantage of the grizzly developments of 1672. Wittist regents were replaced by Orangist followers in the major town and provincial offices of Holland and Zeeland. The three provinces occupied by the French were treated with greater severity. As William and the Dutch armies turned back the French and forced them to leave Dutch soil in 1673–1674, the liberated provinces were treated as if they

12. See also Chapter 8, pp. 229–230.

had seceded. In order to "rejoin" the Dutch state, they had to agree to William's terms. Even more than in Holland and Zeeland, William was able to dictate the choice of personnel and policies. Before the Dutch War was over, William capped his triumphs by becoming hereditary *Statholder* of five provinces, while a relative held the Statholderates of the remaining two. William's power was as great as that achieved by Frederick Henry over a longer period of time.

The Orangist "restoration" of 1672 resembled the Glorious Revolution of 1688 in England in two important respects. First, it was accomplished with a minimum of bloodshed and disorder. The de Witts had been murdered, but for the most part there was simply a purging of anti-Orangists from their offices. As in England, a strange turn of events and unexpected opportunities had much to do with the mildness of the transition. In the second place, the Orangist coup enhanced the authority of the state within the framework of existing institutions. William had no intention of overthrowing the regent class as such. His purging of regents was more thorough than any previous purges by his family, and his control over the States General, provincial assemblies and town governments was more direct than his bribery of the English parliamentarians after 1688. Nevertheless, William's policy was basically one of replacing hostile regents with friendly persons from the same social background. He ruled with and through the commercial interests and the small native nobility of the Dutch Republic, just as the Regime of True Liberty had. The cooperation between the prince of Orange and the political-social establishment was such that the state's financial position remained strong. Through the semi-state Bank of Amsterdam and other institutions of credit, William was able to finance the war of 1688–1697 with France and even to pour money into England and the German states allied with the Dutch. At the end of the seventeenth century, the Dutch state had an enormous debt of 250,000,000 florins. It could not bear the strain, and such a debt was symptomatic of the state's economic decline. Nevertheless, the fact that it could amass a debt of such size with the backing of an annual revenue of only 13,000,000 florins attests to the political strength of the Orangist regime.

Like the English, the late seventeenth-century Dutch establishment went its own way in matters which most concerned it. The same corruptibility and desire for easy living which are to be found in post-revolutionary England can easily be detected in the reformed regent class after 1672. If there was a difference, it was largely due to the decline of Dutch commercial power in contrast to the emerging commercial greatness of England. For the Dutch regents became more addicted to living on their past greatness, enjoying the income from their estates and the safe financial investments which they had accumulated during brighter days. Their attitude to the lower classes of the Dutch Republic, while not so openly hostile as that of the English, was certainly one of superiority. Along with William III, the regents put down all attempts to give a voice in public decisions to their inferiors. The gradual increase of religious and intellectual toleration which made the Dutch Republic the most open society of continental Europe was achieved against the bitter complaints and occasional counterattacks of the orthodox Calvinists in churches and universities. The Whig John Locke found temporary exile in the Dutch Republic before 1688, and the heterodox Pierre Bayle fled from France to breathe free Dutch air. But Bayle was harassed by the orthodox Calvinists, and Locke's circle of friends was shunned by many influential Dutchmen.

After William III persuaded the regent class to let him invade England in 1688, he became increasingly engrossed in the grand alliance against Louis XIV. Dutch internal affairs were left more and more to the regents, although in foreign affairs the Dutch were guided by William's staunch supporter, Heinsius, Advocate of Holland. When William III died in 1702 without direct heirs, there was another relatively peaceful transfer of power from Orangist regents to regents of a republican bent. The military machine which William had assembled, plus the backing of English naval and financial power, helped the Dutch through the War of Spanish Succession without an Orangist head. Attempts were made by the lower echelons of society to broaden the base of political power after 1702, but they were short lived. The regents ruled the eighteenth-century republic just as the landed and mercantile elite did in Georgian England.

IV.

European Thought and Culture in Metamorphosis

While Europe's secular states were weathering the mid-century crises, its intellectual–cultural heritage was being profoundly altered by the shock waves of post-Reformation thought. We have already described the nature of those shocks, which between 1540 and 1640 undermined the prevailing conceptions of God, man and the world.[1] It remains to be seen how that initial, destructive phase of an intellectual revolution gave way to a second, constructive phase during the Age of Louis XIV and Sir Isaac Newton.

The destructive phase had been a many-faceted one. Theological squabbles among Christians, criticisms of Christianity from the frontiers of religious belief, the challenge of natural science and the dangers of an exaggerated supernaturalism had all played their role in unhinging the belief in the theocentric, hierarchical world-view of early modern men. The rebuilding of European thought and culture on new foundations was also the work of many men. Scientists and artists, philosophers and writers of fiction, biblical scholars and secular political theorists all made their contributions. However, it was the fate of natural science, especially physics and astronomy, to play the dominant role in bringing new intel-

1. See Chapter 3.

lectual order out of seeming cultural chaos. Scientists provided the suggestive picture of a mechanistic, physical world. Out of the assumptions of a rational universe and a deity who did not interfere in its operation, intellectuals fashioned a new set of secular conclusions about human destiny. Philosophers spun out new systems which related man to his natural environment and nature's God. Political theorists described how man's self-made institutions conformed to nature. Even in the realms of art, literature, music and history, science played a role in reshaping the human vision of the world.

The road from old, religious absolutes to new, secular ones was by no means a smooth one. Often the language of science had to be mistranslated to make it fit the mysteries of human existence. The arts were especially obstinate in resisting the "geometric spirit" and the concept of nature's fixed laws. Nor was it easy to tame the destructive intellectual fury of the century's first decades, to divert it to the new task of reconstruction. The continuing criticism of religious universals led inexorably to the question of whether any absolutes existed in the world of man. Only by inventing new myths did Europe's intellectual elite prevent a complete breakdown of all intellectual order, and avoid falling into complete cultural relativism. Meanwhile, the intellectual chasm between the elite who accepted the ways of science and the mass of Europeans who clung to old beliefs grew wider and deeper.

13.

Science:
The Mechanistic Universe

B y the middle of the seventeenth century, science was begging for
someone who could make sense of the physical universe. Copernicus,
Kepler, Galileo and Descartes had each undermined part of the medieval
cosmology, but no one had as yet put together all their findings in a
satisfactory new synthesis.[1] In view of the destructive work of scientists
between 1540 and 1640, it was becoming increasingly difficult to accept a
finite, hierarchical universe stretching outward from the central Earth to
Heaven. But the new conception of an infinite, centerless universe was
difficult to grasp, and still more difficult to explain. The old scheme had
the merit of providing God's creation with meaning and purpose, since
each part had its particular place, form and quality. If there were no
objects with special functions but only "matter in motion," as scientists
were suggesting, it would not be easy to show why a particular object
moved or how its movements were coordinated with those of others. It
was particularly difficult to explain why planets moved around the Sun.
In the old cosmology, the Earth was the obvious center of planetary
activity; in the new scheme, neither Sun nor Earth could claim any right
to such a role. Nor was motion on the Earth intelligible. Earthly objects

1. On early seventeenth-century science, see Chapter 3, pp. 85–95.

no longer had an urge to move downward if they were heavy or upward if they were light. Above all, how could the elliptical movement in the heavens be reconciled with the very different movements on Earth if the universe were really a unit? Scientists had to struggle with a world where quantity and not quality counted, where law and not capricious spirits held sway. There was great need of a geometer who could read the entire book of nature and find universal laws and mathematical relationships to explain how this infinite universe was held together.

The Newtonian Synthesis

It was the Englishman Isaac Newton who managed to fit together the pieces of the mathematical-mechanical universe. He did so in his justly famous *Mathematical Principles of Natural Philosophy* (1687), better known as the *Principia*. From virtual obscurity as a professor at Cambridge University and a quarrelsome associate of the Royal Society of London, this strange figure emerged as a genius of the highest rank. In the succeeding decades the Newtonian synthesis became accepted as the final word on science, first in England and more slowly on the continent. That an Englishman accomplished all this was astonishing, since in the early 1600's continental scientists had been the giants of astronomy and physics. That Newton should have been the person to make the breakthrough was still more surprising. Many men were on the verge of the discovery in the 1660's, 1670's and 1680's. And Newton was such a curious scientist. His greatest work was accomplished in two brief periods of eighteen months each, first in 1665–1666 and then in 1685–1686. For years he put aside his early studies of dynamics and celestial mechanics, only to become so engrossed in them again that he would wander towards the dining hall, become distracted and return to work unaware that he had meant to go to dinner. Yet he had to be goaded into finishing the task. A rival, Robert Hooke, tormented him into frenzied activity by claiming that he had the answers Newton was searching for. A friend, Edmund Halley, had to coax Newton to continue working until his findings could be placed before a publisher. At one point, Halley discovered that Newton had worked out precise calculations and carelessly mislaid his notes, while everyone else was still trying to do what he had forgotten. Newton's wild speculations in his unpublished studies and his caution in publishing only what he considered absolutely verifiable hypotheses, also make one wonder how he managed to combine imagination and accuracy in the right proportions for his major treatise. And yet his pride, erratic habits and paranoic distrust of rivals produced a picture of the physical universe which came to be accepted virtually *in toto* for generations. This Newtonian world remains the scientific truth for the average person today and scientists still consider it valid for all but the very small and very fast phenomena in nature.

Newton's key to understanding the world of the new science was the principle of universal gravitation. In the early seventeenth century, several scientists edged towards this idea. Kepler showed how the planets swept around the Sun, but instead of positing a mutual attraction between Sun and planet he thought of the Sun as a driving force. Galileo arrived at the idea of inertial motion on the Earth, assuming that a body continued in a straight line without the need of any special quality or force. However, he did not show how inertial movement could lead a planet into an elliptical orbit or a ball to the Earth. Descartes went further. He took as the starting point on Earth and in the heavens the same inertial movement in a straight line. He went on to describe how planets departed from their inertial path, although his solution was inadequate. Instead of gravitation acting across empty space between planet and Sun, Descartes assumed a space filled with matter—particles which in jostling each other formed whirlpools that swept the planets around the sun. While some scientists struggled with Descartes' fanciful vortices, an Italian, Alfonso Borelli, suggested in 1665 that it was centripetal force which bent planets from their inertial path into orbits around the Sun and kept moving objects from leaving the Earth. And in 1673 a Dutchman, Christiaan Huygens, actually calculated the force required to keep a planet in orbit. In England, the same principle was being developed by Robert Hooke, Edmund Halley, Christopher Wren and Isaac Newton.

The mere idea of gravitation was not enough to clinch the point, however. Huygens' calculation placed planets in circular orbits. It remained to be shown whether gravitation could account for the actual movement of planets in elliptical orbits. It was also necessary to prove whether the same principle of gravitation actually applied to earthly objects. Proof of both hypotheses could come only through eleborate mathematical calculations which demanded powers of concentration and mathematical insight rare in human beings. Even given the advances that had been made in higher mathematics since the early seventeenth century, the outcome was uncertain. Newton invented a form of calculus to determine the direction and acceleration of motion. With the calculus, the Englishman explained to his own satisfaction that two bodies are mutually attracted according to the product of their masses and inversely as the square of the distance between their centers. He felt that these laws explained actual motion in the heavens and on the Earth. The Newtonian synthesis may or may not have been the result of a youthful comparison of a falling apple and the revolving Moon. Nevertheless, Newton had linked the apple with the Moon, the planetary system and the infinite universe.

For Newton, the law of gravitation was proof that everything in the physical world was a product of motion, acting either by inertia or by some natural force operating across the distances of space. Newton did not of course explain all the forces which operate in the world, although he speculated on them. For the most part, he kept secret his thoughts about motion when he was not on firm ground. He set aside a draft of the *Principia* which was as imaginative and hypothetical as the published work was solid and convincing. In that suppressed draft, the great scientist described motions internal to objects as the product of repulsion and attraction among "insensible particles." And in it he also called upon scientists to account for "the motions of the particles in hot bodies, in fermenting bodies, in putrescent bodies, in growing bodies, in the organs of sensation and so forth." These comments show how far Newton was capable of taking his view of the universe. It was fortunate that his self-protective instinct excluded these speculations from his great work. The book which the world saw confined itself so rigidly to absolutely verifiable hypotheses in physics and astronomy that it made the Newtonian universe very convincing.

The reception of Newton's *Principia* was quite different from the response of the erudite world to early seventeenth-century attacks on traditional cosmology. There were strong reservations among scientists, philosophers and clergymen, but even those reservations showed how far Europe had strayed from the Aristotelian-Christian world-view of previous centuries. Newton had not invented a new system out of nothing, but had worked within the framework of assumptions which had gradually captured the minds of the intelligentsia since Galileo's unfortunate clash with religious authority. Between 1633 and 1687 most literate Europeans, including devout Christians, had come to accept the heliocentric viewpoint and the mathematical-mechanical description of the universe. Hooke's criticism of Newton was little more than the product of a jealous, narrow-minded man. Newton's rival thought that he had prior claim to the "essential" idea of gravitation and that Newton's mathematical demonstrations were unnecessary footnotes. There were other barriers to the book's acceptance, however. The *Principia* was very difficult to read, and perhaps no more than a handful of scientists could understand all its arguments. In the early eighteenth century Voltaire quipped: No one understands Newton but everyone talks about him.

Unfortunately, Newton suppressed the demonstrations which he had worked out with the calculus, and fell back on archaic geometry in his published account. As a result scientists had to "translate" the *Principia* back into the new language of the calculus, in order to make it useful. Much of the reluctance of foreigners to accept Newton was due to national pride. The English philosopher Locke asked only whether Newton's mathematics could be accepted, and once assured on that score, took the *Principia* on faith. But Frenchmen proudly clung to Descartes' vortices into the eighteenth century. Many Germans became involved in the emotional argument over whether Newton or Leibniz had first discovered the calculus, and took their revenge on Newton's claim to priority by questioning his work on universal gravitation.

Strangely enough, the followers of Descartes also objected that Newton's system was not mechanical enough! They held that there must be a physical, material cause of celestial movement. Descartes had supplied that material cause with his whirlpools. But Newton had only his mysterious gravity which somehow reached across empty space to hold the planets in orbit. The Cartesians understandably felt that gravity was really an "occult quality" like those of Aristotle, which seventeenth-century scientists were banishing from the universe. Newton had a difficult time explaining that he was no Aristotelian, that he meant only to describe a "principle of motion" which showed how the planets were kept in position and was far more satisfactory in that respect than Descartes' vortices. The author of the *Principia* did not know and did not pretend to know the "cause" of gravity. How, not why, was all-important to him. "It is enough that gravity does really exist, and act according to the laws we have explained, and abundantly serves to account for all the motions of the celestial bodies, and of our sea," he wrote. Still the Cartesians remained unconvinced until well on into the eighteenth century. These true believers in the Cartesian world-machine failed to observe that Newton's system was also essentially mechanical. Nor did they acknowledge Newton's thought that space might be filled with an "ether," serving as a medium for gravitational force. The dispute between Newton and the Cartesians was in part a quibble over the composition of the physical universe: whether it was a molasses-like Cartesian continuum or a Newtonian sand pile of separate atoms. In the late seventeenth century this question was more important for philosophy than for science, since virtually every scientist established the laws of physical nature by using both assumptions.

Criticisms by the English philosopher Bishop Berkeley and the German philosopher-scientist Leibniz were closer to the religious objections which Galileo had faced. But Berkeley and Leibniz were not really objecting to Newton's science as such. They simply feared that Newton had slighted God and deified nature in his *Principia*. Leibniz and his followers agreed with the Cartesians that gravity was too pat a solution to the problems of celestial and terrestrial physics. But while the Cartesians said that Newtonian gravitation was too mysterious and unmechanical, followers of Leibniz contended that it implied a soulless, deterministic world-machine. Moreover, Leibniz agreed with Berkeley's *Principles of Human Knowledge* (1710), which criticized Newton's belief in absolute time, space and motion. For the Anglican bishop, this implied "that Real Space is God, or else that there is something beside God which is eternal, uncreated, infinite, invisible, immutable."

Newton responded in the second edition of his *Principia*, which appeared in 1713, but his inserted comments on God did not satisfy these critics. He argued that "this most beautiful system of the sun, planets, and comets, could only proceed from the counsel and dominion of an intelligent and powerful Being." In his treatise on *Opticks* (1704), Newton declared without reservation that the world could not have arisen "out of Chaos by the mere laws of Nature." Newton really believed that God was alive in the universe. He, like his critics, wanted both a living God and a universe of matter in motion. However, the more he argued the more they misunderstood him. We can sample his efforts in the following extract from his revised *Principia:*

> This Being governs all things, not as the soul of the world, but as Lord over all. . . . He is not eternity and infinity, but eternal and infinite; he is not duration and space, but he endures and is present. He endures forever, and is everywhere present; and by existing always and everywhere, he constitutes duration and space.

Unfortunately, Newton ran into problems also by discovering that mechanical difficulties sometimes occur in the universe. Quite plausibly, he argued that God had to intervene to set the world-machine back in order. To Leibniz this was the last straw: Newton had made God into a bungling workman. Newton could not even attempt to answer this charge; it was only after his death that French scientists showed how the machine corrected its own quirks.

Despite all these objections, Newton added immeasurably to the triumph of the new science. Charles C. Gillispie sums up the Newtonian achievement: "Newton's critics, in short, wanted more out of science than he found there." While they sought a "system . . . which accounted at once for the behavior and the cause of phenomena, the 'how' and the 'why' of nature . . . Newton only said how it is and how it works."[2]

2. C. C. Gillispie, *The Edge of Objectivity* (1960), 146–150.

Scientific Method and the Search for Certain Knowledge

Newton not only culminated the quest for knowledge about the physical world; he also showed how the scientist could arrive at such knowledge. He not only described, but indicated how one could describe. His work on scientific method was a synthesis of the various methodologies which had been advanced during previous decades, notably by the English Lord Chancellor, Francis Bacon, and René Descartes, the noted French scientist and philosopher. While theologians argued about religious truth and free-thinking skeptics used ancient pagan arguments to question the attainability of any certain knowledge,[3] scientists developed theories to show that at least in the physical realm human beings could know the truth. God might not have revealed why he made the world or how he was achieving his ends through human existence and history. But while theologians had to fall back repeatedly on the assumption that God's ways with men were mysterious, the scientist discovered that His ways with the physical world were not. Given the right method, man could understand how God's creation worked.

The influence of Francis Bacon on the scientific spirit of the Age of Newton and the eighteenth century is surprising in view of his lack of scientific credentials. We know that he rejected Copernicus, Kepler and Gilbert, quarreled with Harvey and misunderstood Galileo. Who can forget Harvey's acid comment that Bacon philosophized like a Lord Chancellor? Yet, as a prophet of empirical and utilitarian science, he inspired the Royal Academy of London in the late seventeenth century and continental scientists in the eighteenth. Bacon joined in the early seventeenth-century criticism of intellectual authority without falling into the trap of skepticism. He complained of excessive reliance on the methods, first principles and systems of the ancients, especially Aristotle; but he railed equally against those who were too timid or overawed by God to attempt the search for scientific truth. The task, for him, was simply to begin the work of science without the encumbrances of past errors or present misplaced humility, and to proceed with the proper method. His unfinished *Great Instauration,* or "Great Renewal," begins with the call "to commence a total reconstruction of sciences, arts and all human knowledge, raised upon the proper foundations." That man was meant to know God's creation he did not doubt; human error alone had held man back. "Human intellect makes its own difficulties," he stated boldly. "The entire fabric of human reason which we employ in the

3. See Chapter 3, pp. 72–82.

inquisition of nature is badly put together and built up, and like some magnificent structure without foundation."

In his *Advancement of Learning* (1605) and more elaborately in the portion of his *Great Instauration* entitled the *New Organon* (1620), the Lord Chancellor blithely enumerated the intellectual traps which man must avoid. In a series of sparkling aphorisms, Bacon described these "Idols." The Idols of the Market Place and the Theater are especially censured. The former stem from the loose use of language, "imposed according to the apprehension of the vulgar." It is not surprising that "the ill and unfit choice of words wonderfully obstructs the understanding . . . and throws all into confusion, and leads men away into numberless empty controversies and idle fancies." The Idols of the Theater are the "playbooks of philosophical systems and the perverted rules of demon-stration" which tyrannize over men and blind their vision of the real world. Bacon ranted not only against Aristotle but also against the system-builders of his own day, and against those who mixed science with theology and superstition. For the new prophet of science it was equally wrong to take "either a great deal of a few things, or a very little out of many things." In both cases, he felt, science was "based on too narrow a foundation of experiment and natural history," a charge which applied even to the scientists of Bacon's day belonging to the "empirical school of philosophy."

Bacon also attacked what he called the Idols of the Tribe and the Cave. The Idols of the Tribe are the product of human nature itself. In general the tribe of man looks at the world from his peculiar perspective, not as it is. "The human understanding," Bacon declared, "is like a false mirror, which receiving rays irregularly, distorts and discolors the nature of things by mingling its own nature with it." The Idols of the Cave are the prejudices and inclinations of individual men. Some persons are ad-dicted to novelty, others to antiquity; some always see similarities in things, others their differences.

Bacon was convinced that science could smash these idols with the help of a correct scientific method. His method was essentially an in-ductive one—the careful development of generalizations based upon systematic and thorough observation as well as experimentation or artifi-cial reproduction of nature. Instead of starting with assumed first princi-ples and spinning out logical conclusions, or starting with a few facts and racing to generalizations, Bacon exhorted scientists to build slowly from the particular to the general. Historians have been quick to point out that Bacon's approach to science was one-sided, that it emphasized the empiri-cal, experimental side and frowned on the use of mathematics and intui-tion. Doubtless, no scientist made important generalizations with Bacon's method. The Royal Academy was certainly overly Baconian in its grubbing for curious and inconsequential facts, to the point of inquiring about the river in Java which turned wood into stone. However, his critics miss the point that Bacon's greatness was in making science factual and utilitarian. Bacon's vision was one of useful knowledge grounded in empiricism. His concern for practical rather than pure science ignored the fact that one was dependent on the other. But it was his emphasis on the practical which made both his work and science in general popular in succeeding decades. He declared that "the true and lawful goal of the sciences is none other than this: that human life be endowed with new discoveries and power." In stressing science's potential contribution to agriculture and cooking, industry, trade, shipping and in general the "mechanical arts," he struck a responsive chord which fired the imagination and enthusiasm of Europeans. He was prophetic when he proclaimed that he was "laboring to lay the foundations, not of any sect or doctrine, but of human utility and power." In an age of rival religious sects and contending scientific systems, Bacon's call to action was a welcome addition to the babble of tongues. It was comforting to "know" that Bacon's method opened knowledge and power to the common man. As Bacon himself stated, his approach "leaves but little to the acuteness and strength of wits, but places all wits and understandings nearly on a level."

While Bacon opened up the frontiers of knowledge to all, he did not succeed in showing how either the gifted scientist or the common man could overcome all the Idols which blocked his vision. If the Idols of the Tribe and the Cave (i.e. man's senses and prejudices) stood in the way, it was naive of Bacon to believe that a method grounded in the senses was sufficient. Seventeenth-century scientists were acutely aware of the problem. From Galileo to Newton, astronomer-physicists struggled with the fact that the world the scientist describes and reduces to law differs from the one which impinges on his senses. Galileo talked about man's "rape of the senses" as the path to true knowledge. The Italian scientist partially resolved the apparent contradiction between the world of science and that of the senses by distinguishing between primary and secondary qualities. The world which the scientist investigates should be one of material bodies stripped of all qualities except those essential to it: extension, number and motion. It is a world of "triangles, circles and other geometric figures" to be known by man through quantitative, mathematical description. Galileo could dispense with the world of secondary qualities—the colors, tastes, odors and textures which play tricks on the senses—as being irrelevant for the scientist. He felt that although they excite certain sensations, they are really modes of perception rather than essential properties of objects. Remove the human being and the feather remains while the tickle disappears. "If ears, tongues and noses were removed, shapes and numbers and motions would remain, but not odors or tastes or sounds."

It was this world of primary qualities which was the background of Descartes' scientific method. But Descartes' fusion of his own peculiar philosophy and Galileo's mathematical treatment of geometric space made the Cartesian method far more convincing than Galilean or Baconian science. Like Bacon, Descartes objected to past and present philosophical and scientific systems. Like Bacon, he knew that the senses deceived. But unlike Bacon, he turned to abstract mathematics rather than empiricism to guide him to absolute truth about the world. Mathematics was the key because of the "certitude and evidence of their reasonings." In mathematics there were axioms and principles which were "clearly and distinctly seen" to be true. From these self-evident truths or premises, one could draw logical conclusions, or theorems. Descartes' ambition and accomplishment was to reduce all knowledge, including that of the physical world, to this procedure.

In reducing physics to mathematics, Descartes put contemporary, destructive skepticism to work on behalf of certainty. He said that he would "reject as absolutely false anything of which [he] could have the least doubt." Initially this meant denying not only the existence of the world and of his own body, since the senses deceive, but even his geometrical discoveries, since anyone could make logical slips in reasoning. However, it also meant arriving at self-evident truths, from which Descartes could build a true picture of the universe.

Descartes decided to "see whether anything would be left after this procedure which could be called wholly certain." It is somewhat surprising that the first truth he hit upon was his own existence, inferred from the fact that he was doubting and that thought could not be separated from existence. It is still an exciting if weird experience to follow Descartes' intellectual journey from his "I think, therefore I am" to his world-system of vortices. As we shall see, he argued from his own existence and his idea of a perfect Being to the existence of that Being (God).[4] It was a simple matter for Descartes to proceed logically from this deity to the world which was His creation. He assumed that God did not deceive, and hence the world which we see through our senses cannot be a figment of our imagination. Assured on this point, Descartes could go on to examine the primary qualities which hid behind the secondary qualities of the senses.

In his examination of the laws controlling Galilean matter in motion,

4. See Chapter 14, p. 345.

Descartes did not rely exclusively on purely mathematical reasoning divorced from observation and experiment. He had to start with self-evident truths about the world, which he intuited in part from empirical knowledge. But it is accurate to describe the Cartesian method as essentially rational-geometrical. Once Descartes had established these self-evident truths as his premises, he deduced the laws of the Cartesian universe without looking back at the physical world. It is interesting that Descartes' laws were inferred in part from his assumptions about God's nature. For example, since Descartes' God is immutable, it is unthinkable that His material creations could pass of themselves from motion to rest or from rest to motion. There can be only one conclusion, namely that matter remains at rest, or if moving, continues its motion unless some external object intervenes. Thus Descartes arrived at the principle of inertia from the premise of God's immutability, without even a glance at the world of inertial matter!

Whatever one thinks of Descartes' method of acquiring knowledge, the fact remains that it gave the appearance of certitude. The "geometric spirit" of Cartesian rationalism for a while swept across continental Europe like a prairie fire. Its flaw was that it tended to equate mathematics with science. While mathematics is the language of science, a means of expressing quantity, Descartes "mistook the language for the subject," as Gillispie notes.[5] Relying partly on the senses at the start of his journey to the truth, Descartes tended to forget the facts somewhere along the way. By proceeding with a rigid logic and failing to verify the results of his deductions, he built an inflexible system which had to be corrected by Newton. Newton's method also corrected Descartes' method, wedding Baconian empiricism with Cartesian rationalism. Newton took the Cartesian view of the world as a mathematical-mechanical order. He accepted Bacon's insistence on adhering to the facts. But he rejected Bacon's simple fact-mongering and Descartes' confidence in unverified hypotheses. As Newton succinctly summarized his views, "The whole burden of [science] seems to consist in this—from the phenomena of motions to investigate the forces of nature, and from these forces to demonstrate the other phenomena."

Science in Popular Dress

While scientists discovered the mechanistic universe and scientist-philosophers explained how it could be known, a host of writers set out to bring the vision of science's potential before the literate public of Europe.

5. C. C. Gillispie, *The Edge of Objectivity*, 93.

It is certainly true, as G. N. Clark argues, that a gulf was created between the few who were captivated by the new science and the many who clung to the old.[6] But those who accepted the new science were, by and large, those who dominated public and private life. Through them, the "geometric spirit" of Cartesianism and the idea that nature could be understood and used by man came to play a key role in the eighteenth century.

There were many who used their literary talents to explain the latest discoveries and the mechanistic scheme of the universe to those who could not fathom Descartes' theorems or Newton's *Principia*. While the *Principia* was "translated" into the language of calculus for the erudite, it was watered down for the less learned. In the early eighteenth century there was even a book entitled *Newtonism for Ladies!* The most charming book on popular science was *Conversations on the Plurality of Worlds* (1686). In the introduction, the author, Bernard de Fontenelle, explained that he had selected from the new science precisely that part "which is most likely to excite curiosity." But he made doubly certain that his work would not bore the reader, by explaining the Cartesian universe in a free-wheeling dialogue between himself and a fashionable lady. In the lady's garden, Fontenelle discusses astronomy for six evenings, patiently and wittily turning her fears and doubts about the whirling earth into fascination and belief. The countess wonders whether Indian elephants might be a better prop for the earth than Descartes' celestial matter and vortices. However, as she begins to realize how the universe works, her tone changes: "I value it the more since I know it resembles a Watch, and the whole order of Nature the more plain and easy it is, to me it appears the more admirable."

The amateur rubbed shoulders with the scientist not only through books but also in the social world of science. In addition to ladies investigating cadavers in their carriages, and kings, princes and nobles puttering in their botanical gardens and chemical laboratories, there was more substantial contact through the growing numbers of scientific academies. In western Europe, the popularizing role of these academies seems to have been more pronounced in the early decades of the seventeenth century. The "curiosi" who mingled with the "virtuosi" in London, Oxford, Paris, Rome and Florence during the days of Galileo drop out of the picture in the Age of Newton. The amateurs were attracted by debates about broad, rival theories, and must have lost interest as these debates became repetitive and the serious scientists turned to more detailed studies and to complicated mathematical demonstrations. However, the scientific societies of western Europe continued to play an important role

6. G. N. Clark, *The Seventeenth Century* (Galaxy, 1961), 251.

by combining the efforts of individual scientists in a single institution and by disseminating new ideas from one institution to another. Whether or not amateurs were included, these societies continued to popularize scientific knowledge by presenting popular lectures and allowing the public to attend open meetings, by printing "memoirs" and by reviewing scientific books in their journals. The Royal Society of London, chartered in 1662, and its publication, *Philosophical Transactions*, became famous on the continent as well as at home, although the English state gave little more than the official stamp of approval to its work. The more closely supervised and subsidized creation of the French monarchy known as the Royal Academy of Sciences (founded in 1666) also achieved greatness. Through the *Journal des Savants* and a reprint of that periodical in Amsterdam, and after 1699 by means of a series of *Mémoires*, the French academy broadcast scientific knowledge. The central and eastern European states also established scientific societies and scholarly journals as the century neared its end. The Saxon, Prussian, Austrian, Danish, Swedish and Russian enterprises tended to appeal more narrowly to the scholars of pure science. At the same time, however, their interest in knowledge was often more sweeping than that of their western counterparts. They delved into history, law, philology, theology and economics, as well as the natural sciences.

Through academies, journals, books of popular science and the more popularly written treatises on pure science, the scientific revolution introduced Europe to the idea of material progress. We have seen Francis Bacon discoursing on the "human utility and power" which science could provide. Descartes was still bolder in proclaiming the material advantages of science. With the help of science, he wrote, men could make themselves "masters and possessors of nature." Inventions would not only improve agriculture and reduce labor, but eradicate maladies of mind and body. Man would become wiser and healthier and eventually push back the time of senility. The noble patron of the Lyncean Academy, Frederico Cesi, made a similar prediction in an address to Roman scientists in 1616. And even Bacon allowed his imagination to stray from empiricism in his utopian *New Atlantis* (1627). In Solomon's House on an imaginary South Sea island, Bacon placed rain and snow makers, wonder drugs, music amplifiers, wrecking machines, airplanes, submarines, perpetual-motion clocks and illusion-making funhouses.

As science became more self-confident, it began to challenge the long-accepted idea that the Golden Age of man lay in the past. Descartes thought that he lived in a corrupt age, a belief probably derived from his reading of the ancients. A generation later, the Quarrel of the

Ancients and Moderns saw Descartes' scientific successors aligned with those who thought corruption lay in the past.

The argument was most evident in France and in England. It began over the merits of ancient and contemporary literature, but quickly spread to scientific subjects. Fontenelle's *Digression on the Ancients and Moderns* (1688) assumes that men of all ages are made of the same "paste." Since Plato and Homer were no more intelligent than modern men and since knowledge accumulates, the Moderns obviously knew more than the Ancients about the world. The famous writer of Mother Goose stories, Charles Perrault, sketched out a poem on behalf of the Moderns during the succeeding decade. Being assured by Huygens that science had uncovered many of nature's deepest secrets during the previous eighty years, Perrault used poetic license to attack the Ancients. "Within the last twenty or thirty years," he stated baldly, "more discoveries have been made in natural science than were made throughout the whole period of learned antiquity."

> Fair antiquity was always venerable
> But I never deemed her adorable.
> I look on the Ancients, without bending my knee;
> They are great, it is true, but men, like we.
> And one can compare, without fear of injustice
> The Age of Louis to the fair Age of Augustus.[7]

In England, an Anglican clergyman and member of the Royal Society, Joseph Glanvill, summed up his position in the title of his work, *Plus Ultra: or, the Progress and Advancement of Knowledge since the days of Aristotle, in an account of some of the most remarkable late improvements of practical, useful knowledge* (1668).

Defenders of the Ancients remained, to be sure. The most famous of these, Jonathan Swift, propounded his views in his scurrilous poem *The Battle of the Books* (1710), and more elaborately in the third book of *Gulliver's Travels*, in which the Grand Academy of Lagado is lampooned. Swift made some telling points. We can laugh with him at the academicians who confused the mental with the physical and thought that by swallowing propositions written on wafers they were digesting knowledge. But his treatment of the Lagadan experimenters does not strike us today as anything more telling than a caricature of science. Satire finds its mark only when the satirized object is objectionable. We are more inclined to laugh at Charles II of England than to laugh with him at the scientists who were "weighing air." And we are a little amused at William Temple's *Essay upon Ancient and Modern Learning* (1690), when that

---

7. C. Perrault, *Comparison of the Ancients and Moderns* (1688–1696).

defender of the Ancients declared that "there is nothing new in astronomy to vie with the Ancients, unless it be the Copernican system."

It is interesting to note that as the ideas of material progress and the mechanistic universe took hold, science itself began to slacken its pace. The authority of Newton and the tyranny of Cartesian geometry probably deterred scientists from launching bold, new investigations in physics and astronomy. The rigid space-time machine of late seventeenth-century thought also made it difficult for men to probe into chemistry, geology and biology. Both Descartes and Newton speculated on an evolutionary theory of the Creation, but even they agreed that the created world was mechanistic, and not subject to change. Many discoveries were made concerning heat, air, fossils, plant cells, spermatozoa and bacteria. But they do not tell the story of the striking changes in physics and astronomy which were at the heart of the scientific revolution.

14.

Philosophy: God, Man and the Mechanistic Universe

Medieval intellectuals made theology the key to understanding other branches of knowledge. The term "science" embraced all learning, and theology was the Queen of the Sciences. The erosion of religious absolutes during the post-Reformation period of 1540–1640 undermined, but did not dethrone the queen. The scientific revolution accomplished that feat, unintentionally but decisively. Instead of natural and human sciences being subordinated to religion, theological and human sciences had to be reconciled with natural science. The mechanistic view of the universe as matter in motion raised awkward questions about the Biblical God and Adam's descendants. What role was left for God in a world governed by fixed laws of nature? Were human beings the fallen but special creatures of God who could be saved only by divine grace, or were they cogs in the world machine? The growing acceptance of scientific methodology as a certain guide to truth stood in sharp contrast with hopeless confusion about the truths of Christianity. It was but a step to the conclusion that religious knowledge should be pursued with the methods which science was using so effectively in its own realm. To be sure, many scientists and those close to science shrank from treating human nature and divine attributes the way they treated planets and stars. Many held back due to the ingrained habit of placing theology on a pedestal. Many clung tenaciously to the God of Christianity who constantly intervened in the world, and to the Christian belief in frail human nature fettered by Original Sin. An equal number maintained a residual belief in revelation as a vehicle of knowledge superior to the human senses and reason, and a reluctance to second-guess Biblical truth. Nevertheless, it proved impossible to separate God and man from natural science. There was compartmentalization of knowledge, but there was also a marked tendency to combine God, man and the mechanistic world in new philosophical syntheses. And as philosophers and philosopher-scientists went about this work, they could hardly escape the temptation to remake God and man in the image of science. Even where compartmentalization continued, assumptions about the physical universe crept into seventeenth-century views of Christian God and man.

The leading philosophical reconstruction was the work of Descartes. Cartesianism was the rage of seventeenth-century Europe. Throughout the middle and last decades of the century, the giants of philosophy and many a second-rate commentator contended with Descartes' philosophical system. His views not only caused an uproar in the universities of the Spanish and Dutch Netherlands as well as in his native France, but also inspired lively debates in England, Italy and Sweden. In Germany, Leibniz struggled with the dilemmas posed by Descartes' synthesis; in the Dutch Netherlands, Spinoza had his peculiar answer. In England Hobbes took issue with Cartesianism and Locke was clearly influenced by it. It is easy to lose sight of Descartes' primary place in the debate, since there was a vast amount of correspondence among the giants of seventeenth-century philosophy. But a glance at the detailed objections to Descartes and his replies, which were published together with his *Meditations*, will quickly restore perspective.

The most curious product of Cartesianism was the common-sense philosophy of John Locke. A wretched, confused and slip-shod philosopher, whose works can easily be torn apart by college undergraduates, Locke nevertheless made more sense at the end of the century than more brilliant and logical philosophers like Leibniz, Spinoza, Hobbes and Descartes himself. Locke may have been confused, but he was not confusing. He may have been simplistic; he certainly was not abstruse, far-fetched or difficult. People did not have to talk about Locke as they did about Newton. They could read Locke, understand him and accept his common-sense approach to human knowledge and human capabilities in the mechanistic world. It is revealing that Paul Hazard, who makes clear his dislike of the secular tendency of *fin-de-siècle* thought, makes Locke the hero of his book on the "crisis of European conscience." [1] Locke was

1. P. Hazard, *The European Mind, 1680–1715* (Meridian, 1963), 239–251.

secularist in his outlook, and his God and man were not those of Christian tradition; but he brought Europe back to its senses, reassuring his contemporaries that the philosophical implications of the new science were not as confusing and destructive as was commonly assumed.

The furor over Descartes and the development of Lockean common sense were part of a general drift towards belief in a "natural religion." The subject is far more complex than many textbooks imply. Pagan free-thinking, differing theological positions within the churches of Christian Europe and even religious "enthusiasm" had already played a role in stripping Christianity of its mysteries. But science added a strong and, it would seem, decisive voice to the movement towards the do-nothing God and secular man of eighteenth-century Deism. So strong was the voice that many late seventeenth-century Europeans with impeccable Christian credentials became unconscious supporters of natural religion while still flaying religious enthusiasts and free-thinkers.

Of those who took into account the achievements of science and yet rejected the syntheses of God, man and the mechanistic world, the most interesting and influential was Blaise Pascal. Pascal's rejection was the closest that Christianity came to finding a satisfactory rebuttal to the intellectual trend of the seventeenth century. In the eighteenth century, Voltaire wrote many bitter and unfair critiques of Pascal's *Pensées*. He could not bypass Pascal, but he could never meet him head-on. If we want to understand the seventeenth century, we cannot ignore the man whose answers to its philosophical problems were to haunt generations of men long after his death.

Descartes' Philosophy

Descartes has been described in many ways: as a skeptic who tore down Christian beliefs without finding a satisfactory substitute, as a rationalist liberating man from religious orthodoxy and Aristotelian logic, as a dogmatist and most recently as a conservative who tried to revamp traditional thought in the light of contemporary skepticism and the scientific revolution. All these points of view can be supported, as they were in his own day. Richard Popkin's description of Descartes as a would-be conservative is the most interesting.[2] If we keep in mind the fact that Descartes failed in his attempt and that his views were actually non-Christian and potentially anti-Christian, this approach is a useful one.

The young Descartes was strongly influenced by the skeptical cir-

2. R. H. Popkin, *History of Scepticism from Erasmus to Descartes* (1960), 175.

cles in which he moved. He was particularly well acquainted with Montaigne's doubts about man's ability to find absolute truth in religion, science and philosophy.[3] Towards the end of the 1620's Descartes turned against skepticism, and the staunchly orthodox Cardinal Bérulle suggested that the youthful French thinker use his talents to combat it. The religious aims of Bérulle's protégé can be inferred from the *Discourse on Method* (1637). They are explicit in *The Meditations Concerning First Philosophy* (1640). There Descartes stated that "It does not seem possible ever to persuade those without faith to accept any religion, nor even perhaps any moral virtue, unless they can first be shown these two things [the existence of God and the immortal soul] by means of natural reason." Revelation tells us these truths, he maintained, but the atheist, the doubter, the man without faith will accept them only when convinced by reason. Some scholars argue that Descartes was simply trying to protect himself from the Catholic authorities by such statements. But it is more likely that he was sincere, if naïve, in thinking that his rational treatment of God and man could be reconciled with revealed Christian truth.

REVELATION ≠ RATIONALISM

God had a curious place in Descartes' philosophy. As we have already seen, Descartes deduced his mechanistic universe from the existence and attributes of God.[4] But God was not the starting point of Descartes' philosophy. His nature and His existence were deduced in turn from the existence of man. Two comments need to be made about this cavalier treatment of the deity. In the first place, the God of Descartes was a convenience, a link in the chain of logic by which he spun out his philosophy. God was a tool of rational thought, not a being important in His own right. The second point is that Descartes did not assume the existence of God: He proved it by human reasoning. The idea that all knowledge, including religious knowledge, had to be attained or rejected by reason, was a radical departure from traditional Christianity. It is true that Descartes' rational proofs for the existence of God differ only slightly from ones that medieval theologians had employed. For example, the ontological argument used by Anselm in the eleventh century is reflected in the following Cartesian proof: I am aware of my imperfection since I am subject to doubts; but I also have an idea of perfection (God); perfection must include existence; therefore God exists. What distinguishes Anselm from Descartes is that the former did not rely solely on rational proofs of the existence of God. He also took it on faith, through revelation.

MAN

3. On Montaigne, see Chapter 3, p. 81.
4. See Chapter 13, pp. 336–337.

A DEDUCTION

ATTRIBUTES OF GOD

MECHANISTIC UNIVERSE

By insisting on human reason as the true path to certain knowledge, Descartes infuriated many Christian thinkers, even though he never explicitly ruled out revelation. His dogmatism was not their dogmatism. Many also suspected that the path to Cartesian truth through systematic doubt of everything which was not "clearly and distinctly perceived" furthered the cause of skepticism. The Dutch Calvinist Voet and the French Jesuit Bourdin believed that Descartes' initial doubt gave away so much that no religious truth could ever be reestablished. They felt that he had dissolved all secure bases of knowledge, including the senses, human judgment and reliance on God. Descartes also aroused the fury of Christian and quasi-Christian skeptics who were willing to settle for probable knowledge, based on what is perceived through the frail senses. Gassendi, noted popularizer of an ancient theory of a universe composed of atoms, caustically wrote "Each person thinks that he clearly and distinctly perceives that proposition which he defends." Dogmatism based on intuition, he maintained, was false dogmatism. Late in the century Bishop Huet returned to this theme, parodying Descartes' "I think, therefore I am" as "I thought, then perhaps I was."

Did Descartes' conceivable but scarcely credible God play any role in the universe? The answer is a very slight role. Pascal correctly stated that Descartes employed God only to start the world, and commented "I cannot forgive Descartes: he would have liked, throughout his philosophy, to be able to dispense with God." Descartes' God was assumed to have created the world, but Descartes did not even care to use the argument from design to prove God's existence. That argument holds that the beautiful design of the universe presupposes an intelligent creator, a final cause. But since final causes were not relevant to Descartes' mechanistic explanation of nature, they were excluded from his philosophy. Nor could the Frenchman find any room for intervention by God in human life. Of course, he believed in the Christian God, but in his writing, he conveniently compartmentalized to such an extent that the God of his philosophy was devoid of Christian traits. It was a God of "infinite substance, eternal, immutable, independent, omniscient, omnipotent"; it was certainly not the deity who sent His Son to die on the Cross for men's sins, who loved and forgave men, and saved them through divine grace. In the quest for certain knowledge and a synthesis of God, man and the universe, Descartes placed God at a distance from the world and human existence.

For those of us who live in the twentieth century, Cartesian man is infinitely more interesting than Cartesian God. When referring to the deity, Descartes talks like a closet philosopher; when he discourses on man, we come face to face with the living Descartes, who had a law degree as well as a smattering of ancient learning, who joined the Dutch army, tramped across central Europe as a soldier during the Thirty Years' War, dedicated one book to a Protestant German princess and ended his days conversing with the queen of Sweden at five in the morning.

Man was much more important to Descartes than God. From his "I think, therefore I am," he inferred that man was a thinking being. This came close to saying that men were rational creatures. That human beings were imperfect was obvious to Descartes, since only God was perfect. And yet he insisted that man had sufficient free will and understanding to be able to know the world and to find his proper place in it. Sin was not innate since Adam's Fall; it was merely due to the improper use of understanding. In short, man did not use the Cartesian method to truth, "and thus it happens that I make mistakes and that I sin." Descartes may have picked up this idea unconsciously from his Jesuit teachers who believed that God made allowances for sin. If so, he went far beyond his preceptors, for there was not even a hint in Descartes' writings of the need for God's forgiveness, or that sin was more than a simple error in thought. It is true that, for Descartes, man's understanding came by means of "clear and distinct conceptions" or intuitions, each of which "must have God for its author," and that "divine Grace" came to the assistance of human understanding as well. Yet Cartesian thought was simply a natural faculty, what Descartes eventually called "natural understanding." Divine grace in Descartes' words was God guiding his private thoughts, acting as a rather nebulous conscience.

For all his emphasis on human understanding, Descartes had difficulty connecting man with the world. By assuming that man was a thinking being, he placed himself in an intellectual blind alley. As a thinking being, man was immaterial; yet he was attached to his own material body and placed in a material world. This famous Cartesian dualism, which sharply separated mind or soul from body and world, raised a question which was to plague philosophers ever after. How can matter and mind communicate and interact? Cartesian man in the Cartesian world might be likened to a dog in a library. Men might receive moral ideas from their intuition. They might know that the physical world really existed, because God did not deceive man. But how could man's immaterial soul actually function in the material world? In his *Passions of the Soul* (1649), Descartes suggested that the pineal gland in the human brain was the intermediary between soul and body. This was a clever suggestion, since that particular gland does not exist in animals. It gave the human soul a bridge to the material world and yet retained the uniqueness of human beings. But since the pineal gland was material, its discovery evaded rather than answered the question of how pure mind is connected with pure matter. Descartes could have solved his dilemma by making man an integral part of nature. He believed that the world was mechanical in operation. From Harvey's principle of the circulation of the blood he inferred that animals were machines. He was willing to concede that the human body as such was mechanical in its actions. Why not make the whole man a material entity and end the dualism between soul and body? But this Descartes could not do. To take such a step would be degrading to man and an outrage to God. Man would no longer be a creature whose essence and greatness were thought, and his materialized soul would no longer be immortal. Thus Descartes failed in his effort to find a cohesive synthesis of God, man and the mechanistic universe. It was left for others to continue the search, starting with Cartesian assumptions about the world.

Cartesianism Interpreted: Malebranche, Spinoza, Leibniz

Many Christians accused Descartes' dualism of being atheism in disguise, and his works were placed on the Catholic Index of Prohibited Books in 1663. But he could not be dismissed so easily. Defenders and interpreters appeared throughout western and central Europe. Particularly strong were the attempts to place Cartesianism within the framework of Christianity. The most famous Christian Cartesian was Nicholas Malebranche. Upon reading Descartes in the mid-1660's, he became inspired to make Cartesianism buttress Christian faith. Malebranche combined Cartesian rationalism and Christian mysticism in an extraordinary synthesis. Although he firmly believed in Descartes' rationalism, Malebranche was a more fervent Christian than the man he took as his master. He was a priest of the Oratorian order in France, and one who placed Moses above Aristotle and Saint Augustine over the pagan free thought of his own day.

Malebranche retained Descartes' emphasis on rational argumentation and dualism, but he made God the central figure of his philosophy. According to the Cartesian priest, finite beings could not act on their own, whether they were human souls or material substances. Only infinite God could be the real cause of anything in the universe. Finite beings were merely the occasion for carrying out His will. Human thought, the interaction of body and mind and even the movement of matter were to be considered merely "occasional causes." The God of Malebranche was very much alive and active throughout the universe, connecting mind and matter, running the physical world, giving man all his knowledge through divine illumination. Nor did Malebranche neglect the role of grace and the mediation of God's Son. Jesus was the sole occasional cause of grace, dispensing forgiveness according to a divine plan.

Many Christians refused to see Malebranche's "occasionalism" as any more satisfactory than pure Cartesian dualism. God may have been the cause of all in Malebranche's philosophy, but He caused everything in accordance with general, fixed laws, not by His own free will. Jesus' mediation was undertaken in accordance with a general plan of God, not through special divine orders concerning each occasion. If occasionalism was infused with mysticism, it was deterministic nonetheless. Moreover, it was discomforting to many that Malebranche could take the Cartesian method to the point of proving by human reason not only the existence of God and the immortality of the soul, but also the divinity of Christ. The staunchly orthodox Catholic Bishop Bossuet said of Malebranche: "How I hate those philosophers who, measuring the designs of God by their own thoughts, make of Him nothing but the author of a certain general order, from which the rest develops as it can."

Thus Christian Cartesianism inflamed rather than snuffed out the controversy over Descartes. In France, England and the Netherlands there were refutations of Malebranche and rebuttals of those refutations. One supporter of Malebranche's *Search for Truth* (1674–1675) had to settle for the cumbersome title *Critique of the Critique of the Search for Truth*. Malebranche's writings were placed on the Index alongside Descartes' works. Still they continued to circulate, in edition after edition. Before he died the quiet Malebranche became something of a celebrity, appearing before polite French society to interpret Cartesianism, receiving visits from curious foreigners, and known as far away as China.

Outside Christian Cartesian circles, two great thinkers developed their own distinctive philosophies under the shadow of Cartesianism. One was Benedict Spinoza, a Sephardic Jew by upbringing and an inhabitant of the Dutch Netherlands. Treated as a free-thinker and an untouchable by both the local Jewish community and the major Christian churches, Spinoza lived a quiet life of contemplation on the fringes of Dutch academic society. To the end he refused to give up his independence for the sake of respectability or security. He turned down an offer to teach philosophy at the University of Heidelberg, and kept himself alive by making optical lenses. This occupation may have aggravated an inherited chest disease, which caused his early death in 1677 at the age of forty-four. The gentle, kindly philosopher was cursed to the end by the many who misunderstood him and loved by the few who knew him personally.

In striking contrast was Gottfried Wilhelm Leibniz, a native German, a broad-minded Lutheran and an inveterate activist and traveller.

He lived in the capital of one European state after another, became librarian for the Elector of Hanover, tried to unite the Christian churches and achieved the distinction of being the last human being to master all branches of knowledge. Neither Spinoza nor Leibniz was fully appreciated in his own day, and many of their important writings either were dismissed out of hand or lay undiscovered for several generations. Although they did not directly influence intellectual developments in the seventeenth century, they are important for two reasons. First, both grappled with the intellectual problems of their day. Secondly, their ideas were sufficiently known to disturb lesser minds and to cause further controversy in the intellectual world of the late seventeenth century.

Spinoza was strongly influenced by Descartes' works, and even wrote a book expounding Cartesian principles. But while he adhered to the latter's rational-geometrical approach to knowledge, he could accept neither the separation of mind and matter, nor the seeming separation of infinite God from finite substances. For the Dutch philosopher, God was no mere creator of the universe. He was the sole substance, who was everything and in everything. What others saw as God's creatures, Spinoza believed were mere modes of the divinity. God had an infinity of attributes, although man was able to perceive only two of these, thought and extension. Spinoza also argued logically that God had to establish the world as it exists, and make it run according to the immutable laws which man can see in operation. For if God acted out of caprice or free will to achieve some special end, He would be admitting that He was not perfect in Himself. Therefore He acted out of necessity, by His very nature.

This pantheistic philosophy, expounded in Spinoza's *Ethics Demonstrated in the Geometrical Manner* (1677), had distinct merits. The problem of connecting mind and matter did not exist in the united, Spinozist universe. And Spinoza's God had worthier attributes than the convenient deity of Descartes or the anthropomorphic God of the common man. Clearly, a deity who was everything and everywhere was superior to the Cartesian God of mathematical truths. Just as clearly, the Nature-God of Spinozist thought was meant to be a corrective to common misconceptions about divinity. The Dutch philosopher pitied the human prejudice which placed nature at man's disposal, "eyes for seeing, teeth for mastication, vegetables and animals for food, the sun for giving light, the sea for breeding fish." Nor could he condone the efforts of the individual to manipulate God, worshipping the deity so that "God may love him above the rest and direct the whole of nature for the gratification of his blind cupidity and insatiable avarice." Spinoza was sure that God did not act with man in mind, using His power to create phenomena such as earthquakes to express His anger at human misdeeds or incorrect worship. Such a deity was to the Dutchman "as mad as men."

One might think that this God-in-Nature had no relevance to human existence. On the contrary, to Spinoza, pantheism gave man hope of finding his place in the universe and of leading a happy, useful and full life. To be sure, men would have to rid themselves of their narrow and selfish view of God and the world. Man was not "situated in nature as a kingdom within a kingdom." It was false for writers on ethics to consider as "good" what was most useful and pleasing to the senses and to attribute "sin" to human frailty, to "infirmities and fickleness," rather than to natural causes. Far from disturbing nature's order, man was part of it, and the "passions of hatred, anger, envy and so on, considered in themselves, follow from the same necessity and efficacy of nature." Although his view of reality sounds rigidly deterministic and fatalistic, Spinoza believed that it gave men a certain freedom and greatness. Knowing that they were bound to one another, to nature and to God, human beings would, he hoped, cease to view things from a narrow, self-centered position. Pleasures of the senses were to be enjoyed, but to be seen as far less important than the general scheme of things. Knowledge of that scheme was in itself a much higher pleasure, and also a means to free the mind from momentary interests and emotions. Men would learn to love God and their fellow men, with whom they were connected. Rather than praising or blaming acts which were the product of natural causes, they would understand and sympathize with their neighbors. Rather than bribing God they would be at peace with Him. Spinoza also felt that it was possible for men to regulate their own passions, although this could not be done by sheer will power. Like inertial motion in nature, passions could be counteracted only by external objects. To deal with an impulse, one had to invoke stronger and nobler desires and feelings.

It was not to be expected that Spinoza's contemporaries could understand or accept his sophisticated synthesis of God, man and the universe. Everywhere his pantheism was mistaken for atheism. The Spinozist God was seen to be nothing more nor less than Nature, acting without purpose. The Cartesians reacted as sharply as any other intellectual group. Malebranche, whose Christian Cartesianism was confused with Spinozism, spoke of "the wretched Spinoza." Many were especially bothered by Spinoza's treatment of ethics. The independent-minded Pierre Bayle was horrified that good and evil could both be considered part of the divine substance. He commented: "If men are but modes of one and the same being, if the God that changes himself into a Turk is one and the same as the God that changes himself into an Hungarian, then, that there should be wars and battles between them, is the most outrageous idea ever thought of, surpassing the wildest ravings of the craziest brain that ever found a home in a madhouse." Others were disturbed by Spinoza's method of arriving at moral precepts. Morality to him was not decreed by God's free will and revealed to man through the Bible; it was to be found in nature and known through human reason. Spinoza was certainly understating the case when he declared that some "will doubtless think it strange that I should attempt to treat of human folly geometrically . . . [considering] human actions and desires in exactly the same manner as though I were concerned with lines, planes and solids."

Leibniz, who was perhaps the only man to understand Spinoza, also rejected him. The two were on good terms until the German thinker saw a copy of the manuscript of the *Ethics*. While Leibniz admired Spinoza's rationalism, and tried also to reconcile mind and matter, he rejected the solution of uniting all in a purely mechanical God-Nature. By 1695 Leibniz had arrived at his own solution, published in the widely read *Journal des Savants*, and developed in several later works. The German philosopher-scientist saw the universe as a multitude of individual substances or *monads*, created and sustained by God. These monads were not material atoms, but centers of energy. Each had within itself the germ of everything it would do as it acted and evolved. Instead of a mechanical world of matter in motion, Leibniz saw a world of self-contained organisms; instead of a static world, a dynamic one.

To the layman, this world of self-moving forces seems bizarre and very unreal, a strange anticipation of the post-Newtonian science of the twentieth century. Its strength was in combining mechanism with teleology, the cold world of science with the forgotten traditional world of purposes and meaning. Monads seemed to act like individual machines, but at the same time each had a plan to follow as it developed and changed. And, while each monad acted without reference to any other, God synchronized their activities so that they worked as a whole in a "pre-established harmony." Leibniz's philosophy had a loftier place for God than Spinoza's pantheism or Malebranche's occasionalism, since God acted not out of His nature but of His free will to establish the best of all possible, logical worlds. And man, although seemingly determined in his nature and in his relations with the rest of the universe, was also unique. Unlike most monads, man's soul acted not out of unconscious perception but through memory and conscious thought as well. Realizing that evil was minimal in this best of all possible, logical worlds, and that he could understand his place within it, man could be truly happy with his lot.

Unfortunately for Leibniz, the nuances of his theodicy were cancelled out by a vulgarized version of his optimism which made its way through Europe in the early eighteenth century. Leibniz was partly to blame for this. He was best known through his *Theodicy on the Goodness of God, the Liberty of Man and the Origin of Evil* (1710). In that oversimplification and popularization of his views, the great German thinker tried to counter Pierre Bayle's arguments. Bayle had said that the best philosophical explanation of evil was the Manichean one: two forces, one good and one evil, conflicting in the world. In his slipshod reply, Leibniz made it appear that there was no evil in the world. He knew better: Finite monads, even if connected through preestablished harmony, were in themselves imperfect, and hence some evil must exist. The best of all possible, logical worlds was not the best conceivable one. However, Europeans came to view Leibniz as the man who taught that everything which happens is for the best. This distortion of a penetrating and imaginative synthesis of God, man and the world found its way into Alexander Pope's popular *Essay on Man* (1732–1734):

> All Nature is but Art, unknown to thee;
> All Chance, Direction, which thou canst not see:
> All Discord, Harmony not understood;
> All partial Evil, universal Good;
> And, spite of Pride, in erring Reason's spite,
> One truth is clear, Whatever is, is right.

It was the perverse optimism of Dr. Pangloss in Voltaire's *Candide*. And it brought the equally perverse retort from Candide that optimism "is the mania for pretending that all is well when all is ill."

Cartesianism in Empirical Dress:
Gassendi, Hobbes, Locke

While Malebranche, Spinoza and Leibniz modified Descartes' views of God and man, they all accepted a central feature of Cartesianism, namely rationalism. The empirical "school" of the seventeenth century broke more sharply with the great French philosopher. As much as individual empiricists differed, they agreed that Descartes placed too much faith on pure thought, divorced from the world in which thinking man operated. In Gassendi, Hobbes and Locke, to mention only three empirical writers, there is an insistence on connecting thought with experience, and human beings with their environment. While empirical philosophers agreed with Descartes that the universe was rational, they were concerned with investigating human thinking and human nature in the light of actual experience, rather than assuming from the beginning that man as part of the rational universe must also be rational. In connecting man with the surrounding world, the empiricists had far less interest in God's place in the scheme of things than did the Cartesian rationalists, from Descartes to Leibniz. Man, not God, was revealed by the senses and therefore seemed the proper subject to be studied.

Pierre Gassendi was a second-rate thinker of the early seventeenth century whose influence was more profound than his philosophy. As a member of an intellectual circle in Paris that was in touch with virtually every scientific development of the time, he had an excellent opportunity to disseminate his ideas. He was priest, academician, scientist and philosopher, but above all he was reviver and interpreter of ancient Epicureanism. Gassendi was too orthodox merely to pass on the Epicurean doctrine of a material world composed of uncreated, indestructible atoms. Instead he made this seemingly atheistic world of matter in motion palatable to Christians by a few clever additions. God was made the creator of the atoms, and man's soul was considered to be partly material and partly immaterial. Yet it would seem that for practical purposes, Gassendi's world was still material. Descartes' dualism of soul and body became meaningless in Gassendi's system, in which only the material aspect of the soul communicated with the world. Nor could there be intuitive knowledge as in Cartesianism: All knowledge came from man's senses. Gassendi was also skeptical of man's ability to get beyond the world of the senses. Human beings could not fathom nature's "inner, necessary and infallible causes"; they could only develop probable knowledge of the world and a provisional code of ethics based on seeking pleasure and avoiding pain. Gassendi stopped short of reducing morality to sensualism, and the voluptuous individual was not his ideal. He felt that since pleasure often results in pain, the most prudent life is one in which the individual tries to avoid pain, eliminate fear and achieve tranquility of mind. Gassendi left room in his philosophy for Christian beliefs because human knowledge was imperfect. Unable to go beyond appearances to the inner nature of things, men could accept on faith the traditional Christian answers to ultimate questions. What Gassendi failed to show was how belief in God, miracles, Christian morality and preparation for the afterlife could be reconciled with a world of material atoms which was the source of man's thought and his guide to action.

While Gassendi struggled with two, jarring views of the world, Thomas Hobbes was consistent in his adherence to a coherent philosophical system. When we think of that English philosopher's work, we usually remember his political treatises. But Hobbes' politics cannot be separated from his science and philosophy. Indeed, he combined many vocations and disciplines in his search for truth. For a while, he assisted Francis Bacon as secretary and translator of the latter's works into Latin. He tutored the young Charles II in mathematics, and never lost that king's friendship despite disagreements with the Stuart court over divine-right principles. He was captivated by Euclidean geometry, and his work in that field led him to believe that the axiomatic method could be applied to all realms of knowledge. Yet he was even more impressed with the materialists' approach to science, and became a close friend of Gassendi. His greatest praise was reserved for Galileo, who, he declared, "has been the first to open to us the door to the whole realm of physics, i.e. the nature of motion." Surprisingly, he was equally acquainted with the pagan classics of antiquity and with Europe's Christian heritage. Hobbes' translation of Thucydides' history demonstrated his command of languages and revealed his fascination with power politics. But, although he was constantly accused of being an atheist, his most "anti-religious" book, *Leviathan*, was written at a time when he was a communicating member of the Anglican church. He seriously asserted that nothing in that book was inconsistent with the most famous of Christian documents, the Nicene Creed. In a lighter vein, Hobbes is reputed to have denied the right of English authorities to try him for atheism, on the ground that the revolution of the 1640's had swept aside the extra-legal court which had judged such matters.

Whatever Hobbes' personal religious beliefs may have been, his philosophy was rigidly materialist in tone, and its three parts—matter, man and the state—hang or fall together. They constitute what Harald Höffding has called "the most profound materialistic system of modern times."[5] The Hobbesian philosophy drew on many sources—Galileo, Descartes, Harvey and probably Gassendi. Yet there can be no doubt that it was Hobbes' keen intellect and bold prose which made a striking and unique philosophy of these many ingredients. He developed his ideas slowly, matured late and by his death in 1679 was well known and highly respected, although he had won few converts. His first major work was published while he was in his forties; he was still writing at the age of ninety. His philosophy can be seen in crude form in an early trilogy on matter, man and the state, but it is best known from one of his greatest works, *Leviathan; or the Matter, Form and Power of a Commonwealth, Ecclesiastical and Civil* (1651).

Hobbes would have nothing to do with Descartes' dualism. Like Gassendi, he saw the physical world as matter in motion. More rigorously than the French priest, he combined observation, Cartesian mathematical-logical reasoning, and the findings of contemporary scientists to infer that man was also material. Breaking man down into his simple parts as a scientist would analyze any material object, Hobbes painted a disturbingly mechanistic portrait. He described the heart as a spring, the nerves

5. H. Höffding, *A History of Modern Philosophy*, vol. I (1924), 264.

as "so many strings," the joints "but so many wheels giving motion to the whole body," and life "a motion of the limbs." His description of the way that the senses act is equally interesting. "The cause of sense," Hobbes wrote, "is the external body or object, which presses the organ proper to each sense . . . which pressure, by the mediation of nerves, and other strings and membranes of the body, continued inwards to the brain and heart, causes there a resistance, or counter pressure, or endeavor of the heart, to deliver itself."

Thrust into a world of matter in motion, bombarded by its actions on his senses, man is frighteningly alone in the Hobbesian universe. He can never know the nature of the real world, only the sensations it creates. He cannot even know his fellow man, except by assuming that what occurs in himself occurs in others. Nor is there any certain consolation in religion. In his political writings, Hobbes conceded that God's existence could be proved by tracing back causes of things to the first cause, the deity. But in his scientific-philosophical studies and his critique of Descartes appended to the latter's *Meditations,* the English thinker was more dogmatic. Man could know nothing about the infinite or the beginning of the world, he stated. Nor could he infer from the world that there was a creation or a creator. Religion becomes, for Hobbes, a natural product of human needs, not something revealed to man. Unable to see the causes of things, he said, men look for "some power or agent invisible," as an explanation.

Left on his own, Hobbesian man is matter in motion within a material world in motion. Pleasure is "motion in the heart"; thinking is "motion in the head." Man seeks pleasure and tries to avoid pain. In this "state of nature," there could be no morality, no right or wrong, justice or injustice. It was simply a question of individuals seeking satisfaction of their desires, alone and in competition with others. Since Hobbesian man's uniqueness lay in his memory and his anticipation of the future, human beings were continually driven towards pleasure. It was a frustrating experience: Man's desires were limitless, but competition with others limited the chances of satisfying them. It is debatable whether this bleak state of nature can be deduced from Hobbes' materialism, or was the product of his timid nature and his experience with the English civil wars of the 1640's. In any case, the reader of Hobbes has to be impressed with his unusual insight into human psychology and his attempt to deal with man in the flesh. The Hobbesian solution for man's troubles was also very much of this world, but it was a political solution, and will be treated separately.[6]

6. See Chapter 15.

Most persons turn from Hobbes to Locke with relief. We would like to think that Hobbesian man is a fiction and that Locke's man is the reality. It is intriguing that the two Englishmen could have experienced the same political upheaval in their native land, exposed themselves to the works of the same continental philosophers, reacted against the same traditional knowledge while studying at Oxford University, taken the same empirical approach to truth, and yet arrived at such different conclusions about man. John Locke was strongly influenced by Gassendi and Hobbes, and like them he was familiar with Descartes' writings, which made a great impression on him. He was less well acquainted than either Hobbes or Gassendi with the natural sciences of his day, but he was a serious student of medicine and chemistry. He was in close touch with first-rate scientists in both fields, men who emphasized the empirical side of their subjects. In religious matters, Locke was probably closer than Hobbes to orthodoxy. On the other hand, Hobbes was formally an Anglican, and his father a clergyman; and Locke, who wanted to be an Anglican priest, was barred because his views were considered too independent. There was a "generation gap" of forty-four years between the two men, but that in itself was probably not important. Perhaps the decisive difference was in temperament, personality and intellect. Hobbes was pessimistic about human nature and precise in his logic; Locke was more of an optimist and less penetrating in his analysis of man.

Unlike Hobbes, Locke's fame rests on his philosophical as well as his political thought. His great work on philosophy *An Essay Concerning Human Understanding* (1690), was the product of at least twenty years' thought. Its genesis lay in a discussion with friends on the principles of morality and revealed religion, which occurred when Locke was in his thirties. Since they could not agree, Locke thought it appropriate to determine precisely what subjects human beings were capable of understanding. His ideas on that question appeared in abbreviated form in a Dutch journal during 1688. The finished essay, if a rambling seven-hundred-page book can be called that, was in Locke's own words "begun by chance, continued by intreaty, written by incoherent parcels, and after long intervals of neglect resumed again as my humor or occasions permitted."

Locke's ambition in philosophy was a modest one. He had no intention of establishing what the universe was like, nor of developing his own philosophical synthesis of God, man and the world. Although inspired by Descartes' emphasis on the geometrical-rational method, the English philosopher would have nothing to do with system-building based on a few intuitive truths. Although he became addicted to the Newtonian world-machine and was influenced by Hobbesian materialism, Locke would not follow mechanical materialism logically to the conclusion that man was merely a cog in the system. In his *Essay* he stated: "It shall suffice to my present purpose to consider the discerning faculties of a man, as they are employed about the objects which they have to do with." What Locke did not realize was that in undertaking this limited study, he would in fact find a peculiar place for man in the universe, a place of great promise and hope.

Bypassing Hobbes' treatment of how the material world acts on man's senses, Locke was satisfied with the principle that human knowledge comes from "experience." "Our observation, employed either about external sensible objects or about the internal operations of our minds perceived and reflected on by ourselves, is what supplies our understandings with all the materials of thinking." This was not of itself a novel view. Locke probably took it from Gassendi, with whose ideas he was familiar. It was what he ruled out by that dictum and the way he dealt with "experience" that made the English empiricist so influential. He labored the point that man had no "innate ideas" or "innate principles" stamped on his mind at birth. The mind was like a blank slate or "white paper, void of all characters, without any ideas." Whenever Locke harped on a negative argument we can be sure that he meant to demolish a popular idea and was not simply setting up a straw man. In this case, he had in mind Descartes' popular idea of intuitive knowledge. Descartes had argued that anything which is clearly and distinctly perceived constitutes true knowledge, and he had occasionally referred to this type of knowledge as "innate." Locke saw that Cartesian intuition or innate ideas had to be demolished if there were to be any firm basis for human understanding. The English empiricist had seen how men disagree about God, about morality and even about simple ideas. If men's disagreements were based on knowledge indelibly stamped on their minds, they could never find a common ground comparable to the uniform laws of the physical world. As Alfred Cobban notes, divergent ideas would have to be accepted as a basic element of human nature, and not subject to question.[7]

Having reduced the source of knowledge to experience, Locke went on to divide experience into two types: "sensation" and "reflection." He was sure that most ideas came directly from the senses. But to these he added reflective ideas, the products of the human mind's sorting and expanding on the simple ideas that stem from sensation. Locke was far from precise in showing what the mind was or how it acted on the raw material of sensation. He was too much of a Cartesian to break with Descartes' separation of mind and body, of immaterial and material substances. Yet,

7. A. Cobban, *In Search of Humanity* (1960), 70.

he had too much common sense to be worried by Descartes' inability to connect these opposites. By combining Descartes' rationalism and Gassendi's materialism, the English empricist was able to give man greater hope than either approach warranted. By stressing the senses, as Gassendi had done, Locke opened the way for the belief in environmental change. If, as Locke said, the difference between a Hottentot and an Englishman was education, the savage could be civilized by substituting a superior environment. But if environment were all, man would be as rigidly molded as if he had innate ideas. By adding Cartesian reflection to sensation, Locke allowed men to draw lessons freely from nature and to arrive at general principles useful for human conduct, rather than being completely at the mercy of their environment.

It is interesting that Locke had his ready-made notions of general principles, which he thought were perceived through the senses and reason. They are to be found in his *Second Treatise of Government* (1690). There, Locke declared:

> The state of nature has a law of nature to govern it which obliges everyone; and reason, which is that law, teaches all mankind who will but consult it that, being equal and independent, no one ought to harm another in his life, health, liberty or possessions.

One cannot help coming to the conclusion that Locke destroyed innate ideas while unconsciously holding to the principle of man's innate rationality. Leibniz saw this when he wrote: "There is nothing in the mind which is not first in the senses, except the mind itself." But the German philosopher's critique of Locke's *Essay* went unnoticed until it was published late in the eighteenth century. The delay was probably fortunate; it certainly allowed Locke, though imprecise in his thought, to be convincing in his view of human understanding. By making rationality seem not innate, but the product of human effort, Locke gave Europeans ground for hope. A Europe which was accustomed to the irrational and the perverse in human society and institutions could now believe that human reason was within reach. To the scientists' belief in material progress, Lockean philosophy added the idea of potential progress in human society.[8]

Locke's treatment of religion was tucked into the back pages of his *Essay*, where its apparent inconsistency with his views of human understanding could remain undetected. There, Locke declared that human ideas were either "according to reason," "above reason" or "contrary to

---

8. On the idea of material progress, see Chapter 13, pp. 339–341. On the problem of applying both that idea and Locke's theory of knowledge to history, see Chapter 16, pp. 418–420.

reason." He ruled out the last category, much as Descartes had done. The existence of more than one God was "irreconcilable to our clear and distinct ideas," and hence should be denied. The resurrection of the body belonged in the second category, and was more difficult for Locke to evaluate. Although it was "above reason," it had to be considered a true idea since it had been revealed by God. However, Locke did not stop with this facile explanation. He obviously was bothered by his principle that all knowledge came from the senses and reason. He therefore tried to reconcile revelation with "experience" by the following argument: If the revelation is clear, and our doubts are based only on "opinions, prejudices, and interest," we must accept revelation. Unfortunately, this does not place revelation "above reason," but above conjecture. When Locke turned directly to the subject of reason versus revelation, he seemed to place the former above the latter. He stated that "whether it be a revelation or no, reason must judge." There Locke left the reader, understandably confused. He was convinced in his own mind that he could keep his belief in miracles, Original Sin and the reconciliation of God and man through the mediation of Jesus. Yet the tenor of his philosophy and his awkward treatment of revelation made him the popular expounder of a very secular view of human nature and conduct. Lockean man seems capable of acting on his own, without the burden of Original Sin or the help of divine grace. This can be seen even in a statement Locke made about religion in general. For Locke, religion "should most distinguish us from beasts, and ought most peculiarly to elevate us, *as rational creatures, above brutes.*" [9] While some Christians were outraged by Locke's ambivalence on religious matters, he quickly became *the* interpreter of human nature for Europeans. In the eighteenth century, Voltaire singled out two men for the highest praise. One was Newton. The other was Locke.

Natural Religion, Superstition and Christian Mysteries

While the great seventeenth-century philosophers varied in their treatment of God and man, they left Europe with a picture of the world which filled the void created by the weakening of traditional belief. This world was one of order and rationality, devoid of constant supernatural disturbances. Whether God was the Creator, nature itself or nonexistent, the orderliness of nature remained. Man was both part of nature and sufficiently unique to be able to make the world serve his ends. In essence,

9. Italics have been added for emphasis.

the philosophical interpreters of seventeenth-century science developed a sophisticated "natural religion," which amounted to a code of conduct discovered through man's reason and senses. There was sharp disagreement over what form this "natural religion" took,[10] but it was clearly not supernatural in origin. And it was to be accepted precisely because it was natural, not because it was dictated by God. Above all, natural religion left little or no room for Christian belief in Original Sin, divine grace and predestination.

The idea of a natural religion which was explicit in the philosopher's books was implicit in the works of the scientists. We have already seen how Newton described God.[11] As much as he saw God as the lord of nature, it was nature, not God, which was the guide for Newtonian man. Newton and his fellow scientists constantly used their discoveries to buttress belief in God, but their praises of the God of nature only served to reinforce the idea of natural religion. The very titles of their books betray this tendency: *The Existence of God demonstrated by the Marvels of Nature; Theology of Insects; Wisdom of God in the Creation; The Astronomical Principles of Religion; The Christian Philosopher: a Collection of the Best Discoveries in Nature, with Religious Improvements.* Whether the scientist was refuting atheism, praising natural religion or supporting Christianity, the effect was the same. Thus we can turn from Walter Charleton's *The Darkness of Atheism dispelled by the Light of Nature: a Physico-Theological Treatise* to John Wilkins' *Of the Principles and Duties of Natural Religion* and then to Robert Boyle's *The Christian Virtuoso*, without losing the train of thought. Boyle's will provided for a series of annual lectures by Anglican clerics, designed to use science to prove Christian doctrines against the attacks by "atheists, theists, pagans, Jews and Mohammedans." One wit commented that nobody questioned God's existence until the Boyle lectures tried to prove it. The remark is too glib to be accurate; what the Boyle lectures undermined was not God but the Christian God. What the English scientists were doing was not unique. The philosopher-scientist Leibniz, a German Lutheran, was performing the same "service" on the continent. On the one hand he wrote to the Catholic Jansenist Arnauld that the spread of scientific curiosity was "strengthening atheism, or at least naturalism, and subverting the Christian faith." On the other he wrote several treatises on behalf of Christianity, such as his *Testimony of Nature against Atheists*, which furthered the cause he was attacking.

It is true that scientists often believed in supernaturalism and accepted miracles, even as they discovered the immutable laws of nature.

10. See Chapter 16, for numerous examples.
11. See Chapter 13, pp. 331–332.

Members of the Royal Society and many others spoke of God's "extraordinary providence" as well as his "ordinary providence." They argued that God usually acted through the laws which He had established, but that He could suspend those laws and intervene personally when He chose to do so. Thus the Biblical story of Daniel's companions miraculously escaping the fiery furnace was perfectly plausible for Boyle: "The author of nature was pleased to withdraw his concourse to the operation of the flames, or supernaturally to defend against them the bodies that were exposed to them." Isaac Newton could not accept the Trinity, since a united universe implied one God, not three persons in one. Yet Newton accepted Jesus as the divinely inspired mediator between God and man.

This combination of naturalism and supernaturalism was not destroyed overnight. As Francis Oakley shows,[12] the combination had been accepted in European intellectual circles as far back as the late thirteenth century. In the seventeenth, it was believed by Catholics, Lutherans, Calvinists and Old and New World Puritan divines. However, it was almost inevitable that the new science's assumption of an orderly, rational world and the discovery of more and more immutable laws of nature would cast increasing doubt on divine intervention after the Creation. Even the scientists of the late seventeenth century who believed in God's intervention made nature the norm and supernature the exception.

Other scientists and popularizers of science cast doubts on non-Christian supernaturalism.[13] Comets, astrology, witchcraft, oracles and many other supernatural matters turned out to be either purely natural or very human activities. The comet of 1680 was "the outstanding event" of the months following its appearance, according to the *Journal des Savants*. While the *Journal* reported that "everyone says it portends all manner of disasters," scientists were charting its natural course. The controversy over its "effects" on man raged in a pamphlet war from the Dutch Netherlands to Spanish America. In one pamphlet after another, Pierre Bayle dismissed these "effects," using his trenchant wit and his knowledge of natural causes. Bayle did not miss the opportunity to laugh at his opponents. He wryly commented that superstitious attitudes towards comets had aided paganism and harmed Christianity: Pagans terrified by comets increased their worship of false gods, while comet-fearing Christians seldom transferred their fear into respect for God. But Bayle also relied heavily on science in his arguments. Comets conformed to the laws of motion, and like all heavenly phenomena could not be concerned about the birth or death of a mere earthly prince. In empirical fashion, he

12. F. Oakley, "Christian Theology and the Newtonian Science: the Rise of the Concept of the Laws of Nature," *Church History*, vol. XXX (1961), 433–457.
13. On early modern superstition, see Chapter 3.

clinched his point by saying that years when comets appeared were not unusually disastrous. The best books against superstition were often too dull and involved to be read, but their arguments were plagiarized and expressed wittily by other authors. Thus no one remembers the Dutchman Van Dale's book on oracles, but Fontenelle's cribbed version, *The History of Oracles and the Cheats of the Pagan Priests* (1687), makes delightful reading even today. In England, Jonathan Swift made an astrologer look ridiculous by "predicting" his death and later describing how he had actually died close to the time predicted. Of course, the victim of Swift's wit was still very much alive, but his embarrassment was acute, particularly when the English authorities actually claimed the "dead" man's publication rights.

As the literate public laughed with the critics of pagan superstition, they also found themselves turned by the critics against Christian supernaturalism. Fontenelle used his attack on oracles to insinuate that Christian belief was similar to pagan superstition. Bayle's comet studies also included barbs at Christian conduct. In his opinion, Christianity was so seldom practiced that atheists might be more moral in their actions. It was one thing for a judge to dismiss the last case of witchcraft in England by saying that there was no law against flying by broomstick between Oxford and London. It was quite another matter to take the mystery out of Christianity by glorifying nature and reducing all religion to natural principles.

Few knew how to keep the mysteries of Christianity in the face of science and philosophy. Hundreds of moral and religious tracts were written proclaiming the faith, and must have been widely read. But these ignored the intellectual challenges of the age, and were forgotten by later generations. A few writers took the other extreme. They used science not only to prove the existence of God the lawgiver, but to reveal the Christ of the Cross. Their attempt to prove Christian truths by scientific methods and principles alone was like mixing oil and water. One of the most intriguing of these attempts was John Craig's *Mathematical Principles of Christian Theology* (1699). It was modeled on Newton's *Principia,* from which the author obviously lifted not only the method but also the title. Craig's mathematical demonstration of the date of Christ's Second Coming (3153 A.D.) raises eyebrows, but is empirically impossible to disprove. When we read that the truth of "the story of Christ" can be reduced to the formula, $cz + (n-1)f + (T^2/t^2)k$, we wonder how many contemporaries took him seriously.

The only way to win the minds of the literate public to true Christianity was to make use of both the weaknesses and the strengths of scientific thought. Christian skeptics, from Montaigne in the late sixteenth century to Bayle at the end of the seventeenth, made the attempt, but rejected science too quickly and took the leap of faith too soon. Their "fideism" was unconvincing because it made religion and science into opposites.[14] In the early seventeenth century fideism tended to discredit both man's senses and revealed truth. Towards the end of the century, it could no longer weaken faith in the senses, reason and science, but it continued to shake men's belief in Christianity. The attempt by philosophers like Gassendi to superimpose Christian doctrines on a mechanistic world were equally ineffective: Once the world of matter in motion was accepted as the whole truth, there was no room left for the miracle of Jesus' life, death and resurrection.

Blaise Pascal was almost unique in placing the natural and supernatural worlds in perspective. He proved that it was possible to combine science and Christianity against intellectual critics from without and unconscious enemies from within. In his short life of thirty-nine years, Pascal combined many careers. He read Montaigne, gambled, and consorted with free-thinkers. His mathematical achievements drew the praise of one of the greatest mathematicians of the century, Leibniz. His experiments to disprove Aristotle's assumption that nature abhors a vacuum furthered his reputation as a scientist, although Descartes caustically complained that the only vacuum was in Pascal's head. Pascal also wrote polemics on behalf of Catholic Jansenists against Catholic Jesuits, and at the age of thirty-one experienced a religious vision which convinced him of his worthlessness and of God's forgiveness of men's sins. Although he never completely rejected science and philosophy, he turned increasingly to religious matters, scribbling his thoughts on paper in striking epigrams. Constant pain and premature death prevented the completion of his attempt to defend Christianity. The rough notes were first published in 1670 as *The Thoughts of M. Pascal*. However, the text was at best a jumble, and the publishers of the early editions mangled it almost beyond recognition by deleting and adding to suit their particular purposes. Seventeenth and eighteenth century Europeans did not have the benefit of modern editions of the *Pensées*, which arrange all Pascal's thoughts in some semblance of order. Even so, the real Pascal could not be completely edited out of his work.

Pascal shrewdly used Descartes' rationalism and Montaigne's skepticism to counteract each other. By making man a creature whose very nature was to think, Pascal blunted the edge of skepticism. By making man a frail creature who was deceived by his senses, misled by his reason and victimized by his passions, Pascal struck at the heart of Cartesian

14. On Montaigne's fideism, see Chapter 3, p. 81. On Bayle, see Chapter 16, pp. 404–407.

certainty. For the scientist-turned-mystic, man was not everything nor was he nothing. He was "incapable of both certain knowledge or absolute ignorance." Because of his insatiable curiosity, he felt, man has to ask basic questions, but as a finite being he cannot know the answers.

This argument sets the stage for Pascal's Christian answer. The logical step for Pascal would have been to flee from reason and doubt to faith. But he refused to take that step, at least initially. He was determined to show that the Christian religion was "not contrary to reason" and that it was "attractive." By dwelling on the dual nature of man as a "thinking reed," who was great and also miserable, Pascal sought to show that man's actual nature conformed with the Christian view of him. Essentially, he was arguing that only Christianity took into account the two opposite human traits. For Christianity saw man as God's special creation and also as fallen Adam. Those who saw only human rationality were the hopelessly naïve victims of false pride. Those who saw only man's troubles were the hopelessly pessimistic victims of despair. The Christian alone had hope.

> Knowledge of God without knowledge of man's wretchedness leads to pride.
> Knowledge of man's wretchedness without knowledge of God leads to despair.
> Knowledge of Jesus Christ is the middle course, because by it we discover both God and our wretched state.

To convince the skeptics, Pascal was forced into an argument which he must surely have considered inferior. Yet he knew the skeptic well and he combined this knowledge with his own mathematical work on calculating probabilities. The result was Pascal's famous Wager: God is a good bet. Men should gamble that God exists and act accordingly. If they are correct in their belief, they win all; if they are wrong, they lose nothing.

Pascal relied heavily on science to provide a picture of man's place in the universe, but he refused to use the scientists' world of order and rationality to bring men to God. He showed that man was lost in the physical world, "fixed in one corner of this vast space," unable to fathom his origins or his ultimate end. God was clearly not revealed in such a world. Pascal's deity was, indeed, a "hidden God," a mystery to finite man. It would not help to say that He could be seen through the "works of nature." Natural religion could never reveal a God who cared for man and acted through the mediation of Jesus.

Ultimately, after arguing for the necessity and plausibility of Christian belief, Pascal took his leap of faith. He probably was proudest of his argument that man's reason could take him only so far, and that the only intelligible way to conduct oneself was as a Christian. One could argue all one wished, but only by acting like a Christian could man prove that Christianity worked. Pascal the thinker and the mystic was also Pascal the pragmatist.

Pascal coaxed the doubter along by other arguments, but one wonders how he could have considered them convincing for the rationalist or the skeptic. He declared that miracles, the Biblical story, the "fact" that Christianity was the oldest religion all attested to the truth of Christian doctrine. At the very time he was writing these arguments, others were questioning the occurrence of miracles, the divine nature of the Bible and the claim that Adam was the first man.[15] It is strange that almost one half of Pascal's *Pensées* was devoted to traditional defenses of Christianity, which were becoming obsolete.

Pascal did not succeed in bridging the widening chasm between traditional faith on the one side and the new science and philosophy on the other. Some historians have argued that the course of western thought might have been far less secular than it has become, if only the churches had embraced and publicized his views. It is certainly true that no Christian apologist with Pascal's understanding of science's contributions and limitations filled the void created by his death in 1662. Thus at the very time when the new science was passing from its uncertain, destructive phase in Galileo's day to its more positive and popular phase in Newton's time, organized religion allowed the debate between Christian man and secular man to go by default.

This does not mean that Christian beliefs were discarded by the end of the seventeenth century, nor that the churches were in danger of losing members. It does mean that unconsciously, many of the intellectual, political and social elite were beginning to think and act on the basis of secular rather than religious assumptions. Locke, Leibniz, Boyle, Newton and their reading public would have been astounded and dismayed had they known that their Christianity was more formal than real. There is a tragic irony in their life work, for in trying to bring religion up to date they unwittingly deprived western civilization of the very beliefs which had made its political and social institutions intelligible. In their own day, Locke and his fellow-philosophers were already confronted with the awesome problem of discovering how secular man in the natural world could organize society without using religious guidelines.

15. See Chapter 16, pp. 400–416.

15.

Political Thought:
Nature, Man and Human Society

The century which produced such ferment in science and philosophy was equally creative in its political ideas. We have seen how the theorists of divine-right monarchy combatted religious rebellion by modernizing medieval conceptions of government.[1] In its turn, divine right slowly yielded ground to yet another way of looking at human society. Instead of accepting rulers as quasi-divine creatures responsible only to God, some intellectuals began to view government as a human institution, created by man and responsible for meeting his secular needs. The existence of the state itself, which had been threatened by religious revolts, was increasingly taken for granted. But within that context, individual rights were considered to stand above state necessity. The very idea of a mythical "state of nature," in which man supposedly had existed before he instituted government and laws, underlined the new view that the state and its laws were artificial developments. Rulers were considered to be bound by a "social contract" between themselves and their subjects, established to preserve the "natural rights" and "natural law" which individuals had enjoyed in the state of nature. We should be wary of seeing the *avant-garde* political thought of the seventeenth century simply

1. See Chapter 2, pp. 36–43.

as a repudiation of divine-right absolute monarchy. But it is proper to describe it as an attempt to put the growing power of the state to constructive use, serving its members rather than its head.

The new way of looking at human society and government sowed the seeds of a sharp break with the political past. It is true that the vast majority of Europeans remained immune to the political ferment, deferring to the judgment of a narrow political-social elite. But within that elite, several great writers tried to justify the new political philosophy, and many more read their books. By 1715, the top echelons of society and government were becoming converted to the idea of natural rights, or at least of a responsible absolutism acting in accordance with natural law. We should not be misled by the fact that many of the new ideas were expressed in traditional phrases. The terms "natural law" and "social contract" had a long and distinguished history, and at the beginning of the seventeenth century were used to rationalize rebellion against the state. But during the course of the century these terms changed their meaning, and became weapons to control the state rather than to destroy it. Other words *were* new. Emphasis on the "estates" gradually went out of fashion; and the terms "state" and "individual" became the common coin of political treatises which discussed how those two abstractions could be accommodated. Divine-right theory still viewed the political world as a hierarchical structure, with the ruler standing above the various political-social estates. But the political thought which emerged as its new rival dispensed with the hierarchical assumption and concentrated on individuals as the basic ingredients of the body politic.

❧ The Intellectual Origins of New Political Thought

The changing political conditions of the seventeenth century encouraged men like Hobbes, Pufendorf and Locke to raise fundamental questions about contemporary politics. The secularization of politics and the strengthening of the secular state forced thoughtful persons to frame their political philosophy around its existence. The weakening of political estates despite the continuity of social ones compelled theoreticians to find new checks on government. And the stability which the body politic was gradually achieving meant that it no longer had to concentrate solely on repressing rebellion: Its power could well be used for other purposes.

The questions suggested by these political developments were easier to ask than to answer. It was an awesome task to analyze political man once secularization stripped him of traditional religious ideals and controls. If the state were simply a human creation, was it a product of force, its laws mere expediency and its actions proof that might was right? How could traditional conceptions of natural law and the social contract check the emerging power of the state, if those conceptions were tied so closely to the very religious base which secular governments were discarding? In previous times, it was assumed that God was an invisible third party to contracts between ruler and subject. If God were now a silent partner, would monarchs recognize any notion of a binding contract? For centuries, natural law was assumed to be an ideal dictated by God. Were kings who considered themselves quasi-divine subject to any guidelines? Contemporary rulers and their subjects might insist that kings were accountable to God, but the temptation for sovereign princes to make laws suit their own purposes was great. In the face of these difficulties, one cannot help being impressed by the provocative suggestions of Althusius, Grotius and Hobbes in the early seventeenth century, and the more comprehensive political systems of Spinoza, Pufendorf and Locke in later decades. But one wonders where they found the inspiration for their solutions.

The most natural reservoir of ideas was the ancient past. In seeking answers, the great political philosophers turned to the Bible and the writers of Graeco-Roman antiquity. University training exposed seventeenth century intellectuals to the thought of Cicero, Tacitus, Thucydides, Plato and Aristotle. As members of an overwhelmingly Christian society, they all knew Biblical history, chapter and verse; and many of them reinforced that background with advanced university courses in sacred history. They found in the ancient Stoics a secularized form of natural law, and in Plato the notion of a philosopher-king who patterned his conduct on eternal ideals. Aristotle taught that man was by his very nature a political animal, while Tacitus found the key to politics in the state's self-interest, or "reason of state." The ancient categorization of government as either monarchical, aristocratic or democratic was well known. Yet, as Sir George Clark notes, "One after another the writers of the century discovered that the traditional principles did not cover the new facts." [2] It is true that Grotius was fond of the Stoics, but when he actually applied their brand of natural law to seventeenth-century states he became hopelessly muddled in his thinking. The ancients could provide hints, but their ideas had to be taken out of context and drastically altered before they could blend with the seventeenth-century political scene. When the Spanish thinker Alamos de Barrientos tried to apply ancient maxims to contemporary Spain, he found himself constantly de-

2. G. N. Clark, *The Seventeenth Century* (Galaxy, 1961), 209.

parting from his text to add more revelant illustrations from recent
Spanish history.

Even the "reason of state" principle was not as practical as it appeared to be. At the beginning of the seventeenth century, Justus Lipsius
collected aphorisms from Tacitus and other classical authors on the subject. His books were reprinted several times, found their way into university lectures and many libraries, and probably influenced the Spanish
statesman Olivares. From Italy, France, England and Germany came
similar works on "reason of state." But that principle was no more satisfactory to the new political writers than was divine-right monarchy. It
had the advantage of being a secular doctrine, but the disadvantage that
it begged the very questions which the age was posing. Divine right
asked men to leave the judgment of kings to God. Reason of state suggested mysteriously that the state acted in its own interest, thereby cutting off the debate on what that interest should be.

Still less fruitful were suggestions from Scripture. Apart from visionaries who attempted to realize the Fifth Monarchy foretold in the book
of Daniel, Old Testament verses were more useful for illustrating a point
than making one. John Locke could actually make God's gift of the
world for common use look like a justification of private property.

Contemporary political experience was more relevant, but it could
blind as well as broaden man's vision. It forced men into asking questions,
but it did not necessarily provide any answers. In its original form,
Locke's famous *Second Treatise of Government* was a call to future rebellion, not a commentary on the system of government produced by a
successful revolution.[3] Political upheaval was accompanied by some original political thought in England, but not in Spain. The Dutch-German
borderland of Friesland provided a very calm setting for Althusius'
thought. And it was the cloistered life of provincial towns, university
communities and sedate princely courts which surrounded Pufendorf as
he wrote. Moreover, Pufendorf was influenced most directly by the most
atypical state of the age, the Holy Roman Empire, which he called an
indefinable monster. To be sure, actual political experience inspired hundreds of dull legal studies, comparative works on various states and inflammatory partisan pamphlets. But something else was needed to produce
great political philosophy. Cardinal de Retz feared that the rebellion of
the Fronde might bring about anarchy; it never crossed his mind that
the debate between French royal authority and those who tried to limit
it could produce any constructive answers.

That the most original treatises should have been written in Prot-

3. See Chapter 12, p. 314.

estant countries is probably no more than a coincidence. Those historians who like to link Protestantism with the "progressive" developments of early modern Europe find the germs of new political thought in Calvinism. But Hobbes was an Anglican with a materialist's viewpoint, Pufendorf a strong Lutheran, Spinoza a renegade Jew, and Locke an Anglican whose Calvinistic background was probably cancelled out by his close relationship with Dutch sectarians and free-thinkers. The subject needs careful study, as does the question of the interplay between political experience and political thought. At the present time there is no reason to believe that either religious faith or geography had a necessary bearing on the development of new political ideas. Indeed, political philosophy easily crossed religious and political frontiers. Pufendorf drew on Grotius and Hobbes, Locke on Pufendorf.

More alluring is the thesis that capitalistic individualism lay behind the work of several prominent thinkers. This is the subject of C. B. Macpherson's brilliant and exciting analysis of Hobbes, Locke, the political Levellers and Harrington. Macpherson argues that these currents of English political thought were based on the assumption of a "possessive market society." The individual was assumed to be "the proprietor of his own person or capacities, owing nothing to society for them." If this assumption actually came from seventeenth-century English society, it would help to explain the drift of contemporary thought away from the estates and towards individual rights. For it would follow that natural society "consists of relations of exchange between proprietors," possessive individuals clashing in a free market. Political society would become "a calculated device for the protection of . . . property and for the maintenance of an orderly relation of exchange."[4]

We cannot dismiss out of hand what may well be the most original book of several decades on the seventeenth century. But serious reservations are in order. Seventeenth-century English society seems too closely wedded to the idea of hierarchy and too far removed from the nineteenth-century belief in individual property to fit neatly its role as the source of modern liberal-democratic principles. Nor was England sufficiently close to a laissez-faire, competitive economy to allow an historian to talk of a "market society" in a modern sense. Moreover, the emphasis on the individual and on individual-state relations can be found not just in seventeenth-century England, but in the thought of continental writers like Pufendorf. Even if one accepts Macpherson's view of the "market society" in England, we can scarcely agree that Pufendorf had the slightest notion of such a dog-eat-dog economy.

4. C. B. Macpherson, *The Political Theory of Possessive Individualism* (Oxford, 1964), 3–4.

By default, we must fall back on the conventional opinion that the new science was the key to the new political philosophy. Difficulties remain, and historians have been reluctant to go beyond sweeping generalizations on the subject. The most frequently quoted passage is from the late seventeenth-century writer of popular science Fontenelle: "A work on politics, on morals, a piece of criticism, even a manual on the art of public speaking would, other things being equal, be all the better for having been written by a geometrician." But Fontenelle was referring to the precision of thought and clarity of style in science, rather than to its methodology and results. Many historians have also quoted passages from Sir William Temple, without realizing that he was skeptical of many of the contributions made by seventeenth-century science.[5] Although he may well have been unconsciously influenced by the new science, one passage taken out of context does not clinch the point.

The connection between the scientific "laws of nature" and political "natural law" is no less open to critical examination. Seventeenth-century men knew that the laws of science were in constant operation. By contrast, traditional natural law was assumed to be the ideal—what men should do rather than what they actually did. The confusion over this subject is compounded when one turns to individual thinkers. It is well known that John Locke's treatment of natural law in his political works contradicted the general philosophy which he derived from science. In his philosophical *Essay Concerning Human Understanding*, Locke assumed that man's ideas came from experience. This assumption demolished the idea of law as an ideal, since men merely did what was useful for themselves: pursuing pleasure and avoiding pain. But in Locke's *Second Treatise of Government* we find law as an ideal once more. Human beings are asked to govern themselves by ideal natural laws which are eternally true.

Despite these qualifications, there is no doubt that science was admirably suited to the needs of the new political thought. In fact, it appears that only the assumptions of science could have given the great political philosophers the answers which they were seeking. Whether they acknowledged their debt or based their political ideas on unstated or even unconscious premises derived from the natural sciences, does not concern us. It is enough to show the hidden relationship between the two disciplines. The best treatment on the subject is George H. Sabine's *History of Political Theory*, which suggests that science changed the political idea of natural law. However, Sabine never developed his hypothesis into a systematic thesis, and his chapters on seventeenth-century

5. See Chapter 13, pp. 340–341.

political thought leave the impression that each one was devoted to a different "seventeenth century." The following pages are an attempt to provide some tentative conclusions on a vexing subject.

The most important connection between science and political thought concerned "natural law." The political thinkers of the seventeenth century desperately needed some norm or ideal by which contemporary governments could be judged. Faced with the realization that the old ideal of God-given natural law was becoming irrelevant, and unwilling to admit that government set its own, relative standards, they found a new absolute in science. Scientists were saying that the physical universe was governed by immutable laws, and philosophers were explaining that man was part of that natural world. Some intellectuals dared to say that man could live according to a "natural religion," without the need of divine intervention. Why not assume that individual men in the "state of nature" had a natural set of political principles, a natural law which existed prior to the state and owed nothing to divine decrees? A few bold thinkers made just that assumption. Thus the old transcendental natural law which depended on God was renounced, only to reappear in a secularized and scientific form.

The difficulty with this new natural law was that political theorists interpreted it in two different ways. Sometimes it was viewed as a set of principles or goals by which individuals could judge governments—the old natural law of ideals in secular dress. Sometimes it was considered to be a scientific description of the principles by which human nature operates; that is, a cause of political actions rather than an ethical ideal. Political philosophers never quite reconciled the view of natural law as an end with their conception of it as a cause. Rather they tended to confuse the two. The most satisfying synthesis was accomplished near the end of the century by John Locke. His was a deceptively attractive synthesis, however, since it proposed that actions which were natural were automatically moral. After Locke, Europeans could believe that individual men were both ethical and practical at the same time.

This leads us to the second point which wedded political philosophy to science: namely, the new idea of the individual. If we reject Macpherson's theory that economics lay behind the notion of individual rights we nevertheless have to explain how Europe arrived at a political concept diametrically opposed to its deeply ingrained belief in a hierarchical society in which the group and not the individual was the norm. The answer seems to be in science's treatment of the physical universe as an undifferentiated continuum of individual substances. Seventeenth-century scientists rejected the traditional universe of qualitatively different objects, arranged in a hierarchy. In its place, they substituted a world of matter in motion, and described in mathematical terms how individual substances were related in their movements. Political writers were probably unaware of their inspiration; however, it seems clear that science gave them the radically new idea that all political thought must start with the individual. Even the most daring political thinkers were too conservative to make the individual the norm in social thought. But while they retained hierarchical views in their social theories, they were sufficiently imbued with the new science to make the break in their politics.

When the theoreticians proceeded to link natural law and the individual with the state, science again came to their rescue. Seventeenth-century science looked at the universe as a vast mechanism, whose parts were linked together in harmonious fashion. And seventeenth-century political thought began to envisage the state also as a machine. To be sure, it was somewhat tainted, being an artificial creation of men. In that sense, the state differed from the physical universe, which was obviously natural. Yet there was an analogy in the sense that governments were mechanisms designed to regulate the relations of individuals.

By declaring that governments acted in conformity with natural law, the new political thought completed its break with the existing views. Thus science answered the great political questions posed by the seventeenth century. In the face of the emerging power of the secular state, it suggested that the individual and not the state was the norm, that man in the "state of nature" governed himself by natural law, and that governments were mechanisms which were designed to protect the individual in accordance with that law.

The Secularization of Natural Law: Althusius, Grotius and Hobbes

It is unusual to discuss Althusius, Grotius and Hobbes together, for they make strange bedfellows. Althusius was a died-in-the-wool supporter of the estates in their clashes with the emerging sovereign state. Hobbes was so opposed to this view that he removed even the restrictions of divine-right monarchy from his Leviathan state. Grotius held an uncomfortable middle ground, granting that government was often the result of a contract while freeing it from most restrictions. Yet they had a common interest in natural law, and all three helped to undermine the traditional interpretation of that principle. None of them produced a full-blown modernized version of natural law, and none achieved lasting popularity for his treatment of political thought. Althusius acquired only an ephemeral reputation. Grotius became famous for his treatment of interstate relations, not for his incidental remarks on the developments within states. Hobbes was as detested for his political theory as he was for his materialist philosophy. If we look at the great natural law philosophers of the late seventeenth century, however, we can immediately see that men like Pufendorf, Spinoza and Locke drew much of their inspiration from the suggestions of Althusius, Grotius and Hobbes. Ideas which were half digested or unattractively presented by the earlier thinkers were reconstructed and put into writings which were read and assimilated throughout European society by the opening of the eighteenth century.

Johannes Althusius was the least prominent of the three. He could not completely accept the traditional ways of looking at politics. But he was too conventional to break cleanly with the existing views of natural law, social contracts and political estates. The main points of Althusius' *Systematic Politics* (1603, 1610) fitted neatly with subjects' desires to defend their religious faith and political liberties against a persecuting, tyrannical ruler. As a strong German Calvinist he sympathized with the revolt of the nearby Dutch provinces against Spain, and with efforts by the Germanic Diet to contain the political-religious ambitions of the Holy Roman Emperor. When Althusius sat down to write about these issues, he produced what was essentially a comprehensive textbook of stock answers: Government was the result of an agreement between ruler and subjects, and violations of the compact justified rebellion by the estates as the people's representatives.

Two fresh ideas were inserted in this rather ordinary academic exercise. The first was that human organizations could be explained without reference to religion. Taking his cue from ancient Stoicism, the law professor came close to saying that human beings had an innate social tendency which led them to form families, communities, provinces and finally states. The second notion was that the formation of associations took place in two stages. People agreed to a social compact by which they united as a society, shared its benefits and observed the laws established for its functioning. At the same time, they made a separate governmental compact with their ruler, which defined the limits of his authority.

Although he made these interesting modifications in natural law and the social compact, Althusius refused to take them to their logical conclusion. An orthodox Calvinist, he stopped short of emancipating his politics from religion. For Althusius, society and government were the products of man's natural instincts, but they also conformed with a divine plan. The natural law which guided man turned out to be the Mosaic code revealed by God in his sacred Scriptures. Althusius went so far as to make the state a servant of God's true religion. Rulers were admonished to proclaim the Calvinist faith, protect the state church, establish church-directed schools and censor morals. Thus the writer of *Systematic Politics* saw the handiwork of the Calvinist God in society just as in individual salvation or damnation.

Althusius was equally conservative in his application of the social compact theory. His one distinct break with his contemporaries on that subject was to make the contract a positive doctrine. His contractual arrangement still permitted rebellion if the ruler violated its provisions. However, by separating the social from the governmental contract, Althusius implied that society existed prior to the state. This was important, since it showed that men could continue to live in peace according to the social contract even if the government disintegrated. Unfortunately, Althusius' persistent support of political estates made his two-fold contract superfluous. In his scheme, any breach of the governmental compact resulted not in a reversion to the society based on the social contract, but in the assumption of power by the estates. Only when political thinkers began to dispense with the estates as the intermediary between the ruler and his subjects, did the two-fold contract of Althusius become relevant. In the meantime, Althusius turned his back on both the state and the individual. Although he believed that the people were sovereign, he felt that the officials of the towns and provinces should exercise that sovereign authority through the corporation of political estates. As he said, "what is owed to a corporation is not owed to its individual members."

Althusius' treatise was widely circulated in the Netherlands, the Holy Roman Empire and even in Sweden. Its scholarly and systematic treatment of conventional ideas made it a natural textbook in universities. Its comprehensive apology of government by estates must have appealed to many opponents of strong monarchy. We know, for example, that its merits were debated by supporters of the Swedish national assembly. No less than eight editions of the book appeared, five of them during the first four decades of the seventeenth century. But most readers were impressed by its clarity and its soundness, not by its flashes of inspiration, which seem to have escaped their attention. Althusius' original ideas had to be taken out of their setting before they could become relevant to the problems which the age's great thinkers were pondering.

Conventional supporters of religious rights and group liberties were not the persons to make that transition. The many radical tracts which appeared in England during the religious-political turmoil of the 1640's and 1650's weakened men's acceptance of authority. But not even John Milton's refreshing appeal to the right of individual conscience answered the question of how individual liberty and state necessity could be reconciled. Orthodox Calvinists were probably the most perverse in clinging to outmoded views. The French Huguenot exile Pierre Jurieu was still tracing a well-worn path in the late seventeenth century. He modified Calvinist support of rebellion, but only because he wanted to make the state strong enough to enforce his brand of Christianity. He never budged from the conventional position that the estates and not the individual were the basic components of the state.

Hugo Grotius was the first Calvinist who broke with conventional Calvinist politics, but he was not orthodox in his religious beliefs. Grotius was a Dutch Arminian, who would have nothing to do with the awesome deity of strict Calvinism.[6] He was forced to flee to France because of his moderate religious views, and dedicated his famous work *On the Laws of War and Peace* (1625) to the French monarch, Louis XIII. He was also well read in the ancient pagan classics on politics. And he was particularly influenced by early seventeenth-century science. Indeed, he called Galileo the greatest genius of his age.

Grotius was most interested in reducing the relations between predatory states to some sort of order.[7] By a strange fate his oblique references to order within states made a greater impact on the seventeenth century than did his full-blown theory of harmony between nations. Warrior-kings like Gustavus Adolphus read their Grotius, and continued to conduct their foreign policy according to self-interest. But Grotian views on the origin and practices of governments were picked up and developed by virtually every major political theorist of the next generation. His secularized version of natural law could not be applied to interstate relations where there was no authority to enforce its ideals. Within the state, the situation was different. Governments that rejected any external superior were reaching for sovereignty within their states. Provided Grotian natural law suited their purposes, rulers could use their authority to enforce its principles.

Like Althusius, Grotius provided man with a natural social instinct, and assumed a natural law which governed men in the state of nature. But unlike the German Calvinist, the Dutch Arminian made this law a completely secular one which human beings could know through their reason: "The law of nature is a dictate of right reason, which points out that an act, according as it is or is not in conformity with rational nature, has in it a quality of moral baseness or moral necessity." While Grotius admitted that God was the author of natural law, he contended that He created it not by His arbitrary will but because it was true. As he said, "Just as even God, then, cannot cause that two times two should not make four, so he cannot make what is intrinsically evil not evil." Dramatically, the Dutchman declared that natural law principles "would

6. On the orthodox-Arminian controversy, see Chapter 3, pp. 75–76.
7. See Chapter 2, p. 54.

hold good even if we concede that which we could not do without sinning, [namely] that there is no God, or that the affairs of men are of no
concern to him."

Grotius' secularization of natural law made it possible for men to
reexamine the relations of subjects and rulers without concern for divine
judgment, but his confusion over the actual formation of governments
prevented him from undertaking that task himself. He vacillated between
the principle that government was natural and the idea that it was the
result of mere expediency and convenience. The Grotian state combined
opposite principles without reconciling them. It was a just state, conforming to absolute, natural standards; but it was the product of self-
interested human beings who set their own relative standards. It was
instituted by agreements or social compacts which implied controls on
officials by the subjects who placed them in power; but, because men's
social instinct was so natural, whatever form of government they established seemed to be beyond criticism.

In trying to reconcile these opposites Grotius only succeeded in
subordinating the relative, expedient and libertarian side of the state to
its absolute, natural and authoritarian side. This was understandable for a
man who placed order above division, and religious peace above confessional discord. He was so concerned with establishing order in the relations between sovereign states that he did not want to confuse the picture
by permitting individual or group liberties within them. After making
government a purely human undertaking, he was afraid of the logical
inference that it was the result of convention and whim. From the ancient
skeptical argument that government was merely expediency, Grotius fled
to an extreme Stoicism which made political association a purely natural
and just product of human nature. It is not surprising that while Althusius dedicated his book to the assembly of a nearby Dutch province,
Grotius dedicated his most famous work to a monarch.

However understandable Grotius' sympathy for authority may have
been, it was regrettable. He did provide for some individual rights, and
many scholars have proclaimed him the founder of the modern social
contract argument for limited government. But at best he raised the possibility that natural law implied moral limitations on rulers as well as
subjects. In a book on toleration, the Arminian scholar said that no human
institution could legislate vindictive punishment for activities which were
in conformity with natural law. But one wonders how much individual
freedom his peculiar brand of secularized natural law allowed. Divine-
right absolutism declared that kings would answer to God if they violated
their trust. Having removed divine judgment, Grotius did not go very
far towards finding a secular substitute. He widened the gap between

individual rights and state necessity instead of narrowing it. He granted that government was often the result of a social compact, but contended that the role of subjects in politics was concluded once they made that agreement. And while Grotian natural law stood above ruler and subject alike, Grotius virtually cancelled out its control over the government by treating subjects as if they were the private possession of the ruler. There was to be no sovereignty of the people, and rebellion against a ruler who violated natural law was guarded against by careful qualifications. While Althusius provided the fruitful suggestion that society could link individual and ruler, Grotius proposed only his secularized natural law, which for the moment seemed to control the individual, while permitting government to do whatever was necessary for its preservation.

Thomas Hobbs brought into the open the problems which Althusius and Grotius were too cautious and confused to see clearly. His philosophical materialism made him much less willing than Althusius to see any supernatural influence in the political affairs of men. And his attempt to examine human nature as it existed, rather than as philosophers idealized it, allowed him to attack even the secularized natural law of Grotian thought. The reader of Hobbes' famous *Leviathan* is confronted with a vision of human beings as amoral creatures who act out of self-interest, without regard to any higher principle. As we shall see, the English materialist could not free himself completely from the idea of natural law, but his insertion of his particular brand of the theory came almost as an afterthought.

The scaffolding of Hobbes' political philosophy was provided by his views of contemporary science.[8] He saw the physical universe as matter in motion, and man as simply another material substance. Each individual moved and acted in response to sensations from outside and to his natural desire to follow those sensations which were pleasurable. In the hypothetical "state of nature," Hobbesian man had no "notions of right or wrong, justice and injustice." As Hobbes said, "Justice and injustice are none of the faculties of the body, nor mind. If they were, they might be in a man that was alone in the world, as well as his senses and passions." Hobbes was not even willing to agree with Althusius and Grotius that human beings were innately sociable. To the contrary, he saw the individual moving in pursuit of his pleasure as colliding constantly with other persons who desired the same objects. As men conflicted, they sharpened their competitive instincts, their desire for glory and reputation, their suspicion and fear of each other. This was the scientific law of inertial motion with a peculiar twist. In the rest of the natural world, the

8. On Hobbes' science and philosophy, see also Chapter 14, pp. 354–356.

self-regarding motions of individual substances were coordinated through the laws of nature. But in man's case, without a social instinct or a natural law of absolute principles to guide him, there was only a "war of every man against every man." Life was "solitary, poor, nasty, brutish and short."

It is easy to see why Hobbesian politics had such a profound impact on contemporary Europe. He was the first prominent thinker to give the individual priority over either society or government. Instead of a natural law of ideals standing over human beings, there was only man's natural right to do what was useful for his individual existence. Where Althusius had subordinated the subjects to the estates, Hobbes centered his attention on the individual. Where Grotius had made government so natural that the state's self-preservation appeared to be the highest law, Hobbes implied that all governments had to take into account the basic natural rights of the individuals who established them. In stark outline, Hobbes presented his century with the dilemma of its politics: How to form a new order out of the chaos of secular, amoral and individualistic society.

So sweeping were Hobbes' attacks on conventional assumptions that he nearly made any type of political organization inconceivable. His task was to show how political organization was possible in spite of human nature's selfish acts, its absence of social instincts and its lack of moral principles. The English thinker's solution was in line with his utilitarian analysis of human activity. Men were self-regarding, wishing to do whatever benefitted themselves. Since the state of nature threatened their very existence, they had to escape its clutches. Since men had no sense of right and wrong, and were so unsociable that they could not agree among themselves over a man-made code of conduct, they had to go outside themselves. Their only recourse was to an all-powerful Leviathan state. This was clearly a politics of fear. Men were so afraid for their individual safety that they were willing to give up all their natural rights to an outside power in order to preserve their lives. There was a compact, but it was a one-sided agreement whereby subjects authorized the state to do whatever it deemed necessary to preserve order and life.

The Leviathan state was named by Hobbes after an invincible monster described in the Old Testament. The modern Leviathan was sovereign in every sense. In the absence of any ideal of natural law, it defined what was right and wrong, and laid down laws to enforce its plan of justice. Some historians have denied that the Hobbesian state was totalitarian, but it is difficult to agree with them. For Leviathan had total control over man, his thoughts and his feelings as well as his outward actions. Property was to be regulated, laws interpreted to suit circumstances, universities and churches supervised. Nothing was to be left undone which would be conducive to internal peace. Whether sovereignty was to reside in a king, as Hobbes preferred, or with a legislature, made no difference; the individual was at the sovereign's mercy. Subjects had no right to rebel, since rebellion was self-defeating: It returned man to the insecure state of nature. Without Grotius' secularized natural law, there was not even the possibility of arguing that a sovereign had obligations as well as rights. Without Althusius' dual compact and his estates, there was no middle way between total submission to the state and the chaos of individualism. The single compact of Hobbes was no consolation to subjects. The ruler was not bound by it: His only role was to receive full authority from the contracting individuals.

This brief analysis of Hobbesian politics leaves the impression that Hobbes destroyed conventional assumptions only to rebuild a state more absolutist than that of the divine-right monarchists. But that is only part of the truth. Hobbes undermined existing postulates so successfully that he removed the supports from his own political system as well. His attack on natural law went too far, and he recognized that fact and made a belated effort to restore it. Having reduced government to mere human convention and human nature to sheer expediency, he retraced his path in an effort to show that political institutions were in conformity with an absolute, moral, natural law. He argued that when men in the state of nature began to fear for their lives they miraculously discovered certain "natural laws" which could solve their problems. Reason, which was foreign to natural man, conveniently entered the picture at this point, telling men that they "ought" to do certain things: seek peace, agree to renounce their unlimited rights, and abide by the compact they were making with Leviathan. In general this Hobbesian natural law constituted a golden rule of "doing unto others as we would be done to." The principle is sound enough, but it does not fit with Hobbes' previous treatment of human beings. Historians have noted that the English thinker was confusing principle with utility, the ideal with the actual. Having based government on fear and fear alone, he sought to camouflage the Leviathan state's weak foundations. He was suggesting that, after all, government was not just an expedient but a natural and rational undertaking.

Hobbes did not convince his contemporaries. Even Descartes, who normally kept silent on political matters, thought that the Englishman could have made his thinly veiled apology for absolute monarchy more attractive. Oddly enough, the divine-right monarchists were among Hobbes' most bitter critics. Having joined the exiled royal family in France after the civil wars, Hobbes was compelled to leave when his *Leviathan* appeared in print. The reason was obvious: The philosophical materialist had taken all the mystery out of government, and based its authority on the services it rendered, not on divine sanction. If government were instituted by men and not God, if it were created only to keep peace and prevent bloodshed, subjects could question its every action. Hobbes thought that he had painted the political picture so realistically that subjects would accept his Leviathan more readily than a monarchy protected by God. After all, it was clear to him that human beings had to accept a sovereign state if they desired to save their own lives. What he did not realize was that a very different conclusion could be drawn from his utilitarian politics. He argued that rebellion was illegal and illogical, but he implied that a government was useful only as long as it had the power to maintain order. If the Leviathan ever faltered and lost that power, any individual would logically cease to have any reason for obeying it. Some proponents of divine right tried to save the state by keeping Hobbes' utilitarian rationale, while restoring the supernatural element. For example, the German writer J. C. Becmann argued that the Hobbesian state of nature forced individuals into accepting an absolute monarchy to keep the peace, and then concluded that the sovereign's performance could be judged only by God. The great French apologist of divine-right monarchy, Bossuet, gave a more sophisticated version of this combination, playing down the utilitarian role of the state and stressing its divine element.[9] But most theorists realized that any combination of Hobbesian utility and conventional divine right would tend to undermine rather than buttress royal authority. Hobbes was personally liked and protected by the restored English monarch Charles II, but in 1683 the pro-royalist Oxford University condemned the political philosopher's views as a "damnable doctrine destructive to the sacred person of princes, their state and government, and of all human society."

Those who disliked Hobbes for betraying his own individualist postulates were equally unhappy. They were quick to point out the fallacy of a Leviathan state built on the foundations of natural rights. Few persons were satisfied with a compact theory which gave away all rights in return for mere security of life. They felt that the state must either provide more than security or leave more freedom to the individual. Hobbes did concede that subjects were not compelled to sacrifice their lives for the state, since the very purpose of government was to preserve human life. However, he still believed in capital punishment and military service. All the would-be draft-dodger could do was find someone willing to take his place. The criminal confronted with the executioner was allowed the "right" to become a jailbreaker, but even then he obviously had to leave the state if he wished to avoid the hangman's noose. It has

9. On Bossuet, see Chapter 2, pp. 40–41, 43.

sometimes been noted that Hobbes allowed freedom of employment, cultural interests and other activities which did not adversely affect law and order. However, these were tenuous freedoms which could be revoked if the government decided that they threatened its security. No twentieth-century democracy has resolved these problems. But when forced by Hobbes to grapple with them, seventeenth-century intellectuals refused to accept his facile solutions.

Thus Hobbes completed the breakdown of traditional political thought. His influence was enormous, but his legacy ambiguous. In England, his books were burned by public authorities, and debated incessantly in weighty treatises, as well as in the emerging English newspapers. On the continent, his ideas were condemned by Leibniz as suitable only to a "Utopia of Atheists," but they crept into virtually every major work on politics and many a second-rate political tract. Hobbes brought politics down from the heavens to earth, shattered existing conceptions of natural law, and swept away the debris of all previous political theories. European intellectuals henceforth had to live with secular Leviathan. The task was to reconstruct political thought so that Hobbes' state could be tamed, humanized and if possible brought into line with some new, secular version of the natural law which he had seemingly destroyed.

The Reconstruction of Political Thought: Spinoza, Pufendorf, Locke

Three great political theorists attempted to reconstruct political thought in the light of Hobbes' destructive work. Spinoza took Hobbesian natural rights as far as they could go within the framework of an all-powerful government based on expediency. Pufendorf also relied on natural rights, but attempted to place both the individual and the state under the control of a revived natural law. Locke managed to combine expediency, natural rights and natural law in an illogical but convincing synthesis.

The most brilliant of these late seventeenth-century thinkers was Benedict Spinoza. He began the work of reconstruction by reconciling the principles of state necessity and individual freedom, which Hobbes had made into opposites. Spinoza's influence on his contemporaries is difficult to gauge. His *Theological-Political Treatise* of 1670 aroused controversy because of its secular treatment of the Bible,[10] not because of its secular politics. However, it is likely that those who read the book's passages on Scripture also looked closely at its political message.

10. See Chapter 16, pp. 401–402.

While others burned Hobbes' books and impugned his character, Spinoza challenged him by accepting his premises. The Dutch pantheist [11] agreed with Hobbes that man was part of an amoral nature. He felt that in the state of nature there could be no natural law, no conception of what was right or wrong. Like all other creatures, man simply acted to fulfill his natural instincts. Every being had the right "to exist and act according to its natural condition." Big fishes devoured little ones "by sovereign natural right." Spinoza made man unique in the sense that he possessed reason as well as passion, sympathy and sociableness as well as selfishness. But in the state of nature, Spinozist man acted much like Hobbesian man, victimized by pride, envy, aggressiveness and fear for his life. Human beings were "no more bound to live by the dictates of an enlightened mind . . . than a cat is bound to live by the laws of nature of a lion." The only limitation on man's "natural rights" was his inability to enforce them. Might was right, or at least made right: "Whatever a man does after the laws of nature, he does by the highest natural rights and has as much right over nature as he has power."

In seeking a way out of this nasty and insecure state of nature, Spinoza deftly avoided the traps set by both Hobbes and Grotius. Grotius had argued that once men contracted to live under a government, the state was free to act as it pleased. Hobbes had contended that the social contract bound men to accept whatever the government did, out of fear of the alternative anarchy. Against those contentions, Spinoza raised Hobbes' own assumption that all government is based ultimately on its power. Spinoza conceded that men made a social compact to escape the insecurity of their natural state. But he refused to agree that any such compact was binding on them. Just as the individual's natural rights extended only as far as his power to pursue them, the state's artificial rights were limited to the extent of its power to enforce its decrees.

This conclusion became the premise of the unique Spinozist state. If government commanded obedience because of its superior strength, it had to make certain that it had such strength. To attain it, the state must utilize the hopes and needs of men as well as their fears. No natural or divine law placed such limits on the ruler, but the very survival of the state depended on concessions which would make subjects obedient rather than rebellious. To say that a government had unlimited rights was tantamount to saying it had the right to destroy itself by unpopular acts; this was as irrational as saying a man had the right to be crazy. Thus government, which was created solely to provide security, must for its own sake allow a wide measure of freedom for the individual:

11. For Spinoza's philosophy, see Chapter 14, pp. 349–352.

It follows that the ultimate aim of government is not to rule . . . by fear, not to exact obedience, but to free men from fear, that they may live in all possible security. . . . No, the object of government is not to change men from rational beings into beasts or puppets but to enable them to develop their minds and bodies in security and to employ their reason unshackled; . . . in fact, the true aim of government is Liberty.

Spinoza's reconciliation of the individual and the state was clearly an advance on Hobbes' position, but it could not have satisfied his contemporaries. His political philosophy had the distinct merit of making life in the secular state enjoyable as well as bearable. It made the important point that human beings can realize their full potential only in society, shielded by the state from fear and insecurity, which are debasing. However, Spinoza's reduction of society, government and law to pure expediency was too Hobbesian to be accepted. As J. W. Gough says, Europe clung to "the idea that there was a real criterion, not merely relative to self-interest, by which actions and institutions should be judged." [12] Those who found divine-right principles of responsibility to God unacceptable still wanted to place the individual and the state under some absolute standard. Spinoza, like Hobbes, failed to do this. In his last political work, the posthumously published *Political Treatise* of 1677, he tended also to sacrifice liberty to security, and to minimize even those limitations on the state which were based on expediency. For he admitted that government had the right to check freedom of thought and religion whenever these endangered the state's existence. The emphasis on order over liberty in that work is slight, but it is there: "That dominion is the best where men pass their lives in unity and the laws are kept unbroken. . . . Men are not naturally born for citizenship, but must be made so."

Samuel Pufendorf was far more influential than Spinoza because he managed to combine Hobbesian expediency with Grotius' secularized natural law. Pufendorf's importance was long neglected by scholars since his political solutions were closely identified with continental absolute monarchy. Only in recent years has he received the attention which his influence merits. In his native Germany, the Saxon jurist founded a "school" of political thought which dominated central Europe well into the eighteenth century. His works were translated into French and English and won temporary acclaim in the west. Even John Locke, who rejected Pufendorf's leanings towards absolute monarchy, learned much from reading his books and called his great treatise *On the Law of Nature and Nations* (1672) "the best book of that kind." It was only one of many works which the German scholar wrote on political thought, history,

12. J. W. Gough, *The Social Contract* (1963), 118.

the constitution of the Holy Roman Empire, religious unity and the relations of church and state. What Pufendorf put into his books, he disseminated also by word of mouth, first as a professor at the universities of Heidelberg and Lund, later as historiographer-councilor at the Swedish and Brandenburg-Prussian courts.

Pufendorf's view of human nature drew on many sources, including Christian tradition, Cartesian philosophy and the political thought of Grotius and Hobbes. He rejected Hobbes' gloomy description of human nature and was even more certain than Grotius that man's life in the state of nature was relatively peaceful and secure. Pufendorf was convinced from his reading of Descartes' *Discourse on Method* that human beings were by nature rational creatures. While Grotius thought that natural law was less certain than mathematical demonstrations, Pufendorf asserted that human reason could arrive at certain knowledge in both the scientific and political realms. However, his Christian principles and his realism led him to admit that men did not always follow the dictates of reason. A confirmed Lutheran, he accepted the sinfulness of man resulting from Adam's fall. As he noted in one of his religious treatises, "Due to the corruption of our nature, the observance of the natural law is necessarily imperfect and sullied with many transgressions." Having made this qualification, Pufendorf was ready to draw Hobbesian principles into his political system. Following Hobbes, he declared that natural man needed the political state to counteract the weakness of the state of nature.

This treatment of natural man and the origins of government was clearly a skilfull combination of the Grotian and Hobbesian viewpoints. Since man in the state of nature was aware of natural law ideals, he had a ready-made set of absolute principles which could be transferred to the political state: There was thus no need to let a ruler determine the guidelines for political man. On the other hand, Pufendorf's awareness of man's innate selfishness allowed him to see government as based on expediency. Politics was the art of the possible, which took into account human nature as it actually existed. Pufendorf thus united idealism with realism, natural law with self-centered natural rights.

Pufendorf was the first political theorist to make full use of Althusius' double contract, breaking with the precarious single compact of Hobbes and Grotius. He argued that a social contract among individuals preceded the contract which established the actual government of the state. Thus government came after society and was established only for its welfare. The fact that the social contract laid down the broad aims of government in the light of "natural law" also reinforced the subordination of the state to absolute fixed standards. Moreover, the mechanism by which individuals voted on the goals of the social contract saved individual rights from being submerged completely in the state. The second contract bound all who made it to abide by the decisions of the government. But the government also agreed to follow the goals of the social contract and the principles of natural law. The state could determine how the aims were to be achieved but it could not change the underlying principles.

It has often been argued that Pufendorf's political philosophy was conducive to authoritarian government, despite its emphasis on natural law. Such an interpretation is misleading and fails to take into account the political and intellectual climate of the seventeenth century. To be sure, Pufendorf placed only moral restraint on rulers, who alone were to determine whether their laws and actions conformed to natural law and the aims of the social compact. In a shortened, textbook version of his major work, entitled *The Duties of the Man and the Citizen* (1673), Pufendorf made it clear that "the sovereign power is sacred and inviolable," that it is "evil to resist or disobey it," and that the subject's only recourse is to resignation or flight. But these statements must be viewed in the context of Pufendorf's intention to make government responsible as well as orderly. His stress on the underlying moral principle of natural law and the ruler's duty to be guided by it was far more conducive to responsible authoritarianism than was Spinoza's pure utilitarianism, or Hobbes' politics of fear. In an age when the laws of physical nature were in vogue, it was a step forward, not a step back, to invoke the name of secularized natural law as a check on irresponsible rule.

Followers of Pufendorf in succeeding decades interpreted their master in different ways, but the central idea of benevolent absolutism remained. Like Pufendorf, his students constantly attacked the Hobbesian state. This was true even in the case of Ulrich Huber, a Dutch apologist of royal absolutism. It was most evident in the late seventeenth-century writings of Christian Thomasius, an eminent German publicizer of Pufendorf's politics. Thomasius stressed man's rationality and freedom of thought against divine-right and utilitarian apologists for absolute monarchy. Indeed, he was so persistent in his support of innate popular rights that his writings were burned by the absolutist Danish government. Through Pufendorf and Thomasius the notion of responsible absolutism reached the mid-eighteenth century ruler of Prussia, Frederick the Great, who wrote and believed that "far from being the absolute lord of his people, the king is their first servant." In Frederick's contemporary, Christian Wolff, Pufendorf's apology for enlightened absolutism was almost submerged by the principle of popular sovereignty.

The political thought of John Locke also drew on Pufendorf, but the Englishman's conclusions broke more sharply with the German's views. Locke emphasized and distorted natural law to such an extent that some scholars have looked on his political principles as the opposite of Pufendorf's responsible absolutism. Although this is far from being true, the English philosopher and the German jurist certainly stressed different aspects of their common heritage.

Of Locke's *Two Treatises of Government* (1690), the second is the better known. The first treatise was one of many attempts by English writers to refute the absolutist views of Robert Filmer.[13] The second treatise was more positive in its intent, setting forth Locke's own views on government. As its subtitle says, it was "an essay concerning the true original, extent and end of civil government." There has been no end to the controversy over that work, nor is there likely to be any consensus in the future. Locke has been proclaimed the founder of modern liberal-democratic thought, and denounced as the upholder of narrow propertied interests. Some make him the defender of individual rights, while others see him as the supporter of tyrannical majority rule. To many, he held up the ideal of a stable government acting for the public good; to a few, he preached the right of permanent revolution. In the eighteenth century his name was invoked on behalf of the English status quo, moderate revolution in the American colonies and violent, radical revolution in France. Both liberals and conservatives in the present-day United States can claim Locke as their father. The most plausible interpretation of Locke is that he combined many conflicting principles in an illogical but common-sense philosophy of individual property rights. Locke probably did not realize the tricks he was playing on consistency, but he handled his various ideas in such a way that they seemed to fit together.

There is no doubt that Locke's political philosophy was built on individualism. He accepted with few qualifications Hobbes' notion that the individual in the state of nature had the right to take whatever he could. Locke easily dispensed with the Biblical suggestion that God gave the earth "to mankind in common." It was evident to Locke that God meant men to use His creation, and that to do so they had to appropriate it for individual use. While he initially said that the individual could take only "as much as any one can make use of to any advantage of life before it spoils," he quickly dropped that qualification. With the introduction of money, which did not spoil, the individual was free to enlarge his wealth.

Locke had no intention of praising individual natural rights only to subvert them. He guarded against Hobbes' view that natural rights were virtually useless in the state of nature because they were not respected.

13. On Filmer, see Chapter 2, p. 41.

To do so, Locke had to combine Hobbesian natural rights with the natural law of Grotius and Pufendorf. It was a clever combination, so clever that one suspects that Locke was not fully aware of the implications which could be drawn from the full-blown natural rights philosophy. In order to understand Locke's political system, it is essential to isolate three major ideas which are implied in his fusion of natural rights and natural law.

In the first place, Locke's natural law taught that no one should interfere with any individual's natural right to "life, health, liberty or possessions." This principle, like all natural law principles, was known through man's reason. Since Locke believed that men were naturally reasonable creatures, it seemed logical that they respected one another's natural rights. Thus the state of nature was a peaceful one for Locke, not a state of war.

In the second place, Lockean natural law made the possession of property a moral right. Hobbes had denied that there was any notion of "right" or "wrong" in the state of nature. Man was amoral and simply did what pleased him. Pufendorf had made the sanctity of property part of his natural law, but subordinated it to the idea that natural law stood as a standard above all individual and state interests. Locke virtually equated natural law with natural rights. Starting with Hobbes' assumption that men act simply out of self-interest, Locke added un-Hobbesian natural law, changed its meaning, and made self-interest into a moral principal. This illogical combination was all the more persuasive, since neither Locke, nor his contemporaries, nor future generations realized his confusion of utility with morality.

The third implication of Locke's natural law was the most astounding: Man's acquisition of property and his development owed nothing to society or the state. If the state of nature were as idyllic as the natural rights philosopher contended, it was clear that natural man had everything he needed before he established any formal society or government. Neither Althusius nor Grotius had made such a suggestion, and even Pufendorf shied away from such a glorification of the individual. Christian tradition held that only God was self-sufficient, and even an extreme secularist could see that if man owed nothing to his Creator he certainly owed something to his fellow men. But with Locke we come face to face with the radically new idea that the individual is self-made.

Having made the individual's position secure, moral and self-acquired in the state of nature, Locke was ready to make his peace with the political state. Here, the idealizer of natural man was in logical difficulties, since he had previously implied that no government was necessary. But Locke was not one to place logic above common sense. He had exaggerated man's goodness to emphasize the point that government is for the individual and not the individual for government. Now he dropped hints that the state of nature was not a condition of complete harmony. The reader of Locke's second treatise will be baffled by his confused and contradictory treatment of what went wrong with man's natural state. Locke makes the point that a few bad apples spoil the barrel, only to suggest in another place that most persons are bad. At times, it appears that human nature degenerated following a golden age befitting the Garden of Eden; against this, he argues that natural man simply lacks the impartiality to obey natural law when it is against his interest. This confusion is somewhat beside the point, however. Locke's real objection to the state of nature was that in it man enjoyed everything but security. He concluded that "the great and chief end . . . of men's uniting into commonwealths and putting themselves under government is the preservation of property."

Occasionally, Locke suggested the broader political goal of common welfare, but this thought was not inconsistent with his ideal of government as protecting property. Locke could even place the ultimate control of government in the hands of the majority, and retain his belief in the innate property rights of the individual. Most scholars now believe that Locke's "majority" meant only a majority of the "political nation." Since the "political nation" of late seventeenth-century England consisted exclusively of those subjects who owned property, it was not likely that they would exercise their franchise to tyrannize over property rights. The detective work by C. B. Macpherson on this subject is by far the best, although one can question his identification of property with a capitalistic system.[14] It seems clear that Locke anticipated the modern "bootstrap theory," implying that those individuals who did not pull themselves up and acquire property had only themselves to blame. They were included in the state, but only in the sense that they were under laws which prevented them from encroaching on the political nation's rights.

This analysis of Locke's second treatise should reveal the narrow basis of his political philosophy. But it is necessary to return to the ambiguous Lockean legacy mentioned at the outset of the discussion. Even in criticizing Locke's belief that a little government goes a long way, we should note his healthy criticism of the Leviathan state. If Locke's singular stress on the rights of the few led to the French revolutionary dictum that "the Third Estate is everything," his idea that human rights stand above government necessity was a useful corrective to Pufendorf's optimistic belief that the enlightened state would automatically act

14. See C. B. Macpherson, *The Political Theory of Possessive Individualism*, 247–262.

on behalf of those rights. In the long run, Lockean politics was far more adaptable to changing conditions than Pufendorf's, since Locke left room for individual rights and majority rule to be broadened and deepened.

Perhaps the most important point made by Locke was that popular government, however defined, need not lead to instability or anarchy. Without quite realizing it, Locke employed the dual contract of Althusius and Pufendorf as an argument for stable, popular rule. At the outset of his second treatise, he assumed only a single governmental contract. Towards the end of the book, however, he implied a prior, social contract, saying that one should "distinguish between the dissolution of the society and the dissolution of the government." His argument was that if either the executive or the legislative branch violated the trust placed in it, subjects could overthrow the government and still retain society. There was no danger of anarchy. Locke made the equally perceptive point that the threat of rebellion was usually enough to keep government honest. A man of common sense, he also stated convincingly that rebellions rarely occur, since it takes many grievances to turn people against their rulers.

By the end of the seventeenth century, Locke's natural rights philosophy and Pufendorf's natural law absolutism were beginning to pervade the intellectual climate of Europe. In the eighteenth century they were to enter its council chambers and throne rooms. In his stimulating book on the Enlightenment, Alfred Cobban gives more credit to Locke than to Pufendorf for undermining the theory and practice of royal absolutism. He contends that "the natural law school of thought . . . seemed to be moving toward a justification of absolute sovereignty," and that this intellectual tendency was in danger of making absolute monarchy the dominant form of government in practice as well as theory. Cobban's hero is Locke, who, he believes, saved early eighteenth-century Europe from this fate.[15]

Actually, there is no way to make either Locke or Pufendorf an apologist for a particular political movement after 1715. In England Locke wrote in justification of a revolt which never occurred; later his ideas were used to justify the successful revolution of 1688 and against any further broadening of existing individual rights. As early as 1691 his influence spread to the continent through a commentary in a Dutch periodical. There Lockean natural rights worked like acid to eat away the rationale of irresponsible absolutism. Eventually, his legacy was in the late eighteenth-century revolutions, which forcibly converted states into bastions of inalienable individual rights. Pufendorf had a somewhat calmer

15. A. Cobban, *In Search of Humanity* (1960), 161–162.

and more uniform reception. In some political circles, his ideas were employed to justify irresponsible absolutism. However, his greatest influence was in turning continental absolute monarchy into the so-called enlightened despotism, which attempted to reform from above in the name of subjects' natural rights and immutable natural law.

Whatever their political impact, Locke and Pufendorf found at least a tenuous solution to the question: Is government man-made and mere convention, or is it under an absolute set of standards? Both invoked a refurbished natural law to save Europe from the idea of relativism. However, the very science which inspired their conclusions undermined their confidence in new absolutes. Locke's own natural rights philosophy of politics jarred with his science, which held that all knowledge comes from experience, and that human action is merely based on what is useful, not on what is innately right. Fortunately for the sanity of European society, Locke's generation and those that followed shied away from the relativistic implications of science. They preferred to believe that man was rational, and that what he did was not only utilitarian but also moral. The Europe which had called on divine-right absolutism to counter the weakening of traditional bonds and beliefs, and then refashioned natural law to set standards for the emerging sovereign state, refused to believe that in putting science in the place of religion it had undermined all absolutes.

🙰 Continuity in Economic and Social Thought

One would think that the century which transformed political thought would be equally bold in its treatment of economic and social matters. Such was not the case. The ideas of natural law, utility and individual rights provided the powder for explosive economic and social doctrines, but the spark was lacking. The mercantilistic assumption that the state should regulate economic matters continued in theory as well as in practice.[16] The belief in a hierarchical society of fixed groups controlled the minds of intellectuals as well as the hearts of their less articulate contemporaries. It was probably too much to expect that a generation haunted by economic difficulties could suddenly embrace a laissez-faire economy, acting freely according to "nature." It was certainly inconceivable that the seventeenth-century European, who clung to social stability and political order, would discard the ideal of noble birth for one of commercial wealth and bourgeois individualism. More theoretical

16. On mercantilist thought, see Chapter 2, pp. 50–52, 62–64.

attention was given to the poor than to the possibility that economic and political power could be combined. However, the most advanced ideas on poverty and the poor came not from the new science and the new political thought, but from Christian idealism and mercantilistic realism.

The most striking social and economic criticisms came from the pens of Christian utopians. Many of these visionaries were influenced by both the new science and the common coin of mercantilism. But their ideas were most deeply rooted in the ascetic Christian ideal of a harmonious and simple society fostered by the Christian prince of utopian tradition. Their vision of the ideal society varied considerably from author to author. In mid-century England Gerald Winstanley believed that God was about to usher in a millenium of communal living on the land. In Italy, the priest-scientist Tommaso Campanella wrote of the *City of the Sun* where all individual selfishness was purged by a powerful state. Among the most famous utopian writers was the German Lutheran Johann Valentin Andreae. His *News of a Fraternity* and *Christianopolis* went into edition after edition, and in Dutch, English, French and Italian translations reached the corners of western Europe. Andreae combined a vision of universal education in science, literature and the arts with a program designed to root out the "evils" of his day. In his utopia, all were to live in Christian brotherhood without class distinctions. Material resources were to be supplied to the individual by an elected government. There was to be no absolute monarchy, idle aristocracy, competitive bourgeoisie or harsh legal system which debased instead of rehabilitating the criminal.

Christian utopianism had a diverse legacy. In Louis XIV's France it found a peculiar descendant in Archbishop Fénelon. The famous narrator of Télémache's imaginary travels vacillated between looking for a Louis who would eliminate war, reduce taxes and assist the poor, and dreaming of a never-never land where subjects abolished luxuries and enjoyed an idyllic, bucolic existence. Fénelon is best known, however, as the nobleman who wished to return to a mythical French past where kings were checked by a natural elite of nobles and by traditional political estates.

While Fénelon looked to the past, Veit Ludwig von Seckendorff attempted to grapple with the interplay of Christian ideals and the secular reality. The German Lutheran's ideas were generally Fénelonian. But despite his noble status he was far less aristocratic in his attitudes, and far more elaborate in the public measures he suggested to educate and elevate the poor. Spurred by his fervent religious beliefs, Von Seckendorff broke with many current assumptions about the role of government in economics. He took issue with rulers who put "reason of state" above the interests of their subjects, and public wealth over private welfare. The poor were to be assisted by a wide range of state projects, and these were to be accompanied by other reforms which were laissez-faire in effect if not in principle or intent. Governmental monopolies were to be abolished, the hide-bound guild structure dismantled and state tampering with currency disavowed. These ideas were later purged of their radical content and built into a German variety of mercantilism called cameralism. Von Seckendorff's mid-century treatise on Christian politics had an even greater impact on the academic world. In many German universities it became a standard textbook on politics until late in the eighteenth century. Some professors thought so highly of it that they made it the basis of their lectures.

In addition to this direct link between Christian utopianism and new economic ideas, there was an indirect connection through mid-century English mercantilism. This theme has been developed in a convincing article by Charles Wilson.[17] By the 1670's utopian idealism had been incorporated into the strongly mercantilistic writings of successful businessmen like Josiah Child. The mercantilistic fetish of the favorable balance of trade was maintained, but the achievement of such a balance was connected with social welfare. English "social mercantilists" wanted to raise the mass of unproductive Englishmen to a level at which they could contribute to manufacturing and consumption. It was argued that this policy was good economics, since it would improve English goods in quality, quantity and competitiveness. By 1702, one "social mercantilist" could write a book with the daring title *That the Full Employment of All Hands in the Nation is the Surest Way and Means to bring Bullion into the Kingdom*. Not all members of the political-social elite of England could accept the idea that public workhouses and high wages were either morally good or economically sound. Nevertheless it is revealing that the aggressive, social-climbing merchant Josiah Child could reconcile his lust for personal wealth and family titles with deep concern for the forgotten poor of his native land.

From England, "social mercantilism" spread to the continent, where it was combined with local varieties of Christian utopianism. By the early eighteenth century, economic statism in many German and Italian principalities was undergoing subtle changes, thanks to translations of English treatises and native commentaries on the subject. Earlier still, the German cameralist Joseph Becher was wavering between Christian idealism and the realities of mercantilism. His religious commitment urged him to reject the society of his day, while his visits to England exposed him to the social mercantilists' hope that contemporary society could be improved. In the end, Becher rejected the present for the dream of a utopian future.

17. C. Wilson, "The Other Face of Mercantilism," *Transactions of the Royal Historical Society*, vol. IX (1959), 81–101.

His *Wisdom of the Soul* (1680) envisaged a rural paradise devoid of conflict and private property. However, his more practical side found an outlet in several earlier treatises. His chief work, the *Political Discourses* (1668), stressed mercantilistic regulation of trade, industry, wages and prices as a means to raise the living standard of the masses. Becher died a frustrated and bitter man, but his brand of mercantilism was incorporated into German cameralism by his son-in-law, von Hörnigk.

Outside these circles of social mercantilists, orthodox mercantilism edged towards a natural, unregulated economy, without reaching it. The eighteenth-century idea that "self-love" and "social good" amounted to the same thing was not yet acceptable. When Bernard Mandeville published his doggerel poem, *The Grumbling Hive: or Knaves Turn'd Honest* (1705), he enunciated a laissez-faire idea which shocked his contemporaries. As he expanded on this theme in the *Fables of the Bees: or Private Vices, Public Benefits* (1714), the chorus of protests grew. Undoubtedly the Dutch-English physician made his viewpoint unpalatable by his view of human nature. Mandeville insisted that the hive of bees prospered on account of fraud, pride and luxurious tastes, and that when it was purged of such un-Christian conduct it was ruined. His examples of "good" vice were too distasteful for the reading public; he even suggested that ladies of easy virtue were good for society, since they saved fairer damsels from the clutches of predatory males. Only when Mandeville's vicious individuals were turned into hard-working, conventional persons could Europe believe that each man, acting from self-interest without state interference, contributed to economic prosperity. Locke's natural rights philosophy was an obvious source of a moralized laissez-faire doctrine. However, Locke himself was unable to make the transition from political to economic laissez-faire. He stripped government of major powers in the political realm, but clung to economic statism. Locke rejected state control of the price of money and interference with private property, but he retained an outmoded belief in governmental hoarding of bullion which many orthodox mercantilists had long since abandoned. It is revealing that not even Mandeville could free himself of the notion that the state should ensure a favorable balance of trade. Daniel Defoe, commonly considered a harbinger of eighteenth century free-trade doctrine, also opted for strong protectionism.

Surprisingly, it was a group of French thinkers living during the sunset of Louis XIV's reign who first developed a broad laissez-faire program. While their king was attempting to increase his government's control of economic affairs, a handful of intellectuals argued from the philosophical premises of the new science and political utilitarianism that the state should leave the economy alone. We can find these ideas most clearly in the works of Pierre le Pesant de Boisguilbert, who felt that a truly free economy would work to the benefit of everyone. If left alone, natural laws of supply and demand would check the selfish acts of the individual in favor of the general welfare. Boisguilbert still accepted the Christian view of the Fall of Adam and Original Sin. He was thus closer to Hobbes than to Locke in his view of human nature as depraved. But his Christian view of morality was combined with a secularized treatment of economics. Neither the Christian God nor the mercantilistic state could improve economic conditions. That was the task of "nature," which acted as a secularized version of "providence." Boisguilbert's theory is well illustrated by the following excerpt from his *Dissertation on the Nature of Wealth:*

> A police is required to enforce concord and the laws of justice among so great a number of men who seek only to destroy them, and to deceive and surprise each other from morning to night, seeking continually to establish their opulence upon the ruin of their neighbors. But it is nature alone which can keep this order and maintain the peace; all other authority spoils everything when it mixes in affairs, however well-intentioned it may be.

Seventeenth-century intellectuals were even more cautious in their treatment of social-political relations than they were in their discussion of the connection between politics and economics. Historians often write about that century's bourgeoisie as if they were ready to take over the reigns of power in western Europe by 1715. If we look at the literature of the late 1600's, a very different picture emerges. It is true that in works of fiction the "bourgeois" was beginning to compete with the courtier, hero, soldier and gentleman as the ideal type of man. But even in England, the man of business rarely found his way into major political treatises. Locke was probably too close to the great Whig aristocrats to turn his political system into an open apology for middle-class power. Of all the political writers of the seventeenth century, only two came openly to grips with the question of relating government to changing social conditions.

The most famous was James Harrington, an Englishman who was familiar with both English and Dutch society. His *Commonwealth of Oceana* (1656) provided a utopian land as the backdrop of a provocative and serious examination of the English situation. His argument was that the form of government was determined by socio-economic circumstances: the balance of political power must mirror the balance of property ("land, money or goods"). If a king were the greatest landowner, an absolute monarchy would result. Where the nobility held the lion's share of property, they would dominate a "mixed monarchy." A commonwealth would result if the "people" were blessed with a fairly even distribution of wealth.

Unfortunately, Harrington's scheme broke down when he applied it to contemporary England. His ideal commonwealth turned out to be a regime in which the ordinary people shared their political power with the lesser nobility or gentry. What apparently started out as an apology for middle-class rule, concluded as an aristocratic plea for political and social stability under the leadership of the lesser nobles. Harrington clearly thought of the gentry as economically oriented towards the non-nobles, but in social and political terms he considered them as part of the nobility, the "better sort" who alone knew how to govern a country. His placing of the gentry now with the nobility, now with the "people," obviously mirrored the confusion of his fellow Englishmen about social mobility. Harrington's stimulating treatise was an advance over Locke and Hobbes, who hesitated to look beyond the mass of undifferentiated individuals. And it was far in advance of Althusius' reference to traditional estates. But it was no more an apology for modern middle-class rule than were Locke's more famous treatises on government.

Pieter de la Court's *The Interest of Holland* (1662) was a less schematic work on Dutch politics. On the surface it was an interesting apology for republican government. The Dutchman contended that absolute monarchy harmed the economy, and that a republic consisting of "the generality of the people" alone could provide liberty and prosperity. As one reads into the body of the book, however, it becomes clear that de la Court was an apologist for the narrow aristocracy of wealth which held Dutch commerce and government tightly in its grasp. Not only did he exclude the "rude rabble" from his "popular" government, but he combined that qualification with an implicit support of a political commercial elite, protected against other middle-class interests. Consequently, his work was important only as a period piece, a political tract against the pretensions to absolutism of the Dutch Orangist dynasty.

Apart from Harrington and de la Court, the tendency of political theorists was to write about various forms of government, and then settle on some form of monarchy as the most suitable. Monarchy might be made the creature of the aristocracy, as it was by Fénelon, or the servant of general welfare, as in Pufendorf's and Seckendorff's writings. That was as far as intellectuals would go in their socio-political analysis. Even the word "republican," which could imply a government by the wealthy few or by the less fortunate many, was still anathema to a large segment of the European peoples. By the end of the century the term was starting to become respectable, but as late as 1694 the French Academy's dictionary equated it with sedition. Between 1700 and 1750 only two political utopias of those written by Frenchmen were republican in setting. It should be remembered, too, that "republican government" normally meant a government under law, not necessarily one without a king. In the literal sense, "republic" meant public matters or general welfare. If European intellectuals at the end of the seventeenth century were anxious to have their monarchs rule in the interests of their subjects, they were none too certain that they wanted the "public" to assume power, whether that public was an elite of wealth or birth. Certainly, none wanted the "people" in the broadest sense to usurp the place of the king. Even John Locke's political development reveals only a moderate shift in his ideas on political structure. In 1660 he preferred an absolute monarchy as the best guarantee of property. By the 1680's he was disillusioned with the Stuart dynasty and opted for a monarchy checked by a powerful Parliament and a still more powerful electorate of property owners. But it was still monarchy that he desired. It should not be forgotten that the man who is considered the most modern of seventeenth-century writers on politics prefaced his *Two Treatises of Government* with the hope that they would be "sufficient to establish the throne of our great restorer, our present King William."

16.

The Arts: Cultural Relativism

Anyone familiar with seventeenth-century culture cannot help being dazzled by its achievements in the arts. While the majority of Europeans went about their daily tasks, Biblical scholars, religious and secular historians, literary men, artists and musicians unfolded a brilliant picture of the world for the cultural elite. Of course the arts included much that was old. Many professors taught sacred and secular history without raising new questions. There were old morality plays and older romantic novels for those who wanted merely to be entertained. Many students of non-European culture and travelers in far-away places never bothered to ask themselves how the extra-European world differed from their native lands. Yet, the few who probed deeply make us forget the majority who were more concerned about professionalism than their professions.

The dominant characteristic of the vision of these concerned individuals was its sheer diversity. The world of nature and man was examined from every perspective. One suspects that often there was sheer delight in disorder. The most advanced practitioners of the arts were struck by what appeared to be the relativity of human standards. From one age to another in the past, from one corner of the contemporary world to another and within each individual, there were contradictions which could not be ignored. Neither the fixed laws of the new science nor traditional absolutes could account for the stark, almost chaotic contrasts of life. On canvas and in sound, in stone and on the printed page, cultured Europeans depicted a constant theme—cultural relativism. It was a theme which intensified the seventeenth century's quest for stability and certainty. But in the world of the arts it was much more difficult than in the arenas of politics, science, philosophy and political thought to find any ultimate answers. The fascination with the unique, the urge to examine and tear apart accepted universals, continued to captivate men in the arts as they probed more deeply into the world about them. Even when an individual or a discipline managed to reconcile the existing diversity with the ideal of unity, the cultural relativism that they had uncovered continued to haunt them. Men could obscure reality by a few clever brush strokes or the self-imposed censorship of words, but they could not entirely erase the picture that they had created for themselves and the cultural elite of their day.

The Battle of the Bible

The clearest sign of the times was the critical study of sacred history. If the Bible were no longer beyond scrutiny, nothing remained sacred to Europeans. Very few scholars undertook the task of examining the revealed word of God from a human viewpoint, and only a minority of the European population accepted their criticism. It is safe to say that most of those interested in Biblical scholarship did not intend to destroy anything; they were sincere, God-fearing Christians. Yet the result of their labors was a weakening of the belief in Biblical absolutes.

By far the most important work of Christian "historians" was an edifying and conservative one. The aim was to increase knowledge of the Christian past by making the Bible available to a wider public. Sixteenth-century Protestantism had led the way by Luther's translation of the Bible into German. In the seventeenth century, the famous King James Version was made available to Englishmen, and its unparalleled literary style soon made it one of the world's great classics. While Protestant Bibles in native languages poured off the presses in a number of countries, Catholicism also produced its own, popular translations of the old Latin Vulgate. The Jansenist French Bible was the most famous of these, overcoming initial opposition from the Pope and the king of France, who understandably feared the consequences of letting everyone read into the Bible his own brand of Christianity. But after Louis XIV prohibited Protestant worship, an edition of some 20,000 copies was printed so that Protestant converts to Catholicism could understand their new faith.

The direct consequences of popular Bible-reading are hard to gauge. Undoubtedly it made many a perfunctory Christian more aware of his responsibilities to God and his fellow man. Occasionally, biblicism degenerated into bibliolatry, particularly among some Calvinists and members of a few minor sects who accepted every word of the sacred text as divinely inspired. Among Old and New England Puritans, and even German Lutherans, there was a fad for giving children Biblical names, from Joshua to Mahr-shalal-hash-baz. More than a few persons acquired the habit of opening their Bibles at random to find guidance in times of crisis.

While the public read their popular Bibles, intellectuals were busy producing more scholarly editions, based on the original biblical languages. Their work was the culmination of two centuries of activity. The fifteenth-century Renaissance had been concerned with discovering the best texts of ancient works, both Christian and pagan. By the early sixteenth century, Catholic scholarship had produced two famous "polyglot" Bibles. Their name came from the fact that they were multilanguage editions, including the Greek and Hebrew versions as well as the accustomed Latin Vulgate of medieval Christianity. During the seventeenth century many polyglot Bibles appeared. Perhaps the most spectacular was a mid-century production of several English scholars. The handsome, six-folio work contained an Old Testament in nine languages, and an equally impressive New Testament. The book was also lavishly illustrated with maps, and contained appendices with chronological tables, essays on Biblical coins, weights and measures, discussions of Hebrew expressions and a short history of the major versions of the Biblical text. With this information, seventeenth-century scholars were well prepared to launch a systematic investigation of God's revealed word.

Anyone who had time to reflect on the scholars' Bibles could immediately see that this was no easy task. The sixteenth century had argued over the meaning of key words in Scripture. The seventeenth century discovered that the original recording of those words by biblical scribes posed even more serious problems. The revealed word of God had been handed from person to person before being preserved in manuscripts, and had obviously been embellished by the oral transmitters. By the time the scribes had recorded the story, they were uncertain of many of the facts, and the various accounts of an event frequently contradicted each other. Nor could the recorders resist the temptation to elaborate on the text, adding comments which referred to their own time rather than to the epoch they were discussing.

The intellectual pleasure of the erudite with these Biblical riddles soon turned to horror, as the role of God's all-too-human scribes loomed larger and larger. When the pantheist Spinoza and the materialist Hobbes tried their hand at Biblical detective work, the worst fears of Christian scholars were realized. For Spinoza and Hobbes made the Bible look so human in composition that God appeared to have had no role in inspiring it. Contemporaries must have been as angry with Hobbes' acceptance of the New Testament as with his attacks on Old Testament authorship. The English materialist accepted the Gospel stories of Jesus only because they seemed anti-priestly in tone. He argued that they must be authentic; if priestly scribes had tampered with the text, it would have been much more favorable to their point of view. Spinoza's *Political-Theological Treatise* was even more disturbing. He tried to quiet his critics by declaring that his book dealt "only with the meaning of the Bible, and not with its truth." However, he proceeded from a discussion of the purpose, dating, authorship and historical context of Old Testament books to a rational critique of its miracles. What was not invented by scribes could be explained naturally, he declared. A gale of wind could have parted the waters and allowed the crossing of the Dead Sea, for example. Spinoza concluded that the Jews were not God's chosen people, and that Christianity's triumph was due purely to historical causes.

Leibniz warned that men like Hobbes and Spinoza were digging a grave for Christianity with their subversive suggestions. Still, many Christian scholars could dismiss the work of the materialist Hobbes and the pantheist Spinoza as untrustworthy. This was not the case with Richard Simon's *Critical History of the Old Testament* (1679), written by a devout French Catholic and a member of the Oratorian order. Moreover Simon's aims were conservative and constructive, even if his means were destructive. He had no intention of using the yardstick of human reason to question the divine inspiration of the Bible. His objective was simply to employ philology and history in order to understand the meaning and context of God's revelation. Of course, some of the mystery in Scripture would vanish as a result. But Simon thought it better to understand what the Bible actually said than to rationalize obscure and contradictory passages with meaningless arguments. He would have nothing to do with the jargon of bibliolaters. He felt that they, not he, were the subverters of Christianity. While they made the dubious laugh by their uncritical acceptance of the Bible, he would remove the Scriptural inaccuracies, and give men confidence that what remained could be believed. Simon was convinced that his "critical history" could be reconciled with the view that the Bible was inspired. God's inspiration preserved His scribes from essential errors, but He obviously could not prevent His human servants from making some errors of detail. As Simon was fond of saying, "God's instruments were men, and they did not cease to be men for all that they were prophets."

Simon also employed his scholarship to undermine Protestant Christianity, but again his aim was a constructive one. By destroying the

Biblical foundations of Protestant confessions, he intended to force Protestants to return to the Catholic fold, thereby unifying and strengthening Christianity. His argument was an ingenious one. Protestantism had been born suddenly in the sixteenth century; lacking a long tradition, it relied solely on the Bible to justify its doctrines and organization. By showing that this Bible had undergone many alterations, the Oratorian could reveal how far Protestantism had strayed from God's initial revelation. Such an argument would not harm Catholicism, which had a continuous history since the time of Christ. Simon contended that Catholic "tradition" had maintained contact with the original sense of God's revealed word, although the successive versions of the Bible had wandered further and further from the true meaning of that message. In taking this stand, the French priest was on firm ground, since the sixteenth-century Council of Trent had proclaimed tradition and Scripture to be the twin foundations of Catholicism.

Simon's belief that Christian Europe could accept the abrupt transition from an infallible to a half-human Bible was not shared by his contemporaries. Catholic and Protestant critics joined in a chorus of protest. The controversy of the 1680's reminds us of the treatment which Galileo had received a half-century before.[1] The analogy cannot be pressed too far, however. The Italian scientist had flatly dismissed the Biblical text where it contradicted his scientific hypotheses. The French cleric was far from taking such an adamant position. He did not say that the Bible was wrong in any area of knowledge, rather that its message had to be examined carefully to be understood. Nevertheless, Simon put Christians in an awkward position. They knew that they could not halt criticism of the Bible by silencing one man. Moreover, many recognized the need to purge the sacred text of corrupt passages so that what remained could hold its own against all doubters. On the other hand, many also feared that the admission of any errors would open the floodgates to attacks on everything in the Bible. Their instinctive, conservative fears blotted out the voice of reason. Bishop Bossuet led the counterattack, consigning the first edition of the *Critical History of the Old Testament* to the flames. To ensure their victory, the conservatives had the book placed on the Catholic Index of forbidden literature, and banished the author from the religious order which he had faithfully served. Protestants were even more hostile.

Simon could not be silenced. Taking advantage of the book-burning, he republished his treatise in a more scholarly edition. As the years passed, Simon's pen brought forth many other "critical histories" including those

1. See Chapter 3, pp. 92–95.

dealing with the New Testament, the "versions of the Bible," and its "principal commentators." Bossuet soon realized that he could combat Simon only by arguing with him. Unfortunately for the conservative bishop, this could be done only by meeting his enemy on the latter's ground. Ultimately, Bossuet found himself virtually echoing Simon's position. He admitted that errors had crept into the Bible, but contended that these did not detract from its divine inspiration.

Bossuet's was probably the best of some forty Protestant and Catholic refutations written against the ex-Oratorian scholar. Many of them were far less skillful, and some made Biblical conservatism look absurd. When Simon and others suggested that the first books of the Bible had been composed by a number of writers, the statement was taken as a slur on Moses, who had previously been credited with that accomplishment. In their emotional defense of the Old Testament prophet, some scholars virtually deified him. One such defender proclaimed him the spiritual teacher of the entire world, inferring this status from Moses' acquaintance with the Egyptian god, Teuth, who was shown to be identical with the Mexican deity, Teutl. Other writers became overly literal in defending Biblical passages. A serious debate arose over the way in which God had created Adam and Eve. The story in Genesis simply said that God fashioned Eve from one of Adam's ribs. But did she come from the right or left side of the first man? A tract entitled *Curious Questions Concerning Genesis* claimed to have the definitive answer: The heart was the organ which caused men to love women, and since it was located on the left side, Eve must have been formed from one of Adam's left ribs.

Those whose literal belief in the Bible turned them against Simon's discussions of its "grammar" must have been still more disturbed when Pierre Bayle arrived on the scene. His *Historical and Critical Dictionary* of 1697 was a mine of information about pagan and Biblical antiquity as well as the more recent past. Bayle's biographical sketches encompassed Roman deities, Greek mythological heroes, Old Testament figures, great European philosophers and obscure religious thinkers. While the text was usually innocuous, the author's voluminous footnotes were devastating in their disclosures of the foibles of historical personages and the erroneous accounts of their historians. Nothing was sacred to the French Protestant scholar, who had been converted to Catholicism, relapsed into conventional Calvinism, broken with the orthodox Dutch Calvinists, and taken issue with rationalists like Spinoza. Neither Homer nor Jupiter escaped his scathing wit. However, Bayle's most biting criticisms were reserved for the stories about such Old Testament figures as Adam and Eve, Noah, Abraham and David.

The reader of the *Dictionary* was led to believe that the Old Testament was a tissue of textual errors and confusions. The article on David contained a long footnote that questioned the credibility of the second book of Samuel. Bayle noted wryly:

> If a narrative like this were found in Thucydides or [Livy], all the critics would unanimously conclude that the coypists had transposed the pages, forgotten something in one place, repeated something in another, or inserted additional passages into the author's work.

Bayle then disarmed the reader by averring: "But it is necessary to be careful not to have such suspicions when it is a question of the Bible." After making this qualification, he proceeded to do precisely what he had warned against. One question after another was raised about modern controversies over the Biblical text. Bayle was equally adept in discussing the stories of Adam and Eve in Genesis. Just when the reader thought he was ready to conclude, the indefatigable scholar launched an attack on modern disagreements over the Creation accounts. Most authorities agreed that Eve came from Adam's rib, Bayle stated. However they must be wrong, since a "noted" scholar had proved that Adam came from one of Eve's ribs.

Above all, Bayle suggested that the Old Testament heroes were frail and sinful creatures of God. His criticism of David's extracurricular activities left little to the imagination. In fact Bayle's David looks no different from the frankly immoral pagan god, Jupiter. On David he wrote, "It is commonly believed that his adultery with Bathsheba, the murder of Uriah, and the proscription of the people are the only faults with which he can be charged. But this is a great mistake; for there were many other things in his life that deserve criticism. . . ."

Bayle's purpose in unmasking the sacred past has been disputed ever since his first edition of the *Dictionary* appeared. He was too much of a Pyrrhonist [2] to accept any "inspired" document without examining its credibility. He saw too much of the irrational and absurd in life to adopt any explanation of human nature which glossed over its inconsistencies. His main point seems to have been that human beings are imperfect in their conduct, and that this fact should be admitted regardless of their inspiration. He saw no basic difference in the conduct of a Greek hero or an Old Testament king. Bayle sharply criticized the attempts of Christians to excuse David's sins. He concluded that an action is either moral or immoral, and one cannot change the standard to accommodate a person who "has a share of the inspiration of God."

The trouble with his position is that Bayle was trying to propound absolute and relative standards of morality at the same time. He admitted

2. See Chapter 3, p. 81.

that men did not live by any absolutes, while wanting to judge them absolutely. Furthermore, his attack on Biblical infallibility left him without any traditional account of what man's absolute standards should be. If the Bible were suspect on so many counts, could one accept the Ten Commandments as the truth? Bayle was trapped by his own skepticism, while Simon retained the general inspiration of the Bible and Pascal countered skepticism with his brilliant Christian interpretation of human nature.[3] Bayle tried to flee to blind faith in Christianity, but his previous doubts make one wonder what basis he had for his fideist position. After his attacks on the Bible, it is curious that he could adopt as moral absolutes whatever the Bible proclaimed as such. Nevertheless, this is what he did. He thought that Biblical actions not condemned by God were acceptable, while those which were censured by the God of the Old Testament must be condemned by man. As Bayle asserted, "If Scripture in reporting an action blames or commends it, one is no longer allowed to appeal from that judgment. Everyone ought to regulate his approval or disapproval on the model of Scripture. I have not acted contrary to this rule."

It will be no surprise to the reader that Bayle's *Dictionary* was banned in France. In the Dutch Netherlands, his article on David was rewritten under pressure from the exiled French Calvinist church to which he belonged. Ironically, the French condemnation of the first edition made Bayle's second edition all the more popular. Ironically, too, Calvinist control over the reedited "David" article led Bayle to reprint the original as a separate tract for souvenir-hunters. Anyone who has picked up one of the heavy volumes of the *Dictionary* can tell that it is no mean feat to read through the mass of erudite notes. But in the eighteenth century, hundreds of persons had an edition of the work in their personal libraries, and for those who were too lazy to read Bayle, there were scores of more popular books which turned his skeptical ideas into attractive arguments on behalf of "natural" morality.

Meanwhile, the questions which Bayle raised over Old Testament passages were followed by broader attacks on the Bible. Bayle refused to engage in attacks on the Gospel accounts of Jesus' mission, and seems to have deliberately avoided any reference to the endearing but sinful persons like Mary Magdalene who knew Christ. It would appear that his silence on the New Testament reflected a sincere belief in Christianity, just as his strictures on Old Testament figures indicated his condemnation of individual Christians who failed to follow the standards of Christ's church. But during the decades which followed his death in 1706, there

3. On Pascal, see Chapter 14, pp. 364–366.

were some Europeans who did not adhere to his distinction between Biblical absolutes and the relative conduct of Biblical and post-Biblical man. By the mid-eighteenth century, a few scholars in Germany and elsewhere were circulating unpublished works which suggested that Moses and Jesus were imposters. Bayle would probably have been the first to attack such anti-Christian dogmatism, just as he would have been perplexed by the ability of eighteenth-century rationalists to pervert his skepticism and fideism into arguments on behalf of a natural or man-made morality which owed nothing to God or Biblical tradition.

Church History, Christian Reunion and Religious Toleration

The interest of Christian scholars in the post-Biblical history of Christianity was even greater than their devotion to Biblical scholarship. Those who would not dream of second-guessing Biblical revelation were quite willing to examine the history of the church since New Testament times. Indeed, they could scarcely avoid the subject. Each faith had its own history, its own saints, its own books on the "true" religion. As confession argued with confession, it was inevitable that church history would be used as a weapon of defense and attack. Protestants showed how Catholicism had strayed from the "pure" Christianity of the first centuries A.D. Catholics countered to prove that medieval Christianity had had a continuous and consistent history, culminating in the sixteenth-century Council of Trent which upheld Catholic "tradition" against Protestant aberrations. Before the seventeenth century began, Lutheranism had already produced its famous *Magdeburg Centuries*, a history of Christianity prior to 1300, and Italian Catholics were working on the equally well-known *Ecclesiastical Annals*. Such undertakings helped to make the Christian past better known. Catholic historiography was especially careful to purge the record of many false legends. However, the by-product of historical analysis was skepticism. Protestants were particularly adept at making Popes look like murderers and tyrants. They shamelessly repeated spurious stories about a "Pope Joan" in the hope of casting doubt on the divine inspiration of the Catholic past. The volumes of a scholarly Catholic work on saints' lives, which began to appear in 1643, must have delighted Protestants and scandalized many Catholics. The editors of these *Acts of the Saints* were interested in recounting the saints' actions as models for seventeenth-century men. But in striking out of the text those miraculous occurrences which were obviously flights of fancy, they undermined belief in the saintly acts which remained. The work involved was staggering, and one wonders how twentieth century nation-states or modern political parties could survive such scrupulous debunking of their folk-heroes and "official" biographies.

By the end of the seventeenth century, partisan religious histories had reached a level of sophistication and erudition far superior to the works of the early Reformation. Nevertheless, the aim was still to show the differences between confessional histories, and to discredit rival church traditions. Bishop Bossuet wrote a *History of the Variations of the Protestant Churches* to dramatize the tendency of Protestantism to produce more and more sects in the absence of a common authority. Gilbert Burnet composed a history of the Anglican church, demonstrating that Protestantism had not varied on essentials. One French Calvinist contended that it was the Catholic church which had a history of variations. Another took the controversy to the logical conclusion that variation was the lifeblood of Christianity, and that it was better to question traditions than to accept them uncritically and mechanically.

As historians revealed more and more clearly the disunity within Christendom, there was bound to be a reaction. It became all too clear that Christ had meant his church to be a single body, and that the arguments among his flock were a disgrace to his very name. Thus there developed the strange phenomenon of scholars writing against rival churches and at the same time calling on all confessions to reunite. Tolerance was a bad word, but unity a good one. A rival theological tradition which strayed from "true" Christianity could not be tolerated, but there was also hope that schism could be banished along with heresy. This could be accomplished by bringing together the various branches of Christ's church in a union which would retain the essence of Christianity while purging it of confessional aberrations. French Catholics, Scottish and Dutch Calvinists, German Lutherans, Anglicans and members of the eastern Orthodox churches all expressed the hope described in the New Testament "that they may be one as we are one." The very Peace of Westphalia in 1648, which agreed to religious division in the Holy Roman Empire, proclaimed the goal of eventual reunion. That hope was not thought to be inconsistent with the intolerant principle that each German prince should determine the religion of his subjects. Intolerance, state control of religion and religious union were thus inextricably connected in a way which baffles the twentieth-century observer.

While diplomats were hammering out this bizarre settlement, religious leaders were trying to find the common elements which could actually reunite the churches. Unfortunately the early seventeenth century was still too close to the religious divisions of the previous century to find common ground. The Lutheran George Calixtus tried in vain to unite Lutheranism, Calvinism, Catholicism and Greek Orthodoxy. He hoped that the churches could accept the early Christian creeds as the core of Christianity. This proposal was unacceptable to Catholicism, which had developed many of its great theological, ecclesiastical and liturgical formulas in more recent times. Calixtus found some support among Lutherans and Calvinists in the German and Scandinavian states, but in the end his fellow Protestants accused him of heresy for holding Catholic views. In France, Cardinal Richelieu negotiated amicably with the Huguenots, but continued religious division, not reunion, was the result.

Perhaps the weirdest attempt at reunion was one designed to unite non-Catholics against Catholic military advances during the Thirty Years' War. The proponents of this scheme were sincere Christians. However, they were either unaware that an anti-Catholic union would increase the differences within Christianity, or were too narrow-minded to care. In any case, they failed to unite the participating groups. Included in the scheme were the heads of the Anglican, Greek and Russian Orthodox churches, as well as leading French Huguenots, some Dutch Calvinists and a sprinkling of Bohemian sectarians. Unfortunately these leaders were too divorced from their followers, and could not carry their flock into the common pasture. The Greek Orthodox Patriarch was actually forced into exile, and then strangled by irate followers for introducing Calvinist writings into his church.

The greatest efforts to reverse the sixteenth-century schism took place during the last decades of the seventeenth century. Men like Bossuet, Leibniz and Spinola hoped that at last the memories of recent religious wars would be blurred, and that the separate churches could merge their traditions in a single Christian history. The most spectacular attempt was undertaken by Christobal de Rojas y Spinola, a Spanish Franciscan who was willing to forgive and forget the heretical Protestant past. Spinola made no secret of his desire to woo heretics back to the traditional Catholic faith. Yet he was willing to make substantial alterations in his church's traditions so that Protestants would feel comfortable within its ranks. Negotiations progressed to the point of agreement on some key issues: Protestants would recognize the Pope, and Catholics would suspend the rule that clerics remain unmarried. Spinola also hoped to overcome the obstacle of the Council of Trent. He knew that the Tridentine reaffirmation of Catholic tradition against Protestant heresy could not be repudiated entirely. He suggested that the Protestants give their general approval to the sixteenth-century council's stand, and that the Pope convoke a council of the reunited churches to alter its most anti-Protestant decrees. By 1683, the hopes of Spinola seemed about to become reality. He had the active support or sympathy of an impressive group of people: the Pope, the Holy Roman Emperor, fourteen German princes, some Scandinavian Protestants, leading theologians of the Catholic and Protestant world and the heads of the Jesuit, Dominican, Franciscan and Augustinian orders.

The Council of Trent proved to be the one last hurdle that could not be cleared. The Pope hesitated to admit the need to alter any of its decrees, since to do so would be an admission that Catholic tradition was subject to alteration, and that the Catholic church lacked an infallible, continuous history. While the Pope wavered, the king of France snuffed out the flickering hopes of Christian reunion. Louis XIV put pressure on the Papacy to stand firmly behind Catholic tradition against Protestant heresy. The Sun King was unfortunately playing politics: He wished to make himself more Catholic than the Pope, and rally Catholic princes to his side in case of a European war. The French monarch succeeded only in stiffening the Pope's resistance to Spinola's ecumenical plan. Louis plunged into the War of the League of Augsburg without the hoped-for support of Catholic German princes, and Christian Europe continued to remain divided—theologically, historically and militarily. The greatest opportunity for reunion since Trent had been lost. When Christianity resumed its quest for unity in the twentieth century, it was as a small minority in an alien, secular world which had long since rejected Christian insights into human nature.

Spinola's failure did not immediately still the demands for unity. Two men refused to give up hope—Bossuet and Leibniz. One cannot imagine two less suitable partners for the proposed religious marriage. Bossuet was conciliatory towards Protestants, but adamant against Protestantism. Leibniz was as brilliant in his religious schemes as in his writings in science and philosophy, but he had no real understanding of Christianity. Bossuet wanted to treat Protestants as well-intentioned, lost souls who needed only to accept Catholic tradition to inherit the Kingdom of Heaven. Leibniz admired from afar the Catholic orders, the music, vestments and statues of Bossuet's church, but he was at heart a rationalist. When the French bishop started on the long road to Christian unity in 1671, there was hope. Bossuet's *Exposition of the Catholic Doctrine* went so far towards reconciliation with Protestantism that only the Catholic view of the Mass seemed to divide the confessions. But Louis XIV broke down one bridge by abolishing Huguenot worship in 1685, to the applause of Bossuet! In 1691, the bishop began a long correspondence with Leibniz. As they wrote, the divisions became more and more apparent. Bossuet based his stand on the Council of Trent. Leibniz replied by showing that the history of Catholicism included reversals of conciliar de-

cisions. Indeed, the French monarchy to which Bossuet adhered so un-
swervingly had rejected some Tridentine decrees. As Leibniz continued
to explore the Catholic past, he discovered that books which had been
considered apocryphal by the early medieval church were later accepted
as integral parts of the Catholic Bible. Thus, the Catholic church had
changed, Leibniz declared triumphantly. Catholicism could surely modify
its recent traditions for the sake of Christian unity.

The German philosopher's conclusion applied the *coup de grâce*
to the traditional absolute of Christian history. He made Bossuet's conservatism look like a relic of the past. Twisting the Frenchman's words
around, he sarcastically remarked: "Yesterday we believed such and such
a thing, so we must go on believing it." But Leibniz was better at tearing
down than rebuilding. He believed in brotherhood but he really wanted
to reduce formal Christianity to a few rational principles and let the individual Christian accept or discard the rest. Without realizing it, Leibniz
was saying that it was necessary to destroy Christianity in order to save
it. His correspondence with Bossuet came to a natural close in 1702. There
remained only one solution—toleration.

But toleration was still an unacceptable solution for most Christians
in 1702. Intolerance remained the lingering ideal, long after it became
obvious that if Christians were to live together, they would have to accept
their differences. Tolerance is easier to preach than to practice, whether
it concern the life-and-death matter of salvation, "peaceful coexistence"
between rival global systems, or color-blindness in societies permeated
with racial distinctions. The very word can mean several things. To "tolerate" in a condescending, patronizing manner is not synonymous with
accepting as equals those who differ. Both attitudes are equally removed
from the toleration which stems from sheer indifference.

Seventeenth-century Christianity struggled with all three types of
tolerance. The greatest danger lay in the temptation to flee from the
bondage of intolerance to the blindness of indifference. It was obviously
very difficult to find any common bonds between the existing confessions. There was such diversity in doctrine, organization and ritual that
virtually everything which was essential to Christianity had to be stripped
away before a common ground could be reached. What remained looked
very similar to a secular "natural religion." In fact, those who advocated
such a procedure were accused of Socinianism, a sixteenth-century heresy
which reduced Christianity to a few moral truths found in the Bible and
confirmed by human "reason." Just how many real Socinians there were
in the seventeenth century depended on how narrowly or broadly contemporaries defined that term. Certainly Hugo Grotius' book *On the
Truths of the Christian Religion* leaned towards Socinianism. What the

Dutch Arminian left for the reader to infer was spelled out by an editor when his Latin treatise was translated into English:

> The main object of this work is to place in a clear light the truth of the Gospel, totally unconnected with the bias of any party or sect whatsoever; and that *solely with a view to general virtue, evangelical virtue, in the minds of men.*[4]

Grotius' viewpoint was close to the position held by the Cambridge Platonists. That cluster of intellectuals at Cambridge University tried to avoid the dogmatism of strict Calvinism without falling into the relativism of Hobbes' materialist philosophy.[5] In so doing, they arrived at a mystical version of ancient Platonism which posited moral absolutes known through human reason and divine illumination. Human reason is imperfect, they said, but the individual who practices Christian virtues sharpens his insight into divine matters and "brings such a divine light into the soul, as is more clear and convincing than any demonstration." The Cambridge Platonist, Ralph Cudworth, could declare that it was not his intention "to contend for this or that opinion; but only to persuade men to the Life of Christ as the Pith and Kernel of all Religion." Unfortunately, this position was really begging two questions: How did one arrive at the essentials of the "life of Christ," and was the product really Christianity? Another member of the group, Henry More, said "I am above all sects whatsoever as sects; for I am a true and free Christian." Under the influence of Cudworth and More, Cambridge Platonism seemed to reduce itself to individual mysticism, universal morality and religious anarchy.

The continental Pietists were one group which managed to avoid the watered-down rational Christianity of Grotius and the fuzzy moral precepts of the Cambridge Platonists. While Pietism had a tendency to break away from the existing confessions, many of its adherents managed to retain their membership in Lutheran or Calvinist churches and work for Christian brotherhood from within. Pietists could at times drift into fantasy, anti-intellectualism and maudlin writings about "sighing turtle doves"; but they were also noted for their Bible reading, their university courses on Scripture and their acquaintance with ancient languages. Some fled from the world, while others acted against poverty and illiteracy. Their focus was on leading a pious, upright and useful life. While they played down the churches' emphasis on creeds, they borrowed heavily from any source of mystical piety, Protestant or Catholic. They respected

---

4. Italics have been added for emphasis.
5. On Hobbes' philosophy, see Chapter 14, pp. 354–356.

all religious experiences, provided the individual was sincere. The influence of Pietism on late seventeenth and early eighteenth century Europe was enormous, radiating from the Prussian University of Halle. However, it could not stop the arid argumentation between and within Lutheran and Calvinist circles. The Saxon university of Wittenberg discovered over two hundred and fifty errors in the pronouncements of the great Lutheran Pietist, Philipp Jacob Spener. And the distinguished Lutheran writer of emotional hymns, Paul Gerhard, declared that Calvinists were not Christians.

Where seekers of Christian toleration were not bedevilled by heresy-hunters or the lure of Socinianism, they were frequently thwarted by political considerations. At the end of the century few rulers who reigned over religiously divided subjects cared to impose uniformity for the sake of salvation. But many waved the flag of intolerance in the name of political order. They wished to maintain a state church under their control, and to suppress all other churches on the grounds that they caused religious strife and political unrest. Politically minded members of state churches agreed. Their outlook resembles the modern-day disavowal of prejudice: I have nothing against "them," but. . . . Even John Locke, who pulled together the arguments of earlier English tolerationists, stopped short of advocating complete religious freedom. His *Letter Concerning Toleration* (1689) must have been widely read, since it was quickly translated from Latin into English, French and Dutch. His readers could agree with his refusal to tolerate Catholics, who owed allegiance to a foreign prince (the Pope). And few could quarrel with his intolerance of atheists. They argued that atheists were not bound by oaths to God and hence could not be trusted to obey any laws.

Very different was the sweeping condemnation of all intolerance by Pierre Bayle. A skeptic concerning finite man's ability to know religious truth, Bayle contended that everyone should be allowed to practice his own faith. He went so far as to say that God Himself, who alone knew the full truth, would not punish a heretic or an infidel except "for evil acts that he has committed knowing well that they were evil." Yet Bayle's justification of tolerance stopped short of rejecting Christianity. Indeed, he firmly believed that Christianity and tolerance were compatible, provided Christians lived their faith.

Bayle's eighteenth-century disciples profoundly changed their intellectual master's position. They accepted his belief in tolerance, but were so conscious of lingering Christian narrow-mindedness and "fanaticism" that they equated religion with intolerance and rejected both. They had reason to be critical of the performance by Christian rulers. While some Europeans learned to tolerate or drifted towards religious indifference, most states became more intolerant than ever. During the 1660's, 1670's and 1680's rulers like William III of England and Frederick William of Brandenburg-Prussia tried their best to introduce toleration in the churches of their lands. But by 1715 the trend was towards persecution and intolerance by rulers. Denmark kept Catholic priests out of the country with the threat of capital punishment. Sweden strengthened its anti-Catholic laws. Prussia persecuted and exiled Jesuits. And France continued to harass the Huguenots. Only states like England and the Dutch Netherlands, which had so many sects that none could dominate, came close to realizing Pierre Bayle's ideal. Thus historical divisions and intolerance undermined the old order from within while skepticism and relativism gained more and more converts among Europe's political, social and intellectual elite.

✑ The Secular Past and the Extra-European Present

The scholars who examined Europe's religious past could hardly avoid taking a close look at its secular foundations. Indeed, religious and secular history were closely connected. The Bible was a major source of Europe's intellectual origins, and the very basis of the secular scheme of world history. Most European histories began with Adam and divided the past into distinct epochs. Natural man had existed for two thousand years, from Adam to Moses. Then followed two thousand years under the written Mosaic law or Decalogue. The period of the law was followed by the age of Christianity, beginning with Jesus or the Roman Empire's adoption of Christianity. That epoch was to last for an additional two millenia. Finally, there would be the future millenium ushered in by Christ's Second Coming, culminating in the End of the World. The history of the Greeks and Romans was neatly fitted into the first epochs of this scheme, while the histories of the Egyptian, Moslem and Chinese civilizations were either passed over quickly or ignored.

It was an imposing historical edifice, and one which was bound to flatter European pride. Moreover, the scheme made sense to a Christian world which held to a providential theory of history. The story of man was a continuous drama of the interplay of human sin and divine judgment. History was dynamic in the sense that God used men and nations to prepare the world for the final day of judgment when His ultimate purpose would be revealed. For the most part, however, history was static: God kept giving men the same moral lessons and the same signs, but men continued to relapse into sin. The Graeco-Roman notion of history as cyclical was easily accommodated to the Christian view of life's fluctuations. Even the pagan notion of a primitive Golden Age was acceptable, for it conformed with the Biblical story of the Garden of Eden and man's subsequent fall from grace. The great Greek and Roman historians were also used as models, since they frequently looked at life from an exalted moral perspective. If history were a series of moral lessons, Graeco-Roman antiquity was crammed with secular illustrations.

One of the first sections of this great historical scheme to break down was the history of the ancient Greeks and Romans. While most seventeenth-century scholars used Livy, Tacitus and Sallust as models for their own moralizing histories, a few doubting Thomases took a second look at these models. Dutch and English professors refused to accept the stories about Rome's beginnings which every schoolboy knew by heart. How, they asked, could one take seriously the account of a Vestal Virgin's amorous relations with the god Mars, which resulted in the birth of the twins, Romulus and Remus, their suckling by a wolf and eventually the elevation of Romulus as Rome's first king? Men of previous generations had had their doubts about this and other tales of ancient Greece and Rome, but they had usually kept their thoughts to themselves. Now that historical skepticism was openly embraced, one doubt was piled on top of another. A Frenchman declared confidently: "There is so much that is real to admire in the Roman people, that we do them a disservice in flattering them with fairy-tales." But what could be retained of the past that was admirable, or if admirable, true?

Ancient history, the stories of the origins of European peoples, and recent history all failed to pass muster, one after the other. The same tools used to dismantle the books of Scripture served to take apart secular histories. Several scholars, the most famous being the Catholic Benedictine Jean Mabillon, showed how to identify a forged document. A few archaeologists dug up concrete remnants of the past to set against questionable written accounts or to fill in the gaps between bits of information. Many more began to dissect records from the inside: In addition to asking whether a document was a fraud, they wanted to know to what extent an authentic one was true. Who was the eyewitness, what were his biases, what did he actually see? This was just the beginning of the movement towards historical objectivity which reached its peak in the nineteenth century, but it was enough to cast a cloud on the secular past.

The problem of chronology was one of the most baffling and dangerous to explore. It was difficult enough to fathom the confusion of dates in Greek and medieval European history. The task became staggering when Egyptian, Chinese and Indian records were brought into the picture. One fact was clear. The non-Biblical chronologies revealed that the world was very old when the Old Testament story began. Adam had missed the Creation by several centuries. The flood was nothing more than local history, and its dating obscure.

Many scholars sprang to the defense of Biblical chronology. Joseph Scaliger, the greatest student of dating which the age produced, forgot his scholarship when he tried to determine the world's birthday. His monumental *Restoration of Chronology* (1583) set the beginning as April 23, 3949 B.C., much too close to Luther's 4000 B.C. to square with pagan records. One ingenious scholar after another tried to reconcile the non-Biblical sequence with that of Genesis, producing some two hundred different dates for the Creation by the early eighteenth century. An Englishman explained away the extra Egyptian dynasties by suggesting that they had flourished side by side, rather than one after another. Most literate Europeans finally settled for 4004 B.C. as the starting point, although many wanted to add some fifteen hundred years to accommodate the Egyptians, and geological discoveries were awkwardly hinting at an earthly history which made even the Egyptians late comers.

The tensions between deeply ingrained views of history and the emerging skepticism about the past produced a curious effect. Most men clung so tenaciously to the view of history as a moral story of man's sins and God's judgment that they were unable to grasp any other way of looking at it. When historical skepticism was used as a battering ram to break down the walls of this entrenched belief, the old house collapsed into a heap of ruins that was useless for the task of reconstruction. This negative result can be seen in the work of two great historians of the late seventeenth century, Bishop Bossuet and Pierre Bayle.

Bossuet was the last great writer of traditional world history. His monumental *Discourse on Universal History* (1681) was patterned after the long-accepted Christian periodization. As Bossuet wove his way through the fabric of universal history, he stressed the interaction of God and man, showing how God was using history to teach men moral lessons and to advance His ultimate purpose. However, when the French bishop descended into the mire of facts, he became less certain of the accepted periodization and the role of divine providence. His neat six-thousand-year scheme was thrown out of balance in his third edition, in which he admitted that several centuries had to be added to answer the new chronological findings. The role of God was supplemented by heavy reliance on human causation. As Bossuet admitted, "The true science of history is to note in each age the secret dispositions which prepared for the great changes, and the important conjunctures which made them come to pass." He also acknowledged that the very facts of history were uncertain, and the course of human events often inexplicable. In seeking to shore up the factual foundations of his historical scheme, Bossuet unwittingly embraced a circular argument: the truth of historical fact is based on the Bible's authority, which is certified by the church; but the claim of

Catholicism to be the receptacle of truth is grounded in its traditions, which are based on the very facts with which the argument began!

With Bayle, we are faced with a man who was perfectly willing to start with the facts and never leave them. This meant not that he was a pedant, but that for him historical studies should be factually based. He felt that the person who builds systems without regard for evidence or who accepts reputed facts on faith or authority strays inevitably from the truth. The trouble with this position, as Bayle recognized, is that it makes all system-building impossible. In the first place, there is so much uncertainty about any historical "fact" that the very foundation of history is sand. Secondly, even when one does come to some tentative conclusion as to what happened, it becomes evident that history is merely a collection of events which cannot be forced into any pattern. To go beyond the particular to generalizations is to distort the very diversity of human activity. Bayle made the point forcefully when he declared that "Properly speaking, history is nothing but the crimes and misfortunes of the human race." In short, history made no sense to Bayle.

The modern historian would object that to be useful history must make sense, and that generalizations are legitimate even if they distort and disregard the exceptions to the general rule. But Bayle meant to show that human records reveal no rational pattern, and that this negative knowledge *is* useful. He showed human beings as they were in the flesh, and taught men to be tolerant of their frail fellows and to have faith in a Christian God who made sense in spite of human nonsense. Ultimately, Bayle's historical relativism became one of the building blocks of modern historical studies, just because he insisted on starting with the facts. As Ernst Cassirer notes, Bayle carried out the "Copernican revolution" in historical science, accomplishing for history what Galileo did for science: He demanded independence of authority and adherence to the facts.[6] Nevertheless, in the immediate sense, Bayle was destructive of authority, of the system-builders and of the foundations on which any scheme of history could be built.

Some scholars did attempt to make sense of the confused past. The Venetian, Paolo Sarpi, wrote a brilliant *History of the Council of Trent* which avoided references to supernatural causes and divine guidance. Unfortunately, Sarpi was so interested in attacking papal policies that his work seldom rose above petty considerations. The Tridentine story in Sarpi's version looked very much like a secular history of human crimes and errors. The legal historians were less searching in their treatment of historical causation, but they had the merit of establishing the facts and

6. E. Cassirer, *The Philosophy of the Enlightenment* (1951), 207.

setting them down in chronological order. Their dry-as-dust documents made it virtually impossible for them to see the hand of God in history, while their careful examination of human institutions forced them to realize that history was far from static. It was clear that human beings altered their laws and customs from century to century. In the early eighteenth century, the Italian legist Giambattista Vico even managed to fit historical change into a general scheme. However, his view that human society progressed through three distinct stages as the collective mentality or group mind of man changed was too bold for his contemporaries to accept.

More acceptable to Europeans was the secularization of the religious, millenial theory. Fifteenth-century Renaissance humanists had seen their age as a return to the glories of ancient Greece and Rome. The Reformation had its own version of the Renaissance "rebirth." By the early seventeenth century the Dutch Calvinist Voet was able to divide history into three periods: the age of the primitive church, the "intermediate" period of Catholicism, and the "new age" of Protestantism, which restored the church to its primitive purity. Before the end of the seventeenth century, the German scholar Christian Cellarius combined the Renaissance and Reformation schemes in the pattern which has become popular since that day. Cellarius divided history into the categories of Antiquity, Middle Ages and Modern Times.

Superficially, the work of Sarpi, Vico and Cellarius appears to have revolutionized historical conceptions. Actually, they did little more than camouflage Bayle's view of history as the story of changing customs. Before that idea could be put to constructive use, there had to be some rational theory of the cause and pattern of historical change. Cellarius' scheme of three periods at best implied that history was cyclical. At its worst, it strengthened the relativistic notion that human institutions are constantly changing, and that there are no absolutes in history. The idea that history is a dynamic process could and did lead eventually to the idea that historical change is progressive. But that comforting myth was one which was left for later ages to invent.

Although we can see the germ of the modern progressive theory of history in Newtonian science and Lockean philosophy, the new science could not easily be adapted by the historians. The theory of progress which was implicit in Descartes and Bacon, and which came into the open during the Quarrel of the Ancients and Moderns was actually a non-historical hypothesis.[7] The scientists assumed that man's knowledge of the physical world would improve his physical and mental nature. It was quite

7. On the Quarrel, see Chapter 13, pp. 339–341. On Locke's theory of knowledge, see Chapter 14, pp. 357–359.

another matter to show how such progress could help men solve the problems of society. And while Locke assumed that men can rationally analyze their human environment, it does not necessarily follow that they can actually solve the problems which their society inherits from the past. To make the leap from scientific to historical progress, Europeans had to overlook the fact that the two realms are quite distinct.

To compound the problem, seventeenth-century scientists and historians actually criticized each other's methods, aims and conclusions. Descartes disliked history because it was grounded in uncertainty. He pitied the historians who could not agree on the facts, and who had to make sense of records made by writers who were inaccurate in their observations. Descartes fled from history to science because he felt the scientist had verifiable facts in the form of the primary qualities [8] in physical objects. He knew that the certain language of mathematics permitted scientists to describe the fixed laws governing those objects. Descartes' Christian interpreter, Malebranche, went further. He pointed out that Adam had perfect knowledge without knowing any history. Therefore history was useless. Bayle's position was the very opposite. He accused scientists of being too confident that primary qualities could reveal any truths. His article on Pyrrhonism in the *Dictionary* declared that God could deceive man's senses by primary qualities, just as He did in the case of the secondary qualities of color and taste. Moreover, Bayle was confident that the historian's documents gave man the only true picture of life. The facts might be uncertain, but the confused picture of human crimes and errors was more useful than the hypothetical laws of the physical universe. Bayle was not one to dismiss science completely. In fact he used scientific laws to demolish belief in supernatural occurrences.[9] What he refused to accept was the idea that science described reality.

The hostility between science and history was even more basic than Bayle and Descartes believed. For science posited a static world, governed by fixed laws, while history dealt with changing, particular circumstances. Montesquieu began to bring the two disciplines together with his historical laws, which showed how certain combinations of natural and human conditions led to the rise and fall of certain kinds of governments. But that thesis was closer to an unhistorical concept of "ideal types," than to an historical awareness of the unique development of a particular government. In any case, Montesquieu wrote and lived in the eighteenth century, arriving too late to save the late seventeenth century from its historical skepticism and relativism. History was coming into fashion as a weapon to

8. On primary qualities, see Chapter 13, pp. 335–336.
9. See Chapter 14, p. 362.

criticize the follies of man, his past mistakes and his imperfect present. The eighteenth century itself was to retain much of this negative use of history, although it would add the scientist's hope that future man would overcome the errors of the past.

Doubt and confusion about the European past were complemented by a wave of criticism which reached Europe from across the seas. The broadening of Europe's perspective had begun quite innocently in the fifteenth century, when the so-called Age of Discovery sent Europeans out to explore, convert and exploit the extra-European world. It was a self-contained and relatively complacent Europe which went about the task of Europeanizing the world. By the time the seventeenth century opened, the Spaniards and Portuguese had combined their American and far eastern holdings into a single, impressive empire under Spain's Philip II. The Dutch, English and French followed. They cut into the Iberian powers' trade and established their New Englands and New Frances in North America as proud extensions of European civilization. It was during the seventeenth century that the French founded St. Louis and Québec City, the English, Madras, and the Dutch, Batavia (Jakarta). Where they did not settle, Europeans exploited: the Dutch through their trading posts in the Spice Islands, and one power after another by their conversion of primitive and advanced peoples alike into future Afro-American slaves. Explorations took Europeans to the Arctic and to the fringes of Antarctica. Wandering Russians made contact with the Chinese peoples and gazed at the Pacific Ocean. Western Europeans reached Australasia and the Blue Nile. These were incredible achievements for a small continent just beginning to master the sciences of navigation and ship-building.

Yet that was only one half of the story. Complacent, expansionist Europe "discovered" the extra-European, non-Christian world, only to find that the French, English, Dutch, Spanish, Italian and German peoples had much to learn from their would-be victims. The impact of non-European peoples on the thought and culture of Europe, not the increase of European wealth and real estate, rounds out the contours of seventeenth century European history. The tea, tobacco, "china," cottons, calicos, ginghams, furs, fish, gold, silver and spices of east and west did make some of the luckier Europeans wealthy and more comfortable. But it was an elite market which the non-European products served, and the elite were often simply aping the externals of foreign cultures. The eighteenth century western economy was buoyed by world trade; but in the 1600's, that trade had a greater affect on Europeans' minds than on their pocketbooks.[10] The craze over China was most noticeable. Chinese pot-

10. For the generally bleak picture of Europe's economy, see Chapter 1.

tery, furniture, art, architecture and gardens were imported or copied. The truth was that Europeans could not colonize the well-populated and highly civilized east, and that the priests, traders and travelers who sent reports homeward were overwhelmed by its charms. Even in the Americas, where a tiny Indian population was conquered or pushed into the hinterland, Europeans tended to "go native." The French "forest wanderers," who went out in search of furs, often found themselves adopting native dress, customs and women. The primitive man lost something in translation to European languages, for the travel books soon dubbed him a Noble Savage.

Undoubtedly many factors beyond sheer lack of numbers on the European side and the quaintness of foreign customs are needed to explain the tremendous fad for non-European culture which increased with every generation during the seventeenth century. For the Europeans were not conditioned to accept non-European ways. Certainly the traditional isolation, ignorance and ingrained prejudice of Europe made the new impact a startling one. It may be that Europeans had been held back by circumstances. Previous contact had been mainly with bitter foes who aroused more fear than curiosity. Europe had known the Moslems for centuries, but the military threat and religious rivalry had made Europeans look on them as treacherous infidels rather than as civilized followers of a sophisticated culture and faith. In the seventeenth century, broad-minded individuals like Leibniz still thought it moral to wage a killing crusade against the Terrible Turk. But peoples like the American Indians and the Chinese presented no such problems. Both groups could kill or persecute travelers and colonists, but their military prowess certainly posed no direct threat to Europe, and their deities were not on the level of the Christian God. Then, too, seventeenth-century Europe was literally inundated with knowledge of other societies. A few centuries earlier, China had been known to men like Marco Polo, only to slip out of sight. Now, there was a wealth of information which was simply too massive to be ignored. In addition to travel literature, there were translations of the great works of the Chinese and other civilizations. Confucius was introduced in a Latin translation in 1687, and the *Arabian Nights* reached the French reading public by 1704. It should also be noted that seventeenth-century Europe was in search of new absolutes to replace the old disintegrating ones. As political theorists looked for a secular natural law, travel accounts discovered a model of the natural man in the American natives who were still living in a "state of nature."

Thus Europe saw non-European peoples first as peculiar, then as simply different and in the end they were tempted to consider them superior. There were certainly many tales of cannibalism, sexual indecencies, oriental trickery and primitive knavery. Although these never disappeared, Europe came to prefer the more flattering aspects of other societies. While the English scientist Robert Boyle refused to tolerate Confucianism or Mohammedanism, he boldly declared that the Chinese and East Indians were "the most civilized nations of the world," comparable to the Greeks and Romans of antiquity. Simon Ockley was less reserved. That professor of Arabic at Cambridge University declared that the west had "not added a single iota to the accumulated wisdom of the east," either in its veneration of God or its morality. One French nobleman said that "every nation has its own peculiar type of wisdom," and that Mohammed must take his place at the side of Christ. Another French noble was joined by scores of writers throughout Europe in pronouncing the "natural" Huron Indian better than the civilized Europeans because he was uncorrupted by their religion, law, society, and clothes.

Perhaps the most important result of the foreign craze was that it toppled European customs and ideas from their pedestal. Particularly alarming was the realization that the Chinese people had achieved a great culture, sophisticated philosophy, stable government and superior morality without the benefit of Graeco-Roman antiquity, the Christian religion or divine-right monarchy. Europe could hardly escape recognizing the fact that its traditions were not innately superior. Bayle kept driving home the point that Christians, who ought to be better than others, were in practice superior only in cruelty, bloodshed and intolerance.

The notion that there were universal beliefs held by all peoples also received rough treatment. This was disturbing not only to traditional Christianity, but also to the scientific assumption of universal laws in "nature." Once again, Bayle led the way, pointing out that some inhabitants of Africa and America did not believe in God. It was becoming difficult to tell what was moral, since what was condemned in some societies was permitted in others. As the French writer of brilliant social satire La Bruyère noted, "Some [Europeans] complete their demoralization by extensive travel, and lose whatever shreds of religion remained to them. Every day they see a new religion, new customs, new rites." Even John Locke, whose *Essay Concerning Human Understanding* attempted to find common rational principles, was infected by cultural relativism.

The very attempt of some Europeans to find common denominators in all societies only made matters worse. The efforts of Jesuit missionaries in China to find common ground with their hosts aroused a storm of controversy back in Catholic Europe. The Jesuits calmly pointed out that the Chinese were moral people who believed in a single deity.

They concluded that it would be logical to welcome them into the church, provided their pagan customs were not brought with them. Unfortunately, this noble enterprise had two flaws. In the first place, it was not easy to determine what was pagan and unacceptable, and what was merely "secular" custom and therefore worthy of adoption. The Jesuits were accused of paganizing Christianity so much that it was no longer Christian in content. In the second place, the effort to find a common denominator so reduced religion that there was no religious element left. Ironically, the Jesuits were probably more Christian in their reconciliation of the Chinese ways to Christianity than were their fellow-Catholic opponents.

The papal condemnation of the Jesuit view of "Chinese rites" in 1704 was understandable, but it only envenomed Sino-European relations. It certainly did not resolve the issue of relativism versus universals. The missionaries who had advised the Chinese convert to "cut out error from his mind, but not cut off his pigtail," were confused by the church's decision. St. Paul himself had managed to retain Christian absolutes, while allowing the Greeks to depart from Jewish customs. And while the church tried to maintain absolutes by ignoring differences, Europe continued to be enthralled by the pagan Chinese. The very controversy over the "Chinese rites" did more to undermine traditional absolutes than the Jesuit acceptance of "secular" Chinese customs. In France alone, some two hundred books argued the merits of accepting Chinese ways.

As the seventeenth century closed, Europe was torn between belief in its superiority and the nagging doubt that cultural relativism might be the lot of man. Knowledge of extra-European cultures could serve several masters. The eighteenth century was to turn cultural relativism into a plea for tolerance and raise the hope that behind the differences in human societies lay the common ingredient of "natural," "rational" man. But the eighteenth century also inherited the use of cultural relativism to undermine existing institutions, customs and beliefs. Already in the late seventeenth century, Locke was using the example of Peruvian society to attack the argument that monarchs were benevolent towards their subjects. European monarchs might say that they acted like fathers, but Locke had discovered Peruvian fathers "who begot children on purpose to fatten and eat them." In the face of Locke's relativism, it was difficult to believe in the universal idea of benevolent, patriarchal monarchy. Behind the eighteenth-century myth of the Noble Savage lurked the possibility that cultural relativism could destroy the eighteenth century's secular absolutes of nature and reason, just as it had undermined the old religious absolutes of the seventeenth century.

❦ Art, Music and Literature

The art of any age is complex in its origins and diverse in its achievements. No century proves this generalization better than the seventeenth. The inspiration for its architecture, sculpture, painting, music and fiction came from a bewildering variety of sources. Rome urged Catholics to recapture the grandeur of their faith on canvas and marble. Louis XIV and a host of other princes demanded that palaces, gardens and public squares be planned to glorify their reigns. From antiquity, classical ideals of order, harmony and beauty beckoned the artist and the writer to imitation. The new science offered musicians, painters and architects yet another model for their art in the rationality, movement and boundlessness of Galilean-Cartesian space. The weakening of traditional bonds and beliefs led the cultured elite to search for order in the realm of sounds and sights even as they were driven to revolt against all existing canons of taste. As artists became increasingly emancipated from the tyranny of individual patrons and worked for a larger audience, they were torn between displaying their individual genius and conforming to what the elite demanded of them. When we turn from cause to effect, variety is equally evident. How does one compare the voluptuous flesh of a Rubens painting with the depth of a Rembrandt portrait, the monumental classicism of Versailles with the imposing Baroque dome of St. Peter's in Rome, or Shakespeare's penetrating analysis of Hamlet with the superficial roguishness of Grimmelshausen's Simplicissimus? Differences among generations and national styles help to reduce this confusion to some order. Nevertheless, the underlying diversity of seventeenth-century art forms defies a facile compartmentalization according to time or place.

The attempt to label the culture of the seventeenth century as Baroque has added controversy to the confusion, but it has also revealed a certain cultural unity. The term "Baroque" probably stems from the Portuguese word *barroco*, which refers to pearls that are irregularly shaped and of inferior quality. When first used, the term was meant to imply that seventeenth-century culture was a debasement of Renaissance ideals. In place of the classical canons which the fifteenth century had taken from the Graeco-Roman past, the Baroque had substituted exaggerated, unnatural, even irrational art. Not until the twentieth century did the term free itself from this negative image. In the 1680's the French Academy's dictionary still defined it as "bizarre, both morally and physically." In the meantime, "Baroque" acquired the additional stigma of having been "rejected" by some countries even at the height of its influence. Frenchmen proudly wrote of the classicism of Louis XIV's France, as if the art of his day were a continuation of the Renaissance. In England, the term "Palladian" was employed to show that the seventeenth-century English artists followed the classical ideals laid down by the sixteenth-century Italian architect Andrea Palladio.

In recent decades, the pendulum has swung in the opposite direction. The Baroque is now considered a distinct if complex movement and style, displaying positive and praiseworthy traits. Some have even dared to make it the dominant form of a distinct period, ranging from the late sixteenth to the early eighteenth century, and including even the classicism of England and France. This is justifiable, provided one makes some qualifications. The sixteenth-century "transition" from Renaissance to Baroque, commonly called Mannerism, resists attempts to place it in any rigid mold. Throughout the seventeenth century, there was a strong classicist trend which can be described as part of the Baroque only if we recognize its peculiarities as well. Finally, the Baroque continued well into the eighteenth century in central Europe, while in the west at the end of the seventeenth century it was already shading into a new style, called Rococo.

Just what was the Baroque? In a broad sense it was an extension of Renaissance culture which strayed so far from the classical ideal of the fifteenth century that it became something quite different. The private letters and public pronouncements of seventeenth-century artists and musicians are revealing: The authors said one thing and did another. The Italian sculptor-architect Lorenzo Bernini talked like a fifteenth-century admirer of idealized beauty, which drew on nature but purged it of all its "defects." Yet his quest for the ideal led him to chisel a Saint Teresa and a Louis XIV which expressed very human emotions and tensions lacking in his serene Roman models. The opera stems from a late sixteenth-century attempt by an Italian circle to revive Greek classical drama. Little did Jacopo Peri know that his pro-classical preface to the opera *Eurydice* announced the halting beginnings of the most typical creation of the Baroque. The Renaissance mastery of color, light and shade and proportion led to dramatic, flowing paintings by Rubens and Poussin. In literature, Calderón, Molière and Racine broke through the bonds of acceptable classical form. Had they conformed, they would not be remembered today as literary geniuses.

Quite clearly, Baroque artists, musicians and writers were inspired by a vision of the world which was very different from the one held by the masters whom they so often worshipped. Although they were limited by the musical instruments, building materials and words at their command, they used their talents to unveil a unique vision of the world which suited their age and their individual temperaments.

Baroque artists naturally sought order, harmony and unity in their

The Worship of the Holy Name of Jesus by Giovanni Battista Gaulli from the chapel ceiling of Il Gesu

work, but the turbulence of their times made the classical or Renaissance order seem too shallow and naive to be acceptable. Baroque order was on a much grander scale, for it had much to encompass. It has been said that fifteenth-century painters discovered how to portray the human body, the sixteenth century how to arrange individuals in a group, and the seventeenth century how to connect the group with its setting. The end product was a unique creation which had not only the balance of a Renaissance painting, but a cohesion which was previously lacking. An

Il Gesu facade, Rome

historical tableau by Nicolas Poussin is clear, natural and harmonious, but its figures simply cannot be visualized as individuals. The direction of the eyes, the movements of the hands and the background all blend together to provide a dramatic focal point and create a whole that is greater than its parts. In similar vein, architecture, sculpture and painting were combined to give church interiors a strikingly unified appearance. The most famous example is the Jesuit church in Rome, Il Gesu. The painting of "The Worship of the Holy Name of Jesus" is so skillfully merged with the surrounding chapel ceiling and its sculptured figures that the artistic synthesis is breathtaking. Buildings were also planned to blend with their surroundings. Louis XIV not only built the palace of Versailles, but had gardens, statues, fountains and a Grand Canal arranged to provide an unbelievable unity. If Louis had been able to see his masterpiece from the air, he would have been even more impressed by the victory of order over diversity. The earlier attempt to make St. Peter's basilica in Rome dominate the huge square in front was equally impressive. To the sixteenth-century edifice Bernini added a broken, circular court complete with columns. In its own way, opera was a still more grandiose attempt to combine art forms. What began as a marriage of voice and action grew until opera encompassed singing, instrumental music, acting, scenery, costumes and the inevitable, absurd plot.

The unity of a Baroque masterpiece was rarely achieved by the sacrifice of diversity. Indeed, the ability to combine violent contrasts without destroying their essence was one of the greatest accomplishments of the period. The combination of order and seeming chaos was sometimes developed to the point of absurdity. It was as if the artist knew the world was not so rational as the scientist believed or the politician wanted to think. Poussin declared that "Beauty is at all times based upon a unity imposed upon a chaos of sense perceptions." He sought for that ideal, uniform beauty. Many others made a greater concession to chaos. The late Baroque architecture of central Europe, Spain and Latin America seemed to delight in disorder. The Karlskirche of Leopold II's Danubian monarchy flanked a modest Baroque dome with two towers which were capped by Chinese pagoda roofs. And in front rose two huge columns which resembled Turkish minarets. But the general effect is charming, and somehow escapes the label of eclectic.

The new monodic music of seventeenth-century Italy also accommodated sharp contrasts. A dominant melody replaced the elegantly balanced polyphonic music of previous generations. However, the melody was dramatized by combining pleasant chords with dissonance and chro-

The Expressions by Le Brun

maticism. Claudio Monteverdi's ability to stamp his own genius on this "new music" has led some musicologists to call him the Shakespeare of music.

Those who are affronted by the contrived effects of the Baroque are bound to be horrified by its literature. Many poets sought to overwhelm the reader with irrelevant detail, contorted thought, verbal inversions and sentences which read better backward than forward. In the English metaphysical poetry of John Donne, this style provoked intellectual interest. But it also gave birth to two words of opprobrium: Marinism and Gongorism. "Marinism" comes from the Italian Giambattista Marino, who announced that poetry's purpose was to astonish the reader. The Spanish equivalent is derived from Luis de Gongora y Argote, whose metaphors and allusions often prevent the reader from understanding his lines. At its worst, the piling of word upon word, like the riot of ornaments on some church facades, indicates that Baroque decoration could become an end in itself.

In most instances, Baroque art fell short of this *reductio ad absurdam*. At its best, the attempt to overwhelm the observer with jarring contrasts, the unexpected or the overly ornate was inspired by the artist's wish to probe deeply into the meaning of life. There were endless, insipid romances and epic poems which merely reinforced conventional opinions of knightly honor, moral virtue and Christian charity. Yet beside these appeared fresh, incisive treatments of individual virtues and vices, hopes and fears. Everyone is familiar with Shakespeare's dramatic treatment of human emotions, but in his own lifetime and for some time after his death in 1616, others wrote religious and secular plays which nearly matched his genius. In Spain Pedro Calderón de la Barca wrote religious dramas about the "constant prince" and the Faust-like "excellent magician." Calderón's compatriot, Lope de Vega, may have written as many as two thousand plays on various themes. In France, Pierre Corneille's provocative *Le Cid* portrayed the triumph of honor over all other loyalties and feelings. Jean-Baptiste Molière turned his comedies into devastating attacks on stock characters: the misanthrope, hypocrite, miser, jealous husband, social climber and hypochondriac.

The same incisive analysis of human emotions is evident in other art forms. No age has surpassed the Baroque's mastery of portrait painting. The greatest master of the century was the Dutchman Rembrandt, who used somber backgrounds and the right touch of light to bring out the spiritual depth and introspective qualities of his subjects. In France, Philippe de Champagne made Richelieu come to life on canvas, while Velazquez and Van Dyck did the same for Spanish and English royalty. Nor should we forget the sculptor's chisel, which in the hands of a Bernini

could portray Saint Teresa in Ecstasy to perfection. So intense and provocative was this famous altarpiece in the Roman church of Santa Maria
della Vittoria, that one rakish observer could mutter: "If that is divine
love, it is very familiar to me." Some have argued that the "new music"
was the most suitable vehicle for evoking human passions. Baroque music
was used to heighten the meaning of the words in both opera and oratorio.
In addition to the human voice, Italian musicians placed greater stress on
instruments, realizing that organs, violins and small orchestras could provide tonal shades which no human sound could match.

Baroque artists did not always find answers to their questions about
man and his world. Particularly in the first half of the seventeenth century, one senses that they saw life as a mystery. The raising of great
domes in Rome, Paris, London and Vienna was in part an attempt to show
man's will to dominate the world about him. It was also, one suspects, a
feverish effort to hide the admission that it was all in vain. There is too
much violence in the dramas of the early decades, too much bombast in
its poetry, and too much emotionalism in its writhing columns and in-

*Saint Theresa
in Ecstasy*
by Lorenzo Bernini

The Rape of the Daughters of Leukippos by Rubens (ca. 1618)

tensely alive statues to convince the onlooker that man was in command of himself and his environment.

Sometimes, the bold front was cast aside, and the world treated as unreality. Shakespeare called the world a stage, and life "but a walking shadow, a poor player that struts and frets his hour upon the stage, and then is heard no more." Calderón was equally despondent in his plays *Life is a Dream* and *The Great Theater of the World*. Popular literature in England, Germany, Spain and the Lowlands treated life as a state of constant tension between carnal lust and the quest for salvation. No matter what the ending, the frail human creature lost, whether he was a hero or a villain. The passions were portrayed so vividly that the reader was led to believe that they were both irresistible and excusable. Yet God's vengeance overcame all, suggesting that the damned lost their immortal souls and the saved their worldly pleasures. The great work of Cervantes, *Don Quixote*, has often been described as striking the death-blow to outmoded feudal values. Arnold Hauser is probably closer to the truth when he suggests that Cervantes was torn between the romantic lure of the past and the chilling reality of reason. In *Don Quixote*, we see the saint and fool, the good and bad character, fighting within the soul of the same man.[11]

11. A. Hauser, *A Social History of Art*, vol. II (Vintage, 1951), 147.

Towards the end of the seventeenth century, the Baroque became more subdued and more hopeful as it blended with classicism. The French language was purified of the "filth which it has gathered either in the mouths of the people . . . or in the impurities of chicane . . . or by the abuse of writers and preachers who say the right thing in the wrong way." What the French Academy's dictionary did for France in the 1680's, literary circles were beginning to achieve in England, Germany, Italy and the Netherlands. In England, poetry at the end of the century was purged of its conceits and emotions, until it became another form of prose in the hands of an Alexander Pope. By 1715, flamboyant Baroque music was about to be refined by the young genius Johann Sebastian Bach. The sharp corners and heavy ceilings of Louis XIV's Louvre and Versailles were already being redecorated in the warmer, less severe style of the Rococo. Restful landscapes and pleasing portraits were starting to replace the "Crossing of the Rhine" and the "Rape of the Sabine Women." Musicians began to explore the mathematical relationships which Galileo had earlier seen in the new, monodic music, and Andrea Palladio's rational description of architecture was translated into English. Literary moralists now thought that men could either overcome their passions through their "reason," or give in graciously to what was "natural" and therefore good. Giovanni Lomazzo's *Treatise on the Pictorial, Sculptural and Architectural Arts* became popular after being set aside when published in 1584. Then he had written that "A laughing picture will arouse laughter, grieving cause grief." He wished to enjoy nature, not probe its depths.

Yet, despite the unmistakable shift from the tempestuous Baroque to the more subdued Rococo, there remained an underlying mystery to life for the *fin-de-siècle* artist. Versailles reveals the restlessness as well as the boundless hope of the late seventeenth-century artist. One can certainly describe the Baroque emphasis on movement as a faithful reproduction of the scientist's world of matter in motion. Nevertheless, it is equally valid to see the shimmering of a Baroque facade, and the progression of a sonata or dance suite from one movement to another as the acknowledgement that life cannot be contained or its energies harnessed. We can see that motion in the uniform windows of Versailles which take the eye on and on into the distance. It is tempting to say that the very attempt of Louis XIV to clip his hedges into man-made, geometric forms, was an unconscious effort to hide the natural world which the middle-aged Sun King knew was not grand, noble and delightful. As in the case of the myth of the Noble Savage, late seventeenth-century art found reality too stark to accept in its totality.

Conclusion

In retrospect, seventeenth-century Europe looks almost as baffling to the twentieth-century observer as it did to those who lived during the days of Galileo, Gustav Adolph, Newton and Louis XIV. The political, social and intellectual ferment which was already in process in 1600 continued to plague the last decades of the century and was not halted when Louis XIV died in 1715. As traditional beliefs and bonds weakened, men were torn between the desire to buttress the crumbling foundations of society, government and religion, and the quest for a new order modelled on the certainties of science. The men who lived at the end of the century were probably more hopeful of the future than those who lived through the Thirty Years' War. Yet, along with hope, there remained uncertainty.

The greatest changes had taken place in the realm of ideas. Scientists, philosophers and political theorists in particular had managed to make the transition from old assumptions to new syntheses. However, the vast majority of Europeans clung to old habits of thought and even among intellectuals there was outward conformity to Christianity. The achievements of the new political thought and philosophy armed critics of the old Europe with weapons which the eighteenth century would use to attack what remained of it.

Political changes were less spectacular. The emergence of sovereign secular states was not a repudiation of the old politics. The sovereign state achieved its triumphs only by blunting the edge of its traditional rivals:

loyalty to international religion and attachment to local provinces and estates. The eighteenth century would reveal how strong central government had become, but it would also produce new political tensions, simply because many of the old rivals survived to hamper the work of princes and parliaments from within. Needless to say, enhanced royal power also led to greater international conflicts than Europe had heretofore experienced.

The least change took place in seventeenth-century society. Fears of social instability and mobility in 1600 gave way to the strengthening of society's traditional hierarchy by 1715. This change is not proof that the seventeenth century found a solution to its social ills, however. In fact, the social rigidity of the eighteenth century probably increased the inner tensions of European society, and helped to cause the revolutionary explosions which occurred from the 1760's on. Perhaps Europe might have been able to complete the seventeenth century's political and intellectual transformations without violence, had social changes kept pace.

There is one final note of irony in the story of seventeenth-century Europe. The new intellectual order which was replacing the old religious absolutes could never hope to rival the traditional intellectual synthesis in durability. The pagan-Christian unity of medieval and early modern Europe had lasted for centuries for a variety of reasons. One of the most important stabilizing factors was Christian Europe's ability to reconcile diversity and unity. The hierarchical view of the physical, political, social and intellectual world allowed men to see diversity, and yet feel that everything was in its place. And unifying the entire vision of things was the supreme absolute, the God who created, ordered and sustained the world. Once Europe began to break with the intellectual and political buttresses of that scheme, the entire edifice was in danger of collapsing. The seventeenth century failed to make adjustments which could save the system, and bequeathed to the next generations the task of completing the transformation to a new synthesis. Unfortunately, no secular ideology could accommodate all the diversity and contradictions which had been reconciled by the old. It is true that man had the tools of the new science, and the hope of better things to come. But for all the emphasis of the new thought on rationalism and empiricism, the central figure of the emerging modern world was frail, mortal man. No one can mourn the demise of the popular belief in a deity who treated the world as His private preserve, or the hierarchical view which kept every man in his place. But in shifting the emphasis from the infinite deity to finite man with all his contradictions, Europe gained in freedom by sacrificing meaning. Since that day, modern man has found it increasingly difficult to fit together the pieces of the intellectual, political and social world which once made sense.

Bibliography

Citations normally include the date of the most recent hardcover edition. However, when a book is also available in an inexpensive, paperbound edition, the citation includes the paperback publisher as well. The following books are abbreviated as follows: T. Aston, ed., *Crisis in Europe, 1560–1660* (Anchor Doubleday, 1965) as *Crisis in Europe,* and the *International Congress of Historical Sciences* as *ICHS.* Where a title is followed by (Heath Problems), the parenthetical reference indicates that the volume is part of D. C. Heath and Company's *Problems in European Civilization* series. Each paperback volume in this series includes excerpts from works by leading historians on the subject, an introductory essay by the editor and a good annotated bibliography.

Bibliographical Aids

The best general bibliographical aids are the American Historical Association's *Guide to Historical Literature* (1961) and the annual *International Bibliography of the Historical Sciences.* Also useful are T. Besterman, *A World Bibliography of Bibliographies* (1955–1956); E. M. Coulter and M. Gerstenfeld, *Historical Bibliographies* (1935); and C. M. Winchell, *Guide to Reference Books* (1951). There are very full bibliographical essays in three relevant books in the *Rise of Modern Europe* series edited by W. L. Langer: C. J. Friedrich, *The Age of the Baroque, 1610–1660* (Harper Torchbooks, 1952); F. L. Nussbaum, *The Triumph of Science and Reason, 1660–1685* (Harper Torchbooks, 1953); and J. B. Wolf, *The Emergence of the Great Powers, 1685–1715* (Harper Torchbooks, 1951). Two points should be noted: each of these volumes covers all aspects of the period assigned, the title referring only to the main thesis of the book; and the bibliographies of the recent paperback editions are identical with the original editions, covering works published up to ca. 1950. For recent and current books, it is imperative to look at reviews and lists in the major scholarly periodicals. For all topics, consult the *American Historical Review, Journal of Modern History, English Historical Review, Revue Historique* and *Historische Zeitschrift*. For more specific subjects, see the *Economic History Review, Annales: Économies, Sociétés, Civilisations, Journal of the History of Ideas, Church History* and *Isis* (on science). From time to time, the *Journal of Modern History* and *Revue Historique* include comprehensive bibliographical essays on recent literature pertaining to particular subjects.

Articles in periodicals frequently are superior to lengthy books on the same topic. The reader can always discover a key article on any important subject merely by paying attention to footnotes in books, by looking at the above-listed bibliographical aids (notably the lists of "articles and other books received" in each issue of the *American Historical Review*) or by glancing at the "article" section of the table of contents in a relevant periodical. In addition to the periodicals already noted, one can consult *Past and Present* (devoted to provocative essays on social history), *History, History Today* ("popular" articles by reputable scholars), *Science and Society, French Historical Studies* and *XVIIe Siècle*.

Indispensable for the graduate student, no matter how weak his command of the French language may be, is E. Préclin and V. -L. Tapié, *Le XVIIe Siècle* (1949) from the series *Clio: introduction aux études historiques*. This remarkable book contains a summary of the facts on every aspect of seventeenth-century Europe, an excellent bibliography of primary sources and secondary studies and a superb discussion of past interpretations and suggestions for future research. A *Nouvelle Clio* series (Presses Universitaires de France) is now replacing *Clio* with up-to-date volumes. So far, two volumes on the seventeenth-century have appeared: R. Mandrou, *La France aux XVIIe et XVIIIe Siècles* (1967) and F. Mauro, *L'Expansion Européenne (1600–1870)* (1964). Graduate students should also become acquainted with the *ICHS*, which holds its sessions every five years (Rome, 1955; Stockholm, 1960; Vienna, 1965, etc.) and publishes the papers or résumés orally presented there as well as the debates and criticisms which followed them. The reports and debates are by leading scholars from around the globe and appear in a major western or central European language (English, French, German, Spanish or Italian). Here is a rare opportunity for the alert student to discover the latest interpretations held by every national group and historical "school," without becoming an expert in scores of languages.

🖋 General Histories

There are few single-volume histories of seventeenth-century Europe, still fewer in English, and none by American or Canadian scholars. David Ogg, *Europe in the Seventeenth-Century* (Macmillan Collier Books, 1960) has been revised many times since the original edition of 1928, mainly because it had no competitor in English until the 1960's. It is generally reliable for facts, but the basic viewpoints which prevailed when the book was written have survived seven new editions! Surprisingly enough, an older book by H. O. Wakeman, *The Ascendancy of France, 1598–1715* (1897) is still a firm guide for facts about seventeenth-century political and diplomatic history. D. Maland, *Europe in the Seventeenth Century* (1966) and L. W. Cowie, *Seventeenth Century Europe* (1960) are two recent texts. Both are factually sound, but Maland's book is superior in style and has the added merit of taking into account some current changes in interpretations of the period. Unfortunately, Wakeman, Ogg, Cowie and Maland all follow faithfully the English tradition of omitting England from books on "Europe." G. N. Clark, *The Seventeenth Century* (1947) is a series of thought-provoking essays rather than a text. Although Clark has a habit of judging the continent from the standards of seventeenth-century England, his original ideas and comparative approach have stood the test of time remarkably well. G. Spini, *Storia dell'età moderna dall'Impero di Carlo V all'Illuminismo* (1960) is a masterful synthesis on early modern Europe and deserves to be noted.

There are several good books on seventeenth-century Europe in multi-volume or collaborative series. The old *Cambridge Modern History*, vols. IV and V (1906, 1908) contains some essays which can be used as crutches; but for the most part, the volumes are longwinded, dreary chronicles. Far better is the *New Cambridge Modern History*, edited by G. N. Clark. Only one volume on the seventeenth century has appeared so far: vol. V, *The Ascendancy of France, 1648–1688* (1961). It must be consulted for national history (especially Scandinavia, the Hapsburg lands, the Holy Roman Empire and the Italian peninsula) and is useful for economics, philosophy and political thought. The series of volumes edited by W. L. Langer, previously noted, should be read from cover to cover by graduate students. Together, they provide a total grasp of seventeenth-century European civilization, although the attempt to limit each volume to a generation has led to overlapping and some confusion in their treatment of intellectual history. Wolf's book is the best in this series, especially for inter-state relations and his straightforward treatment of intellectual topics. The Friedrich volume subordinates historical change to the theme of the "Baroque" as a general trait of the age. Nussbaum is heavy but solid reading. The two relevant volumes in the French series *Peuples et Civilisations* subordinate political and intellectual history to the theme of inter-state rivalries. H. Hauser, *La Prépondérance Espagnole, 1559–1660* (1948) is also strong on economic history. P. Sagnac and A. de Saint-Léger, *La Prépondérance Française, 1661–1715* is weighted towards French affairs, although the revised edition entitled *Louis XIV* (1949) is more balanced than the original book of the 1930's. The German counterpart, *Propyläen Weltgeschichte*, vols. V and VI (1930, 1931), redresses the balance by stressing the German scene. The more recent *Historia Mundi, Ein Handbuch des Weltgeschichte*, vol. VII (1957) is interesting because its chapters deal with European problems, not individual national histories. W. Hubatsch, *Das Zeitalter des Absolutismus 1600–1789* (1962) in the *Geschichte der Neuzeit* series emphasizes central and eastern Europe. Finally, every student who can read French should discover the broad sweep of history at its best in the pages of R. Mousnier, *Les XVIe et XVIIe Siècles* (1954 and later editions). This is part of the *Histoire Générale des Civilisations* series edited by M. Crouzet, which is global in scope and daring in its efforts to synthesize all facets of history.

Most general histories of the seventeenth-century plunge into the period without providing background on the Renaissance and Reformation. To supplement one's general knowledge gleaned from "civilization" courses, the reader can consult V. H. H. Green, *Renaissance and Reformation* (1964 edition) or H. J. Grimm, *The Reformation Era* (1965 edition). Both carry the story to the mid-seventeenth century, and Grimm has an extensive, up-to-date bibliography. One can gain further perspective by looking at the well organized, analytical chapters of H. G. Koenigsberger and G. L. Mosse, *Europe in the Sixteenth Century* (1968) and M. S. Anderson, *Europe in the Eighteenth Century* (1961). Despite their titles, these volumes in the *General History of Europe* series edited by D. Hay contain many striking ideas which are relevant to the 1600's.

◈ *Economic and Social History*

S. Clough and C. W. Cole, *Economic History of Europe* and H. Heaton's book of the same title can be used for basic information. The best syntheses of recent work are E. E. Rich and C. H. Wilson, eds., *The Cambridge Economic History of Europe*, vol. IV: *The Economy of Expanding Europe in the Sixteenth and Seventeenth Centuries* (1967) and E. J. Hobsbawm's essay, "The Crisis of the Seventeenth Century," reprinted in *Crisis in Europe*. Some will dispute Hobsbawm's pessimistic conclusions, but his superlative bibliographical apparatus lists the many recent interpretive studies which can be read as a corrective to his dogmatic position. Equally interesting is the seldom noticed essay by F. Braudel, "European Expansion and Capitalism; 1450–1650," which appeared in the third edition of the Columbia University *Chapters in Western Civilization*, vol. I (1961). Braudel has revolutionized the study of early modern economic history through his monumental work on sixteenth-century southern Europe, *La Méditerranée et le monde méditerranéen a l'époque de Philippe II* (1949). Seventeenth-century agriculture, trade and industry are given prominent attention by several distinguished scholars in X *ICHS* (1955), *Relazioni*, vol. IV. For regional and national economies, see especially C. Wilson, *England's Apprenticeship, 1603–1763* (1965), an extraordinarily thorough book; P. Goubert, "The French Peasantry of the Seventeenth Century: A Regional Example," *Crisis in Europe*; J. Meuvret's many articles, including "Les Crises de subsistances et la démographie de la France d'Ancien Régime," *Population* vol. I (1946) and "Circulation monétaire et utilisation économique de la monnaie dans la France du XVI et du XVIIe Siècle," *Études d'Histoire Moderne et Contemporaine*, vol. I (1947); J. Vicens Vives, *Manuel de Historia Económica de España* (1959), now available in an English translation; J. H. Elliott, "The Decline of Spain," *Crisis in Europe*; C. M. Cipolla, "The Decline of Italy," *Economic History Review*, 2nd series, vol. V (1952); R. Romano, "Tra XVI e XVII secolo. Una crisi economica: 1619–1622," *Rivista Storica Italiana*, vol. LXXXIV (1962); A. Klíma and J. Macurek, "La Question de la Transition du Feudalisme au Capitalisme en Europe Centrale (16e–18e Siècles)," XI *ICHS* (1960), *Rapports*, vol. IV; and P. I. Liashchenko, *History of the National Economy in Russia to the 1917 Revolution* (1949).

On international commerce and European expansion, the following are particularly useful: J. H. Parry, *The Establishment of the European Hegemony, 1415–1715* (Harper Torchbooks, 1961); M. Malowist, "Poland, Russia and Western Trade in the 15th and 16th Centuries," *Past and Present*, no. 13 (1950); A. Christensen, *Dutch Trade and the Baltic about 1600* (1940); P. Jeannin, "Les Comptes du Sund comme Source pour la Construction d' Indices Généraux de l'Activité Économique en Europe (XVIe–XVIIIe Siècle), *Revue Historique*, vol. CCXXI (1964); C. R. Boxer, *Four Centuries of Portuguese Expansion, 1415–1825* (1961) and *The Dutch Seaborne Empire: 1600–1800* (1965); F. Mauro, *Le Portugal et l'Atlantique au XVIIe Siècle* (1960); W. Borah, *New Spain's Century of Depression* (1951); and C. Verlinden, *Les Origines de la Civilisation Atlantique. De la Renaissance à l'Age des Lumières*. De L. Jensen, ed., *The Expansion of Europe* (Heath Problems) is a useful collection of essays.

The controversy over the relationship of bullion imports to prices, production and trade is revealed clearly in E. J. Hamilton's summation of his longstanding views in "History of Prices before 1750," XI *ICHS* (1960), *Rapports*, vol. I and in the rebuttals in the same *ICHS, Actes du Congrès*. An enormous amount of controversial literature has been devoted to the broader subject of "capitalism," but see the brief treatments by R. H. Hinton, "Capitalism—What's in a Name?," and P. Vilar, "Problems of the Formation of Capitalism," *Past and Present*, nos. 1 and 10 (1952, 1956); T. Parson's review article in *Journal of Political Economy*, XXXVI, XXXVII (1928, 1929); Max Weber's brilliant short work, *The Protestant Ethic and the Spirit of Capitalism* (Scribner Library, 1958); and R. W. Green, ed., *Protestantism and Capitalism* (Heath Problems).

Social history is a very elusive subject, and systematic treatments are rare. The interested student must peruse relevant sections of economic and national histories in order to piece together a composite picture. Fortunately,

Bernard and Elinor Barber have brought together some typical articles by social historians and added their own introductory essay in *European Social Class; Stability and Change* (Macmillan, 1965). A. Goodwin, ed., *The European Nobility in the Eighteenth Century* (Harper Torchbooks, 1953) is a collection of essays on the nobility in several states and has some relevance for the seventeenth century. J. Blum, *The European Peasantry from the Fifteenth to the Nineteenth Century* (American Historical Association pamphlet) is a brief historiographical discussion. M. S. Anderson's textbook on eighteenth-century Europe is indispensable.

The heated debate over seventeenth-century English society can be followed in J. H. Hexter, *Reappraisals in History* (Harper Torchbooks, 1961); several numbers of *Past and Present;* and C. Wilson's excellent economic and social history of England, cited earlier. Two controversial studies of major importance deserve special mention: L. Stone, *The Crisis of the Aristocracy, 1558–1641* (Oxford U. Press, Galaxy Books, 1965) and P. Laslett, *The World We Have Lost* (Scribner Library, 1966). Stone has also edited a book of readings, entitled *Social Change and Revolution in England 1540–1640*, in the Longmans *Problems and Perspectives in History* series.

The debate over France has been largely carried on between the brilliant rightist French scholar Roland Mousnier and the equally able Russian Marxist Boris Porchnev. Anyone who hopes to master the complexities of seventeenth-century French life should at least be aware of Mousnier's monumental work, *La Vénalité des Offices sous Henri IV et Louis XIII* (1945). Porchnev's major study is *Les Soulèvements populaires en France de 1623 à 1648* (1963). There are two first-rate discussions of this debate: R. Mandrou, "Les Soulèvements populaires et la société française du XVIIe Siècle, *"Annales: E.S.C.,* vol. XIV (1959) and J. H. Salmon, "Venal Office and Popular Sedition in Seventeenth Century France," *Past and Present*, no. 37 (1967).

Social conditions and relations in other states can be examined by reading the following: S. J. Woolf, "Economic Problems of the Nobility in the Early Modern Period: The Example of Piedmont," *Economic History Review*, 2nd series, vol. XVII (1964); J. C. Davis, *The Decline of the Venetian Nobility as a Ruling Class* (1962); J. H. Elliott, *The Revolt of the Catalans* (1963); three essays on the Hapsburg lands, Prussia and the Holy Roman Empire in the *New Cambridge Modern History*, vol. V; H. Rosenberg, *Bureaucracy, Aristocracy and Autocracy: The Prussian Experience, 1680–1815* (Beacon Press, 1958); M. Roberts, "Queen Christina and the General Crisis of the Seventeenth Century," *Crisis in Europe* (on Sweden); and J. Blum, *Lord and Peasant in Russia from the Ninth to the Nineteenth Century* (Atheneum Publications, 1961).

The following provocative studies cannot be easily categorized but are, nevertheless, important: P. Ariès, *Centuries of Childhood: A Social History of Family Life* (Random House Vintage Books, 1962), a brilliant book; W. K. Jordan, *Philanthropy in England, 1480–1660* (1960); M. Foucault, *Madness and Civilization: A History of Insanity* (1965); and G. N. Clark, *War and Society in the 17th Century* (1958), a series of essays.

"Absolute Monarchy" and Interstate Relations

The theory and practice of the so-called absolute monarchy have been closely examined in recent decades. Older works on divine-right theory such as J. N. Figgis, *The Divine Right of Kings* (Harper Torchbooks, 1914) can still be read with profit, but they should not be studied in isolation. W. F. Church, *Constitutional Thought in Sixteenth Century France* (1941) is an excellent study of the evolution of absolutist thought and a good starting point. The intellectual appeal of divine right to early modern men is deftly analyzed by W. H. Greenleaf, *Order, Empiricism and Politics: Two Traditions of English Political Thought, 1500–1700* (1964). The most articulate spokesman for absolutist assumptions is Roland Mousnier; his views are summarized in "Comment les Français voyaient la Constitution au XVIIe Siècle," *XVIIe Siècle*, nos. 25–26 (1955). J. A. Maravall, *La Teoría española del Estado en el Siglo XVII* (1944, French translation in 1955) describes what Spaniards thought about traditional political questions. N. Runeby, *Monarchia Mixta* (1962) is a thorough discussion of various Swedish responses to new theories of absolutism during the period 1611–1660. Although the work is in Swedish, there is a summary in German. For the subversive political thought of religious dissenters which provoked the divine-right counterattack, one can consult J. W. Allen, *A History of Political Thought in the Sixteenth Century* (Barnes and Noble University Paperbacks, 1957). F. Meinecke, *Machiavellism: the Doctrine of Raison d'Etat and its Place in Modern History* (Praeger, 1957) is a famous book on "reason of state," with an emphasis on its sixteenth- and seventeenth-century apologists.

The best study of the connection between absolutist thought and practice is F. Hartung and R. Mousnier, "Quelques problèmes concernant la monarchie absolue," X *ICHS* (1955), *Relazioni*, vol. IV. This indispensable essay looks at the subject from a European perspective and is particularly interesting in its view of England as "absolutist." The article can be compared with J. P. Cooper, "Differences between English and Continental Governments in the Early Seventeenth Century," in *Britain and the Netherlands*, eds. J. S. Bromley and E. H. Kossman (1960). J. Vicens Vives, "Estructura administrativa estatal en los siglos XVI y XVII," XI *ICHS* (1960), *Rapports*, vol. IV is a thoughtful discussion by a great Spanish scholar about the general problem of absolutism. V. G. Kiernan, "State and Nation in Western Europe," *Past and Present*, no. 31 (1965) is crammed with interesting suggestions, while E. Lousse, "Absolutisme, droit divin, despotisme éclairé," *Schweitzer Beitrage zur Allgemeinen Zeitschrift* (1958) and F. Hartung, "Die Epochen der Absoluten Monarchie in der Neueren Geschichte," *Historische Zeitschrift*, vol. CXL (1932) are substantial contributions by distinguished historians. The now famous essay by Hugh Trevor-Roper, "The General Crisis of the Seventeenth Century," *Past and Present*, no. 16 (1959), is an exciting discussion of absolutism's problems; but it should be read along with the criticisms made by Mousnier, Kossman, Elliott, etc. in no. 18 (1960) of the same periodical. The reprint of the Trevor-Roper article in *Crisis in Europe* unfortunately omits some of the best critiques.

Indispensable for an understanding of seventeenth-century relations between states are two contributions by G. Mattingly: *Renaissance Diplomacy* (Penguin, 1955) and "Changing Attitudes towards the State during the Renaissance," in *Facets of the Renaissance*, ed. W. H. Werkmeister (Harper Torchbooks, 1959). There is a good treatment of the entire seventeenth-century military-diplomatic picture by J. B. Wolf, "The Emergence of the European States-System," in *Chapters in Western Civilization*, 3rd. edition, vol. I (1961). The French series *Histoire des Relations Internationales*, edited by P. Renouvin, has made the first serious attempt to place inter-state relations in the context of the totality of contemporary history. Volumes II and III (1953, 1955), by G. Zeller, have sections on the 1600's. Zeller's collection of articles, *Aspects de la Politique Française sous l'Ancien Régime* (1964), is also relevant to the broader European scene.

Many excellent studies on the epoch of the Thirty Years' War have appeared in the last few years, but C. V. Wedgwood, *The Thirty Years War* (Doubleday Anchor Books, 1938) is still basic for presenting an overall picture and discussing the interplay of personalities and issues. The critics of Wedgwood are well represented in T. Rabb, ed., *The Thirty Years' War: Problems of Motive, Extent and Effect* (Heath Problems). C. H. Carter, *The Secret Diplomacy of the Hapsburgs, 1598–1625* (1964) is an excellent work on the background of the conflict. The definitive study of the Peace of Westphalia, F. Dickmann, *Der Westfälische Frieden* (1965), is also useful for obtaining information about the closing war years, 1630–1648. S. H. Steinberg, *The Thirty Years' War and the Conflict for European Hegemony 1600–1660* (Norton, 1966) attempts to connect all the regional conflicts which we collectively call the Thirty Years' War. The often-obscured role of the Baltic and Slavic states is illuminated by two important studies: B. V. Porchnev, "Les Rapports Politiques de l'Europe Occidentale et de l'Europe Orientale à l'Epoque de la Guerre de Trente Ans" and V. Czaplinski, "Le Problème Baltique aux XVIe et XVIIe Siècles," both published in XI *ICHS* (1960), *Rapports*, vol. IV. Interesting articles by J. V. Polišenský and H. Kamen have appeared in *Past and Present*, no. 39 (1968).

J. B. Wolf's Langer series volume is an excellent introduction to late seventeenth-century diplomacy; it is almost unique in its examination of the relationship between the western, southeastern and eastern theaters of war. Wolf's new biography of Louis XIV, cited below, is heavily weighted towards the European power-struggle and contains many new ideas about the diplomatic and military "mind" of the age. S. B. Baxter, *William III and the Defence of European Liberty, 1650–1702* (1966) is of major importance, since it deals with the man who dominated Anglo-Dutch politics and became a leading opponent of Louis XIV. D. M. Vaughan, *Europe and the Turk: A Pattern of Alliances, 1350–1700* (1964) sheds light on the affairs of southeastern Europe. Several studies by the great nineteenth-century scholar Leopold von Ranke are still very pertinent for the foreign policies of individual countries.

Historians who can connect diplomatic or military history with outside factors are in select company. M. Roberts, *The Military Revolution, 1560–1660* (1956) and V. G. Kiernan, "Foreign Mercenaries and Absolute Monarchy," *Crisis in Europe* are first-rate studies. J. U. Nef, "War and Economic Progress, 1540–1640," *Economic History Review*, vol. XII (1942) is a celebrated discussion of the economic effects of war. There is also a very convenient synthesis of historians' views on the subject in Wolf's Langer series book, chapter 7. G. N. Clark's general work on seventeenth-century Europe and L. Dehio, *The Precarious Balance: Four Centuries of the European Power Struggle* (Vintage, 1962) offer contrasting evaluations of the "balance of power" concept. On the diplomatic corps, see D. B. Horn, *The British Diplomatic Service, 1689–1789* (1961) and G. Picavet, *La Diplomatie française au temps de Louis XIV* (1930).

There is a considerable literature on state economic policies, going back to the weighty tomes by E. Heckscher and G. F. von Schmoller. The never-ending dispute over the nature of mercantilism is illustrated in the selections brought together by J. C. Rule in R. E. Sullivan, ed., *Critical Issues in History*, vol. I (D. C. Heath, 1966). The treatments of mercantilism in the economic history textbooks by Clough-Cole and Heaton are sensible and straightforward. C. W. Cole has written three massive volumes on French mercantilism under Colbert and after. They are long on facts and short on interpretation, and the reader can probably learn more from Cole's earlier, short study of French mercantilist thought before Colbert. The German cameralists can be rediscovered in the old book by E. Small (in English) and the recent work by Louise Sommer (in German). It has been left to English scholars to prove that the study of mercantilism can be exciting. One should compare the relevant portions of C. Hill's book on seventeenth-century England, cited below, with C. Wilson's study of English economic history, mentioned earlier. On governmental practices, one can also consult J. U. Nef, *Industry and Government in France and England, 1540–1640* (Cornell U. Press, 1940), while pure theory is briefly discussed in E. Roll, *A History of Economic Thought* (1956).

ᕫ National Histories

English politics of the seventeenth century have attracted the attention of England's greatest scholars. G. E. Aylmer, *A Short History of 17th Century England: 1603–1689* (New American Library Mentor Books, 1963) is a judicious, up-to-date analysis. C. Hill, *The Century of Revolution, 1603–1714* (Norton, 1961) is more controversial but highly stimulating. Together, they provide as balanced and interesting an account as one can hope to find of any seventeenth-century state. There is a wealth of information in the *Oxford History of England* volumes: G. Davies, *The Early Stuarts, 1603–1660* (1959) and G. N. Clark, *The Later Stuarts, 1660–1714* (1955). J. R. Tanner, *English Constitutional Conflicts of the Seventeenth Century* (Cambridge U. Press, 1928) is traditional constitutional history at its best.

In choosing among the many specialized studies, one cannot overlook

W. Notestein, *The Winning of the Initiative by the House of Commons* (1924). The sad story of James I's life is told with charm and grace by D. H. Willson, *James VI and I* (1956). C. V. Wedgwood's studies on Charles I are well-written narratives but reject new interpretations of the reign. By contrast, G. E. Aylmer, *The King's Servants* (1961) is a monumental socio-political study of Charles I's administration which will compel scholars to reevaluate even the latest assessments of the period. T. Ranger, "Strafford in Ireland: A Reevaluation," *Crisis in Europe*, is a valuable essay. C. H. Firth, *Oliver Cromwell and the Rule of the Puritans* (1900) continues to hold its own as a basic study. There is a convenient pamphlet by C. Hill, *Oliver Cromwell* (Historical Association, 1954). Of the many recent books on religious-political issues which engulfed mid-century England, M. Walzer, *The Revolution of the Saints* (1965) is probably the most challenging, even though one suspects that it gives a distorted view. The fundamental studies on the Restoration period are D. Ogg's two books: *England in the Reign of Charles II*, 2 vols. (1956) and *England in the Reigns of James II and William III* (1955). On William III, S. B. Baxter's book is now essential reading, while G. M. Trevelyan, *England under Queen Anne*, 3 vols. (1930–1934) continues to hold its own because of its readability and comprehensiveness. On the important subject of finances, see S. B. Baxter, *The Development of the Treasury 1660–1702* (1957) and P. G. M. Dickson, *The Financial Revolution in England: A Study in the Development of Public Credit, 1688–1756* (1967).

Historians' arguments over the English revolutions are brought together in P. A. M. Taylor, ed., *The Origins of the English Civil War*; R. E. Boyer, ed., *Oliver Cromwell and the Puritan Revolt*; and G. M. Straka, ed., *The Revolution of 1688* (all Heath Problems pamphlets). The standard bibliographies for the century are G. Davies, *Bibliography of British History, Stuart Period* (1928) and A. T. Milne, *Writings on British History* (1937–   ).

The most engaging up-to-date treatment in English of seventeenth-century France is J. M. Wallace-Hadrill and J. McManners, eds., *France: Government and Society* (1957); the essay by Menna Prestwich, entitled "The making of absolute monarchy, 1559–1683," is outstanding. G. R. R. Treasure's *Seventeenth Century France* (Doubleday Anchor Books, 1966) is a good but uneven and overly factual textbook, while J. Lough, *An Introduction to Seventeenth Century France* (1954) is a fine, short study meant to serve the needs of French literature majors but worthwhile for the student of history also. R. Mandrou's book in the *Nouvelle Clio* series, mentioned earlier, is a superb work of synthesis on French political-social-cultural patterns. No one has treated French political-institutional history with as much sureness and insight as G. Pagès' *La Monarchie d'Ancien Régime en France de Henri IV à Louis XIV* (1946). On Louis XIII's reign, the reader should look at G. Rothrock, "Marie de Medici and the Estates General of 1614," *French Historical Studies*, no. 3 (1960) and O. A. Ranum, *Richelieu and the Councillors of Louis XIII* (1963), both perceptive analyses of the monarchy in action. V.-L. Tapié, *La France de Louis XIII et de Richelieu* (1967) is an outstanding work. C. V. Wedgwood, *Richelieu and the French Monarchy* (Macmillan Collier, 1949) is well written and offers an excellent analysis of personalities; however, it is now dated in its interpretation. The turning point in the career and policies of Richelieu is the subject of an excellent article by G. Pagès, "Autour du Grand Orage. Richelieu et Marillac, deux politiques," *Revue Historique*, vol. CLXXIX (1937), and of the provocative book by A. D. Lublinskaya, *French Absolutism: The Crucial Phase, 1620–1629* (1968). By far the best book on the mid-century rebellion of the Fronde is E. H. Kossman, *La Fronde* (1954). The political-institutional background, course and legacy of the upheaval are examined in A. L. Moote, "The French Crown versus its Judicial and Financial Officials, 1615–83," *Journal of Modern History* vol. XXXIV (1962).

Louis XIV has at last been honored with a first-rate biography, J. B. Wolf's *Louis XIV* (Norton, 1968). It is a big but engaging study which brings the Sun King to life as a human being, administrator, military chieftain and mirror of his age's assumptions. V. Cronin, *Louis XIV* (1964) has some excellent chapters and challenges the reader by excusing royal policies which are usually condemned. Students should read Wolf, glance at Cronin and avoid the virtually worthless biographies of older vintage which overflow the stacks of every college library. Two articles on Louis XIV's political ideas should be compared: one by a political scientist, P. W. Fox, "Louis XIV and the theories of absolutism and divine right," *Canadian Journal of Economics and Political Science*, vol. XXVI (1960), and the other by an historian, H. Rowen, "L'Etat c'est à Moi," *French Historical Studies*, vol. II (1961). Three controversial studies on important aspects of the reign are L. Bernard, "French Society and Popular Uprisings under Louis XIV," *French Historical Studies*, vol. III (1964); J. E. King, *Science and Rationalism in the Government of Louis XIV, 1661–1683* (1949); and W. C. Scoville, *The Persecution of the Huguenots and French Economic Development, 1680–1720* (1960).

There are two excellent bibliographical essays on seventeenth-century France: W. F. Church, "Publications on Cardinal Richelieu since 1954: A bibliographical study" and J. B. Wolf, "The Reign of Louis XIV: A Selected Bibliography of Writings since the War of 1914–1918," in *Journal of Modern History*, vols. XXXVI (1965) and XXXV (1964). Both articles include comments on the period, and Church's is particularly useful for new interpretations of Richelieu. W. F. Church, ed., *The Greatness of Louis XIV: Myth or Reality* (Heath Problems) is a handy pamphlet. H. G. Judge, *Louis XIV* (Longmans, 1965) is a helpful collection of sources translated into English, followed by an annotated bibliography and interpretive essay on the reign. W. F. Church, ed., *The Impact of Absolutism in France* (Wiley, 1969) is a very useful source book on Richelieu, Mazarin and Louis XIV.

The study of the Dutch Netherlands has been dominated by the late Pieter Geyl, an extremely able liberal-nationalist historian. Geyl's *The Revolt of the Netherlands, 1559–1609* (Barnes and Noble, 1958) is an excellent study of the artificial separation between the Spanish and Dutch provinces; and *The Netherlands in the Seventeenth Century*, 2 vols. (1961–1964), although less profound, is nevertheless the best account in English of the young republican state. Geyl's talents as an analyst and historiographer were fully utilized in his *Encounters in History* (Meridian, 1961) which includes two essays on Dutch affairs during the 1600's. E. H. Kossman's chapter in the *New Cambridge Modern History*, vol. V is equally brilliant and in some respects more incisive. For detailed treatment of the Dutch people, see P. J. Blok, *History of the People of the Netherlands*, 5 vols. (1898–1912) and H. Brugmans, *Geschiedenis van Nederland*, 8 vols. (1935–1936). The collaborative *Algemene Geschiedenis der Nederlanden*, 12 vols. (1949–1958) treats both the Dutch and Spanish Netherlands, while H. Pirenne, *Histoire de Belgique*, 7 vols. (1950–1952) is a masterful, cosmopolitan work on the Spanish provinces by one of the greatest historians of all time.

Seventeenth-century Spain, neglected or despised by previous generations of historians, can now be studied objectively in J. H. Elliott, *Imperial Spain: 1469–1716* (New American Library Mentor Books, 1963). Elliott accepts the "decline of Spain" as fact but provides a thorough analysis of the reasons rather than falling back on national character as an explanation. The late J. Vicens Vives wrote several outstanding books and articles on Spanish history. His *Approximación a la Historia de España* (1960) is now available in English translation and provides a brief, speculative survey of Spain's evolution. For those who read Spanish, the older histories by R. Altamira y Crevea and A. Ballesteros y Beretta and the recent one by F. Soldevila are highly recommended.

Good, specialized studies in English are rare. C. H. Carter, "The Nature of Spanish Government after Philip II," *The Historian*, vol. XXVI (1963) is brief but informative. J. H. Elliott, "The Count-Duke of Olivares," *History Today*, vol. XIII (1963) provides background on that very puzzling statesman. The pitiable Charles II has attracted no first-rate biographer, although J. Nada, *Carlos the Bewitched* (1962) should be mentioned in order to divert the unwary from worse studies. H. Kamen, "The Decline of Castile: The last Crisis," *Economic History Review*, 2nd series, vol. XVII (1964) is a good attempt to deal with the perplexities of Charles II's reign. Hints that Spanish affairs were improving by 1680 can be found in the chapter by J. Reglá in the *New Cambridge Modern History*, vol. V.

There is a very good bibliographical essay by J. Vicens Vives, J. Reglá and J. Nadal, "L'Espagne aux XVIe et XVIIe Siècles" in *Revue Historique*, vol. CCXX (1958). Current works are listed in the periodicals *Bibliographía histórica de España e Hispano-américa* and *Indice Histórico Español*. Elliott's book on Imperial Spain has a brief annotated bibliography.

The Spanish possessions and native states of the Italian peninsula have not yet received the attention that they deserve. Even Italian scholars tend to assume that nothing happened to Italy during the *seicento* and concentrate instead on the Renaissance and nineteenth-century unification. K. D. Vernon, *Italy from 1494 to 1790* (1909) is cited only because it is in English and because it contains some sound information which can be separated from the capricious judgments displayed by the author. L. Salvatorelli, *A Concise History of Italy* (1940) is worth noting. Among the few superior studies in Italian, A. Visconti, *Italia nell' epoca della controriforma, dal 1516 al 1713* (1958), a beautifully illustrated volume in the *Storia d'Italia* series, is a welcome addition. In the revised *Storia Politica d'Italia* series, R. Quazza, *Preponderanza Spagnuola (1559–1700)* (1950) makes a valiant attempt to treat the 1600's favorably; but it is more useful for facts than for interpretation. The tensions within Spanish-controlled Naples are emphasized by R. Villari, *La Rivolta Antispagnola a Napoli: Le Origini (1585–1647)* (1967). B. Caizza, *Il Comasco sotto il Dominio Spagnola* (1955) sheds light on Spanish fiscal policies in Spain's northern Italian possessions. On Venice, we now have J. C. Davis' study of the Venetian nobility, noted earlier, as well as a book on abortive attempts to reform Venice's political structure, G. Cozzi, *Il Doge Nicolo Contarini: Ricerche sul Patriziato agli Inize del Seicento* (1958). Savoy has attracted the most attention. In addition to the many studies by L. Bulferetti on statebuilding in the late seventeenth-century, there is a monumental work on state reform at the end of the War of Spanish Succession: G. Quazza, *Le Riforme in Piemone nella Prima Meta del Settecento*, 2 vols. (1957).

The study of the German principalities still lacks a comprehensive synthesis. The "rise of Brandenburg-Prussia" is a popular theme, followed by the demise of the Holy Roman Empire as a viable "state"; Austria receives much less attention, and the other states virtually none. The best, overall study is H. Holborn's *History of Modern Germany*. Volume I, *The Reformation* (1959) is centered on the religious issues, while volume II, *1648–1840* (1964) is a fundamental reference work even though it is bedeviled by the lack of a unifying theme. The more restricted F. L. Carsten, *Princes and Parliaments in Germany from the 15th to the 18th Century* (1959) contains information on individual states in addition to a special pleading for their political Estates. E. Erdmansdörffer, *Deutsche Geschichte vom Westfälischen Frieden bis zum Regierungsantritt Friedrichs des Grossen, 1648–1740*, 2 vols. (1892–1893) is a celebrated, older work. F. Hertz, *The Development of the German Public Mind*, vol. II (1962) contains a wealth of detail on the political, social and intellectual conditions of most seventeenth-century German states; but the book tends to be a catalogue rather than a coherent study.

On Prussia, F. L. Carsten, *The Origins of Prussia* (1954) is a major study. H. Rosenberg's previously mentioned book on the Prussian bureaucracy and aristocracy is in some respects a better work due to its greater objectivity and stimulating interpretation. S. B. Fay, *The Rise of Brandenburg-Prussia to 1786* (Holt, Rinehart and Winston, 1937) is a competent survey. F. Schevill, *The Great Elector* (1947) is a substantial work on the reign of the first great Prussian prince. A. Waddington, *Histoire de Prusse*, 2 vols. (divided at 1688) and O. Hintze, *Die Hohenzollern und ihr Werk* are justly famous, older studies. Many of Hintze's articles have been republished as *Regierung und Verwaltung: Gesamelte Abhandlungen zur Staats-, Rechts- und Sozialgeschichte*, 3 vols. (1967).

Today's student of Austria's fantastic development during the seventeenth century must still rely on W. Coxe, *History of the House of Austria* (1847), although F. Hertz's book on the German public mind is useful and contains an extensive bibliography. A. Wandruszka, *The House of Hapsburg:*

Six Hundred Years of a European Dynasty (Doubleday Anchor Books, 1964) is an impressionistic study of the heritage and attitudes of the Hapsburg rulers. The standard political history by A. Huber and O. Redlich, *Geschichte Österreichs*, 7 vols. (1885–1938), is now being republished. Vols. VI and VII on the late seventeenth and early eighteenth centuries (1961–1962) are by Redlich. H. Hantsch, *Die Geschichte Österreichs*, 2 vols. (1953–1959) is a capable study. There is a good study of Ferdinand II's political views, H. Sturmberger, *Kaiser Ferdinand II und das Problem des Absolutismus* (1957). There is no first-rate biography of the enigmatic Leopold I; but T. M. Barker's broad study of the siege of Vienna, *Double Eagle and Crescent* (1967), is a good substitute. F. Frischauer, *The Imperial Crown: The Story of the Rise and Fall of the Holy Roman and Austrian Empires* (1939) sheds light on the personalities of the Hapsburgs. H. F. Schwartz, *The Imperial Privy Council in the Seventeenth Century* (1943); C. A. Macartney, *Hungary: A Short History* (1962); and O. Hintze, "Der österreichische unter der preussische Beamtenstaat," *Historische Zeitschrift*, vol. LXXXVI (1921) are helpful, special studies. There is a good account in English of one additional German principality: C.-P. Clasen, *The Palatinate in European History, 1559–1660* (1963).

Two excellent bibliographies are available. On the Germanies as a whole, see F. C. Dahlmann and G. Waitz, *Quellenkunde der deutschen Geschichte* (1931 edition, now being revised). For Austria there is the recent, fine historiographical survey by A. Lhotsky, *Österreichische Historiographie* (1962).

Of the Scandinavian states, Sweden can now be studied without a working knowledge of Swedish. I. Andersson, *A History of Sweden* (1956) is quite competent on the 1600's, and Michael Roberts has begun to dominate the subject with his brilliant articles and scholarly books. His *Gustavus Adolphus: A History of Sweden 1611–1632*, 2 vols. (1953–1958) is thorough on all aspects of that period, and he has another major study on the period before 1611. Roberts' article on Christina, mentioned in the section on social history, and his "Charles XI," *History*, vol. L (1965) are splendid, wide-ranging essays. F. Bengtsson, *Charles XII* (1960) is competent. On Denmark and its Norwegian territories, see J. Danstrup, *A History of Denmark* (1948); K. Larsen, *A History of Norway* (1948); and the picturesque J. A. Gade, *Christian IV* (1929).

There is no dearth of good, overall studies on eastern and southeastern Europe. See W. H. McNeill, *Europe's Steppe Frontier, 1500–1800* (1964); L. Stavrianos, *The Balkans since 1485* (1958), which includes a good bibliography along with a succinct discussion of the seventeenth century; H. A. R. Gibb and H. Bowen, *Islamic Society and the West*, 2 vols. (1950–1957), which treats Ottoman secular and religious institutions; and O. Halecki, *Borderlands of Western Civilization. A History of East Central Europe.* (1952).

For Russia, V. O. Klyuchevsky, *History of Russia*, 5 vols. (1911–1931) remains fundamental, although only the fourth volume has a good English translation: Klyuchevsky, *Peter The Great* (Vintage, 1958). The best modern synthesis is M. T. Florinsky, *Russia: A History and Interpretation*, 2 vols. (1955). B. Pares, *A History of Russia* (1926) is poorly organized but worth reading. N. Pokrovsky, *History of Russia from the Earliest Times to the Rise of Commercial Capitalism* (1931) deserves attention as an early Marxist interpretation. Peter the Great has several biographers, but one should start with B. H. Sumner's compact *Peter the Great and the Emergence of Russia* (Macmillan Collier, 1950), sample some of Klyuchevsky's chapters and look through M. Raeff, ed., *Peter the Great* (Heath Problems), an excellent pamphlet. Soviet interpretations of Peter are discussed by C. E. Black, "The Reforms of Peter the Great," in Black, ed., *Rewriting Russian History* (Random House Vintage Books, 1956). There are two recent aids to the study of Russian History: A. G. Mazour, *Modern Russian Historiography* (1958) and C. Morley, *Guide to Research in Russian History* (1951). B. Dmytryshyn has edited source books on medieval Russia (to 1700) and Imperial Russia (Holt, Rinehart and Winston).

Polish historical studies suffer from the tendency of Polish scholars to find external reasons for the many disasters in their country's past. Still, one can read with profit both O. Halecki, *A History of Poland* (1956) and W. F. Reddaway *et al.*, *The Cambridge History of Poland*, 2 vols. (1941–1950).

The Ottoman Empire's intriguing system of government is analyzed in the introduction of W. L. Wright, *Ottoman Statecraft: The Book of Counsel for Viziers and Governors* (1935). Other books in English include A. D. Alderson, *The Structure of the Ottoman Dynasty* (1956) and P. Wittlek, *The Rise of the Ottoman Empire* (1958).

Intellectual and Cultural History

There are several good, but no outstanding syntheses on seventeenth-century thought. J. H. Randall, *The Making of the Modern Mind* (1940) is a well-organized, straightforward textbook which has been revised several times since its first appearance in 1926. Unfortunately, its organization has disadvantages as well as merits; intellectual currents are linked a little too glibly with science, and the thought of individual men is fragmented by the topical approach. Randall's *The Career of Philosophy* (1962) is a new exposition of that scholar's viewpoint. J. Bronowski and B. Mazlish, *The Western Intellectual Tradition: from Leonardo to Hegel* (Harper Torchbooks, 1960) is centered on the life and thought of major thinkers; and in many respects it is superior to Randall, although it lacks connecting links between chapters. W. H. Coates, H. V. White and J. S. Schapiro, *The Emergence of Liberal Humanism; an Intellectual History of Western Europe*, vol. I, *From the Italian Renaissance to the French Revolution* (1966) is more comprehensive than either Randall or Bronowski and Mazlish but has not entirely resolved the problem of combining purely intellectual history with broader historical background. Although humorously antiquated in its assumptions, P. Smith's old *History of Modern Culture*, 2 vols. (1930–1934) has a wealth of biographical, factual and anecdotal information. It has been reprinted in a Macmillan Collier paperbound edition of two volumes: *The Origins of Modern Culture* and *The Enlightenment* (divided at 1687). Everyone should read the superbly written masterpiece by P. Hazard, *The European Mind, 1680–1715* (Meridian, 1953). The extensive footnotes in the third volume of the original edition, *La Crise de la Conscience*

Européenne (1935), are missing in the English language editions. The best feature of Hazard's book is its equal stress on traditional and new thought of the age. A. Cobban, *In Search of Humanity* (1960) concentrates on the eighteenth-century, but the early chapters contain hard-to-find information and perceptive comments about the late seventeenth-century.

It is hard to choose among the many fine, interpretive studies of early modern science. H. Butterfield, *The Origins of Modern Science, 1300–1800* (Macmillan Free Press Paperbacks, 1957) is a good starting point, being both provocative and usable for persons having only a layman's acquaintance with science. But many prefer the balanced, solid work by A. R. Hall, *The Scientific Revolution, 1500–1800* (1962). E. A. Burtt, *The Metaphysical Foundations of Modern Science* (Doubleday Anchor Books, 1949) and A. N. Whitehead, *Science and the Modern World* (Macmillan Free Press Paperbacks, 1925) are famous classics on the interplay of ideas and science. Among more recent works are the striking interpretations by C. Gillispie, *The Edge of Objectivity* (Princeton U. Press, 1960); E. J. Dijksterhuis, *The Mechanization of the World Picture* (1961); and A. Koyré, *From the Closed World to the Infinite Universe* (1957).

For those who want a straightforward account of the details about both major and minor scientists, there is A. Wolf, *A History of Science, Technology and Philosophy in the 16th and 17th centuries* (1950). Two fascinating studies, one hostile to Galileo and the other sympathetic, can be compared: A. Koestler, *The Sleepwalkers* (Universal Library, 1959) and G. de Santillana, *The Crime of Galileo* (University of Chicago Phoenix Books, 1955). Koestler's book also has a long section on Kepler. M. Kaspar, *Kepler* (1959); J. F. Scott, *The Scientific Work of René Descartes* (1952); A. E. Bell, *Christiaan Huygens* (1947); M. Boas, *Robert Boyle and Seventeenth Century Chemistry* (1958); and books by E. N. da C. Andrade and F. E. Manuel on Sir Isaac Newton are all good studies of other leading scientists. On scientific organizations, one can consult H. Brown, *Scientific Organization in the Seventeenth Century* (1934); M. Ornstein, *The Role of Scientific Societies in the Seventeenth Century* (1938); and D. Stimson, *Scientists and Amateurs* (1948), a history of the Royal Society of London.

The controversy over the relative importance of Protestantism, technology, socio-economic conditions, etc. in giving "birth" to modern science can be followed in G. Basalla, ed., *The Rise of Modern Science: Internal or External Factors* (Heath Problems). Basalla includes selections from the controversial works by the Marxist Boris Hessen and the American sociologist Robert Merton. The controversy over the reputed religious origins of modern science has unfortunately centered rather narrowly on English scientific circles. The periodical *Past and Present* can be consulted, especially the essays by H. F. Kearney in no. 28 (1964) and T. K. Rabb in no. 31 (1965). The intellectual ability and emotional fervor of the various combatants are fully exemplified by two notable books: C. Hill, *Intellectual Origins of the English Revolution* (1965) and G. N. Clark, *Science and Social Welfare in the Age of Newton* (1949).

Religion was so closely connected with every aspect of the seventeenth century that no single study can reveal all of its ramifications. K. S. Latourette, *A History of Christianity* (1954) is a handy reference. The Pelican *History of the Church*, especially the volume by G. R. Cragg entitled *The Church in the Age of Reason* (Penguin, 1960), is another introduction to the subject. H. Daniel-Rops' church history paints a sympathetic picture of Catholicism's inner vitality and its troubles with Protestantism, scepticism, science and non-European cultures. The following volumes are relevant to the 1600's: *The Catholic Reformation*, vol. II; *The Church in the Seventeenth Century*, 2 vols.; and *The Church in the Eighteenth Century* (all Doubleday Image Books, 1962–1964). L. von Pastor's multivolume work and L. von Ranke's shorter study, both entitled *The History of the Popes*, are older classics. Von Ranke's history is outstanding for the interplay of religion, personality and politics in all geographic areas of seventeenth-century Europe. J. T. McNeill, *The History and Character of Calvinism* (Oxford University Press Galaxy Books, 1954) is thorough, although difficult to use for the 1600's. On Puritanism, see W. Haller, *The Rise of Puritanism* (1938) and *Liberty and Reformation in the Puritan Revolution* (1955). For religious life in central and eastern Europe, see D. Attwater, *The Christian Churches of the East*, 2 vols. (1947–1948); P. Miliukov, *Outlines of Russian Culture*, 3 vols. (1942); and J. B. Neveux, *Vie Spirituelle et Vie Sociale entre Rhin et Baltique au XVIIe Siècle* (1967), a massive sociological study of theology, religious and secular institutions, and religious individuals and groups. Several fine studies of specific religious problems have appeared recently. R. Knox, *Enthusiasm* (Oxford University Press Galaxy Books, 1950) is a critical but humane examination of Quakers, Jansenists and Quietists. Several provocative essays on the "church" appeared in X *ICHS* (1955), *Relazioni*, vol. IV. P. Chaunu, "Le XVIIe Siècle Religieux: Réflexions Préalables," *Annales: E. S. C.* (1967) will introduce the reader to some of the startling new attempts to look at organized religion from a non-partisan perspective. On witchcraft, one should at least read H. Trevor-Roper's stimulating articles, "Witches and Witchcraft," *Encounter*, vol. XXVIII, nos. 5 and 6 (1967), or his book on the European witch-craze. Early modern scepticism has been turned upside down by scholars like Elisabeth Labrousse and Richard H. Popkin. Popkin's major work is the *History of Scepticism from Erasmus to Descartes* (1960). Of his many articles, the one on late seventeenth-century sceptics is perhaps the most instructive: "The High Road to Pyrrhonism," *American Philosophical Quarterly*, vol. II (1965). Labrousse has an exhaustive monograph: *Pierre Bayle*, 2 vols. (1963–1964). The excellent source book Pierre Bayle, *Historical and Critical Dictionary: Selections*, ed. R. H. Popkin (Bobbs-Merrill Library of Liberal Arts, 1965) has a representative bibliography for those who wish to decide between the "sceptical" and "religious" interpretations of Bayle. J. S. Spink, *French Free-thought from Gassendi to Voltaire* (1960) can also be consulted.

Historians are deeply indebted to other academic disciplines for their knowledge of the new science's intellectual effects. Among the many fine histories of philosophy, the first volume of H. Höffding's *History of Modern*

Philosophy merits special consideration even though it first appeared in 1900. The surveys by W. Windelband, G. Boas, B. Russell and R. Copleston are also helpful guides. Strangely enough, literary scholars have contributed as much as students of philosophy to our understanding of seventeenth-century philosophical issues. Historians of philosophy have usually judged philosophers with the criteria of logic and consistency, while the student of literature has tried to see the same men in the context of their age's assumptions. E. M. W. Tillyard, *The Elizabethan World Picture* (Random House Vintage Books, 1950) is an excellent portrayal of the early modern assumptions as they were undergoing a transformation. A. O. Lovejoy, *The Great Chain of Being* (Harper Torchbooks, 1936) is a classic on the alterations of the basic chain of being concept. There are some excellent chapters on intellectual adjustments in B. Willey, *The Seventeenth Century Background: Studies of the Thought of the Age in Relation to Poetry and Religion* (Doubleday Anchor Books, 1953). Also available are several first-rate studies by Marjorie Hope Nicolson on the impact of science on literature, as well as a work dealing with the effect of science on art: H. H. Rhys, ed., *Seventeenth Century Science and the Arts* (1961). On the concept of progress, see J. B. Bury, *The Idea of Progress* (1920); R. F. Jones, *Ancients and Moderns* (1936); and the essays by M. E. Prior on Francis Bacon and L. M. Marsak on Fontenelle in Marsak's collection of articles entitled *The Rise of Science in Relation to Society* (Macmillan, 1964). On individual philosophers and their influence, the following are informative: S. V. Keeling, *Descartes* (1934); S. Hampshire, *Spinoza* (Penguin, 1951); R. Peters, *Hobbes* (Penguin, 1956); S. Mintz, *The Hunting of Leviathan: Seventeenth-Century Reactions to the Materialism and Moral Philosophy of Thomas Hobbes* (1962); R. I. Aaron, *John Locke* (1955); and J. Steinmann, *Pascal* (1966).

The best survey of political thought is G. H. Sabine, *A History of Political Theory* (1955). J. Bowle, *Western Political Thought* (1948) is thinner but worth consulting; while W. A. Dunning's older study, *A History of Political Theories from Luther to Montesquieu* (1905), should not be overlooked. For the English political theorists, C. B. Macpherson's *The Politics of Possessive Individualism; Hobbes to Locke* (Oxford Paperbacks, 1962) is a superlative work, one of the few truly original books on political thought in many years. It can be used as a guide to the literature on Hobbes and Locke as well since Macpherson also discusses other interpretations. J. Bowle, *Hobbes and His Critics: A Study in Seventeenth Century Constitutionalism* (1952) also merits special consideration. For continental thought, there is nothing to rival Macpherson's work. J. N. Figgis, *Political Thought from Gerson to Grotius: 1414–1625* (Harper Torchbooks, 1923) and K. Martin, *French Liberal Thought in the Eighteenth Century* (Harper Torchbooks, 1962) are standard but somewhat dated accounts. L. Krieger has filled a void with two perceptive books on German political thought: *The German Idea of Freedom: History of a Political Tradition* (1957), which touches on the seventeenth century, and *The Politics of Discretion: Pufendorf and the Acceptance of Natural Law* (1965), a refreshingly sympathetic study of that maligned thinker. There is also a broader study of central and eastern European political thought during the early modern period: E. Winter, *Frühaufklarung: Der Kampf gegen den Konfessionalismus in Mittel- und Osteuropa und die Deutsch-Slawische Begegnung* (1966).

Among the special studies devoted to new economic and social thought in the seventeenth century, C. Wilson's "The Other Face of Mercantilism," *Transactions of the Royal Historical Society*, 5th series, vol. IX (1959) is the outstanding contribution. E. Troeltsch, *The Social Teachings of the Christian Churches*, vol. II (Harper Torchbooks, 1931) is a monumental book by a great scholar. L. Rothkrug's book on mercantilists and anti-mercantilists, *Opposition to Louis XIV: The Political and Social Origins of the French Enlightenment* (1965), contributes much to our understanding of French political and intellectual circles. J. W. Gough, *The Social Contract* (1963) and O. von Gierke, *Natural Law and the Theory of Society*, 2 vols. (1935) handle difficult subjects with sophistication.

The best study of the relationship between artistic styles and the general traits of the seventeenth century is V.-L. Tapié, *The Age of Grandeur* (1960). F. B. Artz, *From the Renaissance to Romanticism* (1962) is a textbook on art, literature and music from 1300 to 1800. The following are provocative works on art and literature: A. Hauser, *A Social History of Art*, vol. II (Random House Vintage Books, 1951); L. Goldmann, *The Hidden God* (1964) on Racine, Pascal and their socio-political background; P. Bénechou, *Morales du Grand Siècle* (1948) on the views of human nature reflected in literature; G. Duby and R. Mandrou, *A History of French Civilization* (1964), a masterful synthesis; R. Mandrou's suggestive essays entitled "Tragique XVIIe Siècle: A propos de travaux récents," and "Le Baroque Européen: mentalité pathétique et révolution sociale," in *Annales: E. S. C.*, vols. XII, XV (1957, 1960); and P. Francastel's articles on "Versailles et l'architecture urbaine au XVIIe Siècle," and "Baroque et Classique: Une Civilisation," *Annales: E. S. C.*, vols., X, XII (1955, 1957).

The following is a very select listing of additional studies on the various "arts." On art in the strict sense, the classic works are by H. Wöllflin: *Principles of Art History* (Dover) and *Renaissance and Baroque* (Cornell University Press). On music, consult A. Harman and A. Milner, *Late Renaissance and Baroque Music* (1959) and P. H. Lang, *Music in Western Civilization* (1941). For literature, see I. Buffum, *Studies in the Baroque from Montaigne to Rotrou* (1957); C. J. Friedrich's Langer series book; and J. A. Mazzeo, ed., *Reason and the Imagination* (1962). On patronage, academies and the press, see F. Haskell, *Patrons and Painters* (1963), a study of Baroque art and Italian society; N. Pevsner, *Academies of Art, Past and Present* (1940); J. Frank, *The Beginnings of the English Newspaper, 1620–1660* (1961); P. M. Handover, *Printing in London from 1476 to Modern Times* (1960), which touches on many subjects including royal control of the press; and H. D. MacPherson, *Censorship under Louis XIV* (1929). M. H. Curtis, *Oxford and Cambridge in Transition, 1558–1642* (1959) is an excellent book which helps to compensate for the shocking absence of good studies on early modern university life. The *Commission Internationale pour l'Histoire des Universités* has published the first volume of its *Études et Travaux; Les Universités Européennes du XIVe au XVIIIe Siècle*

(1967); several articles deal with central and eastern European universities in the early modern period. The standard work on classical studies is J. E. Sandys, *A History of Classical Scholarship*, 2 vols. (1906–1908). There is a good account of seventeenth-century historical scholarship in M. A. Fitzsimons, A. G. Pundt and C. E. Nowell, eds., *The Development of Historiography* (1954). Three special studies on historiography should also be mentioned: H. J. Erasmus, *The Origins of Rome in Historiography from Petrarch to Perizonius* (1962); F. S. Fussner, *The Historical Revolution: English Historical Writing and Thought, 1580–1640* (1962); and A. Klempt, *Die Säkularisierung der Universalhistorischen Auffassung: Zum Wandel des Geschichtsdenkens im 16 und 17 Jahrhundert* (1960). There is an interesting monograph on the central figure in seventeenth-century Christianity's reexamination of its common history: S. J. T. Miller and J. P. Spielman, *Cristobal Rojas y Spinola, Cameralist and Irenicist, 1625–1695* (1962). On religious historiography as well as the Christian reaction to non-European societies, one should also consult Paul Hazard's classic on the "European Mind," cited earlier.

Finally, one should note that the great writings of seventeenth-century intellectuals are now quite accessible in many inexpensive editions. Two excellent anthologies are available: A. Lossky, ed., *The Seventeenth Century 1600–1715* (Macmillan Free Press, 1967), which includes a superb introductory essay by the editor, and R. T. Vann, *Century of Genius: European Thought 1600–1700* (Prentice-Hall Spectrum Books, 1967). Two outstanding source books on science and its intellectual results are S. Drake, ed., *Discoveries and Opinions of Galileo* (Doubleday Anchor Books, 1957) and H. S. Thayer, ed., *Newton's Philosophy of Nature* (Hafner Library of Classics, 1953). There is a careful selection of writings by seventeenth-century philosophers in S. Hampshire, ed., *The Age of Reason* (New American Library Mentor Books, 1956). The many-faceted career of Blaise Pascal is well represented in R. W. Gleason, ed., *The Essential Pascal* (Mentor-Omega Books, 1966). A. T. S. Goodrick's *The Adventurous Simplicissimus* (University of Nebraska Bison Books, 1962) is the best paperbound edition of the great seventeenth-century picaresque novel by Grimmelshausen. It brings twentieth-century man as close as he can come to the superstitions, society and life of his seventeenth-century ancestors. Absolutist and natural-rights political thought are conveniently combined in a single volume edited by T. I. Cook, entitled *Two Treatises of Government by John Locke, with a Supplement, Patriarcha, by Robert Filmer* (Hafner Library of Classics, 1947). The second volume of Elizabeth G. Holt's splendid *Documentary History of Art* (Doubleday Anchor Books, 1947) reveals what the painters, sculptors and architects of the seventeenth-century were thinking about their art and their society. The Bobbs-Merrill Library of Liberal Arts is an outstanding series of classics with editions of major works by Arnauld, Bayle, Descartes, Grimmelshausen, Grotius, Harrington, Hobbes, Locke, Molière, Shaftesbury and Spinoza. In a new *Documentary History of Western Civilization* edited by E. C. Black and L. W. Levy (Harper Torchbooks), several volumes related to the political, diplomatic, economic, social, religious and scientific aspects of the seventeenth century will soon be published.

ஃ Imperial, Royal and Princely Dynasties

with dates of individual reigns

HOLY ROMAN EMPIRE

Austrian Hapsburgs:
Rudolph 1576–1612
Matthias (brother) 1612–1619
Ferdinand II (cousin) 1619–1637
Ferdinand III (son) 1637–1657
Leopold I (son) 1658–1705
Joseph I (son) 1705–1711
Charles VI (brother; claimed
  to be Charles III in
  Spain, 1700–1714) 1711–1740

SPAIN

Spanish Hapsburgs:
Philip II 1556–1598
Philip III (son) 1598–1621
Philip IV (son) 1621–1665
Charles II (son) 1665–1700

Spanish Bourbons:
Philip V (grandnephew;
  grandson of Louis XIV) 1700–1746

FRANCE

French Bourbons:

Henry IV (succession
  in question until 1595) 1589–1610
Louis XIII (son) 1610–1643
Louis XIV (son) 1643–1715

SAVOY

*House of Savoy (dukes;
  kings after 1713):*
Emanuel Philibert 1553–1580
Charles Emanuel I (son) 1580–1630
Victor Amadeus I (son)........1630–1637
Charles Emanuel II (son) 1637–1675
Victor Amadeus II (son) 1675–1730

ENGLAND
(Great Britain after 1707)

Tudors:
Elizabeth I 1558–1603

Stuarts (also kings of Scotland):
James I (cousin; James VI
  in Scotland after 1567) 1603–1625
Charles I (son) 1625–1649
Interregnum 1649–1660
Charles II (son; claimed
  to be king in 1649)..........1660–1685

James II (brother) 1685–1688
William III (nephew and
  son-in-law) 1689–1702
  Joint rule with his
  wife, Mary II 1689–1694
Anne (Mary's sister) 1702–1714

Hanoverians:
George I (cousin; great-
  grandson of James I) 1714–1727

DUTCH REPUBLIC

House of Orange
  (statholders):
Maurice 1586–1625
Frederick Henry (brother) 1625–1647
William II (son) 1647–1650
Regime of True Liberty 1650–1672
William III (son; also
  William III in England
  after 1689) 1672–1702

BRANDENBURG
(Prussia after 1701)

Hohenzollerns (electors;
  kings after 1701):
Joachim Frederick 1598–1608
John Sigismund (son) 1608–1619
George William (son) 1619–1640
Frederick William (son;
  the Great Elector) 1640–1688
Frederick I (son;
  Frederick III as elector) 1688–1713
Frederick William I (son) 1713–1740

POLAND-LITHUANIA
Polish Vasas:
Sigismund III (king of
  Sweden, 1592–1604) 1587–1631
Ladislas IV (son) 1631–1648
John II Casimir (half brother)...1648–1668
Michael Wisniowiecki
  (Polish noble) 1669–1673
John III Sobieski
  (Polish noble) 1674–1696
Augustus II (called the Strong;
  also elector of Saxony) 1697–1704
Stanislas Leszczinski
  (Swedish puppet) 1704–1709
Augustus II (restored) 1709–1733

MUSCOVY (RUSSIA)
House of Rurik:
Ivan IV (called the Dread
  or the Terrible) 1533–1584
Fedor I (son) 1584–1598
Boris Godunov
  (brother-in-law) 1598–1605
Time of Troubles
  (pretenders) 1605–1613
Romanovs:
Michael (Ivan's grandnephew)..1613–1645
Alexis (son) 1645–1676
Fedor III (son) 1676–1682
Ivan V (brother) 1682–1696
Peter I (the Great; half brother
  and co-Tsar until 1696).......1682–1725

SWEDEN
Swedish Vasas:
Erick IV 1560–1568
John II (brother) 1568–1592
Sigismund (son) 1592–1604
Charles IX (uncle; in
  control after 1598)...........1604–1611
Gustav II Adolph (son)........1611–1632
Christina (daughter) 1632–1654
Charles X (cousin) 1654–1660
Charles XI (son) 1660–1697
Charles XII (son) 1697–1718

DENMARK
Oldenburgs:
Christian IV 1588–1648
Frederick III (son) 1648–1670
Christian V (son) 1670–1699
Frederick IV (son) 1699–1730

OTTOMAN EMPIRE
Sultans:
Mohammed III 1595–1603
Ahmed I (son) 1603–1617
Mustapha I (brother) 1617–1618
Osman II (nephew) 1618–1622
Mustapha I (restored) 1622–1623
Murad IV (nephew) 1623–1640
Ibrahim I (brother) 1640–1648
Mohammed IV (son) 1648–1687
Suleiman II (brother) 1687–1691
Ahmed II (brother) 1691–1695

Mustapha II (nephew) 1695–1703
Ahmed III (brother) 1703–1730
*Grand Viziers of the
Kiuprili line:*
Mohammed Kiuprili 1656–1661
Ahmed Kiuprili (son) 1661–1676
Kara Mustapha
(brother-in-law) 1676–1684
Mustafa Kiuprili
(son of Mohammed) 1689–1691
Houssein Zadé (cousin) 1697–1702

THE PAPACY

*Popes (also rulers of
the Papal States):*
Clement VIII
(Ippolito Adlobrandini) 1592–1605
Leo XI
(Alessandro de' Medici) 1605
Paul V
(Camillo Borghese) 1605–1621

Gregory XV
(Alessandro Ludovisi) 1621–1623
Urban VIII
(Maffeo Barberini) 1623–1644
Innocent X
(Giambattista Pamfili) 1644–1655
Alexander VII
(Fabio Chigi) 1655–1667
Clement IX
(Giulio Rospigliosi) 1667–1669
Clement X
(Emilio Altieri) 1670–1676
Innocent XI
(Benedetto Odescalchi) 1676–1689
Alexander VIII
(Pietro Ottoboni) 1689–1691
Innocent XII
(Antonio Pignatelli) 1691–1700
Clement XI
(Giovanni Francesco-Albani)..1700–1721

Index

Abbas the Great (Shah: Persia), 149

Absolutism, 36, 42, 232–233; biblical, 400; Catholic, 153, 156; Christian, 411; Denmark, 303; despotism and, 43; Dutch Netherlands, 305; England, 305, 306; of Frederick William, 281; Hapsburgs, 153, 156; monarchical, 119; religious, 326, 342; responsible, 368; of the state, 378; Sweden, 300, 301, 302

Act of Seclusion (Holland), 229, 230

Act of Union (England-Scotland), 320

Adam: fall of, and predestination, 77; in theology, 70

Aggressor state, domination by, 65

Agrarian revolution, 9; in England, 14

Agricultural improvements, 8

Agricultural techniques, antiquated, 8

Agriculture: basic livelihood, 7; industry and, 10; overcoming depression, 14; trade and, 4

Air, in universe, debate on, 86

Aix-la-Chapelle, Treaty of, 240

Alais, peace of, 191, 205, 268

Albemarle, Duke of, 223

Albert V (Duke: Bavaria), 38

Alcala, University of, 73

Alexander III (Pope), public humiliation of, 60

Alexis (Tsar: Muscovy), 171, 181, 193; foreign policy, 173

Alsace: French occupy, 245; Protestantism in, 274

Althusius, Johannes, 369; secularization of natural law, 374, 375–377

Altmark, Treaty of (1629), 138

Ambassadors: ambivalence among, 54; initial use of, 53; institution of, perfecting, 65

Americas: bullion from, 5; 17th century trade, 11

Amsterdam: religious persecution, 124; siege of, 228

459

Spanish war, 191; Hungarian interests, 170; local government, 46; Ottoman Empire, 146; Sweden, war with, 163–167; Thirty Years' War, 158, 159; Turkish interests, 170
Austrian Succession, war of the, 291
Austrian-Swedish war, 159, 163–167
Austro-Turkish war, 244, 269–250, 258. *See also* Holy League, war of.
Authoritarianism, in England, 214, 224
Authority: acceptance of, 376; Grotius on, 378
Autocracy, Tsarist, 182
Autonomous provinces, 33
Autonomy, governmental, 32
Azov, 250, 251, 254, 293, 294

Bacon, Francis, 339; historical theory, 418; Hobbes and, 354; impeachment of as Lord Chancellor, 118; influence of, 333–335.
Baghdad, fall of, 149
Baius, Michael, 74
Balance of power, 60–67, 233, 235, 248; and complexity of war, 66; concept of, 61, 64; French interference, 253; and status quo, 65; war and, 64
Balance of trade: Europe/Asia, 11; rivalry for, 63
Balkan conflict (1600's), 7, 236
Balkans, peace deteriorating, 246
Baltic area: civil strife, 132–138; commerce in, 164; international insecurity, 132–138; Swedish imperialism, 159; trading company, 161
Baltic countries, trade with, 51
Baltic islands, Sweden gains, 167
Baltic Sea: control of, 132; Russian interest in, 294; trade routes, 132
Bank of Amsterdam, 17
Bank of England, 17, 50, 249, 316–317
Bank notes, issuance of, 17
Bank of Stockholm, 17
Banking industry: establishment of, 17; in France, 275; rise of, 4

Bankruptcy: France, 276; governmental, 49
Baptists, as Enthusiasts, 82
Barclay, Robert, 83
Baroque period, 424–432
Barrientos, Alamos de, 369–370
Bavaria, Catholicism in, 156, 160
Bavaria, Duke of, 151
Baxter, Richard, 83
Bayle, Pierre, 323, 351–352, 362, 364; and the Bible, 404–407; history and, 417; religious toleration, 413
Becher, Joseph, 394
Bekkar, Balthasar, 97
Bellarmine, Cardinal, 93
Berkeley, Bishop, 331, 332
Berlin, city of, 284, 285
Berlin Academy of Sciences and Arts, 285
Bernard, Samuel, 275
Bernini, Lorenzo, 425, 427, 429
Berullé, Cardinal, 345
Bible: absolutism and, 400; awkwardness of, accepting, 342; Catholic version, 400; clarification of, 80; cosmology and, 87; critical study of, 400–414; individual interpretation of, 53; literal acceptance, 93; political philosophy and, 369; Protestantism and, 400, 403; Reformation and, 408; translating presents problems, 401; witch-hunting and, 97
Biblical chronology, 416
Biblical truth, 343
Big government: emergence of, 52; growth of, 43–52
Bill of Rights (England: 1689), 314, 318
Black Death, 12
Black Sea, Russia and, 251, 294
Blenheim, battle of, 66, 254
Blood, circulation theory, 91
Blood ties, universality of, 21
Bloodless Revolution (England). *See* Glorious Revolution.
Bodin, Jean, 39

Osiander, Andreas, 75
Ottoman Empire, 146–150; Balkan power, 243; bureaucracy, 148; commerce in, 148; and Danubian Monarchy, 250; fear of, 235; Hapsburg interest in, 170; Holy League war, 128, 249; Louis XIV and, 244; military system, 147; and Muscovy, 251; Persia challenges, 149, 150; Poland, war with, 149; Russo-Swedish war, 254; strength of, 148; Thirty Years' War, 149. *See also* Turkey, Porte.
Oudenarde, battle of, 255
Oxenstierna, Axel, 135, 136, 165

Paganism: Christianity and, 84; morality and, 84; worship, 362
Paintings, Baroque school, 429–430
Palatinate: Catholics sieze, 156–157; Spanish troops in, 105
Palatinate, Elector of, 151
Palermo, revolt in, 126
Palladian style, 425
Palladio, Andreas, 425
Pantheism, 350–352, 384
Papacy: anti-Jansenist, 268; and College of Cardinals, 127; expansion halted, 127; irresponsible leadership, 74; Louis XIV and, 267; patronage, 128; power and prestige reduced, 130
Papal authority, and monarchical authority, 37
Papal Bull (1631), astrology condemned, 98
Papal States: internal crises, 130; military power, 127; stability of, 127
Parlement (France), 45, 109; financial pressures, 206; and the Fronde, 207, 273; Louis XIII and, 203; political power, 273–274; reforms in, 208; Richelieu and, 202
Parlementary Fronde, 207
Parliament (Great Britain): Cavalier Parliament, 307, 309; Charles I dissolves, 213, 217; the Crown, coopera-

tion with, 36; James I dissolves, 118; and law courts, 114; Long Parliament, 218, 221; nobility in, 35; Nominated Parliament, 221; obstructionism in, 212, 221; orthodoxy determined, 224; power of, 308; Presbyterians expelled, 220; press censorship, 307; religious and political reform, 218; Rump Parliament, 220, 221, 223; Short Parliament, 217; social status and, 20; and the Stuarts, 115; William III and, 315
Parliamentary rights (England), 116
Pascal, Blaise: on Descartes, 346; philosophy of, 344; on supernatural world, 364–366
Passarowitz, Treaty of (1718), 258
Paternalism, in England, 214
Patronage, 26
Paulette, 46, 109, 111–112, 273
Pazmany, Archbishop, 156
Peace, 55; international, upholding of, 54
Peace congresses, 65
Peasantry, 22
Peasants, financial pressure on, 5
Penn, William, 55
Perrault, Charles, 340
Persecutions, Catholic, 227, 248; of Huguenots, 248, 264, 268, 269; of Puritans, 214; Quakers, 308
Peter the Great (Tsar: Russia), 50, 61; and Augustus the Strong, 251; Baltic Sea, 294; and Charles XII, 254; industry and, 15; military-political state, 298; nationalizing process, 61–62; navy and, 66; personality, 292; reforms by, 296; War of the North, 252, 294; westernization of Muscovy, 291
Petition of Right (England: 1628), 213
Persia: challenges Ottoman Empire, 149, 150; Turkey, war with, 166
Petrine Era, 292
Petrine Revolution, 294–295
Philanthropy, and class status, 27